Patterns of
World History

Patterns of World History

VOLUME TWO from 1400

Brief Third Edition

Peter von Sivers
University of Utah

Charles A. Desnoyers
La Salle University

George B. Stow
La Salle University

New York   Oxford
OXFORD UNIVERSITY PRESS

Oxford University Press is a department of the University of Oxford.
It furthers the University's objective of excellence in research,
scholarship, and education by publishing worldwide. Oxford is a
registered trade mark of Oxford University Press in the UK and
certain other countries.

Published in the United States of America by Oxford University Press
198 Madison Avenue, New York, NY 10016, United States of America.

For titles covered by Section 112 of the US Higher Education
Opportunity Act, please visit www.oup.com/us/he for the
latest information about pricing and alternate formats.

Library of Congress Cataloging-in-Publication Data
Names: Von Sivers, Peter, author. | Desnoyers, Charles, 1952– author. | Stow,
George B., author.
Title: Patterns of world history / Peter von Sivers, University of Utah;
Charles A. Desnoyers, La Salle University; George B. Stow, La Salle
University.
Description: Third brief edition. | New York : Oxford University Press,
2017. | Includes bibliographical references and index.
Identifiers: LCCN 2017013736| ISBN 9780190697310 (pbk. : alk. paper) | ISBN
9780190697327 (pbk. : alk. paper)
Subjects: LCSH: World history—Textbooks.
Classification: LCC D21 .V66 2017 | DDC 909—dc23 LC record available at https:
//lccn.loc.gov/2017013736

9 8 7 6 5 4
Printed by LSC Communications, United States of America

Coniugi Judithae dilectissimae

—PETER VON SIVERS

To all my students over the years,
who have taught me at least as much as I've taught them;
and most of all to my wife, Jacki, beloved in all things,
but especially in her infinite patience and fortitude
in seeing me through the writing of this book.

—CHARLES A. DESNOYERS

For Susan and our children, Meredith and Jonathan.

—GEORGE B. STOW

—I hear and I forget; I see and I remember; I do and I understand
(Chinese proverb) 我听见我忘记;我看见我记住;我做我了解

Brief Contents

MAPS xv
STUDYING WITH MAPS xvii
PREFACE xviii
**NOTE ON DATES
AND SPELLINGS** xxvi
ABOUT THE AUTHORS xxvii

PART 3:

The Formation of Religious Civilizations
600–1450 CE 212

15. The Rise of Empires in the Americas, 600–1550 CE
337

PART 4:

Interactions across the Globe
1450–1750 356

16. Western European Overseas Expansion and the Ottoman–Habsburg Struggle, 1450–1650
358

17. The Renaissance, New Sciences, and Religious Wars in Europe, 1450–1750
380

18. New Patterns in New Worlds, 1500–1800
406

19. African Kingdoms, the Atlantic Slave Trade, and the Origins of Black America, 1450–1800
432

20. The Mughal Empire: Muslim Rulers and Hindu Subjects, 1400–1750
456

21. Regulating the "Inner" and "Outer" Domains: China and Japan, 1500–1800
476

PART 5:

The Origins of Modernity

1750–1900 500

22. Patterns of Nation-States and Culture in the Atlantic World, 1750–1871
502

23. Creoles and Caudillos: Latin America in the Nineteenth Century, 1790–1917
528

24. The Challenge of Modernity: East Asia, 1750–1910
553

25. Adaptation and Resistance: The Ottoman and Russian Empires, 1683–1908
576

26. Industrialization and Its Discontents, 1750–1914
598

27. The New Imperialism in the Nineteenth Century, 1750–1914
624

PART 6:

From Three Modernities to One

1914–Present 648

28. World Wars and Competing Visions of Modernity, 1900–1945
650

29. Reconstruction, Cold War, and Decolonization, 1945–1962
679

30. The End of the Cold War, Western Social Transformation, and the Developing World, 1963–1991
707

31. A Fragile Capitalist-Democratic World Order, 1991–2017
732

FURTHER RESOURCES R-1
CREDITS C-1
SUBJECT INDEX I-1

Contents

MAPS	XV
STUDYING WITH MAPS	XVII
PREFACE	XVIII
NOTE ON DATES AND SPELLINGS	XXVI
ABOUT THE AUTHORS	XXVII

PART THREE

Chapter 15
600–1550 CE

Features:

Patterns Up Close:
Human Sacrifice and
Propaganda   352

Against the Grain:
Amazon Rain Forest
Civilizations   355

The Rise of Empires in the Americas	337
The Legacy of Teotihuacán and the Toltecs in Mesoamerica	338
Militarism in the Mexican Basin	338
Late Maya States in Yucatán	339
The Legacy of Tiwanaku and Wari in the Andes	341
The Expanding State of Tiwanaku	341
The Expanding City-State of Wari	343
American Empires: Aztec and Inca Origins and Dominance	344
The Aztec Empire of Mesoamerica	344
The Inca Empire of the Andes	346
Imperial Society and Culture	350
Imperial Capitals: Tenochtitlán and Cuzco	350
Power and Its Cultural Expressions	351
Putting It All Together	353

PART FOUR

Chapter 16
1450–1650

Features:

Patterns Up Close:
Shipbuilding   364

Against the Grain:
Tilting at Windmills   379

Interactions across the Globe	
1450–1750	356
Western European Overseas Expansion and the Ottoman–Habsburg Struggle	358
The Muslim–Christian Competition in the East and West, 1450–1600	359
Iberian Christian Expansion, 1415–1498	359
Rise of the Ottomans and Struggle with the Habsburgs for Dominance, 1300–1609	363
The Centralizing State: Origins and Interactions	371
State Transformation, Money, and Firearms	371
Imperial Courts, Urban Festivities, and the Arts	374
The Ottoman Empire: Palaces, Festivities, and the Arts	374
The Spanish Habsburg Empire: Popular Festivities and the Arts	375
Putting It All Together	377

Chapter 17
1450–1750

The Renaissance, New Sciences, and Religious Wars in Europe 380

Cultural Transformations: Renaissance, Baroque, and New Sciences 381
  The Renaissance and Baroque Arts 381
  The New Sciences 383
  The New Sciences and Their Social Impact 386
  The New Sciences: Philosophical Interpretations 389

Centralizing States and Religious Upheavals 390
  The Rise of Centralized Kingdoms 390
  The Protestant Reformation, State Churches, and Independent Congregations 393
  Religious Wars and Political Restoration 395

Putting It All Together 403

Features:

Patterns Up Close:
  Mapping the World 390

Against the Grain:
  The Digger Movement 404

Chapter 18
1500–1800

New Patterns in New Worlds: Colonialism and Indigenous Responses in the Americas 406

The Colonial Americas: Europe's Warm-Weather Extension 407
  The Conquest of Mexico and Peru 407
  The Establishment of Colonial Institutions 411

The Making of American Societies: Origins and Transformations 419
  Exploitation of Mineral and Tropical Resources 419
  Social Strata, Castes, and Ethnic Groups 422
  The Adaptation of the Americas to European Culture 426

Putting It All Together 428

Features:

Patterns Up Close:
  The Columbian Exchange 420

Against the Grain:
  Juana Inés de la Cruz 430

Chapter 19
1450–1800

African Kingdoms, the Atlantic Slave Trade, and the Origins of Black America 432

African States and the Slave Trade 434
  The End of Empires in the North and the Rise of States in the Center 434
  Portugal's Explorations along the African Coast and Contacts with Ethiopia 437
  Coastal Africa and the Atlantic Slave Trade 438

American Plantation Slavery and Atlantic Mercantilism 441
  The Special Case of Plantation Slavery in the Americas 441
  Slavery in British North America 444
  The Fatal Triangle: The Economic Patterns of the Atlantic Slave Trade 446

Culture and Identity in the African Diaspora 449
  A New Society: Creolization of the Early Atlantic World 449

Putting It All Together 452

Features:

Patterns Up Close:
  Voodoo and Other New World Slave Religions 450

Against the Grain:
  Oglethorpe's Free Colony 454

Chapter 20
1400–1750

The Mughal Empire: Muslim Rulers and Hindu Subjects 456

History and Political Life of the Mughals 457
From Samarkand to Hindustan 457
The Summer and Autumn of Empire 461

Administration, Society, and Economy 466
Mansabdars and Bureaucracy 466
The Mughals and Early Modern Economy 467
Society, Family, and Gender 468

Science, Religion, and the Arts 470
Science and Technology 470
Religion: In Search of Balance 470
Literature and Art 471

Putting It All Together 473

Features:
Patterns Up Close:
Akbar's Attempt at Religious Synthesis 464
Against the Grain:
Sikhism in Transition 475

Chapter 21
1500–1800

Regulating the "Inner" and "Outer" Domains: China and Japan 476

Late Ming and Qing China to 1750 477
From Expansion to Exclusion 477
The Spring and Summer of Power: The Qing to 1750 482
Village and Family Life 486
Science, Culture, and Intellectual Life 488

The Long War and Longer Peace: Japan, 1450–1750 489
The Struggle for Unification 489
The Tokugawa Bakufu to 1750 490
Growth and Stagnation: Economy and Society 493
Hothousing "Japaneseness": Culture, Science, and Intellectual Life 495

Putting It All Together 496

Features:
Patterns Up Close:
The "China" Trade 480
Against the Grain:
Seclusion's Exceptions 498

PART FIVE

The Origins of Modernity
1750–1900 500

Patterns of Nation-States and Culture in the Atlantic World 502

Chapter 22
1750–1871

Origins of the Nation-State, 1750–1815 503
The American, French, and Haitian Revolutions 503

Enlightenment Culture: Radicalism and Moderation 512
The Enlightenment and Its Many Expressions 512
The Other Enlightenment: The Ideology of Ethnic Nationalism 513

The Growth of the Nation-State, 1815–1871 515
Restoration Monarchies, 1815–1848 515
Nation-State Building in Anglo-America, 1783–1900 519

Features:
Patterns Up Close:
The Guillotine 508
Against the Grain:
Defying the Third Republic 526

Romanticism and Realism: Philosophical and
Artistic Expression to 1850 522
   Romanticism 523
   Realism 523

Putting It All Together 524

Chapter 23
1790–1917

Creoles and Caudillos: Latin America in the Nineteenth Century 528

Independence, Constitutionalism, and Landed Elites 529
   Independence in the Southern Cone: State Formation in Argentina . . . 529
   Brazil: From Kingdom to Republic 531
   Independence and State Formation in Western and Northern South America . . . 533
   Independence and Political Development in the North: Mexico 535

Latin American Society and Economy in the Nineteenth Century . . . 541
   Rebuilding Societies and Economies 542
   Export-Led Growth 545
   Culture, Family, and the Status of Women 549

Putting It All Together 550

Features:

Patterns Up Close:
Slave Rebellions in
Cuba and Brazil   542

Against the Grain:
Early Industrialization
in Chile?   551

Chapter 24
1750–1910

The Challenge of Modernity: East Asia 553

China and Japan in the Age of Imperialism 554
   China and Maritime Trade, 1750–1839 554
   The Opium Wars and the Treaty Port Era 557
   Toward Revolution: Reform and Reaction to 1900 561
   In Search of Security through Empire: Japan in the Meiji Era 564

Economy and Society in Late Qing China 566
   The Seeds of Modernity and the New Economic Order 567
   Culture, Arts, and Science 568

Zaibatsu and Political Parties: Economy and Society in Meiji Japan . . . 569
   Commerce and Cartels 569
   "Civilization and Enlightenment": Science, Culture, and the Arts 572

Putting It All Together 572

Features:

Patterns Up Close:
Interaction and Adaptation:
"Self-Strengthening" and
"Western Science and Eastern
Ethics"   560

Against the Grain:
Reacting to Modernity   574

Chapter 25
1683–1908

Adaptation and Resistance: The Ottoman and Russian Empires 576

Decentralization and Reforms in the Ottoman Empire 577
   Ottoman Imperialism in the 1600s and 1700s 577
   The Western Challenge and Ottoman Responses 578
   Iran's Effort to Cope with the Western Challenge 586

Westernization, Reforms, and Industrialization in Russia   587
Russia and Westernization   588
Russia in the Early Nineteenth Century   588
The Great Reforms   591
Russian Industrialization   592
The Abortive Russian Revolution of 1905   594

Putting It All Together   595

Features:

Patterns Up Close:
Sunni and Shiite Islam   584

Against the Grain:
Precursor to Lenin   596

Chapter 26
1750–1914

Industrialization and Its Discontents   598
Origins and Growth of Industrialism, 1750–1914   599
Early Industrialism, 1750–1870   599
The Spread of Early Industrialism   601
Later Industrialism, 1871–1914   603

The Social and Economic Impact of Industrialism, 1750–1914   608
Demographic Changes   608
Industrial Society   610
Critics of Industrialism   612
Improved Standards of Living   613
Improved Urban Living   614
Big Business   615

Intellectual and Cultural Responses to Industrialism   617
Scientific and Intellectual Developments   617
Toward Modernity in Philosophy and Religion   619
Toward Modernity in Literature and the Arts   619

Putting It All Together   620

Features:

Patterns Up Close:
"The Age of Steam"   604

Against the Grain:
The Luddites   622

Chapter 27
1750–1914

The New Imperialism in the Nineteenth Century   624
The British Colonies of India and Australia   625
The British East India Company   625
Direct British Rule   629
British Settler Colonies: Australia   631

European Imperialism in the Middle East and Africa   632
The Rising Appeal of Imperialism in the West   633
The Scramble for Africa   636

Western Imperialism and Colonialism in Southeast Asia   640
The Dutch in Indonesia   640
Spain in the Philippines   641
The French in Vietnam   644

Putting It All Together   645

Features:

Patterns Up Close:
Military Transformations and
the New Imperialism   632

Against the Grain:
An Anti-Imperial
Perspective   647

PART SIX	**From Three Modernities to One**
	1914–PRESENT 648
	World Wars and Competing Visions of Modernity 650
Chapter 28	**The Great War and Its Aftermath** 651
1900–1945	A Savage War and a Flawed Peace 651
	America First: The Beginnings of a Consumer Culture
	and the Great Depression 654
Features:	Great Britain and France: Slow Recovery and Troubled Empires 659
Patterns Up Close:	Latin America: Independent Democracies and Authoritarian Regimes 663
The Harlem Renaissance and	
the African Diaspora 658	**New Variations on Modernity: The Soviet Union and Communism** 664
Against the Grain:	The Communist Party and Regime in the Soviet Union 664
Righteous among the	The Collectivization of Agriculture and Industrialization 665
Nations 677	
	New Variations on Modernity: Supremacist Nationalism
	in Italy, Germany, and Japan 666
	From Fascism in Italy to Nazism in the Third Reich 666
	Japan's "Greater East Asia Co-Prosperity Sphere" and China's Struggle for Unity 671
	Putting It All Together 675
Chapter 29	**Reconstruction, Cold War, and Decolonization** 679
1945–1962	**Superpower Confrontation: Capitalist Democracy and Communism** 680
	The Cold War Era, 1945–1962 680
	Society and Culture in Postwar North America, Europe, and Japan 688
	Populism and Industrialization in Latin America 689
Features:	Slow Social Change 689
Patterns Up Close:	Populist-Guided Democracy 691
Bandung and the Origins	
of the Non-Aligned	**The End of Colonialism and the Rise of New Nations** 692
Movement (NAM) 698	"China Has Stood Up" 692
Against the Grain:	Decolonization, Israel, and Arab Nationalism in the Middle East 693
Postwar Counterculture 705	Decolonization and Cold War in Asia 696
	Decolonization and Cold War in Africa 701
	Putting It All Together 704
Chapter 30	**The End of the Cold War, Western Social Transformation,**
1963–1991	**and the Developing World** 707
	The Climax of the Cold War 708
	The Soviet Superpower in Slow Decline 708
	Transforming the West 714
	Civil Rights Movements 714

From "Underdeveloped" to "Developing" World, 1963–1991   718

China: Cultural Revolution to Four Modernizations   718

Vietnam and Cambodia: War and Communist Rule   720

The Middle East   722

Africa: From Independence to Development   725

Latin America: Proxy Wars   728

Putting It All Together   729

Chapter 31

1991–2017

A Fragile Capitalist-Democratic World Order   732

Capitalist Democracy: The Dominant Pattern of Modernity   733

A Decade of Global Expansion: The United States and the
World in the 1990s   733

Two Communist Holdouts: China and Vietnam   740

Pluralist Democracy under Strain   741

The Environmental Limits of Modernity   754

Putting It All Together   756

FURTHER RESOURCES   R-1

CREDITS   C-1

SUBJECT INDEX   I-1

Features:

Patterns Up Close:
From Women's Liberation to
Feminism   716

Against the Grain:
The African National
Congress   730

Features:

Patterns Up Close:
Social Networking   752

Against the Grain:
North Korea: Lone Holdout
against the World   758

Maps

Map 15.1	North America and Mesoamerica, ca. 1100	340
Map 15.2	Tiwanaku and Wari, ca. 1000	343
Map 15.3	The Aztec Empire, ca. 1520	346
Map 15.4	The Inca Empire, ca. 1525	348
Map 15.5	Tenochtitlán and the Mexican Basin	350
Map 16.1	Africa, the Mediterranean, and the Indian Ocean, 1415–1498	361
Map 16.2	The Ottoman Empire, 1307–1683	367
Map 16.3	Europe and the Mediterranean, ca. 1560	368
Map 16.4	Ottoman–Portuguese Competition in the Indian Ocean, 1536–1580	370
Map 17.1	Centers of Learning in Europe, 1500–1770	387
Map 17.2	European Warfare, 1450–1750	392
Map 17.3	The Protestant Reformation, ca. 1580	395
Map 17.4	Europe in 1648	400
Map 17.5	The Expansion of Russia, 1462–1795	402
Map 18.1	The European Exploration of the Americas, 1519–1542	410
Map 18.2	The Colonization of Central and South America to 1750	413
Map 18.3	The Colonization of North America to 1763	417
Map 18.4	The Columbian Exchange	421
Map 19.1	Peoples and Kingdoms in Sub-Saharan Africa, 1450–1750	435
Map 19.2	Regions from which Captured Africans Were Brought to the Americas, 1501–1867	442
Map 19.3	Regions in which Enslaved Africans Landed, 1501–1867	444
Map 19.4	The North Atlantic System, ca. 1750	447
Map 19.5	Slave Revolts in the Americas, 1500–1850	453
Map 20.1	Area Subjugated by Timur-i Lang, 1360–1405	458
Map 20.2	The Conquests of Babur	459
Map 20.3	Mughal India under Akbar	460
Map 20.4	European Trading Ports in India and Southeast Asia, ca. 1690	468
Map 21.1	China in 1600	478
Map 21.2	World Trade Networks, ca. 1770	479
Map 21.3	Silver Flows and Centers of Porcelain Production	480
Map 21.4	China during the Reign of Qianlong	483
Map 21.5	The Campaigns of Hideyoshi	491
Map 21.6	Urban Population and Major Transport Routes in Japan, ca. 1800	493
Map 22.1	British North America in 1763	504
Map 22.2	Napoleonic Europe, 1796–1815	510
Map 22.3	Europe after the Congress of Vienna	516
Map 22.4	Europe in 1871	519
Map 22.5	The Expanding United States in 1900	520
Map 23.1	The New Nation-States of Latin America and the Caribbean, 1831	538
Map 23.2	Mexico's Loss of Territory to the United States, 1824–1854	539
Map 23.3	The Economy of Latin America and the Caribbean, ca. 1900	544
Map 23.4	Non-Western Migrations in the Nineteenth Century	548
Map 24.1	The Opium Trade: Origins, Interactions, Adaptations	556
Map 24.2	Treaty Ports and Foreign Spheres of Influence in China, 1842–1907	558
Map 24.3	The Taiping Rebellion, 1851–1864	559
Map 24.4	Japanese Territorial Expansion, 1870–1905	566
Map 24.5	The Modernization of Japan to 1910	570
Map 25.1	The Decline of the Ottoman Empire, 1683–1923	580
Map 25.2	The Territorial Expansion of the Russian Empire, 1795–1914	589
Map 26.1	Industrializing Britain in 1850	602
Map 26.2	The Industrialization of Europe by 1914	603
Map 26.3	World Population Growth, 1700–1900	608
Map 26.4	European Population Movements, 1750–1914	610
Map 27.1	The Expansion of British Power in India, 1756–1805	627
Map 27.2	The British Empire in India, 1858–1914	630
Map 27.3	Competitive Imperialism: The World in 1914	634
Map 27.4	The Scramble for Africa	637
Map 27.5	Western Imperialism in Southeast Asia, 1870–1914	642
Map 28.1	Europe, the Middle East, and North Africa in 1914 and 1923	655
Map 28.2	European Empires, 1936	661
Map 28.3	World War II in Europe, 1939–1945	672
Map 28.4	World War II in the Pacific, 1937–1945	676
Map 29.1	The Cold War, 1947–1991	682
Map 29.2	The Cuban Missile Crisis	687
Map 29.3	Urbanization and Population Growth in Latin America and the Caribbean, ca. 1950	690

Map 29.4   Decolonization in Africa, the Middle
                East, and Asia since 1945   694
Map 29.5   The Palestine Conflict, 1947–1949   695
Map 30.1   Communist Eastern Europe, 1945–1989   710
Map 30.2   The Fall of Communism in Eastern
                Europe and the Soviet Union   713
Map 30.3   Governmental Participation by Women   716

Map 30.4   The Vietnam War   721
Map 30.5   The Arab–Israeli Wars, 1967 and 1973   723
Map 31.1   The Global Distribution of Wealth, 2012   734
Map 31.2   The Global Balance of Trade, 2008   735
Map 31.3   US Security Commitments since 1945   738
Map 31.4   World Map of Climate
                Change Performance   756

Studying with Maps

MAPS

World history cannot be fully understood without a clear comprehension of the chronologies and parameters within which different empires, states, and peoples have changed over time. Maps facilitate this understanding by illuminating the significance of time, space, and geography in shaping the patterns of world history.

Global Locator

Many of the maps in *Patterns of World History* include *global locators* that show the area being depicted in a larger context.

Projection

A map *projection* portrays all or part of the earth, which is spherical, on a flat surface. All maps, therefore, include some distortion. The projections in *Patterns of World History* show the earth at global, continental, regional, and local scales.

Topography

Many maps in *Patterns of World History* show *relief*—the contours of the land. Topography is an important element in studying maps, because the physical terrain has played a critical role in shaping human history.

Scale Bar

Every map in *Patterns of World History* includes a *scale* that shows distances in both miles and kilometers, and in some instances, in feet as well.

Map Key

Maps use symbols to show the location of features and to convey information. Each symbol is explained in the map's *key*.

One map in each chapter is accompanied by an icon that indicates that the map can be analyzed in an interactive fashion (see pages xxiii–xxiv).

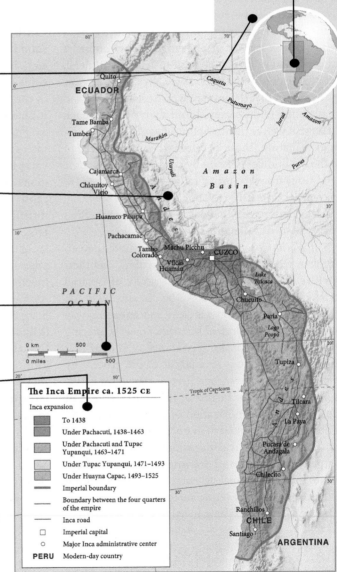

The Inca Empire ca. 1525 CE

Inca expansion
- To 1438
- Under Pachacuti, 1438–1463
- Under Pachacuti and Tupac Yupanqui, 1463–1471
- Under Tupac Yupanqui, 1471–1493
- Under Huayna Capac, 1493–1525
- Imperial boundary
- Boundary between the four quarters of the empire
- Inca road
- □ Imperial capital
- ○ Major Inca administrative center
- **PERU** Modern-day country

Preface

The response to the first two editions of *Patterns of World History* has been extraordinarily gratifying to those of us involved in its development. The diversity of schools that have adopted the book—community colleges as well as state universities; small liberal arts schools as well as large private universities—suggests to us that its central premise of exploring *patterns* in world history is both adaptable to a variety of pedagogical environments and congenial to a wide body of instructors. Indeed, from the responses to the book we have received thus far, we expect that the level of writing, timeliness and completeness of the material, and analytical approach will serve it well as the discipline of world history continues to mature. These key strengths are enhanced in the third edition of *Patterns* by constructive, dynamic suggestions from the broad range of students and instructors who are using the book.

It is widely agreed that world history is more than simply the sum of all national histories. Likewise, *Patterns of World History*, Third Edition, is more than an unbroken sequence of dates, battles, rulers, and their activities, and it is more than the study of isolated stories of change over time. Rather, in this textbook we endeavor to present in a clear and engaging way how world history "works." Instead of merely offering a narrative history of the appearance of this or that innovation, we present an analysis of the process by which an innovation in one part of the world is diffused and carried to the rest of the globe. Instead of focusing on the memorization of people, places, and events, we strive to present important facts in context and draw meaningful connections, analyzing whatever patterns we find and drawing conclusions where we can. In short, we seek to examine the interlocking mechanisms and animating forces of world history, without neglecting the human agency behind them.

The *Patterns* Approach

Our approach in this book is, as the title suggests, to look for patterns in world history. We should say at the outset that we do not mean to select certain categories into which we attempt to stuff the historical events we choose to emphasize, nor do we claim that all world history is reducible to such patterns, nor do we mean to suggest that the nature of the patterns determines the outcome of historical events. We see them instead as broad, flexible organizational frameworks around which to build the structure of a world history in such a way that the enormous sweep and content of the past can be viewed in a comprehensible narrative, with sound analysis and ample scope for debate and discussion. In this sense, we view them much like the armatures in clay sculptures, giving support and structure to the final figure but not necessarily preordaining its ultimate shape.

From its origins, human culture grew through interactions and adaptations on all the continents except Antarctica. A voluminous scholarship on all regions of the world has thus been accumulated, which those working in the field have to attempt to master if their explanations and arguments are to sound even remotely persuasive. The sheer volume and complexity of the sources, however, mean that even the knowledge and expertise of the best scholars are going to be incomplete. Moreover, the humility with which all historians must approach their material contains within it the realization that no historical explanation is ever fully satisfactory or final: As a driving force in the historical process, creative human agency moves events in directions that are never fully predictable, even if they follow broad patterns. Learning to discern patterns in this process not only helps novice historians to appreciate the complex challenges (and rewards) of historical inquiry; it also develops critical thinking abilities in all students.

As we move through the second decade of the twenty-first century, world historians have long since left behind the "West plus the rest" approach that marked the field's early years, together with economic and geographical reductionism, in the search for a new balance between comprehensive cultural and institutional examinations on the one hand and those highlighting human agency on the other. All too often, however, this is reflected in texts that seek broad coverage at the expense of analysis, thus resulting in a kind of "world history lite." Our aim is therefore to simplify the study of the world—to make it accessible to the student—without making world history itself simplistic.

Patterns of World History proposes the teaching of world history from the perspective of the relationship between continuity and change. What we advocate in this book is a distinct intellectual framework for this relationship and the role of innovation and historical change through patterns of origins, interactions, and adaptations. Each small or large technical or cultural innovation originated in one geographical center or independently in several different centers. As people in the centers interacted with their neighbors, the neighbors adapted to, and in many cases were transformed by, the innovations. By "adaptation" we include the entire spectrum of human responses, ranging from outright rejection to creative borrowing and, at times, forced acceptance.

Small technical innovations often went through the pattern of origin, interaction, and adaptation across the world without arousing much attention, even though they had major consequences. For example, the horse collar, which originated in the last centuries BCE in China and allowed for the replacement of oxen with stronger horses, gradually improved the productivity of agriculture in eleventh-century western Europe. More sweeping intellectual–cultural innovations, by contrast, such as the spread of universal religions like Buddhism, Christianity, and Islam and the rise of science, have often had profound consequences—in some cases leading to conflicts lasting centuries—and affect us even today.

Sometimes change was effected by commodities that to us seem rather ordinary. Take sugar, for example: It originated in Southeast Asia and was traded and grown in the Mediterranean, where its cultivation on plantations created the model for expansion into the vast slave system of the Atlantic basin from the fifteenth through the nineteenth centuries, forever altering the histories of four continents. What would our diets look like today without sugar? Its history continues to unfold as we debate its merits and health risks and it supports huge multinational agribusinesses.

Or take a more obscure commodity: opium. Opium had been used medicinally for centuries in regions all over the world. But the advent of tobacco traded from the Americas to the Philippines to China, and the encouragement of Dutch traders in the region, created an environment in which the drug was smoked for the first time. Enterprising rogue British merchants, eager to find a way to crack closed Chinese markets for other goods, began to smuggle it in from India. The market grew, the price went down, addiction spread, and Britain and China ultimately went to war over China's attempts to eliminate the traffic. Here, we have an example of an item generating interactions on a worldwide scale, with impacts on everything from politics to economics, culture, and even the environment. The legacies of the trade still weigh heavily on two of the rising powers of the recent decades: China and India. And opium and its derivatives, like morphine and heroin, continue to bring relief as well as suffering on a colossal scale to hundreds of millions of people.

What, then, do we gain by studying world history through the use of such patterns? First, if we consider innovation to be a driving force of history, it helps to satisfy an intrinsic human curiosity about origins—our own and others. Perhaps more importantly, seeing patterns of various kinds in historical development brings to light connections and linkages among peoples, cultures, and regions—as in the aforementioned examples—that might not otherwise present themselves.

Second, such patterns can also reveal differences among cultures that other approaches to world history tend to neglect. For example, the differences between the civilizations of the Eastern and Western Hemispheres are generally highlighted in world history texts, but the broad commonalities of human groups creating agriculturally based cities and states in widely separated areas also show deep parallels in their patterns of origins, interactions, and adaptations. Such comparisons are at the center of our approach.

Third, this kind of analysis offers insights into how an individual innovation was subsequently developed and diffused across space and time—that is, the patterns by which the new eventually becomes a necessity in our daily lives. Through all of this we gain a deeper appreciation of the unfolding of global history from its origins in small, isolated areas to the vast networks of global interconnectedness in our present world.

Finally, our use of a broad-based understanding of continuity, change, and innovation allows us to restore culture in all its individual and institutionalized aspects—spiritual, artistic, intellectual, scientific—to its rightful place alongside technology, environment, politics, and socioeconomic conditions. That is, understanding innovation in this way allows this text to help illuminate the full range of human ingenuity over time and space in a comprehensive, evenhanded, and open-ended fashion.

Options for Teaching with *Patterns of World History*

For the sake of continuity and to accommodate the many different ways schools divide the midpoint of their world history sequence, Chapters 15–18 overlap in both volumes; in Volume 2, Chapter 15 is given as a "prelude" to Part Four. Those using a trimester system will also find divisions made in convenient places, with Chapter 10 coming at the beginning of Part Two and Chapter 22 at the beginning of Part Five.

Patterns of Change and Six Periods of World History

Similarly, *Patterns* is adaptable to both chronological and thematic styles of instruction. We divide the history of the world into six major time periods and recognize for each period one or two main patterns of innovation, their spread through interaction, and their adoption by others. Obviously, lesser patterns are identified as well, many of which are of more limited regional interactive and adaptive impact. We wish to stress again that these are broad categories of analysis and that there is nothing reductive or deterministic in our aims or choices. Nevertheless, we believe the patterns we have chosen help to make the historical process more intelligible, providing a series of lenses that can help to focus the otherwise confusing facts and disparate details that comprise world history.

Part One (Prehistory–600 BCE): Origins of human civilization—tool making and symbol creating—in Africa as well as the origins of agriculture, urbanism, and state formation in the three agrarian centers of the Middle East, India, and China.

Part Two (600 BCE–600 CE): Emergence of the axial-age thinkers and their visions of a transcendent god or first principle in Eurasia; elevation of these visions to the status of state religions in empires and kingdoms, in the process forming multiethnic and multilinguistic polities.

Part Three (600–1450): Disintegration of classical empires and formation of religious civilizations in Eurasia, with the emergence of religiously unified regions divided by commonwealths of multiple states.

Part Four (1450–1750): Rise of new empires; interaction, both hostile and peaceful, among the religious civilizations and new empires across all continents of the world. Origins of the New Science in Europe, based on the use of mathematics for the investigation of nature.

Part Five (1750–1900): Origins of scientific-industrial "modernity," simultaneous with the emergence of constitutional and ethnic nation-states, in the West (Europe and North America); interaction of the West with Asia and Africa, resulting in complex adaptations, both coerced as well as voluntary, on the part of the latter.

Part Six (1900–Present): Division of early Western modernity into the three competing visions: communism, supremacist nationalism, and capitalism. After two horrific world wars and the triumph of nation-state formation across the world, capitalism remains as the last surviving version of modernity. Capitalism is then reinvigorated by the increasing use of social networking tools, which popularizes both "traditional" religious and cultural ideas and constitutionalism in authoritarian states.

Chapter Organization and Structure

Each part of the book addresses the role of change and innovation on a broad scale in a particular time and/or region, and each chapter contains different levels of exploration to examine the principal features of particular cultural or national areas and how each affects, and is affected by, the patterns of origins, interactions, and adaptations:

- *Geography and the Environment*: The relationship between human beings and the geography and environment of the places they inhabit is among the most basic factors in understanding human societies. In this chapter segment, therefore, the topics under investigation involve the natural environment of a particular region and the general conditions affecting change and innovation. Climatic conditions, earthquakes, tsunamis, volcanic eruptions, outbreaks of disease, and so forth all have obvious effects on how humans react to the challenge of survival. The initial portions of chapters introducing new regions for study therefore include environmental and geographical overviews, which are revisited and expanded in later chapters as necessary. The larger issues of how decisive the impact of geography on the development of human societies is—as in the commonly asked question "Is geography destiny?"—are also examined here.

- *Political Developments:* In this segment, we ponder such questions as how rulers and their supporters wield political and military power. How do different political traditions develop in different areas? How do states expand, and why? How do different political arrangements attempt to strike a balance between the rulers and the ruled? How and why are political innovations transmitted to other societies? Why do societies accept or reject such innovations from the outside? Are there discernible patterns in the development of kingdoms or empires or nation-states?

- *Economic and Social Developments:* The relationship between economics and the structures and workings of societies has long been regarded as crucial by historians and social scientists. But what patterns, if any, emerge in how these relationships develop and function among different cultures? This segment explores such questions as the following: What role does economics play in the dynamics of change and continuity? What, for example, happens in agrarian societies when merchant classes develop? How does the accumulation of wealth lead to social hierarchy? What forms do these hierarchies take? How do societies formally and informally try to regulate wealth and poverty? How are economic conditions reflected in family life and gender relations? Are there patterns that reflect the varying social positions of men and women that are characteristic

of certain economic and social institutions? How are these in turn affected by different cultural practices?

- *Intellectual, Religious, and Cultural Aspects:* Finally, we consider it vital to include an examination dealing in some depth with the way people understood their existence and life during each period. Clearly, intellectual innovation—the generation of new ideas—lies at the heart of the changes we have singled out as pivotal in the patterns of origins, interactions, and adaptations that form the heart of this text. Beyond this, those areas concerned with the search for and construction of meaning—particularly religion, the arts, philosophy, and science—not only reflect shifting perspectives but also, in many cases, play a leading role in determining the course of events within each form of society. All of these facets of intellectual life are in turn manifested in new perspectives and representations in the cultural life of a society.

Features

- **Seeing Patterns/Thinking Through Patterns:** "Seeing Patterns" and "Thinking Through Patterns" use a question–discussion format in each chapter to pose several broad questions ("Seeing Patterns") as advance organizers for key themes, which are then matched up with short essays at the end ("Thinking Through Patterns") that examine these same questions in a sophisticated yet student-friendly fashion.

- **Patterns Up Close:** Since students frequently apprehend macro-level patterns better when they see their contours brought into sharper relief, "Patterns Up Close" essays in each chapter highlight a particular innovation that demonstrates origins, interactions, and adaptations in action. Spanning technological, social, political, intellectual, economic, and environmental developments, the "Patterns Up Close" essays combine text, visuals, and graphics to consider everything from the pepper trade to the guillotine.

- **Against the Grain:** These brief essays consider counterpoints to the main patterns examined in each chapter. Topics range from visionaries who challenged dominant religious patterns, to women who resisted various forms of patriarchy, to agitators who fought for social and economic justice.

- **Marginal Glossary:** To avoid the necessity of having to flip pages back and forth, definitions of key terms are set directly in the margin at the point where they are first introduced.

Today, more than ever, students and instructors are confronted by a vast welter of information on every conceivable subject. Beyond the ever-expanding print media, the Internet and the Web have opened hitherto unimaginable amounts of data to us. Despite such unprecedented access, however, all of us are too frequently overwhelmed by this undifferentiated—and all too often indigestible—mass. Nowhere is this more true than in world history, by definition the field within the historical profession with the broadest scope. Therefore, we think that an effort at synthesis—of narrative and analysis structured around a clear, accessible, widely applicable theme—is needed, an effort that seeks to explain critical patterns of the world's past behind the billions of bits of information accessible at the stroke of a key on a computer keyboard. We hope this text, in tracing the lines of transformative ideas and things that left their patterns deeply imprinted into the canvas of world history, will provide such a synthesis.

Changes to the New Edition

Streamlined narrative To facilitate accessibility, we have shortened the text by approximately 25 percent for this Brief Edition. This reduction has not come at the expense of discarding essential topics. Instead, we have tightened the narrative, focusing even more on key concepts and (with the guidance of reviewers) discarding extraneous examples. We are profoundly grateful to the reviewers who pointed out errors and conceptual shortcomings. Factual accuracy and terminological precision are extremely important to us.

Updated scholarship All chapters were revised and updated, in accordance with recent developments and new scholarship. Here is a chapter-by-chapter overview that highlights the changes we made in the third edition:

- **Part One** Chapter 1 includes three major changes: a discussion of the new stone tool finds in Kenya, dated to 3.3 million years ago; revisions to our understanding of the Neanderthals, on the basis of the new Bruniquel Cave finds; and revisions to our understanding of the human settlement of the Americas, resulting from new genetic studies (2015–2016). Chapter 2 clarifies the conceptual transition from nature spirituality to what is commonly called polytheism. Chapter 3 updates the material on ancient India and Harappans, and the "Patterns Up Close" in Chapter 5 adds the results of a new 2016 genetic study on corn.

- **Part Two** The title of Chapter 7 has been changed to "Interaction and Adaptation in Western Eurasia: Persia, Greece, and Rome" to more emphatically show the interactions among these cultural zones. Chapter 8 contains a revised section on Jainism, and Chapter 9 adds a survey of the contemporary debate about the "Han Synthesis."

- **Part Three** Chapter 10 offers clearer discussions of the Arab conquests of the Middle East, North Africa, and Iberia during the 600s and early 700s as well as of the composition of Islamic salvation history in the 800s, including the biography of the Prophet Muhammad. The coverage of Byzantium has been improved with a discussion of iconoclasm and the split between Catholicism and Greek Orthodoxy in 1054. Chapter 12 focuses more strongly on the Mongol interval and adds specificity to the discussion of Neo-Confucian philosophy. The new chapter subtitle, "Contrasting Patterns in India and China," reflects these changes.

- **Part Four** In Chapter 17 we eliminated considerable detail from the presentation of the European religious wars and broadened the focus in the English case to include the War of the Three Kingdoms. Chapter 21 updates the discussion of the Chinese rural economy and the debate about the High Level Equilibrium Trap. It also improves the discussion of Qing concepts of multicultural empire.

- **Part Five** In Chapter 22 the basic concepts of modern nationalism are reformulated: We now distinguish between the patterns of constitutionalism and ethnic nationalism as keys for the understanding of political modernity. In addition, the process of Italian ethnic nationalist unification is presented more clearly. Chapter 23 is completely reorganized, emphasizing in addition the significance of the Paraguayan War of 1864–1870. In Chapter 24, the role of the Hakkas in the Taiping movement is described more clearly. Chapter 26 emphasizes the importance of the steam engine in the Industrial Revolution more strongly and reconceptualizes the nineteenth-century class structure in the emerging industrial societies. Chapter 27 defines more sharply the pattern of the New Imperialism during the nineteenth century.

- **Part Six** Chapter 29 updates the "Patterns Up Close" feature on the Non-Aligned Movement. In Chapter 30 we shortened the text so as to create room for an improved coverage of the Lebanese civil war, the Iranian Islamic Revolution, the US Vietnam War, and the Brazilian economic miracle. In Chapter 31, we similarly removed text and replaced it with paragraphs on the travails of the Arab Spring, the new military regime in Egypt, the "Islamic State" of Iraq and Syria, the failed coup d'état in Turkey, as well as the new populist anti-globalism, complete with "Brexit" in Europe and Donald J. Trump's electoral victory in the United States. The "Patterns Up Close" essay on information technology was updated to include IT's misuse by terrorists.

Ensuring Student Success

Oxford University Press offers instructors and students a comprehensive ancillary package for qualified adopters.

- **Dashboard:** Simple, informative, and mobile, Dashboard is an online learning and assessment platform tailored to your textbook that delivers a simple, informative, and mobile experience for professors and students. It offers quality content and tools to track student progress in an intuitive, web-based learning environment; features a streamlined interface that connects students and instructors with the most important course functions; and simplifies the learning experience

to save time and put student progress first. Dashboard for *Patterns of World History*, Third Edition, includes:

- An embedded e-book that integrates multimedia content, providing a dynamic learning space for both students and instructors. Each chapter in *Patterns of World History* includes:

image analysis   document analysis

map analysis, interactive timelines, and interactive concept maps   Many chapters also include video analysis

audio flashcards

- Three sets of quizzes per chapter for both low stakes and high stakes testing. The quizzes are aligned according to Bloom's Taxonomy: quiz 1 tests basic concepts and terminologies; quiz 2 provides questions that test both basic facts and ability to apply concepts; quiz 3 tests ability to evaluate and analyze key concepts.
- The complete set of questions from the testbank (1,500 questions), that provide for each chapter, approximately 40 multiple-choice, short-answer, true-or-false, and fill-in-the-blank as well as approximately 10 essay questions.
- **Ancillary Resource Center (ARC):** This online resource center, available to adopters of *Patterns of World History*, includes:
- **Instructor's Resource Manual:** Includes, for each chapter, a detailed chapter outline, suggested lecture topics, learning objectives, map quizzes, geography exercises, classroom activities, "Patterns Up Close" activities, "Seeing Patterns

and Making Connections" activities, "Against the Grain" exercises, biographical sketches, and suggested Web resources and digital media files. Also includes for each chapter approximately 40 multiple-choice, short-answer, true-or-false, and fill-in-the-blank as well as approximately 10 essay questions.

- **Oxford World History Video Library:** Includes short, two- to three-minute videos that offer overviews of such key topics as the the Golden Age of Islam, Genghis Khan, the steam engine, and the atomic age.
- **PowerPoints:** Includes PowerPoint slides and JPEG and PDF files for all the maps and photos in the text, an additional 400 map files from *The Oxford Atlas of World History*, and approximately 1,000 additional PowerPoint-based slides from OUP's Image Bank Library, organized by themes and topics in world history.
- **Computerized testbank:** Includes approximately 1,500 questions that can be customized by the instructor.
- **Course cartridges:** containing student and instructor resources are available for the most commonly used course management systems.

Additional Learning

- *Sources in Patterns of World History:* **Volume 1: To 1600:** Includes approximately 75 text and visual sources in world history, organized by the chapter organization of *Patterns of World History*. Each source is accompanied by a headnote and reading questions.
- *Sources in Patterns of World History:* **Volume 2: Since 1400:** Includes approximately 90 text and visual sources in world history, organized by the chapter organization of *Patterns of World History*. Each source is accompanied by a headnote and reading questions.
- *Mapping Patterns of World History,* **Volume 1: To 1600:** Includes approximately 50 full-color maps, each accompanied by a brief headnote, as well as blank outline maps and Concept Map exercises.
- *Mapping Patterns of World History,* **Volume 2: Since 1400:** Includes approximately 50 full-color maps, each accompanied by a brief headnote, as well as blank outline maps and Concept Map exercises.
- *Now Playing: Learning World History Through Film:* Designed specifically to accompany *Patterns of World History*, this free supplement examines thirty-two films to show how key themes in world history play out in a variety of time periods and contexts.
- **Open Access Companion Website (www.oup .com/us/vonsivers):** Includes quizzes, note-taking guides, and flashcards.
- **E-book for Patterns of World History:** E-books of all the volumes, at a significant discount, are available for purchase at www.redshelf.com or www.vitalsource.com.

Bundling Options

Patterns of World History can be bundled at a significant discount with any of the titles in the popular Very Short Introductions, World in a Life, or Oxford World's Classics series, as well as other titles from the Higher Education division world history catalog (www.oup.com/us/catalog/he). Please contact your OUP representative for details.

Acknowledgments

Throughout the course of writing, revising, and preparing *Patterns of World History* for publication we have benefited from the guidance and professionalism accorded us by all levels of the staff at Oxford University Press. John Challice, vice president and publisher, had faith in the inherent worth of our project from the outset and provided the initial impetus to move forward. Meg Botteon guided us through the revisions and added a final polish, often helping us with substantive suggestions. Katherine Schnakenberg carried out the thankless task of assembling the manuscript and did so with generosity and good cheer, helping us with many details in the final manuscript. Carrie Crompton copyedited the manuscript with meticulous attention to detail, and Keith Faivre steered us through the intricacies of production with the stoicism of a saint.

Most of all, we owe a special debt of gratitude to Charles Cavaliere, our editor. Charles took on the daunting task of directing the literary enterprise at a critical point in the book's career. He pushed this project to its successful completion, accelerated its schedule, and used a combination of flattery and hard-nosed tactics to make sure we stayed the course. His greatest contribution, however, is in the way he refined our original vision for the book with several important adjustments that clarified its latent possibilities. From the maps to the photos to the special features, Charles's high standards and concern for detail are evident on every page.

Developing a book like *Patterns of World History* is an ambitious project, a collaborative venture in which authors and editors benefit from the feedback provided by a team of outside readers and consultants. We gratefully acknowledge the advice that the many reviewers, focus group participants, and class testers (including their students) shared with us along the way. We tried to implement all of the excellent suggestions. We owe a special debt of thanks to Evan R. Ward, who provided invaluable guidance for the revision of the coverage of Latin America and the Caribbean in Part 5, and to Jonathan S. Perry, who deftly assembled the documents. Of course, any errors of fact or interpretation that remain are solely our own.

Reviewers of the New Edition
Kevin Eoff, Palo Verde College

Christina Firpo, CalPoly University

Aaron Hagler, Troy University

Ephraim Harel, Montgomery College, Rockville

Michael Markus, Alabama State University

Scott Merriman, Troy University

Curtis Morgan, Lord Fairfax Community College

Joanna Neilson, Lincoln Memorial University

Jahan Salehi, Central Piedmont Community College

William Skiles, California State University, San Marcos

Marika Snider, Miami University

Daniel Stephen, Colorado State University

Jason Tatlock, Armstrong State University

Michael Thensted, Mississippi Gulf Coast Community College

Walter Ward, University of Alabama at Birmingham

Paul Tenkotte, Northern Kentucky University

Daniel R. Pavese, Wor-Wic Community College

and one anonymous reviewer.

Please let us know your experiences with *Patterns of World History* so that we may improve it in future editions. We welcome your comments and suggestions.

Peter von Sivers
pv4910@xmission.com

Charles A. Desnoyers
desnoyer@lasalle.edu

George B. Stow
gbsgeorge@aol.com

Note on Dates and Spellings

In keeping with widespread practice among world historians, we use "BCE" and "CE" to date events and the phrase "years ago" to describe developments from the remote past.

The transliteration of Middle Eastern words has been adjusted as much as possible to the English alphabet. Therefore, long vowels are not emphasized. The consonants specific to Arabic (alif, dhal, ha, sad, dad, ta, za, `ayn, ghayn, and qaf) are either not indicated or rendered with common English letters. A similar procedure is followed for Farsi. Turkish words follow the alphabet reform of 1929, which adds the following letters to the Western alphabet or modifies their pronunciation: c (pronounced "j"), ç (pronounced "tsh"), ğ (not pronounced but lengthening of preceding vowel), ı ("i" without dot, pronunciation close to short e), i/İ ("i" with dot, including in caps), ö (no English equivalent), ş ("sh"), and ü (no English equivalent). The spelling of common contemporary Middle Eastern and Islamic terms follows daily press usage (which, however, is not completely uniform). Examples are "al-Qaeda," "Quran," and "Sharia."

The system used in rendering the sounds of Mandarin Chinese—the northern Chinese dialect that has become in effect the national spoken language in China and Taiwan—into English in this book is *hanyu pinyin*, usually given as simply pinyin. This is the official romanization system of the People's Republic of China and has also become the standard outside of Taiwan, Republic of China. Most syllables are pronounced as they would be in English, with the exception of the letter *q*, which has an aspirated "ch" sound; ch itself has a less aspirated "ch" sound. *Zh* carries a hard "j" and *j* a soft, English-style "j." Some syllables also are pronounced—particularly in the regions around Beijing—with a retroflex r so that the syllable *shi*, for example, carries a pronunciation closer to "shir." Finally, the letter *r* in the *pinyin* system has no direct English equivalent, but an approximation may be had by combining the sounds of "r" and "j."

Japanese terms have been romanized according to a modification of the Hepburn system. The letter *g* is always hard; vowels are handled as they are in Italian—*e*, for example, carries a sound like "ay." We have not, however, included diacritical markings to indicate long vowel sounds for *u* or *o*. Where necessary, these have been indicated in the pronunciation guides.

For Korean terms, we have used a variation of the McCune-Reischauer system, which remains the standard romanization scheme for Korean words used in English academic writing, but eliminated any diacritical markings. Here again, the vowel sounds are pronounced more or less like those of Italian and the consonants, like those of English.

For Vietnamese words, we have used standard renditions based on the modern Quoc Ngu ("national language") system in use in Vietnam today. The system was developed by Jesuit missionaries and is based on the Portuguese alphabet. Once more, we have avoided diacritical marks, and the reader should follow the pronunciation guides for approximations of Vietnamese terms.

Latin American terms (Spanish, Nahua, or Quechua) generally follow local usage, including accents, except where they are Anglicized, per the *Oxford English Dictionary*. Thus, the Spanish-Quechua word "Tiahuanacu" becomes the Anglicized word "Tiwanaku."

We use the terms "Native American" and "Indian" interchangeably to refer to the peoples of the Americas in the pre-Columbian period and "Amerindian" in our coverage of Latin America since independence.

In keeping with widely recognized practice among paleontologists and other scholars of the deep past, we use the term "hominins" in Chapter 1 to emphasize their greater remoteness from apes and proximity to modern humans.

Phonetic spellings often follow the first appearance of a non-English word whose pronunciation may be unclear to the reader. We have followed the rules for capitalization per *The Chicago Manual of Style*.

About the Authors

Peter von Sivers is associate professor of Middle Eastern history at the University of Utah. He has previously taught at UCLA, Northwestern University, the University of Paris VII (Vincennes), and the University of Munich. He has also served as chair of the Joint Committee of the Near and Middle East, Social Science Research Council, New York, 1982–1985; editor of the *International Journal of Middle East Studies*, 1985–1989; member of the board of directors of the Middle East Studies Association of North America, 1987–1990; and chair of the SAT II World History Test Development Community of the Educational Testing Service, Princeton, NJ, 1991–1994. His publications include *Caliphate, Kingdom, and Decline: The Political Theory of Ibn Khaldun* (1968), several edited books, and three dozen peer-reviewed chapters and articles on Middle Eastern and North African history, as well as world history. He received his Dr. phil. from the University of Munich.

Charles A. Desnoyers is professor of history and director of Asian Studies at La Salle University in Philadelphia. He has previously taught at Temple University, Villanova University, and Pennsylvania State University. In addition to serving as History Department chair from 1999–2007, he was a founder and long-time director of the Greater Philadelphia Asian Studies Consortium and president (2011–2012) of the Mid-Atlantic Region Association for Asian Studies. He has served as a reader, table leader, and question writer for the AP European and World History exams. He served as editor of the organization's *Bulletin* from 1995–2001. In addition to numerous articles in peer-reviewed and general publications, his work includes *Patterns of Modern Chinese History* (2016, Oxford University Press) and *A Journey to the East: Li Gui's "A New Account of a Trip Around the Globe"* (2004, University of Michigan Press). He received his PhD from Temple University.

George B. Stow is professor of ancient and medieval history and director of the graduate program in history at La Salle University, Philadelphia. His teaching experience embraces a variety of undergraduate and graduate courses in ancient Greece and Rome, medieval England, and world history, and he has been awarded the Lindback Distinguished Teaching Award. Professor Stow is a member of the Medieval Academy of America and a Fellow of the Royal Historical Society. He is the recipient of a National Defense Education Act Title IV Fellowship, a Woodrow Wilson Foundation Fellowship, and research grants from the American Philosophical Society and La Salle University. His publications include a critical edition of a fourteenth-century monastic chronicle, *Historia Vitae et Regni Ricardi Secundi* (University of Pennsylvania Press, 1977), as well as numerous articles and reviews in scholarly journals including *Speculum*, *The English Historical Review*, the *Journal of Medieval History*, the *American Historical Review*, and several others. He received his PhD from the University of Illinois.

The Rise of Empires in the Americas

J ust outside Lima lies the shantytown of Túpac Amaru, named after the last Inca ruler, who died in 1572. People fleeing the Maoist Shining Path guerillas southeast of Lima settled here during the 1980s. Archaeologists knew that the site was an ancient burial place called Puruchuco (Quechua "Feathered Helmet") but could not prevent the influx of settlers. By the late 1990s, the temporary shantytown had become an established settlement. However, residents realized that archaeologists had to be consulted before the shantytown could be officially recognized.

During excavations from 1999 to 2001, archaeologists unearthed one of the most astounding treasures in the history of American archaeology. The team discovered some 2,200 mummies, most of them bundled up in blankets and perfectly preserved. Many bundles also contained burial gifts of food and jewelry.

Scholars hope that when all of the mummies have been unwrapped, more will be learned about the social characteristics of the buried people, as so much about the Inca Empire that ruled the Andes from 1438 to 1533 remains unknown.

T he Inca Empire and the Aztec Empire (1427–1521) grew from patterns that began to form around 600 CE in Mesoamerica and the Andes (see Chapter 5). After 600, kingdom formation spread across Mesoamerica

ABOVE: **This kind of knotted string assembly (a quipu) was used in the Andes from ca. 2500 BCE onward for the recording of taxes, population figures, calendar dates, troop numbers, and other data.**

Seeing
Patterns

≫ Within the patterns
of state formation basic
to the Americas, which
types of states emerged
in Mesoamerica and
the Andes during the
period 600–1550? What
characterized these
states?

≫ Why did the Tiwanaku
and Wari states have
ruling classes but no
dynasties and central
bureaucracies? How were
these patterns expressed
in the territorial
organization of these
states?

≫ What patterns of
urban life characterized
the cities of Tenochtitlán
and Cuzco, the capitals
of the Aztec and Inca
Empires? In which ways
were these cities similar
to those of Eurasia and
Africa?

and arose for the first time in the Andes. These kingdoms were states with military ruling classes that could conquer larger territories than was possible prior to the 600s. Military competition prepared the way for the origin of empires. Even though empires arrived later in the Americas than in Eurasia, they demonstrate that humans, once they had adopted agriculture, followed similar patterns of social and political formation across the world.

The Legacy of Teotihuacán and the Toltecs in Mesoamerica

The city-state of Teotihuacán had dominated northern Mesoamerica from 200 BCE to the late 500s CE. After its collapse, the surrounding towns and villages perpetuated the cultural legacy of Teotihuacán. Employing this legacy, the conquering state of the Toltecs unified part of the region from 900 to 1180. At the same time, after an internal crisis, the southern Maya kingdoms on the Yucatán Peninsula reached their late flowering, together with the northern state of Chichén Itzá.

Militarism in the Mexican Basin

After the ruling class of Teotihuacán disintegrated at the end of the sixth century, the newly independent small successor states of Mesoamerica continued Teotihuacán's cultural heritage. The Toltecs, migrants from the north, militarized the Teotihuacán legacy and transformed it into a program of conquest.

Ceremonial Centers and Chiefdoms   In the three centuries after the end of Teotihuacán, the local population declined from some 200,000 to about 30,000. However, other places around the Mexican Basin and beyond rose in importance. The region to the northwest of the valley had an extensive mining industry that produced a variety of gemstones. Independent after 600, inhabitants built small states and traded their gemstones to their neighbors.

To the north were the Pueblo cultures in today's southwestern United States. These cultures, which flourished between 700 and 1500, were based on irrigated farming systems and are known for their painted pottery styles. These cultures might have been in contact with the Mississippi cultures, of which the city of Cahokia (650–1400) near modern St. Louis is the best-known site (see Map 15.1).

To the south, in western Mesoamerica, chiefdoms flourished on the basis of metallurgy (especially copper), which arrived with Ecuadoran seaborne merchants ca. 600–800. Copper, too soft for agricultural implements or military weapons, was used mostly in household objects and as jewelry. A number of small, fortified hilltop states also flourished in the south. More than in other Mesoamerican states, the ruling classes in the west were embroiled in fierce wars during 600–900.

The Toltec Conquering State   Soon after the collapse of Teotihuacán, craftspeople and farmers migrated north to Tula. They founded a ceremonial center and town with workshops known for tools fabricated from the local Pachuca obsidian. Around 900, new migrants arrived from northwest Mexico as well as the Gulf Coast. The northerners spoke Nahuatl [NAH-huaw], the language of the later Aztecs, and after taking possession of Tula, they made it their ancestral city.

The integration of the new arrivals resulted in the abandonment of the temple and the departure of a defeated party of Tulans.

The new Tula of 900 developed quickly into a large city with a new temple. It later became the capital of the conquering state of the Toltecs, whose warrior culture influenced Mesoamerica from around 900 to 1180 (see Map 15.1).

The Toltecs introduced two innovations in weaponry that improved the effectiveness of hand-to-hand combat: a short sword made of hardwood with inlaid obsidian edges could slash as well as crush; and obsidian daggers with wooden handles worn inside a band on the left arm. Traditional dart throwers and slings for stone projectiles completed the offensive armament of the warriors.

The Toltec army was sufficiently large to engage in battles of conquest within 4 days' march from Tula. Any target beyond this range was beyond their capabilities, given the logistics—and, of course, Toltecs did not have the benefit of wheeled vehicles. Thus, the only way of projecting power beyond the 4-day range was to establish colonies and to have troops accompany traders. As a result, the Toltec state projected its power through the prestige of its large military, rather than through an administrative imposition of governors, tributes, and taxes.

Trade   The Toltecs established a large trade network based on Tula's obsidian. Merchants moved southward into the cacao, vanilla, and bird-feather production centers of Chiapas and Guatemala; to the north into gemstone mining regions; and westward into centers of metal mining. Metallurgy advanced around 1200 with the development of the technology of bronze casting. Bronze was preferable to copper for axes and bells; both were prized by the elites in Tula.

The Late Toltec Era   Toltec military power declined in the twelfth century when the taxable grain yield around the city diminished. Sometime around 1180, foraging peoples from the northwest invaded, attacking Toltec communication lines. The disruptions caused an internal revolt, which brought down the ceremonial center and its palaces. By 1200, Mesoamerica relapsed into a period of small-state coexistence.

Late Maya States in Yucatán

Teotihuacán's demise at the end of the sixth century was paralleled by a realignment of the balance of power among the Maya kingdoms in the southern Yucatán lowlands of Mesoamerica. This realignment was resolved by around 650. A period of late flowering spanned the next two centuries, followed by a shift of power from the southern to the northern part of the peninsula.

The Southern Kingdoms   At its height during the fourth and fifth centuries, Teotihuacán had interjected itself into the balance of power among the Maya kingdoms of southern Yucatán. Alliances shifted, and wars racked the lowlands, destroying

Chapter Outline

• The Legacy of Teotihuacán and the Toltecs in Mesoamerica

• The Legacy of Tiwanaku and Wari in the Andes

• American Empires: Aztec and Inca Origins and Dominance

• Imperial Society and Culture

• Putting It All Together

Mayan ceremonial ball game scene, Late Classic Period

interactive timeline

600	600–900	850–1000	1427–1521
End of city-state of Teotihuacán in Mexican Basin	Late Maya kingdoms in Yucatán Peninsula	City-state of Chichén Itzá in northern Yucatán Peninsula	Aztec Empire in Mesoamerica

600–1100	700–1000	900–1170	1438–1533
Conquering state of Tiwanaku in Andes (southern Peru/Bolivia)	Conquering state of Wari in Andes (central Bolivia)	Toltec conquering state, north of Mexican Basin	Inca Empire in Andes

MAP 15.1 **North America and Mesoamerica, ca. 1100.**

North America and
Mesoamerica, ca. 1100 CE

- Pueblo cultures
- Mississippian cultures
- Movement of trade goods north from Mesoamerica
- Sea route from Mesoamerica to Mississippi River valley
- Mayan trade route
- Toltec conquests

Chontal Peoples
UTAH Modern-day state

▷

Mayan city-state
of Palenque

several older states. A dozen new kingdoms emerged and established a new balance of power among themselves. After a lengthy hiatus, Maya culture entered its final period (650–900).

The final period in the southern, rain forest–covered lowlands and adjacent highlands was marked by agricultural expansion and ceremonial monument construction. The rain forest on hillsides was cut down and terraces were built for soil retention. The largest kingdoms grew to 50,000–60,000 inhabitants and reached astounding rural population densities of about 1,000 persons per square mile. Although the late Maya states were geographically small, they were administratively the most centralized polities ever created in indigenous American history.

The late Maya states did not last long. Torrential downpours washed the topsoil from the newly built hillside terraces. Malnutrition resulting from the shrinking agricultural surface began to reduce the labor force. In the end, even the ruling classes suffered, with members killing each other for what remained of agricultural surpluses. By about 900, the Maya kingdoms in southern Yucatán had shriveled.

Chichén Itzá in the North   A few small Maya states on the periphery survived. The most prominent among them was Chichén Itzá [chee-CHEN eet-SAH], which flourished from about 850 to 1000. The region would appear to be inhospitable, as the climate was very dry and the surface was rocky or covered with thin topsoil. There were no rivers, but many sinkholes in the porous limestone underneath the soil held water. Cisterns to hold additional amounts of water for year-round use were cut into the limestone; this water, carried in jars to the surface, supported a productive garden agriculture.

Chichén Itzá was founded during the phase of renewed urbanization in 650. The population was composed of local Maya as well as the Maya-speaking Chontal from the Gulf Coast farther west. Groups among these people engaged in long-distance trade, both overland and in boats along the coast. Since trade in the most lucrative goods required contact with people outside even the farthest political reach of either Teotihuacán or Tula, merchants traveled in armed caravans.

Chontal traders adopted Toltec culture, and in Chichén Itzá around 850 they superimposed their adopted culture over that of the original Maya. At the very end of the period of Teotihuacán, Maya, and Toltec cultural expansion, the three cultures finally merged on the Yucatán Peninsula. This merger did not last long: Already around 1000 the ruling-class factions left the city-state for unknown reasons, and the city-state diminished in size and power.

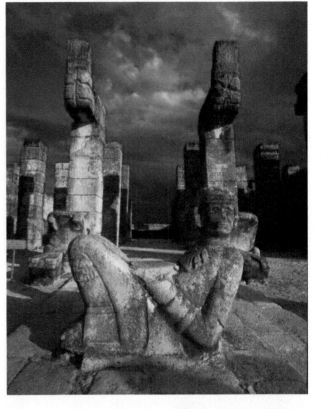

Chacmool (Offering Table) at the Entrance to the Temple of Warriors, Chichén Itzá. Chacmools originated here and spread to numerous places in Mesoamerica, as far north as Tenochtitlán and Tula. Offerings to the gods included food, tobacco, feathers, and incense. Offerings might have included also human sacrifices. The table in the form of a prostrate human figure is in itself symbolic of sacrifice.

The Legacy of Tiwanaku and Wari in the Andes

Mesoamerica and the Andes shared the tradition of regional temple pilgrimages. In the Andes, the chiefdoms remained mostly coastal. Around 600 CE, the two conquering states of Tiwanaku in the highlands of what are today southern Peru and Bolivia and Wari in central Peru emerged. Both states represented a major step in the formation of larger, militarily organized polities.

The Expanding State of Tiwanaku

Tiwanaku was a political and cultural power in the south-central Andes during the period 600–1100. It began as a ceremonial center and developed into a state

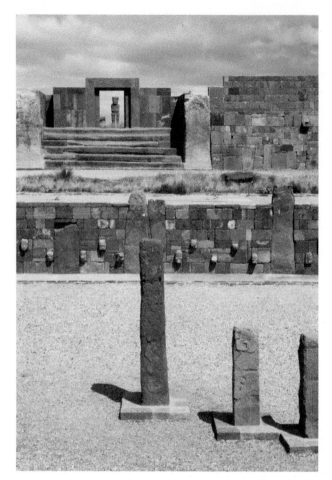

Tiwanaku, Kalassaya Gate. Within the Temple of the Sun, this gate is aligned with the sun's equinoxes and was used for festive rituals. Note the precise stone work, which the Incas later developed further.

dominating the region around Lake Titicaca. At its apogee it planted colonies in regions far from the lake and conveyed its culture through trade to peoples even farther away.

Agriculture on the High Plain The Andes consist of two parallel mountain chains along the west coast of South America. In southeastern Peru and western Bolivia an intermountain plain, 12,500 feet above sea level, extends as wide as 125 miles. At its northern end lies Lake Titicaca, which has one outlet at its southern end, a river flowing into Lake Poopó [po-PO], a salt lake 150 miles south. The Lake Titicaca region receives winter rains sufficient for agriculture and grazing.

The region around Lake Titicaca offered nearly everything necessary for an advanced urbanization process. The lake's freshwater supported fish and resources such as reeds from the swamps, which served for the construction of boats and roofs. The food staples were potatoes and quinoa. The grasslands of the upper hills served as pastures for llama and alpaca herds. Llamas were used as transportation animals, and alpacas provided wool; the meat of both animals was a major protein source.

Farmers grew their crops on hillside terraces or on raised fields close to the lake. The raised-field system, which farmers adopted from peoples of the Maya lowlands, consisted of a grid of narrow strips of earth, separated from each other by channels. Mud from the channels, heaped onto the strips, replenished their fertility. By 700, the city of Tiwanaku had 20,000 inhabitants.

Ceremonial feasts brought together elite lineages and clients, or ordinary craftspeople and villagers. Elites and clients cohered through **reciprocity**—that is, communal labor by clients rewarded by the elites with feasting. Forced labor through conscription or taxation did not appear until shortly before the collapse of the state.

Reciprocity: In its basic form, an informal agreement among people according to which a gift or an invitation has to be returned after a reasonable amount of time; in the pre-Columbian Americas, an arrangement of feasts instead of taxes shared by ruling classes and subjects in a state.

Expansion and Colonization The region around southern Lake Titicaca housed related but competing elite–client hierarchies. Ruling clans and ordinary farmers comprised a state capable of imposing military power beyond the center. Counterbalancing clans at the head of similar hierarchies prevented the rise of permanent, unified central administrations and military forces.

The hallmark of Tiwanaku authority was the prestige of its ceremonial center, rather than military might. Tiwanaku feasting ceremonies could be considered expressions of Tiwanaku authority—and pilgrims who partook in the feasts came into its orbit.

Yet military force did play a role in the western valleys of the Andes. Merchants accompanied by warriors traveled hundreds of miles. Settler colonies were additional forms of power projection, especially those established in the Moquegua [mow-KAY-gah] valley to the west. Here, Tiwanaku emigrants established villages, which

MAP 15.2 **Tiwanaku and Wari, ca. 1000.**

sent some of their corn or beer to the capital in return for salt and obsidian tools. Although overall less militarily inclined than the Mesoamerican states of the same time period, Tiwanaku wielded a visible influence over southern Peru (see Map 15.2).

The Expanding City-State of Wari

Little is known about early settlements in central Peru. The state of Wari emerged around 600, and expansion to the south put Wari into direct contact with Tiwanaku. The two states came to some form of mutual accommodation, and it appears that neither embarked on an outright conquest of the other. Their military postures remained limited to their regional spheres of influence.

Origins and Expansion   Wari was centered on the Ayacucho valley, a narrow plain in the highlands of northern Peru. The land is mountainous, interspersed with valleys and rivers. Farmers grew potatoes, corn and cotton. In the seventh century, Wari grew to 30,000 inhabitants and brought neighboring cities under its control. It also expanded terrace farming. Like Tiwanaku, Wari became the center of a developed urbanism and a diversified agriculture.

In addition to maintaining control over the cities in its vicinity, Wari constructed new towns with plazas, housing for laborers, and halls for feasting. Outside the core area, Wari elites established colonies. It appears that Wari exercised much stronger political control over the chiefs of its core region than Tiwanaku and was more active in founding colonies.

The Wari–Tiwanaku Frontier Wari established a colony upstream in the Moquegua valley with extensive terraces, canals, and protective walls. This building activity coincided with the establishment by Tiwanaku of downstream farming colonies. It is possible that there was tension with Tiwanaku during the initial period (650–800), but during 800–1000 the two agricultural communities developed closer ties. Very likely, the Moquegua valley was politically so far on the periphery of both states that neither had the means to impose itself on the other.

Wari, like Tiwanaku, was an expanding state. Both were governed by elite clans who benefited from reciprocal patron–client organizations. However, there is evidence of increased internal tension after 950 in the two states. Groups defaced sculptures, destroyed portals, and burned down edifices. Scholars have argued that it was perhaps the fragility of power based on an increasingly unequal sharing that caused the rift between elites and subjects.

Why would elites allow reciprocity to be weakened? Some suggest that climatic change made large feasts no longer possible. A more convincing explanation suggests environmental degradation as the result of agricultural expansion. As in the late Maya kingdoms, the exhausted land could perhaps no longer sustain an increasing population. Unfortunately, an ultimate explanation for the disintegration of Tiwanaku and Wari remains elusive.

American Empires: Aztec and Inca Origins and Dominance

States in the Andes and Mesoamerica gave way in the early fifteenth century to empires. As in Eurasia, they were centralized multireligious, multiethnic, and multilinguistic polities: empires in every sense of the word.

The Aztec Empire of Mesoamerica

The ancestors of the Aztecs left Tula and arrived at the Mexican Basin at an unknown time. They eventually conquered the Mexican Basin, the site of today's Mexico City. In the fifteenth century they conquered an empire that encompassed Mesoamerica from the Pacific to the Gulf of Mexico and from the middle of modern northern Mexico to the Isthmus of Panama.

The Founding of
Tenochtitlán

Settlement in the Mexican Valley According to the Aztecs' founding myth, the first Aztec was born on an island in a lake or in a mountain cave northwest of the Mexican Basin. This Aztec ancestor and his descendants migrated south, guided by their hunter–warrior patron god Huitzilpochtli [hoo-it-zil-POSHT-lee] to a land of plenty.

When the ancestors arrived at the Mexican Basin, an eagle perched on a cactus commanded the Aztecs to settle and build a temple to their god. In this temple, they were to sacrifice to the god the blood of humans captured in war.

The historical record in the Mexican Basin becomes clearer in the fourteenth century, during which the Aztecs appeared as clients of two Toltec-descended overlords in city-states on the southwestern shore. Here, they created two islands, founded a city with a ceremonial center and rendered military service to their overlords. Aztec leaders married into the elites of the neighboring city-states and gained the right to have their own ruler presiding over a council of the elite and priests.

The Rise of the Empire   After the successful rebellion in 1428 of a triple alliance among the Aztec city-state and two other vassal states against the reigning city-state in the Mexican Basin, the Aztec leader Itzcóatl [its-CO-aw] (r. 1428–1440) emerged as the dominant figure. Tenochtitlán, the Aztec city on one of the islands, became the capital of an empire that consisted of a set of six "inner provinces" in the Mexican Basin. Local elites were required to attend ceremonies in Tenochtitlán, bring and receive gifts, leave their sons as hostages, and intermarry with the elites of the triple alliance. Farmers had to provide tribute, making the imperial core self-sufficient.

After further conquests by the middle of the fifteenth century, the triple alliance created an imperial polity from the Pacific to the Gulf (see Map 15.3). This state was more centralized than the Teotihuacán and Toltec city-states. In this empire, local ruling families were generally left in place, but commoners had to produce tributes of goods and materials.

In some provinces, Aztec governors replaced the rulers; in others, Aztec tribute collectors (supported by troops) held local rulers in check and supervised the transportation of the tributes. Although reciprocity continued, it was now clearly subordinate to military considerations.

The resulting multiethnic, multireligious, and multilinguistic empire was still developing in the early sixteenth century when the Spanish arrived. The state of Tlaxcala [tlash-KAH-lah], held out in opposition, together with enemy states on the periphery. Although the triple alliance did everything to expand, pockets of anti-Aztec states survived and eventually became allies of the Spanish.

The key policy of continued expansion of Aztec central control was the threat of warfare. This fear-inducing tactic was an integral innovation in the imperialism of the Aztecs.

The Military Forces   The triple alliance ruled 1.5 million inhabitants in the Mexican Basin. This number yielded up to a quarter of a million potential soldiers. Initially, the army was recruited from among the elite of the Aztecs and their allies. But toward the middle of the fifteenth century, Aztec rulers set up separate military school systems for the sons of the elite and the commoners. After graduation, soldiers rose in the army hierarchy on the basis of merit, particularly their success in the capture of enemies for future sacrifice.

The Aztecs inherited the weaponry and armor of the Toltecs, and they also made innovations, including the bow and arrow, which arrived from northwest Mexico at the end of Toltec rule, and the obsidian-spiked broadsword, derived from the Toltec short sword. Clubs, maces, and axes declined in importance in the Aztec arsenal. Body armor, consisting of quilted, sleeveless cotton shirts, thick

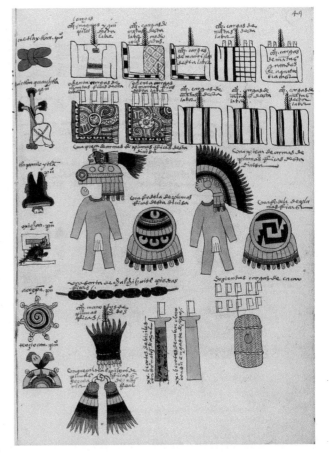

List of Tributes Owed to the Aztecs. The list includes quantities of cotton and wool textiles, clothes, headgear with feathers, and basketry. The Aztecs did not continue the complex syllabic script of the Maya, but used instead images, including persons with speech bubbles, for communication. Spanish administrators and monks who copied the Aztec manuscripts added their own explanations to keep track of Native American tributes.

image analysis

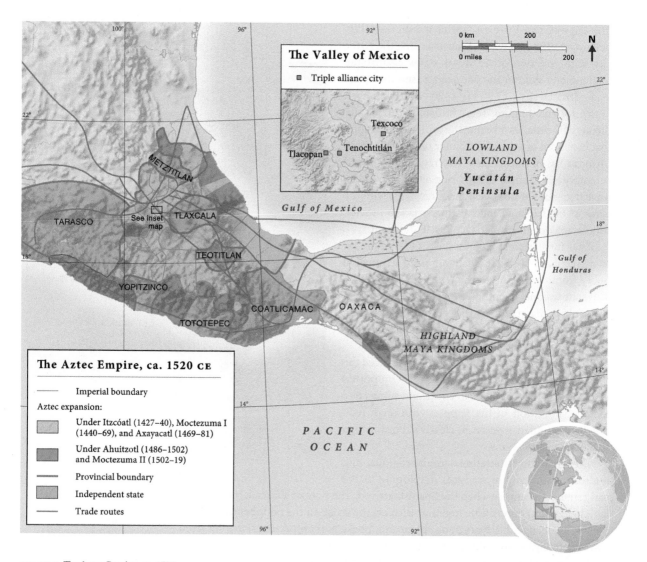

MAP 15.3 **The Aztec Empire, ca. 1520.**

cotton helmets, and round wooden or cane shields, was adopted from the Toltecs. With the arrival of the Aztecs, the Americas had acquired the heaviest infantry weaponry in their history.

The Inca Empire of the Andes

After the disintegration of Tiwanaku and Wari around 1100, the central Andes returned to local chiefdoms in small city-states with ceremonial centers and agricultural hinterlands. Tiwanaku cultural traditions, however, remained dominant.

The southern Peruvian city-state of Cuzco, with its Inca elite, emerged in the early fifteenth century at the head of a militaristic conquering polity. Within another century, the Incas had established an empire, called Tawantinsuyu [ta-wan-tin-SOO-yuh] (Quechua "Four Regions"), symbolizing its geographical expanse. It stretched from Ecuador in the north to central Chile in the south, with extensions into the upper Amazon and western Argentina (see Map 15.4).

The Incas, like the Aztecs, have a founding myth. In one version, the creator god Viracocha [vee-rah-KO-chah] summoned four brothers and four sisters, pairing them as couples and promising them a land of plenty. They would find this land when a golden rod would get stuck in the soil. Alternatively, the sun god Inti [IN-tee] did the pairing of the couples before sending them with the golden rod to their promised land. In Cuzco, where the rod plunged into fertile soil, the Incas drove out the existing farmers.

In the fourteenth century, Cuzco became a serious contender in the city-state competition. Eight rulers are said to have succeeded each other in the consolidation of Cuzco as a regional power, although little is known about them. Firm historical terrain is reached with the ninth ruler, Pachacuti (r. 1438–1471). The history of the Incas from 1438 onward is known much better, primarily because of the records of the Spanish conquerors.

Aztec Weapons. Aztec weapons were well-crafted hardwood implements with serrated obsidian edges, capable of cutting through metal, including iron. As slashing weapons they were highly effective in close combat.

Imperial Expansion   The system of reciprocity that characterized earlier Mesoamerican and Andean history continued under the Incas. *Ayllu* [AY-yoo], the Quechua term for a household with an ancestral lineage, implied mutual obligations among groups of households, neighborhoods, villages, and city-states. The most important social expression of reciprocity remained the feast. In the Incan Empire, the state collected more from the *ayllus* than Tiwanaku and Wari had done, but whether it returned comparable amounts through feasts and celebrations was a matter of contention, often leading to armed rebellion.

The earliest conquests under Pachacuti were around Lake Titicaca, as well as the north of the former Wari state. The Incas then expanded 1,300 miles northward to southern Ecuador and 1,500 miles southward to Chile. The final provinces, added in the early sixteenth century, were in northern Ecuador as well as on the eastern slopes of the Andes. The capital, Cuzco, with some 100,000 inhabitants in the early sixteenth century, was laid out in a grid of four streets. Symbolically, the capital reached out to the four regions of the empire—coast, north, south, and Amazon rain forest.

Administration   Ethnic Inca governors administered the four regions, which were subdivided into provinces, each with an Inca subgovernor. Most provinces were composites of former city-states, which remained under their local elites. A system of population organization was imposed by the Inca rulers. According to this system, members of the local elites commanded 10,000, 1,000, 100, and 10 household heads for the *mit'a* [MIT-ah] ("to take a turn," in reference to service obligations rotating among the subjects). The services were owed by subjects to the empire as a form of taxes.

The ***mit'a*** was an important innovation the Incas contributed to the history of the Americas. In contrast to the Aztecs, who shipped taxes in kind to their capital by boat, the Incas had no efficient means of transportation for long distances. The only way to make use of the taxes in kind was to store them locally. The Incas built storehouses and required subjects to deliver a portion of their goods and harvests under *mit'a* obligations to the nearest storehouse. These supplies enabled the Incas to conduct military campaigns far from Cuzco. In addition, it was through the *mit'a* that

Mit'a: Innovation of the Incas in which subjects were obligated to deliver a portion of their harvests, animal products, and domestically produced goods to nearby storehouses for use by Inca officials and troops. The *mit'a* also provided laborers for construction projects as well workers on state farms or mines.

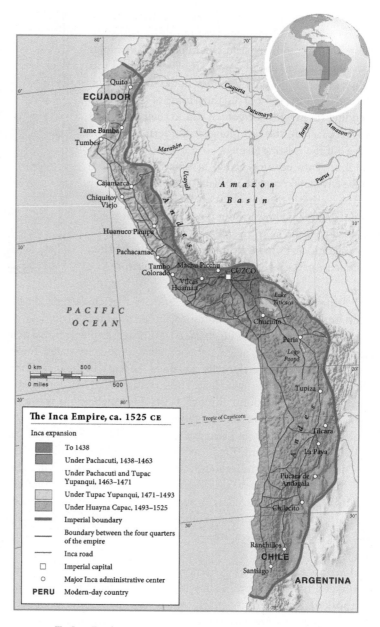

MAP **15.4** **The Inca Empire, ca. 1525.**

map analysis

laborers were assembled for construction projects, often far from the urban center. Finally, *mit'a* provided laborers for mines, quarries, farms, and colonies.

To keep track of *mit'a* obligations, officials used bundles of knotted cord (**quipu**, or *khipu* [KEE-poo], "knot"). The numbers of knots on each cord in the bundles contained information on population figures and service obligations. The use of *quipus* was widespread in the Andes long before the Inca. Although some 700 have been preserved, attempts to decipher them have so far failed.

Military Organization   Under the *mit'a* system of the Inca empire, men were required to serve in the military. As in the Aztec Empire, administrators made sure that

Quipu: Knotted string assembly, used in the Andes from ca. 2500 BCE onward for the recording of taxes, population figures, calendar dates, troop numbers, and other data.

Inca Roads. Inca roads were paths reserved for runners and the military. They were built on beds of rocks and rubble and connected strategic points in the most direct line possible.

enough laborers remained in the villages to take care of their other obligations of farming, herding, transporting, and manufacturing. Intermediate commanders came from the local and regional elites, and the top commanders were members of the two upper and lower Inca ruling elites.

Inca weaponry was comparable to that of the Aztecs, consisting of bows and arrows, dart throwers, slings, clubs with spiked bronze heads, wooden broadswords, bronze axes, and bronze-tipped javelins. The Incas also used a snare to entangle the enemy's legs. Protective armor consisted of quilted cotton shirts, copper breastplates, cane helmets, and shields.

During the second half of the fifteenth century, the Incas turned from conquest to consolidation. Faced with rebellions, they deemphasized the draft and recruited longer-serving troops from a smaller number of trusted peoples. These troops garrisoned forts throughout the empire and were part of the settler colonies in rebellious provinces and border regions. Personal guards recruited from non-Inca populations accompanied leading ruling-class members. The professionalization of the Inca army, however, lagged behind that of the Aztecs, since the Incas did not have military academies open to their subjects.

Communications   The Incas created an excellent imperial communication and logistics structure. They improved on the road network that they inherited from Tiwanaku, Wari, and other states. Roads extended from Cuzco nearly the entire length of the empire. The roads often required extensive grounding, paving, staircasing, and tunneling. In many places, the 25,000-mile road network still exists today.

The roads were reserved for troops, officials, and runners carrying messages. For their convenience, every 15 miles, or at the end of a slow 1-day journey, an inn provided accommodation. Larger armies stopped at barracks or pitched tents. Despite the fact that they did not have wheeled transport, the Incas were aware of how crucial paved and well-supplied roads were for infantry soldiers.

Imperial Society and Culture

As Mesoamerica and the Andes entered their imperial age, cosmopolitan capitals with monumental ceremonial centers and palaces emerged. Ceremonies and rituals impressed on enemies and subjects alike the irresistible might of the empires.

Imperial Capitals: Tenochtitlán and Cuzco

In the fifteenth century, the Aztec and Inca capitals were among the largest cities of the world, encompassing between 100,000 and 200,000 inhabitants. Although their monumental architecture followed different artistic traditions, both emphasized platforms and sanctuaries atop large pyramid-like structures as symbols of elevated power as well as closeness to the gods.

Tenochtitlán as an Urban Metropolis   More than half of the approximately 1.5 million people living during the fifteenth century in the Mexican Basin were urban dwellers. Such an extraordinary concentration of urban citizens was unique in the agrarian world prior to the industrialization of Europe, when cities usually held no more than 10 percent of the total population (see Map 15.5).

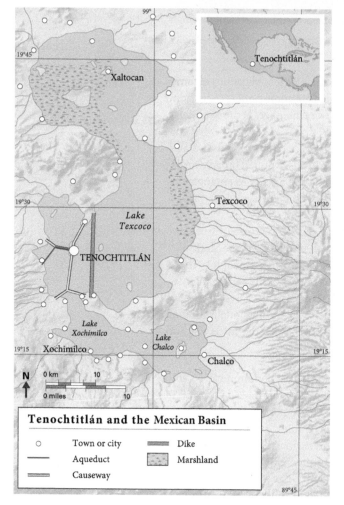

The center of Tenochtitlán, on the southern island, was a large platform. In an enclosure on this platform were the main pyramid, with temples to the Aztec gods on top, and smaller ceremonial centers. Also on the platform were a food market, palaces of the ruling elite, courts of law, workshops, a prison, and councils for teachers and the military. Aztecs and visitors assembled each day to pay respect to the ruler and to trade in the market.

In 1473, the southern island was merged with the northern island. At the center of the northern island was the principal market of the combined islands, which attracted as many as 40,000 people each day. The sophistication of the market was comparable to that of any market in Eurasia during the fifteenth century.

Causeways linked the capital with the lakeshore, and people traveled inside the city on a system of canals. Dikes with sluices regulated both the water level and the salinity of the lake. Potable water arrived from the shore via an aqueduct on one of the western causeways. Professional water carriers took fresh water from the aqueduct to commoners in the city; professional waste removers collected human waste from urban residences and took it to farmers for fertilizer.

The two city centers—the pyramid and palaces in the south and the market in the north—were surrounded by residential

MAP 15.5 Tenochtitlán and the Mexican Basin.

quarters, many of which were inhabited by craftspeople of a shared profession. The rooms of the houses surrounded a central patio—an architectural preference common to Meso-america and the Andes, as well as the Middle East and Mediterranean.

Residents of quarters farther away from the center were farmers. Here, a grid of canals encased small, rectangular islands devoted to housing compounds and/or farming. A raised-field system prevailed, whereby farmers dredged the canals and heaped the fertile mud on top of the rectangular islands, called *chinampas*. In contrast to the luxurious palaces of the elite, housing for farmers consisted of humble plastered huts. As in all agrarian societies, farmers—subject to high taxes or rents—were among the poorest folk.

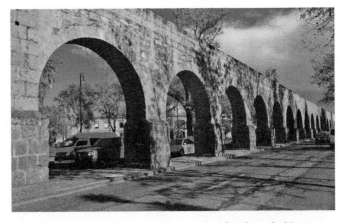

Aqueduct from the Western Hills to Tenochtitlán. This aqueduct, still standing today, provided fresh water to the palace and mansions of the center of the island, to be used as drinking water and for washing.

On the surface of the *chinampas*, farmers grew seed plants as well as *maguey* [mag-AY], a large succulent agave. This evergreen plant has a large root system, which stabilizes the ground, and produces fiber for weaving and pulp for making *pulque* [POOL-kay], a fermented drink.

Ownership of the *chinampas* was vested in clans, which, under neighborhood leaders, were responsible for the allocation of land and adjudication of disputes as well as the payment of taxes in kind to the elite. There were also members of the elite who possessed estates and employed managers to collect rents from the farmers. Whether there was a trend from taxes to rents is unknown.

Chinampas: Small, artificial islands in Lake Texcoco created by farmers for raising agricultural crops.

Cuzco as a Ceremonial-Administrative City   The site of the Inca city of Cuzco was a triangle formed by the confluence of two rivers. At one end was a hill on which were built the imperial armory and a temple dedicated to the sun god. Enormous stone walls followed the contours of the hill.

Below, the city was laid out in a grid pattern. The residents of the city, all belonging to the Inca ruling class, lived in adobe houses arranged in a block-and-courtyard pattern similar to that of Wari. Squares and temples served as ceremonial centers. The Coricancha [co-ri-CAN-tsha], the city's main temple, stood near the confluence of the rivers. This temple was a walled compound set around a courtyard. Each year priests of the empire's ceremonial centers sent a sacred object to the Coricancha, to demonstrate their obedience to the central Inca temple.

Across the rivers were settlements for commoners with markets and store-houses. In the fields, interspersed stone pillars and shrines were aligned on sight lines radiating from the Coricancha, tying the countryside closely to the urban center. Farther away were imperial estates with unfree laborers from outside the *mit'a* system. In contrast to the Aztec elite, which allowed meritorious generals to rise in the hierarchy, the Inca elite remained exclusionary, allowing no commoners to reside in Cuzco.

Power and Its Cultural Expressions

Ruling elites emphasized the display of power during the period 600–1500. This was particularly true with the Aztecs and Incas during the fifteenth century.

Human Sacrifice and Propaganda

In the first millennium CE, Mesoamerica and the Andes evolved from their early re-ligious spirituality to polytheism. The spiritual heritage, however, remained a strong undercurrent, as seen in human as well as animal and agricultural sacrifices. Rulers appeased the gods also through self-sacrifice—that is, the piercing of tongue and penis. The feathered serpent god Quetzalcóatl was the Mesoamerican deity of self-sacrifice, revered in the city-states of Teotihuacán (200 BCE–570 CE) and Tula (ca. 900 CE). Under the Toltecs and the Aztecs, this god receded, in favor of warrior gods such as Tezcatlipoca and Huitzilpochtli. The survival of traditional blood ritu-als within polytheism was a pattern that distinguished the early American empires from their Eurasian counterparts.

Whether human sacrifices were prolific under Aztec and Inca imperialism is questionable. Archaeological evidence does not support the impression created by

Human Sacrifice. Human sacrifice among the pre-Columbian Mesoamericans and Andeans was based on the concept of a shared life spirit or mind, symbolized by the life substance of blood. In the American spiritual-polytheistic conceptualization, the gods sacrificed their blood, or themselves altogether, during creation; rulers pierced their earlobes, tongues, or penises for blood sacrifices; and war captives lost their lives when their hearts were sacrificed.

Inca Ruling-Class Gender Relations The greatest honor for Inca girls in Cuzco and provincial colonies was to enter at age 10–12 into the service of a "House of Chosen Women." An inspector from Cuzco visited villages to select attractive young girls for the service. These houses had female instructors who provided the girls with an education in cooking, beer making, weaving, and officiating in the cere-monies of the Inca religion. After their graduation, the young women became virgin temple priestesses, were given in marriage to non-Incas honored for service to the rule, or became servants or concubines of the Inca elite. The collection of this girl tribute was separate from the reciprocity system.

The form of agriculture in Mesoamerica and the Andes gave males fewer op-portunities to accumulate wealth and power than plow agriculture did in Eurasia. Nevertheless, the gradual agrarian–urban diversification of society, even if it was slower in the Americas than in Eurasia, proceeded along similar paths of increasing male power concentration. An emphasis on gender differences, therefore, should be viewed as a characteristic phenomenon arising in imperial contexts.

Inca Mummy Veneration Other houses in Cuzco were ghostly residences in which servants catered to the needs of deceased, mummified Inca emperors and their principal wives. During the mummification process, attendants removed the ca-daver's internal organs, placed them in special containers, and desiccated the bodies until they were completely mummified. Servants dressed the mummies in their finest clothing and placed them back into their residences amid their possessions, as if they had never died. The mummies received daily meals and were carried around by their retinues for visits to their mummified relatives. On special occasions, mummies were lined up according to rank on Cuzco's main plaza to participate in ceremonies and processions. In this way, they remained fully integrated in the daily life of the elite.

the Spanish conquerors and encourages doubts about the magnitude of human sacrifices in temple ceremonies.

Could it be that there was no significant increase in human sacrifice under the Aztecs and Incas, as the self-serving Spanish conquerors alleged? Were there perhaps, instead, imperial propaganda machines in the Aztec and Inca Empires, employed in the service of conquest and consolidation who sought to intimidate their enemies? If the answer to these questions is yes, the Aztec and Inca Empires would be but two typical examples of the general world-historical pattern of competitive militaristic states during the early agrarian era using propaganda to further their imperial power.

Questions

- In examining the question of whether empires such as the Inca and the Aztec employed human sacrifice for propaganda purposes, can this practice be considered an adaptation that evolved out of earlier rituals, such as royal bloodletting?

- If the Aztec and the Inca did indeed employ human sacrifice for propaganda purposes, what does this say about the ability of these two empires to use cultural and religious practices to consolidate their power?

In Andean society, mummies were a crucial ingredient in the religious heritage, in which strong spiritual elements survived underneath the polytheistic overlay of astral gods. In the spiritual tradition, a dead person's spirit, while no longer in the body, remains nearby and needs daily nourishment in order not to be driven away. Hence, even though non-Incan Andean societies removed the dead from their daily living spaces, descendants had to visit tombs regularly with food and beer.

The expenses for the upkeep of the mummy households were the responsibility of the deceased emperor's bloodline, headed by a surviving brother. As heirs of the emperor's estate, the members of the bloodline formed a powerful clan within the ruling class. The new emperor was excluded from this estate and had to acquire his own new one in the course of his rule. In the early sixteenth century, however, this mechanism of keeping the upper and lower rungs of the ruling class united became counterproductive. Emperors lacking resources had to contend with brothers richly endowed with inherited wealth and ready to engage in dynastic warfare—as actually occurred shortly before the arrival of the Spanish (1529–1532).

>> Putting It All Together

The Aztec and Inca Empires unleashed extraordinary creative energies. Sculptors, painters, and (after the arrival of the Spanish) writers recorded the traditions as well as the innovations of the fifteenth century. Aztec painters produced codices, or illustrated manuscripts, that present the cultural and administrative activities of their societies in exquisite detail. Today, a handful of these codices survive, preserved in Mexican and European libraries.

interactive concept map

The Aztec and Inca Empires were polities that illustrate how humans not in contact with the rest of the world developed patterns of innovation that were remarkably similar. On the basis of an agriculture that produced ample surpluses, humans made the same choices as their cousins in Eurasia and Africa. Specifically, in the period 600–1500, they created temple-centered city-states, just like their Sumerian and Hindu counterparts. Their military states were not unlike the Chinese warring states. And, finally, their empires were comparable to those of the New Kingdom Egyptians or the Assyrians. The Americas had their own unique variations of these larger historical patterns, but they nevertheless displayed the same humanity as found elsewhere.

Review and Relate

> Within the patterns of state formation basic to the Americas, which types of states emerged in Mesoamerica and the Andes during the period 600–1550? What characterized these states?

> Why did the Tiwanaku and Wari states have ruling classes but no dynasties and central bureaucracies? How were these patterns expressed in the territorial organization of these states?

> What patterns of urban life characterized the cities of Tenochtitlán and Cuzco, the capitals of the Aztec and Inca Empires? In which ways were these cities similar to those of Eurasia and Africa?

Thinking Through Patterns

Examine the ways historians approach the big questions of this chapter.

The basic pattern of state formation in the Americas was similar to that of Eurasia and Africa. Historically, it began with the transition from foraging to agriculture and settled village life. As the population increased, villages became chiefdoms, which in turn became city-states. American city-states often became conquering states, beginning with the Maya kingdoms and Teotihuacán. Military states in which ruling classes sought to expand territories, such as Tula and Tiwanaku and Wari, were characteristic of the early part of the period 600–1550. Their successors—the Aztec and Inca Empires—were multiethnic, multilinguistic, and multireligious polities that dominated Mesoamerica and the Andes before the Spanish conquest brought them to a premature end.

The states of Tiwanaku and Wari had cohesive ruling classes but no dynasties or centralized bureaucracies. These ruling classes and their subjects were integrated through systems of reciprocity. Over time, tensions arose, either between stronger and weaker branches of the ruling classes or between rulers and subjects over questions of obligations and justice. When these tensions erupted into internal warfare, the states disintegrated, often in conjunction with environmental degradation and climate change.

Tenochtitlán and Cuzco, the capitals of the Aztec and Inca Empires, were urban centers organized around temples and associated residences of the ruling dynasties and their priestly classes. They also contained quarters inhabited by craftspeople, and large central markets. Armed caravans of merchants and porters transported luxury goods across hundreds of miles. Tenochtitlán had an aqueduct for the supply of drinking water, and Cuzco was traversed by a river. Both capitals had agricultural suburbs in which farmers used irrigation for their crops.

Against the Grain

Consider this as a counterpoint to the main patterns examined in this chapter.

Amazon Rain Forest Civilizations

For years, scholarly opinion held that the Amazonian river basin, covered by rain forest, was too inhospitable to allow for more than small numbers of widely dispersed foragers. Even farmers, living in populated villages, could not possibly have founded complex societies. Slash-and-burn agriculture prevented the advance of urban life: After exhausting the soil, whole villages had to pack up and move.

However, scholars now realize that this belief was erroneous. Modern farmers, encroaching on the rain forest, noticed two hitherto neglected features. First, these farmers found in stretches of forest and savanna a black soil so fertile that it did not require fertilizers. Second, as they slashed and burned the rain forest and savanna with their modern tools, the farmers exposed monumental earthworks that had previously escaped attention. The two features were connected. *The black soil* was the result of centuries of soil enrichment by indigenous people who also built the earthworks. Instead of slashing and burning, these people had engaged in "slashing and charring"—that is, turning the trees into nutrient-rich charcoal rather than quickly depleted ash.

Scholars have now documented large-scale settlements in areas along the southern tributaries to the Amazon. In the Purus region, for example, researchers employing aerial photography revealed a huge area home to perhaps 60,000 inhabitants during a period around the late thirteenth century. This area is adjacent to the farthest northeastern extension of the Inca Empire into the Amazon. Thus, when the Incas expanded into the rain forest, they clearly did so to incorporate advanced societies into their empire. Thanks to scholars who challenged the orthodoxy of the "empty rain forest," we are rediscovering the Amazonian past.

- Which is more important: to save the rain forest or uncover its archaeological past? Can the two objectives be combined?
- Compare the Amazonian earthworks to those of Benin in Africa during the same period (Chapter 14). Which similarities and differences can you discover?

Key Terms

Chinampas 351	*Quipu* 348
Mit'a 347	Reciprocity 342

🔊))

audio flashcards

For additional resources, please go to
www.oup.com/us/vonsivers.
Please see the Further Resources section at the back of the book for additional readings and suggested websites.

PART FOUR

Interactions across the Globe

1450–1750

A round 1450, important changes occured in the patterns of world history. While religious civilizations continued to evolve, the competing states that constituted these civilizations began to give way to new empires. Smaller European countries were creating the first global seaborne empires. The new empires reorganized themselves as centralized polities based on money economies, large bureaucracies, and professional armies possessed of firearms. Competing for resources, markets, and ideological influence, they interacted with each other with increasing intensity.

Two new phenomena appeared between 1450 and 1750 that would have far-reaching implications: the New Sciences (or Scientific Revolution) and the Enlightenment. Attempts to found an understanding of the universe on mathematics and experimentation would lead to science as the chief mode of interpreting the physical realm. Attempts to apply principles of science to understanding human societies would lead to the concepts of individual rights, natural law, and popular sovereignty. The combination of these two trends created the foundations of the *scientific–industrial society* that dominates contemporary global culture.

The process by which this formation of *scientific–industrial society* took place was extremely complex, and it is impossible for us to do more than suggest some of the larger patterns of it here. Moreover, because of the long-standing argument

1440–1897 Benin kingdom, West Africa	**1492** Spanish conquest of Granada, expulsion of Jews, and discovery of the Americas	**ca. 1500** Beginning of Columbian Exchange	**1514** Nicolaus Copernicus formulates the heliocentric model
1453 Ottoman capture of Constantinople	**1498** Vasco da Gama's circumnavigation of Africa and journey to India	**1511** First African slaves taken to Caribbean	**1517** Martin Luther publishes his 95 theses; beginning of Protestant Reformation

in Western historiography for European exceptionalism, we must be careful to explore this process without easy assumptions about their inevitability. For example, one question is "To what extent did the societies of western Europe (what we have termed the 'religious civilization' of Western Christianity) part ways with the other religious civilizations of the world?" Aspects of the question have recently been the subject of debate:

- On one hand, there appears to have been no movement comparable to that of the European Renaissance or Reformation arising during this time in the other parts of the world to create a new culture similar to that of Europe. The Middle East, India, and China for the most part continued ongoing cultural patterns, although often on considerably higher levels of refinement and sophistication.

- On the other hand, Europe, like much of the rest of the world, remained rooted in agrarian–urban patterns until the effects of the Industrial Revolution began to be felt sometime after 1800. Furthermore, through nearly this entire period, China and India were more populous and at least as wealthy and diversified in their economies and social structures as their European counterparts. Nonetheless, the overall wealth of European countries involved in the conquest and exploitation of the resources of the Americas and the development of global trading systems advanced immensely. Thus, while India and China had possessed these resources for a long time, European countries were now utilizing them at an accelerating rate. This wealth and the patterns of its acquisition and distribution would eventually have far-reaching consequences.

For the great majority of people, even in 1750, much seemed to go on as before. Everywhere in the world empires continued to grow and decline, religious tensions continued to erupt into warfare, and rulers continued to ground their authority not in their peoples but in the divine. Thus, for a full understanding of world history during 1450–1750, one has to keep in mind that although change was certainly occurring, it was often too imperceptible for contemporaries to detect.

Thinking Like a World Historian

≫ What new and different patterns characterized the development of states and empires in the period 1450–1750?

≫ How did the emergence of centralizing states lead to more intensive and frequent interactions among empires in the period 1450–1750?

≫ How did the New Sciences and the Enlightenment lay the foundation for the scientific–industrial society that dominates our global culture today?

≫ To what extent did the societies of western Europe diverge from other civilizations in the period 1450–1750? Why is the notion of "exceptionalism" problematic in examining this question?

interactive timeline

1521, 1533
Spanish conquest of the Aztec and Inca Empires

1577
Matteo Ricci, first Jesuit missionary to arrive in China

1607
Founding of Jamestown, Virginia

1720
Edo, capital of Japan, world's largest city

1542–1605
Akbar, the most innovative of the Mughal rulers (India)

1604
Galileo Galilei formulates the mathematical law of falling bodies

1687
Isaac Newton unifies physics and astronomy

1736–1795
Reign of Qianlong emperor, China

>> Chapter 16 1450–1650

Western European Overseas Expansion and the Ottoman–Habsburg Struggle

A l-Hasan Ibn Muhammad al-Wazzan (ca. 1494–1550) was born in Muslim Granada soon after the Christian conquest of this kingdom in southern Iberia in 1492. Unwilling to convert to Christianity, Hasan's family emigrated to Muslim Morocco around 1499–1500. Here, Hasan received a good education and entered the administration of the Moroccan sultan, traveling to sub-Saharan Africa and the Middle East on diplomatic missions.

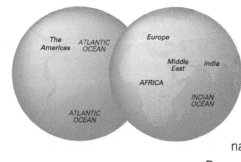

In 1517, as he was returning home from a mission to Istanbul, Christian **corsairs** kidnapped him. Like their Muslim counterparts, these corsairs roamed the Mediterranean to capture travelers, whom they then held for ransom or sold into slavery. For a handsome sum of money, they turned Hasan over to Pope Leo X (1513–1521), who ordered Hasan to convert to Christianity and baptized him with his own family name, Giovanni Leone di Medici. Hasan became known in Rome as Leo Africanus ("Leo the African"). He stayed for 10 years

ABOVE: This 1630 map by João Teixeira Albernaz the Elder (late 1500s–ca. 1662), member of a prominent family of Portuguese map makers, shows Arabia, India, and China.

in Italy, initially at the papal court and later as a scholar in Rome. During this time, he taught Arabic to Roman clergymen and compiled an Arabic–Hebrew–Latin dictionary. His most enduring work was a travelogue, *Description of Africa*, which was for years the sole source of information about sub-Saharan Africa in the Western Christian world.

In 1527 Charles V (r. 1516–1558), king of Spain and emperor of the Holy Roman Empire of Germany, invaded Italy and sacked Rome. Hasan survived but departed for Tunis sometime after 1531, seeking a better life in Muslim North Africa. Unfortunately, all traces of Hasan after his departure from Rome are lost. It is possible that he perished in 1535 when Charles V attacked and occupied Tunis (1535–1574), although it is generally assumed that he lived there until around 1550.

The world in which Hasan lived was a Muslim–Christian world composed of the Middle East, North Africa, and Europe. Although Muslims and Christians traveled with relative freedom in much of this world, the two religious civilizations were locked in a pattern of fierce competition. During 800–1050, the Muslims justified their conquests as holy wars (*jihads*), and during 1050–1300 the Christians retaliated with their Crusades and the reconquest (*Reconquista*) of Iberia.

By the fifteenth century, the Christians sought to rebuild the crusader kingdom of Jerusalem, which had been lost to the Muslims in 1291. Searching for a route that would take them around Africa, they hoped to defeat the Muslims in Jerusalem with an attack from the east. In the process, the Christians discovered the Americas. For their part, the Muslims sought to conquer eastern and central Europe while defending North Africa and driving the Portuguese out of the Indian Ocean. After a hiatus of several centuries, imperial polities reemerged in the form of the Ottoman and Habsburg Empires.

The Muslim–Christian Competition in the East and West, 1450–1600

In the second half of the fifteenth century the Christian kings resumed the *Reconquista* of Iberia. During the same period, the small principality of the Ottomans took advantage of Mongol and Byzantine weakness to conquer lands in both Anatolia and the Balkans. After the Muslim conquest of Constantinople in 1453 and the Western Christian conquest of Granada in 1492, the Ottoman and Habsburg Empires emerged.

Iberian Christian Expansion, 1415–1498

Portugal resumed its *Reconquista* policies by expanding to North Africa in 1415. Looking to circumnavigate the Muslims, collect West African gold, and reach the Indian spice coast, the Portuguese established fortified harbors along the African

Seeing Patterns

≫ What patterns characterized Christian and Muslim competition in the period 1300–1600? Which elements distinguished them from each other, and which elements were similar? How did the pattern change over time?

≫ How did centralizing states in the Middle East and Europe function in the period 1450–1600? How did economics, military power, and imperial objectives interact to create the centralizing state?

≫ Which patterns did cultural expressions follow in the Habsburg and Ottoman Empires? Why did the ruling classes of these empires sponsor these expressions?

Corsairs: In the context of this chapter, Muslim or Christian pirates who boarded ships, confiscated the cargoes, and held the crews and travelers for ransom; they were nominally under the authority of the Ottoman sultan or the pope in Rome, but operated independently.

Chapter Outline

• The Muslim–Christian Competition in the East and West, 1450–1600

• The Centralizing State: Origins and Interactions

• Imperial Courts, Urban Festivities, and the Arts

• Putting It All Together

map of the known world by Martellus, ca. 1489

Military orders: Ever since the early 1100s, the papacy encouraged the formation of monastic fighting orders, such as the Hospitalers and Templars, to combat the Muslims in the crusader kingdom of Jerusalem; similar *Reconquista* orders, such as the Order of Santiago and the Order of Christ, emerged in Iberia to eliminate Muslim rule.

Apocalypse: In Greek, "revelation"—that is, the unveiling of events at the end of history, before God's judgment; during the 1400s, expectation of the imminence of Christ's Second Coming, with precursors paving the way.

coastline. Castile and Aragon conquered Granada in 1492, occupied ports in North Africa, and sent Columbus to discover an alternate route to India. Columbus's discovery of America, instead, delivered the prospect of a new continent to the rulers of Castile and Aragon (see Map 16.1).

Maritime Explorations   In 1277–1281, mariners of the Italian city-state of Genoa pioneered commerce by sea between the Mediterranean and northwestern Europe. In Lisbon, Portuguese shipwrights and their Genoese teachers developed ships suited for Atlantic seas. In the early fifteenth century they developed the *caravel*, a ship with upward-extending fore and aft sides, a stern rudder, and square as well as triangular lateen sails. The Portuguese became important traders between England and the Mediterranean countries.

The sea trade stimulated an exploration of the eastern Atlantic. By the early fifteenth century, the Portuguese had discovered the Azores and Madeira, while the Castilians began a conquest of the Canary Islands. Here, the indigenous inhabitants, the Guanches, put up a fierce resistance. But settlers carved out colonies on conquered parcels of land, enslaving the Guanches to work in sugarcane plantations. They thus introduced the sugarcane plantation system from the eastern Mediterranean, where it had Byzantine and Crusader roots on the island of Cyprus, to the Atlantic.

Apocalyptic Expectations   The loss of the crusader kingdom in Palestine to the Muslim Mamluks in 1291 stirred deep feelings of guilt among Western Christians. Efforts to reconquer Jerusalem failed, however, because rulers in Europe were warring against each other for territorial gain. The failure did not dampen spiritual revivals, however, especially in the Franciscan and **military orders** of Iberia. These monks, often well connected with the Iberian royal courts, were believers in apocalypse— that is, the imminent end of the world and the Second Coming of Christ.

According to the **Apocalypse**, Christ's return could happen only in Jerusalem. This made it urgent for the Christians to reconquer the city. Christians as well as Muslims saw no contradiction between religion and military conquest. A providential God, so they believed, justified the conquest of lands and the enslavement of the conquered. The religious justification of military action, therefore, was a declaration by believers that God was on their side to help them convert and conquer.

In Portugal, political claims in the guise of apocalyptic expectations guided the military orders in "reconquering" Ceuta, a northern port city of the Moroccan sultans. Accordingly, a fleet under Henry the Navigator (1394–1460) took Ceuta in 1415, capturing a stock of West African gold. Henry, a brother of the ruling Portuguese king, was searching for the West African source of Muslim gold. By the middle of the fifteenth century, Portuguese mariners had reached the "gold coast" of West Africa, where local rulers imported gold from the interior Akan fields.

Reforms in Castile   The Portuguese renewal of the *Reconquista* stimulated a similar revival in Castile, which occurred after the dynastic union of Castile and Aragon–Catalonia under their respective monarchs, Queen Isabella (r. 1474–1504) and King Ferdinand II (r. 1479–1516). The two monarchs used the reconquest ideology to speed up political and religious reforms.

MAP **16.1** **Africa, the Mediterranean, and the Indian Ocean, 1415–1498.**

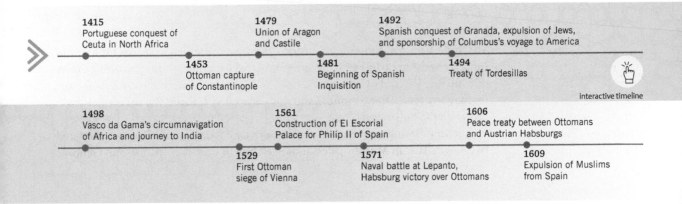

1415
Portuguese conquest of
Ceuta in North Africa

1453
Ottoman capture
of Constantinople

1479
Union of Aragon
and Castile

1481
Beginning of Spanish
Inquisition

1492
Spanish conquest of Granada, expulsion of Jews,
and sponsorship of Columbus's voyage to America

1494
Treaty of Tordesillas

interactive timeline

1498
Vasco da Gama's circumnavigation
of Africa and journey to India

1529
First Ottoman
siege of Vienna

1561
Construction of El Escorial
Palace for Philip II of Spain

1571
Naval battle at Lepanto,
Habsburg victory over Ottomans

1606
Peace treaty between Ottomans
and Austrian Habsburgs

1609
Expulsion of Muslims
from Spain

Among the political reforms was the recruitment of urban militias and judges to check the military and judicial powers of the aristocracy. Religious reform focused on education for the clergy and enforcement of Christian doctrine among the population. The institution entrusted with the latter was the Spanish Inquisition, a body of clergy appointed in 1481 to discover and punish those deemed to be in violation of Christian theology and church law. These reforms laid the foundations for increased state power.

The Conquest of Granada   The *Reconquista* culminated in a 10-year campaign (1482–1492) that resulted in Granada falling into Christian hands. The last emir of Granada negotiated terms for an honorable surrender. According to these terms, Muslims who stayed as subjects of the Castilian crown were permitted to worship in their own mosques.

The treaty did not apply to the Jews of Granada, however, who were forced to either convert to Christianity or emigrate. Many emigrated in 1492 to Portugal and the Ottoman Empire. Portugal adopted its own expulsion decree in 1497. This ended the nearly millennium-and-a-half-long Jewish presence in Sefarad, as Spain was called in Hebrew.

After the expulsion of the Jews, it did not take long for the Christians to violate the Muslim treaty of surrender. The church forced conversions, burned Arabic books, and transformed mosques into churches. In 1499 the Muslims of Granada rebelled. Christian troops crushed the uprising, and Isabella and Ferdinand abrogated the treaty of surrender. During the early sixteenth century, Muslims were forced to convert, disperse to other provinces, or emigrate.

Columbus's Journey to the Caribbean   In early 1492, Isabella and Ferdinand authorized the mariner Christopher Columbus (1451–1506) to build two caravels and a larger carrack and sail across the Atlantic. Columbus promised to reach India ahead of the Portuguese. Money for the construction of ships came from Castilian and Aragonese Crusade levies on the Muslims.

In September, Columbus and his mariners departed from the Castilian Canary Islands, catching the favorable South Atlantic easterlies. After a voyage of a little over a month, Columbus landed on one of the Bahaman islands, mistakenly assuming that he was close to the Indian subcontinent. After 3 months, he left a colony of settlers behind and returned to Iberia with seven captured Caribbean islanders and some gold.

Although disappointed by the meager returns of Columbus's first and subsequent voyages, Isabella and Ferdinand were delighted to have acquired new islands in the Caribbean, in addition to the Canaries. In one blow they had drawn even with Portugal.

Vasco da Gama's Journey to India   Portugal continued to search for a way to India around Africa. In 1498, the king appointed a member of the crusading Order of Santiago, Vasco da Gama (ca. 1469–1524), to command four caravels for the journey to India. After 6 months, the ships arrived in Calicut, the main spice trade center on the Indian west coast.

The first Portuguese mariner sent ashore by da Gama in Calicut encountered two North African Muslims, who addressed him in Castilian Spanish and Genoese

Italian: "The Devil take you! What brought you here?" The mariner replied: "We came to seek Christians and spices." The Muslim and Hindu merchants were uninterested in the goods designed for the African market offered by da Gama and demanded gold or silver, which the Portuguese had only in small amounts. As rumors spread about a Muslim and Hindu plot against him, da Gama prudently sailed home.

However, Portugal soon mastered the India trade. The Portuguese crown organized regular journeys around Africa, and when Portuguese mariners ventured in the other direction to northeast Brazil, they claimed it for their expanding commercial network. During the early sixteenth century, as the Portuguese India fleets brought considerable amounts of spices from India back to Portugal, the project of retaking Jerusalem receded into the background.

Pedro Reinel's map of East Africa and the Indian Ocean, ca. 1507

Rise of the Ottomans and Struggle with the Habsburgs for Dominance, 1300–1609

While Muslim rule was disappearing from the Iberian Peninsula in the late fifteenth century, the opposite was happening in the Balkans. Here, the Ottoman Turks expanded Islamic rule over Christians. By the late sixteenth century, when conflict between the Habsburgs and Ottomans reached its peak, entire generations of Croats, Germans, and Italians feared a Muslim conquest of all of Christian Europe.

Late Byzantium and Ottoman Origins   The rise of the Ottomans was related to the decline of Byzantium. The emperors of Byzantium had reclaimed their "empire" in 1261 from its Latin rulers and Venetian troops. This empire was a mid-size kingdom with modest agricultural resources. But it was still a valuable trading hub, given Constantinople's strategic position. Thanks to its commercial wealth, Byzantium experienced a cultural revival that influenced the Western Renaissance in Italy (see Chapter 10).

Both Balkan Slavs and Anatolian Turks appropriated Byzantine provinces in the late thirteenth century, further reducing the empire. One of the lost provinces was Bithynia, where, in 1299, the Turkish warlord Osman (1299–1326) declared himself an independent ruler. Osman and other Turkish lords in the region were nominally subject to the Seljuks, the Turkish dynasty that had conquered Anatolia from the Byzantines two centuries earlier but by the early 1300s was disintegrating.

During the first half of the fourteenth century, Osman and his successors conquered further Anatolian provinces from Byzantium. In 1354, the Ottomans gained their first European foothold on a peninsula about 100 miles southwest of Constantinople. Thereafter, it seemed only a matter of time before the Ottomans would conquer Constantinople.

Through skillful mixture of defense and diplomacy, however, the Byzantine emperors salvaged their rule for another century. They were also helped by Timur the Great (r. 1370–1405), a Turkish-descended ruler from central Asia who sought to rebuild the Mongol Empire. He defeated the Ottomans in 1402. Timur and his successors were unsuccessful with their dream of Mongol world rule; the Ottomans needed nearly two decades (1402–1421) to reconstitute their empire in the Balkans and Anatolia. Under Mehmet II, "the Conqueror" (r. 1451–1481), they finally laid siege to the Byzantine capital.

Patterns Up Close | Shipbuilding

With the appearance of empires during the Iron Age, four regional but interconnected shipbuilding traditions—Mediterranean, North Sea, Indian Ocean, and China Sea—emerged.

In the Mediterranean, around 500 BCE, shipwrights began to use nailed planks for their war galleys as well as for cargo transports. In the Roman Empire (ca. 200 BCE–500 CE), nailed planking allowed the development of the roundship (image *a*), a large vessel 120 feet in length with a capacity of 400 tons of cargo for the transport of grain from Egypt to Italy. The roundship and its variations had double planking, multiple masts, and multiple square sails. After 100 BCE, the triangular (lateen) sail allowed for tacking (zigzagging) against the wind, greatly expanding shipping during the summer sailing season.

The Celtic North Sea tradition adapted to the Mediterranean patterns of the Romans. Shipwrights in Celtic regions shifted to frame-first construction for small boats in the 300s. At the same time, Norsemen, or Vikings, innovated by introducing overlapping (clinkered) plank joining for their seagoing boats. The North Sea innovations, arriving as they did at the end of the western Roman Empire, remained local for nearly half a millennium.

China made major contributions to ship construction. In the Han period (206 BCE–220 CE) there is evidence from clay models for the use of nailed planks in riverboats. One model, dating to the first century CE, shows a central steering rudder at the end of the boat. At the same time, similar stern rudders appeared in the Roman Empire. Who adopted what from whom, if there was any borrowing at all, is still an unanswered question.

Patterns of Shipbuilding. Left to right: (*a*) Hellenistic-Roman roundship, (*b*) Chinese junk, (*c*) Indian Ocean dhow.

From Istanbul to the Adriatic Sea   Mehmet's siege and conquest of Constantinople (April 5–May 29, 1453) is one of the stirring events of world history. The Byzantines were unable to defend the land walls that protected the city. Using their superiority in troop strength, the Ottomans bombarded Constantinople's walls with heavy cannons. A weak section was on the northeastern side, along the harbor in the Golden Horn, where the walls were low. Here, the Byzantines had blocked off the entrance to the Golden Horn with a huge chain. Mehmet circumvented the chain by having troops drag ships on rollers over a hillside into the harbor. The soldiers

Shipbuilding innovations continued after 600 CE. In Tang China, junks with multiple bulkheads (watertight compartments) and layers of planks appeared. The average junk was 140 feet long, had a cargo capacity of 600 tons, and could carry on its three or four decks several hundred mariners and passengers (see image *b*). Junks had multiple masts, and their trapezoidal (lug) and square sails made of matted fibers were strengthened (battened) with poles sewed to the surface. The Middle Eastern, eastern African, and Indian dhow was built with sewed or nailed planks and rigged with lateen and square sails, traveling as far as southern China (see image *c*).

In western Europe, the patterns of Mediterranean and North Sea shipbuilding merged during the thirteenth century. At that time, northern shipwrights developed the cog, a ship of some 60 feet in length and 30 tons in cargo capacity, with square sails and flush planking below and clinkered planking above the waterline. Northern European crusaders traveled during 1150–1300 on cogs via the Atlantic to the Mediterranean. Builders adapted the cog's clinker technique to the roundship tradition that Muslims as well as Eastern and Western Christians had modified in the previous centuries. Genoese clinkered roundships pioneered the Mediterranean–North Sea trade in the early fourteenth century (see image *d*).

Lisbon shipwrights in Portugal developed the caravel around 1430. The caravel was a 60-foot-long ship with a 50-ton freight capacity, a stern rudder, square and lateen sails, and a magnetic compass (of Chinese origin). The caravel and, after 1500, the similarly built but much larger galleon were the main vessels the Portuguese, Spanish, Dutch, and English used during their oceanic voyages from the mid-fifteenth to mid-eighteenth centuries (see image *e*).

(d)

(e)

Patterns of Shipbuilding (*Continued*). From top: (*d*) Baltic cog, (*e*) Iberian caravel. These ships illustrate the varieties of shipbuilding traditions that developed over thousands of years.

Questions

- How does the history of shipbuilding demonstrate the ways in which innovations spread from one place to another?

- Do the adaptations in shipbuilding that flowed between cultures that were nominally in conflict with each other provide a different perspective on the way these cultures interacted?

massed on these ships were ready to assault the walls with the help of ladders. On the first sign of cracks in the northeastern walls, the Ottoman besiegers stormed the city. The last Byzantine emperor, Constantine XI, perished in the massacre that followed the Ottoman occupation of the city.

Mehmet repopulated Constantinople ("Istanbul" in Turkish) and appointed a new patriarch at the head of the Eastern Christians, to whom he promised full protection as his subjects. He ordered the construction of the Topkapı Palace (1459), the transfer of the administration to Istanbul, and the resumption of expansion in

Siege of Constantinople, 1453. Note the soldiers on the left pulling boats on rollers and wheels over the Galata hillside. With this maneuver, Sultan Mehmet II was able to circumvent the chain stretched across the entrance to the Golden Horn (in place of the anachronistic bridge in the image). This allowed him to speed up his conquest of Constantinople by forcing the defenders to spread their forces thinly over the entire length of the walls.

a Safavid battle tunic

the Balkans, where he forced the majority of rulers into submitting to vassal status.

Mehmet's conquests brought him to the Adriatic Sea, from where the Ottomans were poised to launch a full-scale invasion of Italy. When the sultan died unexpectedly, his successor turned back, preferring instead to consolidate the Ottoman Empire in the Middle East, North Africa, and the Balkans.

Imperial Apogee   Between 1500 and 1600 the Ottomans consolidated their empire. In 1514, they defeated the Persian Safavids in Iran, who had risen in 1501 to form a rival Shiite empire in opposition to the Sunni Ottomans. In the southern Middle East, tensions between the Ottomans and the Mamluk Turks erupted in war in 1517. The Ottomans defeated the Mamluks and took control of western Arabia, including the holy pilgrimage city of Mecca. A year later, in 1518, Sultan Süleyman I, "the Magnificent" (r. 1520–1566), drove the Spanish from much of North Africa, which the latter had conquered in the name of the *Reconquista* in the 1490s and early 1500s.

In the Balkans, the Ottomans completed their conquests of Serbia and Hungary with the annexation of Belgrade and Buda (now part of Budapest) as well as a brief siege of Vienna in 1529. By the second half of the sixteenth century, the Ottoman Empire was a vast multiethnic and multireligious state of some 15 million inhabitants extending from Algeria in the Maghreb to Yemen in Arabia and from Upper Egypt to the Balkans and the northern shores of the Black Sea (see Map 16.2).

Morocco and Persia   In the period 1450–1600, the Ottomans and Indian Mughals dominated Islamic civilization. Two smaller realms existed in Morocco and Persia, ruled by the Saadid (1509–1659) and Safavid (1501–1722) dynasties, respectively. The Saadid sultans defended themselves successfully against the Ottoman expansion and liberated themselves from the Portuguese occupation of Morocco's Atlantic ports. In 1591, the Saadids sent an army to West Africa in an unsuccessful attempt to revive the gold trade. Moroccan army officers assumed power in Timbuktu, and their descendants, the Ruma, became provincial lords independent of Morocco. The Saadids split into provincial realms. The still-reigning Alaouite dynasty of Moroccan kings replaced them in 1659.

The Safavids grew in the mid-1400s from a mixed Kurdish-Turkish mystical brotherhood in northwestern Iran into a Shiite warrior organization that carried out raids against Christians in the Caucasus. In 1501, the leadership of the brotherhood put forward a 14-year-old boy named Ismail as the Hidden Twelfth Imam. According to Shiite doctrine, the Hidden Imam, or Messiah, was expected to arrive and establish a Muslim apocalyptic realm of justice at the end of time, before God's Last Judgment. This realm would replace the "unjust" Sunni Ottoman Empire. The Ottomans, however, crushed the Safavid challenge in 1514 at the Battle of Chaldiran. Ismail dropped his claim to messianic status, and his successors assumed the more modest title of king (Persian *shah*) as the head of state.

The Safavids recruited a standing infantry from among young Christians on lands conquered in the Caucasus. They held fast to Shiism, thereby continuing their

MAP **16.2 The Ottoman Empire, 1307–1683.**

map analysis

opposition to the Sunni Ottomans, and made this form of Islam dominant in Iran. They moved the capital from Tabriz to the centrally located Isfahan in 1590, and built a palace, administration, and mosque complex in the city. They also held the monopoly in the production of Caspian Sea silk, a high-quality export product.

Not everyone accepted Shiism, however. An attempt to force the Shiite doctrines on the Afghanis backfired badly when enraged Sunni tribes formed a coalition, defeated the Safavids, and ended their regime in 1722.

Rise of the Habsburgs   On the Iberian Peninsula, Castile-Aragon evolved into the center of a vast empire. A daughter of Isabella and Ferdinand married a member of the Habsburg dynastic family, which ruled Flanders, Burgundy, Naples, Sicily, and Austria, as well as Germany (the "Holy Roman Empire of the German Nation," as this collection of principalities was called). Their son, Charles V (r. 1516–1558), not only inherited Castile–Aragon, now merged and called "Spain," and the Habsburg territories but also became the ruler of the Aztec and Inca Empires in the Americas. In both Austria and the western Mediterranean the Habsburgs were direct neighbors of the Ottomans (see Map 16.3).

After a victorious battle against France in 1519, Charles V also won the title of emperor from the pope, which made him the overlord of all German principalities and supreme among the monarchs of Western Christianity. He was now the titular political head of Western Christianity and thereby the direct counterpart of Sultan Süleyman in the struggle for dominance in the Christian–Muslim world of Europe, the Middle East, and northern Africa. Both the Habsburgs and the Ottomans renewed the traditional Islamic–Christian imperialism which had characterized the period 628–950 and which had been replaced by the Muslim and Christian commonwealths of 950–1450.

MAP 16.3 **Europe and the Mediterranean, ca. 1560.**

Habsburg Distractions   Charles V faced a daunting task in his effort to prevent the Ottomans from advancing against the Christians in the Balkans and the Mediterranean. Problems in his European territories diverted his attention from what Christians in most parts of Europe perceived as a pervasive Ottoman–Muslim threat. During the first three decades of the sixteenth century, revolts in Iberia, the Protestant Reformation in the German states, and renewed war with France commanded Charles's attention.

The emperor's distractions increased further in 1534 when, in an attempt to drive the Habsburgs out of Italy, France forged an alliance with the Ottomans. While this alliance horrified western Europe, it demonstrated that the Ottomans had become crucial players in European politics.

Habsburg and Ottoman Losses   These diversions strained Habsburg resources against the Ottomans, who pressed ahead on the two fronts of the Balkans and North Africa. Although Charles V deputized his younger brother Ferdinand I to shore up the Balkan defenses, he was unable to send him enough troops. After a series of defeats, Austria had to pay the Ottomans tribute and, eventually, sign a humiliating truce (1562). On the western Mediterranean front, by 1556, at the end of Charles V's reign, only two of eight Habsburg garrisons had survived Ottoman onslaught.

A third frontier of the Muslim–Christian struggle for dominance was the Indian Ocean. After Vasco da Gama had returned from India in 1498, the Portuguese kings sought to break into the Muslim-dominated Indian Ocean trade. In response, the Ottomans protected existing Muslim commercial interests in the Indian Ocean. They blocked Portuguese military support for Ethiopia and strengthened their ally, the sultan of Aceh on the Indonesian island of Sumatra, by providing him with troops and weapons. War on land and on sea raged in the Indian Ocean through most of the sixteenth century.

In the long run, the Portuguese were successful in destroying the Ottoman fleets sent against them, but smaller convoys of Ottoman galleys continued to harass Portuguese shipping interests. By 1570 the Muslims traded as much via the Red Sea route to the Mediterranean as the Portuguese did by circumnavigating Africa. In addition, the Ottomans now benefited from the trade of coffee, produced in Ethiopia and Yemen. Both Portugal and the Ottomans reduced their by now unsustainable military presence in the Indian Ocean, which allowed the Netherlands in the early seventeenth century to overtake both Portugal and the Ottoman Empire in the Indian Ocean spice trade (see Map 16.4).

Portuguese trading posts in the Indian Ocean, 1630

Habsburg–Ottoman Balance   In the 1550s, Charles V decided to ensure the continuation of Habsburg power through a division of his western and eastern territories. Accordingly, he bestowed Spain, Naples, the Netherlands, and the Americas on his son Philip II (r. 1556–1598). The Habsburg possessions of Austria, Bohemia, and the remnant of Hungary not lost to the Ottomans, as well as the Holy Roman Empire (Germany), went to his brother Ferdinand I (r. 1558–1564). Charles hoped that his son and brother would cooperate and help each other militarily against the Ottomans.

When Philip took over the Spanish throne, he realized that most of the Habsburg military was stationed outside Spain, leaving that country vulnerable to attack—especially as the Ottomans had recently conquered Spanish strongholds in North Africa. Fearful of **morisco** support for an Ottoman invasion of Spain, Philip's administration and the Inquisition renewed their decrees of conversion.

This sparked a revolt among the moriscos of Granada in 1568–1570, which Philip was able to suppress only after recourse to troops and firearms from Italy. To break up the large concentrations of Granadan moriscos in the south of Spain, Philip ordered them to be dispersed throughout the peninsula. At the same time, to alleviate the Ottoman naval threat, Philip, the pope, Venice, and Genoa formed a Holy Christian League. The fleet succeeded in 1571 in destroying the entire Ottoman navy at Lepanto, in Ottoman Greece.

The Ottomans, however, rebuilt their navy and captured the strategic port city of Tunis in 1574 from the Spaniards. After this date, Venice was the only naval enemy of the Ottomans. The Ottomans turned their attention to the rival Safavid Empire,

Moriscos: From Greek *maurus* ("dark"); Castilian term referring to North Africans and to Muslims under Spanish rule.

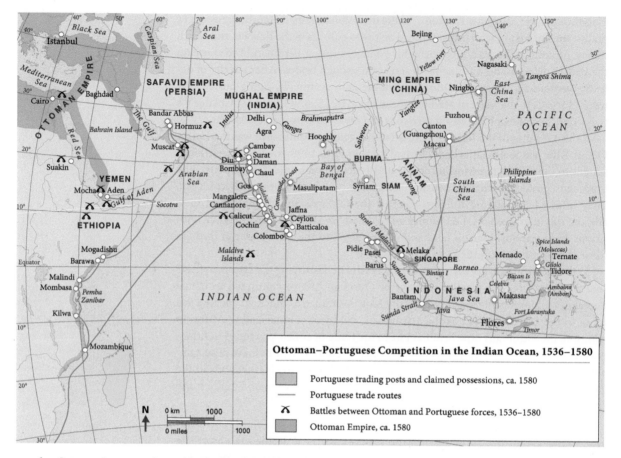

MAP 16.4 **Ottoman–Portuguese Competition in the Indian Ocean, 1536–1580.**

where they exploited a period of dynastic instability for the conquest of territories in the Caucasus (1578–1590). The Catholic Philip II, for his part, was faced with the Protestant war of independence in the Netherlands. This war was so expensive that Philip II had to declare bankruptcy and sue for peace with the Ottomans (1580).

The Limits of Ottoman Power After their victory over the Safavids, the Ottomans looked again to the west, where a long peace with Ferdinand I in Austria (since 1562) was ready to collapse. A series of raids and counter-raids at the Austrian and Transylvanian borders had inflamed tempers, and in 1593 the Ottomans went on the attack.

Eventually, the Ottomans were only able to draw on the battlefield with the Austrians. In 1606, the Ottomans and Austrian Habsburgs made peace again. With minor modifications in favor of the Austrians, the two sides returned to their earlier borders. The Austrians made one more tribute payment and then let their obligation lapse. Officially, the Ottomans conceded nothing, but in practical terms Austria was no longer a vassal state.

Expulsion of the Moriscos Although the peace between the Ottomans and Spanish Habsburgs held, Philip and his successors were aware of the possibility of renewed Ottoman aid to the Iberian Muslims, or moriscos, who continued to resist conversion. The church advocated the expulsion of the moriscos, arguing that the allegedly high Muslim birthrate was a serious threat.

Fierce resistance against the proposed expulsion, however, rose among the Christian landowners in the southeastern province of Valencia. These landowners benefited from the skills of morisco tenant farmers. Weighing the potential Ottoman threat against the possibility of economic damage, the government decided in 1580 in favor of expulsion.

It took until 1609, however, before a compensation deal with the landowners in Valencia was worked out. In the following 5 years, some 300,000 moriscos were forcibly expelled from Spain, under often appalling circumstances: As in the case of the Jews a century earlier, Spain's loss was the Ottoman Empire's gain, this time mostly in the form of skilled irrigation farmers.

The Centralizing State: Origins and Interactions

The major technological change in the Middle East and Europe during 1250–1350 was the use of firearms. It took until the mid-1400s, however, before cannons and muskets were effective enough to make a difference in warfare. At this time, a pattern emerged whereby rulers created centralized states to finance their shift to firearm-bearing infantries. They resumed the policy of conquest and imperialism. Both the Ottomans and the Habsburgs raised immense amounts of silver and gold to spend on cannons, muskets, and ships for achieving world rule.

State Transformation, Money, and Firearms

In the early stages of their realms, the kings of Iberia (1150–1400) and the Ottoman sultans (1300–1400) compensated military commanders for their service with land grants. Once the Iberian and Ottoman rulers had conquered cities and gained control over long-distance trade, however, patterns changed. Rulers began collecting taxes in cash, with which they paid regiments of personal guards to supplement the army of land-grant officers. This centralizing state was the forerunner of the absolutist state of the early seventeenth century.

The Land-Grant System   In the 1300s, Ottoman military lords created personal domains on lands they had conquered and took rents in kind from villagers to finance their dynastic households. Members of their clan or adherents (many of whom were holy warriors and/or adventurers), received other conquered lands, from which they collected rents. As the Ottomans conquered Byzantine cities, they gained access to the **money economy**. They collected taxes in coins from the markets and tollbooths at city gates, as well as from the Christians and Jews subject to the head tax.

After the conquest of the southern Balkans by the Ottoman Empire in the fifteenth and sixteenth centuries, both the land-grant system and the money economy expanded. A military ruling class of grant holders emerged, cavalrymen who

Paolo Veronese, *Battle of Lepanto*, altar painting with four saints beseeching the Virgin Mary to grant victory to the Christians (ca. 1572). In the sixteenth century, the entire Mediterranean, from Gibraltar to Cyprus, was a naval battleground between Christians and Muslims. The Christians won the Battle of Lepanto thanks to superior naval tactics. At the end of the battle "the sea was entirely covered, not just with masts, spars, oars, and broken wood, but with an innumerable quantity of blood that turned the water as red as blood."

Money economy: Form of economic organization in which mutual obligations are settled through monetary exchanges; in contrast, a system of land grants obliges the landholders to provide military service, without payment, to the grantee (sultan or king).

Janissaries: Infantry soldiers recruited among the Christian population of the Ottoman Empire and paid from the central treasury.

Devşirme: The levy on boys in the Ottoman Empire; that is, the obligation of the Christian population to contribute adolescent males to the military and administrative classes.

lived with their households of retainers in the interior of Anatolia and the Balkans. Most of the time, they were away on campaign with the sultans, leaving managers in charge of the collection of rents. By the early years of the sixteenth century, the landed ruling class of cavalrymen constituted a reserve of warriors for the mobilization of troops each summer.

The Janissaries The military institution of the **Janissaries**—troops who received salaries from the central treasury—is first documented in 1395. It was based on a practice (called ***devşirme*** [dev-SHIR-meh]) of conscripting young boys from the empire's Christian population. Boys between the ages of 6 and 16 were sent to Istanbul, where they were converted to Islam and trained as future soldiers and administrators. The youth then entered the system of manumitted palace slaves under the orders of the sultan and his ministers.

The practice of *devşirme* contradicted Islamic law, which forbade the enslavement of "peoples of the Book" (Jews, Christians, and Zoroastrians). Its existence, therefore, documents the extent to which the sultans reasserted the Roman–Sasanid–Arab imperial traditions of the ruler making doctrine and law.

Boy Levy (*devşirme*) in a Christian Village. This miniature graphically depicts the trauma of conscription, including the wailing of the village women and the assembly of boys waiting to be taken away by implacable representatives of the sultan.

Toward the first half of the fifteenth century, the sultans equipped their Janissaries with cannons and matchlock muskets. By this point, firearms had undergone some 150 years of development in the Middle East and North Africa. By the mid-1400s, gigantic siege cannons and slow but reliable matchlock muskets were the standard equipment of Ottoman and other armies, and the sultans relied on indigenous, rather than European, gunsmiths.

Revenues and Money The maintenance of a salaried standing army and a central administration would have been impossible without precious metals. Therefore, the Ottoman imperial expansion was driven by the need to acquire mineral deposits. During the fifteenth century the Ottomans captured the silver, lead, and iron mines of Serbia and Bosnia. Together with Anatolian copper, iron, and silver mines, the Balkan mines made the Ottomans the owners of the largest precious metal production centers prior to the Habsburg acquisition of the Mexican and Andean mines in the mid-1500s.

The sultans left the Balkan mining and smelting operations in the hands of preconquest Christian entrepreneurs who were integrated into the Ottoman imperial money economy as tax farmers. **Tax farming** was the preferred method of producing cash revenues for the central administration. The holders of tax farms delivered the profits from the production of minerals to the state, minus the commission they were entitled to subtract for themselves. Thus, tax farmers were crucial members of the ruling class.

The right to mint silver was part of the tax-farm regime, as were the market, city gate, and port duties. The tax-farm regime was dependent on a strong sultan or chief minister, the grand vizier. Without close supervision, this regime could easily become decentralized, which indeed eventually happened in the Ottoman Empire.

Süleyman's Central State   The Ottoman state reached its apogee under Sultan Süleyman I, "the Magnificent." The sultan financed a massive expansion of the military and bureaucracy and formed a centralized state, the purpose of which was to project power and cultural splendor toward its subjects as well as Christian enemies outside the empire.

The bureaucrats were recruited from two population groups. Most top ministers and officers in the fifteenth and sixteenth centuries came from the *devşirme* among the Christians. The empire's other recruits came from colleges to which the Muslim population of the empire had access. Ambitious villagers far from urban centers could gain upward mobility through the colleges. Muslims of Christian parentage made up the top layer of the elite, while Muslims of Islamic descent occupied the middle ranks.

Under Süleyman, the Janissaries comprised musket-equipped troopers, a cavalry, and artillery regiments. Most were stationed in Istanbul, while others served in provincial cities and border fortresses.

Typical military campaigns required sophisticated logistics. Wages, gunpowder, weapons, and foodstuffs were carried on wagons and barges, since soldiers were not permitted to provision themselves from villagers, whether friend or foe. Although the state collected heavy taxes, it had a strong interest in not destroying village productivity.

Charles V's Centralizing State   The centralizing state began in Iberia with the reforms of Isabella and Ferdinand and reached its mature phase under Charles V. From the late fifteenth century onward, Castile and Aragon shared fiscal characteristics with the Ottomans, such as tax farming. In addition, Muslims paid head taxes in cash. Most of the money taxes were also enforced in Flanders, Burgundy, Naples, Sicily, and Austria, after Iberia's incorporation into the Habsburg domain in 1516. Together, these taxes were more substantial than those of Spain.

From 1521 to 1536, the Spanish crown enlarged its money income from looted Aztec and Inca gold and silver. Under Charles V, Habsburg imperial revenues doubled, reaching about the same level as those of the Ottomans. At the height of their struggle for dominance in the Muslim–Christian world, the Habsburgs and the Ottomans expended similar resources in wars with each other.

In one significant respect, however, the two empires differed. The cavalry ruling class of the Ottoman Empire was nonhereditary. By contrast, Iberian landholders possessed a legal right to inheritance. When Isabella and Ferdinand embarked on state centralization, they had to wrestle with a powerful, landed aristocracy that had taken over royal jurisdiction and tax prerogatives on their vast lands. The two monarchs took back much of the jurisdiction but were unable to do much about the taxes.

Ottoman Siege of a Christian Fortress. By the middle of the fifteenth century, cannons had revolutionized warfare. Niccolò Machiavelli, ever attuned to new developments, noted in 1519 that "no wall exists, however thick, that artillery cannot destroy in a few days." Machiavelli could have been commenting on the Ottomans, who were masters of siege warfare. Sultan Mehmet II, the conqueror of Constantinople in 1453, founded the Imperial Cannon Foundry shortly thereafter; it would go on to make some of the biggest cannons of the period.

Tax farming: Governmental auction of the right to collect taxes in a district. The tax farmer advanced these taxes to the treasury and retained a commission.

The Habsburgs sought to overcome their lack of power over the aristocracy and the weakness of their Spanish tax base by exploiting the Italian and Flemish cities and the American colonies. But in the long run their finances remained precarious. Spanish aristocrats seldom fulfilled their obligation to unpaid military service. As a result, the kings hired as many Italians, Flemings, and Germans as possible, and at times, they deployed these mercenaries to Spain in order to maintain peace there.

Although the Ottoman and Habsburg patterns of centralized state formation bore similarities to patterns in the earlier Roman and Arab Empires, the centralizing states of the period after 1450 were much more potent enterprises because of firearms. They were established polities, evolving into absolutist and eventually national states.

Imperial Courts, Urban Festivities, and the Arts

Ottoman and Habsburg rulers projected the splendor of their states to subjects at home as well as enemies abroad. Although Christian and Muslim artists and artisans belonged to different religious and cultural traditions, their artistic achievements were inspired by the same impulse: to glorify their states through religious expression.

The Ottoman Empire: Palaces, Festivities, and the Arts

The Ottomans built palaces and celebrated public feasts to demonstrate their imperial power and wealth. Many mosques were built during the sixteenth century. Painting and illustration was found only inside the privacy of the Ottoman palace and wealthy households. Theater and music were enjoyed on the popular level, in defiance of religious restrictions.

The Topkapı Palace　When the Ottoman sultans conquered the Byzantine capital Constantinople in 1453, it was dilapidated and depopulated. The sultans initiated large construction projects and populated the city with craftspeople and traders from across their empire. By 1600 Istanbul was again an imposing metropolis, easily the largest city in Europe at that time.

One of the construction projects was a new palace for the sultans, the Topkapı Sarayı, or "Palace of the Gun Gate," begun in 1459. The Topkapı complex included the main administrative school, military barracks, an armory, a hospital, and living quarters, or harem, for the ruling family.

The institution of the harem arose during the reign of Süleyman. At that time, sultans no longer pursued marriage alliances with neighboring Islamic rulers. Instead, they chose slave concubines (often Christian) for the procreation of children. A concubine who bore a son to the reigning sultan acquired privileges.

The head eunuch of the harem guard evolved into a powerful intermediary for diplomatic and military decisions between the sultan's mother, who was confined to the harem, and those she sought to influence. In addition, the sultan's mother arranged marriages of her daughters to high-ranking officials. In the strong patriarchal order of the Ottoman Empire, such women exercised considerable power.

Public Festivities   As in Habsburg Spain, feasts and celebrations were events that displayed the state's largesse. Typical festivities commemorated Muslim holidays. Other feasts were connected with the birthday of the Prophet Muhammad and his journey to heaven and hell. Processions and communal meals commemorated the birthdays of local Muslim saints in many cities. As in Christian Spain, these feasts attracted large crowds.

Wrestlers, ram handlers, and horsemen performed in the Hippodrome, the stadium for public festivities. At the harbor of the Golden Horn, tightrope artists performed high above the water. Court painters recorded the procession and performance scenes in picture albums. The sultans incorporated these albums into their libraries, together with history books recording their military victories against the Habsburgs.

Imperial Hall, Topkapı Palace. The Ottomans never forgot their nomadic roots. Topkapı Palace, completed in 1479 and expanded and redecorated several times, resembles in many ways a vast encampment, with a series of enclosed courtyards. At the center of the palace complex were the harem and the private apartments of the sultan, which included the Imperial Hall, where the sultan would receive members of his family and closest advisors.

image analysis

Popular Theater   The evenings of the fasting month of Ramadan were filled with festive meals and a special form of entertainment, the Karagöz ("Black Eye") shadow theater. This form of theater came from Egypt, although it probably had Javanese–Chinese roots. For boys, a performance of the Karagöz theater accompanied the ritual of circumcision, a rite of passage from the ancient Near East adopted by Islamic civilization. Circumcision signified the passage from the nurturing care of the mother to the educational discipline of the father.

Mosque Architecture   During the sixteenth century, the architect Sinan (ca. 1492–1588) filled Istanbul and the earlier Ottoman capital Edirne with imperial mosques, defined by their slender minarets. Sultan Süleyman, wealthy officials, and private donors provided the funds. Sinan was able to hire as many as 25,000 laborers, enabling him to build each of his mosques in six years or less.

Sinan's most original contribution to architecture was the replacement of the highly visible and massive four exterior buttresses, which marked the square ground plan of the Hagia Sophia, with up to eight slender pillars as hidden internal supports of the dome. His intention was not massive monumentality but elegant spaciousness.

The Spanish Habsburg Empire: Popular Festivities and the Arts

The culture of the Habsburg Empire was strongly religious, and both state-sponsored spectacles and popular festivities displayed devotion to the Catholic faith. More secular tendencies, however, emerged as a result of the Renaissance. Originating in Italy and the Netherlands, Renaissance aesthetics emphasized pre-Christian Greek and Roman heritages.

Capital and Palace   The Habsburgs were relatively late in establishing a capital city and a palace. Catholicism was the majority religion by the sixteenth century and a powerful unifying force, but there were strong linguistic differences among the provinces of the Iberian Peninsula. Charles V resided for a while in a palace in

Granada next door to the formerly Muslim Alhambra palace—but Granada was too Moorish and, geographically too far away from the north for many Spanish subjects to be properly awed.

Only a few places in Spain were suited for the location of a central palace and administration. Philip II eventually found such a place near the city of Madrid, which had once been a Muslim provincial capital. There, royal architect Juan Bautista de Toledo (ca. 1515–1567) built the Renaissance-style palace and monastery complex of El Escorial (1563–1584). As a result, Madrid became the seat of the administration and later of the court.

Christian State Festivities   Given the close association between the state and the church, the Spanish crown expressed its glory through the observance of feast days of the Christian calendar. These feasts were the occasion for processions and/or **passion plays**, during which urban residents affirmed their Catholic faith. During Holy Week, the week preceding Easter, Catholics marched through the streets, carrying heavy crosses or shouldering wooden platforms with statues of Jesus and Mary. The physical rigors of the Holy Week processions were collective reenactments of Jesus's suffering on the Cross.

By contrast, the processions that took place several weeks after Easter were joyous celebrations. Costumed marchers participated in jostling and pushing contests, played music, performed dances, and enacted scenes from the Bible.

Passion play: Dramatic representation of the trial, suffering, and death of Jesus Christ; passion plays are still an integral part of Holy Week in many Catholic countries today.

The Auto-da-Fé   The investigation or proceeding of faith (Portuguese *auto-da-fé*, "act of faith") was a show trial in which the state, through the Spanish Inquisition, judged a person's commitment to Catholicism. The Inquisition employed thousands of state-appointed church officials to investigate anonymous denunciations of individuals failing to conform to the Catholic faith.

Suspected offenders, such as Jewish or Muslim converts to Catholicism or perceived deviants from Catholicism, had to appear before a tribunal. In secret trials, officials determined the offense and the appropriate punishment. These trials often employed torture. However, scholarship has emphasized that in the great majority of cases the punishments were minor, or the investigations did not lead to convictions.

Popular Festivities   *Jousts* (mock combats between contestants mounted on horseback) were secular, primarily aristocratic events. Contestants rode their horses into the city square and led their horses through a complex series of movements. At the height of the spectacle, contestants galloped past each other, hurling their javelins at one another while protecting themselves with their shields. The joust evolved eventually into exhibitions of dressage ("training"), cultivated by the Austrian Habsburgs, who in 1572 founded the Spanish Court Riding School in Vienna.

Bullfights often followed the jousts. During the Middle Ages, bullfights were aristocratic pastimes that drew spectators from local estates. Bullfighters, armed with detachable metal points on 3-foot-long spears, tackled several bulls in a town square. The bullfighter who stuck the largest number of points into the shoulders of the bull was the winner.

Theater, Literature, and Painting   The dramatic enactments of biblical scenes in the passion plays and religious processions were the origin of secular theater in Italy and Spain. Stationary theaters appeared in the main cities of Spain during the

Auto-da-Fé, Madrid. This detail from an 1683 painting by the Italian-born painter Francisco Rizi shows a huge assembly in the Plaza Mayor of Madrid. It captures the solemn spectacle of the trial: In the center, below a raised platform, the accused stand in the docket waiting for their convictions to be pronounced; ecclesiastical and civil authorities follow the proceedings from grandstands. On the left, an altar is visible: The celebration of mass, often lasting for hours, was a common feature of the auto-da-fé.

sixteenth century. A performance typically began with a musical prelude and a prologue describing the piece, followed by the three acts of a drama or comedy. Many were hugely successful, enjoying the attendance or even sponsorship of courtiers, magistrates, and merchants.

An important writer of the period was Miguel de Cervantes (1547–1616). His masterpiece, *Don Quixote*, describes the adventures of a poverty-stricken knight and his attendant, the peasant Sancho Panza, as they wander around Spain searching for the life of bygone *Reconquista* chivalry. *Don Quixote* is an example of a new literary form: the novel.

The outstanding painter of Spain during Philip II's reign was El Greco (Domenikos Theotokopoulos, ca. 1546–1614), a native of the island of Crete. El Greco's works reflect the spirit of Spanish Catholicism, with its emphasis on strict obedience to traditional faith and fervent personal piety. His characteristic style represents a variation of Mannerism (with its perspective exaggerations), which succeeded the Renaissance style in Venice during the later sixteenth century.

Putting It All Together

The Ottoman–Habsburg struggle can be seen as another chapter in the long history of competition that began when the Achaemenid Persian Empire expanded into the Mediterranean and was resisted by the Greeks in the middle of the first millennium BCE. There were obvious religious and cultural differences between the Islamic and Western Christian civilizations as they encountered each other during this period. But their commonalities are equally interesting. Both Ottomans and Habsburgs were representatives of the return to imperialism, and in the pursuit of their imperial goals, both adopted the policy of the centralizing state with its firearm infantries and

interactive concept map

urban money economy. Both found it crucial to project their glory to the population and to sponsor artistic expression. In the long run, however, the imperial ambitions of the Ottomans and Habsburgs exceeded their ability to raise cash. Although firearms and a monetized urban economy made them different from previous empires, they were as unstable as all their imperial predecessors. Eventually, around 1600, they reached the limits of their conquests.

Review and Relate

Thinking Through Patterns

Examine the ways historians approach the big questions of this chapter.

⟫ **What patterns characterized the Christian and Muslim imperial competition in the period 1300–1600? Which elements distinguished them from each other, and which elements were similar? How did the pattern change over time?**

I n 1300, the Ottomans renewed the Arab-Islamic tradition of jihad against the Eastern Christian empire of Byzantium, defeating the empire with the conquest of Constantinople in 1453. They also carried the war into the western Mediterranean and Indian Ocean. In Western Christian Iberia, the rekindling of the reconquest was more successful. Invigorated by a merging of the concepts of the Crusade and the *Reconquista*, the Iberians expanded overseas to circumvent the Muslims and trade for Indian spices directly. The so-called Age of Exploration is rooted in the Western traditions of war against Islamic civilization.

⟫ **How did the centralizing state in the Middle East and Europe function in the period 1450–1600? How did economics, military power, and imperial objectives interact to create the centralizing state?**

I n the mid-1400s, the Middle East and Europe returned to the pattern of imperial state formation after a lull during which states had competed against each other within their respective commonwealths. The element which fueled this return was gunpowder weaponry. The use of cannons and handheld firearms became widespread during this time but required major financial outlays on the part of the states. The two empires became states based on a money economy: Bureaucracies maintained centralized departments that regulated the collection of taxes and the payroll of soldiers.

⟫ **Which patterns did cultural expressions follow in the Habsburg and Ottoman Empires? Why did the ruling classes of these empires sponsor these expressions?**

T he rulers of these empires were concerned to portray themselves, their military, and their bureaucracies as highly successful and just. The state had to be as visible and benevolent as possible. Rulers, therefore, were builders of palaces, churches, or mosques. They celebrated religious and secular festivities with great pomp and encouraged ministers and the nobility to do likewise. In the imperial capitals, they patronized architects, artists, and writers, resulting in a veritable explosion of intellectual and artistic creativity. In this regard, the Ottomans and the Habsburgs followed similar patterns of cultural expression.

Against the Grain

Consider this as a counterpoint to the main patterns examined in this chapter.

Tilting at Windmills

Cervantes's *The Ingenious Gentleman Don Quixote of La Mancha* contributed to the rise of the novel as a characteristic European form of literary expression. Cervantes composed his novel in opposition to the dominant literary conventions of his time—as he wrote, to "ridicule the absurdity of those books of chivalry, which have, as it were, fascinated the eyes and judgement of the world, and in particular of the vulgar."

Every episode in this novel parodies one or another absurdity in society. The frame is provided by the fictional figure of Cide Hamete Benengeli, a purportedly perfidious Muslim and historian who might have been lying when he chronicled the lives of the knight Don Quixote and his squire Sancho Panza. Don Quixote's joust, or "tilting," against windmills has become a powerful metaphor for rebelling against the overpowering conventions of society.

Don Quixote is today acclaimed as the second-most-printed text after the Bible. Over the past four centuries, each generation has interpreted the text anew. Revolutionary France saw Don Quixote as a doomed visionary; German Romantics, as a hero destined to fail; Communists, as an anti-capitalist rebel before his time; and secular progressives, as an unconventional hero at the dawn of modern free society. For Karl Marx, Don Quixote was the hidalgo who yearned for a return to the feudal aristocracy of the past. Sigmund Freud saw the knight-errant as "tragic in his helplessness while the plot is unraveled." In our own time, Don Quixote has become the quintessential postmodern figure; in the words of Michel Foucault, his "truth is not in the relation of the words to the world but in that slender and constant relation woven between themselves as verbal signs." As a tragic or comic figure, Don Quixote continues to be the irresistible symbol of opposition.

- What explains the lasting literary success of Don Quixote?

- Why has the phrase "tilting at windmills" undergone a change of meaning from the original "fighting imaginary foes" to "taking on a situation against all seeming evidence" in our own time?

Key Terms

audio flashcards

Apocalypse 360	Janissaries 372	Moriscos 369
Corsairs 358	Military orders 360	Passion play 376
Devşirme 372	Money economy 371	Tax farming 372

For additional resources, please go to
www.oup.com/us/vonsivers.
Please see the Further Resources section at the back of the book for additional readings and suggested websites.

>> Chapter 17   1450–1750

The Renaissance, New Sciences, and Religious Wars in Europe

URBAN POPULATION OF EUROPE IN 1700

London • • Amsterdam
Paris •
Naples •

- Over 30%
- 25–30%
- 10–15%
- 5–10%
- 1–5%
- 0–1%
- city with population over 200,000

O ne of the most remarkable scientific minds of the seventeenth century was Maria Cunitz (ca. 1607–1664). Under the tutorship of her father, a physician, she became accomplished in six languages, the humanities, and the sciences. During the Thirty Years' War (1618–1648), as Cunitz and her Protestant family sought refuge in a Cistercian monastery, she wrote *Urania propitia* (*Companion to Urania*), in praise of the Greek muse and patron of astronomy. When the family returned home, Cunitz continued to devote her life to science through her careful astronomical observations.

Cunitz's book is a popularization of the astronomical tables of Johannes Kepler (1571–1630), who discovered the elliptical trajectories of the planets. Cunitz's book, published privately in 1650, makes corrections in Kepler's tables and offers simplified calculations of star positions. It was generally well received, although there were a few detractors who found it hard to believe that a woman could succeed in the sciences.

Cunitz lived in a time when Western Christianity had entered the age of early global interaction, from 1450 until 1750. Europe remained

ABOVE: In his *Principia Mathematica*, first published in 1687, Isaac Newton (1643–1727) unified physics and astronomy into a single mathematic system.

institutionally similar to the other parts of the world, especially the Middle East, India, China, and Japan. Rulers throughout Eurasia governed by divine grace. All large states followed patterns of political centralization, and their economies depended on the productivity of agriculture.

Culturally, however, northwestern Europe began to move in a different direction from Islamic, Hindu, Neo-Confucian, and Buddhist civilizations after 1500. New developments in the sciences and philosophy in Europe initiated new cultural patterns. As significant as these patterns were, these new mathematized sciences remained limited to a relatively few educated persons, largely outside the ruling classes. Their ideas diverged substantially from those represented by the Catholic and Protestant ruling classes and resulted in tensions or even repression of scientists by the authorities. The new scientific and intellectual culture broadened after 1750 and eventually led to the Industrial Revolution.

The European Renaissance, Baroque, and New Sciences began with the appropriation of the Greek and Roman cultural heritage, allegedly absent from the Middle Ages, by an educated elite. However, this elite overestimated the extent of their break from the Middle Ages. Scholars today understand this break as far less radical, with much in culture remaining unchanged. Similarly, the political and social changes of the period 1400–1750 have to be balanced against inherited continuities. While the seeds of a departure of Western Christianity from the general patterns of agrarian–urban society were planted around 1500, the "great divergence" from the agrarian–urban patterns of Islamic, Hindu, and Chinese civilizations began only after 1750.

Cultural Transformations: Renaissance, Baroque, and New Sciences

The **Renaissance** was a period of cultural transformation in the fifteenth century that followed the scholastic Middle Ages in Western Christianity. Its thinkers and artists considered their period a time of "rebirth" (which is the literal meaning of "renaissance" in French). They were powerfully influenced by the writings of Greek and Hellenistic-Roman authors who had been unknown during the scholastic age. In the sixteenth century, the Renaissance gave way to the Baroque in the arts and the **New Sciences**.

The Renaissance and Baroque Arts

An outpouring of learning, scholarship, and art began around 1400 in Italy and spread through northwestern Europe. Thinkers and artists benefited from Greek and Hellenistic-Roman texts that scholars had discovered in Byzantium. The emerging cultures of the Renaissance and Baroque were creative adaptations of those Greek

Seeing Patterns

≫ What were the reasons for the cultural change that began in Europe with the Renaissance around 1400? In which ways were the subsequent patterns of cultural change different from those in the other religious civilizations of Eurasia?

≫ When and how did the mathematization of the sciences begin, and how did it gain popularity in northwestern Europe? Why is the popularization of the sciences important for understanding the period 1500–1750?

≫ What were the patterns of centralized state formation and transformation in the period 1400–1750? How did the Protestant Reformation and religious wars modify these patterns?

Renaissance: "Rebirth" of culture based on new publications and translations of Greek, Hellenistic, and Roman authors whose writings were previously unknown in Western Christianity.

New Sciences: Mathematized sciences, such as physics, introduced in the 1500s.

Chapter Outline

• **Cultural Transformations: Renaissance, Baroque, and New Sciences**

• **Centralizing States and Religious Upheavals**

• **Putting It All Together**

Humanism: Intellectual movement focusing on human culture, in such fields as philosophy, philology, and literature, and based on the corpus of Greek and Roman texts.

and Hellenistic-Roman writings to the cultural heritage of Western Christianity. This vibrant mixture led to the movement of **humanism**.

New Manuscripts and Printing   Eastern Christian Byzantium experienced a cultural revival between 1261 and the 1453 Muslim Ottoman conquest of Constantinople. Italian scholars, aware of how much of Greek literature was still absent from Western Christianity, invited Eastern Christian scholars to bring manuscripts to Italy for teaching and translation. Their students became fluent in Greek and translated Hesiod and Homer, Greek plays, Plato and the Neo-Platonists, the works of Aristotle, Hellenistic scientific texts, and the Greek church fathers.

The dissemination of these works was helped by the development of paper. Experimentation in the 1430s with movable metal typeface led to the printing press. A half century later, a printing revolution had taken place in Europe.

Philology and Political Theory   This examination of manuscripts encouraged the study of Greek, Latin, and Hebrew philology. The best-known philologist was the Dutchman Desiderius Erasmus (1466–1536), who published an edition of the Greek and Latin New Testaments in 1516.

Another approach emerged as a central element in political thought. In *The Prince*, Niccolò Machiavelli (1469–1527) argued that what Italy needed was a unifier who possessed what Aristotle discussed in Book 5 of his *Politics*: a person of indomitable spirit (Italian, *virtù*) to take the proper steps when political success was to be achieved. Many Renaissance scholars preferred Plato, but Machiavelli remained faithful to Aristotle—an Aristotle later esteemed by the American founding fathers.

The Renaissance Arts   In Italy, a new artistic way of looking at the Roman past and the natural world emerged. The first artists to adopt this perspective were the sculptor Donatello (ca. 1386–1466) and the architect Filippo Brunelleschi (1377–1446), who received their inspiration from Roman imperial statues and ruins. The artistic triumvirate of the high Italian Renaissance was composed of Leonardo da Vinci (1452–1519), Michelangelo (1475–1564), and Raphael (1483–1520). Inspired by the Italian creative outburst, the Renaissance flourished also in Germany, the Netherlands, and France.

For musical composers of the Renaissance, the difficulty was that the music of the Greeks or Romans was completely unknown. A partial solution for this difficulty

interactive timeline

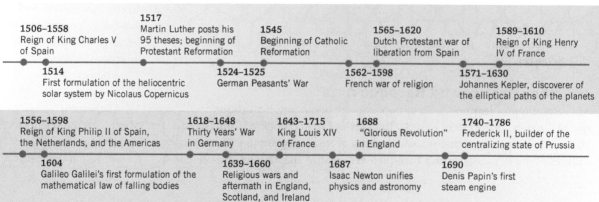

1506–1558 Reign of King Charles V of Spain	1517 Martin Luther posts his 95 theses; beginning of Protestant Reformation	1545 Beginning of Catholic Reformation	1565–1620 Dutch Protestant war of liberation from Spain	1589–1610 Reign of King Henry IV of France
1514 First formulation of the heliocentric solar system by Nicolaus Copernicus		1524–1525 German Peasants' War	1562–1598 French war of religion	1571–1630 Johannes Kepler, discoverer of the elliptical paths of the planets

1556–1598 Reign of King Philip II of Spain, the Netherlands, and the Americas	1618–1648 Thirty Years' War in Germany	1643–1715 King Louis XIV of France	1688 "Glorious Revolution" in England	1740–1786 Frederick II, builder of the centralizing state of Prussia
1604 Galileo Galilei's first formulation of the mathematical law of falling bodies		1639–1660 Religious wars and aftermath in England, Scotland, and Ireland	1687 Isaac Newton unifies physics and astronomy	1690 Denis Papin's first steam engine

was found through emphasizing the relationship between the word—that is, rhetoric—and music. In the sixteenth century this emphasis coincided with the Protestant and Catholic demand for liturgical music, such as hymns and masses.

The theater was a relatively late expression of the Renaissance. The popular mystery, passion, and morality plays from the centuries prior to 1400 continued in Catholic countries. In Italy, in the course of the fifteenth century, the *commedia dell'arte* (a secular popular theater) emerged. In England during the sixteenth century, theater troupes became stationary and professional. Sponsored by the aristocracy and the Elizabethan court, the best-known playwright was William Shakespeare (1564–1616).

Albrecht Dürer, *The Fall of Man (Adam and Eve)*, 1504

The Baroque Arts   The Renaissance gave way around 1600 to the Baroque, which dominated the arts until about 1750. Two factors influenced its emergence. First, the Protestant Reformation, Catholic Reformation, and religious wars changed the nature of patronage, on which artists depended. Many Protestant churches, opposed to imagery as incompatible with their view of early Christianity, did not sponsor artists for the adornment of their buildings with religious art.

Second, the predilection for Renaissance balance and restraint gave way to greater spontaneity and dramatic effect. Church and palace architecture shifted to the "baroque" voluptuousness of forms and decorations seen in Bavarian and Austrian Catholic churches, the Versailles Palace, and St. Paul's Cathedral in London, all completed between 1670 and 1750. Baroque composers, as exemplified by the Italian Antonio Vivaldi (1678–1741) and the German Johann Sebastian Bach (1685–1750), benefited from ample church and palace patronage.

The New Sciences

Italian Renaissance scholars were divided between those who continued to adhere to the scholastic Aristotelian scientific method and those (such as Copernicus) who were more interested in newly translated Hellenistic mathematical, astronomical, and geographical texts. In the 1600s, two scientists—Galileo and Newton—abandoned much of the *qualitative* scientific method of Aristotelian scholasticism in favor of the *mathematized* science of physics. In the eighteenth century, Newton's science of a mechanical, deterministic universe became the foundation of modern scientific–industrial society.

Copernicus's Incipient New Science   Nicolaus Copernicus (1473–1543) was born in Torún, a German-founded city under Polish rule. He studied at the University of Kraków, the only eastern European school to offer courses in astronomy. During the years 1495–1504, he continued his studies at Italian universities. In 1500 he taught mathematics in Rome and perhaps read Greek astronomical texts translated from Arabic. After he graduated with a degree in canon law, Copernicus took an administrative position at the cathedral of Torún, which allowed him time to pursue astronomical research. One text Copernicus did read, the *Geography* written by the Hellenistic cosmographer Ptolemy, proposed the geographical concept of Earth as a globe composed of a single sphere of intermingled earth and water.

Between 1507 and 1514 Copernicus realized that the discovery of the Americas in 1492 provided empirical proof for the theory of the world as a single earth-water sphere. It is likely that he saw the new world map by the German cartographer

Renaissance Art. Brunelleschi's cupola for the cathedral of Florence, completed in 1436, was one of the greatest achievements of the early Renaissance (a). Raphael's School of Athens (1509–1510) depicts some 50 philosophers and scientists, with Plato (in red tunic) and Aristotle (blue) in the center of the painting (b).

Copernicus's heliocentric universe

Martin Waldseemüller (ca. 1470–1520), which made him aware of the Americas as hitherto unknown inhabited lands on the other side of the world.

As a result, Copernicus firmly espoused the Ptolemaic theory of the single intermingled water-earth sphere. A globe with well-distributed water and landmasses is a perfect body that moves in perfect circular paths, he argued further. He formulated a hypothesis, according to which the earth is a body that has the same appearance and performs the same motions as the other bodies in the planetary system, especially the sun with its similar path. This revolutionary idea removed the earth from the center of the planetary system and made it revolve around the sun.

Galileo's Mathematical Physics   In the decades between the births of Copernicus and Galileo Galilei (1564–1642), mathematics improved considerably. Euclid's *Elements* was retranslated correctly from the original Greek in 1543. A translation in 1544 of a text on floating and descending bodies by the Hellenistic scholar Archimedes (287–212 BCE) also attracted intense scholarly attention.

In 1604, Galileo combined geometry, algebra, and Archimedean physics to formulate his mathematical "law of falling bodies." While earlier scholars reflected on the logical and/or geometric properties of motion only "according to imagination," Galileo systematically combined imagination with empirical research and experimentation. He thereby established what we now call the (mathematized) New Sciences.

Running Afoul of the Church   Galileo was one of the first astronomers to use a telescope, which had been recently invented in Flanders. On the basis of his astronomical work, in 1610 he became chief mathematician and philosopher at the court of the Medici, the ruling family of Florence. But his increasing fame also attracted the enmity of the Catholic Church.

As a proponent of Copernican heliocentrism, Galileo seemed to contradict the passage in the Hebrew Bible where God recognized the motion of the sun around

Waldseemüller's 1507 World Map. The German mapmaker Martin Waldseemüller was the first western Christian to draw a world map which included the newly discovered Americas. He gave them the name "America" after the Italian explorer Amerigo Vespucci (1454–1512), who was the first to state that the Americas were a separate landmass, unconnected to Asia. The single copy of Waldseemüller's map still extant is among the holdings of the US Library of Congress.

image analysis

the earth. (In Joshua 10:12–13, God stopped the sun's revolution for a day.) In contrast to the more tolerant pope at the time of Copernicus, the Roman Inquisition favored a strictly literal interpretation of this passage. In 1632 Galileo was condemned to house arrest and forced to make a public repudiation of heliocentrism.

The condemnation of Galileo had a chilling effect on scientists in countries where the Catholic Reformation was dominant. During the seventeenth century, interest in the New Sciences shifted to France, Germany, the Netherlands, and England. In these countries, no single church authority was sufficiently dominant to enforce the literal understanding of scripture. As a result, these countries produced mathematicians, astronomers, physicists, and inventors, Catholic as well as Protestant. It was this relative intellectual freedom, not sympathy on the part of religious authorities for the New Sciences, which allowed the latter to flourish, especially in the Netherlands and England.

Galileo's views of the moon

Iberian Natural Sciences   Southern European countries were still well situated to make substantial scientific contributions, even if not in the New Sciences. Botanists, geographers, ethnographers, physicians, and metallurgists fanned out across the new colonies to research the new plants, diseases, peoples, and mineral resources of the New World, Africa, and Asia. They used the traditional methods of the natural sciences and accumulated a voluminous amount of knowledge. For long periods, the Habsburg monarch kept these discoveries hidden, fearful that colonial competitors would benefit from them. It is only recently that the Iberian contributions to the sciences in the 1500s and 1600s have become more widely known.

Isaac Newton's Mechanics   In the middle of the English struggles between the Protestants and the Catholic/Catholicizing Stuart monarchs, Isaac Newton (1643–1727) brought the New Sciences of Copernicus and Galileo to their culmination. As a professor at the University of Cambridge, his primary early contribution was calculus, which he developed at the same time as the German philosopher Gottfried Wilhelm Leibniz (1646–1716). Later in his career, Newton unified the fields of physics and astronomy, establishing the so-called Newtonian synthesis. His *Mathematical Principles of Natural Philosophy*, published in 1687, established a deterministic universe following mathematical rules and formed the basis of science until the early twentieth century, when Albert Einstein's theory of relativity superseded Newtonianism.

The New Sciences and Their Social Impact

Scientists in the seventeenth century met each other in scientific societies or residential salons. Popularizers introduced the public to the New Sciences. Scientific instruments such as telescopes, microscopes, thermometers, and barometers were constantly improving. Experimentation with barometers, vacuum chambers, and cylinders operating with condensing steam culminated with the invention of the steam engine in England in 1712.

New Science Societies   When the Catholic Reformation drove the New Sciences to northwestern Europe, chartered scientific societies, such as the Royal Society of London (1660) and the Paris Academy of Sciences (1666), were established. These societies co-opted scientists as fellows, held regular meetings, challenged their fellows to answer scientific questions, awarded prizes, and organized expeditions. They also published their findings. Many societies attracted thousands of members representing an important cross section of seventeenth-century urban society in northwest Europe (see Map 17.1).

The New Science triumphed in northwestern Europe in a large, scientifically and technically interested public of experimenters, engineers, instrument makers, artisans, business people, and lay folk. Popularizers lectured to audiences of middle-class amateurs, instrument makers, and craftspeople, especially in England and the Netherlands. Coffeehouses allowed the literate urban public to meet, hear lectures, read the daily newspapers (first appearing in the early seventeenth century), and exchange ideas. Wealthy businessmen endowed public lectures and supported elaborate experiments and expensive laboratory equipment. Male urban literacy is estimated to have exceeded 50 percent in England and the Netherlands during this period, although it remained considerably lower in France, Germany, and Italy.

Women, Social Salons, and the New Science   Women were part of this scientifically inclined public. In the fields of mathematics and astronomy, Sophie Brahe (1556–1643), sister of the Danish astronomer Tycho Brahe (1546–1601), and Maria Cunitz (p. 380) made contributions to the new astronomy of Copernicus and Kepler. According to estimates, in the second half of the seventeenth century some 14 percent of German astronomers were women. A dozen prominent female astronomers practiced their science privately in Germany, Poland, the Netherlands, France, and England.

MAP 17.1 **Centers of Learning in Europe, 1500–1770.**

map analysis

Another institution that helped in the popularization of the New Sciences was the salon. As the elegant living room of an urban residence, the salon was a meeting place for the urban social elite to engage in conversations, presentations, and experiments. The culture of the salon emerged first in Paris. Since the Catholic French universities were hostile to many new ideas, educated urban aristocrats and middle-class professionals turned to the salons as places to learn about new scientific developments. Furthermore, French universities and scientific academies refused to admit women, in contrast to Italian and German institutions. The French salon, therefore, became a bastion of female scholars.

One example of a French woman scientist was Gabrielle-Émilie du Châtelet (1706–1749). In a Paris salon she met François-Marie Arouet, known as Voltaire (1694–1778), a writer, skeptic, satirist, and amateur Newtonian. Although Voltaire published prolifically, Châtelet eventually outstripped him in both research and scientific understanding. Her lasting achievement was the translation of Newton's *Mathematical Principles* into French, published in 1759.

Discovery of the Vacuum   Of all the scientific instruments available at the time, it was the barometer that would prove crucial for the exploration of the properties of the vacuum and condensing steam, eventually leading to the invention of the steam engine. The scientist who laid the groundwork for the barometer was Evangelista Torricelli (1608–1647), an assistant of Galileo. He experimented with mercury-filled glass tubes, demonstrating that atmospheric pressure produced a vacuum inside these tubes.

A few years later, the French mathematician and philosopher Blaise Pascal (1623–1662) used a mercury barometer to demonstrate lower air pressures at higher altitudes. Soon thereafter, scientists discovered the connection between changing atmospheric pressures and the weather. The discovery of the vacuum was an important step toward the practical application of the New Sciences to mechanical engineering in the eighteenth century.

The Steam Engine   The French Huguenot scientist and engineer Denis Papin (ca. 1647–1712) made the first step from the vacuum chamber to the steam engine. In 1690, Papin constructed a cylinder with a piston. Weights, via a cord and two pulleys, held the piston at the top of the cylinder. When heated, water in the bottom of the cylinder turned into steam. When subsequently cooled through the injection of water, the steam condensed, forcing the piston down and lifting the weights up. The Royal Society of London held discussions of his papers, thereby alerting engineers, craftspeople, and entrepreneurs in England to the steam engine as a labor-saving machine. In 1712, the mechanic Thomas Newcomen built the first steam engine to pump water from coal mine shafts.

Altogether, it took a little over a century for Europeans to apply the New Sciences to engineering—that is, to the construction of the steam engine. Prior to 1600, mechanical inventions—such as the wheel, the compass, the stern rudder,

Vacuum Power. In 1672, the mayor of Magdeburg, the New Scientist Otto von Guericke, demonstrated the experiment that made him a pioneer in the understanding of the physical properties of the vacuum. In the presence of German emperor Ferdinand III, two teams of horses were unable to pull the two sealed hemispheres apart. Guericke had created a vacuum by pumping out the air from the two sealed copper spheres.

and the firearm—had been constructed by anonymous tinkerers. By 1700, engineers needed at least a basic understanding of mathematics and such abstract physical phenomena as inertia, gravity, vacuums, and condensing steam in order to build a steam engine or other complex machinery.

The New Sciences: Philosophical Interpretations

The New Sciences engendered a pattern of radically new intellectual, religious, and political thinking. This thought evolved into a powerful instrument of critique of Christian doctrine and the constitutional order of the absolutist states. Through the new concept of the social contract, these ideas became a potent political force in the course of the 1700s.

Descartes's New Philosophy   The first major New Scientist who started a radical reconsideration of philosophy was the Frenchman René Descartes (1596–1650). In the service of the Dutch and Bavarian courts, he bore witness to the atrocities committed in the name of religious doctrines during the Thirty Years' War. He spent two decades in the Netherlands, studying and teaching the New Sciences. His principal innovation in mathematics was the discovery that geometry could be converted, through algebra, into analytic geometry.

Descartes, selections from *A Discourse on Method* (1637)

Descartes was shocked by the condemnation of Galileo and decided to abandon all traditional propositions and doctrines of the church. Realizing that the five senses of seeing, hearing, touching, smelling, and tasting were unreliable, he determined that the only reliable body of knowledge was thought, especially mathematical thought. As a person capable of thought, he concluded—bypassing his unreliable senses—that he existed: "I think, therefore I am" (*cogito ergo sum*). A further conclusion from this argument was that he was composed of two radically different substances, a material substance consisting of his body (that is, his senses) and another, immaterial substance consisting of his thinking mind.

Variations on Descartes's New Philosophy   Descartes's radical distinction between body and mind stimulated a lively debate. Was this distinction only conceptual, while reality was experienced as a unified whole? If the dualism was real as well as conceptual, which substance was more fundamental, sensual bodily experience or mental activity, as the creator of the concepts of experience? The answers of three philosophers—Baruch Spinoza, Thomas Hobbes, and John Locke—set the course for two major directions of philosophy during the so-called Enlightenment of the 1700s (see Chapter 23), one Continental European and the other Anglo-American.

For Baruch Spinoza (1632–1677), Descartes's distinction between body and mind was to be understood only in a conceptual sense. He therefore abandoned Descartes's distinction and developed a philosophical system that sought to integrate Galilean nature, the ideas of God, the Good in ethics, and the Just in politics into a unified whole. The Jewish community of Amsterdam, into which he had been born, excommunicated him for heresy, since he seemed to make God immanent in the world.

Both Thomas Hobbes (1588–1679) and John Locke (1632–1704) not only accepted Descartes's radical distinction; they furthermore made the body the fundamental reality and the mind a dependent function. Consequently, they focused on the bodily passions, not reason, as the principal human character trait. Hobbes

Mapping the World

In 1400, no accurate map of the world existed anywhere. Prior to the first Portuguese sailing expeditions down the west coast of Africa in the 1420s and 1430s, mariners relied upon local knowledge of winds, waves, and stars to navigate. The Portuguese were the first to use science to sail, adapting scholarship in trigonometry, astronomy, and solar timekeeping developed by Jewish and Muslim scientists in Iberia.

Crucial to this approach was latitude, which required precise calculations of the daily changes in the path of the sun relative to the earth and determination of the exact height of the sun. The invention of the nautical astrolabe in 1497 by the Jewish scientist Abraham Zacuto aided this process. To determine longitude, Jewish scientists in Portugal adapted a method based on the work of the Islamic astronomer al-Biruni (973–1048).

The new maps of the fifteenth century also drew upon an innovation from another part of the world: the compass. Originating in China, the compass was used as a navigational instrument by Muslim sailors during the twelfth century. In the thirteenth century, mapmakers in the Mediterranean began to include compasses

frontispiece to *Leviathan*

Locke, *An Essay Concerning Human Understanding* (1690)

speculated that individuals in the primordial state of nature were engaged in a "war of all against all." To survive, they forged a social contract in which they transferred all power to a sovereign. Hobbes's book *Leviathan* (1651) can be read as a political theory of absolute rule, but his ideas of a social contract and transfer of power nevertheless move toward constitutionalism.

Locke focused on the more benign bodily passion of acquisitiveness. Primordial individuals, so he argued, engaged as equals in a social contract for the purpose of erecting a government that protected their properties and established a civil society governed by law. With Hobbes and Locke a line of new thought came to its conclusion, leading from Descartes's two substances to the ideas of absolutism as well as democratic constitutionalism.

Centralizing States and Religious Upheavals

The pattern of the centralizing state transforming the institutional structures of society was characteristic not only of the Ottoman and Habsburg Empires during 1450–1750, but also of other countries of Europe, the Middle East, and India. The financial requirements for such a state required a reorganization of the relationship between rulers, ruling classes, and regional forces. Although the Protestant Reformation and religious wars slowed the pattern of central state formation, two types of states eventually emerged: the French, Russian, and Prussian landed centralizing state and the Dutch and English naval centralizing state.

The Rise of Centralized Kingdoms

The shift from feudal knights to firearm-equipped professional infantries led to states whose rulers sought to strengthen their administrations. Rulers centralized state on portolans, or nautical charts, enabling sailors to follow their direction on a map.

With an accurate science for fixing latitude and improved knowledge for longitude, the science of cartography was transformed in the fifteenth and sixteenth centuries. Any place on earth could be mapped mathematically in relation to any other place, and the direction in which one place lay in relation to another could be plotted using compass lines. By 1500 mapmakers could locate any newly discovered place in the world on a map.

Portolan by Pedro Reinel. Drawn in 1504 by the great Portuguese cartographer Pedro Reinel (ca. 1462–ca. 1542), this nautical chart (portolan) shows compass lines and is the earliest known map to include lines of latitude.

Questions

• How were adaptations from various cultural traditions essential to the transformation of cartography in the fifteenth and sixteenth centuries?

• How are developments in cartography in this time period an example of the shift from descriptive science to mathematical science?

power, collected taxes, and curbed the decentralizing forces of the nobility, cities, and local institutions. Not all city-states, city-leagues, and religious orders dating to the previous period (600–1450) survived the race to centralization. A winnowing process during 1450–1550 left only a few kingdoms in control of European politics.

The Demographic Curve   Following the demographic disaster of the Black Death, the population of the European states expanded again after 1470 and continued to grow until about 1600, when it entered a half century of stagnation during the coldest and wettest period in recorded history, the Little Ice Age (1550–1750).

During 1650–1750, the population rose slowly at a moderate rate from 105 to 140 million. The overall population figures for Europe demonstrate that Western Christianity had risen by 1750 to demographic equivalence to the two leading religious civilizations of India (155 million) and China (225 million).

A Heritage of Decentralization   Bracketed between the two empires of the Ottomans and Habsburgs, Western Christian Europe during the second half of the fifteenth century was comprised of independent or autonomous units, including the centralizing kingdoms of France and England; the Hanseatic League of trading cities; the territory ruled by the Catholic crusading order of Teutonic Knights; and the small kingdoms of Denmark, Sweden, Norway, Poland–Lithuania, Bohemia, and Hungary. It furthermore comprised the principalities and cities of Germany, the duchy of Burgundy, the republic of Switzerland, and the city-states of Italy. At the northeastern periphery was the Grand Duchy of Moscow, representing Eastern Christianity after the fall of Byzantium to the Ottomans in 1453. These units competed with each other.

Military and Administrative Capacities   In the course of the sixteenth century, some kingdoms turned their mercenary troops into standing armies and stationed them in star-shaped forts. Habsburg imperial as well as Dutch troops introduced the line infantry in the course of the sixteenth century. Since the line formation required peacetime drills and maneuvers, the regimental system came into use. Soldiers formed permanent regiments and wore standardized uniforms.

The French-invented flintlock gradually replaced the matchlock musket during 1620–1630. Similarly, during 1660–1700 the French introduced and improved the bayonet. By 1750, armies in the larger European countries were more uniform in their armaments and increased to tens of thousands of soldiers (see Map 17.2).

The military forces were expensive, and taxes expanded during the period 1450–1550. But rulers could not raise taxes without the assent of the ruling classes and cities. Villagers simply moved when taxes became too oppressive. The taxation limits were reached in most European countries in the mid-sixteenth century, and for the next two centuries rulers could raise finances only to the detriment of their central powers, such as by borrowing from merchants and selling offices.

MAP **17.2 European Warfare, 1450–1750.**

The Netherlands was an exception. Only there did the urban population rise from 10 to 40 percent, willing to pay higher taxes on expanded urban manufactures and commercial suburban farming. The Dutch government also derived revenues from charters granted to overseas trading companies. Given the severe limits on revenue-raising measures in most of Europe, the eighteenth century saw a general deterioration of state finances, which eventually contributed to the American and French Revolutions.

The Protestant Reformation, State Churches, and Independent Congregations

Parallel to the centralism of the kings, the popes restored the central role of the Vatican in the church hierarchy. The popes undertook expensive Vatican construction projects that aroused criticism, especially in Germany, where the leading clergy was strongly identified with Rome. Growing literacy and lay religiosity nurtured a profound theological dissatisfaction, leading to the **Protestant Reformation**. The Reformation began as a movement in the early sixteenth century that demanded a return to the simplicity of early Christianity. The movement quickly engulfed the kingdoms and resulted in religious wars. The divisions mark the culture of Europe even today.

Protestant Reformation: Broad movement to reform the Roman Catholic Church, the beginnings of which are usually associated with Martin Luther.

Background to the Reformation   Religious and political changes in the fifteenth century led to the Protestant Reformation. One religious shift was the growth of popular theology, a consequence of the introduction of the printing press (1454/1455). Devotional tracts catered to the spiritual interests of ordinary people. Many Christians attended Mass daily. Wealthy Christians endowed saint cults and charitable institutions; poor people studied scripture on their own.

A key political change was an increasing inability of the popes to appoint archbishops and bishops outside Italy. The kings of France, Spain, England, and Sweden were transforming their kingdoms into centralized states, reducing the influence of the popes. (The popes' influence remained strong in a politically splintered Germany.) What remained to the popes was the right to collect dues, which they used to finance their expensive administration in Rome. One of the dues was the sale of **indulgences**, which, in popular understanding, were tickets to heaven. Those disturbed by the discrepancy between declining papal power and the remaining financial privileges demanded reforms.

Erasmus, *Julius Excluded from Heaven* (1514)

Indulgence: Partial remission of sins after payment of a fine or presentation of a donation. Remission would mean the forgiveness of sins by the Church, but the sinner still remained responsible for his or her sins before God.

Luther's Reformation   One such observer was the German monk, priest, and professor Martin Luther (1483–1546). In 1517 he wrote his archbishop a letter with 95 theses in which he condemned the indulgences and other matters as contrary to scripture. What was to become the Protestant Reformation had begun.

News of Luther's protest traveled across Europe. Sales of indulgences fell off sharply. In a series of writings, Luther spelled out further reforms. One reform was the elevation of original New Testament scripture over canon law and papal decisions. Another reform was the declaration of the priesthood of all Christians, doing away with the privileged position of the clergy. A third reform was a call to German princes to begin church reform through their power over clerical appointments, even if the Habsburg emperor was opposed. Finally, by translating the Bible into German, Luther made the text available to all.

Reaction to Luther's Demands   Both the emperor and the pope failed to arrest Luther and suppress his call for church reform. Emperor Charles V, a devout Catholic, was distracted by the Ottoman-led Islamic threat in eastern Europe and the western Mediterranean. In addition, his rivalry with the French king precluded the formation of a common Catholic front against Luther. People in Germany exploited Charles's divided attention and abandoned both Catholicism and secular obedience. A savage civil war, called the Peasants' War, engulfed Germany from 1524 to 1525.

Luther and other reformers were horrified by the war. They drew up church ordinances that regulated preaching and other church matters. In Saxony, the duke endorsed this order in 1528, creating the model of Lutheran Protestantism as a state religion with the rulers as protectors and supervisors of the churches in their territories.

Other German princes and the kings of Denmark and Sweden followed suit. In England, Protestants gained strength when Henry VIII (r. 1509–1547) broke with Rome and took over church leadership in his kingdom. Although remaining Catholic, he proclaimed an Anglican state church that combined elements of Catholicism and Protestantism. Switzerland and Scotland also adopted reforms. Thus, most of northern Europe followed a pattern of alliances between Protestant reformers and the state (see Map 17.3).

Calvinism in Geneva and France   In France, King Francis I controlled all church appointments but did not create an independent state church. Since he competed with Charles V of the Habsburg Empire for dominance over the papacy in Italy, he had to appear especially loyal and devout. When Protestants in France demanded church reform, Francis I gave them the choice of exile or burning at the stake.

One reformer who chose exile was John Calvin (Jean Cauvin, 1509–1564). During his exile in Geneva, he began a stormy career as the city's religious reformer. Geneva was unsure about which path of reform to embrace. It was not until the 1550s that Calvin's form of Protestantism prevailed in the city.

A crucial doctrine of Calvin's was *predestination*. According to this doctrine, God has "predestined" each human prior to birth for heaven or hell. Believers could only hope, through faith alone, that they would receive a glimpse of their fate. In contrast to Luther, however, Calvin made the enforcement of a moral code by local authorities, part of his version of Protestantism.

Interestingly, this code did not prohibit the taking of interest on loans. While Luther as well as the Catholic Church, in accordance with scripture, condemned all interest as usury, Calvin placed moneylending into the increasingly urban context of the 1500s. Acquiring wealth with the help of money and thereby perhaps gaining a glimpse of one's fate became a hallmark of Calvinism. Wealth began to become respectable in Christian society.

Calvinist preachers went to France and the Netherlands in the mid-1500s. Under the protection of local magistrates, they organized the first independent Calvinist congregations. Calvinist religious self-organization by independent congregations became an alternative to Lutheran state religion.

The Catholic Reformation   The rivalry between Spain and France made it difficult for the popes to address Catholic reforms in order to meet the Protestant challenge. Finally, at the Council of Trent (1545–1563), they abolished payment for indulgences and phased out other church practices considered to be corrupt.

MAP 17.3 **The Protestant Reformation, ca. 1580.**

These actions launched the **Catholic Reformation**, an effort to gain back dissenting Catholics. Supported by the kings of Spain and France, however, the popes made no changes to the traditional doctrines of faith together with good works, priestly mediation between believer and God, and monasticism. They even revived the papal Inquisition and promulgated a new Index of Prohibited Books.

The popes also furthered the work of the priest Ignatius Loyola (1491–1556). At the head of the Jesuits, Loyola devoted himself to the education of the clergy, the establishment of a network of Catholic schools and colleges, and the conversion of Protestants as well as non-Christians by missionaries to the Americas and eastern Asia. Thanks to Jesuit discipline, Catholics regained self-assurance against the Protestants.

Religious Wars and Political Restoration

The growth of Calvinism led to a civil war in France and a war of liberation from Spanish Catholic rule in the Netherlands in the later sixteenth century. In England,

Catholic Reformation: Also known as Counter-Reformation. Reaffirmation of Catholic papal supremacy and the doctrine of faith together with works as preparatory to salvation. Such practices as absenteeism (bishops in Rome instead of their bishoprics) and pluralism (bishops and abbots holding multiple appointments) were abolished.

the slow pace of reform in the Anglican Church erupted in the early seventeenth century into a civil war. In Germany, the Catholic–Protestant struggle turned into the Thirty Years' War (1618–1648). The centralizing states evolved into polities based on absolutism, tempered by provincial and local administrative practices.

Civil War in France   During the mid-1500s, Calvinism in France grew mostly in the western cities, where literate merchants and craftspeople were receptive to Protestant publications. Calvinism was an urban denomination; and peasants, rooted more deeply in traditional ways of life, did not join in large numbers. Some 10 percent of the population were Huguenots, as the Protestants were called in France. The Huguenots posed a formidable challenge to French Catholicism; and although the government persecuted them, it was impossible to imprison or execute them all.

In many cities, relations between Huguenots and Catholics were uneasy. From time to time, groups of agitators crashed each other's church services. Hostilities escalated after 1560, when the government weakened under a child king and was unable to deal with the increasingly powerful Huguenots. In four western cities the Huguenots achieved self-government and full freedom of religious practice from the crown. Concerned to find a compromise, in 1572 the now reigning king married his sister to the leader of the Huguenots, King Henry III of Navarre (later King Henry IV of France, 1589–1610), a Protestant of the Bourbon family in southwestern France. Henry detested the fanaticism that surrounded him.

Only 6 days after the wedding, on St. Bartholomew's Day (August 24, 1572), outraged members of the Catholic aristocracy perpetrated a wholesale slaughter of thousands of Huguenots. This massacre, in response to the assassination of a French admiral, occurred with the apparent connivance of the court. For over a decade and a half, civil war raged, in which Spain aided the Catholics and Henry enrolled German and Swiss Protestant mercenaries. A turning point came only when Henry of Navarre became King Henry IV in 1589. It was 9 years before he was able to calm the religious fanaticism of the French people. With the Edict of Nantes in 1598, he decreed freedom of religion for Protestants. However, Catholic adherents were deeply offended by the edict as well as by the alleged antipapal policies of Henry IV, and the king was assassinated in 1610. In 1685, King Louis XIV revoked the edict and triggered the emigration of Huguenots to the Netherlands, Germany, England, and North America. At last, France was Catholic again.

The Dutch War of Independence   In the Netherlands, the Spanish overlords were determined to keep the country Catholic. When Charles V resigned in 1556 (effective 1558), his son Philip II (r. 1556–1598) became king of Spain and the Netherlands. Like his father, Philip supported the Catholic Reformation. He asked the Jesuits and the Inquisition to aggressively persecute the Calvinists. Philip also subdivided the bishoprics into smaller units and recruited clergymen in place of members of the nobility.

In response, in 1565 the nobility and Calvinist congregations rose in revolt, triggering what was to become a Protestant war of Dutch liberation from Catholic Spanish overlordship (1565–1620). Philip suppressed the liberation movement, reimposed Catholicism, and executed thousands of rebels, many of them members of the Dutch aristocracy.

first Dutch national atlas, 1622

In 1579, rebels renewed the war of liberation. Spain kept fighting the rebellion until acute Spanish financial difficulties prompted the truce of 1609–1621. Although drawn into fighting again during the Thirty Years' War, the Netherlands gained its full independence eventually in 1648.

Civil War in England   The prevalent form of Protestantism in England was Calvinism. During the sixteenth century, the majority of people in England, including Calvinists, belonged to the Anglican Church. English Catholics were a small minority. The percentage of Calvinists was the same as in France before 1685, but the partially reformed Anglican Church under the tolerant queen Elizabeth I (1533–1603) was able to hold them in check.

The Calvinists encompassed moderate and radical tendencies that neutralized each other. Among the radicals were the Puritans, who demanded the abolition of the Anglican clerical hierarchy and a new church order of independent congregations. When Anglican Church reform slowed with the arrival of the Stuart monarchs on the throne of England (1603–1685), unfortunately the balance among the religious tendencies unraveled. As rulers of England, the Stuarts were officially heads of the Anglican state church, but except for the first king, the 3 successors were either Catholics or Catholic sympathizers. Since they were furthermore rulers of what was called the England of the Three Kingdoms they found it impossible to maneuver among the demands of the English Puritans, Scottish Presbyterians (self-governing regional Calvinists), and Catholic Irish. The issue of how little or how far the Anglican Church had been reformed away from Catholicism and how dominant it should be in the three realms became more and more divisive (see Source 17.1).

In addition, the Stuarts were intent on building a centralized state. They collected taxes without the approval of Parliament. Many members of Parliament resented being bypassed. A slight majority in the House of Commons was Puritan, and what they considered the stalled church reform added to their resentment. Eventually, when all tax resources were exhausted, the king had to call Parliament back together. The two sides were unable to come to an agreement, however, and civil war broke out. Since this war was also a conflict among the Three Kingdoms, it had both religious and regional aspects (1639–1651).

Because of widespread pillage and destruction, the indirect effects of the war for the rural population were severe. The New Model Army, a professional body of 22,000 troops raised by the Puritan-dominated English Parliament against the royal forces, caused further upheavals by cleansing villages of their "frivolous" local traditions. In the end, the monarchy was replaced with a republican theocracy, the "Commonwealth of England."

Republic, Restoration, and Revolution   The ruler of this theocracy, Oliver Cromwell (r. 1649–1658), was a Puritan member of the lower nobility and a commander in the New Model Army. After dissolving Parliament, Cromwell handpicked a new parliament but ruled mostly without its consent. Since both Scotland and Ireland were opposed to the English Puritans, Cromwell waged a savage war of submission against the two. The Dutch and Spanish, also opponents of the Puritans, were defeated in naval wars that increased English power in the Atlantic. But fear in Parliament of a permanent centralized state led to a refusal of financial subsidies for the military. After Cromwell's death in 1658, it took just 3 years to restore the Stuart monarchy and the Anglican state church.

The recalled Stuart kings, however, resumed the policies of centralization. As before, the kings rarely called Parliament together and raised funds without its authorization. But their standing army was intended more to intimidate the parliamentarians than to subjugate them. In the "Glorious Revolution" of 1688, a defiant Parliament deposed the king and made his daughter and her Dutch husband the new co-regents.

The Thirty Years' War in Germany   Continuing religious tensions in Germany erupted into the Thirty Years' War. Rulers of the German principalities had made either Catholicism or Protestantism their state religion, though most tolerated minorities or even admitted them to offices. The Jesuit-educated Ferdinand II (r. 1619–1637), ruler of the Holy Roman Empire, however, refused to appoint Protestants in majority-Protestant Bohemia. In response, Protestant leaders in 1618 renounced Ferdinand's authority and made the Calvinist prince of the Palatinate in the Rhineland their new king.

In a first round of war (1619–1630), Ferdinand and the Catholic princes suppressed the rebellion and advanced toward northern Germany, capturing Lutheran territories for reconversion to Catholicism and defeating Denmark. In 1630, however, the Lutheran king Gustavus II Adolphus (r. 1611–1632) of Sweden intervened. By aiding the German Lutherans, he hoped to consolidate his predominance in the region. Louis XIII (r. 1610–1643) of France granted Sweden financial subsidies, since he was concerned that Ferdinand's victories would further strengthen the Habsburg grip around France. With the politically motivated alliance between Sweden and France, the German Catholic–Protestant war turned into a war for state dominance in Europe.

The Swedes were initially successful, but withdrew when Gustavus II Adolphus fell. Ferdinand compromised with the Protestant princes of Germany, by reestablishing the prewar divisions, in order to keep the French out of the war. But Louis XIII entered anyway and occupied Habsburg Alsace. Swedish armies, exploiting the French successes against the Habsburgs, fought their way back into Germany. In 1684, the Austrian–German Habsburgs agreed to the Peace of Westphalia.

The agreement provided for religious freedom in Germany and ceded Habsburg territories in Alsace to France and the southern side of the Baltic Sea to Sweden. It granted territorial integrity to all European powers. The Spanish Habsburgs continued their war against France until their defeat in 1659, which accelerated the decline of Spain's overseas power. France emerged as the strongest country in Europe, and the Spanish-dominated Caribbean became an area of open rivalry (see Map 17.4).

Absolutism: Theory of the state in which the unlimited power of the king, ruling under God's divine mandate, was emphasized. In practice, it was neutralized by the nobility and provincial and local communities.

Absolutism in France?   During its period of greatest political dominance, France came under the rule of its longest-reigning monarch, King Louis XIV (1643–1715). He made Versailles—a gigantic palace and gardens near Paris, populated with 10,000 courtiers, attendants, and servants—into a site of almost continuous feasting, entertainment, and intrigue. It was here that Louis, the "Sun King," exercised his "absolute" divine mandate upon his aristocracy and commoners alike.

In practice, the **absolutism** of Louis XIV, as well as absolutism in other European countries, was a mixture of centralized and decentralized forces. On one

Centralizing States at War. German imperial troops besiege Swedish troops in the northern German city of Stralsund in 1628. The etching shows typical features of the centralizing state, from top to bottom: galleon-style warships (successors of the caravel); a star-shaped fort (an Italian innovation) designed to withstand artillery barrages; the medieval walls of the city; musket-equipped infantry troops; field cannons; and the colorful Baroque uniforms worn by the musketeers of the period.

hand, after the end of the religious wars in 1648, mercenary armies under autonomous dukes and counts were replaced by permanent armies or navies under the central command of royal relatives or favorites. The kings no longer called assemblies together to have new taxes approved (in France from 1614 to 1789), and thus, many of the nobility's tax privileges disappeared.

On the other hand, kings were aware that true absolutism was possible only if the taxes were collected by centrally salaried employees. However, a centrally paid bureaucracy would have required a central bank with provincial branches, using

MAP **17.4** **Europe in 1648.**

a credit and debit system. The failed experiment with such a bank in Paris from 1714 to 1720 demonstrates that absolute central control was beyond the powers of the kings.

Instead, the kings had to rely on subcontracting out the collection of taxes to the highest bidders, who then helped themselves to the collection of their incomes. Under Louis XIV anyone who had money or borrowed it from financiers was encouraged to buy an office. The government often forced these officers to grant additional loans to the crown. To retain their loyalty, the government rewarded them with first picks for retaining their offices within the family. They were also privileged to buy landed estates or acquire titles of nobility. By selling offices and titles, the king sought to bind the financial interests of the two nobilities to those of his own.

Louis XIV sent salaried *intendants* to the provinces to ensure that collecting taxes, rendering justice, and policing functioned properly. About half of the provinces had *parlements*—appointed assemblies for the ratification of decrees from Paris—whose officeholders, drawn from the local noble, clerical, and commoner classes, frequently resisted the intendants.

In later years, when Louis XIV was less successful in his wars against the rival Habsburgs and Protestant Dutch, the crown overspent and had to borrow heavily. Louis's successors in the second half of the eighteenth century were saddled with crippling debts.

The Rise of Russia   The ideological embodiment of absolutism in the Versailles of Louis XIV spawned adaptations across Europe. These adaptations were most visible in eastern Europe, which had far fewer towns and cities. Without a large population of urban commoners to aid them in building the centralized state, rulers there had to make do with the landowning aristocracy. As a result, rulers and aristocracy connived to finance state centralization through an increased exploitation of farmers. In the 1600s, the legal status of farmers deteriorated, their tax liabilities increased, and they became serfs.

In Russia, **Tsar** Peter I, "the Great" (r. 1682–1725), of the Eastern Christian Romanov dynasty, sought to establish the French-type centralized state. Peter invited western European soldiers, mariners, administrators, craftspeople, scholars, and artists into his service. He built ports on the Baltic Sea and established the new capital of St. Petersburg, with beautiful palaces and official buildings.

The Russian military was completely reorganized by the tsar. Peter made the inherited firearm regiments part of a new army recruited from the traditional Russian landed nobility. Soldiers received education at military schools and academies and were required to provide lifelong service. A census was taken to facilitate the shift from the inherited household tax on the villagers to a new capitation tax collected by military officers. In the process, many farmers now found themselves classified and taxed as serfs, unfree to leave their villages. The result of Peter's reforms was a powerful, expansionary centralizing state (see Map 17.5).

The Rise of Prussia   Similar to Russia, the principality of Prussia-Brandenburg was underurbanized. When the Lutheran Hohenzollern rulers embarked on the construction of a centralized state in the later seventeenth century, they first broke the tax privileges of the landowning aristocracy and raised taxes themselves through agents. As in Russia, farmers who worked on estates held by landlords were serfs. Since there were few urban middle-class merchants and professionals, the kings enrolled members of the landlord aristocracy in the army and civilian administration.

The Hohenzollern monarchs enlarged the army, employing it during peacetime for drainage and canal projects as well as palace construction in Berlin, the capital. Under Frederick II, "the Great" (1740–1786), Prussia pursued an aggressive foreign policy. Frederick also sought to attract immigrants, intensify agriculture, and establish manufacturing. Prussia emerged as a serious competitor of the Habsburgs in the Holy Roman Empire of Germany.

English Constitutionalism   In contrast to Prussia, France, Spain, Austria, and other European states, England had since 1450 a political system ruled by a king or a queen, with a parliament composed of the aristocracy as well as representatives of towns and cities. Only in England did the interests of the nobility and the urban merchants gradually converge: Younger sons, unable to inherit the family estate, sought their fortunes in London. English cities allied with the aristocracy in resisting indirect tax increases and forcing the throne to use the revenues of its royal estates to pay

Peter the Great, "Decree on the Invitation to Foreigners" (1702)

Tsar (or Czar): Derived from "Caesar," title used by the Russian rulers to emphasize their imperial ambitions.

MAP **17.5** **The Expansion of Russia, 1462–1795.**

Prussian Military Discipline. The Prussian line infantry made full use in the mid-1700s of flintlock muskets, bayonets, and drilling.

soldiers. Efforts of the Stuart kings to create a centralized state based on firearm infantries failed. Instead, the ruling class preferred to build a centralized naval state. After the Glorious Revolution of 1688, England became the world's dominant naval power.

After its victory over the Stuart kings, Parliament consolidated its financial powers through the creation of the Bank of England in 1694. When Mary and William died without children, England continued in 1714 with a king from the principality of Hannover in Germany distantly related to the previous royals. Around the same time, England and Scotland united, creating the United Kingdom. Parliament collected taxes and, through its bank, was able to keep its debt service low during the early 1700s. The navy grew twice as large as that of France and was staffed by a well-salaried, disciplined military, while the few land troops were mostly low-paid Hessian-German mercenaries. A two-party system of two aristocracy–merchant alliances emerged. The two parties were known as the Tories and the Whigs, with the Whigs in power for most of the first half of the eighteenth century.

» Putting It All Together

Prior to 1500, all religious civilizations possessed mathematics and qualitative sciences. Trigonometry-based astronomy existed in the Islamic, Hindu, and Christian religious civilizations and was practiced also in China. Physics became the second mathematical science in the early 1500s, but only in Western Christianity. This transformation of the sciences had no practical consequences prior to the invention of the steam engine in the 1700s. Furthermore, the mathematization of physics did little to influence the continued prevalence of qualitative description as the methodology of the other sciences.

Interactive concept map

Most importantly, the rise of the New Sciences should not be confused with the vast changes, called "modernity" after 1800, which propelled the West to world dominance. Although the West began to acquire its scientific and philosophical identity with the introduction of the mathematical sciences in the century between Copernicus and Galileo (1514–1604), the impact of these sciences on the world was felt only after 1800 when they were applied to industry. Once this application gathered momentum in the nineteenth century, Asia and Africa had no choice but to adapt to modern science and industrialization.

Review and Relate

| Thinking Through Patterns

Examine the ways historians approach the big questions of this chapter.

Located far from the traditional agrarian–urban centers of Eurasia, Western Christianity adapted its culture in response to outside stimuli coming from Islamic and Eastern Christian civilizations. Without these stimuli, the Renaissance, Baroque, New Science, and Enlightenment would not have developed. In contrast,

» What were the reasons for the cultural changes that began in Europe around 1450? In which ways were the patterns of cultural changes during

1450–1750 different from those in the other religious civilizations of Eurasia?

≫ When and how did the New Sciences begin, and how did they gain popularity in northwestern European society? Why is the popularization of the New Sciences important for understanding the period 1450–1750?

≫ What were the patterns of centralized state formation and transformation in the period 1450–1750? How did the Protestant Reformation and religious wars modify these patterns?

the Middle East, Byzantium, India, and China, originating within the traditional agrarian–urban centers, received far fewer outside stimuli prior to the scientific–industrial age. Scholars and thinkers in these religious civilizations did not feel the same pressure to change their cultural heritage and adapt as their colleagues in Western Christianity did.

The discovery of the two new continents of the Americas prompted Nicolaus Copernicus to posit a sun-centered planetary system. Copernicus's new approach to science continued with Galileo Galilei's discovery of the mathematical law of falling bodies in physics and was completed when Isaac Newton unified physics and astronomy. The New Sciences became popular in educated urban circles in northwestern Europe, where Catholic and Protestant church authorities were largely divided. In southern Europe, where the Catholic Reformation was powerful and rejected Galileo, the adoption of the New Sciences occurred more slowly. Scientists in northwestern Europe discovered the practical applicability of the New Sciences as they experimented with steam engines, a catalyst for the launching of the scientific–industrial age.

European kingdoms expanded their powers of taxation to the detriment of the nobility. With these funds, they hired and salaried mercenary infantries equipped with firearms, using them to conquer land from their neighbors. The religious wars of the 1500s and 1600s strengthened centralization efforts and hastened the demise of the nobility as an obstacle to the centralized state. In England, Parliament blocked the Stuart kings from building a landed central state and instead pursued the construction of a naval state.

| Against the Grain

Consider this as a counterpoint to the main patterns examined in this chapter.

The Digger Movement

- Was Winstanley hopelessly utopian in his efforts to establish farmer communities on common land in England?

- How have other figures in world history sympathized with the lot of poor and landless farmers and attempted reform (or revolution) on their behalf?

In April 1649, toward the end of the English Civil War and just 3 months after the execution of King Charles I, a group of farmers and day laborers occupied "common" (public) land south of London to establish a colony. As the farmers and laborers dug up the soil, they came to be called the "Diggers."

Driven off by small landowners who benefited from the use of common land for grazing sheep and cutting timber, a smaller group of Diggers moved on to common land in nearby Cobham in August 1649. This time it was the gentry with their manor rights to the common land who destroyed the Diggers' cottages and fields in the winter of 1650. The Diggers made a much-publicized statement that public land was "the treasure of all people" and should not be reserved for the benefit of anyone—a bold demand that ran counter to the rapidly increasing privatization of land and commercialization of agriculture.

The leader of the group was Gerrard Winstanley (1609–1670), a former cloth merchant in London who had had to abandon his trade in 1643 after he became insolvent. He struggled to regain his solvency in the countryside of Surrey, at one point working as a grazier of cattle. Parts of Surrey had suffered substantial hardship during the Civil War, having been forced to provision and quarter troops. In pamphlets between 1648 and 1650, Winstanley explained the motives and goals of the Diggers, making these affairs relevant, in the religious idiom of Protestantism, for England as a whole. He was the first to identify the problem of the rising numbers of rural landless laborers victimized by the increasing commercialization of agriculture in England—a labor force that continued to increase until the industrializing cities of the later 1700s eventually absorbed them.

Key Terms

audio flashcards

Absolutism 398	Indulgence 393	Renaissance 381
Catholic Reformation 395	New Sciences 381	Tsar (or Czar) 401
Humanism 382	Protestant Reformation 393	

For additional resources, please go to
www.oup.com/us/vonsivers.
Please see the Further Resources section at the back of the book for additional readings and suggested websites.

New Patterns in New Worlds

COLONIALISM AND INDIGENOUS RESPONSES IN THE AMERICAS

ATLANTIC OCEAN

PACIFIC OCEAN

THE AMERICAS IN 1750

- Spanish
- Portuguese
- British
- French
- Dutch

Alonso Ortíz fled from his creditors in Spain in the early 1770s to find a new life in the Americas. In Mexico City, he set up shop as a tanner. Eight Native American employees did the actual labor of stomping the hides in the vats filled with tanning acids. A black slave was the supervisor. Ortíz concentrated on giving instructions and hustling his flourishing business.

Ortíz's situation in Mexico City was not entirely legal, however. He had left his wife and children alone in Spain, though the law required that families should be united. The authorities rarely enforced this law, but that was no guarantee for Ortíz. Furthermore, he had not yet sent his family any remittances. And then there was still the debt. Ortíz had reasons to be afraid of the law.

To avoid prosecution, Ortíz wrote a letter to his wife. In this letter, he described the comfortable position he had achieved. He announced that his business partner was sending her a sum of money sufficient to begin preparations for her departure from Spain. To his creditors, Ortíz promised to send 100 tanned hides within a year. Evidently aware of her reluctance

ABOVE: In his monumental Historia de la conquista de México, *written more than 150 years after the events described, Antonio de Solís (1610–1686) depicted the meeting of Moctezuma and Cortés.*

to join him in Mexico, Ortíz closed his letter with a request to grant him 4 more years abroad and to do so with a notarized document from her hand. Unfortunately, we do not know her answer.

The Ortíz family drama gives a human face to European colonialism and emigration to the "New World" of the Americas. Like Alonso Ortíz, some 300,000 other Spaniards left the "Old World" (Europe, contiguous with Asia and Africa) between 1500 and 1800. A few hundred letters by emigrants exist, giving us glimpses of their lives in the parts of the Americas conquered by the Spanish and Portuguese in the sixteenth century. These relatively privileged immigrants hoped to build successful enterprises using the labor of Native Americans as well as black slaves imported from Africa. The example of Ortíz shows that even in the socially not very prestigious craft of tanning, a man could achieve a measure of comfort by having people of even lower status working for him.

Seeing Patterns

≫ What is the significance of western Europeans acquiring the Americas as a warm-weather extension of their northern continent?

≫ What was the main pattern of social development in colonial America during the period 1500–1800?

≫ Why and how did European settlers in South and North America strive for self-government, and how successful were they in achieving their goals?

Beginning in the sixteenth century, the Americas became an extension of Europe. European settlers extracted mineral and agricultural resources from these new lands. A pattern emerged in which gold and silver, as well as agricultural products, were intensively exploited. In this role, the Americas became a crucial factor in Europe's changing position in the world. First, Europe acquired precious metals, which its two largest competitors, India and China, lacked. Second, with agricultural commodities pouring in from the Americas, Europe rose to a position of agrarian autonomy similar to that of India and China.

The Colonial Americas: Europe's Warm-Weather Extension

The European extension into the Americas followed Columbus's pursuit of a sea route to India that would circumvent the Mediterranean and its dominance by Muslim traders. The Spaniards financed their imperial expansion as well as their wars against Ottoman and European rivals with American gold and silver, leaving little for domestic investment. A pattern evolved in which Iberian settlers transformed the Americas into mineral-extracting and agrarian colonies based on either cheap or forced labor.

The Conquest of Mexico and Peru

The Spanish conquerors of the Aztec and Inca Empires exploited internal weaknesses in the empires. They eliminated the top of the power structures, paralyzing the decision-making apparatuses long enough for their conquests to succeed. Soon after the conquests, the Old World disease of smallpox ravaged the Native American population and dramatically reduced the indigenous labor force. To make up for this reduction, colonial authorities imported black slaves from Africa. A three-tiered society of European immigrants, Native Americans, and black slaves emerged in the Spanish and Portuguese Americas.

Bartolomé de las Casas, from *A Short Account of the Destruction of the Indies* (1542)

Chapter Outline

• The Colonial Americas: Europe's Warm-Weather Extension

• The Making of American Societies: Origins and Transformations

• Putting It All Together

Land-labor grant (*encomienda*): Land grant by the government to an entrepreneur, entitling him to use forced indigenous or imported slave labor on that land for the exploitation of agricultural and mineral resources.

Cultural Intermediary. The Tabascans gave Malinche, or Doña Marina, to Hernán Cortés as a form of tribute after they were defeated by the Spanish. Malinche served Cortés as a translator and mistress, playing a central role in Cortés's eventual victory over the Aztecs. She was in many respects the principal face of the Spanish and is always depicted center stage in Native American visual accounts of the conquest.

From Trading Posts to Conquest Columbus had discovered the Caribbean islands under a royal commission, which entitled him to build fortified posts and to trade with the indigenous Taínos. Trade relations with the Taínos, however, deteriorated into exploitation, with the Spaniards usurping the traditional entitlements of the Taíno chiefs to the labor of their fellow men. With the help of **land-labor grants** (Spanish *encomiendas*), the Spanish took over from the Taíno chiefs and, through forced labor, amassed quantities of gold. What had begun as trade-post settlement turned into full-blown conquest of land.

The Spaniards conquered the Caribbean islands not only through force. Much more severe in its consequences was the indirect conquest through disease. Smallpox wiped out an estimated 250,000 to 1 million Taínos as well as the Caribs. Isolated from the rest of humankind, Native Americans possessed no immunity against smallpox and other introduced diseases.

Protests, mostly among some members of the clergy, arose against both the labor exploitation and the helplessness of the Taínos against disease. The land-labor grant system finally came to an end after 1542 with the introduction of the *repartimiento* system (see p. 414 below).

First Mainland Conquests Hernán Cortés (1485–1547), upon arriving on Hispaniola in 1504, advanced from governmental scribe in Hispaniola to mayor of Santiago in Cuba. Thanks to labor grants, he became rich. When the Cuban governor asked him in 1518 to lead an expedition for trade and exploration to the Yucatán Peninsula in Mexico, Cortés enthusiastically agreed. He assembled 300 men, considerably exceeding his contract. The governor tried to stop him, but Cortés departed quickly for the American mainland.

As the Cuban governor had feared, Cortés did not bother with trading posts in Yucatán. The Spanish had learned of the existence of the Aztec Empire, with its immense silver and gold treasures. In a first encounter, Cortés's small Spanish force defeated a much larger indigenous force at Tabasco. The Spaniards' steel weapons and armor proved superior in hand-to-hand combat against the defenders.

Among the gifts presented by the defeated Native Americans in Tabasco was Malinche, a Nahuatl [NAH-huaw]-speaking woman. Malinche quickly learned Spanish and became the consort of Cortés. As a translator, Malinche was nearly as decisive as Cortés in shaping events. With Tabasco conquered, Cortés quickly moved on; he was afraid that the Cuban governor would otherwise force him to return to Cuba.

Conquest of the Aztec Empire On the southeast coast of Mexico, Cortés founded the city of Veracruz. He had his followers elect a town council, which made Cortés their head and chief justice, allowing Cortés to claim legitimacy for his march inland. Marching inland, the Spaniards ran into resistance from indigenous people, suffering their first losses of horses and men. They pressed onward with thousands of Native American allies, most notably the Tlaxcalans, traditional enemies of the Aztecs. The support from these indigenous peoples proved essential when Cortés and his army reached the court of the Aztecs.

When Cortés arrived at the city of Tenochtitlán on November 2, 1519, the emperor Moctezuma II (r. 1502–1519) was unsure of how to react to the invaders. To gain time, Moctezuma greeted the Spaniard in person and invited him to his palace. Cortés and his company, now numbering some 600 Spaniards, took up quarters in the palace precincts. After a week of deteriorating discussions, Cortés suddenly put the incredulous emperor under house arrest and made him swear allegiance to Charles V.

However, Cortés was diverted by the need to march back east, where troops from Cuba had arrived to arrest him. After defeating those troops, he pressed the remnants into his own service and returned to Tenochtitlán. During his absence, the Spaniards who had remained in Moctezuma's palace had massacred Aztec nobles. As an infuriated crowd of Tenochtitlán's inhabitants invaded the palace, Moctezuma and some 200 Spaniards died. The rest of the Spanish retreated east to their Tlaxcalan allies. There, after his return, Cortés devised a new plan for capturing Tenochtitlán.

After 10 months of preparations, the Spaniards returned to the Aztec capital. In command now of about 2,000 Spanish soldiers and assisted by some 50,000 Native American troops, Cortés laid siege to the city. After nearly 3 months, much of the city was in ruins, water and food became scarce, and smallpox began to decimate the population. On August 21, 1521, the Spaniards and their allies stormed the city and looted its gold treasury. They captured the last emperor, Cuauhtémoc [coo-aw-TAY-moc] and executed him in 1525, thus ending the Aztec Empire (see Map 18.1).

Conquest of the Inca Empire   A relative of Cortés, Francisco Pizarro (ca. 1475–1541), planned to conquer the Andean empire of the Incas. Pizarro, like Cortés born in Spain, but uneducated, arrived in Hispaniola as part of an expedition in 1513 that went on to discover Panama and the Pacific. He became mayor of Panama City, acquired some wealth, and heard rumors about an empire of gold and silver to the south. After a failed initial expedition, he captured some precious metal from an oceangoing Inca sailing raft. Upon receiving a permit from Charles V to establish a trading post, Pizarro and a team departed in late December 1530.

▷ Cortés and the conquest of the Aztec Empire

🖼 "The Capture of Tenochtitlán"

👆 interactive timeline

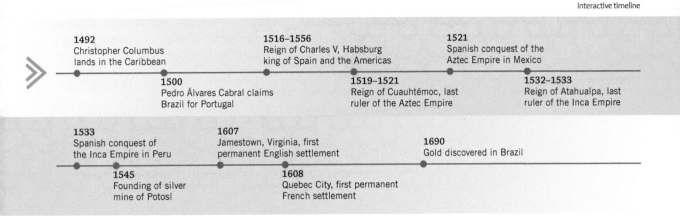

1492 Christopher Columbus lands in the Caribbean	1516–1556 Reign of Charles V, Habsburg king of Spain and the Americas	1521 Spanish conquest of the Aztec Empire in Mexico
1500 Pedro Álvares Cabral claims Brazil for Portugal	1519–1521 Reign of Cuauhtémoc, last ruler of the Aztec Empire	1532–1533 Reign of Atahualpa, last ruler of the Inca Empire

1533 Spanish conquest of the Inca Empire in Peru	1607 Jamestown, Virginia, first permanent English settlement	1690 Gold discovered in Brazil
1545 Founding of silver mine of Potosí	1608 Quebec City, first permanent French settlement	

MAP 18.1 **The European Exploration of the Americas, 1519–1542.**

In the years before Pizzaro's expedition, smallpox had ravaged the Inca Empire, killing the emperor and his heir apparent and leading to a protracted war of succession between two surviving sons. When Pizarro entered the Inca Empire, one of those sons, Atahualpa, was encamped with an army of 40,000 men near the town of Cajamarca.

Arriving at Cajamarca, Pizarro arranged an unarmed audience with Atahualpa. On November 16, 1532, Atahualpa came to this audience, surrounded by several thousand unarmed retainers, while Pizarro's soldiers hid nearby. At a signal, these soldiers rushed forward, capturing Atahualpa and massacring his retainers. Not one Spanish soldier was killed.

The ambush paralyzed the Inca Empire at the very top. Atahualpa offered his captors a room full of gold and silver as ransom. In the following 2 months, Inca administrators delivered immense quantities of precious metals to Pizarro. But Spanish officers executed Atahualpa anyway on July 26, 1533, hoping to keep the Incas disorganized.

The Spaniards then captured the Incan capital, Cuzco, massacring the inhabitants and stripping the city of its immense gold and silver treasures. In 1535 Pizarro founded a new capital, Lima, which was more conveniently located on the coast. Although Incas in the south rebuilt a kingdom that held out until 1572, the Spanish eventually gained full control of the Inca Empire.

ATAHUALLPA, INCA XIIII.

Conquest by Surprise. The Spanish conqueror Francisco Pizarro captured Emperor Atahualpa in an ambush. Atahualpa promised a roomful of gold in return for his release, but the Spaniards collected the gold and murdered Atahualpa before generals of the Inca army could organize an armed resistance.

The Portuguese Conquest of Brazil Navigators from both Spain and Portugal had first sighted the Brazilian coast in 1499–1500, and the Portuguese quickly claimed it for themselves. The majority of Brazil's indigenous population at that time lived in villages based on agriculture, fishing, and hunting.

The Portuguese were interested initially in trade with villagers, mostly for brazilwood, which was used to make a red dye. When French traders appeared, ignoring the Portuguese commercial treaties with the tribes, the Portuguese crown shifted to trading-post settlements. Land grants were made with the obligation to build fortified coastal villages for settlers and to engage in agriculture and friendly trade. By the mid-sixteenth century, inhabitants of some of these villages intermarried with local indigenous chieftain families and established sugarcane plantations.

Explanations for the Spanish Success The stupendous victories of handfuls of Spaniards over huge empires defies easy explanation. Four factors invite consideration. First, the conquistadors went straight to the top of the imperial pyramid. The emperors expected diplomatic deference, but confronted instead with arrogance and brutality, they were thrown off balance by the Spaniards. Second, in both the Aztec and Inca Empires, individuals and groups contested the hierarchical power structure. The conquistadors either found allies among the subject populations or encountered a divided leadership. Third, European-introduced diseases took a devastating toll. In both empires, smallpox hit at critical moments during or right before the Spanish invasions. Finally, thanks to horses and European steel weapons and armor, small numbers of Spaniards were able to hold large numbers of attacking Aztecs and Incas at bay in hand-to-hand combat. Cannons and matchlock muskets were less important, since they were useless in close encounters.

Malinche directing Spanish forces, from the *Lienzo de Tlaxcala* (1552)

The Establishment of Colonial Institutions

The Spanish crown established administrative hierarchies in the Americas, with governors at the top and lower ranks of functionaries. Some settler autonomy was permitted through town and city councils, but the crown was determined to make the Americas a territorial extension of the European pattern of centralized state formation.

Several hundred thousand settlers found a new life in the Americas. By the early seventeenth century, an elite of Spaniards who had been born in America, called **Creoles** (Spanish *criollos*), first assisted and later replaced most of the administrators sent from Spain (see Map 18.2).

From Conquest to Colonialism The riches of Cortés and Pizarro inspired further expeditions into Central and North America, Chile, and the Amazon. These expeditions, however, yielded only modest amounts of gold and earned more from selling captured Native Americans into slavery. In the north, expeditions penetrated as far as Arizona, New Mexico, Texas, Oklahoma, Kansas, and Florida, but encountered only relatively poor villagers and Pueblo towns. No new golden kingdoms beyond the Aztec and Inca Empires were discovered in the Americas.

In the mid-sixteenth century, the conquistadors shifted from looting to the exploitation of Native American labor in mines and in agriculture. Explorers discovered silver in Bolivia (1545) and northern Mexico (1556), gold in Chile (1552), and mercury in Peru (1563).

Indigenous peoples occasionally resisted incorporation into the Spanish colonies. Notably, the Mapuche in southern Chile repulsed all attempts by the Spanish to subdue them. Initially, in 1550–1553 the Spanish succeeded in establishing forts and opening a gold mine, but they failed to gain more than a border strip with an adjacent no-man's-land. In 1612 they agreed to a temporary peace that left the majority of the Mapuche independent.

Another Native American people who successfully resisted the Spanish conquest were the Asháninka in the Peruvian rain forest. The Asháninka exploited hillside salt veins in their region and were traders of goods between the Andes and the rain forest. It was only in 1737 that the Spanish finally built a fort in the region—a first step toward projecting colonial power into the rain forest.

Bureaucratic Efficiency During the first two generations after the conquest, Spain maintained an efficient colonial administration to deliver revenues to Spain. In addition, the viceroyalty of New Spain in Mexico remitted another 25 percent of its revenues to the Philippines, the Pacific province for which it was administratively responsible from 1571 onward. Settlers in New Spain had to pay up to 40 different taxes and dues. The only income tax was the tithe to the church, which the administration collected and, at times, used for its own budgetary purposes. Altogether, however, for the settlers the tax level was lower in the New World than in Spain, and the same was true for the English and French colonists in North America.

Brazil in 1519. This early map is fairly accurate for the northern coast, but increasingly less accurate as one moves south. First explorations of the south by both Portuguese and Spanish mariners date to 1513–1516. Ferdinand Magellan passed through several places along the southern coast on his journey around the world in 1520–1521. The scenes on the map depict Native Americans cutting and collecting brazilwood, the source of a red dye much in demand by the Portuguese during the early period of colonization.

Creoles: American-born descendants of European, primarily Spanish, immigrants.

MAP 18.2 **The Colonization of Central and South America to 1750.**

map analysis

Labor assignment (*repartimiento*): Obligation by villagers to send stipulated numbers of people as laborers to a contractor, who had the right to exploit a mine or other labor-intensive enterprise; the contractors paid the laborers minimal wages and bound them through debt peonage (repayment of money advances) to their businesses.

In the 1540s the government introduced rotating **labor assignments** (*repartimientos*) to phase out the *encomiendas*. This institution of rotating labor assignments was a continuation of the *mit'a* system, which the Incas had devised as a form of taxation (see Chapter 15). Rotating labor assignments meant that a percentage of villagers had to provide labor to the state. Private entrepreneurs could also contract for indigenous labor assignments, especially in mining regions.

In Mexico the *repartimiento* fell out of use in the first half of the seventeenth century due to the toll of smallpox on the Native American population. The replacement for the lost workers was wage labor. In highland Peru, where the effects of smallpox were less severe, the assignment system lasted to the end of the colonial period. Wage labor expanded there as well. Wages for Native Americans and blacks remained everywhere lower than for those for Creoles.

The Rise of the Creoles   Administrative and fiscal efficiency did not last very long. The wars of the Spanish Habsburg Empire cost more than the crown was able to collect in revenues. In order to make up the financial deficit, the crown began to sell offices in the Americas to the highest bidders. By the end of the century, Creoles had purchased life appointments in city councils as well as other important sinecures that allowed them to collect fees and rents. Local oligarchies emerged, effectively ending participatory politics in Spanish colonial America.

The effects of the change from recruitment by merit to recruitment by wealth on the functioning of the bureaucracy were far-reaching. Creoles advanced on a broad front in the administrative positions, while fewer Spaniards found it attractive to buy their American positions from overseas. The only opportunities which European Spaniards still found enticing were positions that gave their owners the right to subject the Native Americans to forced purchases of goods, yielding huge profits. By 1700, the consequences of the Spanish crown selling most of its American administrative offices were a decline in the competence of officeholders, the emergence of a Creole elite able to bend the Spanish administration to its will, and a decentralization of the decision-making processes.

Northwest European Interference   As Spain's administrative grip on the Americas weakened during the seventeenth century, the need to defend the continents militarily against European interlopers arose. European privateers, holding royal charters, harassed Spanish silver shipments and ports in the Caribbean. In the early seventeenth century, the French, English, and Dutch governments occupied the smaller Caribbean islands not claimed by Spain. Privateer and contraband traders stationed on these islands further damaged Spain's monopoly of shipping between Europe and the Caribbean.

Conquests of Spanish islands followed in the second half of the century. England captured Jamaica in 1655, and France colonized western Hispaniola (Saint-Domingue) in 1665. Along the Pacific coast, the galleons of the annual Acapulco–Manila fleet were the targets of English privateers. Over the course of the seventeenth century, Spain allocated one-half to two-thirds of its American revenues to the defense of its annual treasure fleets and Caribbean possessions.

Bourbon Reforms   After the death of the last, childless Habsburg king of Spain in 1700, the new French-descended dynasty of the Bourbons made major efforts to regain control over their American possessions. Fortunately, population increases among the settlers as well as the Native Americans offered opportunities to Spanish manufacturers and merchants. By the middle of the eighteenth century, the Bourbon reform program began to show results.

The reforms aimed to improve naval connections and administrative control between the mother country and the colonies. The monopolistic annual armed silver fleet was reduced. Instead, the government authorized more frequent single sailings. Newly formed Spanish companies, receiving exclusive rights at specific ports, reduced contraband trade. Elections took place again for municipal councils. Spanish-born salaried officials replaced many Creole tax and office farmers. The original two viceroyalties were subdivided into four, to improve administrative control. The sale of tobacco and brandy became state monopolies. Silver mining and cotton textile manufacturing were expanded. By the second half of the eighteenth century, Spain had regained a measure of control over its colonies.

As a result, government revenues rose substantially. In the end, however, the reforms remained incomplete. Since the Spanish economy was not also reformed, the changes did not much diminish the English and French dominance of the import market. Spain failed to produce goods at competitive prices for the colonies; thus the level of English and French exports to the Americas remained high.

Early Portuguese Colonialism   In contrast to the Spanish Americas, the Portuguese overseas province of Brazil developed only slowly during the sixteenth century. The first governor-general arrived in 1549. He and his successors (after 1640 called "viceroys," as in the Spanish colonies) were members of the high aristocracy, but their positions were salaried and subject to term limits. As the colony grew, the crown created a council in the capital of Lisbon for all Brazilian appointments and established a high court for all judicial affairs in Bahia in northern Brazil. In the early seventeenth century, offices became as open to purchase as in the Spanish colonies, although not on the city council level, where an electoral process survived.

Jesuits converted the Native Americans, whom they transported to Jesuit-administered villages. Colonial cities and Jesuits repeatedly clashed over the slave raids of the "pioneers" (*bandeirantes*) in village territories. Although the Portuguese crown and church had, like the Spanish, forbidden the enslavement of Native Americans, the bandeirantes exploited a loophole. The law was interpreted as allowing the enslavement of Native Americans who resisted conversion to Christianity. For a long time, Lisbon and the Jesuits were powerless against this interpretation.

Expansion into the Interior   In the middle of the seventeenth century, the Jesuits and Native Americans pushed many bandeirantes west and north, where they switched from slave raiding to prospecting for gold. In the far north, however, the raids continued until 1680, when the Portuguese administration finally ended Native American slavery, almost a century and a half after Spain.

As a result of gold discoveries in Minas Gerais in 1690 by bandeirantes, the European immigrant population increased rapidly. Brazilians imported slaves from Africa, to work at first in the sugar plantations and, after 1690, in the mines, where their numbers increased to two-thirds of the labor force. The peak of the gold boom came in the 1750s, when the importance of gold was second only to that of sugar among Brazilian exports to Europe.

Early in the gold boom, the crown created the new Ministry of the Navy and Overseas Territories, which greatly expanded the administrative structure in Brazil, and moved the capital from Bahia to Rio de Janeiro in 1736. The ministry in Lisbon ended the sale of offices, increased the efficiency of tax collection, and encouraged Brazilian textile manufacturing to render the province more independent from English imports. By the mid-1700s, Brazil was a flourishing overseas colony of Portugal.

Samuel de Champlain's map of the northeast coast of North America, ca. 1607

North American Settlements   Efforts at settlement in North America in the sixteenth century were unsuccessful. Only in the early part of the seventeenth century did French, English, and Dutch merchant investors succeed in establishing small communities of settlers on the coast: Jamestown (founded in 1607 in today's Virginia), Quebec (1608, Canada), Plymouth and Boston (1620 and 1630, respectively, in today's Massachusetts), and New Amsterdam (1625, today's New York). Subsistence agriculture and fur, however, were not enough for growth. The settlements struggled through the seventeenth century, sustained either by Catholic missionary efforts or by the Puritans who had escaped persecution in England. Southern places like Jamestown survived because they adopted tobacco as a cash crop for export to Europe. In contrast to Mexico and Peru, the North American settlements were not followed— at least, not at first—by territorial conquests (see Map 18.3).

Native Americans   European arrivals in North America soon began supplementing agriculture with trade, exchanging metal and glass wares, beads, and seashells for furs with the Native American groups of the interior. As a result, smallpox, already a menace during the 1500s in North America, became devastating as contacts intensified.

The introduction of guns contributed an additional lethal factor to trading arrangements, as traders provided Native American trading partners with flintlocks in order to increase the yield of furs. As a result, during the 1600s the Iroquois in the northeast were able to organize themselves into an armed federa-

Mine Workers. The discovery of gold and diamonds in Minas Gerais led to a boom, but did little to contribute to the long-term health of the Brazilian economy. With the Native American population decimated by disease, African slaves performed the backbreaking work.

tion, capable of inflicting heavy losses on rival groups as well as on European traders and settlers.

Farther south, in Virginia, the Jamestown settlers encountered the Powhatan confederacy. These Native Americans dominated the region between the Chesapeake Bay and the Appalachian Mountains. Initially, the Powhatan supplied Jamestown with foodstuffs and sought to integrate the settlement into their confederation.

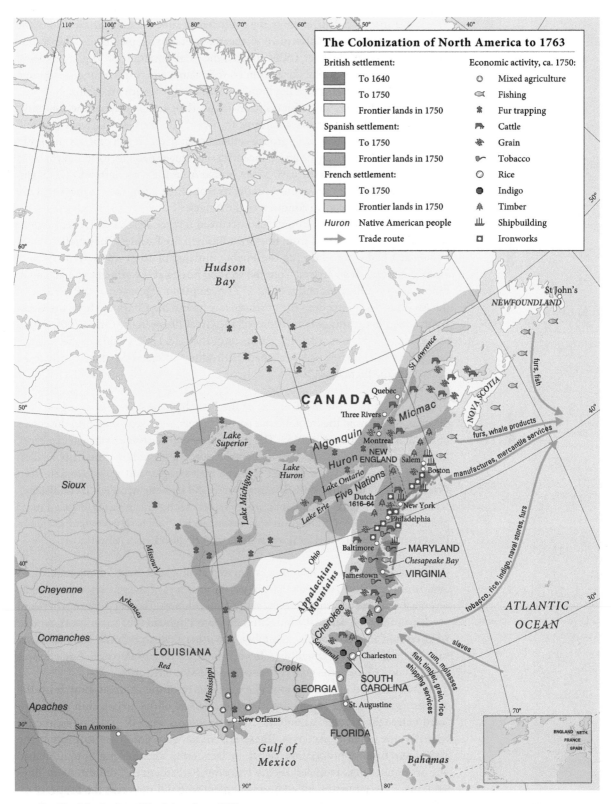

The Colonization of North America to 1763

British settlement:

	To 1640
	To 1750
	Frontier lands in 1750

Spanish settlement:

| | To 1750 |
| | Frontier lands in 1750 |

French settlement:

| | To 1750 |
| | Frontier lands in 1750 |

Huron Native American people

⟶ Trade route

Economic activity, ca. 1750:

- ⊙ Mixed agriculture
- 🐟 Fishing
- ✳ Fur trapping
- 🐂 Cattle
- 🌾 Grain
- 🚬 Tobacco
- ○ Rice
- ● Indigo
- 🌲 Timber
- ⛭ Shipbuilding
- ◻ Ironworks

MAP 18.3 **The Colonization of North America to 1763.**

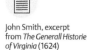

John Smith, excerpt
from *The Generall Historie
of Virginia* (1624)

When this attempt failed, however, the confederacy raided Jamestown twice. But the settlers defeated the Powhatan in 1646, thereafter occupying their lands. The decline of the Powhatan in the later 1600s allowed the English settlers of Virginia to move westward, in contrast to the Puritans in New England, where the Iroquois, although allied with the English against the French, blocked any western expansion.

The Iroquois were determined to maintain their dominance of the fur trade, driving smaller Native American groups westward into the Great Lakes region and Mississippi plains, where these groups settled as refugees. French officials and Jesuit missionaries sought to create an alliance with the refugee peoples, to counterbalance the powerful Iroquois to the east. Many Native Americans converted to Christianity, creating a Creole Christianity similar to that of the Africans of Kongo and the Mexicans after the Spanish conquest of the Aztecs.

Major population movements also occurred further west on the Great Plains, where the Apaches arrived from the Great Basin in the Rockies. They had captured horses that had escaped during the Pueblo uprising of 1680–1695 against Spain. The Comanches, who arrived from the west on horses at the same time, had, in addition, acquired firearms and around 1725 began their expansion at the expense of the Apaches. The Sioux from the northern forests and the Cheyenne from the Great Basin added to the mix of federations on the Great Plains in the early 1700s. Smallpox epidemics did not reach the Plains until the mid-1700s, while in the east the ravages of this epidemic had weakened the Iroquois so much that they concluded a peace with the French in 1701.

French Canada   The involvement of the French in the Great Lakes region with refugees fleeing from the Iroquois was part of a program of expansion into the center of North America, begun in 1663. The governor of Quebec had dispatched explorers, fur traders, and missionaries into the Great Lakes region and the Mississippi valley. The French government then sent farmers, craftspeople, and single women from France to establish settlements. The most successful settlement, called "La Louisiane," was at the mouth of the Mississippi, where settlers with African slaves founded sugar plantations. Because immigration was restricted to French subjects and excluded Protestants, Louisiana had far fewer settlers than English North America.

Colonial Assemblies   As immigration to New England picked up, the merchant companies in Europe, which had financed the journeys of the settlers, were initially responsible for the administration of settlement colonies. The first settlers to demand participation in the colonial administration were Virginian tobacco growers, who in 1619 created an early popular assembly. The other English colonies soon followed suit, creating their own assemblies. In contrast to Spain and Portugal, England was initially uninvolved in the governance of the overseas territories.

When England eventually took the governance of the colonies away from the charter merchants and companies in the second half of the seventeenth century, it faced entrenched settler assemblies. Many governors were deputies of aristocrats who never traveled to America. These governors were powerless to prevent the assemblies from appropriating rights to levy taxes and making appointments. The assemblies thus modeled themselves after Parliament in London. As in England, these assemblies excluded poorer settlers who did not meet the property requirements to vote or stand for elections.

Territorial Expansion Steady immigration encouraged land speculators in the British colonies to cast their sights beyond the Appalachian Mountains. In 1749, the Ohio Company of Virginia received a royal permit to develop land, together with a protective fort, south of the Ohio River. The French, however, also claimed the Ohio valley. Tensions over the valley soon erupted into open hostility. Initially, the local encounters went badly for the Virginian militia and British army. In 1755, however, the British and French broadened their clash into a worldwide war for dominance in the colonies and Europe, the Seven Years' War of 1756–1763.

powder horn, ca. 1757

The Seven Years' War Both France and Great Britain borrowed heavily to finance the war. England had the superior navy and France the superior army. Since the British navy succeeded in choking off French supplies to its increasingly isolated land troops, Britain won the war overseas. In Europe, Britain's failure to supply the troops of its ally Prussia against the Austrian–French alliance caused the war on that front to end in a draw. Overseas, the British gained most of the French holdings in India, several islands in the Caribbean, all of Canada, and all the land east of the Mississippi. The costs, however, proved to be unmanageable for all concerned. The unpaid debts became the root cause of the American, French, and Haitian constitutional revolutions that began 13 years later.

The Making of American Societies: Origins and Transformations

The patterns which made the Americas an extension of Europe emerged gradually and displayed characteristics specific to each region. On one hand, there was the slow transfer of the plants and animals native to each continent, called the **Columbian Exchange** (see "Patterns Up Close"). On the other hand, Spain and Portugal adopted different strategies of mineral and agricultural exploitation. In spite of these different strategies, however, the settler societies of the two countries in the end displayed similar characteristics.

Columbian Exchange: Exchange of plants, animals, and diseases between the Americas and the rest of the world.

Exploitation of Mineral and Tropical Resources

The pattern of European expansion into subtropical and tropical lands began with the Spanish colonization of the Caribbean islands. When the Spanish crown ran out of gold in the Caribbean, it exported silver from Mexico and Peru to finance a centralizing state. By contrast, Portugal's colony of Brazil did not at first mine for precious metals, and consequently the Portuguese crown pioneered the growing of sugar on plantations. The North American colonies of England and France had, in comparison, little native industry at first. By moving farther south, however, they adopted the plantation system for indigo and rice.

Silver Mines Two main mining centers emerged in the Spanish colonies: Potosí in southeastern Peru (today Bolivia) and Zacatecas and Guanajuato in northern Mexico. During the eighteenth century, gold mining in Colombia and Chile rose to importance as well.

Innovations such as the "patio" method, which facilitated the extraction of silver through the use of mercury, and the unrestrained exploitation of indigenous labor

The Columbian Exchange

Few of us can imagine an Italian kitchen without tomatoes or an Irish meal without potatoes or Chinese or Indian cuisine without chilies, but until fairly recently each of these foods was unknown to the Old World. Likewise, for millennia apples, as well as many other common fruits, were absent from the New World. It was not until the sixteenth century that new patterns of ecology and biology changed the course of millions of years of divergent evolution.

When considering the long list of life forms that moved across the oceans in the Columbian Exchange, the impact of European weeds and grasses on American grasslands, which made it possible for the North American prairie and the South American pampas to support livestock, should not be overlooked. By binding the soil together with their long, tough roots, the "empire of the dandelion" provided the conditions for the grazing of sheep, cattle, and horses, as well as the planting of crops like wheat.

The other silent invader that accompanied the conquistadors was disease. Thousands of years of mutual isolation between the Americas and Afro-Eurasia rendered the immune systems of Native Americans vulnerable to the scourges that European colonists unwittingly brought with them. By some estimates, the native populations of Mesoamerica and the Andes plummeted by 90 percent in the period 1500–1700. In comparison, the contagions the New World was able to reciprocate upon the Old World—syphilis and tuberculosis—did not unleash nearly the same devastation, and the New World origin of these diseases is still debated.

Therefore, the big winner in the Columbian Exchange was western Europe, though the effects of the New World bounty took centuries to be fully discerned. While Asia and Africa also benefited from the Columbian Exchange, the Europeans got a continent endowed with a warm climate in which they could create new and improved versions of their homelands. The Native Americans were nearly wiped out by disease, their lands appropriated, and the survivors either enslaved or marginalized. The precipitous drop in the population of Native Americans, combined with the tropical and semitropical climate of much of the Americas, created the

made American silver highly competitive in the world market. Conditions among the Native Americans and blacks employed as labor were abominable. Few laborers lasted through more than two forced recruitment (*repartimiento*) cycles before they were incapacitated or dead.

Since the exploitation of the mines was of central importance, for the first century and a half of New World colonization, the Spanish crown organized its other provinces around the needs of the mining centers. The main function of Hispaniola and Cuba in the Caribbean was to feed and protect Havana, the collection point for Mexican and Peruvian silver and the port from where the annual Spanish fleet shipped the American silver across the Atlantic.

A second region, Argentina and Paraguay, was colonized as a bulwark to prevent the Portuguese and Dutch from accessing Peruvian silver. Once established, the two colonies produced goods and foodstuffs to supply the miners in Potosí.

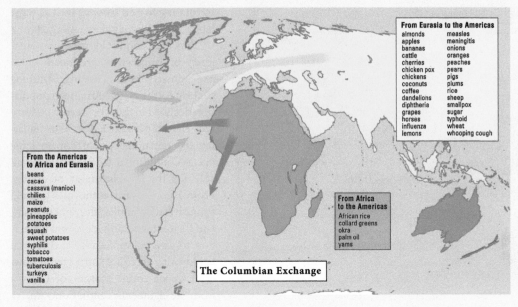

From Eurasia to the Americas

almonds	measles
apples	meningitis
bananas	onions
cattle	oranges
cherries	peaches
chicken pox	pears
chickens	pigs
coconuts	plums
coffee	rice
dandelions	sheep
diphtheria	smallpox
grapes	sugar
horses	typhoid
influenza	wheat
lemons	whooping cough

From the Americas to Africa and Eurasia

beans
cacao
cassava (manioc)
chilies
maize
peanuts
pineapples
potatoes
squash
sweet potatoes
syphilis
tobacco
tomatoes
tuberculosis
turkeys
vanilla

From Africa to the Americas

African rice
collard greens
okra
palm oil
yams

The Columbian Exchange

MAP 18.4 **The Columbian Exchange.**

necessary conditions for the Atlantic slave trade. The population losses from this trade were monumental.

Questions

- Can the Columbian Exchange be considered one of the origins of the modern world? How? Why? How does the Columbian Exchange demonstrate the origins, interactions, and adaptations model that is used throughout this book?

- Weigh the positive and negative outcomes of the Columbian Exchange. Is it possible to determine whether the overall effects of the Columbian Exchange on human society and the natural environment were for the better or for the worse?

A third colonial region, Venezuela, began as a grain and cattle supply base for Cartagena, the port for the shipment of Colombian gold, and Panama and Portobelo, ports for the transshipment of Peruvian silver from the Pacific to Havana. Thus, three major regions of the Spanish overseas empire in the Americas were mostly peripheral as agricultural producers during the sixteenth century. Only after the middle of the century did they begin to specialize in tropical agricultural goods, and they were exporters only in the eighteenth century.

Wheat Farming and Cattle Ranching   To support the mining centers and administrative cities, the Spanish colonial government encouraged the development of agricultural estates (*haciendas*). Native American tenant farmers were forced to grow wheat and raise livestock for the conquerors, who were now agricultural entrepreneurs. In the latter part of the sixteenth century, the land grants gave way

map of Mexican town drawn by indigenous artists, 1579

The Silver Mountain of Potosí.
Note the patios in the left
foreground and the water-driven
crushing mill in the center,
which ground the silver-bearing
ore into a fine sand that then
was moistened, caked, amalgam-
ated with mercury, and dried
on the patio. The mine workers'
insect-like shapes reinforce the
dehumanizing effects of their
labor.

to rotating forced labor as well as wage labor. A landowner class emerged.

Like the conquistadors before, a majority of landowners produced wheat and animals for sale to urban and mining centers. As the Native American population declined in the seventeenth century and the church helped in consolidating the remaining population in large villages, additional land became available for the establishment of estates. From 1631 onward, authorities granted Spanish settler families the right to maintain their estates undivided from generation to generation. Secular and clerical landowning interests supported a powerful upper social stratum of Creoles from the eighteenth century onward.

Plantations and Gold Mining in Brazil   Brazil's economic activities began with brazilwood, followed by sugar plantations, before gold mining rose to prominence in the eighteenth century.

These gold-mining operations were less capital-intensive than the silver mines in Spanish America. Most miners were relatively small operators with a few black slaves as unskilled laborers. Many entrepreneurs were indebted for their slaves to absentee capitalists, with whom they shared the profits. Since prospecting took place on the land of Native Americans, bloody encounters were frequent. Brazil's gold production was a welcome bonanza for Portugal at a time of low agricultural prices.

Plantations in Spanish and English America   The expansion of plantation farming in the Spanish colonies was a result of the Bourbon reforms. Although sugar, tobacco, and rice had been introduced early into the Caribbean and southern Mexico, it was only in the plantation system of the eighteenth century that these and other crops were produced for export to Europe. The owners of plantations invested in African slave labor, with the result that the slave trade hit full stride beginning around 1750.

English Northeast American settlements in Virginia and Carolina exported tobacco and rice beginning in the 1660s. Georgia joined southern Carolina as a major plantation colony in 1750. In the eighteenth century, New England exported timber for shipbuilding and charcoal production in Great Britain. These timber exports illustrate the importance of the Americas as a replacement for dwindling fuel resources across much of northern Europe. Altogether, it was thanks to the Americas that mostly cold and rainy Europe rose into the ranks of the wealthy Indian and Chinese empires.

Social Strata, Castes, and Ethnic Groups
Given the small settler population of the Americas, the temptation to develop a system of forced labor in agriculture and mining was irresistible. Since the Native Americans and African slaves pressed into labor were ethnically so different from

the Europeans, however, a social system evolved in which the latter two not only were economically underprivileged but also made up the ethnically nonintegrated lowest rungs of the social ladder. A pattern of legal and customary discrimination evolved which prevented the integration of American ethnicities into settler society.

The Social Elite   The heirs of the Spanish conquistadors and estate owners maintained city residences and employed managers on their agricultural properties. In Brazil, cities emerged more slowly. During the seventeenth century, estate owners intermarried with the Madrid- and Lisbon-appointed administrators, creating the top tier of settler society known as Creoles. They formed a relatively closed society in which descent, intermarriage, landed property, and a government position counted more than money and education.

In the seventeenth and eighteenth centuries, the estate owners farmed predominantly with Native American forced labor. In contrast to the black slave plantation estates of the Caribbean and coastal regions of Spanish and Portuguese America, these farming estates did not export their goods to Europe.

As local producers with little competition, farming and ranching estate owners did not feel market pressures. They exploited their estates with minimal investments and usually drew profits of less than 5 percent of annual revenues. As a result, they were often heavily indebted.

Lower Creoles   The second tier of Creole society consisted of privileged European settlers who, as craftspeople and traders, theoretically worked with their hands. In practice, many of them were owner-operators who employed Native Americans and/or black slaves. Many strove to rise into the ranks of the landowning Creoles.

Wealthy weavers ran textile manufactures mostly concentrated in the cities of Mexico, Peru, Paraguay, and Argentina. On a smaller scale, manufactures also existed for pottery and leather goods. On the whole, the urban manufacturing activities of the popular people, serving the poor in local markets, remained vibrant until well into the nineteenth century, in spite of massive European imports. Prior to the arrival of railroads, the transportation of imports into the interior of the Americas was prohibitively expensive.

Mestizos and Mulattoes   The mixed European–Native American and European–African population had the collective name of "caste" (*casta*), or ethnic group. The two most important castes were the *mestizos* (Spanish), or *mestiços* (Portuguese), who had Iberian fathers and Native American mothers, and *mulatos*, who had Iberian fathers and black mothers. By 1800 the castas as a whole formed the third largest population category in Latin America. In both Spanish and Portuguese America, there were also a small percentage of people descended from Native American and black unions. These inter-mediate population groups played important neutralizing roles in colonial society, as they had one foot in both the Creole and subordinate social strata (see Figure 18.1).

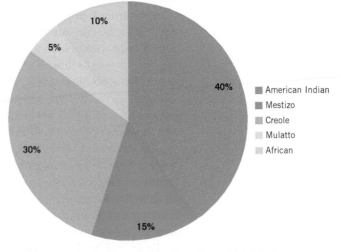

Figure 18.1 **Ethnic Composition of Latin America, ca. 1800.**

Mestizos and mulattoes filled lower levels of the bureaucracy and the lay hierarchy in the church. They held skilled and supervisory positions in mines and on estates. In addition, in the armed forces mulattoes dominated the ranks of enlisted men; in the defense militias, they even held officer ranks. In Brazil, many mulattoes and black freedmen were farmers. Much of the craft production was in their hands. Many laws kept mestizos and mulattoes in their intermediate social and political positions.

Women   The roles played by women depended on their social position. Elite Creole households followed the Mediterranean tradition of secluding women from men. Within the household, Creole women were the owners of substantial dowries and legally stipulated grooms' gifts. Often, they actively managed the investment of their assets. Outside the household, however, even elite women lost all protection. Husbands and fathers could banish daughters or wives to convents for alleged lapses in chastity, or even kill them without punishment. Thus, even elite women were bound by limits set by a patriarchal society.

On the lower rungs of society, gender separation was much less prevalent. Men, women, and children shared labor in the fields and workshops. Girls or wives took in clothes to wash or went out to work as domestics in wealthy households. Older women dominated retail in market stalls. Working families with few assets suffered abandonment by males. Women headed one-third of all households in Mexico City, according to an 1811 census. Among black slaves in the region of São Paulo, 70 percent of women were without formal ties to the men who fathered their children. The most pronounced division in colonial society was that of a patriarchy among the Creoles and a slave society dominated by women, with frequently absent men.

Native Americans   In the immediate aftermath of the conquest, Native Americans could be found at all social levels. Social distinctions, however, disappeared during the first 150 years of Spanish colonialism as disease reduced the Native American population by nearly 80 percent. It was only in the twentieth century that population figures reached the preconquest level again in most parts of Latin America.

Apart from European diseases, the Native Americans in the Amazon, Orinoco, and Maracaibo rain forests were the least affected by European colonials during the period 1500–1800. Not only were their lands economically the least promising, but they also defended those lands successfully. In many arid or semiarid regions, such as Patagonia, southern Chile, the Argentine grasslands (*pampas*), the Paraguayan salt marshes and deserts, and northern Mexican mountains and steppes, the semi-nomadic Native Americans quickly adopted the European horse and became highly mobile warrior peoples in defense of their mostly independent territories.

The villagers of Mexico, Yucatán, Guatemala, Colombia, Ecuador, and Peru had fewer choices. When smallpox reduced their numbers in the second half of the sixteenth century, authorities razed villages and concentrated the survivors in *pueblos de indios*. Initially, the Native Americans put up strong resistance against these resettlements. From the middle of the seventeenth century, however, the pueblos were self-administering units, with councils (*cabildos*), churches, schools, communal lands, and family parcels.

The councils were important institutions of legal training and social mobility for Native Americans. Initially, the traditional "noble" chiefly families descending from

Illustration from an Indian Land Record. The Spaniards almost completely wiped out the Aztec archives after the conquest of Mexico; surviving examples of Indian manuscripts are thus extremely rare. Although the example shown here, made from the bark of a fig tree, claims to date from the early 1500s, it is part of the so-called Techialoyan land records created in the seventeenth century to substantiate native land claims. These "títulos primordiales," as they were called, were essentially municipal histories that documented in text and pictures local accounts of important events and territorial boundaries.

the preconquest Aztec and Inca ruling classes were in control as administrators. The many village functions, however, for which the *cabildos* were responsible allowed commoners to move up into auxiliary roles. Native American villages were closed to settlers, and the only outsiders admitted were Catholic priests. Contact with the Spanish world remained minimal, and acculturation went little beyond official conversion to Catholicism. Thus, even in the heartlands of Spanish America, Native American adaptation to the rulers remained limited.

Unfortunately, however, tremendous demographic losses made the Native Americans in the pueblos vulnerable to the loss of their land. Estate owners expanded their holdings, and when the population rebounded, many estates had grown to immense sizes. Villages began to run out of land for their inhabitants. Increasing numbers of Native Americans had to rent land from estate owners or find work on estates as farmhands. They became estranged from their villages, fell into debt peonage, and entered the ranks of the working poor.

New England Society   In the early modern period, the small family farm remained the norm for the majority of New England's population. An acute lack of money and cheap means of transportation hampered the development of market networks in the interior well into the 1770s. The situation was better in the agriculturally more favored colonies in the Mid-Atlantic, especially in Pennsylvania. The number of plantations in the south rose steadily, demanding a substantial increase in numbers of slaves, although world market fluctuations left planters vulnerable. Except for boom periods in the plantation sector, the rural areas remained largely poor.

Real changes occurred during the early eighteenth century in the urban regions of New England. Large port cities emerged which shipped in goods from Europe in return for timber. A wealthy merchant class formed, spawning urban strata of professionals. Primary school education was provided by municipal public schools as well as by some churches, and evening schools for craftspeople also existed. By the middle of the eighteenth century, a majority of men could read and write. Finally, in contrast to Latin America, social ranks in New England were less elaborate.

The Adaptation of the Americas to European Culture

European settlers brought two distinct cultures to the Americas. In the Mid-Atlantic, Caribbean, and Central and South America, they brought with them the Catholic Reformation, a culture that resisted the New Science and the Enlightenment until the late eighteenth century. In the northeast, colonists implanted dissident Protestantism as well as the Anglicanism of Great Britain and the Presbyterianism of Scotland.

Catholic Missionary Work Spanish and Portuguese monarchs relied on the Catholic Church for their rule in the new American provinces. A strong motive driving many in the church and society was the belief in the imminent Second Coming of Jesus. This belief was one inspiration for the original Atlantic expansion (see Chapter 16). When the Aztec and Inca Empires fell, members of the Franciscan order, the main proponents of the belief in the imminence of the Second Coming, interpreted it as a sign of the urgent duty to convert the Native Americans to Christianity.

Thousands of preaching monks, later followed by the Jesuits, fanned out among the Native Americans. They baptized them, introduced the sacraments, and taught them basic theological concepts. The missionaries learned native languages, translated the catechism and New Testament into those languages, and taught the children of the ruling native families how to read and write.

The role and function of saints formed one element of Catholic Christianity to which Native Americans acculturated early. Good works as God-pleasing human efforts to gain salvation in the afterlife formed another. The veneration of images of the Virgin Mary and pilgrimages to the chapels and churches where they were kept constituted a third element. On the other hand, the Spanish Inquisition also operated in the Spanish and Portuguese colonies, seeking to limit the degree to which Catholicism and traditional religion mingled.

Education and the Arts The Catholic Reformation also influenced the organization of education. The Franciscans and Dominicans had offered education to the children of settlers early on and, in colleges, trained graduates for missionary work. New World universities taught theology, church law, and Native American languages. Under the impact of the Jesuits, universities broadened the curriculum. Although the universities did not teach the New Sciences and Enlightenment of northwestern Europe, there was nevertheless scientific research on tropical diseases, plants, and animals. The extent of this research was long kept secret by the Spanish and Portuguese monarchs from their European competitors.

Furthermore, missionary monks collected and recorded Native American manuscripts and oral traditions, such as the Aztec *Anales de Tula* and the Maya *Popol Vuh*. Others wrote histories and ethnographies of the indigenous peoples.

Jesuit missionaries, from the Church of San Pedro in Lima, Peru, ca. 1700

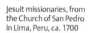

earliest representation of the Madonna and Child created by Indians in the New World (1531)

Spanish Cruelty to Incas. Felipe Guamán Poma de Ayala, a Peruvian claiming noble Inca descent, was a colonial administrator, well educated and an ardent Christian. He is remembered today as a biting critic of the colonial administration and the clergy, whom he accused of mistreating and exploiting the Andean population, as in this colored woodcut print.

A number of Native American and mestizo chroniclers, historians, and commentators on the early modern state and society are similarly noteworthy. Felipe Guamán Poma de Ayala (ca. 1535–1616), a native Peruvian, is of particular interest. He accompanied his 800-page manuscript, entitled (in English translation) *The First New Chronicle and Good Government*, with some 400 drawings of daily-life activities in the Peruvian villages. Unfortunately, King Philip II of Spain forbade in 1577 the publication of all manuscripts dealing with what he called idolatry and superstition. Many manuscripts lay hidden in archives until modern times.

Illustration from Willem Piso's *Natural History of Brazil* (1637)

Protestantism in New England   Religious diversity was a defining cultural trait of English settlements in North America. The spectrum of Christian denominations ranged from English and continental European versions of Protestantism to Anglicanism and a minority of Catholics. Dissenters frequently split from the existing denominations, moved into new territory, and founded new settlements.

An early example of religious splintering was the rise of an antinomian ("anti-law") group within Puritan-dominated Massachusetts. The preachers and settlers represented in the General Court, as their assembly was called, were committed to the Calvinist balance between "inner" personal grace obtained from God and "outer" works according to the law. The antinomian group, however, advocated an exclusive commitment to inner grace through spiritual perfection.

Their leader was Anne Hutchinson, an early proponent of women's rights and an inspiring preacher. She was accused of arguing that she could recognize those believers in Calvinist Protestantism who were predestined for salvation and that these believers would be saved even if they had sinned. After a power struggle, the General Court prevailed and forced the antinomians to move to Rhode Island in 1638.

The example of Hutchinson is noteworthy because it led to the founding of Harvard College in 1636 by the General Court. Harvard was the first institution of higher learning in North America.

New Sciences Research   As discussed in Chapter 17, the New Sciences had their most hospitable home in northwestern Europe, where the rivalry between Protestantism and Catholicism had left enough of an authority-free space for the New Sciences to flourish. Under similar circumstances—intense rivalry among denominations—English North America also proved hospitable to the New Sciences. An early practitioner was Benjamin Franklin (1706–1790), who began his career as a printer, journalist, and newspaper editor. Franklin founded the University of Pennsylvania (1740), the first secular university in North America, and the American Philosophical Society (1743), the first scientific society. This hospitality for the New Sciences in North America was in contrast to Latin America, where a uniform Catholic Reformation prevented its rise.

Witch Trial. In the course of the 1600s, in the relatively autonomous English colonies of Northeast America, more persons were accused, tried, and convicted of witchcraft than anywhere else. Of the 140 persons coming to trial between 1620 and 1725, 86 percent were women. Three witch panics are recorded: Bermuda, 1651; Hartford, Connecticut, 1652–1665; and Salem, Massachusetts, 1692–1693. This anonymous American woodcut of the early 1600s shows one method used to try someone for witchcraft: The accused would swim or float, if guilty—or sink, if innocent.

Witch Hunts   In the last decade of the seventeenth century, religious intensity was at the root of a witchcraft frenzy that seized New England. Witches, male and female, were believed to be persons exerting a negative influence, or black magic, on their victims. In medieval Europe, the church had kept witchcraft hidden, but in the wake of challenges to church authority, it had become more visible. In the North American colonies, with no overarching religious authority, the visibility of witch-craft was particularly high.

This sensitivity erupted into hysteria in Salem, Massachusetts, in 1692. Tituba, a Native American slave from Barbados, worked in the household of a pastor. She prac-ticed voodoo, the West African–originated, part-African and part-Christian religious practice of influencing others. When young girls in the pastor's household suffered from convulsions, mass hysteria broke out, in which 20 women accused of being witches were executed. (Tituba, ironically, survived.) A new governor finally re-stored order.

Revivalism   Religious fervor expressed itself also in periodic Protestant renewal movements, such as the "Great Awakening" of the 1730s and 1740s. The main im-pulse for this revivalist movement came from the brothers John and Charles Wesley, two Methodist preachers in England who toured Georgia in 1735. Preachers from other denominations joined, all exhorting Protestants to literally "start anew" in their relationship with God. Thus, revivalism, recurring with great regularity to the present, became a potent force in Protestant America, at opposing purposes with secular founding-father constitutionalism.

❯ Putting It All Together

interactive concept map

During the period 1500–1800 the contours of a new pattern in which the Americas formed a resource-rich extension of Europe took shape. During this time, China and India continued to be the most populous and wealthiest agrarian–urban regions of the world. In 1500, Europe was struggling to defend itself against the push of the Ottoman Empire into eastern Europe and the western Mediterranean. But its suc-cessful conquest of Iberia from the Muslims led to the discovery of the Americas. Possession of the Americas made Europe similar to China and India in that it now encompassed, in addition to its northerly cold climates, subtropical and tropical re-gions that produced cash crops as well as precious metals. Over the next 300 years, Europe narrowed the gap between itself and China and India.

However, because of fierce competition both with the Ottoman Empire and internally, much of the wealth Europe gained in the Americas was wasted on war-fare. The centralizing state, created in part to support war, ran into insurmountable budgetary barriers. Even mercantilism, a logical extension of the centralizing state, had limited effects. Its centerpiece, state support for the export of manufactures to the American colonies, functioned unevenly. The Spanish and Portuguese govern-ments, with weak urban infrastructures and low manufacturing capabilities, were unable to enforce this state-supported trade until the eighteenth century and even then only in very limited ways. France and England practiced mercantilism more successfully, but were able to do so in the Americas only from the late seventeenth century onward, when their plantation systems began to take shape. Although the American extension of Europe had the potential of making Europe self-sufficient, this potential was realized only partially during the colonial period.

Debate continues over the question of the degree of wealth the Americas added to Europe. On one hand, research has established that the British slave trade for sugar plantations added at best 1 percent to the British gross domestic product (GDP). The profits from the production of sugar on the English island of Jamaica may have added another 4 percent to the British GDP. Without doubt, private slave-trading and sugar-producing enterprises were immensely profitable to individuals and groups. However, these profits were smaller if one takes into account the immense waste of revenues on military ventures—hence, the doubts raised by scholars today about large gains made by Europe through its American colonial acquisitions.

On the other hand, the European extension to the Americas was clearly a momentous event in world history. It might have produced dubious overall profits for Europe, but it definitely encouraged the parting of ways between Europe on one hand and Asia and Africa on the other, once a new scientific–industrial society began to emerge around 1800.

Review and Relate

Thinking Through Patterns

Examine the ways historians approach the big questions of this chapter.

In their role as subtropical and tropical extensions of Europe, the Americas had a considerable impact on Europe's changing position in the world. First, Europe acquired large quantities of precious metals, which its two largest competitors, India and China, lacked. Second, with its new access to warm-weather agricultural products, Europe rose to a position of agrarian autonomy similar to that of India and China. In terms of resources, compared with the principal religious civilizations of India and China, Europe grew between 1550 and 1800 from a position of inferiority to one of near parity.

>> What is the significance of western Europeans acquiring the Americas as a warm-weather extension of their northern continent?

Because the numbers of Europeans who emigrated to the Americas was low for most of the colonial period, they never exceeded the numbers of Native Americans or African slaves. The result was a privileged settler society that held superior positions on the top rung of the social hierarchy. In principle, given an initially large indigenous population, labor was cheap and should have become more expensive as diseases reduced the Native Americans. In fact, labor always remained cheap, in part because of forced labor and in part because of racial prejudice.

>> What was the main pattern of social development in colonial America during the period 1500–1800?

≫ **Why and how did European settlers in South and North America strive for self-government, and how successful were they in achieving their goals?**

Two contrasting patterns characterized the way in which European colonies were governed. The Spanish and Portuguese crowns, interested in extracting minerals and warm-weather products from the colonies, were motivated to exercise centralized control over their possessions in the Americas. In contrast, the British crown granted self-government to the Northeast American colonies from the start, in part because the colonies were far less important economically and in part because of a long tradition of self-rule at home. Nevertheless, even though Latin American settlers achieved only partial self-rule in their towns and cities, they destroyed central rule indirectly through the purchase of offices. After financial reforms, Spain and Portugal reestablished a degree of central rule through the appointment of officers from the home countries.

| Against the Grain

Consider this as a counterpoint to the main patterns examined in this chapter.

Juana Inés de la Cruz

- Why were the Latin American colonies more socially conservative than Europe?
- Was de la Cruz right to stop her correspondence with the Mexican clergy in 1693?

In the wake of the Protestant and Catholic Reformations of the 1500s, it was no longer unusual for European women to pursue higher education. In the more conservative Latin American colonies of Spain, Juana Inés de la Cruz (1651–1695) was less fortunate, even though her fame as the intellectually most brilliant figure of the seventeenth century in the colonies endured.

De la Cruz was the illegitimate child of a Spanish immigrant father and a Creole mother. She grew up on the hacienda of her maternal grandfather, in whose library she secretly studied Latin, Greek, and Nahuatl, and also composed her first poems. Unable, as a woman, to be admitted to the university in Mexico City, de la Cruz was fortunate to receive further education from the wife of the vice regent of New Spain. In order to continue her studies, she entered a convent in 1668. Here, she continued to study and write hundreds of poems, comedies, religious dramas, and theological texts. Her seminars with courtiers and scholarly visitors were a major attraction.

In 1688, however, she lost her protection at court with the departure of her viceregal supporters for Spain. Her superior, the archbishop of Mexico, was an open misogynist. A crisis came in 1690 when the bishop of Puebla published de la Cruz's critique of a famous sermon of 1650 by the Portuguese Jesuit António Vieira on Jesus's act of washing his disciples' feet, together with his own critique of de la Cruz. De la Cruz viewed Vieira's interpretation as more hierarchical/male and her own interpretation as more humble/female.

A year later, in 1691, de la Cruz wrote a spirited riposte to the bishop's apparently well-meaning advice to her in his critique to be more conscious of her status as a woman. Her message was clear: Even though women had to be silent in church, as St. Paul had taught, neither study nor writing was prohibited for women. Before the church could censor her, in 1693 Juana Inés de la Cruz stopped writing. She died two years later.

Key Terms

audio flashcards

Columbian Exchange 419	Labor assignment	Land-labor grant
Creoles 412	(*repartimiento*) 414	(*encomienda*) 408

For additional resources, please go to
www.oup.com/us/vonsivers.
Please see the Further Resources section at the back of the book for additional readings and suggested websites.

African Kingdoms, the Atlantic Slave Trade, and the Origins of Black America

I t was a claim the Catholic Capuchin monks of the kingdom of Kongo denounced as a heretical abomination: that Dona Beatriz Kimpa Vita (1684–1706) had been reborn as St. Anthony of Padua. For many subjects of the kingdom, this claim was perfectly reasonable as part of an African Christian spirituality in which a gifted person could enter other people's minds and assume their identity. But the monks prevailed. The king of Kongo had Dona Beatriz condemned after a trial and burned at the stake.

Dona Beatriz had been intellectually precocious. In her childhood, her family had her initiated as a *nganga marinda* (a Kikongo word derived from "knowledge" or "skill"). In her initiation ceremony, Dona Beatriz was put into a trance that enabled her to recognize and repel troubling forces that might disturb a person or the community.

The people in Kongo were aware, however, that not all *ngangas* were benevolent. Some *ngangas* were thought to engage in witchcraft. For the missionary Capuchin monks, preaching the Catholic Reformation in the 1500s and 1600s, all *ngangas* were seen as witches. Whether the

THE ATLANTIC
WORLD,
1500–1800

ABOVE: In this watercolor by Capuchin monk Antonio Cavazzi (1621–1678), a European monk and Kongo natives participate in a religious procession.

young Dona Beatriz was intimidated by the monks' denunciations or not, she renounced her initiation, married, and pursued the domestic life of any other young woman in Kongo society.

But Dona Beatriz's spiritual path did not end here. In 1704, she underwent another religious transformation; she "died," only to be reborn as St. Anthony of Padua (1195–1231), one of the patron saints of Portugal. In her new saintly and male identity, more powerful than her earlier one as a *nganga*, Dona Beatriz preached that she had arrived to restore the Catholic faith and reunify the kingdom of Kongo, after nearly half a century of dynastic disunity and civil war (1665–1709).

After her spiritual rebirth, Dona Beatriz went to Pedro IV, king of Kongo (r. 1695–1718), and his Capuchin ally, the chief missionary Bernardo da Gallo, and accused them of failing to restore the faith and unity of the kingdom. Bernardo angrily interrogated Dona Beatriz, and she responded with an attack on the Catholic cornerstone of the sacraments. Intention or faith alone, she argued, not the sacraments of the church, would bring salvation. She derived her convictions from her *nganga* initiation: It was her good intentions that distinguished her from a malevolent witch.

After the king and Bernardo let Beatriz go, she led a crowd of followers to the ruined capital of Kongo, M'banza (called São Salvador by the Portuguese). There, she trained "little Anthonies" as missionaries to convert the Kongolese to her new Antonian-African Christianity. Beatriz was at the pinnacle of her spiritual power when everything unraveled. Though already married, she gave birth to a child conceived with one of her followers. Allies of King Pedro arrested the lovers and brought them before the king. After a state trial—the church stayed out of the proceedings—Beatriz, her companion, and the baby were executed by burning at the stake.

Seeing Patterns

❯❯ What was the pattern of kingdom and empire formation in Africa during the period 1500–1800?

❯❯ How did patterns of plantation slavery evolve in the Atlantic and the Americas?

❯❯ What are the historic roots from which modern racism evolved?

The story of Dona Beatriz illustrates a pattern discussed in this chapter: the process by which Africans adapted their religious heritage to the challenge of European Christianity. Europeans arrived on the western coast of Africa in the late fifteenth century as missionaries and merchants—and also as slave traders and slave raiders. Africans responded with gold, goods, and their own adaptive forms of Christianity, as well as efforts to limit the slave trade. Elsewhere, however, Africans also exploited and adapted indigenous systems of slavery to profit from the developing Atlantic human traffic. The unprecedented massive transfer of African slaves to the Americas brought to both continents a complex array of peoples representing a wide variety of religious experiences—including those of both Islam and Christianity. In many cases, these cultures would not only survive in the Americas but become foundational in the new societies being created there.

African States and the Slave Trade

Chapter Outline

• African States and the Slave Trade

• American Plantation Slavery and Atlantic Mercantilism

• Culture and Identity in the African Diaspora

• Putting It All Together

In the north of sub-Saharan Africa, the pattern of Islamic and Christian dynastic state formation continued to dominate herder and village societies in the period 1500–1800. An invasion by Muslim forces from Morocco during the sixteenth century, however, ended the trend toward empire building in West Africa and strengthened the forces of decentralization. By contrast, in the savanna and Great Lakes regions of central Africa, improved agricultural wealth and intensified regional trade helped perpetuate the kingdom formation already under way. Slavery existed in the chiefdoms and states of Africa, though it was far different from the chattel slavery that would characterize the Americas. The implications of the new trade provided both enormous opportunities and horrific challenges for African traders and local leaders. While the growing Atlantic slave trade appealed to some West African rulers as a path to enhanced wealth and power, more often, rulers tried to resist what ultimately became the greatest forced migration in human history.

The End of Empires in the North and the Rise of States in the Center

Mali (1240–1460), which united peoples of many different religions, languages, and ethnic affiliations, was the first African empire that was similar to the empires of Eurasia in this respect. Mali's successor state, the focus of this section, was the even larger Songhay Empire (1460–1591). Though vast, it lasted only a short time.

Origins of the Songhay   Songhay was initially a tributary state of Mali. It was centered on the city of Gao, downstream on the Niger River from Jenné-jeno and Timbuktu. Gao's origins dated to 850, when it emerged as the end point of the eastern trans-Saharan route from Tunisia and Algeria. Gao was located at the northern end of the Songhay Empire and was inhabited by the Songhay, an ethnic grouping composed of herders, villagers, and fishermen.

At the end of the eleventh century, the leading clans of the Songhay, profiting from the trans-Saharan trade, converted to Islam. Two centuries later the warriors among them assumed positions of leadership as vassals of the *mansa*, or emperor, of Mali.

The Songhay Empire   The Songhay began their imperial expansion in the mid-1400s. Mali lost its northern outpost, Timbuktu, to the Songhay in 1469. In the following decades, Mali slowly retreated, eventually becoming a minor vassal of the Songhay. At its height, the Songhay Empire stretched from Hausaland in the savanna southeast of Gao all the way westward to the Atlantic coast (see Map 19.1).

The factor that elevated the Songhay emperors above their vassals was their taxation of the gold trade. The gold fields of the Upper Niger, Senegal, and Black Volta Rivers were outside the empire, but merchant clans transported the gold to Timbuktu and Gao. Here, North African merchants exchanged their Mediterranean manufactures and salt for gold and slaves. Agents of the emperors in these cities collected market taxes in the form of gold. Agricultural taxes and tributes supported kingdoms; long-distance trade was needed for an empire to come into being.

Songhay's Sudden End   After the initial conquests, the Songhay Empire had little time to consolidate its territory. After just over a century, the Songhay Empire

Peoples and Kingdoms in Sub-Saharan Africa, 1450–1750

- Ethiopia
- Mali (1240–1460)
- Songhay
- Benin
- Kongo
- *Hausa*   People
- - - - Indian Ocean trade route
- ——— Trans-Saharan trade route
- ⟶ Portuguese African coastal slave trade, 1450–1650
- ········ Extent of Portuguese exploration of West African coast up to 1487

MAP 19.1 **Peoples and Kingdoms in Sub-Saharan Africa, 1450–1750.**

map analysis   interactive timeline

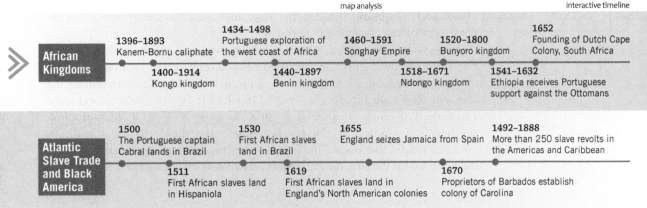

African Kingdoms

- 1396–1893 Kanem-Bornu caliphate
- 1434–1498 Portuguese exploration of the west coast of Africa
- 1460–1591 Songhay Empire
- 1520–1800 Bunyoro kingdom
- 1652 Founding of Dutch Cape Colony, South Africa
- 1400–1914 Kongo kingdom
- 1440–1897 Benin kingdom
- 1518–1671 Ndongo kingdom
- 1541–1632 Ethiopia receives Portuguese support against the Ottomans

Atlantic Slave Trade and Black America

- 1500 The Portuguese captain Cabral lands in Brazil
- 1530 First African slaves land in Brazil
- 1655 England seizes Jamaica from Spain
- 1492–1888 More than 250 slave revolts in the Americas and Caribbean
- 1511 First African slaves land in Hispaniola
- 1619 First African slaves land in England's North American colonies
- 1670 Proprietors of Barbados establish colony of Carolina

ended in 1591,when a Moroccan force invaded from the north. The invasion was prompted by Moroccan sultans concerned about Portuguese involvement in the African gold trade. They wanted to find the West African gold fields in the rain forest themselves, thus depriving the Portuguese of their supply.

However, after defeating Songhay, they were unable to march any farther. Although the officers initially turned the region into a Moroccan province, within a generation they had assimilated into the West African royal clans. As a result, imperial politics in West Africa disintegrated, together with much of the trans-Saharan gold trade.

The Eastern Sahel and Savanna   The area between Songhay in the west and Ethiopia in the northeastern also was home to Islamic regimes. Kanem-Bornu (1396–1893) was a long-lived Islamic realm, calling itself a caliphate, but with a majority of subjects following African religious traditions. It was based on a slave and ivory trade with the Mediterranean and on agriculture and fishing for its internal organization on the south side of Lake Chad. Kanem-Bornu waged wars with the neighboring kingdoms of Hausaland.

The Hausa kingdoms had formed during the height of the Mali-dominated trans-Saharan trade. During the period 1500–1800, many of the ruling clans converted to Islam. They maintained cavalry forces for both military and trade purposes. The Hausa kings collected taxes on traders and dues from the villagers. Craftspeople manufactured a range of goods, and miners and smiths smelted and forged copper, iron, and steel.

Farther east, between Lake Chad and the Nile, the Fur and the Funj, cattle-breeding clan-lineage federations, converted fully to Islam. In contrast, in West Africa, only the dynasties and merchants became Muslim. Their leaders adopted the title "sultan" and became increasingly Arabized in the period 1500–1800, while Christianity along the Upper Nile disappeared.

South Central Africa   On the southern side of the rain forest, the eastern part of the southern savanna and the Great Lakes area in central Africa remained outside the reach of the slave trade. Farmer and cattle herder groups, organized in chiefdoms, inhabited these regions. In the eastern savanna, the kingdom of Luba emerged before 1500, while others followed thereafter.

An increase in regional trade enabled chieftain clans to enlarge their holdings into kingdoms. Living in enclosures and surrounded by dense ruling-class settlements, kings maintained agricultural domains worked by slaves. Villages delivered tribute of foodstuffs. From the mid-seventeenth century onward, the American-origin staples corn and cassava were cultivated. Tributaries at some distance delivered prestige goods. At times, the kings mobilized thousands of workers for construction projects around their courts.

In the Great Lakes region, to the north, south, and west of Lake Victoria, agriculture, cattle breeding, and trade supported political competition. Small agricultural–mercantile kingdoms shared the region, but sometime in the sixteenth century the Luo, who were cattle breeders, arrived and shook up the existing political and social structures. Pronounced disparities in cattle ownership emerged. Cattle lords, bolstered by their wealth and status, rose as competitors of the kings.

North of Lake Victoria, the Bunyoro kingdom held the cattle lords at bay, while on the south side of the lake, the cattle lords created new small kingdoms. After a while dominant cattle breeders and inferior farmers settled into relations of mutual dependence. Under the colonial system in the nineteenth century, these unequal relations froze into a caste system in which the dominant but minority Tutsi cattle breeders were continually at odds with the majority Hutu farmers. Farther south, the interaction of Africa with Portugal set the kingdoms on a different historical trajectory.

Portugal's Explorations along the African Coast and Contacts with Ethiopia

The Portuguese expansion into North Africa and the exploration of the African coast were outgrowths of both the *Reconquista* and religious crusading impulses. Mixed in with these religious motives was the necessity of financing the exploration through trade. The combination of the two guided Portugal within a single century around the African continent to India. Along the coast, the Portuguese established forts to protect their merchants. They protected the Ethiopian Christian kingdom against the Ottomans in Yemen.

Chartered Explorations in West Africa Henry the Navigator (1394–1460), brother of the ruling king, occupied the Moroccan port of Ceuta in 1415 under the pretext that Ceuta was once Christian. He also wished to renew crusading for the reconquest of Jerusalem. But the Lisbon court was wary of military expenditures. During the fifteenth century, campaigns for the military occupation of other cities of Morocco alternated with voyages financed by Portuguese merchants and aristocrats for commerce along the West African coast.

Between 1434 and 1472, Portuguese mariners explored the West African coast as far east as the Bight of Benin. They traded European woolens and linens for gold, cottons, and Guinea pepper. Some African slaves were traded, mostly through purchases from chieftains and kings. The Portuguese used slaves to establish sugar plantations on islands off the African coast, and shipped other slaves to Europe for domestic employment.

excerpt from Gomes Eannes de Azurara, *The Chronicle of the Discovery and Conquest of Guinea* (1453)

Portugal and Ethiopia In the second half of the fifteenth century, the military wing of the Portuguese court revived crusading. From 1483 through 1486 the king organized state expeditions for further expansion from the Bight of Benin south to the Congo River. Here, mariners sailed upstream and encountered the ruler of the kingdom of Kongo, who converted to Christianity and established close relations with Portugal.

A few years later, the Portuguese crown continued the search for a way to Ethiopia or India. Eventually, Vasco da Gama circumnavigated the southern tip of Africa, established trade outposts in the Swahili city-states of East Africa, and reached India in 1498. From this point, Portuguese development of the Indian spice trade grew in importance.

The Portuguese discovered in the early sixteenth century that the Ethiopian kingdom was weak in the face of the Muslim sultanate of Adal, on the Red Sea to the east. Until the end of the fifteenth century, Ethiopia had been a powerful Coptic Christian kingdom. Its people practiced a productive agriculture, and its kings controlled a trade of gold, ivory, animal skins, and slaves. Ethiopia and Adal struggled to possess a Red Sea port for this trade during the first half of the sixteenth century.

excerpt from *The Fetha Nagast* (ca. 1450)

A Christian incursion into Muslim territory in 1529 triggered a destructive Muslim holy war with Adal. Ethiopia would have been destroyed had a Portuguese fleet with artillery and musketeers not arrived in 1541. For its part, Adal received Ottoman Muslim support from Yemen, but the Christians eventually prevailed.

Ethiopia paid a high price for its victory, however. Adal Muslim power was destroyed, but in its place, the Ottomans took over the entire west coast of the Red Sea. Non-Christian cattle breeders from the southwest occupied the Rift Valley, which separated the northern and southern Ethiopian highlands, and Christians in the southern highlands were left to their own devices. Small numbers of Portuguese stayed in Ethiopia, with Jesuit missionaries threatening to dominate the Ethiopian church. In 1632 the Ethiopian king expelled the Jesuits and consolidated the kingdom.

From about 1700 Ethiopia decentralized into provincial lordships. Only in the mid-nineteenth century did the kings take back their power from the provincial lords.

Coastal Africa and the Atlantic Slave Trade

Portuguese mariners initially focused on developing their spice trade with India. Gradually, however, they also built their Atlantic slave trade. To understand the pattern underlying the slave trade from 1500–1800, it is crucial to be aware of the importance of slavery within the African historical context. In many places, a form of slavery existed in the place of land ownership. The more slaves a household, clan leader, chief, or king owned, the wealthier he was. This form of **household slavery** was the most common variety.

Household slavery: African chiefs and kings maintained large households of retainers, such as administrators, soldiers, domestics, craftspeople, and farmers; many among these were slaves, acquired through raids and wars but also as a form of punishment for infractions of royal, chiefly, or clan law.

Trade Forts   In the 1440s, Portuguese mariners raided the West African coast for slaves. But they suffered losses, since their muskets were not yet superior to the poisoned arrows of the Africans. Furthermore, West African warriors paddled along the coast and picked off the mariners from their caravels with their arrows if they approached the coast in a hostile manner. The Portuguese thus took a different approach, developing a lucrative coastal fort trade in a variety of items, including slaves.

Through treaties with local African leaders, Portugal acquired the right to build forts from which to trade. Africans involved in this trade produced items such as cloth and metal that were soon to be in demand in Europe. In particular, Africans smelted iron and forged steel that was of higher quality than that of iron-poor Portugal.

Trade was for luxury goods, not ordinary articles of daily life. Merchants had to be able to achieve high profits while carrying comparatively little to weigh down their ships. African rulers purchased luxuries in order to enhance their status and cement power relations. They sold slaves to the Europeans in a similar fashion, as luxuries in return for luxuries.

African Slavery   Sub-Saharan Africa offered enormous hurdles to a shift in patterns from local self-sufficiency to exchange agriculture and urbanization.

Outer defensive walls of Elmina. This town in present-day Ghana was, along with the village of São Jorge da Mina, the first Portuguese fortified trading post on the African coast, from 1482 until it passed to the Dutch in 1637. Merchants used it for storing the goods they traded and for protection in case of conflicts with Africans. It was staffed by a governor and 20–60 soldiers along with a priest, surgeon, apothecary, and a variety of craftspeople. Throughout the first half of the sixteenth century, Elmina was also the center of Portuguese slaving activities.

Inland exchanges of food for manufactured goods over long distances were prohibitively expensive. Because of the tsetse fly (see Chapter 6), human portage or animal transport were limited to highly valuable merchandise. Everything else was manufactured within self-sufficient households.

Such self-sufficiency required large households. In villages with limited outside trade, the polygamous household with the largest number of people employed at home and in the fields was the wealthiest. To increase his wealth further, a household master often raided neighboring villages and acquired captives, to be enslaved and put to work inside and outside the household. Slave raiding and household slavery were common in sub-Saharan African societies. The more stratified slaveholding societies were, the more slaves rose into positions of responsibility and, frequently, autonomy. Thus, as in many societies outside of Africa, the varieties of slavery in sub-Saharan Africa tended to be highly complex in structure and function.

Limited Slave Trade from Benin   When Portugal began the slave trade, African chiefs and kings had to evaluate the comparative value of slaves for their households or for sale. The kingdom of Benin west of the Niger delta was an example of this calculation. The ruler Ewuare (r. 1440–1473) was the first to rise to dominance over chiefs and assume the title of king. Through conquests, Ewuare acquired slaves who were employed in his army and for the construction of earthworks protecting the capital, Benin City.

Portuguese Traders. This brass plaque, from about the middle of the sixteenth century, decorated the palace of the Benin *oba* and shows two Portuguese traders. The fact that they are holding hands suggests they could be father and son.

Early trade contacts between Portuguese mariners and Benin intensified when the successor of Ewuare granted permission to build a fort on the coast in 1487. But the king closely controlled the exchange of goods and slaves. A generation later, when the kings prohibited the sale of male slaves, the Portuguese abandoned their fort. A compromise was reached whereby a limited number of slaves were traded in return for firearms. The kingdom admitted missionaries and members of the dynasty acculturated to the Portuguese. Benin became economically diversified and culturally complex.

Slave exports remained restricted while Benin was a strong, centralized state. Under weak kings and during times of civil war, more slaves were sold as more weapons were purchased. But overall, compared to the slave trade farther west on the West African coast, the large centralized kingdom of Benin with its high internal demand for slave labor remained a modest exporter of slaves and thus retained a considerable degree of autonomy and agency.

The Kingdom of Kongo   Farther south, on the central West African coast, the Portuguese established trade relations with the Kongo and Ndongo kingdoms. Kongo, the oldest and most centralized kingdom in the region, emerged about 1400. By the sixteenth century, its capital, M'banza (São Salvador), was comparable in size to London, Amsterdam, Moscow, and Rome. M'banza also contained a large palace population and a royal domain farmed by slaves.

To defend their rule, the kings relied on a standing army of 5,000 troops. They appointed members of the royal family as governors, who were entitled to rents but were also obliged to deliver taxes in kind to the palace. In addition, the kings collected a head tax. This region of direct rule was marked by a unified law and administration. Vassal kings, called dukes (Portuguese *duque*), governed and sent tribute or gifts to the capital. They sometimes rebelled and broke away; thus, the territory of Kongo, similar to that of Songhay, shifted constantly in size.

The kings of Kongo converted to Christianity early and sent members of the ruling family to Portugal for their education. Portuguese missionaries converted the court and a number of provincial chiefs. Among the ruling class, many read and wrote Portuguese and Latin fluently. Kongolese royalty wore Portuguese dress, listened to church music and hymns, and drank wine imported from Madeira. Lay assistants converted many commoners to Catholicism, and schoolmasters instructed children at churches and chapels. The result was an African Creole culture, in which the veneration of territorial and ancestral spirits was combined with Catholicism.

Kongo began to sell slaves to Portuguese traders as early as 1502. By the mid-1500s, the kings permitted the export of a few thousand slaves a year. But Portugal wanted more slaves, and in 1571 the crusader king Sebastião I (r. 1557–1578) chartered a member of the aristocracy to create a colony in the adjacent kingdom of Ndongo for the mining of salt and silver by slaves. At first, this holder of the charter assisted the king of Ndongo in defeating rebels; but when his colonial aims became clear, the king turned against him, and a full-scale Portuguese war of conquest and for slaves erupted.

In this war (1579–1657), the Portuguese allied themselves with the Ibangala, fierce warriors from the eastern outreaches of Kongo and Ndongo into central Africa who raided in both kingdoms. Together, a few hundred Portuguese musketeers and tens of thousands of Ibangalas raided the kingdoms of Ndongo and Kongo for slaves, often capturing as many as 15,000 a year.

Portuguese and allied Ibangala troops also exploited a long civil war (1665–1709) in Kongo. That war expanded further when the Dutch West India Company, mistakenly assumed that the small numbers of Portuguese troops would be unable to defend the coastal forts. Thanks to Brazilian help, however, Portugal was able to drive out the Dutch. The latter decided to return to a more peaceful trade for slaves from other fortified strongholds on the African west coast.

The Dutch in South Africa

In 1652, the Dutch built a fort on the South African coast to supply ships traveling around the Cape of Good Hope. Employees of the company grew wheat and bought cattle from the Khoi, local cattle breeders. A few wealthy landowners imported the first black slaves in 1658 to convert the original Dutch smallholdings into larger plantations. Gradually, a culturally Dutch settler society emerged.

The majority of these settlers were urban craftspeople and traders, while most of the actual farmers employed slaves. Around 1750, there were about 10,000 *Boers* (Dutch for "farmer") in the Cape Colony, easily outnumbered by slaves. Through expansion into the interior, ranchers destroyed the Khoi, forcing their absorption into other local groups. The Boers governed themselves, and their descendants, who called themselves "Afrikaners," would one day create the system of apartheid in South Africa.

Kongolese Cross of St. Anthony. Considered an emblem of spiritual authority and power, the Christian cross was integrated into Kongo ancestral cults and burial rituals and was believed to contain magical protective properties. In Antonianism, the religious reform movement launched by Dona Beatriz Kimpa Vita, in 1704, St. Anthony of Padua, a thirteenth-century Portuguese-born saint, became known as Toni Malau, or "Anthony of Good Fortune," and was the patron of the movement. His image was widely incorporated into religious objects and personal items, such as this cross.

American Plantation Slavery and Atlantic Mercantilism

While European slave traders exploited existing African slave systems, the American plantation slave system had its roots in the Eastern Christian religious civilization of Byzantium. There, the Roman institution of agricultural estate slavery had survived. Imperial estates on the Mediterranean islands of Cyprus and Crete employed Muslim prisoners as well as captives as slaves for the cultivation of labor-intensive crops. After 1191, crusader landlords and Venetian and Genoese merchants expanded into sugar production, which had been introduced from Iran to the eastern Mediterranean by the Muslims.

map analysis: the spread of sugar cultivation

The Special Case of Plantation Slavery in the Americas

In examining the patterns of American **plantation slavery**, a number of questions arise: How many Africans were forcibly taken from Africa to the Americas? Who were they, and who were the people who exploited their labor? What institutions were created to capture, transport, supply, and work slaves? What did the labor of the African slaves help to build? Why did this system develop the way it did—and last so long?

Plantation slavery: Economic system in which slave labor was used to grow cash crops such as sugarcane, tobacco, and cotton on large estates.

Numbers   The enslavement of Africans for labor in the Western Hemisphere constituted the largest human migration in world history before the latter nineteenth century. While the figures have been debated, estimates put the numbers of Africans shipped out of Africa at around 12.5 million. An estimated 1.4 million, or 12 percent, may have died between their initial capture and transfer to the African coast, or at sea. Nearly half of the surviving slaves, 5.8 million, were sent to Brazil. These figures exclude the numbers killed in the African slave raids and wars themselves, which will probably never be precisely known (see Map 19.2).

Chattel Slavery   By the mid-eighteenth century African slaves in the New World had been reduced to the status of **chattel**. A significant difference between chattel slavery and earlier kinds of slavery was what came to be known as the "color line." By the eighteenth century, color was the determining factor in American slavery. The equation of blackness with slavery created the basis for the modern expression of the phenomenon of racism, a problem that has plagued all societies touched by the institution of African slavery to this day.

Chattel: Literally, an item of moveable personal property; chattel slavery is the reduction of the status of the slave to an item of personal property of the owner, to dispose of as he or she sees fit.

Historians debate the role of present-day sensibilities and issues in the study of the past. The practice of looking at the past through the lens of the present is called **presentism**. Historians try to distance themselves from their biases while attempting to empathetically enter the past. Nowhere is this problem more evident than in considering the origins of the plantation system and African slavery. While those origins are distant in time, what they led to remains repellent to our present sensibilities.

Presentism: A bias toward present-day attitudes, especially in the interpretation of history.

Caribbean Plantations   Following the first European voyages to the Americas, indigenous populations were decimated by smallpox. To replenish the labor force, as early as 1511, the Spanish crown authorized the importation of 50 African slaves for gold mining on the island of Hispaniola. In the following decades thousands more

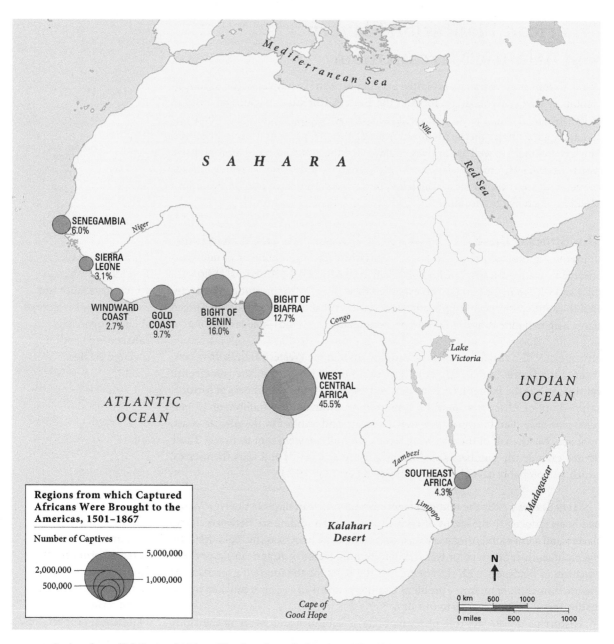

MAP **19.2** **Regions from which Captured Africans Were Brought to the Americas, 1501–1867.**

engraving showing African slaves working in the mines of Hispaniola (1595)

followed for work on newly established sugar plantations. By the late sixteenth century, African slaves outnumbered Europeans on the Spanish-controlled islands and in Mexico and Peru, where they were primarily involved in mining.

Apart from mining, plantation work for sugar production is among the most arduous forms of labor. The average slave field hand on a sugar plantation was estimated to live just 5 or 6 years. Early on, the workforce was largely male, which meant that there were relatively few children to replenish the slave population. With the price of slaves low and the mortality rate high, it was economically more desirable to literally work slaves to death and buy more than to make the investments necessary to cultivate families. Not surprisingly, revolts, work slowdowns, and sabotage were frequent, with punishments being severe and public.

Mercantilism in Action in the Caribbean   With the decline of Spanish power and the rise of the North Atlantic maritime states during the seventeenth century, a profound shift of the political balance in the Caribbean took place. Portugal, Spain, the Netherlands, Great Britain, and France all followed the path of **mercantilism**— that is, when the wealth of the state depends on having the maximum amount of gold and silver in its treasury. Thus, states should keep their economies blocked off from competitors and import as little and export as much as possible. Colonies were seen as vital to this economic system, because they supplied raw materials to the European homeland and provided safe markets for goods manufactured in the home country.

One way to enhance riches was to capture those of rivals. Thus, from the late sixteenth through the early eighteenth centuries, the navies of the Dutch, English, French, Spanish, and Portuguese all attacked each other's shipping interests and maritime colonies. Moreover, all of these governments issued "letters of marque" allowing warships owned by **privateers** to prey on the shipping of rival powers for a share in the prize money they obtained.

The trade in plantation commodities from the Caribbean compelled Spain's European competitors to oust the Spanish from their sugar islands. England seized Jamaica from Spain in 1655; a decade later, France seized the western part of Hispaniola, which came to be called Saint-Domingue.

Two developments enhanced the mercantilist economies of both powers. First, English and French merchants became involved in the African slave trade. Second, the growing demand for molasses (a by-product of sugar refining) and the even greater popularity of its fermented and distilled end product, rum, pushed both sugar planting and slavery to heights that would not reach their peak until after 1750. Sugar, slaves, molasses, and rum formed the triangular trade that sustained the Atlantic economic system.

The demand for labor quickly became gargantuan. Barbados, for example, was settled initially in 1627 by English planters who employed English and Irish **indentured laborers**. After planters began cultivating sugarcane around 1640, however, English and Irish indentured laborers proved so unwilling to go to Barbados that law courts in England and Ireland resorted to convicting them on trumped-up charges and sentencing them to "transportation." But even then planters had to resort to slave imports from Africa, at the rate of two slaves to one indentured laborer, to satisfy the demand.for workers.

The Sugar Empire: Brazil   The Portuguese first planted sugarcane as a crop in Brazil in the 1530s. Also in the 1530s, the Portuguese trading network on the central African coast began to supply the colony with African slaves. By the end of the century, a dramatic rise in demand for sugar in Europe increased the importation of African slaves. The insatiable demand of the sugar industry for slaves received a further boost in 1680 when enslavement of Indians was finally abolished, and in 1690 the discovery of gold in Minas Gerais further increased demand for labor. Brazil ultimately went on to be the largest slave state in the world, with about two-fifths of its entire population consisting of people of African descent, and was the last country in the Americas to give up the institution of slavery, in 1888 (see Map 19.3).

Mercantilism: Political theory according to which the wealth derived from the mining of silver and gold and the production of agricultural commodities should be restricted to each country's market, with as little as possible expended on imports from another country.

Privateers: Individuals or ships granted permission to attack enemy shipping and to keep a percentage of the prize money the captured ships brought at auction; in practice, privateers were often indistinguishable from pirates.

Indentured laborers: Poor workers enrolled in European states with an obligation to work in the Americas for 3–7 years in return for their prepaid passage across the Atlantic.

slaves working in a sugar mill in Brazil, ca. 1658

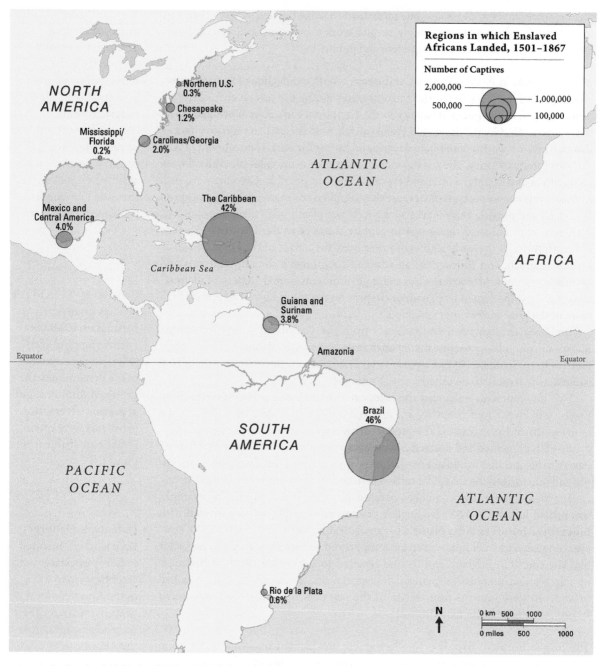

MAP **19.3** **Regions in which Enslaved Africans Landed, 1501–1867.**

Slavery in British North America

In 1750, a plantation zone extended unbroken from the Chesapeake Bay in England's North American colonies to Brazil, embracing the entire Caribbean. This zone represented a pattern unprecedented in world history. It created the largest demand for human labor yet seen, which after 1700 was satisfied almost exclusively through the African slave trade. This in turn created a color line that defined a permanent underclass and identified blackness with slavery and inferiority. At one time, legal slavery extended far beyond the plantation zone into what is now Canada.

The "Sot Weed" Enterprise   The first permanent English settlements in the Americas were the for-profit enterprise at Jamestown in 1607 and the religious "errand in the wilderness" of the initial settlements in Massachusetts from 1620. Both would soon count Africans among them. In August of 1619 the first slaves were sold in the English colonies of North America. They would be far from the last. Though only about 3–5 percent of the slaves shipped from Africa ended up in North America, through procreation on the continent their numbers grew to more than 4 million by the eve of the American Civil War.

Their labor was needed for a new crop: tobacco. The local Native Americans already grew tobacco, but it was considered by European smokers to be inferior to the varieties grown in the Caribbean. The English acquired some of the Caribbean plants and began cultivation of this "sot weed," as it came to be called. Indentured labor was widely used, but as those workers were bound to stay only until they had worked off the cost of their passage, slaves became the preferred labor source in Virginia. Though a surprising number of Africans earned **manumission** from their owners, even on occasion starting their own plantations with their own slaves during the seventeenth century, the colonial authorities eventually passed laws fixing the slave underclass as one based on color.

Manumission: The process by which slaves are legally given freedom.

Sugar, Rice, and Indigo in the Lower South   The colony of Carolina came under the purview of the Lords Proprietors in Barbados, who began sending settlers in 1670. In the seventeenth and early eighteenth centuries, these settlers enslaved tens of thousands of Native Americans. Native resistance to slaving resulted in war between the settlers and a Native American alliance in 1715–1717 that almost lost the colony for the Lords Proprietors. The settlers, angry with what they considered the mismanagement of the Lords Proprietors, appealed to the crown, and South Carolina was split off in 1719 and set up as a royal colony. Deprived of Native Americans for slaves, the colonies began to import West African slaves as the Dutch dominance of the trade gave way to the British. Ultimately, South Carolina became the only North American colony, and later state, in which African Americans outnumbered those of European descent.

South Carolina produced many of the same plantation commodities as Brazil and the Caribbean (such as sugarcane, molasses, and rice), along with indigo, which was destined to become the colony's most important cash crop until the cotton boom of the nineteenth century. The indigo plant was used to produce a dark blue dye popular in Europe. The need for labor in planting indigo, stripping the leaves, fermenting,

TO BE SOLD, on board the Ship *Bance-Island*, on tuesday the 6th of *May* next, at *Afhley-Ferry*, a choice cargo of about 250 fine healthy NEGROES, juft arrived from the Windward & Rice Coaft. —The utmoft care has already been taken, and fhall be continued, to keep them free from the leaft danger of being infected with the SMALL-POX, no boat having been on board, and all other communication with people from *Charles-Town* prevented. *Auftin, Laurens, & Appleby.*

N. B. Full one Half of the above Negroes have had the SMALL-POX in their own Country.

Advertisement for a Slave Auction. In this notice from 1766, potential slave buyers in Charleston, South Carolina, are informed of the time and place for the sale of a "choice cargo" of recently arrived Africans. As Charleston was undergoing a smallpox epidemic at the time, potential customers are reassured that the captives are healthy and likely to be immune to the disease.

cleaning, draining, scraping, and molding the residue into balls or blocks drove the slave trade even further.

The last new English possession in southern North America prior to 1750 was Georgia. The southern regions of what was to become the colony of Georgia had been claimed by the Spanish as early as 1526. Attempts by the French to found a colony near present-day Jacksonville in the 1560s failed. With the expansion of the English presence in the seventeenth century and the French concentrating on their vast claims in Canada and the Mississippi valley, the territory between Carolina and the Spanish fort at St. Augustine became increasingly disputed.

Into this situation stepped James Oglethorpe (1696–1785), whose vision was to set up a colony for England's poor, debtors, and dispossessed. He obtained a royal charter and in 1733 arrived at the site of the modern city of Savannah. After buying land from the local Native Americans, he began to develop the colony as a free area in which slavery was banned. The Spanish attempted to claim Georgia in 1742, but were repulsed. Pressed by settlers bringing their slaves in from South Carolina, Georgia's ban on slave labor was soon rescinded. By the end of Oglethorpe's life, Georgia had developed its own slave-based plantation economy, which included cotton—the commodity that would ensure slavery's survival in the United States until 1865.

The Fatal Triangle: The Economic Patterns of the Atlantic Slave Trade

The European countries that dominated the transportation of slaves from the West African coast moved in a pattern that paralleled their naval and merchant marine power. During the fifteenth and sixteenth centuries, Portugal had an effective monopoly on the trade from African outposts including Elmina. The success of Dutch and English privateers encouraged the seizure by the Dutch of Elmina in 1637. Now it was the Dutch who became the principal slave carriers, part of a pattern of aggressive colonizing that made the Netherlands the world's richest country through much of the seventeenth century. The rise of England's naval power at the expense of the Dutch and the fading of the Spanish and Portuguese naval presence next allowed the English to dominate the slave trade. By the mid-eighteenth century, the slave trade had become the base of the world's most lucrative economic triangle (see Map 19.4).

Rum, Guns, and Slaves England's colonies in the Americas were by the eighteenth century producing valuable crops for export to the Old World. Tobacco was raised mainly in England's North American colonies, along with some cotton for export to England. So profitable were these exports that, in keeping with the policy of mercantilism, the crown passed the Navigation Acts in 1651 and 1660. These acts required that all goods imported to England from American colonies had to be transported only on English ships, thereby guaranteeing a virtual monopoly on transatlantic trade.

British merchants acquired enormous profits through their colonial trading practices, particularly with the Atlantic colonies. An analysis of the **Atlantic system**, or the "triangular trade," illustrates how this system worked. In general terms, British ships would leave home ports in either their North American colonies or Britain

Atlantic system: Economic system in which European ships would exchange goods for slaves in West Africa and slaves would then be brought to America and exchanged for goods that would be carried back to the home port.

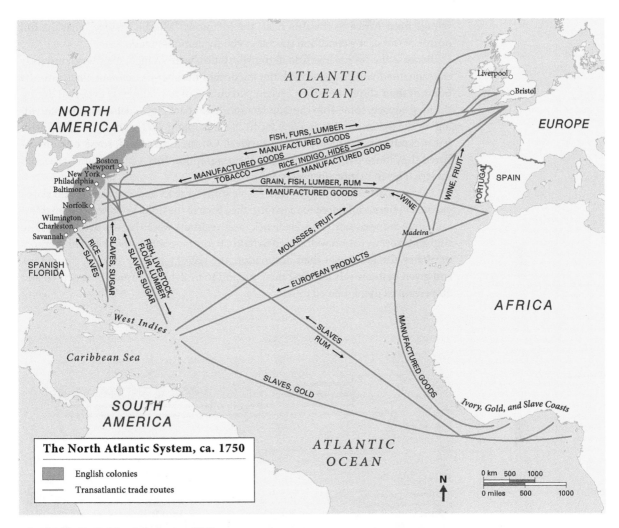

MAP 19.4 **The North Atlantic System, ca. 1750.**

with trade goods, then travel to ports along the western coast of Africa, where these goods would be exchanged for African slaves; these ships would then cross the Atlantic, where slaves would be exchanged for goods produced in western Atlantic colonies; and finally, these goods would be carried back to the home port.

One common pattern involved the following: An English ship loaded with rum would sail from Europe to the western coast of Africa, where the rum would be exchanged for slaves; laden with slaves, the ship would then cross the Atlantic to sugar colonies in the Caribbean, where the slaves would be exchanged for molasses; the ship would sail to New England, where the molasses would be processed into rum.

The Middle Passage Following capture in Africa, prisoners were usually marched to slave markets and embarkation ports. Slave lots were then wholesaled to middlemen or auctioned directly to foreign factors. From this point they would be imprisoned until the next ship bound for their sale destination arrived. But it was on the

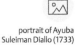

portrait of Ayuba
Suleiman Diallo (1733)

voyage from Africa to the Americas, the infamous "Middle Passage," that the full horror of the slave's condition was most vividly demonstrated.

Because the profits involved in transportation were so high, mariners constantly experimented with ways to pack the maximum number of human beings into the holds of their ships. Because a certain percentage of mortality was expected during the long voyage, some ship captains favored "tight packing"—deliberate overcrowding on the assumption that a few more captives might survive than on a ship with fewer captives but a higher rate of survival. On the other hand, some captains favored the "loose pack" method, with the assumption that a higher number would survive if given marginally more room.

Fearing slave mutiny, the holds of slave ships were locked and barred, and slaves chained in tiers configured to maximize the space of the hold. Food was minimal and sanitation nonexistent. The dead, sick, and resistant were thrown overboard. The ship and crew were also well armed to fight off mutineers and attacks by competitors or pirates. On landing at their destination, the slaves were imprisoned, cleaned up, and given better meals pending their auction to individual buyers. Between 10 and 30 percent of them died en route.

Plan of a Slave Ship, 1789. This image, based on the *Brooks*, a Liverpool slave ship, was one of the first to document the horrors of the slave trade. It shows the captives laid out like sardines below deck. In such conditions, slaves perished at the rate of 10–30 percent during the Middle Passage. The engraving was widely distributed by British abolitionists, who eventually succeeded in banning the trade in 1807.

Culture and Identity in the African Diaspora

The term "diaspora" is used by scholars for the wide dispersal by forced or voluntary migration of any large group. In the case of the **African diaspora**, in which Africans moved to nearly all parts of the Americas primarily through the slave trade, the story is far too complex for us to do more than note some general patterns related to culture and identity.

African diaspora: Dispersal of African peoples throughout the world, particularly the Americas, as part of the transatlantic slave trade.

A New Society: Creolization of the Early Atlantic World

An effect of the Portuguese trade forts and colonies in coastal Africa was the adaptation of African societies to Western Christianity and Portuguese culture. Clan- or lineage-based societies welcomed trade with outsiders; others were militarily oriented and saw the new arrivals as unwelcome competitors; still others were kingdoms, some of which cooperated intermittently or permanently with the Portuguese and other Europeans. In the interactions of these societies with Portuguese Christianity, African Creole cultures of different characters emerged.

While earlier scholarship described this creolization as the uneasy grafting of an alien, colonizing culture onto "genuine" Africanness, Creole culture is now understood as an "authentic" phenomenon in its own right. This is similarly true for black Creole cultures in the Americas, where Africans arrived with either their own local spiritual traditions or as Christians and Muslims. African slaves adapted to plantation life through creolization or, as African Christian or Muslim Creoles, through further creolization, a process that expressed itself in distinct languages or dialects as well as synthetic (or hybrid) religious customs. Adaptation was a creative transformation of cultural elements to fit a life of forced labor abroad.

A key element in the development of culture and identity of Africans in the Americas lay in the influence of the central African Creoles from Kongo and Ndongo up to the middle of the seventeenth century. The Christianity of some believers and its later variants helped to nurture this religion among Africans in the new lands, especially when it was reinforced by the religious practices of the slave owners. The mix of language and terms similarly gave the early arrivals a degree of agency in navigating the institutions of slavery as they were being established.

An example of a Creole language that has survived for centuries is Gullah, used by the isolated slave communities along the coastal islands of South Carolina and Georgia and still spoken by their descendants today. In Haiti, Creole (*Kreyòl*) is not only the daily spoken language but one also used in the media and in literary works. Creole cultures thus typically involve not only adaptation but also multiple identities—in language, religion, and culture.

Music and Food   The roots of most popular music in the Americas are African. African slaves brought with them musical instruments, songs, and chants, all of which contributed to shaping the musical tastes of their owners and society at large. The widespread use of drumming and dance in African celebrations, funerals, and even coded communications was the basis for Brazilian samba, Cuban and Dominican rumba and meringue, New Orleans jazz, and American blues, rock and roll, soul, and hip-hop. American country-and-western music and bluegrass feature

Voodoo and Other New World Slave Religions

Altar and Shrine from the Interior of the Historic Voodoo Museum in New Orleans.

One prominent pattern of world history is the way indigenous elements shape the identity of imported religions. Buddhism in China and Japan, for example, adopted elements from Daoism and Chinese folk beliefs as well as spirits and demons from Shinto. Christianity added Roman and Germanic elements to its calendar of holidays, architecture, and cult of saints. Islam in Iran and India and Christianity in Africa underwent similar processes. This trend of interaction continues today, where we find the African Christian churches among the fastest growing in the world.

In the Americas three main strains of interaction and adaptation of imported and indigenous traditions developed: Santeria, which is found primarily in Cuba, among the Spanish-speaking Africans of the Caribbean, and in cities of North America with communities of Caribbean immigrants; vodoun, usually written as "voodoo," which developed in Haiti and old Saint-Domingue and is widely practiced among African-descended French speakers around the Caribbean and in areas of Louisiana; and Candomblé, which is found mostly in Brazil.

the banjo, descended from a West African stringed instrument. The chants of field hands, rhyming contests, and gospel music also contributed to these genres.

Like music, cuisine passed easily across institutional barriers. Many dishes that most Americans consider "Southern" have African roots. The first rice brought to the Carolinas was a variety native to West Africa. Africans brought with them the knowledge of setting up an entire rice-based food system, which was established in the Carolina lowlands and Gulf Coast. The yam, the staple of West African diets, also made its way to the Americas. The heart of Louisiana Creole cooking, including gumbos, "dirty rice," and jambalaya, relies on the African vegetable okra and a mixture of African, American, and Asian spices along with rice.

Plantation Life and Resistance   Although nineteenth-century apologists for slavery frequently portrayed life under it as tranquil, the system was in fact one of constant violence.

Most slaves navigated their condition as best they could, but were constantly reminded of their status. Those who endured the Middle Passage had violence thrust upon them immediately upon capture. Even those born into slavery lived in squalid shacks or cabins; ate inadequate rations; and spent most of their waking hours at labor.

House servants had a somewhat easier life than field hands. In some cases, they were the primary guardians, midwives, wet nurses, and even confidants of their masters'

All three are syncretic religions composed of elements which practitioners see as part of an integrated whole. They intermingle Roman Catholic saints with West African natural and ancestral spirits and gods, see spiritual power as resident in natural things, and incorporate images of objects to represent a person or thing whose power the believer wants to tap or disperse (as in the use of so-called voodoo dolls). They also hold that ritual and sacrifices by priests and priestesses can tune in to the spirits of the natural world. Such innovations allowed the slaves to create a religious and cultural space in which they carved out autonomy from their masters— indeed, in which they *were* the masters. They also provided alternate beliefs that could be invoked alongside more mainstream Christian practices. In a real sense, they provided a precious degree of freedom for people who had almost no other form of it.

Questions

- How do black Christianity and voodoo religion show the new patterns of origins, interaction, and adoption that emerged after 1500?

- Can you think of more recent examples of syncretic religions? If so, which ones? Why are they syncretic?

Mami Wata. Both a protector and a seducer, Mami Wata is an important spirit figure throughout much of Africa and the African Atlantic. She is usually portrayed as a mermaid, a snake charmer, or a combination of both. She embodies the essential, sacred nature of water, across which so many African Americans traveled in their diaspora.

Slave Culture. This ca. 1790 painting from Beaufort, South Carolina, shows the vibrancy of African American culture in the face of great hardship. Note the banjo, whose origins lie in West Africa and which would have a great impact on the development of American music.

families. Often, there was affection between the household slaves and the master's family. But more often, this was tempered by the knowledge that they or their family members could be sold at any time, and that infractions would be severely punished.

Field hands led a far harder and shorter life. The price of slavery for the master was eternal vigilance; his nightmare was slave revolt. A variety of methods kept slaves in line and at their work. Overseers ran the work schedules and supervised punishments; drivers kept slaves at their work with a bullwhip to beat the slow. Slaves leaving plantations on errands had to carry passes, and precautions were taken to discourage escape or even unauthorized visits to neighboring plantations. Runaways were relentlessly pursued and flogged, branded, maimed, or castrated when returned.

Given these conditions, slaves tried to manage their work on their own terms or to get back at their owners. Slaves staged work slowdowns, feigned illnesses, sabotaged tools and equipment, or pretended not to understand how to perform certain tasks. Despite the risks, runaways were common. Later, in the United States in the 1850s, enforcement of the Fugitive Slave Act would be a prime factor driving the country toward civil war.

Slave owners faced the constant prospect of slave insurrection. The most famous of these revolts in the United States was that of Nat Turner in Virginia in 1831. In 2016 a feature-length drama titled *Birth of a Nation* about Turner's rebellion was released—its title meant to counter the racist sentiments of the famous film of that name released a century before. In some cases, these rebellions were successful enough for the slaves to create their own settlements where they could, for a time, live in freedom. These escapees were called *Maroons*. Three of the more successful Maroon settlements existed in Jamaica, Colombia, and Surinam. Map 19.5 lists some of the larger slave insurrections from 1500 to 1850.

❯ Putting It All Together

interactive concept map

Portugal, the Netherlands, England, France, and Spain built up a pattern of trading for plantation slaves on the Atlantic coast of Africa in the course of the sixteenth and seventeenth centuries. The trade took off toward the end of the sixteenth century, and by 1700 it had reached 80,000 annually, where it stayed until the early nineteenth century, when the slave trade was abolished. As for the patterns of state formation in Africa, the more powerful a kingdom was, the fewer slaves it sold, given its own labor requirements. Conversely, the more conducive the circumstances were to the collapse of chiefly or royal rule and the emergence of raider societies, the more damaging the impact was on a given population. The period marked a profound transformation for Africa, with many areas depopulated by the slave trade, some enhanced through the trade and the introduction of new food crops, and others undergoing creolization.

The interaction and adaptation patterns of Europeans and Africans in Africa and Europeans, Africans, and Native Americans in the Caribbean and Americas during the period 1500–1800 created not just a new world system of trade but a new kind of society as well. The Atlantic slave trade was the foundation of the mass production of cash crops and commodities, the first world pattern of its kind. This economic sphere was the richest of its kind in the world, but with it came the creation of an enduring social underclass and the emergence of modern racism.

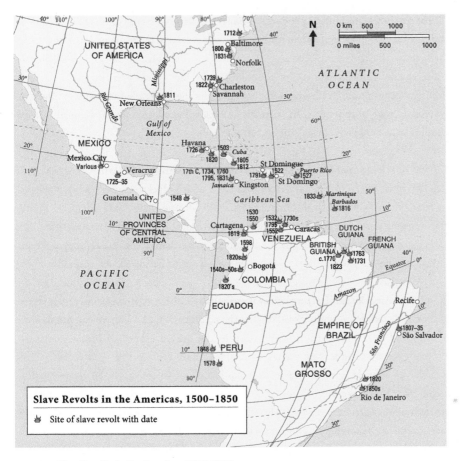

MAP **19.5 Slave Revolts in the Americas, 1500–1850.**

Yet even as early as the 1750s, one finds the origins of the abolition movement—the international movement to end first the slave trade and ultimately slavery itself. Among the leaders of Europe's Enlightenment, thinkers were already calling for the end of the trade and institution. Elsewhere, it would take a revolution, as in Haiti, or a civil war, as in the United States, for abolition to occur. In the Atlantic world, slavery finally ended in Brazil in 1888. But it persists informally in India, Africa, and the Middle East even today.

Review and Relate

Thinking Through Patterns

Examine the ways historians approach the big questions of this chapter.

A frica during these 300 years continued its pattern of kingdom and empire formation at an accelerated pace, on the basis of increased intra-African trade. In the interior of Africa, the pattern continued in spite of the demographic effects of the Atlantic slave trade.

> On what was the pattern of kingdom and empire formation in Africa based during the period 1500–1800?

The pattern of plantation production was transplanted to the islands of the Atlantic and the Caribbean as well as the Americas. It was a system for growing labor-intensive cash crops—indigo, sugar, tobacco—that relied increasingly on African slave labor. By 1800, the demand for plantation commodities by Europeans and the guns, textiles, rum, and other manufactured goods that Africans took in trade for slaves swelled the system to huge proportions. In turn, the mercantilist economics of western Europe regulated the trade within an efficient triangular system.

≫ How did the patterns of slave trade and plantation slavery evolve in the Atlantic and the Americas?

The domination of African slavery in the Americas and Caribbean over other kinds of servitude created a pattern of racism, in which blackness was permanently associated with slavery. As the economics of slavery became entrenched, the participants in the system answered the criticism of slavery on moral grounds by claiming that black Africans were inherently inferior. The argument was essentially circular: They were enslaved because they were inferior, and they were inferior because they were slaves.

≫ What are the historic roots from which modern racism evolved?

In North America, long after slavery was abolished, these attitudes were preserved in law and custom and reinforced during the colonization of Africa in the nineteenth century and in the practice of segregation in the United States. In Latin America—although racism is no less pervasive—racial views are more subtle. People describing themselves as *mulato*, *sambo*, or *pardo* have had a better chance to be recognized as members of their own distinct ethnic groups than in the United States, where until recently the census classified people simply as either black or Caucasian. The 2010 census form, however, expanded its choices to 14 racial categories and allowed people to check multiple boxes. Clearly, the complexities of race and ethnicity in the Americas are continuing to evolve.

| Against the Grain

Consider this as a counterpoint to the main patterns examined in this chapter.

Oglethorpe's Free Colony

- Why were institutions of slavery so prevalent in so many places in the world?
- Even though many people found slavery to be immoral on humanitarian and even economic grounds, the institution persisted for centuries in

Set against the backdrop of both expanding colonial slavery and the hardening of the so-called color line, James Oglethorpe's dream of a colony of Georgia in which both slavery and rum were to be banned, and where the colonists were to consist of the "worthy poor" freed from the threat of debtor's prison, would appear to defy the patterns of the times. Oglethorpe, as a young member of the House of Commons, was appalled by the practice of imprisoning debtors and forcing them to pay for their own upkeep while incarcerated. Appointed to a parliamentary committee investigating the situation, he developed a scheme to address problems plaguing English society: indebtedness on the part of the working poor and the jobless; alcoholism fueled by cheap rum and gin; and migration to cities by the landless.

His solution was to found a colony for those afflicted by these ills. He bought land at fair prices from the Creek people, ensured that skilled craftsmen and laborers were among the initial settlers, and laid out what became the city of Savannah in a design that included a farm outside the city for self-sufficiency and common areas to create close-knit neighborhoods. To ensure that the labor of the immigrants would be valued, slavery was forbidden, as was the slave-produced product of rum. While scholars differ on whether he was a true abolitionist, he did declare slavery to be "immoral" and felt that it violated English law.

As we saw in this chapter, however, his visionary aims were ultimately defeated by the colony's position on the border with Spanish Florida. With Oglethorpe's retirement to England in 1750, his fellow trustees returned control of the colony to the British crown, and the ban on slavery was rescinded. Soon, cotton would become the most valuable export in the world and the bulwark of the US economy. And as cotton became king, the slave state of Georgia would be at the epicenter of its expansion.

the Atlantic world. Why do you think it proved so difficult to dismantle?

Key Terms

🔊))
audio flashcards

African diaspora 449	Indentured laborers 443	Presentism 441
Atlantic system 446	Manumission 445	Privateers 443
Chattel 441	Mercantilism 443	
Household slavery 438	Plantation slavery 441	

For additional resources, please go to
www.oup.com/us/vonsivers.
Please see the Further Resources section at the back of the book for additional readings and suggested websites.

The Mughal Empire

MUSLIM RULERS AND HINDU SUBJECTS

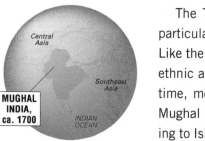

When Mumtaz Mahal, the wife of the Mughal emperor Shah Jahan, died in childbirth in 1631, the royal family was plunged into mourning.

Inconsolable for months, Shah Jahan finally resolved to build a magnificent tomb complex for Mumtaz Mahal over her burial site along the Jumna (or Yamuna) River near the fortress at Agra. This tomb, with its balance of deceptively simple lines, harmony of proportion, and technical skill, would become the most recognized symbol of India throughout the world: the Taj Mahal.

The Taj Mahal illustrates the circumstances of Mughal rule in India, particularly the attempted syncretism of Muslim rulers and Hindu subjects. Like their predecessors, the Mughals discovered the difficulties of being an ethnic and religious minority ruling a diverse population. By Shah Jahan's time, moreover, religious revival was sweeping Islamic India, and earlier Mughal rulers were subject to criticism about their laxity in ruling according to Islamic law. Shah Jahan devoted himself to a study of the Quran and resolved to rule according to Islamic precepts. The resulting policy changes would raise tensions between Hindus and Muslims.

ABOVE: The Taj Mahal (1631–1653), a magnificent architectural synthesis of Hindu and Muslim influences and Persian classicism.

S hah Jahan's architectural masterpiece is at the center of a much larger complex that serves as an **allegory** of Allah's judgment in paradise on the day of the resurrection. In the end, Mughal ambition to create an empire as the earthly expression of this vision lent itself to that empire's ultimate decline. The drive to bring the remaining independent Indian states under Mughal control strained imperial resources. Dynastic succession almost always resulted in internal wars. By the eighteenth century, rebellion and the growing influence of the European powers would send the dynasty into a downward spiral from which it never recovered.

History and Political Life of the Mughals

Relations between Muslims and India's other religions were *syncretic*, coexisting on occasionally difficult or hostile terms, but remaining largely separate from the other traditions. Yet the political and social systems created by the Mughals were in many respects a successful *synthesis*. That is, the Mughals brought with them a tradition that blended the practices of conquest and plunder with several centuries of ruling more settled areas by peaceful means. This legacy would guide them as they struggled to create an empire centered on one religion. The Mughals created a flexible bureaucracy with a hierarchy of ranks and separation of powers but with ultimate power concentrated in the hands of the emperors. Like those of the Chinese and Ottomans, the system was easily expanded into newly conquered areas, gave free rein to the ambitious, and weathered major political storms until its decline during the eighteenth century.

From Samarkand to Hindustan

The rise to prominence of speakers of Turkic languages of the Altaic group took many centuries. From at least the time of the Huns, these groups regularly coalesced into potent raiding and fighting forces, most importantly those of the Mongols in the twelfth and thirteenth centuries. When the Mongol Empire fell apart, the central Asian heartland of the Turkic peoples evolved into a patchwork of smaller states, many of whose rulers claimed descent from Genghis Khan. With the ousting of the Mongol Yuan dynasty from China in 1368, the eastern regions of this territory were thrown into further disarray, which set the stage for another movement toward consolidation.

The Empire of Timur Islam, by the fourteenth century, was the dominant religion among the central Asian Turkic peoples. In the interior of central Asia, the memory of the accomplishments of the Mongol Empire among the inhabitants of Chagatai—the area given to Genghis Khan's son of that name—was still fresh. Their desire for a new Mongol Empire, now coupled with Islam, created opportunities for military action to unite the settled and nomadic tribes of Chagatai. The result was the stunning rise of Temur Gurgan (r. 1370–1405), more widely known by the Persian rendering of his name, Timur-i Lang, or Tamerlane.

Though Timur came close to matching the conquests of Genghis Khan, his forebears were not direct descendants of the conqueror. He therefore devised genealogies connecting him to the dominant Mongol lines to give him legitimacy as a ruler,

>> What were the strengths and weaknesses of Mughal rule?

>> What was the Mughal policy toward religious accommodation? How did it change over time?

>> What factors account for the Mughal decline during the eighteenth century?

Allegory: A literary, poetic, dramatic, pictorial, or architectural device in which the parts have symbolic value in depicting the meaning of the whole.

Chapter Outline

- History and Political
  Life of the Mughals

- Administration, Society,
  and Economics

- Science, Religion, and
  the Arts

- Putting It All Together

and he even found a direct descendant of Genghis Khan to use as a figurehead for his regime.

From 1382, when he secured the region of his homeland around the capital, the Silk Road trading center of Samarkand, until his death in 1405, Timur ranged through western central Asia, Afghanistan, northern India, Iran, Anatolia, and the eastern Mediterranean (see Map 20.1). Like his model, Genghis Khan, he proved surprisingly liberal in his treatment of certain cities that surrendered peacefully. Many more times, however, he reduced cities to rubble, slaughtered the inhabitants, and erected pyramids of skulls as a warning to others to submit.

Shortly after his death in 1405, Timur's empire, like that of Genghis Khan, fell apart. The Chagatai peoples resumed their feuds, once again leaving the way open for a strong military force to impose order.

Babur and the Timurid Line in India   By the beginning of the sixteenth century, the region from Samarkand south into the Punjab in northern India had become the province of feuding Turkic tribes and clans of Afghan fighters. Into this volatile environment was born Zahir ud-Din Muhammad Babur (1483–1530, r. 1526–1530), more commonly known as simply Babur. Babur's claims to legitimate rule were considerable: His father was a direct descendant of Timur, while his mother claimed the lineage of Genghis Khan.

In 1504, Babur moved into Afghanistan, captured Kabul, and went on to raid points farther south over the following decade. By 1519, he raided northern India with a view to subjugating and ruling it. After 7 more years of campaigning, this goal was achieved. In 1526, Babur's army met the forces of Sultan Ibrahim Lodi at Panipat, near Delhi. Though the sultan's forces were much larger, Babur's forces employed the new technologies of matchlock muskets and field cannon to devastating effect. In the end, the Lodi sultan was killed, and Babur's way was now clear to consolidate his new Indian territories.

Victory at Panipat was followed by conquest of the Lodi capital of Agra and further success over the Hindu Rajputs in 1528. At his death in December 1530, Babur controlled territory extending from Samarkand in the north to Gwalior in India in the south (see Map 20.2). For Babur and his successors, their ruling family would always be the "House of Timur." Because of their claims to the legacy of Genghis Khan, however, they would be better known to the world as the Mughals (from "Mongols").

Loss and Recovery of Empire   Babur's son, Humayun (r. 1530–1556) was now faced with the problem of consolidating, organizing, and administering this vast domain

Area Subjugated by Timur-i Lang, 1360–1405

Area under Timur-i Lang's control, 1405

MAP 20.1 **Area Subjugated by Timur-i Lang, 1360–1405.**

MAP 20.2 **The Conquests of Babur.**

Unfortunately, Humayun was more interested in literature (and, at times, wine and opium) than responsible leadership.

A chronic problem was the **institutionalization** of traditional nomadic succession practices among the Mughal rulers. Though only one son was designated as the ruler's successor, the others were given territories within the empire, which led to conflict. Humayun also faced hostile military forces in unconquered areas of northern India and Afghanistan. When an Afghan leader named Sher Khan Sur invaded the extreme eastern region of Bengal, Humayun, twice routed, fled to Persia, where he was forced to convert to Shia Islam. As distasteful as this was for him as a Sunni Muslim, he now at least had Persian backing and proceeded to move into Afghanistan and, ultimately, to Delhi. By 1555, the dynasty was restored. For Humayun, however, the peace brought only a brief respite. In a final irony for this scholarly man, he made a misstep with a pile of books in his arms: as he was descending the stairs from the roof terrace of his palace library with the books, he heard the sound of the muezzin's call to prayer. As he went to kneel on the staircase, he tripped on his robe. After several days he died of his injuries in January 1556.

Institutionalization: The creation of a regular system for previously improvised or ad hoc activities or things, such as law codes to replace local customs.

interactive timeline

1336–1405 Timur (Tamerlane), founder of Timurid line of rulers	**1542–1605** Akbar, most innovative of Mughal rulers	**1618–1707** Aurangzeb, last powerful Mughal ruler	**1739** Invasion by Persians; looting of Delhi; taking of Peacock Throne
1483–1530 Babur, founder of Timurid line in India—the Mughals	**1627–1657** Shah Jahan, builder of the Taj Mahal	**1707–1858** Ebbing of Mughal power in India; rise of British influence	

Portrait of Babur. This imagined portrait of Babur was done about 60 years after his death. He is shown receiving representatives of the Uzbeks of Central Asia and the Rajputs of India in an audience dated December 18, 1528.

Consolidation and Expansion   Humayun's death was kept secret while the court worked out plans for a **regency** for the emperor's son, 14-year-old Jalal ud-Din Akbar (r. 1556–1605). His military education began quickly as Humayun's old enemy, Sher Khan Sur, sent an army to attack Delhi in 1557. The Mughal forces triumphed, and went on to secure the eastern, southern, and western flanks of their lands, once again anchoring Islam in the former areas of its influence—"Hindustan."

Akbar plunged into renewed campaigning in quest of more territory. Although determined to master all India by any military means necessary, Akbar, who abhorred religious violence, worked to reconcile the different religious traditions of his empire. But his attempts would prove futile, earning him the enmity of many of his fellow Muslims, who felt he had become an unbeliever.

As a warrior Akbar was far more successful. Through the 1560s, Mughal armies continued to push the boundaries of the empire west, south, and east. This string of victories continued into the next decade, with the long-sought conquest of Gujarat taking place in 1573. Turning eastward, Akbar set his sights on Bengal, which, along with the neighboring regions of Bihar and Orissa, fell to the Mughals by the mid-1570s. They remained, however, volatile and hostile to Mughal occupation. Both Muslim and Hindu princes in the region continued their resistance into the following decades (see Map 20.3).

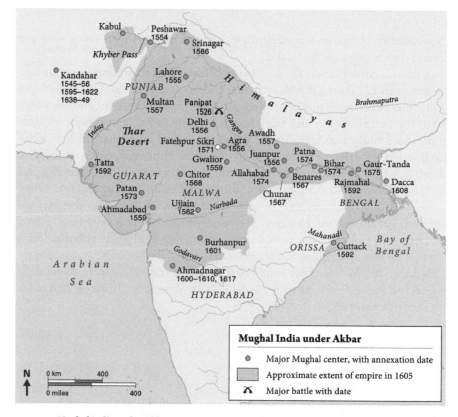

MAP **20.3 Mughal India under Akbar.**

Resistance and rebellion plagued other areas of the empire. In order to keep the old Islamic heartland of northern India—Hindustan—under Mughal control, the Mughals built fortresses throughout their inner domains as well as along the frontier. Among the most important of these were Allahabad, Lahore (in modern Pakistan), Ajmer (the Amber Fort in Jaipur), and the Red Fort in Delhi.

The New City   In addition to fielding large armies and maintaining forts, the immense revenues of the Mughal lands allowed for other monumental projects. In an effort to show solidarity with his non-Muslim subjects, Akbar had married a Hindu Rajput princess named Manmati. Akbar consulted a Sufi holy man named Salim Chishti (sometimes spelled as Chisti), who told Akbar that he would ultimately have a son. When that son—named Salim in honor of the holy man—was born, Akbar built a city on the site of Salim Chishti's village of Sikri. Akbar's instincts for dynastic propaganda were everywhere evident within Fatehpur Sikri, as the city was known. At its center was the mosque, which housed the tomb of Salim Chishti and became an object of veneration and pilgrimage for Indian Sufis. However, the city was ultimately abandoned because there was not enough water to sustain the population.

The Summer and Autumn of Empire

The saga of Fatehpur Sikri reflects Mughal fortunes over the next century. The military accomplishments of the dynasty are spectacular, but they were eventually worn down by internal rebellion; the immense fortunes of the rulers were depleted by the needs of defense and demonstration of power; and new economic and military competitors arrived with the coming of the Europeans.

The Revolt of the Sons   In 1585, Akbar left Fatehpur Sikri with his army for Lahore, which he made his temporary capital. Once again, the Afghan princes were chafing under Mughal domination and intriguing with the Uzbeks and Safavid Persians to wrest local control for themselves. For Akbar, it was vital to maintain a hold over these areas because of their connection to the peoples of Chagatai and the need to keep control of the essential Silk Road trade. Now the key city of Kandahar, in modern Afghanistan, was in Safavid Persian hands, disrupting Mughal control of the trade. For the next 13 years, Akbar and his generals fought to subdue the Afghans and roll back the Safavids. In the end, the Mughals acquired Sind and Kashmir, subdued for a time the region of Swat, and, with the defection of a Safavid commander, occupied Kandahar. By 1598, the regions in question were secure enough for Akbar to move back to Agra.

In 1600, Akbar embarked on his last great campaign against the remaining free Muslim sultanates of central India. These were reduced within a year, but Akbar was now faced with a domestic crisis. His son Salim launched a coup and occupied the fort at Agra. Salim declared himself emperor and raised his own army. In the end, one of Akbar's wives and a group of court women were able to reconcile Akbar and Salim, and upon Akbar's death on October 25, 1605, Salim acceded to the throne as Jahangir (r. 1605–1627).

Humayun Being Received by the Persian Shah Tahmasp. This gouache rendering of a pivotal moment in Mughal dynastic history is by the late sixteenth-century Indian painter Sanwalah. Although all seems cordial between the two men and Humayun was treated well by the Shah, a number of accounts claim that he was threatened with execution if he did not covert to Shia Islam.

a Jesuit describes Akbar (1582)

Visions of Akbar. A depiction of Akbar from ca. 1630 (*above*) shows him in all of his religious glory: surrounded by a luminous halo, surmounted by angels glorifying him and holding his crown, and graced with the holiness to make the lion lie down with the heifer.

Renewed Expansion of the "War State" Jahangir continued the tradition of conquest and expansion. This now meant pushing south into the Deccan and periodically resecuring Afghanistan and its adjacent regions. A move into Bengal, however, foreshadowed a major clash with a very different kind of enemy: the Shan people of Southeast Asia called the Ahoms. Though they had converted to Hinduism, the Ahoms had no caste system and drew upon a legacy of self-confident expansion. With little fixed territory to defend because of their mobility, the Ahoms proved the most stubborn enemies the empire had yet encountered. Though both sides employed troops armed with matchlocks and cannon, neither side could obtain a clear tactical edge, and their wars dragged on for decades.

A different threat to the Mughals was posed by the empire to their west, Safavid Persia. Both sides periodically went to war, and there was also intense religious rivalry, with the predominantly Sunni Mughals and Shiite Safavid Persians each denouncing the other as heretical unbelievers. For the Mughals, it was particularly galling that they owed the survival of their dynasty in part to the Persian shah Tahmasp, who had forced Humayun to convert to Shiism.

In addition, many Persians and Shiites within the Mughal elites felt that the Persian culture, language, and literature were superior to those of the Turks and Muslim India as a whole. In some respects, both Persians and "Persianized" Indians saw Muslim India as a kind of cultural colonial outpost. This made for complex relations between the two empires, with both vying for power in religious and cultural terms as much as in the political and military realm.

Salim Chishti's Tomb at Fatehpur Sikri. The tomb of the Sufi mystic Salim Chishti shows the sense of restrained flamboyance that marks the mature Mughal architectural style. The Chishtis had long been revered by India's Sufis, and Salim's simple, elegant tomb, with its domed sarcophagus, multihued marble, and Quranic inscriptions, quickly became a favorite pilgrimage site. Surrounding it is one of the red sandstone courtyards of Akbar's Fatehpur Sikri.

New Directions in Religious Politics   After Jahangir died in October 1627, his oldest son, Khurram, reigned as Shah Jahan (r. 1627–1657). His rule coincided with the high point of Mughal cultural power and prestige, as reflected in the Taj Mahal. However, his record is less spectacular in political and military terms. The Mughal obsession with controlling the northern trade routes coincided with the need to take back the fort at Kandahar, once again in Persian hands. Thus, Shah Jahan spent much of his reign on the ultimately fruitless drive to finally subdue the northwest.

The reigns of Akbar and of Jahangir were marked by extraordinary religious tolerance. The attraction of both men to the Sufi school of Salim Chishti created a favorable emotional environment for religious pluralism. It also made Muslims, for whom strict adherence to Sunni doctrine was necessary to guard against Persian Shia influence, apprehensive. Others, noting that Hindus incorporated the beliefs of other faiths into their own, feared that the ruling Muslim minority might ultimately be assimilated into the Hindu majority.

With Shah Jahan, however, we see a turn toward a more legalistic tradition. Under the influence of Sunni theologians, Shah Jahan began to block construction and repair of non-Muslim religious buildings, instituted more state support for Islamic festivals, and furnished subsidies for Muslim pilgrims to Mecca. The ideal of a unified Muslim world governed by Quranic law gained ground at the Mughal court and would see its greatest champion in Shah Jahan's son Aurangzeb.

The Pinnacle of Power   The ascendancy of Aurangzeb (r. 1658–1707) was marked by the familiar pattern of princely infighting. In this case it was brought on by the extended illness of Shah Jahan in 1657. A four-way struggle broke out among the sons of Shah Jahan. By 1661 three had been killed, leaving Aurangzeb in control of the empire. Shah Jahan lived on in captivity until 1666.

Aurangzeb's long rule seemed to begin auspiciously when his armies fought the Ahoms to a standstill in the early 1660s and made them Mughal clients. When Mughal control of the area around Kabul and the Khyber Pass was threatened by local tribesmen, Aurangzeb fought to retain control of the region and bought off other troublesome groups with gifts.

With these campaigns, the political power of the Mughals reached perhaps its greatest extent. But the period also marked a watershed in several respects. First, it launched decades of wars with the Hindu Marathas in which the empire's cohesion was eroded. In addition, European trading companies expanded their own fortified outposts in Indian ports outside Mughal domains. As Mughal power was sapped by the revolts of the eighteenth century, the companies' armed forces became important players in regional politics.

The other watershed was Aurangzeb's bid for a more effective "Islamification" of Mughal India ruled by Islamic Sharia law. As an Islamic state, connected to the larger commonwealth of Islamic states, he believed that Mughal rule should be primarily for the benefit of Muslims. This was an almost complete repudiation of his great-grandfather Akbar's vision of religious transcendence. While Aurangzeb stopped short of forcible conversion, elites who converted to Islam were given gifts and preferential assignments, while those who did not convert found themselves isolated. Muslim judges prompted protests from Hindus regarding their rulings. Aurangzeb further ordered the demolition of Hindu temples. Finally, he reinstated the *jizya* tax on unbelievers, which had been abolished by Akbar.

Patterns Up Close | Akbar's Attempt at Religious Synthesis

The Mughals as Muslim rulers in India were faced with an array of diverse religious and cultural traditions. Akbar's innovation within the world-historical pattern of religious civilizations was to create a new religion that would encompass these traditions and bind his followers directly to him as emperor and religious leader: to create an Indian "religious synthesis."

Akbar was resistant to the strictures of Sunni Islam or any other organized religion. He developed an extraordinary memory for literature and poetry, and his tastes within Islam centered on Sufi mysticism, which had a long tradition of tolerance and eclecticism. This openness encouraged him to study the mystical traditions of the Hindus, Parsis (Zoroastrian immigrants from Persia), and Christians. After establishing himself at Fatehpur Sikri, he sponsored regular theological debates, mostly among Muslim scholars but gradually including Hindus, Parsis, and in 1578 Catholic missionaries. He honored many of the cultural traditions of India's various religions as well: He wore his hair long under his turban like the Sikhs and some Hindus, coined emblems of the sun to honor the Parsis, and kept paintings of the Virgin Mary as a nod to the Christians.

During a lavish and bloody hunting party in 1578, he had a sudden, intense mystical experience. Like Ashoka so long before him—of whom Akbar

Akbar Presiding Over a Religious Debate. Akbar's distaste for religious orthodoxy manifested itself most dramatically in his conducting regular debates among theologians from many of India's faiths. Here, a discussion is taking place with two Jesuit missionaries, Fathers Rudolph Aquaviva and Francis Henriquez (dressed in black) in 1578. Interestingly, the priests had unfettered access to Akbar, were free to preach, and even gave instruction to members of Akbar's family at his request.

The new religious policies created problems with self-governing, non-Muslim groups within the empire. The distrust of the Mughals among the Sikhs was inflamed by Aurangzeb's attempts to intervene in the selection of a new Sikh religious leader, and by the destruction of some Sikh temples. These conditions would soon lead to a full-blown Sikh revolt.

The Maratha Revolt Aurangzeb conquered areas that had long eluded Mughal efforts: Bijapur, Golconda, and much of the Maratha lands of south central India. Yet here, too, the preconditions were already in place for a rebellion.

The Hindu Marathas had evolved working relationships with the old Muslim sultanates that, over time, were annexed by the Timurids. For the earlier Mughal rulers, it was often enough for these small states to remit tribute and supply troops in order to retain their autonomy. For Aurangzeb, however, commitment to a more legalistic Islam also meant political expansion of the Mughal state. Hence, Aurangzeb spent many years campaigning to bring central India under his sway.

Despite the tenacity of Maratha resistance, Aurangzeb's strategy—supporting pro-Mughal factions among the Maratha leaders, lavishing money and gifts on Maratha converts and deserters, and fielding large armies to attack Maratha was completely unaware—he was now appalled by the destruction and waste in which he had participated. He developed a personal philosophy he called *sulh-i kull*—"peace with all." While this did not end his military campaigns, which he saw as ordained by God, it did push him to develop a new religion he called *din-i ilahi* (divine faith). Akbar directed the movement at those aspiring to gain favor from the regime. He devised rituals in which adherents swore loyalty to him not only as emperor but as the enlightened religious master of the new sect. Borrowing from Sufi mysticism, Persian court protocols, Zoroastrian sun and fire veneration, and even Muslim- and Christian-influenced spiritualism, he sought to at once limit the power of Sunni Islamic clerics and draw followers of other religions to what he taught was a "higher" realm, one that embraced all religions and provided the elect with secret insights into their ultimate truths.

In the end, however, despite its merging of the needs of state and religion to overcome religious and cultural divisions, Akbar's attempt must be considered a failure. While some Hindu and Muslim courtiers embraced *din-i ilahi* for its perceived religious truths, many did so for opportunistic reasons, and it was condemned by most Sunni theologians. Akbar's successors not only repudiated it but swung increasingly in the direction of stricter Sunni Islam.

Questions

- How does Akbar's attempt at religious syncretism demonstrate the pattern of origins–innovations–adaptations that informs the approach of this book?

- Why was Akbar's attempt to create a new divine faith doomed to failure?

fortifications—was successful. Yet prolonged fighting also led to problems at court and in the interior of the empire.

The demands of constant campaigning reduced the flow of money and goods across central India. Moreover, by the early eighteenth century, the Maratha frontier, was actually expanding into Mughal areas. The Marathas had set up their own administrative system and encouraged raids on Mughal caravans and pack trains. Persia exploited the weakening of the Mughal interior, sacking Delhi in 1739 and carrying off Shah Jahan's fabled Peacock Throne—associated since with the monarchs of Persia and Iran, rather than with India and the Mughals.

The East India Companies   Soon after Vasco da Gama's first voyage to India in 1498, armed Portuguese merchant ships seized the port of Goa in 1510. Other European maritime countries began to imitate Portugal's spice trade, building their own fortified bases from which to conduct business. For the English, Dutch, and French, these enterprises were conducted by royally chartered companies, which were given a monopoly over their country's trade within a certain region. These companies acted much like independent states. They maintained fortified warehouses, their armed merchant ships functioned as naval forces, and they assembled their own mercenary armies.

Throughout the seventeenth century English, French, and Dutch enterprises largely supplanted Portuguese influence in the region, while the location of their trading ports outside Mughal lands allowed them considerable freedom. As the companies grew richer and more powerful, they increasingly found themselves involved in local politics. For the English, the acquisition of Bombay (Mumbai) from Portugal in the 1660s gave the company a superb harbor. In 1690, British traders began building a trading station called Calcutta (not to be confused with the port of Calicut, on the west coast of India). By 1750, the power of the Dutch in India had been eclipsed by that of the British and French East India Companies. With the victory of the British East India Company over French forces in 1757 came British domination of Bengal and, by century's end, much of northern India.

Administration, Society, and Economy

A characteristic pattern of the period under consideration in this section is a trend toward centralization. The creation of states and empires requires power at the center to hold the state together, ensure consistent governance, provide for revenues, and maintain defense. What is noteworthy, however, is that in widely separate regions throughout Eurasia a variety of states concurrently reached a point where their governments, with armies now aided by firearms, made concerted efforts to focus more power than ever at the center. As part of this effort, some form of enforcement of approved religion or belief system legitimating the rulers was also present. For Mughal India, the system that attempted to coordinate and balance so many disparate and often hostile elements of society is sometimes called "autocratic centralism." Its policies and demands influenced the lives of its inhabitants in often unexpected ways.

the ideal of a Muslim ruler: excerpt from *Rulings on Temporal Government* by Barni (ca. 1358)

Mansabdars and Bureaucracy

Babur and his successors attempted to govern a largely settled society whose traditions, habits, and (for the majority) religious affiliations were different from their own. The nomadic Timurids initially felt more comfortable in adapting their own institutions and then grafting them onto the existing political and social structures. The result was hybrid institutions that, given the tensions within Indian society, worked well when the empire was guided by tolerant rulers but became increasingly problematic under more dogmatic ones.

Political Structure   The Timurids sought to create a uniform administrative structure that did not rely on a single, charismatic ruler. Thus, Akbar created four principal ministries: one for army and military matters; one for taxation and revenue; one for legal and religious affairs; and one for the royal household.

Under the broad central powers of these ministries, provincial governors held political and military power and were responsible directly to the emperor. In order to prevent their having too much power, however, the fiscal responsibility for the provinces was in the hands of officers who reported to the finance minister. Thus, arbitrary or rebellious behavior could, in theory at least, be checked by the separation of financial control.

Administrative Personnel   One key problem faced by the Mughals was how to impose a centralized administrative system on a state whose nobles were used to wielding power themselves. For the Mughals, India's diversity and patchwork of small states meant that competition among the ambitious for imperial favor was intense. The Timurid rulers were careful to avoid overt favoritism toward particular groups; and though most of their recruited nobility were Sunni Muslims, Hindus and even Shiite Muslims were also represented.

The primary criteria were military and administrative skills. A system of official ranks was created in which the recipients, called *mansabdars*, were awarded grants of land and the revenues those working the land generated. In turn the mansabdars were responsible for remitting taxes and, above a certain rank, for furnishing men and materiel for the army. The positions in the provincial governments and state ministries were filled by candidates from this new mansabdar elite chosen by the court. Thus, although the nobles retained considerable power in their own regions, they had no hope of political advancement if they did not get court preferment.

The Mughals and Their Early Modern Economy

Mughal India had a vigorous trade and manufacturing economy, and Hindu, Muslim, Buddhist, and Jain traditions reserved an honored place for commerce and those who conducted it. Thus, Mughal economic interests sought to promote the flow of goods moving around the empire while maintaining import and export trade and safeguarding access to the Silk Road routes.

Agriculture and Rural Life   The basic administrative unit of rural India at the time of the Mughals was the *pargana*, a unit comprising a town and up to 100 villages. It was in the pargana that the lowest levels of officialdom had met the network of clan and caste leaders of the villages under both the Hindu rajas and the Muslim sultans before the Timurids, and this pattern continued over the coming centuries, with village life going on much as it had before the conquest. Thus, the duties of the local chiefs and headmen were to channel the local clans, castes, and ethnic and religious groups into activities the Mughals considered productive, such as clearing forests for farmland, harvesting tropical products for market, and driving off bands of foragers from the forests and hills.

Agricultural expansion required systematic integration of the rural and urban economies. One enormous obstacle facing the Mughals was efficiency and equity in rural taxation. Agricultural commodities provided the bulk of Indian tax revenues, but differences in regional soil conditions, climate, and productivity made uniform tax rates difficult to enforce. During Akbar's reign, surveys of local conditions were conducted to monitor harvests and grain prices. These data were used by local officials to calculate expected harvests and tax obligations. Imperial and local officials would sign agreements as to grain amounts to meet tax obligations over a set period. These obligations would then be paid in silver or copper coin.

The net effect of rural economic expansion in Mughal India allowed for a population increase from about 150 million in 1600 to 200 million in 1800. Moreover, the acreage under cultivation increased by perhaps as much as one-third over this same period. Preferential tax rates on coveted trade items meant that their supply would be secure. India began a burgeoning silk industry during this time, as well. Revenues more than doubled between Akbar's and Aurangzeb's reigns, while the increase in population meant that the per capita tax burden actually went down.

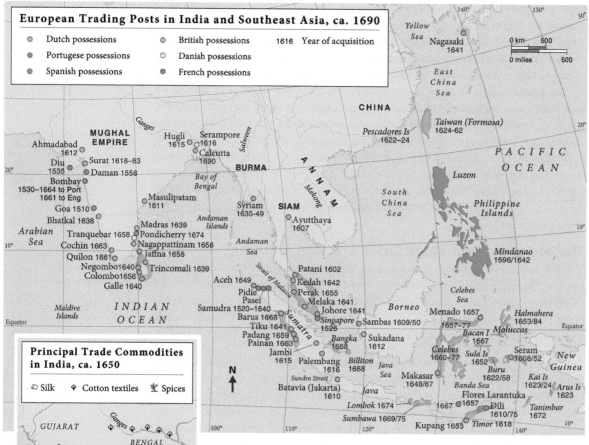

European Trading Posts in India and Southeast Asia, ca. 1690

Principal Trade Commodities in India, ca. 1650

MAP 20.4 European Trading Ports in India and Southeast Asia, ca. 1690.

map analysis

1630 Portuguese map of Asia

International Trade   The intense and growing competition among the English, Dutch, and French East India Companies meant that Indian commodities were now being shipped globally, while imports of American silver and food and cash crops were growing annually. By the mid-seventeenth century, the Dutch and English dominated maritime trade in Indian spices. An often added bonus was Indian saltpeter, a vital component of gunpowder, used as ships' ballast (see Map 20.4).

Perhaps of even more long-term importance, however, was the growth of India's textile trade, especially the rapid rise of Indian cotton exports. Lighter and more comfortable than wool or linen, Indian cotton *calicoes* (named for Indian port of Calicut) proved popular for underwear and summer clothing.

Society, Family, and Gender

Though much of this chapter describes the activities of the Muslim Timurids in India, it must be kept in mind that the majority of people in India were Hindus rather than Muslims. Thus, although the laws and customs of the areas controlled by the Mughals had an effect on Indian society, most of the everyday lives of Indians at the pargana, village, clan, and family levels went on much as it had before the arrival of the Mughals—or, for that matter, before the arrival of Islam.

Caste, Clan, and Village   The ties of family, clan, and caste were the most important for the majority of Indians (most of whom were Hindu), particularly in rural society. Indeed, many new converts to Islam retained their caste and clan affiliations.

Nevertheless, even in areas under Muslim control for centuries, religious and cultural tensions as well as local friction with central authority were present. Thus, during the reign of Akbar, whose tolerant rule eased tensions somewhat, clan archives are relatively quiet; in contrast, during Aurangzeb's long rule and periods of internal conflict, these same archives bristle with conflict. In areas only marginally under Mughal control, clan councils offered resources for potential rebels.

Family and Gender   For the Indian elites outside the areas of Mughal control, family life of the higher castes also went on largely as it had from the time of the Guptas. Women spent most of their lives in seclusion. Whether among the highest castes or the lowest, their primary duties still included the running of the household and childrearing. Among the elites, where education in literature, poetry, and basic mathematics was also available to certain women, maintaining the household accounts, supervising servants, as well as education were also considered part of a wife's proper knowledge. In all cases, however, the "inner" world of the household and the "outer" world of business, politics, warfare, and so on were clearly defined by gender. In rural areas, the lives and work of peasant families, though generally guided by traditional gender roles, were more flexible in that large collective tasks such as planting and harvesting required the participation of both men and women.

image analysis

The conquests of the Mughals brought with them a somewhat different temperament among their elites. The nomadic Turkic peoples of the Asian steppes had not developed the class, caste, and gender hierarchies of their settled neighbors. Women could, and often did, enjoy a greater degree of power and influence than among the Hindu, Sikh, or Muslim elites in India.

Even after the conversion of these nomadic peoples to Islam, this tradition of female independence continued among the Timurids. Moreover, since marriages played a vital role in cementing diplomatic and internal relations, women wielded influence in terms of the extension of imperial power. Nur Jahan (d. 1645), the Persian princess married to Jahangir, played a leading role in court politics and in mediation during the succession wars at the end of Jahangir's reign. Indeed, Jahangir occasionally turned the running of the empire over to her.

As the Mughals assimilated local Muslim elites, the court set up the harem as an institution of seclusion and protection for court women. Within the harem, women constructed their own hierarchies and celebrated their own holidays and ceremonies largely insulated from the influence of men. It was a kind of alternative women's society, in which distinct values were instilled in daughters and women newly married into the household.

Jahangir's Influential Wife, the Former Persian Princess Nur Jahan, in Her Silk Gauze Inner-Court Dress.

For these women, navigating the harem's social relationships was of critical importance, since the inner harmony of the court depended on it.

Science, Religion, and the Arts

Lahore fort, a masterpiece of Mughal architecture

Mughal India achieved noteworthy developments in weaponry, mathematics, and astronomy. In terms of religion, the great theological differences between Hindus and Muslims persisted—and with the reign of Aurangzeb increased. However, the tendency of Hinduism to assimilate other traditions and the compatibility of Islamic Sufi practices with other mystical traditions did sometimes decrease tensions. Finally, the attempts of language, literature, art, and architecture to reconcile religions left a brilliant legacy of cultural synthesis.

Science and Technology

Muslim scholars in India continued to draw upon the rich scientific history of the subcontinent, merging it with their efforts at preserving the ancient Greco-Roman and Persian achievements. Among the most important developments in this regard was the spreading of the Indian decimal number system and the use of zero as a placeholder in mathematical computations. Among the developments that fostered the rise of Muslim empires, the most important was gunpowder weapons.

New Directions in Firearms in the Gunpowder Empires   By the beginning of the sixteenth century, the armies of the major European kingdoms, Ming China, Ottoman Turkey, and Persia had all become accustomed to employing cannons and explosive charges for besieging fortresses. They were developing more convenient small arms for their infantries and were beginning to employ portable cannons as field guns for pitched battles. The use and effect of these weapons became so important that scholars often refer to the states of the Mughals, Persians, and Ottomans as the **gunpowder empires**.

Gunpowder empires: Muslim-ruled empires of the Ottomans, Safavids, and Mughals that used cannons and small arms in their military campaigns, 1450–1750.

Mathematics and Astronomy   A century before Akbar, Indian mathematicians had pushed their calculations of the value of pi to nine decimal places and expanded their facility with trigonometry to the point where some of the fundamental concepts of infinite series and calculus had been worked out.

Dependent on an accurate calendar for the yearly agricultural and ceremonial cycle, Mughal rulers had a vital interest in knowing when unusual celestial phenomena such as comets, eclipses, and meteor showers were due. Using extremely fine calculations and careful observation, the astronomers of the Kerala school had calculated elliptical orbits for the visible planets a century in advance of Johannes Kepler and suggested systems of planetary orbits similar to those of both Tycho Brahe and Copernicus (Chapter 17).

Religion: In Search of Balance

Indian Islam went through relatively open, inclusive, and Sufi-oriented cycles, and phases in which a more rigorous attention to orthodox Sunni practices and the desire to connect with Muslim communities beyond India prevailed. These latter periods played an important role in mandating which forms of Islam would be most influential in Mughal India and the relations of the Mughals with the Muslims of other regions.

The Position of Non-Muslims in Mughal India   As we have seen, despite profound theological differences between the monotheism of Islam and the polytheism of Hindu religious traditions, there was a degree of attraction between the adherents of the two religions. The mystical and devotional sects of both saw a commonality in their ways of encountering the profound mysteries of faith. Thus, Akbar's grounding in Islamic Sufi mysticism made him interested in, and receptive to, Hindu mystical traditions. For their part, in addition to the mystical elements of Islam, Hindus of the lower castes were attracted to the equality before God of all Islamic believers. Thus, like Buddhism before it, Islam promised emancipation from the restrictions of the caste system.

More generally, however, the religious divisions remained difficult to reconcile. From the first occupation of territories by Muslim armies in the seventh century, nonbelievers had been granted the legal status of protected peoples (Chapter 10). There were also inducements and penalties aimed at conversion to Islam. For their part, Hindus considered Muslims to be ritually unclean, and upper-caste members underwent purification rites after contact with them.

Yet the presence of a vastly larger Hindu population also meant that rulers had to make accommodations in order to run the empire effectively. In addition, the financial skills of Hindus and Jains were increasingly sought by the court, and their status rose further when Akbar made a Hindu his finance minister and employed Hindu court astrologers. Perhaps of even more symbolic and political importance was the habit of Mughal rulers of occasionally marrying Hindu women.

The position of Christians was similar. They, along with Jews, were protected but were still subject to the same taxes and impediments as before the reign of Akbar. While the position of Christian missionaries in Mughal lands was often precarious, the reverence with which Muslims regarded the biblical prophets and Jesus also helped to smooth diplomatic relations at court. Akbar even invited Jesuits to his debates.

After Akbar, the pendulum soon began to swing back toward less openness. Mughal receptiveness of Islamic mysticism and other religions offended more orthodox Sunni Muslims, whose influence was felt at court during the reigns of Jahangir and Shah Jahan, reaching its zenith during Aurangzeb's reign. Aurangzeb reimposed the taxes on unbelievers and purged many Hindus from his court.

Mughal painting showing the crucifixion and the Virgin Mary (1600)

Islamic Developments   While the majority of India's Muslims remained adherents of the Sunni branch of Islam, there was an influential Shiite presence in India. For centuries, Shiites had migrated into Hindu areas of southern India, where they generally escaped the discrimination at the hands of Sunnis characteristic of the north. In addition, Mughal relations with Safavid Persia, where Shia Islam was the official state religion, meant that a certain influence on the Mughal court was unavoidable. Hence, Akbar studied mystical elements of Shiism, while Jahangir married the Safavid princess Nur Jahan.

Literature and Art

During the Mughal period, India's rich multicultural environment fostered arrestingly synthetic works of literature, art, and architecture.

New Literary Directions   Arabic and Persian were the principal literary languages of Islamic India. The use of both, however, was enlivened by the introduction of Turkic terms by the Chagatai–Turkic Mughals. Chagatai itself remained in use among the elites until the nineteenth century, while many of its loan words, along with Persian and Arabic vocabulary, were grafted onto the base of Sanskrit to form the modern languages of Hindi and Urdu. Regional languages, such as Kashmiri and Bengali, were also in literary and general use.

Ironically, the catalysts for the explosion of literary work from the mid-sixteenth to the mid-seventeenth centuries came from the Mughals's most humiliating period. The exile of Humayun to Persia in the 1540s coincided with the Persian Shah Tahmasp embarking on reforms in response to criticism about the worldliness of his court. Writers, painters, and poets who suddenly found themselves out of favor at the Persian court followed Humayun to India. Their classical Arab and Persian verse forms were ultimately adopted into Urdu.

Sufi scholarship proliferated under Akbar, borrowing concepts and terminology from non-Islamic sources. By Aurangzeb's reign, the pendulum had swung back to the more Mecca-centered strain in Indian Islam. Thus, the works tended to be more often treatises on Islamic law, interpretation of *hadith*—the traditions of the Prophet—and Sunni works on theology and philosophy.

Art and Painting   One of the more interesting aspects of Islam as practiced by the Mughals—as well as the Safavid Persians and Ottomans—is that the injunctions against depicting human beings in art were often ignored in the private rooms of the court.

Akbar had a direct hand in the creation of what is considered to be the first painting in the "Mughal style"—a combination of the delicacy of Persian miniature work with the vibrant colors and bold themes of Hindu painters. Akbar inherited two of the master painters who accompanied Humayun from Persia, and the contact they acquired with Hindu works under Akbar's patronage resulted in hundreds of Mughal **gouache** works, including the colossal illustrated *Hamzanama* of 1570. Mughal artists often passed their skills on within their families and represented an important subset of members at the imperial court and among the entourages of regional elites.

Gouache: Watercolors with a gum base.

By the end of the sixteenth century, the realistic approach of European artists and their use of perspective began to influence painters at the courts of Akbar and Jahangir. One prominent female artist, Nadira Banu, specialized in producing Flemish-style works. The period of Akbar's religious experiments also prompted Mughal painters to try their hand at representing Christian religious figures. A picture of the Virgin Mary even appears in a portrait of Jahangir.

Architecture   Nowhere was the Mughal style more in evidence than in the construction of tombs and mausoleums. The ethereal lightness of the Taj Mahal and the perfection of its layout make it the most distinctive construction of its kind. The chief architect, Ustad Ahmad Lahori (d. 1649), also designed the famous Red Fort of Shah Jahan's city, Shahjahanabad. During the high point of Mughal wealth and power, several Mughal emperors built entire cities. By far the most famous of these, as we have previously seen, was Akbar's Fatehpur Sikri.

Mosques were among the empire's most important constructions. Once again, a distinctive style emerged in which the basic form of the dome and the minaret interacted with central Asian, Persian, and even Hindu architectural influences. The largest Mughal mosques, like the Jama Masjid (the "Friday" mosque) in Shahjahanabad (Old Delhi) and Aurangzeb's huge Badshahi Mosque in Lahore, contain immense courtyards surrounded by cloisters leading to small rooms for intimate gatherings, separate domed areas for men and women, and distinctive minarets with fluted columns and bell-shaped roofs. Like some cathedrals in Europe, many of the largest mosques were built adjacent to government buildings in order to demonstrate the seamless connections of these religious civilizations.

The *Hamzanama* (Book of Hamza). Akbar so enjoyed the *Hamzanama*, a heroic romance about the legendary adventures of the Prophet Mohammad's uncle Amir Hamza, that he commissioned an illustrated version in 1562. This painting from Akbar's version shows the prophet Elijah rescuing Hamza's nephew.

⟫ Putting It All Together

The rise of the Turkic Central Asian peoples to prominence and power, from the borders of successive Chinese dynasties to Anatolia and the domains of the Ottomans, including the rise of the Timurids—the Mughals—in India, is one of the most dramatic sagas of world history. In India, these outside conquerors grappled with the question of how to create a viable state out of so many long-standing religious traditions. With the arrival of Islam, a new religion that stood in opposition to the older Hindu pattern of assimilation of gods and favored instead the conquest and conversion of opponents, a divide was created, which persists to this day. The later development of Sikhism, an attempt at a syncretic bridge across India's religious divide, sometimes added to efforts for greater tolerance and at other times contributed to religious tensions.

Against this backdrop, the accomplishments of the Mughals must be weighed as significant in terms of statecraft and artistic and cultural achievement, and perhaps less so in religious areas. At its height, Mughal India was the most populous, wealthy, politically powerful, and economically vibrant empire in the world next to China. Yet, for all its wealth and power, the Mughal dynasty was plagued by problems that ultimately proved insoluble. The old nomadic succession practices of the Timurids repeatedly led to palace revolts by potential heirs. These wars in turn encouraged conflict with internal and external enemies who sensed weakness at the core of the regime. Protracted conflicts in Afghanistan, with Safavid Persia, and in Bengal also bled this centralized state of resources. Finally, the Maratha wars slowly wore down even the semblance of unity among the rulers following Aurangzeb.

But perhaps an equally important factor in the ultimate dissolution of the empire was that of Hindu–Muslim syncretism. Despite the flexibility of the early rulers in trying to deemphasize the more oppressive elements of Islamic rule in Hindu India, the attempt at a stricter orthodoxy under Aurangzeb hardened Hindu–Muslim and Sikh divisions for centuries to come.

Throughout the period, one other factor loomed as the dynasty went into decline. The well-financed and well-armed trading companies of the Europeans gradually moved into positions of regional power. By 1750, they were on the cusp of changing the political situation completely.

interactive concept map

Review and Relate

Thinking Through Patterns

Examine the ways historians approach the big questions of this chapter.

> **What were the strengths and weaknesses of Mughal rule?**

Two weaknesses are immediately apparent: first, the position of the Mughals as an ethnic and religious minority ruling a larger majority population and, second, the conflict-prone succession practices of the older central Asian Turkic leaders. The minority position of the Mughals aggravated tensions between Hindu subjects and Muslim rulers in India, of which the Mughals were to be the last line. Central Asian Turkic succession practices almost always guaranteed conflict when it was time for a new ruler to accede the throne. Nearly every Mughal successor during this period ended up having to fight factions and family to gain the empire.

In some respects, the strengths of Mughal rule developed in reaction to these problems. Babur and Akbar, in particular, were extraordinarily tolerant rulers in terms of religion. When later rulers like Aurangzeb returned to strict Sunni Islamic policies, they met with resistance, especially among Hindus. Also, while Mughal rulers were never able to completely free themselves from succession struggles, they succeeded in setting up a well-run fiscal–military state, largely undercutting old local and regional loyalties and tying the new loyalty to the state.

> **What was the Mughal policy toward religious accommodation? How did it change over time?**

Mughal rulers faced the problem confronted by nearly all religious civilizations: Religious orthodoxy was seen as an element of loyalty to the state. But for the Mughals, the desire for strict adherence to Muslim law was always tempered by the problem of Islam being a minority religion in India. Early Mughal rulers upheld Sunni Islam as the approved state religion but refrained from forcing Muslim practices on other religious groups. Akbar went so far as to create a new religion and met with leaders of other religions to find ways to satisfy the desires of all. Shah Jahan, however, enforced more strict practices, which peaked during the long reign of Aurangzeb. By the end of Aurangzeb's reign, the Sikhs were near revolt and the long Hindu Maratha revolt was in full swing. But even during this period, local religious customs remained largely intact and, indeed, often thrived.

> **What factors account for the Mughal decline during the eighteenth century?**

At the beginning and for much of the eighteenth century, Mughal India was the second richest and most prosperous empire in the world, after China. But by 1750 it was already in pronounced decline. A large part of this was due to rebellions by the Sikhs, Rajputs, and especially the Marathas. By the 1750s, the European trading companies were becoming locally powerful. Here, the great milestone would take place during the Seven Years' War (1756–1763), when the British East India Company eliminated its French competitors and in essence took over the rule of Bengal from its headquarters in Calcutta. Within 100 years it would take over all of India.

Against the Grain

Consider this as a counterpoint to the main patterns examined in this chapter.

Sikhism in Transition

As we saw in Chapter 13, Zen Buddhism affords an example of a pacifistic religious tradition that was taken up by warrior classes. In some respects, Sikhism underwent a similar transformation, although one that took place for very different reasons. The Sikhs had started from an avowedly peaceful premise: that the conflict between Hindus and Muslims must somehow be transcended. Influenced by poets and mystics and drawing upon the emotional connections experienced by Muslim Sufis and Hindu Bhakti devotees, the Sikhs had emerged during the sixteenth century as an entirely new religious movement.

Yet, far from providing a model for the two contending religions to emulate, Sikhs were viewed with suspicion by both. Although they attracted enough of a following to remain vital to the present day, their attempts at transcendence were viewed in much the same light as Akbar's attempts at a new religious synthesis were. Though they were awarded the city of Amritsar, the Golden Temple of which became their religious center, Mughal repression of the Sikhs under Aurangzeb in the seventeenth century turned them into a fierce fighting faith in self-defense. The Sikhs established control of most of the Punjab region during the eighteenth-century decline of the Mughals. During the days of British control, the reputation of the Sikhs as fighters prompted the British to employ them as colonial troops and policemen throughout their empire. Even after independence, smoldering disputes between the government and Sikhs urging local autonomy for Punjab led to the assassination of Indian prime minister Indira Gandhi in 1984, in retaliation for a government operation to forcibly remove a Sikh splinter group from the Golden Temple.

• Why would both Hindus and Muslims express hostility toward a religion that claims to want to transcend the differences between them? Did the Sikhs appear to have any alternatives to becoming a fighting faith in order to ensure their survival?

• Why does it seem that, on the whole, what we have termed "religious civilizations" have difficulty tolerating different religious traditions within their domains? Does loyalty to a state require loyalty to its approved religion(s) as well? Why?

audio flashcards

Key Terms

Allegory   457
Gouache   472

Gunpowder empires   470
Institutionalization   459

For additional resources, please go to
www.oup.com/us/vonsivers.
Please see the Further Resources section at the back of the book for additional readings and suggested websites.

Chapter 21   1500–1800

Regulating the "Inner" and "Outer" Domains

CHINA AND JAPAN

CHINA AND JAPAN, 1500–1800

The time seemed right for a letter home. In only 2 weeks the Japanese invasion force had captured the Korean capital of Seoul, and the skill and firepower of the Japanese warriors seemed to let them brush their opponents aside at will. The Japanese commander, Toyotomi Hideyoshi, was a battle-hardened commoner who had embarked on an audacious campaign to extend his power to the Asian mainland. Six years before, he had written his mother that he contemplated nothing less than the conquest of China. Now seemed like a good time to inform her that his goal might actually be within his grasp.

However, the Japanese soon faced a massive Chinese and Korean counterattack and became mired in a bloody stalemate, their guns and tactics barely enough to compensate for the determination and numbers of their enemies. After 4 more years of negotiation punctuated by bitter fighting, Hideyoshi finally withdrew to Japan. One final invasion attempt of Korea in 1597 collapsed when his death the following year set off

ABOVE: This scene, one of 15 from the handscroll painting A *Visit to the Yoshiwara* by Hishikawa Mononobu (ca. 1625–1694), depicts the "floating world" of Tokugawa Japan.

a bloody struggle for succession, which ultimately placed in power the Tokugawa family, who would go on to rule Japan for more than 250 years.

Seeing Patterns

≫ Why did late Ming and early Qing China look inward after such a successful period of overseas exploration?

≫ How do the goals of social stability drive the policies of agrarian states? How does the history of China and Japan in this period show these policies in action?

≫ In what ways did contact with the maritime states of Europe alter the patterns of trade and politics in eastern Asia?

≫ How did Neo-Confucianism in China differ from that of Tokugawa Japan?

The rise of Japanese power represents a vitally important pattern of world history, which we have seen in other areas, such as the Mediterranean and the expanding kingdoms of Europe: A state on the periphery absorbs innovation from a cultural center, in this case China, and then becomes a vital center itself. And like the other states in the region, Japan had absorbed the structures of "religious civilizations," as we have termed them—in this case, the Chinese philosophical system of Neo-Confucianism.

Hideyoshi's invasion was made possible in part by the appearance in the sixteenth century of the first Europeans in the region. By the middle of the nineteenth century, their presence would create a crisis of power and acculturation for all of East Asia. European intrusions provided powerful incentives for both China and Japan to turn inward to safeguard their own security and stability.

Late Ming and Qing China to 1750

Proclaimed as a new dynasty in 1368, the Ming at first followed the pattern of the "dynastic cycle" of previous dynasties. Having driven out the Mongol remnant, the Hongwu emperor and his immediate successors consolidated their rule, elevated the Confucian bureaucracy to its former place, and set up an administrative structure more focused on the person of the emperor than in previous dynasties. In 1382, the Grand Secretariat was created as the top governmental board below the emperor. Under the Grand Secretariat were the six boards, the governors and governors-general of the provinces, and lower-level officials down to the district magistrate.

In this section we will also take up the question of China's retreat from its greatest period of maritime expansion in the early 1400s—and sudden withdrawal to concentrate on domestic matters. Why such an abrupt change in policy? What factors led to the ultimate decline of the Ming dynasty and the rise to power of the Manchus? By what means did the Manchus create a state that endured into the twentieth century? Finally, what hints of the dynasty's problems appeared during the mid-eighteenth century?

From Expansion to Exclusion

During the late fourteenth and early fifteenth centuries, while China was rebuilding from the war to drive out the Mongols, the problems of land distribution and tenancy had abated somewhat. The depopulation of some areas from fighting, banditry, and the Black Death had raised the value of labor, depressed the price of land, and increased the amount of money in circulation. In addition, the Columbian Exchange introduced new food that had a substantial impact on the world's agricultural productivity, including China (see Chapter 18).

New Food Crops   In addition to new, higher-yielding rice strains from Southeast Asia, the Chinese began to cultivate crops that came from Africa and the Americas by way of the Spanish in the Philippines and the Portuguese at Macau. Corn and potatoes swiftly became staples, while peanuts, sugarcane, indigo, and tobacco established themselves as important cash crops.

Aided by the productivity of these new crops, China's population more than doubled between the beginning of the Ming period and 1600. Urbanism increased as market

Chapter Outline

• Late Ming and Qing
  China to 1750

• The Long War and
  Longer Peace: Japan,
  1450–1750

• Putting It All Together

towns multiplied. The efficiency of Chinese agriculture, the incorporation of marginal lands into production, and the empire's internal trade all contributed to another doubling of the population, to perhaps 300 million, by 1800. This accelerating growth began China's movement toward what some historical demographers have argued was a *high-level equilibrium trap*—a condition in which the land was approaching its maximum potential for feeding an increasing population but the economy had not reached a point of disequilibrium that could only be corrected by a technological and/or institutional change. In this schema, for example, the unbalanced nature of England's economy in the mid-eighteenth century created an environment favorable to the innovations in the textile industry that began the Industrial Revolution. China, which continued to have abundant labor, no large pool of capital in search of investment, and no obvious need for more efficient agriculture or labor-saving machinery would go through the nineteenth century in a "balanced" state but one in which the growing population was slowly squeezed into impoverishment (see Map 21.1). Though the outlines of this theory were drawn in the early 1970s, its viability and fine points are still under debate today.

MAP **21.1** **China in 1600.**

China and the World Commercial Transformation

China's rapid recovery placed the late Ming and Qing Empires in the center of an increasingly complex worldwide commercial transformation (see "Patterns Up Close"). The competition for markets among the emerging maritime Atlantic states of Europe pushed them to develop trade networks in the Indian and Pacific Oceans, along the African coast, and in the Americas. In all of these regions (except the Americas) they faced competition from local traders, particularly in the Indian Ocean, among the many ports of what is now Indonesia.

Among the European states, commercial, political, and religious competition resulted in policies of mercantilism. Similarly, China and Japan sought to tightly control imports, regulate the export trade, and keep potentially subversive foreign influences in check. China's production of luxury goods, the seclusion policies of Japan and Korea, and the demand for porcelain, tea, silk, paper, and cotton textiles made the Chinese empire the world's dominant economic engine until the nineteenth century (see Map 21.2).

MAP 21.2 **World Trade Networks, ca. 1770.**

In the midst of this growth, the government simplified land taxation. Corvée labor was effectively abolished. Land was assessed and classified according to its use and relative productivity. Land taxes were then combined into a single bill, payable in silver by installments over the course of the year: the so-called single-whip tax system. The system reduced the need for peasants to borrow at high rates from moneylenders at crucial times of the yearly cycle. The requirement that the payments be in silver played a role in the increasing monetization of the economy. This was aided considerably by the increasing amounts of silver entering the Chinese economy by means of the Manila trade. Merchants from south China exchanged spices and Chinese luxury goods in Manila in the Spanish-controlled Philippines for Spanish silver from the Americas. Spanish (and later Mexican) silver continued to be used by Chinese merchants for centuries.

Regulating the Outer Barbarians   By the late fifteenth century, Ming China had made progress toward establishing peace and stability. The view of the empire cultivated by China's elites placed it at the center of a world order defined by Neo-Confucian philosophy and supported by a host of Chinese cultural assumptions.

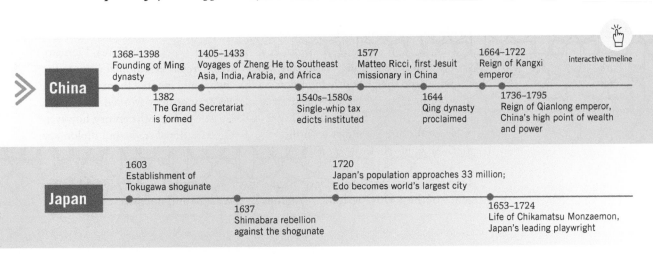

China

| 1368–1398 Founding of Ming dynasty | 1405–1433 Voyages of Zheng He to Southeast Asia, India, Arabia, and Africa | 1577 Matteo Ricci, first Jesuit missionary in China | 1664–1722 Reign of Kangxi emperor | interactive timeline |

1382 The Grand Secretariat is formed

1540s–1580s Single-whip tax edicts instituted

1644 Qing dynasty proclaimed

1736–1795 Reign of Qianlong emperor, China's high point of wealth and power

Japan

1603 Establishment of Tokugawa shogunate

1720 Japan's population approaches 33 million; Edo becomes world's largest city

1637 Shimabara rebellion against the shogunate

1653–1724 Life of Chikamatsu Monzaemon, Japan's leading playwright

Patterns Up Close | The "China" Trade

Ming and Qing China are at the heart of two innovations of enormous importance to the patterns of world history. The first is in the development of ceramics, culminating in the creation of true porcelain during the Song period (960–1279). The early Ming period saw the elaboration of the use of kaolin white clays with minerals, metals, and compounds that can be used to form durable glazes and striking artistic features. The Song and Yuan periods were characterized by pure white and celadon green wares, while by the Ming period, highly distinctive blue and white ware set the world standard for elegance.

The artistic excellence of Chinese porcelain spawned imitations throughout the Chinese periphery. By 1500, porcelain works in Korea, Japan, and Vietnam supplied a burgeoning market both at home and throughout East and Southeast Asia. Thus, there was already a highly developed

Porcelain Vase, Ming Period. Porcelain ware of the Song and Ming periods is among the most coveted Chinese art objects even today. Here we have a Ming vase showing characteristically vibrant colors and a degree of technical perfection indicative of the best Chinese pottery works, such as Jingdezhen. The motif of the grass carp on the vase is symbolic of endurance and perseverance, and thus associated with the god of literature and scholarship.

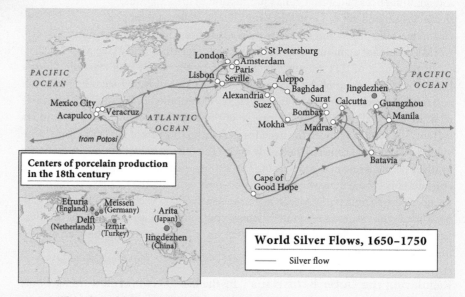

MAP 21.3 **Silver Flows and Centers of Porcelain Production.**

East Asia and Southeast Asia as shown in a 1625 Chinese map

Hence, successive rulers placed restrictions on maritime trade and conceived of diplomatic relations primarily in commercial terms. Emissaries from Korea, Vietnam, the Ryukyu Islands, and occasionally Japan traveled to pay ceremonial visits to the emperor, who then bestowed presents on the envoys and granted them permission to trade in China. This diplomatic-commercial arrangement worked within the hierarchy of the Confucian cultural sphere. By the late eighteenth century, however, it came into direct conflict with the system of international trade and diplomacy that had evolved in the West.

The Ming in Decline Despite the attention directed at the Mongol resurgence of the 1440s, periodic rebellions in the north and northwest punctuated regional market for what was, at the time, arguably the world's most highly developed technology.

The second great innovation was the world market for porcelain. China's wares had found customers for centuries in Eurasia and North and East Africa. Shipwrecks have been found in the Straits of Malacca laden with Ming porcelain; traders in the Swahili cities along the East African coast were avid collectors, while Africans farther inland decorated their graves with Chinese bowls.

Before the sixteenth century, a trickle of Ming porcelain also made its way to Europe. With the establishment of the first European trade empires, however, the demand for porcelain skyrocketed. From 1500 to 1800 it was arguably the single most important commodity in the unfolding world commercial revolution. Such was the prominence of this "export porcelain" in the furnishings of period homes that scarcely any family of means was without it (see Map 21.3).

With the rise of mercantilist theory and protectionism toward home markets during the seventeenth and eighteenth centuries, foreign manufacturers sought to break the Chinese monopoly. During Tokugawa times, the Japanese, for example, forced a group of Korean potters to labor at the famous Arita works to turn out Sino–Korean designs; the Dutch marketed delftware as an attempt to copy Chinese "blue willow" porcelain. It was not until German experimenters in Saxony happened upon a workable formula for hard-paste porcelain that their facility at Meissen began to produce true porcelain in 1710. Josiah Wedgwood set up his own porcelain factory in 1759 in England. But Chinese manufacturers would still drive the market until the end of the nineteenth century. And fine porcelain would forever carry the generic name of "china," regardless of its origins.

Porcelain Candlestick for the Export Market, Qing Period. By the early 1700s, luxury exports from China such as porcelain, lacquerware, and, of course, tea had become important staples of European maritime trade. Export porcelain—either items made to order by Chinese porcelain works for overseas buyers or generic ones made to suit European and colonial tastes—had become such a big business that cheaper pieces were sometimes actually used as ship's ballast on the homeward voyages. Shown here is a candlestick for use in a European home with Chinese motifs of vessels at the top. The cobalt blue color is characteristic of the Ming and Qing designs.

Questions

- How does the development of porcelain serve as an example of Chinese leadership in technical innovation during the premodern and early modern periods?

- How did the emergence of a global trading network after 1500 affect both the demand for porcelain and its impact on consumer tastes?

the late fifteenth and sixteenth centuries. The commitment of Chinese troops in Korea against the forces of the Japanese leader Hideyoshi from 1592 to 1598 weakened the dynasty further during a period that saw the rise of another regional power: the Manchus. By the turn of the seventeenth century, the Manchus, an Altaic-speaking nomadic people related to the Jurchens inhabiting the northeastern section of the Ming domain, had become the prime military force of the area, and dissident Chinese sought them as allies. In 1642, in the midst of factional warfare among the Ming, the Chinese general Wu Sangui invited the Manchu leader Dorgon to cross the Great Wall. The Manchus occupied Beijing in 1644 and declared the founding of a new regime, the Qing, or "pure," dynasty.

The Spring and Summer of Power: The Qing to 1750

The Manchus now found themselves in the position of having to rule. Preparation for this had already taken place within the state they had created for themselves in south Manchuria. Long exposure to Chinese culture and Confucian administrative practices provided models that soon proved adaptable by Manchu leaders within the larger environment of China proper.

Banner system: The organizational system of the Manchus for military and taxation purposes; there were eight banners under which all military houses were arranged, and each was further divided into blocks of families required to furnish units of 300 soldiers to the Manchu government.

The Banner System   The **banner system**, under which the Manchus were organized for military and tax purposes, was also expanded under the Qing to provide for segregated Manchu elites and garrisons in major cities and towns. Under the banner system, the Manchu state had been divided into eight military and ethnic divisions, each represented by a distinctive banner. The system eventually became the chief administrative tool of the Manchu leadership

Minority Rule   As a ruling minority in China, the Manchus, like the Mongols before them, walked a fine line between administrative and cultural adaptation and complete assimilation. Chinese and Manchus were recruited in equal numbers for high administrative posts, Manchu quotas in the examination system were instituted, edicts were issued in both Chinese and Manchu, Qing emperors sought to control the empire's high culture, and Manchu "bannermen" had their own special quarters. In addition, the Manchu conqueror Dorgon instituted the infamous "queue edict" in 1645: All males, regardless of ethnicity, were required on pain of death to adopt the Manchu hairstyle of a shaved forehead and long pigtail in the back—the queue—as the sign of loyalty to the new order.

The results, however, were bloody and long-lasting. The queue edict provoked revolts in several cities, and the casualties caused by its suppression may have numbered in the hundreds of thousands. For the remainder of the Qing era, rebels and protestors routinely cut their queues.

As the Manchus consolidated their rule, however, their conception of their empire grew far more expansive. That is, while the Han Chinese were by far the largest ethnic group, the Manchus conceived of their state as one embodying in a more or less egalitarian sense all of the peoples within it. By the time of the Kangxi, Yongzheng, and Qianlong emperors, Qing concepts of the state had become remarkably inclusive, embracing nearly all of the minorities recognized by the People's Republic today. While rebellions were put down ruthlessly, and conquest of western lands proceeded apace, the incorporated peoples were seen as partners in a world empire.

excerpts from the Kangxi emperor on ruling (1717)

Creating the New Order   Though the Qing kept the centralized imperial system of the Ming largely intact, they made one significant addition to the uppermost level of the bureaucracy. While retaining the Ming Grand Secretariat, the emperor Kangxi's successor, Yongzheng, set up an inner advisory body called the Grand Council in 1733. Over the succeeding decades the Grand Council became the supreme inner advisory group to the emperor, while the Grand Secretariat was relegated to handling less crucial "outer" matters.

As had been the case in past dynasties, the Qing sought to safeguard the borders of the empire by bringing peoples on the periphery into the imperial system. This meant a final reckoning with the Mongols in the 1720s, and the intervention of the Qing in religious disputes regarding Tibetan Buddhism, which had also been adopted by a number of Mongols. Toward this end, the Qing established a protectorate over Tibet in 1727, with the Dalai Lama as the approved temporal and religious leader.

The Qianlong Emperor The reign of the Qianlong [chi-en-LUNG] emperor, from 1736 to 1795, marked both the high point and the beginning of the decline of the Qing dynasty—and of imperial China itself.

The Qing army was many times larger than that of any potential competitor, and Qianlong wielded this power successfully, with expeditions against pirates and rebels on Taiwan and in punitive campaigns against Vietnam, Nepal, and Burma between 1766 and 1792 (see Map 21.4). Under his direction, the state also

map analysis

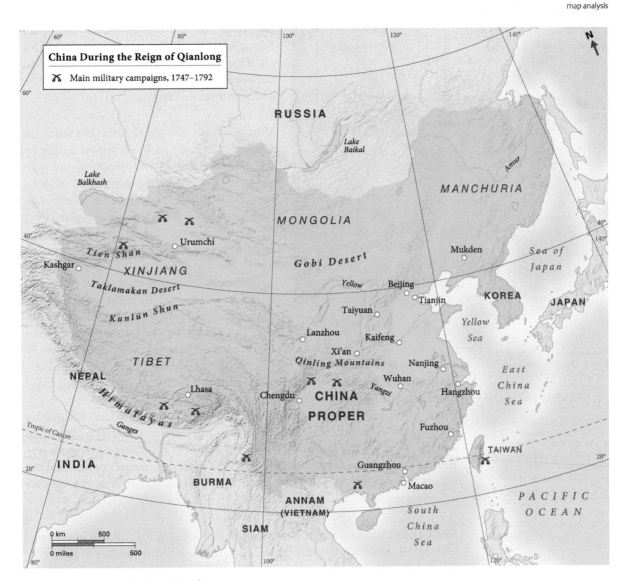

MAP 21.4 **China during the Reign of Qianlong.**

sponsored monumental literary enterprises. Based on the information on the Qing empire circulating around Europe, it seemed to some that the Chinese had solved several problems of good government and might provide models of statecraft for Europeans to emulate.

Matteo Ricci and Li Paul. The cross-cultural possibilities of sixteenth- and seventeenth-century Sino–Western contact were perhaps best exemplified by the activities of the Jesuit Matteo Ricci (1552–1610). Ricci predicated his mission in China on a respectful study of the language and the classical canon of the empire coupled with a thorough knowledge of the new mathematics and astronomy of the West. Here, he is pictured with one of his most prominent converts, a literatus and veteran of the war against the Japanese in Korea, Li Yingshi. Upon his conversion in 1602, Li took the Christian name of Paul.

Early European Contacts Just as China was abandoning its oceanic expeditions, Portugal surmounted its first big hurdle in pursuit of a worldwide maritime trade empire. By the 1440s, Portuguese navigators had opened commercial relations with the coastal kingdoms of West Africa. Scarcely a decade after Vasco da Gama arrived in Calicut in 1498, the first Portuguese ships appeared in Chinese waters. By 1557, the Portuguese had wrested the first European colony from the Chinese at Macau. From this point on, through merchants and missionaries, the contacts would frequently be profitable—and, sometimes, disastrous.

Missionaries The arrival of the first European merchants in East Asia was followed shortly by that of the first Catholic missionaries, who were quick to realize the vast potential for religious conversions in China and Japan. Franciscan, Dominican, and Jesuit missionary orders set up headquarters in Malacca, and in 1549 the Franciscan Francis Xavier landed in Japan.

In China, the Ming at first refused entry to missionaries. Once admitted, the Franciscans and Dominicans, with their limited training in Chinese language and culture, made little headway. The Jesuits, led by Matteo Ricci (1552–1610), tried a different strategy. They immersed themselves in the classical language and high culture of the empire and gained recognition through their expertise in mathematics, astronomy, military science, and other European learning sought by the imperial court.

The papacy, however, had long considered Jesuit adaptations to local sensibilities problematic. In the case of China, the Jesuits's acquiescence to ancestor veneration and the use of tea and rice in the Eucharist, instead of bread and wine, was a particular concern. After several decades, Kangxi's successor, Yongzheng, banned the order's activities in China in 1724. Christianity and missionary activity were thus driven underground.

The Canton Trade While China's commerce with the maritime Atlantic states grew rapidly in the eighteenth century, the Europeans had not yet been fully incorporated into the Qing diplomatic system.

Canton Factories, ca. 1800. Under the "Canton system" begun in 1699, all maritime trade with the Europeans was tightly controlled and conducted through the single port of Canton, or Guangzhou. Foreign merchants were not allowed to reside within the walled city, so they constructed their own facilities along the Pearl River waterfront. Though it kept profits high for the concerned parties, the restrictiveness of the system caused nineteenth-century merchants and diplomats to push the Chinese to open more ports to trade, which proved to be a major sticking point in Sino–Western relations.

The British East India Company, having established its base at Calcutta in 1690, soon sought to expand its operations to China. At the same time, the Qing sought to control contact with foreign and overseas Chinese traders as much as possible, while keeping their lucrative export trade at a sustainable level. Their solution, implemented in 1699, was to permit overseas trade only at the southern port of Guangzhou [GWAHNG-joe], more widely known as Canton. The local merchants' guild, or *cohong,* was granted a monopoly on the trade and was supervised by a special official from the imperial Board of Revenue. The Qing permitted only a small number of foreigners, mostly traders from the English, French, and Dutch East India Companies, to reside at the port. They were confined to a small compound of foreign "**factories**," were not permitted inside the city walls, and could not bring their families along. Violations of the regulations could result in a suspension of trading privileges, and all infractions and disputes were judged according to Chinese law. Finally, since foreign affairs under these circumstances were considered a dimension of trade, all diplomatic issues were settled by local officials in Canton.

Factory: Here, the place where various "factors" (merchants, agents, etc.) gathered to conduct business.

The eighteenth century proved to be a boom time for all involved in the Canton trade. After 1784, the United States joined the trade; but despite the growing American presence, it was the British East India Company that dominated the Canton factories. Both the cohong and foreign-chartered companies carefully guarded their respective monopolies, and the system kept competition low and profits high on all sides.

Village and Family Life

Just as the effort toward greater centralization was visible in the government and economy of China during the Ming and Qing, it also reverberated within Chinese village life. While local custom among the peasants still revolved around family, clan, and lineage, institutions perfected under the Ming and Qing had a lasting impact.

Organizing the Countryside

During the sixteenth century, the consolidation of the tax system into the single-whip arrangement led to the creation of the *lijia* system. All households were placed into officially designated villages for tax purposes; 10 households made up a *jia*, and 100 households composed a *li*, whose headmen, appointed by the magistrate, were responsible for keeping tax records and labor dues.

While the lijia system was geared primarily toward more efficient tax collection and record keeping, the *baojia* (see Chapter 12) system functioned as a more far-reaching means of government surveillance and control. The baojia system required families to register all members and be organized into units of 10 families, with one family in each unit assuming responsibility for the other nine. Each of these responsible families was arranged in groups of 10, and a member of each was selected to be responsible for that group of 100 households, and so on up to the *bao*, or 1,000-household level. Baojia representatives at each level were to be chosen by the families in the group. These representatives were to report to the magistrate on the doings of their respective groups and held accountable for the group's behavior.

Glimpses of Rural Life

Both the scholar-gentry and, starting in the seventeenth century, Westerners traveling in China wrote about peasant life. Based on these accounts, some generalizations can be made about rural and family life in Ming and Qing times.

First, while the introduction of new crops led to cultivation of more land, population increase, and the commercialization of agriculture, the overall rhythms of peasant life changed little over the centuries.

Second, some early signs of economic stress were already present toward the end of Qianlong's reign. Chief among these was the problem of absentee landlordism. This would grow increasingly acute as the gentry were drawn away from the countryside by urban opportunities and amenities.

Third, pressures on patterns of village life tended to be magnified in the lives of women and girls. Elite women were routinely educated to be as marriageable as possible. Women were expected to be modest and obedient and were usually separated from and subordinate to men. The custom of foot binding had long since become institutionalized, and the sale of infant girls—and, in extreme cases, female infanticide—rose markedly in rural areas during times of social stresses. While the

Chinese Commercial Enterprises. The growing volume and profits of the export trade encouraged further development and specialization of long-standing Chinese domestic industries during the eighteenth and nineteenth centuries. Moneychangers, known as *shroffs* (a), were involved in testing the quality of silver taken from foreign concerns in exchange for Chinese goods. A worker and overseer demonstrate the operation of a silk reeling machine (b). Women worked to sort tea; in this photograph (c), packing chests for tea are stacked behind the sorters. The hairstyle of the men in these photos—shaved foreheads with long braid called a queue—was mandatory for all Chinese males as a sign of submission to the Qing.

dominance of women over the "inner realm" of the family remained largely complete, this realm was never considered equal in importance to the outer sphere of men's activities.

Science, Culture, and Intellectual Life

The Ming dynasty marked the high point as well as the beginning of the decline of China's preeminent place as a world technological innovator. One area in which this became evident by the eighteenth and nineteenth centuries was in military matters.

Superpower   The Ming at their height have been described by some Chinese scholars as a military superpower. By the mid-fifteenth century the Ming arsenal was producing thousands of cannon, handguns, and "fire lances" every year; in 1450 over half of the Ming frontier military units had cannon and one-third of all troops carried firearms. As early as the 1390s large shipborne cannon were already being installed in naval vessels. Court historians of the late Ming credited nearly all the military successes of the dynasty to their firearms. By the Qing period, however, continual improvement of arms was seen as both too costly and unnecessary.

Science and Literature   In geography, mathematics, and astronomy, a fruitful exchange was inaugurated between European Jesuit missionaries and Chinese officials in the seventeenth and eighteenth centuries. The most lasting legacy of this meeting was the observatory in Beijing and new maps of the world based on sixteenth- and seventeenth-century explorations.

The centralizing tendency of the government of China led to control in the cultural realm through patronage, monopoly, and licensing. The Kangxi, Yongzheng, and Qianlong emperors set the tone in matters of aesthetics and used cultural projects (such as dictionaries and encyclopedias) to direct the energies of scholars into approved areas. At the same time, they sought to quash unorthodox views through lack of support and, more directly, through literary inquisitions.

Neo-Confucian Philosophy   In the sixteenth century new directions in Neo-Confucianism were being explored by Wang Yangming (1472–1529). While Wang's school remained popular, his intuitive approach to enlightenment placed his more radical followers increasingly on the fringes of intellectual life. In addition, the Qing victory ushered in an era of soul-searching among Chinese literati and a questioning of the systems that had failed in the face of foreign conquest.

Two of the most important later figures in Qing philosophy were Huang Zongxi [hwang zung-SHEE] (1610–1695) and Gu Yanwu [goo yen-WOO] (1613–1682). Both men's lives spanned the Qing conquest, and both concluded that the collapse of the old order was in part due to a retreat from practical politics and too much indulgence in the excesses of the radicals of the Wang Yangming school. With a group of like-minded scholars, they devoted themselves to reconstituting an activist Confucianism based on rigorous self-cultivation and on remonstrating with officials and even the court. One outgrowth of this development was the so-called Han learning movement, which sought to recover the original meaning of classic Confucian works. Though on the fringe of approved official activities, the movement successfully uncovered a number of fraudulent texts.

The Arts and Popular Culture   Official patronage ensured that approved schools and genres of art would be maintained. The Qianlong emperor, motivated by a life-long quest to master the fine arts, collected thousands of paintings, rare manuscripts, jade, porcelain, lacquerware, and other objets d'art. Because the force of imperial patronage was directed at conserving past models rather than creating new ones, the period is not noteworthy for stylistic innovation.

Local Custom and Religion   Chinese villages often featured storytellers, corner poets, spirit mediums, diviners, and other entertainers. Popular village culture was also dominated by Daoism, Buddhism, and older traditions of local worship, including beliefs in ancestral spirits, "hungry ghosts" (roaming spirits of those not properly cared for in death), fairies, and demons. These beliefs were enhanced over the centuries by tales of Daoist adepts and "immortals," *yijing* diviners, Buddhist bodhisattvas, and underworld demons.

A glimpse into local society comes from Pu Songling's (1640–1715) *Strange Tales from the Make-Do Studio*. Pu traveled extensively, collecting folktales, accounts of local curiosities, and especially stories of the supernatural. His grandson published the stories in 1740. In Pu's world, "fox-fairies" appear as beautiful women, men are transformed into tigers, the young are duped into degenerate behavior, and crooked mediums and storytellers take advantage of the unwary.

excerpts from Pu Songling, *Strange Tales from a Chinese Studio* (1740)

The Long War and Longer Peace: Japan, 1450–1750

In 1185, struggles by court factions in Japan's capital of Heian-Kyo (Kyoto) resulted in the creation of the office of the *shogun*, the chief military officer of the realm. By the fourteenth century the emperor had become the puppet of his first officer. When Emperor Go-Daigo attempted to reassert his prerogatives in 1333, his one-time supporter Ashikaga Takauji expelled him and set up his own headquarters in the capital. A debilitating civil war would ravage the capital until it ended with Japan's unification.

The price of unification, however, was high. The first of Japan's unifiers, Oda Nobunaga, was assassinated; the invasions of Korea undertaken by his successor Hideyoshi resulted in massive loss of life. The final custodians of Japanese unification, the Tokugawa family, created a system that they hoped would preserve Japan in a state of unity and seclusion. Yet over the two and a half centuries of the Tokugawa peace, forces were building that would allow Japan to vault into the modern world with unprecedented speed.

The Struggle for Unification

The instability of the Ashikaga regime led to battles for the shogun's office among the daimyo, or regional warlords. In 1467, these factional conflicts erupted into a civil war that would last for more than a century. The opening phase of this struggle devastated the city of Kyoto. With no real center of power, a bitter struggle among the daimyos continued into the 1570s.

Toyotomi Hideyoshi (1536–1598). Portraits of Japanese daimyo and shoguns tend to position them in similar ways, looking to the front left, with stiff, heavily starched official robes that reflect their austerity and dignity. In this 1601 portrait, done several years after his death, Hideyoshi is shown in a typical pose, with the signs of his adopted family and imperial crests around the canopy to denote his role of imperial guardian.

Oda Nobunaga and Toyotomi Hideyoshi By the mid-sixteenth century, some daimyo began to consolidate their power and secure allies. A factor in deciding the outcome of these wars was intrusion from the outside. By the 1540s, the first Portuguese and Spanish merchants and missionaries had arrived in southern Japan. One daimyo, Oda Nobunga, was quick to use the newcomers and their improved small arms to his advantage. Oda employed newly converted Christian musketeers to secure the area around Kyoto and had largely succeeded in unifying the country when he was assassinated in 1582. His second in command, Hideyoshi, systematically brought the remaining daimyo under his sway over the next nine years.

Hideyoshi viewed a foreign adventure as a way to cement the loyalties of the daimyo. In addition, the army he had put together might prove dangerous to disband. Hence, as early as 1586 he announced his plans to conquer China itself. In 1592 he set out with a massive expeditionary force for Korea. The Japanese made good progress up the peninsula until massive Chinese counterattacks slowly eroded their gains and decimated large stretches of Korea.

Hideyoshi's turned homeward to Japan with the remnants of his army in 1596. His stature kept his coalition of daimyo together until his death during his troubled second Korean campaign in 1598.

The coalition then broke in two, and a civil war began between Tokugawa Ieyasu, the leader of the eastern coalition of daimyos, and their western counterparts. After a decisive Tokugawa victory, Ieyasu, who claimed to be a descendant of the original shoguns, was officially invested with the office in 1603. His accession marked the beginning of Japan's most peaceful, most secluded, and perhaps most thoroughly regulated and policed interval in its history. The Tokugawas would create a hereditary shogunate, organized along Chinese Neo-Confucian models of morality and government, which would last until 1867 (see Map 21.5).

The Tokugawa *Bakufu* to 1750

The realm that Tokugawa Ieyasu (1542–1616) now led had been scarred by warfare and social disruption. The daimyo and samurai employed advanced military technology, but their depredations had broken old alliances. The intrusion of European missionaries and merchants contributed to the social ferment.

Ieyasu's assumption of the shogunate in 1603 began a process of centralization and stabilization in Japan that would last until 1867. Initially, however, seclusion did not figure among its principles. The immediate priority was to erect a system for the daimyo that would reward the loyal and keep an eye on the defeated.

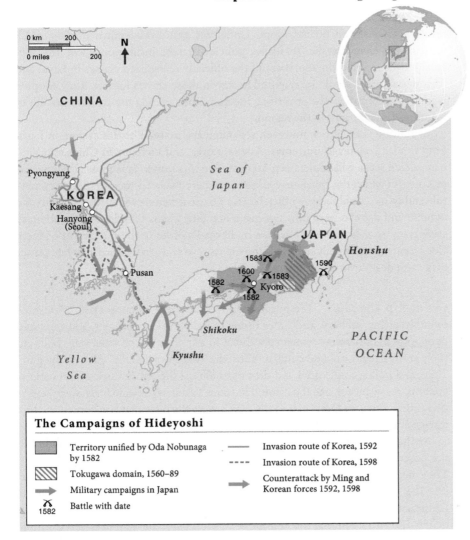

MAP 21.5 **The Campaigns of Hideyoshi.**

The legend reads:

The Campaigns of Hideyoshi

- Territory unified by Oda Nobunaga by 1582
- Tokugawa domain, 1560–89
- Military campaigns in Japan
- Battle with date (1582)
- Invasion route of Korea, 1592
- Invasion route of Korea, 1598
- Counterattack by Ming and Korean forces 1592, 1598

"Tent Government"   The system devised under the Tokugawa *bakufu* ("tent government," referring to the shogun's official status as the emperor's mobile deputy) was called *sankin kotai*, the "rule of alternate attendance." The shogunate placed its new headquarters in the Tokugawa castle in Edo (Tokyo). In order to ensure their loyalty, all daimyo who had been defeated by Ieyasu were required to reside in the capital in alternate years and return to their domains during the off years. Members of their families were required to stay as permanent hostages in Edo. Almost from the beginning, the main roads to Edo spurred commerce and services to meet the needs of the constant traffic of daimyo households coming and going. Although the providers of the goods and services prospered, the daimyo found both their power and their purses increasingly depleted.

Freezing Society   In turning the office of shogun over to his son Hidetada in 1605, Ieyasu made it legally hereditary for the first time. Given the possibility of revolt, Ieyasu stayed on as regent. Under his grandson Iemitsu (1604–1651), most of the characteristic Tokugawa policies became institutionalized. The shogunate declared that the members of the officially recognized classes in Japan and their descendants would be required to stay in those classes forever. They adopted Neo-Confucianism as the governing ideology, thus joining the commonwealth of Confucian civilizations in the region.

Significant differences, however, separated the practice of this system in Japan from similar, concurrent systems in China, Korea, and Vietnam. In China and Vietnam, a civil service had long been in place. The situation in Japan was closer to that of Korea, in which the *Yangban* were already a hereditary aristocracy in the countryside and so monopolized the official classes. Japan differed even further because the samurai and daimyo were now not just a hereditary class of officials but a military aristocracy as well. The low position traditionally given to the military in Chinese Confucianism was totally reversed, and the daimyo and samurai had absolute power of life and death over commoners.

Giving Up the Gun   The government required the samurai class to practice swordsmanship, archery, and other forms of individual martial arts. But the rapid development of firearms remained a threat to any class whose skills were built entirely around hand-to-hand combat. Thus, the Tokugawa literally "gave up the gun." Tokugawa police confiscated and destroyed almost the entire stock of the nation's firearms. A few pieces, like the cannon in some Tokugawa seaside forts, were kept as curiosities. Thus, weapons cast in the 1600s were the ones that confronted the first foreign ships nearly 250 years later in 1853.

As the shogunate strove to impose peace on the daimyo and bring stability to the populace, it became increasingly anxious to weed out disruptive influences. They began to restrict the movements of foreigners, particularly missionaries. The influence of the missionaries on the growing numbers of Japanese Christians was worrisome to those intent on firmly establishing Neo-Confucian beliefs and rituals among the commoners. Moreover, the duel between Catholic and Protestant missionaries and merchants carried its own set of problems for social stability.

Tokugawa Seclusion   Ultimately, therefore, missionaries were ordered to leave the country, followed by their merchants. The English and Spanish withdrew in the 1620s, while the Portuguese stayed until 1639. Only the Dutch, Koreans, and Chinese were allowed to remain, in small numbers and at the pleasure of the shogunate. Further, in 1635 it was ruled that Japanese subjects would be forbidden to leave the islands and that no oceangoing ships were to be built. Foreign merchants would be permitted only in designated areas in port cities and could not bring their families with them. The Dutch were restricted to a tiny island in Nagasaki harbor. In return for the privilege, they were required to make yearly reports to the shogun's ministers on world events. This "Dutch learning" eventually found a small readership among educated Japanese, and along with the accounts of Chinese and Korean observers formed the basis of the Japanese view of the outside world for over two centuries.

Trampling the Crucifix   Much less tolerance was shown to Japan's Christian community. Dissatisfaction with the new Tokugawa strictures provoked a rebellion in 1637 by Christian converts and disaffected samurai. As the revolt was suppressed, those who were captured were roasted to death inside a ring of fire. Subsequently, remaining missionaries were sometimes crucified upside down, while suspected converts were given an opportunity to "trample the crucifix" to show they had discarded the new faith. However, thousands continued to practice in secret until Christianity was declared legal again during the reign of Emperor Meiji (r. 1867–1912). Though foreign ships would occasionally attempt to call at Japanese ports, by the eighteenth century Europeans generally steered clear of the islands.

Growth and Stagnation: Economy and Society

By 1750, Japan had become the most urbanized society on earth. Edo had a population of one million, making it arguably the world's largest city, and as much as 10 percent of Japan's population lived in cities with populations above 10,000 (see Map 21.6).

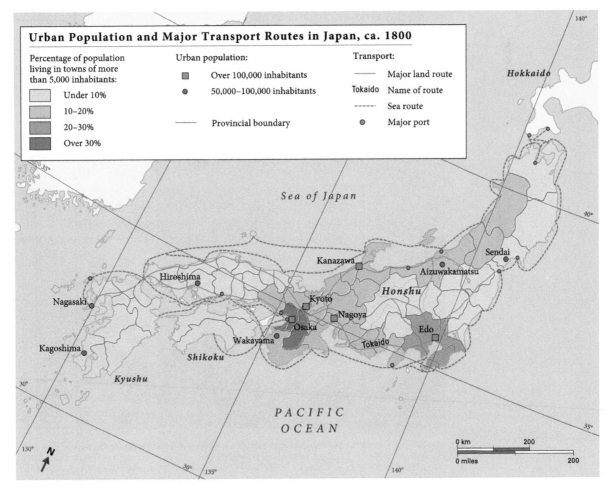

MAP 21.6 **Urban Population and Major Transport Routes in Japan, ca. 1800.**

The law of alternate attendance ensured growing traffic in and out of the major cities along the major routes into Edo. Services required to support that traffic aided urban and suburban growth and spread the wealth.

Population, Food, and Commerce   One cause of this urbanization was the growth of the population as a whole. The efficiency of small-scale, intensive rice and vegetable farming, aided by simple machines, made Japanese agriculture the most efficient in the preindustrial world.

Tokugawa policies aimed at stabilizing the country had the unanticipated effect of spurring the economy. The Tokugawa tax structure set quotas of rice for each village and left the individual daimyos responsible for remitting these to the capital. Thus, traffic in bulk rice spurred the carrying trade. In addition to guaranteeing provisions for the cities, the need to convert rice to cash for the treasury contributed to a banking and credit infrastructure.

The tastes of the three largest cities—Edo, with its high concentration of the wealthy and well connected; Kyoto, with its large retinue of the imperial household; and Osaka, the chief port—created a demand for sophisticated consumer goods and services. Such enterprises as sake brewing, wholesaling dried and prepared foods, running bathhouses, and managing large studios of artisans all became booming businesses. Books, porcelains, lacquerware, and objets d'art were exchanged for Japanese hard currency, and what was once the province of the elite was now widely available to anyone who had the money and interest to afford it.

Woodblock Print of the Fish Market at the East Side of Nihonbashi (The Bridge of Japan). The Tokugawa period, with its long interlude of peace and prosperity, was Japan's first great age of urban life. The constant traffic of daimyo progressions along the main roads and the large coasting trade along the Inland Sea ensured a growing middle class of artisans, tradespeople, and merchants. The capital, Edo, had ballooned to over a million people on the eve of the American intrusion. The bustle of the capital is illustrated in this panel depicting a famous fish market.

Rural Transformations   Life in rural areas also changed. As they had with the military houses, the Tokugawa promulgated Neo-Confucian rules for village families and their individual members. Buddhist temples kept registers of the villagers in their districts. Weddings, funerals, travel, rents, taxes, and so forth were subject to official permission through either the village headman or the samurai holding a position equivalent to a magistrate. Within these strictures, however, and subject to the hereditary occupation laws, families, clans, and villages were relatively autonomous.

This was especially true of rural families, in which families commonly worked together on their plots. While the "inner domain," so central to Neo-Confucian thought as the strict province of women, retained a good deal of that character, Japanese women were not entirely secluded, and men routinely helped with childrearing. Women in cities and larger villages ran businesses, especially those involved in entertainment, such as geisha houses, bathhouses, taverns, restaurants, and retail establishments. By the eighteenth century, merchants utilized the spinning and weaving talents of rural women in parceling textile manufacturing—a Japanese version of the English "putting-out system."

The Samurai in Peacetime   The samurai's position evolved as his role as an official and Neo-Confucian role model became paramount. Samurai were not necessarily prosperous, and by the later eighteenth century many samurai lived in genteel poverty. In many rural areas, they founded village academies in the local temples for the teaching of literacy and correct moral behavior, which would result, by the mid-nineteenth century, in what was probably the world's highest level of functional literacy.

By the middle of the eighteenth century there were signs of tension among the aims of the government in ensuring peace and stability, the dynamism of the internal economy, and the boom in population. Signs of rural impoverishment and social unrest were often noted by commentators. Inflation in commodity prices outpaced efforts to increase domain revenues, squeezing those on fixed incomes and stipends. Efforts to keep rural families small enough to subsist on their plots led to an increasing frequency of infanticide. Famines in 1782 and 1830 compounded these problems. By the early nineteenth century, the government was gradually losing its ability to care for the populace.

Hothousing "Japaneseness": Culture, Science, and Intellectual Life

Painting, poetry, and calligraphy flourished among the daimyo and samurai, while attracting the new middle classes. Zen-influenced **monochrome** painting, the ideals of the tea ceremony, the austere Noh theater, and principles of interior design and landscape gardening were becoming "Japanese."

Monochrome: Single-color; in East Asian painting, a very austere style popular in the fourteenth and fifteenth centuries, particularly among Zen-influenced artists.

New Theater Traditions   Traditional cultural elements coexisted with new forms, such as *bunraku*, the puppet theater still popular in Japan today. The facile movements and facial expressions of Bunraku puppets proved effective in popularizing the older Noh plays. But renowned playwrights soon wrote special

Two Courtesans. The new genre of *ukiyo-e*, "pictures of the floating world," developed in the late seventeenth century and remained popular through the nineteenth century. Finely wrought woodblock prints in both monochrome and color, they take their name from the pleasure districts whose people and scenes were favorite subjects. This work is from a series by the noted artist Kitagawa Utamaro (ca. 1753–1806) on famous courtesans of the "Southern District," part of the Shinagawa section of Edo.

interactive concept map

works for these theaters as well. The most revered was Chikamatsu Monzaemon [chick-ah-MAT-soo mon-ZAE-mon] (1653–1724), who skillfully transferred the tragically noble sentiments of the best Noh works into contemporary themes. His most well-known work, *The Forty-Seven Ronin*, written in 1706, is based on a 1703 incident in which the daimyo of 47 samurai was killed by a political opponent, leaving them as *ronin*—masterless. The ronin killed the daimyo's assassin out of loyalty to their leader, knowing they would pay for the deed with their own lives.

Originally written for the bunraku theater, *The Forty-Seven Ronin* was adapted a few decades later as a work for *kabuki*, the other great mass entertainment art of Tokugawa Japan. Kabuki remained by far the most popular Japanese mass entertainment, and *The Forty-Seven Ronin* remained the most frequently performed play throughout the Tokugawa period.

The era also marked the golden age of the poetic form of *haiku*, the most famous practitioner of which was Matsuo Basho (1644–1694). As a poet he used a dozen pen names; he took "Basho" from the banana plant he especially liked in his yard. Haiku compressed unbearable emotion and release in a way that has made them a treasured form in Japan.

In the visual arts, fine woodblock printing allowed popular works to be widely duplicated. The new genre was called *ukiyo-e*, "pictures of the floating world," a reference to the pleasure quarters on the edge of the cities that furnished many of its subjects. During Tokugawa times, one of the most famous practitioners of the art was Kitagawa Utamaro (1753–1806), whose studies of women became forever associated with Japanese perceptions of female beauty. These and other such works formed many of the first popular images that nineteenth-century Westerners had of Japan.

Putting It All Together

During the late Ming and early Qing periods, imperial China achieved social and political stability and developed the world's largest economy. Yet by the second part of the eighteenth century, internal problems emerged that would erupt in succeeding decades. In the following century, these problems would have a profound impact on China's fortunes.

The arrival of foreign traders who brought with them the new technologi[es of the] first scientific–industrial societies, combined with China's self-confidence in [its] culture and institutions, added more pressure to an already volatile interna[l situa-] tion and ultimately created an unprecedented challenge for China. Over the c[oming] decades, Chinese expectations of being able to assimilate all comers would dis[...]

along with the hope that a renewed faithfulness to Confucian fundamentals would produce the leaders necessary to navigate such perilous times. But at the halfway mark of the eighteenth century, the Chinese still expected that they would successfully regulate the "inner" and "outer" domains of their empire and keep pernicious foreign influences at arm's length.

Ravaged by a century of warfare and foreign intrusion, Japan also sought to regulate its inner and outer domains and minimize outside influences. As in China, however, the stability of the seventeenth and eighteenth centuries would be threatened in the nineteenth by the commercial power of the Europeans and Americans. Before the nineteenth century was finished, China would be rent by civil war, while Japan would emerge from its own civil war to install a unified government under an emperor for the first time since the twelfth century. In the final years of the nineteenth century, Japan would once again invade Korea to attack China—this time with very different results. In the process, the historical relationship of more than two millennia between the two countries would be altered forever.

Review and Relate

Thinking Through Patterns

Examine the ways historians approach the big questions of this chapter.

While the commercial prospects for China's fleets grew in prominence, maritime trade was simply not essential to the Chinese economy at that point. Moreover, urgent defense preparations were needed in the overland north against the resurgent Mongols. Although the discontinuing of the fleets seems like a mistake in hindsight, because of what happened to China hundreds of years later due to a lack of adequate naval defenses, these measures seemed both rational and appropriate to the Chinese and outside observers at the time.

> ≫ Why did late Ming and early Qing China look inward after such a successful period of overseas exploration?

One almost universal pattern of world history among agrarian states is that their governments adopt policies aimed at promoting social stability. This is because nearly everything depends on having reliable harvests. Given the agricultural techniques and technology of preindustrial societies, the majority of the population must be engaged in food production to ensure sufficient surpluses. If such a society places a premium on change and social mobility, it risks chronic manpower shortages and insufficient harvests. Thus, social classes are carefully delineated, and the state directs its policies toward eliminating social upheaval.

> ≫ How do the goals of social stability drive the policies of agrarian states? How does the history of China and Japan in this period show these policies in action?

In both China and Japan, these connections resulted in severe restrictions on maritime trade: the Canton system in China and the seclusion policies of the Tokugawa

---

❯ In what ways did contact with the maritime states of Europe alter the patterns of trade and politics in eastern Asia?

❯ How did Neo-Confucianism in China differ from that of Tokugawa Japan?

in Japan. Earlier, the Chinese emperor had welcomed Jesuit missionaries and even considered conversion to Catholicism. But the backlash against "subversive" influence induced the Qing to drive Christianity underground. In Japan such contact had earlier injected European influences into Japan's civil wars, and the reaction against this was Tokugawa seclusion.

The fundamental difference was that Japan was a military society, which adopted the forms and structures of Neo-Confucianism to make the daimyo and samurai into officials. They therefore were expected to maintain this civil role as bureaucrats but also to stand ready to fight. The low esteem in which the military was held in China was just the inverse of that of the martial elites of Japan. Another key difference was that officials in China were selected on the basis of competitive examinations, thus creating some social mobility. In Japan, the social classes were frozen, and no exams were offered for potential officials.

Against the Grain

Consider this as a counterpoint to the main patterns examined in this chapter.

Seclusion's Exceptions

- While the attempts by China, Korea, and Japan to keep out foreign influences may strike us as impractical, many nations today still seek to limit foreign influences, particularly in the realm of culture. What are the advantages and disadvantages of such policies? Are they inevitably self-defeating?

- Were the policies of turning inward among these agrarian–urban societies part of larger historical patterns at work during this time? Why or why not?

Despite Japan's policies of seclusion during the Tokugawa era, the country was more porous than is popularly supposed. Chinese and Korean merchants continued to do business in Japan. Formal relations with Korea were maintained by the Tokugawa through the lord of the Tsushima feudal domain, who also maintained a trading post in the Korean port of Pusan. Korean vessels, like those of the Chinese, were permitted to put in at Nagasaki, and the shogunate's attempts to curtail silver exports were generally waived for Korean trade. More than a dozen Korean trade missions traveled to the shogun's court during the Tokugawa period.

No official exchanges with Chinese representatives took place, since neither side wanted to be seen as the junior partner in the Neo-Confucian hierarchy of diplomacy by the so-called tribute mission system. In addition to the predominance of Chinese ships at Nagasaki, however, both Chinese and Japanese merchants took advantage of a loophole in the sovereignty of the Ryukyu Islands to trade there. China and Japan both insisted that the islands were under their protection, though the Japanese domain of Satsuma had captured Okinawa in 1609. The leaders in Okinawa, however, sent trade and tribute missions to both China and Japan in order to safeguard their freedom of action, thus keeping the conduit for trade semiofficially open for both sides.

The Dutch established an exclusive relationship with Japan. Warning the Tokugawa about the sinister religious intentions of Iberians the Dutch alone should handle Japan's European trade. Though their power in European markets ebbed during the eighteenth and early nineteenth centuries, their influence among the small but vital circle of Japanese leaders engaged in "Dutch learning" remained strong right up to the time of the coming of Perry's "Black Ships" in 1853.

Key Terms

audio flashcards

Banner system   482   Factory   485   Monochrome   495

For additional resources, please go to
www.oup.com/us/vonsivers.
Please see the Further Resources section at the back of the book for additional readings and suggested websites.

PART FIVE

The Origins of Modernity

1750–1900

What we have termed "modernity" in this section begins around 1800 in western Europe and may be characterized as the product of two revolutions of the late eighteenth century. One of these was the new political landscape resulting from constitutional revolutions in North America, France, and Haiti, which challenged the concept of monarchical rule by divine right and introduced popular sovereignty as the new justification for political power. The other was the Industrial Revolution, which began in England with the introduction of steam-driven machine–produced goods. Scientific–industrial modernity, with values marked by experimentation; political, social, and technological progress; social mobility; and secularism began to displace the older agrarian–urban patterns of religious civilizations that had been characterized by hierarchy, natural order, patriarchy, and divinely ordained morality and law.

The Origins of Modernity

The discovery of the Americas, as well as the Copernican revolution in astronomy, provided powerful incentives for the introduction of new patterns of science and political philosophy. For more than two centuries, however, these ideas remained the province of only a small intellectual elite.

Political and Industrial Revolutions

By the 1700s, adherents of the new science and philosophy in northwestern Europe had become influential in society. In Britain, the *theory* of the social contract entered into the *practice* of constitutionalism following the Glorious Revolution of

1765
James Watt perfects the steam engine

1776–1804
American, French, and Haitian Revolutions

1798–1801
Napoleon's occupation of Egypt

1815
Congress of Vienna

1832
Greece wins independence from the Ottomans

1839–1876
Tanzimat reforms in the Ottoman Empire

1848
Karl Marx and Friedrich Engels publish *The Communist Manifesto*

1853–1854
Commodore Perry opens trade and diplomatic relations with Japan

1688. During the eighteenth-century Enlightenment, these ideas inspired the American, French, and Haitian Revolutions. These were narrow revolutions in the sense of ending monarchical–aristocratic rule, but set the emancipation of humanity from the confining traditions of the past as a goal. In Haiti, the Enlightenment idea that "all men are created equal" formed the basis of a successful slave rebellion against revolutionary France itself.

The Industrial Revolution was a socially transformative sequence of technical inventions and their commercial applications. Britain industrialized during the first half of the 1800s, through steam-driven iron foundries, textile factories, overland transportation, and ocean travel. In a second wave, Germany and the United States industrialized, with the introduction of chemicals, electricity, and motorcars into the factory system. The two waves of industrialization created an unequal class system, with a citizenry composed of both landed aristocrats—fading in power as the old agrarian–urban order decayed—and a new urban middle class amassing political and economic power. Members of the equally new industrial working class sought to make good on the promises of the constitutional revolutions.

Resistance and Adaptation to the Western Challenge

The political–industrial revolutions in Europe were a major factor in the mid-nineteenth-century expansion of the existing European empires in Asia and Africa. Postrevolutionary France renewed its competition with Britain, and both later used "gunboat diplomacy" to establish favorable commercial conditions and trade outposts. These two European nations, and others, competed in imperial conquests for strategically important territories across the globe.

The traditional agrarian and religious empires and states of Asia and Africa responded to the European maritime empires and the United States during the 1800s with both resistance and adaptation. Resisting with traditional armies and weapons, however, became more difficult as the industrial development of the West resulted in sophisticated new weaponry. "Adaptation," as it occurred under the duress of imperialism, was a creative process in which states selected elements from the constitutional and industrial revolutions that had made the West powerful and attempted to harmonize them with their inherited traditions.

Thinking Like a World Historian

≫ What were the origins of the "twin revolutions" of the late eighteenth century? How did they combine to create what we call "modernity"?

≫ Why were the values of scientific–industrial society opposed to the older agrarian–urban order? Why does this conflict still persist in many parts of the world today?

≫ What patterns of resistance and adaptation characterized the responses of traditional agrarian and religious empires to European military power and expansion?

interactive timeline

1857	1868–1912	1878–1885	1888	1894–1895	1904–1905
Sepoy Rebellion, India	Reign of Emperor Meiji, Japan	Independence of Serbia, Montenegro, Romania, and Bulgaria	End of slavery, Brazil	Sino-Japanese War	Russo-Japanese War

1861	1869	1884	1900	1905	1908
Emancipation of serfs in Russian Empire	Opening of Suez Canal	Hiram Maxim invents the first fully automatic machine gun	Boxer Rebellion	Albert Einstein publishes theory of relativity	"Young Turks" rise to power in Ottoman Empire

Patterns of Nation-States and Culture in the Atlantic World

THE NORTH ATLANTIC, 1750-1880

Canada
United States
Western Europe
ATLANTIC OCEAN
Haiti

W hen the French Revolution broke out in 1789, a young Caribbean mulatto named Vincent Ogé (ca.1755–1791) was in France on business. His extended family of free light-skinned blacks owned a coffee plantation and a commercial business with black slaves on Saint-Domingue [SAN-doh-MANG] (modern Haiti). Caught up in the excitement, Ogé became an adherent of French constitutionalism. He joined the antislavery Society of the Friends of Blacks in Paris and demanded that French constitutionalism be extended to Saint-Domingue.

The society's efforts soon appeared to bear fruit. In March 1790, the National Assembly granted self-administration to the colonies, and Ogé returned to Saint-Domingue full of hope that he would be able to participate as a free citizen in the island's governance. But the French governor refused to admit mulattoes as citizens. In response, Ogé and a group of freedmen took up arms to carve out a stronghold for themselves by arresting plantation owners and occupying their properties. One plantation owner later testified that Ogé was a man of honor who treated his prisoners fairly and even left him in the possession of his personal arms.

After a few weeks of fighting, government troops pushed the rebels into the Spanish part of the island. Ogé and his followers surrendered after being

ABOVE: Thousands of Polish soldiers joined Napoleon's forces in Haiti in 1802, as depicted here in *Battle on Santo Domingo* by Polish painter January Sucholdoski (1797–1875).

guaranteed their safety. But the Spanish governor betrayed his prisoners, turning them over to the French. After a trial for insurrection in February 1791, Ogé and 19 followers were condemned to death. The execution of Ogé was particularly barbaric: Executioners strapped him spread-eagle on a wagon wheel and systematically broke his bones with an iron bar until he was dead.

The Ogé insurrection was a prelude to the Haitian Revolution, which began in August 1791 and culminated with the achievement of independence under a black government in 1804. It was the third of the great constitutional-nationalist revolutions—after the American and French Revolutions—that inaugurated, with the Industrial Revolution, the modern period of world history.

The events which led to the three constitutional revolutions were parts of a larger cultural ferment called the Enlightenment. The rising urban middle classes embraced the New Sciences and their philosophical interpretations, which provided both the intellectual ammunition for the revolutions and the inspiration for the creative movements of romanticism and realism.

Origins of the Nation-State, 1750–1815

One outcome of the Glorious Revolution of 1688 in England (Great Britain after 1707) was that, for the first time in Europe, the traditional divine rights of a monarch were curbed. A century later, the idea of *subjects* becoming *citizens* with constitutionally guaranteed rights and duties and of Parliament representing the citizens spread from Great Britain to North America, France, and Haiti. The American, French, and Haitian Revolutions were radical in that they rejected the British compromise of royal and parliamentary power and led to republican, middle-class or liberated slave nation-states without traditional divine-right monarchies.

The American, French, and Haitian Revolutions
The American and French Revolutions were, in part, consequences of the Seven Years' War, which left both Great Britain and France deeply in debt. They owed this debt to their wealthy subjects, who formed the ruling class. To pay back the debt, the kings had to raise taxes on all of their subjects. The inequity of this tax burden led many to agitate for political reform and, ultimately, revolution. Once the revolutions were under way, the American and French revolutionary principles of freedom and equality had repercussions in the wider Atlantic world.

Conditions for Revolution in North America   When Britain won the Seven Years' War, it took over French possessions in Canada and the Ohio–Mississippi River valley, and France retreated entirely from the continent of North America. But the British were hugely in debt: The payment of the interest alone devoured most of the country's annual budget. Taxes had to be raised domestically as well as overseas, and in order to do so the government had to strengthen its administrative hand in its empire.

≫ How did the pattern of constitutionalism, emerging from the American and French Revolutions, affect the course of events in the Western world during the first half of the nineteenth century?

≫ In what ways did ethnic nationalism differ from constitutionalism, and what was its influence on the formation of nation-states in the second half of the nineteenth century?

≫ What were the reactions among thinkers and artists to the developing pattern of nation-state formation? How did they define the intellectual–artistic movements of romanticism and realism?

Chapter Outline

• Origins of the Nation-State, 1750–1815

• Enlightenment Culture: Radicalism and Moderation

• The Growth of the Nation-State, 1815–1871

• Romanticism and Realism: Philosophical and Artistic Expression to 1850

• Putting It All Together

By 1763, the 13 North American colonies had experienced rapid growth. Opening lands beyond the Appalachian Mountains into the Ohio valley would relieve some of the pressure of a growing population. But the occupation of new land increased the administrative challenges for the British, who had to employ standing troops to protect settlers and Native Americans from aggression toward each other. The ongoing postwar economic slump created additional hardships (see Map 22.1).

The British government failed to devise a clear plan for strengthening its administration in the North American colonies, and was particularly inept with the imposition of new taxes. In 1765, it introduced the Stamp Act, forcing everyone to pay a tax on the use of paper for any purpose. The tax was to be used for the upkeep of the standing troops, many of which were quartered in the colonies for the enforcement of the increased taxes.

Countdown to War   Protest against the Stamp Act broke out among the urban lower-middle ranks, who organized themselves in groups such as the Daughters of

MAP 22.1 **British North America in 1763.**

Liberty and Sons of Liberty. The Daughters boycotted British goods and promoted homespun textiles. The British Parliament withdrew the Stamp Act in 1766 when exports fell, but replaced it with indirect taxes on other commodities. These taxes were still levied without the colonies' consent.

One such indirect tax was on tea. This tax was a subsidy to keep the near-bankrupt East India Company afloat and had nothing to do either with America or Britain's debt. In 1773 the colonists protested the tax with the dumping of a cargo of tea into Boston Harbor. In response to this "Boston Tea Party," Britain closed the harbor, demanded restitution, and passed the so-called Coercive Acts (called the "Intolerable Acts" in the colonies), which put Massachusetts into bankruptcy. Both sides now moved toward a showdown.

The War of Independence   During the Continental Association of 1774–1776, the colonial assemblies decided on an economic boycott of Britain. In an effort to isolate Massachusetts from the Association, in April 1775 British troops attempted to seize arms and ammunition in Concord. A militia of farmers—"minutemen"—stopped the British. War broke out in earnest, and delegates of the colonies appointed George Washington, a former officer from Virginia, as commander of the colonists' troops. A year later, delegates of the colonies issued the Declaration of Independence. This declaration, steeped in Enlightenment thought, was written by the university-educated Virginian Thomas Jefferson. The great majority of the delegates who signed were also educated men of means.

Thomas Paine,
Common Sense (1776)

Central to the declaration was the idea that the equality of all "men" was "self-evident." As such, all men are entitled to "life, liberty, and the pursuit of happiness"—citizen rights which thus included Hobbes's right to life but not Locke's right to property. Tacitly excluded were the one-fifth of Americans who were black slaves, the one-half who were women, and all Native Americans. When the colonists eventually won the War of Independence in 1783, the founders created a revolutionary federal republic with a Congress that represented a large proportion of the population, though it also excluded many inhabitants.

The Early United States   The new republic's initial years were fraught with organizational difficulties. The governing document, the Articles of Confederation, granted so much power to the individual states that they operated like separate countries. In 1787, a constitutional convention created a more effective federal constitution. Careful to add checks and balances in the form of a bicameral legislature and separation of powers into legislative, executive, and judicial branches, the new constitution seemed to embody Enlightenment ideals—although it sidestepped the issue of slavery. In 1789, under the new system, George Washington was elected the first president of the United States.

The new republic's abolition of the divine right of monarchical rule and its replacement by the sovereignty of the people was a previously unimaginable reversal

interactive timeline

1700–1800	1775–1783	1799–1815	1815	1870
Enlightenment	American Revolution	Napoleonic era	Congress of Vienna	Unification of Italy

1756–1763	1789–1799	1804	1848	1871
Seven Years' War	French Revolution	Beethoven's *Eroica*	Political and economic revolts in Europe	Unification of Germany

of the natural order of things. In this respect, the American and French Revolutions illustrate a new pattern of state formation and the advent of modernity.

Conditions for the French Revolution   King Louis XVI (r. 1774–1792) and the French government had hoped the American War of Independence would provide an opportunity to avenge the kingdom's defeat in the Seven Years' War. France supplied the Americans with money, arms, and officers, and in 1778–1779, in alliance with Spain, waged war on Great Britain. The French–Spanish entry into the war forced Britain into an impossible defense of its colonial empire, and Britain conceded defeat in 1783. However, the French government now had to begin exorbitant payments on the interest for the loans to carry out the war. This crippling debt established the preconditions of the French Revolution.

As in America, the French population had increased sharply during the 1700s. Food production could barely keep up, and inflation increased. The rural economy responded to the rising demand, and colonial trade with the Caribbean colonies boomed. Had it not been for the debt, the government would have been well-financed: It collected direct taxes as well as monies from compulsory loans and the sale of titles and offices to ordinary people of means. Although claiming to be the absolute authority, the king in reality shared power with a ruling class of old and new aristocrats as well as ordinary (if wealthy) urban people.

In 1781, suspicions arose about the solvency of the regime. But the government continued to borrow, especially when bad weather leading to poor harvests in 1786–1787 diminished tax revenues. Without reserves in grain and animals, the peasants suffered severe famine. Government imports intended to help ended up in the hands of profiteers and hoarders.

By 1788, the government was nearly bankrupt, and a reform of the tax system became unavoidable. When a first attempt at reform failed, the king held elections for a general assembly, called the Estates-General, to meet in Versailles. Voters met in constituent meetings in their districts across France, according to their "estate" as clergy, aristocrats, or commoners. Peasants met in the "third estate," or commoner meetings; but the deputies they elected to meet in Paris were overwhelmingly middle- and upper-class. At the request of the king, the deputies listed their grievances to form the basis for the reform legislation.

Amid widespread unrest among peasants in rural France and workers in Paris, the third estate now outmaneuvered the other estates and the king. In June 1789 it seceded from the Estates-General and declared itself the National Assembly. Pressured by the pro-aristocracy faction, the king issued a veiled threat: If the Assembly would not accept his reform proposals, he said, "I alone should consider myself their [the people's] representative." The king then reinforced his troops in and around Paris and Versailles. Parisians, afraid of an imminent military occupation of the city, swarmed through the streets on July 14, 1789. They provisioned themselves with arms and gunpowder and stormed the Bastille, the royal fortress and prison inside Paris.

Three Phases of the Revolution   The French Revolution (1789-1792) went through the three phases: constitutional monarchy (1789–1792), radical republicanism (1792–1795), and military consolidation (1795–1799). The first phase began with near anarchy during July and August 1789. People in the provinces, mostly peasants, chased aristocratic and commoner landlords from their estates. In October, thousands of working women marched from Paris to Versailles, forcing the king to move to Paris. The National Assembly issued the Declaration of the Rights of Man and of the Citizen (1789), subjected the Catholic Church to French civil law (1790), established a constitutional monarchy (1791), and issued laws ending the unequal taxes of the Old Regime (1792).

The second phase, radical republicanism, began as the revolutionaries were unable to establish a stable constitutional regime. After the king tried unsuccessfully in 1791 to flee Paris with his Austrian-born wife, Marie-Antoinette, Austria and Prussia threatened to intervene if the king and queen were harmed. Patriotic feelings were aroused, and in April 1792 the government declared war on its eastern neighbors.

Republicans deposed the king and held elections for a new assembly, the National Convention, to draw up a constitution. In the following year, the republicans executed the royal couple and created a conscript army. A Committee of Public Safety executed some 30,000 real and suspected "reactionaries" during its "Reign of Terror."

The Revolution entered its third phase (1795–1799) after the army had succeeded in securing the borders at the end of 1793. A growing revulsion at the Reign of Terror led to the replacement of the Committee of Public Safety by the Directory in November 1795. A new constitution and bicameral legislature were created, but political and financial stability remained elusive. The Directory depended increasingly on the army, by now the only stable institution in France, to survive.

Within the army, a brigadier general named Napoleon Bonaparte (1769–1821), of Corsican descent, was the most promising commander. From 1796 to 1798 Napoleon scored major victories against the Austrians in northern Italy and invaded Egypt. Thwarted by a pursuing British fleet, he returned to France and overthrew the ineffective Directory in November 1799, thus ending the Revolution.

The French Revolution. After the storming of the Bastille (top left), the French Revolution gained momentum when Parisian women marched to Versailles, demanding that the king reside in Paris and end the famine there (top right). The inevitability of a republic became clear when the king and queen were captured after they attempted to flee (bottom right).

image analysis

Maximilien de Robespierre, "Report of the Principles of Public Morality " (1794)

Patterns Up Close | The Guillotine

During the period of the Terror (June 1793–July 1794) the guillotine was responsible for thousands of executions in Paris and across France. While it is popularly believed that this iconic symbol of public executions was invented by one Dr. Guillotin to speed up the rate of executions during the Reign of Terror, the actual story is far more compelling—and ironic.

The Execution of Marie-Antoinette. During the radical republican period of the French Revolution, the Committee of Public Safety had Queen Marie-Antoinette condemned to death for treason after a show trial. She was executed on October 16, 1793, 9 months after the execution of her husband, Louis XVI.

The first known model of a "decapitation machine" is probably the Halifax Gibbet, in use in England from around 1300 until 1650. Another model, the Scottish Maiden, was derived from the Halifax Gibbet and used from 1565 until 1708. It was turned over to a museum in Edinburgh in 1797 and may have served as a model for the French machine.

When and how did the instrument first appear in France? Ironically, it came as an indirect result of efforts to end the death penalty. During the early days of the Revolution, the National Assembly pondered the abolition of the death penalty in France. On October 10, 1789, the Assembly was addressed by Dr. Joseph Ignace Guillotin (1738–1814), founder of the French

Revival of Empire Napoleon embarked on domestic reforms that restored stability in France. His reform of the French legal system, promulgated in the Civil Code of 1804, established the equality of all male citizens before the law in theory, but in reality it imposed restrictions on many revolutionary freedoms. In 1804 Napoleon crowned himself emperor of the French and began a campaign of conquest in Europe. By 1810, his military victories resulted in the French domination of most of Continental Europe.

Napoleon's goal was the construction of an Enlightenment-influenced but newly aristocratic European empire (see Map 22.2). The failure of Napoleon's Russian campaign in 1812, however, marked the beginning of the end of his grand scheme. An alliance of Great Britain, Austria, Prussia, and Russia ended Napoleon's empire in 1815 and inaugurated the restoration of the pre–French Revolution regimes in Europe.

Conditions for the Haitian Revolution French Saint-Domingue was one of the richest European colonies. It had been a Spanish possession, but as Spain's power slipped during the seventeenth and eighteenth centuries, France established its colony on the western part of the island. In the following century, settlers enjoyed French mercantilist protectionism as they profited from their slave plantations.

In the second half of the 1700s, some 30,000 white settlers, 28,000 mulattos (holding about one-third of the slaves), and about 500,000 black slaves formed an extremely unequal colonial society. When France tightened colonial controls, the

Academy of Medicine and an opponent of capital punishment, who urged the assembly to at least find "a machine that beheads painlessly," if they could not agree to stop executions altogether. Guillotin presented sketches of the kind of machine he had in mind, but his designs were rejected. In 1791 the Assembly finally agreed to retain the death penalty. But instead of adopting Dr. Guillotin's design, the Assembly accepted a model designed by Dr. Antoine Louis, secretary of the Academy of Surgery; Dr. Louis then turned to a German engineer, Tobias Schmidt, who constructed the first version of the "painless" decapitation machine. It was not until April 25, 1792, that the guillotine, nicknamed "Louisette" after Dr. Louis, claimed its first victim. It is not clear when the name was changed to "guillotine" (the final "e" was added later), but Dr. Guillotin's early advocacy of painless executions may have been a factor. As for Dr. Guillotin himself, after fighting a losing battle with the government to change the name of the machine because of embarrassment to his family, he changed his own name.

Questions

- Can the guillotine be viewed as a practical adaptation of Enlightenment ideas? If so, how?

- Why do societies debate the means they use to execute prisoners? What are the criteria by which one form of execution is considered more humane than others?

Punishment of a Slave on the Estate of Charles Balthazar Julien Févret de Saint-Mémin. This watercolor vividly depicts the vast differences between the slave strapped to a frame and the completely unconcerned estate owner on horseback. During the uprising of 1791, slaves occupied the great majority of estates, ended slavery, and drove their owners into exile. Saint-Mémin, whose mother was Creole, waited for a decade in the United States for the return of his estate before giving up and returning to France.

Napoleonic Europe, 1796–1815

France, 1792

Area under direct French rule, 1792–1815:

For more than 10 years

5–10 years

Less than 5 years

Satellite regimes in 1810

Major battles, 1798–1815

MAP 22.2 **Napoleonic Europe, 1796–1815.**

French administrators in Haiti were afraid that the white and mulatto plantation owners would form a united resistance. In order to split the two, they introduced increasingly racist measures to deprive the mulattos of their privileges. It was this split that created the conditions for the slave rebellion once the French Revolution itself was under way.

Revolt of the Slaves   After the failure of Ogé's uprising, resentment continued to simmer among the mulattoes in the south as well as the black slaves in the north of Haiti. The white settler Provincial Assembly refused any concessions even though the French revolutionary National Constituent Assembly in May 1791 granted citizen rights to mulattoes whose parents were free. Aware of the hostility between the mulattoes and whites, slaves seized the opportunity for their own rebellion in August 1791. Almost simultaneously, the mulattoes of the south rose in rebellion as well. Within weeks, the slave and mulatto rebellion encompassed the entire northern and southern provinces of the colony. The overwhelmed settlers suffered heavy losses.

The Assembly in Paris sent commissioners and troops in November 1791 and April 1792 to reestablish order. Neither commission made much headway, largely because of the unrelenting hostility of the whites. In their desperation to gain support, even from the blacks, the second commission abolished slavery in August 1793. This decision, however, failed to rally the black military leaders who had allied themselves with the Spanish, rulers of the eastern half of the island, Santo Domingo. Revolutionary France was embroiled in war against Spain and Britain since early

The Haitian Revolution

1793, and the latter had invaded the French held part in the summer of 1793. Spain and Britain looked like inevitable victors, and the commissioners' emancipation declaration appeared to have been too late.

Both invasions stalled, however. The Assembly in Paris confirmed the emancipation declaration in February 1794, and the French position on the island began to improve. In May 1794, a black rebel leader from the north, François-Dominique Toussaint Louverture (ca. 1743–1803), and his troops abandoned the Spanish and joined the French. Toussaint, grandson of a vassal king (*onto*) in Benin, West Africa, had obtained his freedom in the 1770s. Upon his return to the French, he joined the mulatto faction of the rebellion in the south. The northern blacks and southern mulattoes transformed the rebellion into a full-fledged revolution.

speeches and
letters of Toussaint
L'Ouverture on the
Haitian Revolution
(1793–1800)

Nation-State Building   During the violence of 1791–1794, many plantation owners had fled the colony. Former slaves on deserted plantations grew subsistence crops for their own families. Toussaint remained committed to the plantation system, however, in order to supply revenues for his state-building ambitions. His officers attempted to force former slaves to resume production, with moderate success. In 1801, Toussaint assumed the governorship of Saint-Domingue from the French officials and proclaimed a constitution that incorporated the basic principles of French constitutionalism.

But Toussaint still had to reckon with Atlantic politics. Napoleon Bonaparte, in control of France since 1799, was at that time determined to rebuild the French overseas empire. In the Americas, he purchased Louisiana from Spain in 1800. In 1802, Napoleon dispatched troops to Saint-Domingue to add the colony to Louisiana and revive the French Atlantic empire. Toussaint was prepared for the invasion, but when the French landed, several of his officers surrendered without a fight. As the French advanced into the island against declining resistance, one general, Jean-Jacques Dessalines, betrayed Toussaint. Toussaint was arrested and sent to France, where he died in April 1803. The revolution seemed to be finished.

Jean-Jacques Dessalines (r. 1802–1806) was a former slave from northern Haiti. Seemingly obedient to the French, Dessalines waited for yellow fever to take its toll among the invaders. When more than two-thirds of the French forces were dead by the summer of 1802, Napoleon sold Louisiana to the United States in April 1803 and withdrew from Saint-Domingue in November 1803. On January 1, 1804, Dessalines assumed power and declared the colony's independence.

Subsequently, he made himself emperor, to counter Napoleon, and renamed the country Haiti, its supposed original Taíno name. When he changed the constitution in favor of autocratic rule, he provoked a conspiracy and was assassinated in 1806. The state split into an autocratically ruled black north with a state-run plantation economy and a more democratic mulatto south with a privatized economy of small farms (1806–1821).

Of the three revolutions resulting in the new form of the republican nation-state based on a constitution, that of Haiti realized the Enlightenment principles of liberty, equality, and fraternity most fully. By demonstrating the power of the new ideology of constitutionalism, it participated in the inauguration of a new pattern of state formation in world history not only among the new white and mixed-race urban middle classes but also among the uprooted black African underclass of slaves.

Enlightenment Culture: Radicalism and Moderation

Enlightenment: European intellectual movement (1700–1800) growing out of the New Sciences and based largely on Descartes's concept of reality consisting of the two separate substances of matter and mind.

The American, French, and Haitian Revolutions were embedded in the culture of the **Enlightenment** (ca. 1700–1800). The origins of this culture lay in the new mathematized sciences. The radical interpretation was materialism, according to which all of reality consisted of matter and Descartes's separate substance of mind or reason could either be dispensed with or be explained as a by-product of matter. Moderates held on to Descartes's mind or reason as a separate substance, struggling to explain its presence in reality. The radical Enlightenment tradition evolved primarily in France, while the moderate tradition found adherents in Germany.

The Enlightenment and Its Many Expressions

Writers popularized the new, science-derived philosophy in eighteenth-century France, Holland, England, and Germany. Adherents were still a minority, however, even among the growing middle class, but their voices as radical or moderate "progressives" opposing tradition-bound ministers, aristocrats, and clergy became measurably louder.

It was the late-eighteenth-century generation of this minority that was central to the revolutions in America, France, and Haiti. They translated their New Sciences–derived conception of reality into such "self-evident" ideals as life, liberty, equality, social contract, property, representation, nation, popular sovereignty, and constitution. In the wider culture of the Enlightenment, they fashioned new forms of expression in the arts.

Denis Diderot and the *Encyclopédie*   The idea to bring all knowledge together in an alphabetically organized encyclopedia appeared first in England in 1728. A French publisher decided in 1751 to have it translated. But under the editorship of, for the most part, Denis Diderot (1713–1784) it became a massively expanded work in its own right. Many entries dealt with provocative subjects, such as science, industry, commerce, freedom of thought, slavery, and religious tolerance. The Catholic Church and the French crown banned the project as subversive. But the twenty-eighth and last volume was finally published in 1772.

Jean-Jacques, Rousseau, excerpts from *A Discourse on the Origin of Inequality* (1755)

Philosophy and Morality   Jean-Jacques Rousseau (1712–1778) was a firm believer in the religious morality of the masses. To the consternation of the radicals in France, he argued in his *Social Contract* (1762) that humans had suffered a steady decline from their "natural" state ever since civilization imposed its own arbitrary authority. The radicals held that even though humans had lost their natural state of freedom and equality and had come under arbitrary authority, they were experiencing a steady progress toward freedom and equality. Rousseau, unlike the radicals, had little faith in popular sovereignty, elections, and electoral reforms. Instead, he believed that people, rallying in a nation, should express their unity directly through a sort of direct democracy.

Philosophy and the Categorical Imperative   The philosopher Immanuel Kant (1724–1804) was a believer in the progress of civilization and history, as expressed in his *Perpetual Peace* (1795). Like all Enlightenment thinkers, Kant took Descartes as his point of departure. But he rejected both the two-substance theory of Descartes and the materialist turn of the radical French Enlightenment. Even though he admitted that sensory or bodily experience was primary, he insisted that this experience could be understood only through the categories of the mind or reason that were not found in experience. Reason conditioned experience, but it was not its own substance.

In contrast to Rousseau with his traditional Christian ethics, Kant sought to build morality on reason. He concluded that this morality had to be based on the *categorical imperative*: to act in such a way that the principle of your action can be a principle for any-one's action. This abstract principle later entered modern thought as the basis for concrete human rights, with their claim to universality, as in the Charter of the United Nations (1945).

Economic Liberalism The Enlightenment also saw the birth of the academic discipline of economics. French and British think-ers who were appalled by the inefficient administration of finances, taxes, and trade by the regimes in their countries found the official pursuit of mercantilism wanting. Those opposed to mercantilist state control in France argued that the state should reduce taxes and other means of control to a minimum so that entrepreneurism in the general population could flourish. It should adopt a policy of *laissez-faire* [les-say-FAIR]—that is, "hands-off."

The *Encyclopédie*. Denis Dider-ot's massive work promoted the application of science to practi-cal fields such as glassmaking, illustrated here.

The Scottish economist Adam Smith (1723–1790) developed a British version of laissez-faire economics. In his *Inquiry into the Nature and Causes of the Wealth of Nations* (1776), Smith argued that if the market were largely left to its own devices it would regulate itself through the forces of supply and demand. It would then move in the direction of increasing efficiency as if guided by "an unseen hand." Smith became the founding father of modern economics.

Adam Smith, excerpts from *The Wealth of Nations* (1776)

Literature and Music The Enlightenment also inspired writers and compos-ers. Noteworthy among them were Johann Wolfgang von Goethe (1749–1832) and Wolfgang Amadeus Mozart (1756–1791), sons of a lawyer and a court musician, respectively. Among Goethe's numerous poems, novels, plays, and scientific works was his drama *Faust* about an ambitious scientific experimenter who sells his soul to the devil to acquire mastery of nature. Mozart was a child prodigy who composed symphonies, operas, and chamber music pieces. One of his best-known operas, *The Magic Flute*, displays the influence of the Freemasons, a fraternal association popular in Enlightenment Europe devoted to "liberty, fraternity, and equality"—principles the French Revolution borrowed as its motto.

The imperial turn of the French Revolution under Napoleon effectively ended the Enlightenment. A few years later, with the fall of Napoleon and the restoration of monarchies, the Enlightenment constitutionalists went either silent or underground.

The Other Enlightenment: The Ideology of Ethnic Nationalism

In the revolutions of America, France, and Haiti, ethnic descent and linguistic affili-ations were not significant factors. After 1815, however, these connections began to play increasingly important roles.

Constitutionalism versus Ethnic Nationalism   In Great Britain's North American colonies prior to the Revolution, the great majority of the constitutionalists were "British," which meant that they were primarily Englishmen, with minorities from among the Irish, Welsh, and Scots. In France, the Parisians, who expressed the constitutionalism of the French Revolution in their grammatically complex "high" French, assumed that constitutionalism was nevertheless easily understood and accepted by the provincials. Yet nearly half of the population in the provinces spoke dialects that were often incomprehensible to the Parisians. The other half spoke no French at all and was ethnically either Celtic or German. But no provincials or ethnic Celts and Germans drew support for expressing their separate ethnic identities in the 1700s, nor—in contrast to Britain—even in the 1800s. It was Parisian Frenchness that eventually became the identity of what we call the French nation, and it did so on the basis of the constitutional program of the French Revolution.

Haiti presents the case of a rebellion in favor of French metropolitan constitutionalism. After the Haitians achieved their independence, they elevated their West/Central African ethnic heritage and spoken language, Kreyòl, into their national identity, deemphasizing their French constitutional heritage.

German Cultural Nationalism   In contrast to Great Britain and France, Germany was politically fragmented during the 1700s. In addition, many Germans in eastern Europe were widely dispersed among people with different linguistic, cultural, and even religious heritages. Educated Germans shared a common culture wherever they lived, but in the absence of a strong central state, this culture was largely nonpolitical.

A central figure in shaping this shared culture into a unifying ideology was Johann Gottfried Herder (1744–1803). At college, Herder became familiar with Pietism, a Lutheran version of the medieval Catholic mystical tradition. Employed first as a preacher and then as an administrator at assorted courts in central Germany, he was on close terms with Goethe and other German Enlightenment figures. In his writings, Herder sought to meld the diffuse cultural heritage into a coherent ideology of Germanness combined with the Enlightenment. This ideology, he hoped, would be preached not only to the educated but to the people in general.

The Herder-inspired ethnic version of the Enlightenment received a major boost during the French Revolution, as Germans realized that adoption of French constitutionalism made sense only in a politically united Germany. Before any unification plan could mature, however, Napoleon ended the French Revolution, declared himself emperor, and proceeded to defeat Prussia and Austria. With this, he aroused patriotic passions for liberation from French rule and hopes for a unified Germany under a constitutional government. The figure who decisively advanced in his writings from Herder's cultural Germanness to a fully developed political Germanness was Johann Gottlieb Fichte (1762–1814), a philosophy professor appalled by Napoleon's imperial conquests in Europe. The time seemed ripe for the realization of German political unification on the basis of a marriage of constitutionalism and ethnic nationalism. Instead, the eventual failure of Napoleon's conquests opened the door for a restoration of the pre-1789 monarchies.

Johann Gotlieb Fichte, excerpts from "Addresses to the German Nation" (1807–1808)

The Growth of the Nation-State, 1815–1871

After Napoleon's defeat in Russia in 1812 and the Congress in Vienna of 1815, monarchies and aristocracies reappeared throughout the continent, and only minimal popular representation in parliaments was allowed. By contrast, in Anglo-America, the supremacy of constitutionalism was unchallenged during the 1800s. Here, a pattern of citizen participation in the constitutional process emerged, although its challenges culminated in the American Civil War.

Restoration Monarchies, 1815–1848

As monarchists in Europe sought to return to the politics of absolutism, repression and political manipulation were employed to keep the middle class out of meaningful political participation. A "Concert of Europe" emerged in which rulers avoided intervention in the domestic politics of fellow monarchs, except in cases of internal unrest.

The Congress of Vienna   European leaders met in 1815 at Vienna after the fall of Napoleon in an effort to restore order to a war-torn continent. The driving principle at the session was monarchical conservatism, articulated mainly by Prince Klemens von Metternich (1773–1859), Austria's prime minister. An opponent of constitutionalism, Metternich regarded the still-struggling middle classes outside France with contempt.

To accomplish his objective of reinstituting kings and emperors ruling by divine right, Metternich had the Congress hammer out two principles: legitimacy and balance of power. The principle of legitimacy both recognized exclusive monarchical rule in Europe and reestablished the borders of France as they were in 1789. The principle of the balance of power prevented any one state from rising to dominance over any other. Members agreed to convene at regular intervals in the future in what they called the "Concert," so as to ensure peace and tranquility in Europe. With minor exceptions, this policy of the balance of power remained intact for more than half a century (see Map 22.3).

As successful as the implementation of these two principles was, the solution devised for the German territories was less satisfactory. The Congress of Vienna created a weak confederation of 39 German states, including the empire of Austria and the kingdoms of Prussia, Denmark, and the Netherlands. Prussia and Austria struggled over dominance in the confederation. Constitutionalist and republican Germans disliked the confederation as well, since they had no meaningful voice in it.

Further Revolutions in France   The Congress restored the French Bourbon monarchy with the coronation of King Louis XVIII (r. 1814–1824), a brother of Louis XVI. When Louis died in 1824, the conservatives put Charles X (1824–1830), a second brother of Louis XVI, on the throne. Charles restored the property of the aristocracy lost during the revolution and reestablished the crown's ties to the Catholic Church.

Republican reaction to Charles's restoration policy was swift. In two elections, the republicans won a majority and overthrew the king. But they stopped short of

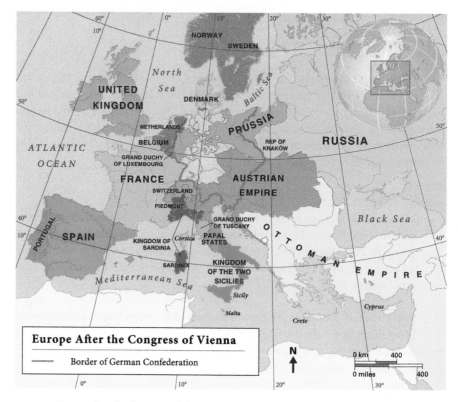

MAP 22.3 Europe after the Congress of Vienna.

abolishing the monarchy and elevated Louis-Philippe (r. 1830–1848), son of a pro-republican duke. Under this "bourgeois king," however, rising income gaps in the middle class as well as difficult living conditions among the industrial working class led to new tensions. In the ensuing revolution of 1848, in which thousands of workers perished, the adherents of restoration and republicanism attempted another compromise: Louis-Philippe went into exile, and the parliament elected Louis-Napoleon Bonaparte (r. 1848–1852; self-declared emperor 1852–1870), a nephew of the former emperor, as president.

Uprisings across Europe   After the revolution in Paris, uprisings occurred in the spring of 1848 in cities across Europe as well as in three Irish counties. In Prussia, the king promised constitutional reforms. In Austria, hit by uprisings in multiple cities, both the emperor and Metternich resigned. The successors, with Russian help, regained military control over the Italians, Czechs, and Hungarians, as well as the Austrians.

In the German Confederation, also hit by uprisings, moderate and republican delegates convened a constitutional assembly in Frankfurt in May 1848. This assembly established the basis for a new, unified state for German speakers and elected a provisional government. The new Austrian emperor, however, refused to let go of his non-German subjects. Therefore, the constitution joined only the German Federation and Prussia (also with non-German minorities) into a unitary state, with the provision for a future addition of German-speaking Austria. Against republican resistance, the delegates offered the Prussian king a new hereditary imperial crown

Rebellion. Following the successful revolution of 1848 that ended the monarchy of Louis-Philippe in France, similar uprisings broke out across Europe. This image shows the Berlin Alexander Square barricades of March 1848.

in the name of the German people. But when the king refused, the tide was turned against the Frankfurt Assembly. Moderate delegates departed, and radical ones instigated revolts. By July 1849, the provisional Frankfurt government had come to an end, and Germany's constitutional experiment was over.

Ethnic Nationalism in Italy   Italy was as fragmented politically as Germany, but unlike Germany, it was also largely under foreign domination. Austria controlled the north and the center through the Habsburgs. The monarchy of Piedmont in the northwest, the Papal States in the center, and the kingdom of Naples and Sicily were independent but weak. After the Metternich restoration, the Italian dynasties had made concessions to constitutionalists, but Austria repressed uprisings in 1820–1821 and 1831–1832 without granting liberties. After the republican Carbonari were defeated in 1831, the remnants formed the Young Italy movement.

Realistic second-generation politicians of the Restoration recognized in the 1860s that by remobilizing the forces of ethnic nationalism, they would be able to make Italy and Germany serious players in the European Concert. Their pursuit of realpolitik—exploitation of political opportunities—resulted in 1870–1871 in the transformations of the Italian kingdom of Piedmont and the German Empire of Prussia into the ethnic nation-states of Italy and Germany.

The Italian politician who did the most to realize Italy's unification was the prime minister of Piedmont-Sardinia, Count Camillo di Cavour (1810–1861). A constitutionalist and supporter of Adam Smith's liberal trade economics, he imported South American guano fertilizer and grew cash crops, like sugar beets, on his estate. As prime minister he was the driving force behind the development of railroads and thereby laid the foundations for the industrialization of northwest Italy.

With the backing of his similarly liberal-minded king, Victor Emanuel II (r. 1849–1878), Cavour began the Italian unification process. With the help of an alliance with France, he was able to provoke Austria, ruler of much of northern Italy, into a war in spring 1859. The allied forces defeated Austria, although not decisively, and in a compromise settlement, Piedmont gained adjoining Lombardy and five regions in north-central Italy. A year later Cavour occupied the Papal States and accepted the offer of Giuseppe Garibaldi (1807–1882) to add adjoining Naples and Sicily to a now largely unified Italy. Garibaldi, a Carbonaro and Young Italy republican nationalist, was an inspiring figure who attracted large numbers of volunteers wherever he went to fight. Cavour died shortly afterward and did not live to see Piedmont transform itself into Italy.

In the years from 1866 to 1870, the expanded Piedmont exploited the Prussian-Austrian war of 1866 to annex Venetia and then took advantage of the Franco-Prussian war of 1870 for the occupation of Rome. (Because of the Prussian threat, Napoleon III recalled his French garrison in Rome which he had sent there against the threat of a campaign by the republican Garibaldi.) Thus, Italy was unified by a king and his aristocratic prime minister, both moderate constitutionalists (though not republicans). As realistic politicians, they tapped into a rising Italian ethnic nationalism to bring about unification.

Bismarck. Bismarck, a Prussian from the aristocratic Junker [YOONK-er] class, was known for his stern, formidable, shrewd, and calculating character and personality; thus, he was nicknamed the "Iron Chancellor." As a consummate practitioner of realpolitik, Bismarck skillfully combined diplomacy with war in order to achieve the unification of Germany in 1871.

Bismarck and Germany   In contrast to Italy, neither King Wilhelm I (r. 1861–1888) nor his chancellor Otto von Bismarck (in office 1862–1890) in Prussia had sympathies for constitutionalism. By forming a coalition, they succeeded in keeping the constitutionalists in the Prussian parliament in check. But they realized they could make use of the ethnic nationalism that had emerged in 1848 for their version of realpolitik.

Bismarck, who was experienced in the diplomacy of the European Concert, realized that Prussia (a weak player in the Concert) would have greater influence only if the kingdom could absorb the German Federation. For Prussia to do so, Bismarck argued, it had to progress from talk about unification to military action. He maneuvered Prussia into an internationally favorable position for the coup that would eventually bring unification: war with France.

First, he exploited a succession crisis in Denmark for a combined Prussian–Austrian campaign to annex Denmark's southern province of Schleswig-Holstein in 1865. Then, when Austria objected to the terms of annexation, he declared war on Austria (1866). After Prussia won, Bismarck dissolved the German Confederation and annexed several German principalities. In France, Louis-Napoleon Bonaparte was greatly concerned about the rising power of Prussia. In a coup d'état in 1852, he ended the Second Republic and, in imitation of his uncle, declared himself emperor. A distraction on his eastern flank was what Emperor Napoleon III did not desire.

But he carelessly undermined his own position. First, he prevented a relative of King Wilhelm from succeeding to the vacant throne of Spain. But when he demanded that Prussia not put forward candidates for any other thrones in the future, Bismarck advised King Wilhelm to refuse the demand. The French, insulted by the refusal, declared war on Prussia but were defeated (1870).

MAP 22.4 **Europe in 1871.**

map analysis

Bismarck on German
nationalism, from his
Memoirs (1899)

Now Bismarck had the upper hand. He annexed Alsace-Lorraine from the French, carried out the final unification of Germany, and elevated the new state to the status of empire in April 1871 (see Map 22.4). In the meantime, French Republicans had proclaimed the Third Republic (September 1870) and deposed Napoleon III (March 1871). While the so-called Second German Empire was consolidated from the start, the French Republic struggled until 1875 to find its republican constitutional order (on this struggle, see "Against the Grain").

Nation-State Building in Anglo-America, 1783–1900

After the independence of the United States in 1783, both the United States and Great Britain pursued their versions of constitutional state development. While the growth of the United States in the 1800s followed its own trajectory, there is no question that the underlying pattern of modern state formation was not unlike that of the other two constitutionally governed countries, France and Great Britain, neither of which was much affected by ethnic nationalism.

The United States During the first half of the nineteenth century, the newly independent North American states began a rapid westward expansion. As this process unfolded, sectional differences developed. Whereas the North developed an industrial and market-driven agricultural economy, the South remained primarily agrarian, relying upon the production of cotton for its economic vitality. Even more, the South relied upon slaves to work the cotton plantations. Cotton not only defined the wealth of the plantation owners but led them to see chattel slavery as the only viable means to remain prosperous. In defense of its stance, the South increasingly relied upon the notion of states' rights in opposition to federal control. With the acquisition of new territory extending to the Pacific coast after the war with Mexico from 1846 to 1848 and the push of settlement beyond the Mississippi, the question of which of the new territories would become "free states" and which would be "slave states" resulted in increasing tensions between North and South.

The result was an attempt by southern states to secede and form a new union, the Confederate States of America. When the new administration of President Abraham Lincoln attempted to suppress this movement, the American Civil War (1861–1865) ensued. Resulting in an enormous loss of life, the Civil War finally ended with a northern victory in 1865. There were several major consequences to the conflict. First, Lincoln's concept of the primacy of national government over individual assertions of states' rights was now guaranteed. Second, slavery was abolished and slaves were granted full citizenship. Third, the rebuilding of the country and opening of the west resulted in a period of remarkable growth, facilitated especially by the expansion of a national network of railroads (see Map 22.5).

The price of reintegrating the old South into the new order was the reversion to an imposition of de facto peonage on its black citizens. Between 1877 and 1914 state legislatures in the South stripped African Americans of voting rights and imposed formal and informal segregation. These were enforced by law and all too often by lynchings and other forms of violence. Most northern policy and opinion makers backed away from the views espoused by champions of racial equality and acquiesced

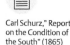

Carl Schurz," Report on the Condition of the South" (1865)

MAP 22.5 **The Expanding United States in 1900.**

to Southern efforts to maintain white hegemony. The drive for full civil rights would occupy American domestic policy debates throughout the twentieth century.

Native Americans Native Americans suffered unmitigated disasters during the 1800s. When the Louisiana Purchase in 1803 nearly doubled the size of the United States, politicians devised strategies to move Native Americans from their eastern homelands to the new territories. For their part, Native Americans realized that only unification would help them to stay put, especially in the South and the Midwest, where white settler encroachment was strong.

In the Midwest, Tecumseh (1768–1812) and his brother Tenskwatawa (1775–1836) worked toward unification. Tecumseh traveled between the Midwest and South, seeking to forge a Native American resistance federation. Tenskwatawa, claiming his authority from visions of the Master of Life, preached that Native Americans needed to reject white culture and return to traditional life. At the battle of Tippecanoe in Indiana, thousands of followers from a variety of nations came together, but suffered a severe defeat at the hands of US troops in 1811. The defeat ended the dream of Native American unity.

A Sauk Indian leader describes relations with Americans (1832)

In the South, discriminatory legislation and brutal assaults made it difficult for Native American nations to survive on their lands. With the declared intention of helping these nations against the states, in 1830 the federal government issued the Indian Removal Act. In fact, however, this act only deepened the sufferings of the Native Americans east of the Mississippi: A quarter died on the "Trail of Tears" to their designated new homeland in Oklahoma. The survivors attempted to reconstruct their agriculture, schools, and councils while accommodating the regular arrival of newly displaced Native Americans.

Destruction of the Buffalo Herds By mid-century, white ranchers and miners were settling farther west of the Mississippi. Again, the federal government passed a law supposedly protecting the Native Americans of the Plains by creating "reservations" (1851). The obligation to stay on reservations rather than to hunt freely was a first aggravation. Further affronts came through the Homestead Act (1862), the construction of the transcontinental railroad (1863–1869), and the construction of towns and cities along the railroad corridors. The worst injury was the destruction of the buffalo (bison), the hunting of which formed the principal livelihood of the Native Americans on the Plains. Within two decades (1865–1884), the herds had been decimated; fewer than 1,000 animals remained.

In the American Indian Wars (1862–1890), the Native Americans defended their homelands tenaciously but in vain. Visionaries sought to unify the various groups through the Ghost Dance, enacting a prophecy of the return of the buffalo herds and the disappearance of the whites. The Native Americans' last stand was at Wounded Knee Creek, South Dakota, in December 1890. Defeated and demoralized by 1900, the remaining indigenous people found themselves on 310 reservations.

Two Girls of the Hopi Nation with Their Characteristic Hairstyles and Blankets. The Hopi live in the American Southwest, today's Arizona. They are best known as sophisticated farmers who live in adobe pueblos, some of which were built into the rock walls of canyons. In 1680, the Hopi rebelled for a dozen years against Spanish missionaries and colonists in their midst, achieving a degree of autonomy as a result. The United States organized the nation in 1882 into the Hopi Reservation.

Reform Measures Rapid industrialization that produced social and labor unrest in the United States led to the reforming initiatives of the Progressive era

(1890–1914). By the 1900s, just a few hundred firms controlled two-fifths of all American manufacturing. The "trust buster" president, Theodore Roosevelt (in office 1901–1909) and Congress ended the monopolies of many such firms. A new Department of Commerce and Labor (1903) and the Pure Food and Drug and Meat Inspection Acts (1906) helped both workers and consumers. With the Federal Reserve Act (1913) and the Federal Trade Commission Act (1914), Congress created an overall framework for the supervision of the financial and business sectors.

Great Britain   The pattern of constitutional nation-state construction that Britain followed in the eighteenth and nineteenth centuries was uninterrupted by wars. Challenges to this pattern came from the rise of linguistic nationalisms outside the English core. The first signs of Irish nationalism, based not only in ethnic and linguistic but also in religious traditions, appeared after the Great Famine of 1845–1849. Rural production and land issues were the main points of contention, leading to demands for home rule or even independence. A Protestant landlord class still controlled most of the land, which was farmed by Catholic tenant farmers. During the worldwide Long Depression of 1873–1896, Irish farmers received low prices for their crops but no reductions in rent. A "land war" (mass protests against tenant evictions) ensued which the British Army sought to quell. This eventually led in 1898 to local government for the Irish and in 1903–1909 to land reform.

Scotland also developed an ethnolinguistic sense of its identity. The development began with the revival of traditional Scottish dress and music. More serious issues came to the fore in 1853 when the Scots, who felt that the British government paid more attention to Ireland, founded an association for the vindication of Scottish rights. But they had to wait until 1885, when the British government appointed the first Secretary for Scotland.

Welsh nationalism arose in the context of industrialization and the development of a Welsh working class, which organized uprisings in the 1830s. Religious issues, mostly related to opposition to the Church of England among nonconformists (e.g., Methodists, Quakers, and Presbyterians), and education issues added to the unrest. It was not until 1925, with the foundation of the Party of Wales, that Welsh nationalism became a force of its own.

During the 1800s, Parliament, the guardian of British constitutionalism, undertook major legal reforms of its constitutional order in recognition of the growing middle and working classes. The Great Reform Bill of 1832 shifted seats from southern districts to the more populated and industrialized center and north. The repeal of the Corn Laws in 1846 liberated imports and made grain cheaper, and the Second Reform Act of 1867 extended the franchise to larger numbers of working-class voters. The end result was not only that Britain escaped the revolutions of 1848 but also that the British electorate was largely united during the Victorian period (1837–1901) in its support for British imperialism around the globe.

Romanticism and Realism: Philosophical and Artistic Expression to 1850

Parallel to the evolution of the patterns of constitutionalism and ethnolinguistic nationalism, the two movements of romanticism and realism patterned the evolution of culture on both sides of the Atlantic.

Romanticism

Inspired by the Enlightenment and the revolutions, many philosophers, writers, composers, and painters of the period of **romanticism** in the early 1800s concluded that humans were free to remake themselves. To them, the mind was entirely independent, creating new aesthetic categories out of its own powers. Indeed, the stereotype of the bohemian creative "genius" crossing new imaginative thresholds became firmly implanted in the public imagination during this time.

Romanticism: Intellectual and artistic movement that emphasized the power of creative genius over matter and sought the sublime in nature.

Philosophers and Artists Building on Kant, the philosopher Georg Wilhelm Friedrich Hegel (1770–1831) postulated the complete freedom of mind or spirit. Hegel asserted that all thought proceeded dialectically from the "transcendental ego" to its opposite, matter, and from there to the spiritualized synthesis of nature. This **dialectic** permeates his entire system of philosophy.

Even more than philosophy, music became the medium for expressing the creative genius. The German Ludwig van Beethoven (1770–1827) and the Frenchman Hector Berlioz (1803–1869) pioneered the new genre of program music, with the *Pastoral Symphony* (Symphony no. 6) and the *Symphonie phantastique*, respectively, emphasizing passion and emotional intensity and the freedom of the musical spirit over traditional form. From among the emerging middle class, eager to play music at home, a veritable explosion of composers erupted during the first half of the 1800s. These musicians were also virtuosi on the violin or piano, playing their own new musical forms and playing concerts across Europe.

Dialectic: The investigation of truth by discussion; in Hegel's thought, the belief that a higher truth is comprehended by a continuous unification of opposites.

The medium of painting also lent itself to the expression of romantic feelings of passion and imagination. The common feature of these painters was that they departed from the established academic practices and styles.

As in the other art forms, romanticism in literature appears in heroines or heroes and their passions and sentiments. In the novels of the British author Jane Austen (1775–1817), educated urbane society shapes the character and sensibilities of young women and prepares them for marriage. Also in Britain, the novels of the three Brontë sisters, Charlotte (1816–1855), Emily (1818–1848), and Anne (1820–1849), placed much greater emphasis on romantic passion, flawed characters, and social ills. The American Edgar Allan Poe (1809–1849) used these themes more explicitly in his Gothic stories and tales, such as "The Fall of the House of Usher" (1839).

Realism

Toward the middle of the 1800s, many artists and writers shifted their focus from the romanticism of the self to the **realism** of the middle classes. In philosophy, thinkers identified stages leading progressively to the rise of middle classes and industrialism. And in literature, the complex relationships that characterized the plots of the romantics were now set in the more prosaic urban world of factories and working classes.

Realism: The belief that material reality exists independently of the people who observe it.

Philosophy of History The French thinker Auguste Comte (1798–1857) published *The Positive Philosophy* (1830–1842), in which he arranged world history into the three successive stages of the theological, metaphysical, and scientific. In his view, the scientific advances of the sciences had all but eclipsed the metaphysical stage and had ushered in the last, scientific era. For Comte this was a sign of Europe's

ASSASSINAT DES OTAGES À LA PRISON DE LA ROQUETTE LE 24 MAI 1871
M. Darboy   Bonjean   Duguerry   Ducoudray   Clerc   Allard

Realism. The documentary power of photography spurred the new impulses of realism that emerged around 1850. The photograph here shows a reenactment of the execution of six hostages by the government of the Commune of Paris on May 24, 1871. This chilling scene was staged several weeks after the collapse of the Commune on May 28 by the photographer Eugène Appert to serve the provisional French government in Versailles in its efforts to expose the crimes of the Commune.

Positivism: A philosophy advocated by Auguste Comte that favors the careful empirical observation of natural phenomena and human behavior over metaphysics.

progress and a "positive" stage. His philosophy, labeled **positivism**, exerted a major influence in Europe as well as in Latin America.

Prose Literature   Realistic writers of fiction moved away from personal sentiments to explore middle-class society. In England, William Makepeace Thackeray (1811–1863) was a supreme satirist, whose novel *Vanity Fair* examines the foibles of the bourgeoisie. Charles Dickens (1812–1870) focused on working- and lower-middle-class characters in his many novels. George Eliot, born Mary Ann Evans (1819–1880), was politically oriented, placing small-town social relations within the context of concrete political events in Great Britain. In France, Gustave Flaubert (1821–1880) featured precise and unadorned descriptions of objects and situations in novels like *Madame Bovary*, 1857. And Henry James (1843–1916), an American living in Britain, in his novel *The Ambassadors* (1903) explored the psychological complexities of individuals whose lives crossed both sides of the Atlantic. In the end, realism, with its individuals firmly anchored in the new class society of the 1800s, moved far from the freedom and exuberance celebrated by the romantics.

Charles Dickens, excerpt from *Hard Times* (1854)

interactive concept map

≫ Putting It All Together

Though the pattern of nation-state building in Europe and North America was relatively slow, it has become the dominant mode of political organization in the world today. The aftermath of World War I and the decolonization movement following World War II spurred the process of nation-state formation. The legacy of European colonialism both planted these ideas among the colonized and, through

Enlightenment ideas of revolution, provided the ideological means of achieving their own liberation from foreign rule. In both cases, the aspirations of peoples to "nationhood" followed older European models as the colonies were either granted independence or fought to gain it from declining empires.

For example, although the United States achieved world economic leadership by 1914, it had faced an early constitutional crisis, endured a prolonged sectional struggle over slavery, fought a civil war that very nearly destroyed it, and remained united in part by acquiescing in segregation and discrimination against the 10 percent of its population that was of African descent. France adopted constitutional nationalism in 1789, but the monarchy bounced back three times. And in Germany, linguistic nationalism diluted the straightforward enthusiasm for the constitution and the symbols accompanying it.

In retrospect, it is impossible to say which of the speed bumps on the way toward the nation-state—slavery/racism, residual monarchism, or the twentieth-century experiments of communism and supremacist nationalism—were responsible for the longest delay.

Review and Relate

Thinking Through Patterns

Constitutionalism emerged as a result of the success of American and French revolutionaries in overthrowing absolute rule. The constitutional revolutionaries replaced the loyalty of subjects to a monarch with that of free and equal citizens to the national constitution. This form of republican constitutionalism called for unity among the citizens regardless of ethnic, linguistic, or religious identity. In the United States, this republicanism had to overcome the adherence to slavery in the South before it gained general recognition after the end of the Civil War. In France, republican constitutionalists battled conservative monarchists for nearly a century before they were able to finally defeat them in the Third Republic.

》 How did the pattern of constitutionalism, emerging from the American and French Revolutions, affect the course of events in the Western world during the first half of the nineteenth century?

Constitutionalists emphasized the principles of freedom, equality, constitution, rule of law, elections, and representative assembly regardless of ethnicity, language, or religion. By contrast, ethnic nationalists in areas of Europe lacking centralized monarchies sought to first unify dispersed members of their nation through ideologies that emphasized common origin, collective history, and shared cultural traditions. In these ethnic (and sometimes also religious) ideologies, constitutional principles were secondary. Only once unification in a nation-state was achieved would the form of government—monarchist, constitutional-monarchist, or republican—then be chosen.

》 In what ways did ethnic nationalism differ from constitutionalism, and what was its influence on the formation of nation-states in the second half of the nineteenth century?

> **What were the reactions among thinkers and artists to the developing pattern of nation-state formation? How did they define the intellectual-artistic movements of romanticism and realism?**

Philosophers and artists in the romantic period emphasized individual creativity. By the 1850s, with the rise of the middle class, individual creativity gave way to a greater awareness, called "realism," of the social and political environment with its class structures and industrial characteristics.

| Against the Grain

Defying the Third Republic

Consider this as a counterpoint to the main patterns examined in this chapter.

- Did the members of the Commune of Paris opponents run counter to the pattern of nation-state formation in the nineteenth century, and if so, how did they want to replace it?

- Did the ideas of small communities and op-position to centralized national governments retain their attraction in the twentieth and twenty-first centuries? If yes, which examples come to mind and for which reasons?

Socialist Parisians despised the government and parliament of the new conservative Third Republic of France (February 1871), headquartered in Versailles and dominated by two monarchist factions. They considered it defeatist against the Prussians who had been victorious in the war of 1870. After two failed protests, the final trigger for an outright revolution was the government's attempt in March 1871 to collect some 400 guns left over from the war and under the command of the Parisian National Guard. The attempt turned into a fiasco. The number of horses sent from Versailles to pull the cannons away was insufficient, and the government troops fraternized with the Parisian crowds. In the melee, however, several soldiers and two generals were killed (the latter probably by army deserters in Paris, not guardsmen). Seizing the opportunity, the central committee of the National Guard declared its independence and held elections for a communal council on March 26 (Commune of Paris: March 18–May 28, 1871).

The council of workers, craftsmen, and professionals issued a flurry of new laws. All deputies were under binding mandates and could be recalled anytime. As a commune of a desired universal republic, Paris considered all foreigners as equals. France itself was to become a federation of communes. Abandoned factories and workshops were to be directed by workers' councils. Church properties were confiscated, and the separation of church and state was declared. Under the auspices of the women-run Union of Women for the Defense of Paris and the Care of the Injured, measures for equal pay and pensions for retired survivors, regardless of marital status, were envisaged. The official symbol of the Commune was the red flag of the radical French Revolution of 1792, not the republican tricolor. The Commune pushed equality much further than the American and French revolutions had ever done, frightening the middle classes to their core.

The Commune had no chance of survival against the superior troops of the Third Republic, and it was bloodily repressed. The symbolical significance of the Commune was immense: Socialists and communists made it the mythical dawn of world revolution, working-class dictatorship, and the eventual withering away of the (national) state in the utopia of a classless society.

Key Terms

Dialectic   523

Enlightenment   512

Positivism   524

Realism   523

Romanticism   523

audio flashcards

For additional resources, please go to **www.oup.com/us/vonsivers.**
Please see the Further Resources section at the back of the book for additional readings and suggested websites.

Creoles and Caudillos

LATIN AMERICA IN THE NINETEENTH CENTURY

LATIN AMERICA AND THE CARIBBEAN

Among the leaders of the Latin American wars of independence (1810–1826) from Spain, a woman named Juana Azurduy de Padilla (1781–1862) stands out for her bravery. Azurduy [asoor-DOO-ee] was a mestiza military commander in what are today the countries of Bolivia and Argentina. With her husband, Manuel Ascencio Padilla, she joined the cause of independence in 1810, creating a mini-republic (*republiquita*) in the mountains.

Azurduy, who was adored by the locals as "Mother Earth" (*pachamama*), had learned swordsmanship, firearms handling, and logistics for fighting guerilla wars. Well versed in Quechua and Aymara, Azurduy and Ascencio recruited some 6,000 locals, armed with the traditional Inca arms of clubs and slings. In 1813, Azurduy, and Ascencio and their men joined a force of independence fighters from Buenos Aires. This force suffered defeat, however, at the hands of Spanish royal troops sent by the vice-regent of Peru. In an effort to recover, Azurduy drilled what she called her "Loyal Battalion" for ambushes and quick retreats. But pressured by the viceregal troops, the battalion suffered a constant loss of men—including Ascencio—in 1816. Azurduy retreated to what is today northwestern Argentina, where she was

ABOVE: **Carts loaded high with sugarcane arrive at a sugar mill in Cuba, late nineteenth century.**

incorporated as a lieutenant colonel in the regular independence army, in recognition of her bravery.

In 1824 Upper Peru gained its independence under the name of Bolivia (in honor of the Venezuelan independence leader Simón Bolívar). Azurduy returned from Argentina to retire. She died in 1862, and in the early 1900s Bolivians named a town near her birthplace after her.

The story of Juana Azurduy illustrates the important role of Amerindians, mestizos, black freedmen, and black slaves in the wars of independence in Latin America. The fact that a woman was able to overcome patriarchal conventions in the early 1800s demonstrates the power of the revolutionary ideas of liberty and of the republican and constitutional nation-state (see Chapter 22).

Independence, Constitutionalism, and Landed Elites

The eighteenth-century Enlightenment was far less influential as an incubator of independence and republican constitutionalism in Latin America than it was in North America. The American and French revolutions had a limited intellectual impact, and the Haitian slave revolution raised apprehension among Creoles. The real catalyst for the majority of Latin Americans to declare independence and introduce republican constitutions was Napoleon's occupation of the Iberian peninsula (1807–1814). This occupation confronted the Spanish-speaking Creoles with the choice of continued loyalty to the deposed absolutist Bourbon dynasty, recognition of Napoleon, or full republican independence. In the end, when Napoleon's regime proved to be shortlived and the restored Bourbon king refused constitutional reforms, the choice was clear: Latin America fought for its full republican independence.

After independence, the four regions governed previously by Spanish viceroys —Rio de la Plata in the south, Peru in the west, New Granada in the center, and New Spain in the north—followed their own political trajectories. The pattern of republican state formation, with states sometimes in fierce competition with each other, unfolded for the most part *within* each of the four regions.

Independence in the Southern Cone: State Formation in Argentina

Independence movements in the viceroyalty of the Río de la Plata formed in June 1810. Under the guise of loyalty to the deposed Fernando VII of Spain, Creoles in the capital Buenos Aires established a junta [HOON-ta] rejecting the viceregal Spanish authorities. Outright independence from Spain was declared in 1816. Even though by this time Spanish loyalists in the south had been defeated, their brethren in the far northwest were still strong. Efforts by troops from Buenos Aires to defeat the loyalists of Upper Peru, part of the viceroyalty of Río de la Plata, had failed. The figure who finally broke the logjam was one of the heroes of Latin American independence, José de San Martín (1778–1850).

Seeing Patterns

≫ Which factors in the complex ethnic and social structures of Latin America were responsible for the emergence of authoritarian politicians, or caudillos?

≫ After achieving independence, why did Latin American countries opt for a continuation of mineral and agricultural commodity exports?

≫ How do the social and economic structures of this period continue to affect the course of Latin America today?

Southern Cone: Geographical term denoting the southern half of South America, comprising the countries of Brazil, Paraguay, Uruguay, and Argentina.

Chapter Outline

• Independence, Constitutionalism, and Landed Elites

• Latin American Society and Economy in the Nineteenth Century

• Putting It All Together

Independence in Argentina   The viceroyalty of La Plata, comprising the modern countries of Argentina, Uruguay, Paraguay, and Bolivia, was the youngest of Spain's colonial units. La Plata, with the port of Buenos Aires as its capital, had grown through contraband trade with Great Britain, and the Bourbon reformers wanted to redirect its trade to Spain.

In 1810, when the first independence movements formed, there was a clear distinction between the Creoles of Buenos Aires, or *porteños*, who favored independence, and the Creoles of the *pampas* (grasslands of the interior of Argentina and Uruguay) and the subtropical plains and hills of Paraguay, who favored continued colonialism.

Uruguay, furthermore, was initially claimed by Brazil and eventually achieved its own independence only in 1828. Upper Peru, or modern Bolivia, was heavily defended by colonial and Spanish troops. Given these circumstances, the porteño independence fighters achieved only a standstill during the initial period of 1810–1816.

The breakthrough for independence eventually came via an experienced military figure, José de San Martín (ca. 1778–1850). San Martín was a Creole from northeastern Argentina. He began service in the porteño independence movement in 1812, where he distinguished himself in the Argentine struggle for independence.

During his service, San Martín realized that success in the struggle for independence in the south would require the liberation of the viceroyalty of Peru. Accordingly, he trained the Army of the Andes, which included mulatto and black volunteers. With this army, he crossed the mountains to Chile in 1818, liberating the country from royalist forces. With the help of a newly established navy, he conquered Lima in Peru. However, San Martín was defied by the local Creoles when he sought to introduce social reforms. When he was also unable to dislodge Spanish troops from Upper Peru and come to terms about the future of Latin America with Simón Bolívar, the liberation hero of central Latin America, he resigned from the army in 1822, to live mostly in Belgium and France for the remainder of his life.

painting commemorating
Chilean independence (1818)

Slow State Formation   After independence, the ruling junta in Buenos Aires solidified into an oligarchy of the city's landowning Creole elite. In the interior, the largely undeveloped areas of the pampas with their small populations of Amerindians and Creole *gauchos*, or cowboys, remained largely outside the new state. But even the core provinces and the port city of Buenos Aires were unable to come to terms. The provinces cherished their autonomy and resented the city's economic superiority and pretensions to political dominance. Uruguay, one of the provinces of the former Spanish viceroyalty of La Plata, strove for independence from the start, but was thwarted by both Argentina, the self-declared heir of the viceroyalty's territories, and Brazil, which claimed it for itself on the grounds of its sizable Portuguese-speaking minority. The independence of Uruguay was recognized by its neighbors in 1828, but even then, meddling in its internal affairs continued.

Interactive timeline

1791–1804 Haitian Revolution	1822–1889 Empire of Brazil	1810–1826 Most of South America achieves independence from Spain	ca. 1870 Beginning of mass immigration to South America	1910–1917 Mexican Revolution
1803 Louisiana Purchase	1810–1821 Mexican war of liberation	1836–1848 Mexico loses Texas and southwest to United States	1888 End of slavery in Brazil	

Political Instability in the Southern Cone
An Argentine constituent assembly finally drew up a definitive federal constitution in 1853, but state formation and territorial consolidation remained in flux. Buenos Aires refused to subscribe to the constitution until 1861. While the constitutional order was settled at this time, the process of territorial consolidation was not and contributed to continued tensions among Paraguay, Uruguay, Argentina, and Brazil.

Tensions among the four countries reached their height during the Paraguayan War of 1864–1870, which proved to be the most devastating in the history of nineteenth-century Latin America. In this war, Paraguay was pitted against a triple alliance among Brazil, Argentina, and Uruguay. The Paraguayan president Francisco Solano López (r. 1862–1870) miscalculated that Argentina would support his idea of a "third force," formed by an alliance between Paraguay and Uruguay, to block Brazil's territorial ambitions. But in spite of their diverging interests, Argentina and Brazil agreed to maintain the traditional policy of keeping Paraguay and Uruguay weak. Paraguay lost the war and suffered terrible destruction. The War of Paraguay contributed to the industrialization and professionalization of modern warfare. In particular, it greatly strengthened the political role of the Brazilian military, which culminated in the army's overthrow of the monarchy (1889). About the only positive outcome was that it finally settled the state formation and territorial consolidation process of Argentina.

Fiercely Independent Gauchos, around 1900. Gauchos, shown here sharpening their long knives (*facónes*), were recognizable by their ponchos or wool blankets, which doubled as winter coats and saddlecloths. As with cowboys in North America, they were expert riders, calf ropers, and—with their dogs, shown in front—cattle herders.

Argentine Demographic Growth   In the years after 1870, the pampas of Argentina were transformed. The land was opened to settlement by European immigrants, driving the gauchos from their independent existence into becoming hired hands. The railroad was spurring settlement, and the remaining Amerindians were driven south to Patagonia or exterminated. The pampas were divided up into huge estates (*estancias*) as the old system of rounding up livestock and driving it to market now gave way to ranching. As in other areas of South America, the new landed Creole elite dominated politics and the economy long into the twentieth century.

While landed interests continued to prevail, the urban center of Buenos Aires grew restless under the rotating presidency that characterized the period of 1880–1900. Spurred by the development of radical politics in Europe, two urban opposition parties took shape: the Radical Party and the Socialists. As the influence of these parties grew, electoral reforms were forced on an unwilling landed oligarchy.

Brazil: From Kingdom to Republic

During the late colonial period, Brazil underwent the same centralizing reforms as the Spanish possessions. Although the Brazilian planters and urban Creoles (Portuguese *crioulos*) resented these reforms, their fear of rebellion by the huge population of black slaves restrained them from openly demanding independence. As it happened, independence arrived through the relocation of the monarchy from Portugal to Brazil in the wake of Napoleon's invasion of Iberia in 1807. Brazil became a monarchically governed empire, striving for expansion into Spanish-speaking territories. When Brazil, under pressure from Britain, finally abolished slavery in 1888, the plantation oligarchy and allied military avenged itself by deposing the emperor, switching to a republican regime under the military in 1889. The regime became solidly federal, making it difficult for authoritarian rulers to succeed.

Relocation of the Dynasty   When Portugal's royal family took refuge in Brazil in 1807, it elevated the colony to the status of a coequal kingdom in union with Portugal but governed from Brazil after Napoleon's defeat in 1815. In 1820, rebels in Portugal adopted a liberal constitution, which demanded the return of Brazil to colonial status as well as the transfer of the dynasty back to Portugal. The reigning king went back but left his son, Pedro I (r. 1822–1831), behind in Brazil. In 1822 Pedro proclaimed Brazil an independent state.

Pedro I's Authoritarianism   Like the restoration monarchs of Europe in the early 1800s, Pedro adhered to his belief in divine right, which was incompatible with constitutionalism. Rejecting an attempt by the landed oligarchy to limit monarchical rule, he promulgated instead his own constitution in 1823, which concentrated most powers in his hands.

In reaction, in 1824 six northeastern provinces attempted to secede. They proclaimed the republican Federation of the Equator and demanded more central government support for the traditional northern sugar and cotton plantations, as British attempts to suppress the slave trade had increased the price for slaves, and the sugar planters could ill afford the higher prices. Given the close ties between Britain and Brazil, Pedro found it difficult to resist the British demands for the abolition of slavery. As a result, early signs of alienation between the crown and the Creole planter elite crept in.

Ultimately, a succession crisis in Portugal in 1830 led to a conservative revolt against Pedro. In 1831 he abdicated, sailing back to Portugal. He left the throne to his 5-year-old son, Pedro II (r. 1831–1889), who required a regent. The landowning elite exploited the opportunity of the temporarily weak monarchy by renewing its demands for federalism.

The Federalist Interlude   In 1834 the government granted the provinces their own legislative assemblies, strengthening the provincial landholding elites with their various regional interests. It also abolished the council of state but created a national guard to suppress slave revolts and urban mobs. Some provinces revolted against these reforms, most dangerously in 1835 in Rio Grande do Sul, a southern province dominated by cattle owners who did not own many slaves and commanded military forces composed of gauchos. These owners established an independent republic that attracted many who were opposed to slavery, and offered refuge to runaway slaves. In reaction to the coexistence of a weakened monarchy and an anti-slavery republic, the centralists reasserted themselves. In 1840 they proclaimed the 14-year-old Pedro II emperor and curbed the powers of the provincial assemblies. In 1845 they negotiated a return of Rio Grande do Sul to Brazil.

The End of Slavery   During the 1830s and 1840s, Brazil made the transition from sugar to coffee as a major export commodity. Both crops required slave labor,

Images from the
Ragamuffin War (1835)

and when the British in 1849 authorized warships to enter Brazilian waters to intercept slave ships, the importation of slaves virtually ceased. Sugar, cotton, and coffee plantation owners began to think of ridding themselves of a monarchy that was unable to maintain the flow of slaves from overseas.

In the 1860s and 1870s, anti-slavery agitation grew as Brazilians became sensitive to their country being isolated in the world on the issue. While the government introduced a few changes, it fell to the provinces to take more serious steps. Planters encouraged their provinces to increase the flow of foreign immigrants, to be employed as wage labor on the coffee plantations. Finally, in 1888 the central government ended slavery.

painting showing a white Brazilian couple being served by black slaves (1839)

The Coffee Boom Little changed in social relations after the abolition of slavery. The coffee growers, enjoying high international coffee prices and the benefits of infrastructure improvements, could afford low-wage hired labor. Although freed, blacks received no land, education, or urban jobs, scraping by with low wages on the coffee and sugar plantations. Economically, however, Brazil expanded its economy in the 5 years following 1888 as much as in the 70 years of slavery since independence.

The monarchy had been thoroughly discredited among the landowners and their military offshoot, the officer corps. During the War of Paraguay (1865–1870) the military had transformed itself into a professional body with its own sense of mission. By the 1880s, officers subscribed to the ideology of *positivism* coming from France (see Chapter 22). Positivists were liberal and republican in political orientation. In 1889, a revolt in the military supported by the Creole plantation oligarchy resulted in the abolition of the monarchy and the proclamation of a republic.

Two political tendencies emerged in the constituent assembly after the proclamation of the republic. The coffee interests favored federalism, with the right of the provinces to collect export taxes and maintain militias. The urban professional and intellectual interests supported a strong presidency with control over tariffs and import taxes as well as powers to use the federal military against provinces in cases of national emergency. The two tendencies resulted in a compromise, which produced provincial authoritarian rulers on the one hand but also regularly elected presidents on the other.

By the 1890s the government was strongly supportive of agricultural commodity exports, which yielded high profits and taxes until 1896, when overproduction of coffee resulted in diminishing returns. The state of São Paulo then regulated the sale of coffee on the world market through a state purchase scheme, which brought some stabilization to coffee production. At the same time, immigrants and foreign investors laid the foundation for **import-substitution industrialization**, beginning with textile and food-processing factories.

Import-substitution industrialization: The practice by which countries protect their economies by setting high tariffs and construct factories for the production of consumer goods (textiles, furniture, shoes, followed later by appliances, automobiles, electronics) and/or capital goods (steel, chemicals, machinery).

Independence and State Formation in Western and Northern South America

Compared to the viceroyalty of La Plata in the south, the Spanish viceroyalty of New Granada in northern South America, with today's countries of Venezuela, Colombia, Ecuador, and Panama, had far fewer Creoles. For its struggle for independence to succeed, leaders had to seek support from the *pardos*, as the majority population of free black and mulatto craftspeople in the cities was called.

Independence eventually came through the building of armies from these diverse elements, mostly by Simón Bolívar, the liberator of northern South America. After independence, however, the Creoles dissolved their coalitions with the lower classes and embraced the **caudillo** [caw-DEE-yoh] politics that were practiced in other parts of South America.

Caudillo: Term referring to authoritarian Latin American rulers who disregard the constitutional limits to their powers. Derived from Latin *capitellum* (little head). Authoritarianism was most pronounced in northern South America.

Creoles and Pardos   New Granada's Creole population was small relative to the population of mestizos and pardos. In 1810, the New Granadans created *juntas*, or committees, among which the junta of Cartagena was the most important, and drove the colonial Spaniards from their administrative positions. Initially, the Creole-led juntas agreed on the equality of all ethnicities and worked on constitutions that provided for elections by all free men. But the juntas were also suspicious of each other. In 1811, cooperation broke down and the majority pardos assumed power. The Creoles struck back a year later when they declared the First Republic of Cartagena. Their power was limited by the pardo-dominated militias, however, and in a compromise the Creoles agreed on the continuation of full voting rights. In the long run, this revolutionary achievement did not last, and the Creoles established oligarchic rule.

Bolívar the Liberator   The junta of Cartagena, together with other juntas, formed the federation of the United Provinces of New Granada in 1811, with a weak executive. The Spanish king, Fernando VII, after returning to the throne in 1813, was determined to reestablish colonial control by dispatching armies to Latin America. The largest forces landed in the United Provinces in 1814 and resurrected the viceroyalty of New Granada.

The eventual liberator of northern South America from renewed Spanish rule in 1819 was Simón Bolívar (1783–1830). Bolívar admired Enlightenment ideals of liberty and popular sovereignty, and he longed to create a constitutional republic in his homeland. In 1816 Bolívar had returned from exile to Venezuela with a military force, partly supplied by Haiti. After some initial difficulties, he succeeded in defeating the Spanish troops. In 1822, he assumed the presidency of "Gran Colombia," an independent republic comprising the later states of Colombia, Venezuela, Ecuador, and Panama.

Liberation of the Slaves in Colombia. As a Creole growing up on his father's cacao plantation, worked by slaves, Bolívar was intimately familiar with slavery. But his exile in post-revolutionary Haiti 1814–1816 demonstrated to him that slavery was incompatible not only with the principles of the American and French Revolutions but also with the revolutions in Spanish America, of which he was one of the main leaders.

The Bolívar–San Martín Encounter   After their defeat in Gran Colombia, Spanish troops continued to hold Upper Peru in the Andes. The Argentinean liberator José de San Martín and Bolívar met in 1822 to deliberate on how to drive the Spanish from Peru and to shape the future of an independent Latin America.

The content of their discussion never became public. San Martín, bitterly disappointed by endless disputes among different groups, apparently favored monarchical rule to bring stability to Latin America. Bolívar, it is believed, preferred republicanism and Creole oligarchical rule. Apart from their awareness of the need for ethnic and racial integration, there was not much common ground between the two independence leaders.

San Martín soon resigned from politics, having perhaps realized that the chances for a South American monarchy were slim. Bolívar more realistically envisioned the future of Latin America as that of relatively small independent republics, held together by strong, lifelong presidencies and hereditary senates. He implemented this vision in the 1825 constitution of independent Upper Peru, renamed Bolivia after him.

Ironically, in his own country of Gran Colombia, Bolívar was denied the role of strong president. Although he made himself a caudillo, he was unable to coax recalcitrant politicians into an agreement on a constitution for Gran Colombia similar to that of Bolivia. Bolívar died in 1830, and in 1831 Gran Colombia divided into its component parts of Colombia, Venezuela, Ecuador, and (later) Panama.

Simon Bolivar, Letter to General Juan Jose Flores, November 9, 1830 ("Ploughing the Sea")

Caudillo Rule   Independent Venezuela became the politically most turbulent Latin American republic. In Carácas, the capital, caudillos from the landowning Creole families displaced each other at a rapid rate. The main issue that kept rival factions at odds was federalism versus tighter central control, with at least one all-out war being fought over the issue during the 1860s.

Venezuela's neighboring countries followed a similar pattern of caudillo politics. Though enjoying longer periods of stability, Colombia—the name adopted in 1861 to replace that of New Granada—also saw a continuing struggle between federalists and centralizers. Panamanian rebels took advantage of the tumult to establish an independent state of Panama in 1903, supported by the United States.

After independence, the administration of Theodore Roosevelt (1901–1909) concluded a treaty with the new country granting the United States control of land for the completion of the Panama Canal.

The Andean States   As with the other new states in South America, it took decades for Peru, Bolivia, and Chile to work out territorial conflicts and complete their respective patterns of state formation. One of these conflicts was the War of the Pacific from 1879 to 1884, resulting in a victorious Chile annexing Peruvian and Bolivian lands. Most devastating for Peru was the destruction that Chilean troops wrought in southern Peru.

Political stability for several decades returned under the presidency of Nicolás de Piérola, who introduced a few reforms during his terms (1879–1881 and 1895–1899). The two most important ones were the stabilization of the monetary system and the professionalization of the army. As the presidency from this time until the 1920s was held by men from the upper landowning Creole class, this Peruvian period is often called the period of the "Aristocratic Republic."

Independence and Political Development in the North: Mexico

In contrast to the central Spanish colony of New Granada, the viceroyalty of New Spain (Mexico and Mesoamerica) had few inhabitants of African descent and large numbers of indigenous Americans. Therefore, mestizos and Amerindians had prominent roles in the political development of the nineteenth century. As in the

Land and Liberty. This enormous mural by Diego Rivera (1886–1957), in the National Palace in Mexico City, shows Father Hidalgo above the Mexican eagle, flanked by other independence fighters. Above them are Emiliano Zapata, Pancho Villa, and other heroes of the Revolution of 1910. The other parts of the mural show historical scenes from the Spanish conquest to the twentieth century.

image analysis

other viceroyalties, however, conservative landowning Creoles were dominant in the political process. Only toward the end of the 1800s did urban white, mestizo, and Amerindian residents acquire a voice. Landless rural laborers entered the political stage in the early twentieth century, during the Mexican Revolution.

The Mexican Uprising   In 1810, Miguel Hidalgo y Costilla (1753–1811), the son of a Creole hacienda estate administrator and his Creole wife, declared his loyalty to the deposed king of Spain, Fernando VII, and launched a movement in opposition to the viceroyalty and its colonial military. A churchman since his youth, Hidalgo was broadly educated, well versed in Enlightenment literature, conversant in Nahuatl, and on the margins of strict Catholicism. As a young adult, he became a parish priest and devoted himself to creating employment opportunities for Amerindians in a province southeast of Mexico City.

Under the leadership of Hidalgo, thousands of poor Creoles, mestizos, and Amerindians marched on Guanajuato (in south-central Mexico). Initially, they were successful in defeating the Spanish troops marching against them, but they were indiscriminate in their looting and killing of both Spaniards and Creoles. Hidalgo, shocked by the violence, called off an attack on Mexico City, and the rebellion was eventually defeated in 1811. Colonial Spanish forces ultimately captured and executed Hidalgo.

War of Independence   After the defeat, associates of Hidalgo failed to make a comeback in the heartland around Mexico City. Here, royalists intent on preserving the union between Spain and Mexico after the return of Fernando VII to power in 1813 remained supreme. In 1813, Hidalgist nationalist rebels adopted a program for independence that envisioned a constitutional government, abolished slavery, and declared all native-born inhabitants of New Spain "Americans." A year later they promulgated a constitution providing for a strong legislature and a weak executive. Both program and constitution, however, still awaited the conclusion of the civil war between nationalists and royalists for their implementation.

The war ended in 1821 with Mexico's independence, based on a compromise between the nationalist Vicente Guerrero (1782–1831) and the royalist Agustín de Iturbide (1783–1824). According to the compromise, Mexico was to become an independent constitutional "empire" (in view of New Spain extending to Mesoamerica), give full citizenship rights to all inhabitants regardless of race and ethnicity, and adhere to Catholicism.

Iturbide became Mexico's first ruler, with the title "emperor," but abdicated in 1823 after a military uprising. By that time, Mexico was no longer an empire, and with a new constitution in 1824, Mexico became a republic. As in other parts of Latin America during the period of early independence, politics remained unstable, pitting federalists and centralists against each other. Centralists eventually triumphed and, for a long period under the caudillo Antonio López de Santa Anna (in office 1833–1836 and 1839–1845), maintained authoritarian rule until 1855.

Northern Mexico and the Comanches

The nominal northern territories of Mexico—Texas, New Mexico, and California—were inhabited by numerous Native American peoples, among whom the Comanches were the most powerful. They had acquired horses during the Pueblo Revolt (1680) against

Revolutionary Women.
Women, such as these *soldaderas* taking rifle practice, played many significant roles in the Mexican Revolution, 1910–1920.

Spain, and as migrants, adapted more readily to horse-breeding and contraband firearms than other, more settled Native American peoples.

In the course of the mid-1700s, the Comanches built an empire from the Arkansas River to just north of San Antonio. They raided into New Mexico and maintained a flourishing trade of horses, cattle, bison hides, and enslaved war captives, including blacks, on their borders. In the last decades of Spanish rule, colonial reformers dispatched troops to check the Comanche expansion. But during the war of Mexican independence, Comanche raids resumed and wiped out the recent gains.

Northern Immigration

To make the northern borderlands more secure against the Comanches, beginning in the early 1820s Mexico supported immigration from the United States. At the same time, the United States entered a period of growth. Settlement of the formerly French Ohio and Mississippi valleys moved quickly. Demand for American cotton in British and American factories drove expansion into Alabama, Mississippi, Louisiana, and Arkansas. Cotton exhausted the soil, and the availability of cheap land made it more efficient to abandon depleted lands and push the realm of "King Cotton" ever westward.

Many US citizens emigrated to Mexico, especially the Mexican province of Texas, to take advantage of its generous land policy and autonomy. While Mexico had outlawed slavery, most slave owners who migrated to Texas ignored these restrictions. The violation of the antislavery laws and the swelling numbers of immigrants to Texas alarmed the Mexican national government by the 1830s.

The US–Mexico War

In 1836, the Mexican president Antonio López de Santa Anna led some 4,000 troops against the militias maintained by the Texans. At first, these troops were successful, decimating Texan militiamen and US volunteers defending the Alamo, a fort near San Antonio. But then Texan forces defeated Santa Anna, and the state declared its independence (1836). Mexico refused to recognize Texas, and nine years later Texas opted for the security of union with the United States. It also settled with the Comanches in 1844 for an end to the raiding.

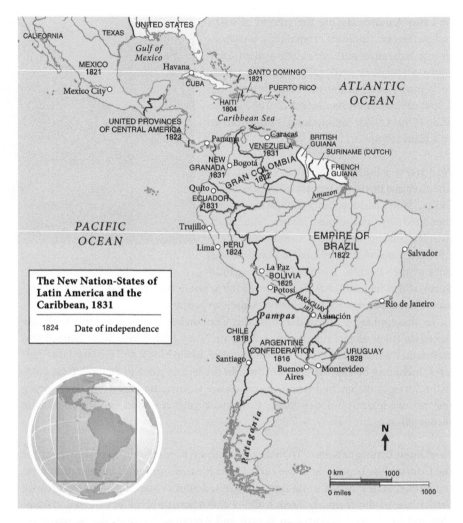

MAP 23.1 **The New Nation-States of Latin America and the Caribbean, 1831.**

The other northern territories of Mexico had also suffered debilitating devastations from Comanche raids. As a result, the government found it impossible to defend itself effectively in 1846 when the United States declared war on Mexico over a Texas border dispute. Within two years, Santa Anna's troops were defeated and Mexico was forced to give up over half of its territory (see Map 23.2).

The French Interlude in Mexico   Santa Anna fell from power, and in 1857 liberals introduced a new constitution that reaffirmed federalism, guaranteed individual liberties, and separated church and state. The conservatives in Mexico detested this new constitution and waged the "Reform War" (1857–1861) to abolish it. They lost, and the liberals elected Benito Juárez (1861–1864) president, the first Amerindian to accede to the office.

Juárez soon discovered that Mexico's financial reserves were depleted, obliging him to suspend payment on the state debt. International reaction was swift, with British, Spanish, and French forces seizing the customs house in the port city of Veracruz in 1861, making a mockery of the US Monroe Doctrine of 1823, according to which no foreign intervention would be tolerated in the Americas. Not wishing to violate the pan-American opposition to European intervention with a prolonged occupation, Britain and Spain withdrew their forces quickly.

The French, however, stayed. Louis-Napoleon III Bonaparte, the self-declared emperor, seized on the debt issue and set in motion an ambitious plan of imposing a pliable ruler in the country. In 1862, he provided military backing to the Austrian prince Maximilian, who installed himself as the emperor of Mexico (1864–1867).

With the defeat of the Confederate states in the US Civil War in April 1865, however, Maximilian's position became precarious. In 1866, aided by the US government, an uprising broke out in Mexico. Maximilian was cut off from any hope of quick support from France. The liberal forces defeated him and executed him by firing squad in 1867.

Díaz's Long Peace   Peace arrived with the withdrawal of most US government troops from Texas and the rise of Mexico's next caudillo, Porfirio Díaz (in office 1876–1880 and 1884–1911).

MAP 23.2 **Mexico's Loss of Territory to the United States, 1824–1854.**

Mexico, 1824–1854

- —— Boundary of Mexico, 1824
- Texas, independent republic 1836–45, 1845 to US
- Ceded 1845, 1850
- Ceded by Treaty of Guadalupe Hidalgo, 1848
- Ceded 1853 (Gadsden Purchase)
- Mexico, 1854

The Execution of Emperor Maximilian of Mexico, June 19, 1867. Édouard Manet has been characterized as the "inventor of modernity," not only for his technique but for the way he portrayed events, even significant political events, in a calm and composed manner. The soldiers who dispatch the hapless emperor come across as casual and professional—what they are doing is ordinary day's work.

This period also coincided with the defeat of the last Amerindians north of the border and the settlement and development of the American West.

Like his contemporary, President Jose Balmeceda of Chile, Díaz favored infrastructural and industrial development. Rail, telegraph, and telephone systems were laid; textile factories and heavy industries were set up; oil was produced in quantity; and agricultural improvements were made. Overall, the economy expanded by 6 percent annually during the Porfiriato, as the period of Díaz's government was called.

Much of Díaz's conservative stability was built on the faction of Creole landowners with whom Díaz had come to power. This faction had grown through the addition of groups of technocrat administrators (*científicos*), financiers, land speculators, and industrialists. The Porfiriato regime was marked by corruption; officials sought self-enrichment while disregarding the law and even resorting to physical violence.

The number of critics among the urban and professional classes rose steadily, however, as they found themselves excluded from economic or even political participation. They demanded a return to the constitution of 1857, but they were arrested, beaten, and exiled as the Porfiriato became increasingly repressive.

Critics also arose among the working classes, who were prohibited from forming trade unions and carrying out strikes. In the early 1900s, an aging Díaz faced an increasingly restless urban population.

The countryside, where the large majority of Mexicans still lived and worked, was just as restless. Ever since colonial times, there had been a profound division between Creole estate (*hacienda*) owners and mestizo and Amerindian rurals. For most of the 1800s, the economy of the countryside had been typified by self-sufficiency: Nearly everything was produced and consumed there, as transportation costs were prohibitive.

But with the construction of the railroad system under Díaz, transportation costs plummeted. Hacienda landlords could now produce crops for the market, and they appropriated farmland from Amerindian villagers who could not show legal titles to the land.

photograph of two *hacendado* (late nineteenth century)

The Early Mexican Revolution Although the elections of 1910 had once more been manipulated in favor of Díaz, the president had declared in 1908 that he would like to have an opposition party in Mexico. Liberals, encouraged, had found a candidate.

This candidate was Francisco Madero (1873–1913), who was committed to the social justice proclaimed in the 1857 constitution. Madero refused to recognize the election and called on the middle classes, working classes, and peasants to rise up against Díaz. By mentioning the right of workers to organize in trade unions and of peasants to receive their own plots of land, he opened the floodgates for revolution.

Among the first to respond was Francisco "Pancho" Villa (1878–1923), a muleteer-cum-cattle rustler who led a rebellion in the northern state of Chihuahua. Another rebel leader was Emiliano Zapata (1879–1919), head of a village in the state of Morelos in south-central Mexico, who had begun with his *campesinos* (tenant farmers, laborers, and village peasants) to occupy sugar plantations and distribute plantation land to them. Victories of Villa and Zapata against federal troops persuaded Díaz to step down in May 1911 and leave for exile in France.

Madero was sworn in as the new president, but it was soon evident that his vision for a constitutional revolution was incompatible with the revolutions pursued by Zapata and Villa. Madero was driven into the arms of Porfiriato officers who, supported by the US government, were nervous about the events in Mexico. The officers, however, deposed and executed him in February 1913.

The Later Revolution Power in Mexico was now disputed between the Porfiriato reactionaries in Mexico City and the Constitutionalists (those faithful to the liberal constitution of 1857) in the wealthy states along the US border. Constitutionalists were opposed to land distribution, but they needed more troops to overthrow the reactionaries. The Constitutionalists, Pancho Villa, and Emiliano Zapata, therefore, forged an alliance that made Venustiano Carranza (1859–1920), from a wealthy but liberal Creole family, their leader. Together, they ended the reactionary regime in Mexico City in July 1914.

Once in power, the Constitutionalists dissolved the reactionary federal army but then broke apart over the issue of land reform. Villa and Zapata, at the head of the pro-reform majority, entered Mexico City but failed to form a functional central government. The working classes and their union representatives threw their support to Álvaro Obregón (1880–1928), a rising commander among the Constitutionalists who had been opposed to Díaz. After the departure of Villa and Zapata for their home states, Obregón entered Mexico City in February 1915.

The Constitutionalists remained deeply divided between a policy of a constitutional revolution under a strong central government with a modest land and labor reform program and a policy of agrarian revolutions in autonomous states. The supporters of the constitutional revolution gained the initiative when Obregón succeeded in driving Villa from power. Carranza followed up by having Zapata eliminated.

Carranza, in office as president of Mexico from 1915 to 1920, removed agrarian revolutionaries from their states and villages and ended all land distributions. But Obregón, more sympathetic to labor and land reform, challenged Carranza for the presidency in the next elections. With the support of the Constitutional army he forced Carranza to surrender and ended the Mexican Revolution late in 1920.

The Mexican Revolution expanded the constitutional process to the urban middle class, workers, farmers, and villagers by bringing about real social and economic gains for men and women other than the landowners. All this happened at tremendous human cost, but by 1920 the Mexican nation was much more cohesive than it had been a century earlier.

Emiliano Zapata and Fellow Revolutionaries in Mexico City, June 4, 1911. Shortly after the fall of Díaz, his opponents Madero, Villa, and Zapata (seated, second from left) entered Mexico City in triumph, to celebrate the end of the regime of Díaz. But already by June 8, Zapata and Madero disagreed on the issue of land reform. The moderate Madero wanted to halt it; Zapata wanted to continue it in his state of Morelos. This disagreement, among other internal rifts in the revolutionary camp, was responsible for the revolution dragging on to 1920.

Platform of the "Socio Political Reform Program of the Revolution," Cuernavaca, Mexico, October 26, 1915

Latin American Society and Economy
in the Nineteenth Century

Independence meant both disruptions and continuities in the economy as well as in politics. In Spanish and Portuguese America, 5 colonial regions eventually became

Patterns Up Close | Slave Rebellions in Cuba and Brazil

Blacks had gained little from the American and French Revolutions, and the pattern of brutal exploitation continued in the Americas. Not surprisingly, therefore, blacks sought to emulate the example of Haiti's successful slave revolt during the first half of the 1800s. However, none of those subsequent revolts were any more successful than previous revolts had been in the 1700s, as a look at rebellions in Cuba and Brazil during the first half of the nineteenth century shows.

In Cuba, the decline of sugar production in Haiti during the revolution encouraged the expansion of plantations and the importation of African slaves. As previously in Haiti, a diversified eighteenth-century society of whites, free mulattoes,

Slave Revolt Aboard Ship. Rebellions aboard ship, such as the famous 1839 mutiny aboard the *Amistad* shown here, were common occurrences. The Amistad was engaged in intra-American slave trafficking, and the slaves overpowered the crew shortly after embarkation in Cuba. After protracted legal negotiations, the slaves were eventually freed and returned to Africa.

21 independent republics, organized around the pattern of constitutionalism. Deep divisions persisted between the small landowning elites and the urban masses, and the Creole landowning elite made participation of the urban classes in the constitutional process increasingly difficult. When trade with Europe resumed, this elite was primarily interested in the export of mineral and agricultural commodities, from which it reaped the most benefits (see Map 23.3).

Rebuilding Societies and Economies

Reconstruction in the independent Spanish-speaking republics and the Brazilian monarchy took several decades. It was only by mid-century that Latin America had overcome the after-effects of the wars of independence.

After Independence The achievement of independence in the 1820s brought an end to Spain's mercantilist monopoly, weak as it had been. The Latin American republics were free to buy or sell and to borrow money anywhere in the world. Initially, however, for Latin Americans the freedom to trade was more hope than reality.

and blacks, as well as urban and rural black slaves, was transformed into a heavily African-born plantation slave society. The black freedman José Antonio Aponte (ca. 1756–1812), a militiaman and head of the Yoruba confraternity in Havana, led an abortive revolt in 1812 that drew support from both sectors. In the subsequent revolts of 1825, 1835, and 1843, the urban element was less evident. Authorities and planters unleashed a campaign of sweeping arrests of free blacks and mulattoes that cut the urban–rural link once and for all.

Brazil, like Cuba, also benefited from the collapse of sugar production on Haiti. It expanded its plantation sector and imported slaves from Africa. But here distrust divided those born in Africa from Brazilian-born slaves, freedmen, and mulattoes. Many freedmen and mulattoes served in the militias that the authorities used to suppress the revolts. Furthermore, in contrast to the island of Cuba, plantation slaves could run away more easily to independent settlements in the Brazilian interior, from where revolts were more easily organized than in cities or on plantations.

Two urban revolts of the period were remarkable for their exceptional mix of insurgents. The first was the Tailor's Rebellion of 1798 in Salvador, Bahia's capital. Freedmen, mulattoes, and white craftspeople cooperated against the Creole oligarchy. The second was the Muslim uprising of 1835, organized by African-born freedmen as well as slaves who had been educated as Islamic clerics in West Africa before their enslavement.

Questions

- Do the slave rebellions in Cuba and Brazil in the early nineteenth century confirm or complicate the pattern of slave revolutions that was manifested first in Haiti?
- What role did geography play in the success or failure of a revolution?

Capital had fled the continent and left behind uncultivated estates and flooded mines. The Catholic Church held huge, uncollectable debts. In many areas taxes could not be collected. Troops helped themselves to payment through plunder. On average, it took until around 1850 for Latin America to fully recover.

Constitutional Nationalism and Society   The Creoles were in many countries the leaders in the wars of independence, and the most powerful among them were large landowners. Independence did not produce much change in agrarian relations: Landowners of self-sufficient estates and plantations continued to employ tenant farmers and slaves. Their interpretation of constitutionalism tended toward *caudillismo*—that is, the same kind of authoritarian and paternalistic form of action that they practiced on their estates.

The majority of the Creoles, however, were not landowners but people who made their money in the cities. They were urban administrators, professionals, craftspeople, and laborers. Their leaders, ardent constitutional nationalists, tended toward political and economic liberalism. In many countries they were joined by

contrasting worlds: photographs of a cholo family, Mexico, and the Rambla at Mar del Plata, Argentina (early twentieth century)

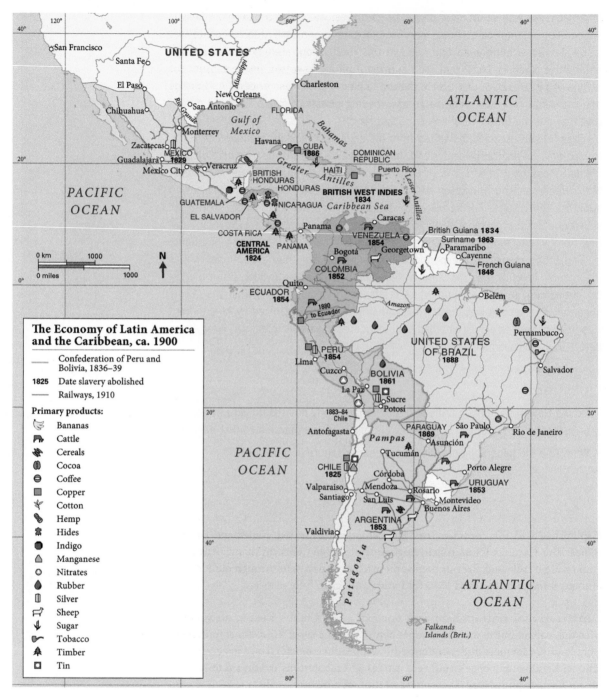

MAP 23.3 **The Economy of Latin America and the Caribbean, ca. 1900.**

map analysis

mestizos, mulattoes, and black freedmen. The main issue dividing the conservatives and liberals in the early years of independence was the extent of voting rights: Conservatives sought to limit the vote to a minority of males through literacy and property requirements, while liberals wanted to extend it to all males. No influential group considered extending voting rights to women.

Political Divisions   Once independence was won, distrust between the two groups set in, and the political consensus fell apart. Accordingly, landed constitutional conservatives restricted voting rights, to the detriment of the urban constitutional liberals. Nevertheless, the expansion of constitutionalism from the landowning oligarchy to larger segments of the population remained a goal for many, especially urban intellectuals and political activists.

Split over State–Church Relations   Conservatives and liberals were especially divided over the relationship between state and church. Initially, Catholicism remained the national religion for all, and education and extensive property remained under church control, as guaranteed by the constitutions.

But the new republics ended the powers of the Inquisition and claimed the right to name bishops. At the behest of Spain, however, the pope left bishoprics empty rather than agreeing to this new form of lay investiture. In fact, Rome would not even recognize the independence of the Latin American nations until the mid-1830s. The conflict was aggravated by the church's focus on its institutional rather than pastoral role.

This hostility of the church was thus one of the factors that in the mid-1800s contributed to a swing back to liberalism, beginning with Colombia in 1849. Many countries adopted a formal separation between church and state and introduced secular educational systems. But the state–church issue remained bitter, especially in Mexico, Guatemala, Ecuador, and Venezuela, where it was often at the center of political shifts between liberals and conservatives.

Economic Recovery   Given the shifts of leadership between conservatives and liberals during the period of recovery after independence (ca. 1820–1850), the reconstruction of a coherent fiscal system to support the governments was difficult to accomplish. For example, governments often resorted to taxation of trade, even if this interfered with declared policies of free trade.

This maneuvering had little effect on the domestic economy, which represented the great bulk of economic activities in Latin America. Grain production on large estates and small farms had escaped the turbulence of the independence war and recovery periods. The distribution of marketable surpluses declined, however, given the new internal borders in Latin America with their accompanying tariffs and export taxes. Self-sufficiency agriculture, and the local economies relying on it, thus remained largely unchanged throughout the 1800s.

The crafts workshops, especially for textiles, suffered from the arrival of cheap British factory-produced cottons. Their impact, however, remained relatively limited to coastal areas. Although there was an awareness in most countries of the benefits of factories, using domestic resources, and linking the agricultural sector to modern industrial development, the necessity of developing a manufacturing industry was not demonstrated until later in the nineteenth century.

Export-Led Growth

The pursuit of a policy of commodity exports—export-led growth—from about 1850 led to rises in the standard of living for many Latin Americans. The industrializing countries in Europe and North America were consumers of Latin American minerals as well as its tropical agricultural products. Productivity was limited, however, by a chronic labor shortage.

religious procession, Mexico, early twentieth century

meatpacking plant, Uruguay, early twentieth century

Raw Materials and Cash Crops   Mining and agricultural cash crop production recovered gradually, so that by the 1850s nearly all Latin American governments had adopted export-led economic growth as their basic policy. Mexican and Peruvian silver production became strong again, although the British adoption of the gold standard in 1821 imposed limits on silver exports. Peru found a partial replacement for silver with guano, which was used as an organic fertilizer and as a source of nitrates for explosives. Chile benefited from guano, nitrate, and copper exports, of crucial importance during the second Industrial Revolution in Germany and the United States.

In other Latin American countries, tropical and subtropical cash crops defined export-led economic growth during the mid-1800s. In Brazil, Colombia, and Costa Rica, coffee growing redefined the agricultural sector. In Argentina, the production of jerked (dried) beef refashioned the ranching economy. Cuba, which remained a Spanish colony until 1898, profited from the relocation of sugarcane plantations from the mainland and Caribbean islands after the British outlawing of the slave trade (1807) and slavery itself (1834) as well as the Latin American wars of independence (1810–1826).

However, cane sugar had a limited future, given the rise of beet sugar production in Europe. While minerals and cash crops were excellent for export-led economic growth, competition on the world market increased during the 1800s, and thus there was ultimately a ceiling, which was reached in the 1890s.

Broadening of Exports   With a focus on mineral and agricultural exports, Latin American governments responded quickly to the increased market opportunities resulting from the Industrial Revolution in Great Britain, the European continent, and the United States. Luxuries from tropical Latin America joined sugar after 1850 in becoming affordable mass consumer items in the industrialized countries. This commodity diversification met not only the broadened demand of the second Industrial Revolution but also the demand for consumer goods among the newly affluent middle classes.

Since the choice among minerals and crops was limited, however, most nations remained wedded to one commodity only. Only two, Argentina and Peru, were able to diversify. They were more successful at distributing their exports over the four main industrial markets of Great Britain, Germany, France, and the United States. Given its own endowments and under the conditions of world trade in the second half of the nineteenth century, the continent's trade was relatively well diversified.

The prices of all Latin American commodities fluctuated substantially during the second half of the nineteenth century, in contrast to the imported manufactured goods, which became cheaper over time. In fact, Brazil's government was so concerned about fluctuating coffee prices in the 1890s that it regulated the amount of coffee offered on the world market, carefully adjusting production to keep market prices relatively stable.

late nineteenth-century photos of Brazilian coffee pickers and farmhands on a Costa Rican banana plantation

Rising Living Standards   In the period from the middle of the 1800s to the eve of World War I, Latin American governments were successful with their choice of export-led growth as their consensus policy. Living standards rose, as measured in gross domestic product (GDP). At various times during 1850–1900, between five and eight Latin American countries kept pace with the living standards in the industrialized countries. Thus, although many politicians were aware that at some point their countries would have to industrialize in addition to relying on commodity export growth, they kept their faith in exports as the engine for improved living standards right up to World War I.

Labor and Immigrants As in the industrialized countries, the profitability of exports was achieved by keeping wages low. Latin America experienced high population increases during the 1800s, although the population remained small in comparison to the populations of Europe, Africa, and Asia. The increases were not large enough to alter the favorable land–person ratio, and the high demand for labor continued during the 1800s. This demand was the reason why the institution of forced labor—revolving labor duties (*mit'a*) among Amerindians in the Andes and slavery—had come into existence in the first place.

Mit'a and slavery continued during the 1800s, liberal constitutionalism notwithstanding, in a number of countries. Even where forced labor was abolished, low wages continued. One would have expected wages to rise rapidly, given the continuing conditions of labor shortage and land availability. Mine operators and landowners, however, were reluctant to raise wages because they feared for the competitiveness of their commodities on the world market. Labor shortages were so severe that governments resorted to measures of selective mass immigration, in order to enlarge the labor pool.

Typical examples of selective immigration were *coolies* (from Urdu *kuli*, hireling)—that is, indentured laborers recruited from India and China. During 1847–1874, nearly half a million Indians traveled to various European colonies in the Caribbean. Similarly, 235,000 Chinese came to Peru, Cuba, and Costa Rica, working in guano pits and silver mines, on sugar and cotton plantations, and later on railroads. Only about 10 percent of the coolies returned home. Coolie migration

Dining Hall for Recently Arrived Immigrants, Buenos Aires. Immigrants, all male, and more than likely all Spanish and Italian, rub shoulders sometime around 1900 in a dining hall in Buenos Aires set up for newly arrived immigrants. By 1914, 20 percent of the population of Argentina had been born in Spain and another 20 percent in Italy.

to Latin America was a part of the pattern of massive migration streams across the world that typified the nineteenth century (see Map 23.4).

Immigration to Latin America from Europe was more regular, and on a much bigger scale. In Argentina, Uruguay, Brazil, and Chile, Italians and Spaniards settled in large numbers from around 1870 on. Most immigrants settled in cities, and Buenos Aires became the first city on the continent with more than a million people. Only here did a semiregular labor market develop, with rising urban and rural wages prior to World War I. Elsewhere in Latin America, governments, beholden to large landowners, feared the rise of cities with immigrant laborers who did not share their interests. Therefore, they opposed mass immigration.

Self-Sufficiency Agriculture   Except for Argentina, Chile, and Uruguay, the levels of commodity exports did not rise sufficiently to reduce the size of the rural labor force engaged in self-sufficiency farming—a major condition for improved living standards. On the eve of World War I, between two-thirds and half of the laborers in most Latin American countries were still employed as tenant farmers or farmhands on large estates. Export-led growth—even though it looked like an effective economic driver—did not have much of a transformative effect on the rural masses in most countries.

Governments paid greater attention to the improvement of rural infrastructures from about 1870 onward, with the development of railroads. Almost everywhere, they looked to direct foreign investment. The foreign investors or consortiums built these railroads primarily for the transportation of commodities to ports. Many self-sufficiency farmers and even landlords, therefore, received little encouragement to produce more food staples for urban markets inland. Overall, the Latin American railroad network represented only about one-fifth to one-third of that in other Western developing settler countries.

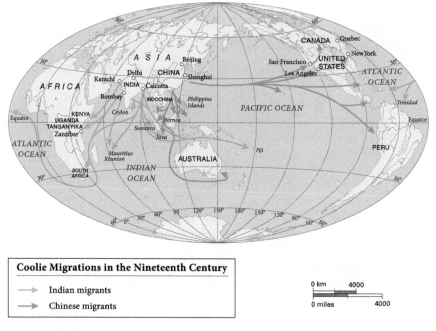

Coolie Migrations in the Nineteenth Century

→   Indian migrants

→   Chinese migrants

0 km   4000
0 miles   4000

MAP 23.4 **Non-Western Migrations in the Nineteenth Century**

Factories   Until about 1870, the handicrafts sector met the demands of the rural and low-earning urban populations. This sector failed in most parts of the world during the 1800s and 1900s to mechanize itself and establish a modern factory system. Latin America was no exception. Most crafts shops were based on family labor, unconnected to the landowning elite and deemed too small by lending banks. There was no path from workshops to factories.

However, even entrepreneurial investors interested in building factories were hampered in their efforts. They had little chance of success prior to the appearance of public utilities in the 1880s, providing water during the dry season and electricity as an energy source, in the absence of high-quality coal in most parts of Latin America. Even then, the risk of engaging in manufacturing, requiring long-term strategies with no or low profits, was so great that the typical founders of factories were not Creoles but European immigrants.

In Argentina and Chile these immigrants saved the start-up capital necessary to launch small but modern textile, food-processing, and beverage factories. Prior to World War I, the only country that took the step from consumer goods to capital goods (goods for building and equipping factories) was Mexico. Full capital goods industrialization had to await the postwar period.

Culture, Family, and the Status of Women

Economic growth and urbanization contributed to the growth of constitutionalist modernity in Latin America. But the absence of industrialization until the end of the nineteenth century slowed the transformation of society and its cultural institutions. The influence of the Catholic Church remained pervasive. In the second half of the nineteenth century, however, with the diversification of the urban population, the idea of separating church and state gained adherents, with legal consequences for social institutions.

Role of the Church   In most countries, repeated attempts by governments after independence to reduce the role of the Catholic Church in society remained unsuccessful. In a number of civil codes, women's rights in inheritance and property control improved; but overall, husbands retained their patriarchal rights over their families. Typically, they were entitled to control the family budget, contractual engagements, choice of husbands for their daughters, and the residence of their unmarried daughters. Only after the middle of the nineteenth century did the influence of the Catholic Church diminish sufficiently to allow legislation for secular marriages and divorce in a number of countries.

Family Relations   In Mexico and South America, despite the long-standing proverb *El hombre en la calle, la mujer en la casa* ("Men in the street, women in the home"), it was often the case that the two spheres were intermingled. In urban areas, women frequently ran shops, managed markets, were proprietors of *cantinas*, and performed skilled and unskilled jobs, particularly in the textile and food trades. In rural areas, farm work was often shared by men and women.

As in Europe and North America, there was a remarkably high level of widowhood and spinsterhood. In areas where the predominant form of employment was dangerous—mining, for example—the incidence of widowhood was very high. Widows often could not or chose not to remarry, especially if they had relatives

Mexican woman making tortillas, Mexico, ca. 1900

to fall back on or were left an income. Many middle-class women chose not to marry at all.

Both of these conditions were common enough that by one estimate, one-third of all the households in Mexico City in the early nineteenth century were headed by women. Widows were entitled to their dowries and half of the community property, while boys and girls received equal portions of the inheritance. Thus, despite society's pressures to marry and raise children, many women did not marry or, after becoming widowed, remained single. In this sense, they achieved a considerable degree of autonomy in a male-dominated society.

The Visual and Literary Arts   The trend in nineteenth-century culture under the aegis of Spanish and Portuguese influences after independence was toward "indigenization," an attempt to break away from European art and literary influences. Along with attempts to form national and regional styles of their own, many countries also engaged in art as a nation-building exercise, celebrating new national heroes or famous historic events through portraiture and landscape painting. Finally, there were also periodic engagements with popular or folk arts in celebration of regional uniqueness.

In literature, an indigenous style developed, called *criollo*, for its inception and popularity in the Creole class. Literature often turned to themes befitting countries trying to establish themselves as nations with distinct historic pasts and great future potential. In some cases, critique of the present was the order of the day.

» Putting It All Together

interactive concept map

Today, although political stability is much greater, many parts of Latin America are still poor and underindustrialized. Were Latin American elites, therefore, wrong to engage in a pattern of export-led growth through mineral and agricultural commodities? And did they collude with elites in the industrial countries to maneuver the continent into permanent dependence on the latter? Indeed, scholars in the twentieth century answered the question in the affirmative and wrote the history of the 1800s in condemnatory tones. They called their analysis "dependency theory."

Contemporary historians, however, compare Latin America not with the United States or western Europe but with the settler colonies of South Africa, Australia, and New Zealand or the old empires of the Middle East and Asia. In these comparisons, Latin America does not appear to have been any more dependent on the industrializing countries than the latter were on Latin America.

Dependence increased only at the very end of the 1800s, when industrial countries like the United States and Britain began to make significant capital investments. It was then that foreign companies, such as those that owned railroads in Nicaragua and Honduras, succeeded in exploiting and controlling production and export. The question we may need to ask, then, is not why Latin America failed to industrialize in the 1800s but, rather, whether Latin America made the right decision when it opted for export-led growth up to about 1890. Did such a choice represent a "third way" toward economic growth, separate from industrial capitalism and attempts to keep economies closed off from the vagaries of world trade? Perhaps it did.

Review and Relate

Thinking Through Patterns

Examine the ways historians approach the big questions of this chapter.

S imilar to the United States and France, which also underwent revolutions in the late 1700s and early 1800s, Latin America's independence movements (1810–1824) did not extend the constitutional revolution beyond a small number of elite property owners. The dominant class of large landlords and plantation owners was conservative and did not favor land reform for the benefit of small farmers. Urban professionals and craftspeople, divided in many places by ethnicity, did not share interests that allowed them to provide an effective opposition to the landed class. Landowning and plantation interests thus protected themselves through authoritarian caudillo politics and sought to keep the opposition weak.

>> **Which factors in the complex ethnic and social structures of Latin America were responsible for the emergence of authoritarian politicians?**

I n colonial times, Latin America sent its mineral and agricultural commodities to Europe. When it acquired its independence and Europe industrialized during the 1800s, these commodities became even more important, and the continent opted for a pattern of export-led development. This meant the systematic increase of mineral and agricultural commodity exports, with rising living standards not only for those who profited directly from the exports but also for many in the urban centers. But even with rising living standards, it became clear by the turn of the century that a supplementary policy of industrialization had to be pursued.

>> **Why did Latin American countries, after achieving independence, opt for a continuation of mineral and agricultural commodity exports?**

M any countries in Latin America are barely richer than they were in the 1800s. Even though industry, mineral and commodity exports, and services expanded in urban centers in the early part of the twentieth century, poor farmers with low incomes continued to be a drag on development. This phenomenon still characterizes many parts of Latin America today.

>> **How do the social and economic structures of this period continue to affect the course of Latin America today?**

Against the Grain

Consider this as a counterpoint to the main patterns examined in this chapter.

Early Industrialization in Chile?

I n the early 1880s, Chilean businessmen explored the idea of moving away from exclusive reliance on the export of coal and copper, as world market prices for those commodities fluctuated widely, and turning instead to industrialization. They founded

• Why and how does rapid urbanization create the demand for industrialization?

- Was Balmaceda too progressive for the Chilean Creole class? Should he have attempted a different course?

the Society for the Stimulation of Manufacturing in 1883, with the purpose of building factories for the transformation of raw materials into finished goods. Their ideas turned into a concrete governmental program under the presidency of José Manuel Balmaceda Fernández (1886–1891), who in 1888 created a ministry for industry and public works.

Chile had experienced a substantial population increase during 1875–1885. The urban population had grown even faster, rising from half to two-thirds the size of the rural population during the same time. Farmers and farmhands were drawn to the mining cities of the north, with their nitrate deposits. Other cities had grown near the existing coal and copper mines farther south. Santiago, Valparaíso, and Concepción had evolved into major urban centers. Although farming still supported the majority of Chileans, urban employments had risen greatly in numbers and importance.

Balmaceda's new ministry for industry and public works engaged in a massive investment program in education, railroads, ports, armaments, and naval ships, financed with the revenue from mining exports, including the northern nitrates. Keeping at least a portion of these nitrates in the country and making them the foundation for a chemical industry became a new option. The second Industrial Revolution had begun during the 1860s in Germany and the United States on the basis of nitrates, crucial for many transformative industries absorbing the urban population of unskilled and skilled laborers.

Unfortunately, Balmaceda's program of import-substitution industrialization fell apart as soon as 1891, without any outside intervention. Perhaps Balmaceda's investment program was too much, introduced too fast. Favoritism in appointments and corruption among officeholders aroused opposition not only among the conservative Creole landowners but also among dissident liberals who disliked Balmaceda's imperious style. The opposition unleashed a civil war, in which Balmaceda was deposed. The indigenous industrialization program ended, apparently still too weak against the dominant policy of export-led economic growth based on mineral extraction.

Key Terms

◁))

audio flashcards

Caudillo   534

Import-substitution Industrialization   533

Southern Cone   529

For additional resources, please go to
www.oup.com/us/vonsivers.
Please see the Further Resources section at the back of the book for additional readings and suggested websites.

The Challenge of Modernity

EAST ASIA

In Asia, our two countries, China and Japan, are the closest neighbors, and moreover have the same [written] language. How could we be enemies? Now for the time being we are fighting each other, but eventually we should work for permanent friendship . . . so that our Asiatic yellow race will not be encroached upon by the white race of Europe.

So commented the Chinese statesman Li Hongzhang to his Japanese counterpart, Ito Hirobumi, as they discussed terms to end the Sino–Japanese War in the Japanese town of Shimonoseki in the spring of 1895. Li was China's most powerful advocate of *self-strengthening*—using new foreign technologies and concepts to preserve China's Confucian society in the face of European and American intrusion. Now he was forced to go to Japan to sue for peace as Japanese troops occupied Korea and southern Manchuria.

For Ito, one of the architects of Japan's rise to power, the victory over China was tinged with sadness. He responded: "Ten years ago when I was at Tientsin [Tianjin], I talked about reform with [you]. . . . Why is it that up to now not a single thing has been changed or reformed? This I deeply regret." This feeling was shared by Li, whose reply betrays a weary bitterness at China's deteriorating position: "At that time when I heard you . . . I was overcome

EAST ASIA
1750–1900

ABOVE: A print depicting Japanese soldiers crushing Chinese troops during the Sino-Japanese War (1894–1895), which completely changed the relationship between these two empires.

Seeing Patterns

≫ What was the impact of Western imperialism on the "regulated societies" of China and Japan?

≫ Why did European empire building in Asia have such dramatically different effects on China and Japan?

≫ How have historians seen the nature of these outside forces and their influences in East Asia?

with admiration . . . [at] your having vigorously changed your customs in Japan so as to reach the present stage. Affairs in my country have been so confined by tradition that I could not accomplish what I desired. . . . I am ashamed of having excessive wishes and lacking the power to fulfill them."

The new Treaty of Shimonoseki imposed a crippling indemnity on the Qing, reduced Korea to a client state, and annexed the island of Taiwan. It also called for the occupation by Japan of Manchuria's Liaodong Peninsula, which guarded the approaches to Beijing. For the Chinese, this marked the most dramatic and humiliating role reversal of the past 1,500 years. China had always viewed Japan in Confucian terms as a younger brother. Like Korea and Vietnam, Japan was considered to be on the cultural periphery of the Chinese world, acculturating to Chinese institutions and following Chinese examples in those things considered "civilized." Now, after barely a generation of exposure to Euro-American influence, Japan had eclipsed China as a military power and threatened to extend its sway throughout the region.

The new order in East Asia brought about by the Sino–Japanese War underscores the larger effects of one of the most momentous patterns of world history: the phenomenon of imperialism growing from the innovations that created scientific–industrial society. In less than a century, European countries and their offshoots—and now Japan—expanded their power so rapidly that on the eve of World War I in 1914 more than 85 percent of the world's people were under their control or influence. How were countries like Japan able to resist and adapt to the broad forces of modernity, while China struggled to cope with its effects through most of the nineteenth and twentieth centuries?

China and Japan in the Age of Imperialism

The reign of the Qing emperor Qianlong (r. 1736–1795) marked the period in which the first hints appeared of trouble to come. Soon after Qianlong stepped down from the throne in 1795, a Buddhist sect called the White Lotus sparked a rebellion that took years to suppress. Less obvious, but perhaps more debilitating for the agrarian imperial order as a whole, were the new directions in economics. China's efforts to retain close control over its export trade in luxury goods coupled with efforts to eradicate the lucrative but illegal opium trade created a crisis with Great Britain in the summer of 1839. This crisis led to the First Opium War, China's first military encounter with the industrializing West.

China and Maritime Trade, 1750–1839

The British government sought to establish diplomatic relations with the Qing in the 1790s. In the summer of 1793, they dispatched Lord George Macartney, an experienced diplomat and colonial governor, to Beijing. He sought to persuade the Qianlong emperor to allow the stationing of diplomatic personnel in the Chinese capital and create a system for the separate handling of ordinary commercial matters and diplomacy. Qianlong, however, rebuffed Macartney's attempts to establish a British embassy. A second British mission in 1816 met with similar results.

Chapter Outline

• **China and Japan in the Age of Imperialism**

• **Economics and Society in Late Qing China**

• **Zaibatsu and Political Parties: Society and Economy in Meiji Japan**

• **Putting It All Together**

The Imbalance of Trade?   Europeans and Americans were anxious to bring the Chinese into their diplomatic system because of the perception that China was benefiting from a huge trade imbalance. Merchants and political economists, convinced that China's control of trade functioned in the same way as European mercantilism, believed that the money paid to Chinese merchants essentially stayed in the "closed" economy of the Qing Empire. However, European merchants offered little that the Chinese needed or wanted.

Thus, by the end of the eighteenth century, European and American traders had become increasingly anxious to find something that Chinese merchants would buy. By the beginning of the nineteenth century, a growing number of merchants were clandestinely turning to a lucrative new commodity, with tragic consequences: opium.

Smugglers and Pirates   By the end of the eighteenth century, the British East India Company's territory in Bengal included a center of medicinal opium production. While company traders were strictly prohibited from carrying opium to China as contraband, some noncompany merchants discovered that they could circumvent Chinese regulations and sell small quantities of the drug for a tidy profit. With success came increased demand, and by the early decades of the nineteenth century, an illicit system of delivery had been set up along the south China coast. Armed ships unloaded their cargoes of opium on sparsely inhabited offshore islands, from which Chinese middlemen picked up the drug and made their rounds on the mainland (see Map 24.1). The profits from this illegal enterprise encouraged piracy along the coast, and the opium trade soon became a major irritant in relations between China and the West.

The relationship that the British East India Company and the government-licensed Chinese merchant guild had developed was increasingly undermined by the new commerce. Moreover, free-trade agitation in England put an end to the East India Company's monopoly on the China trade in 1833. With the monopoly lifted, the number of entrepreneurs seeking quick riches in the opium trade exploded. In

interactive timeline

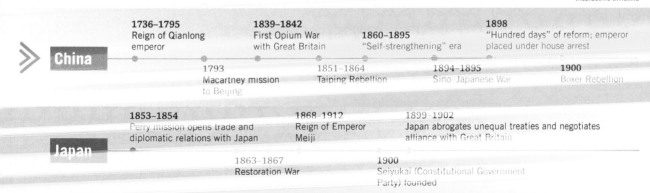

China				
1736–1795 Reign of Qianlong emperor	**1839–1842** First Opium War with Great Britain	**1860–1895** "Self-strengthening" era		**1898** "Hundred days" of reform; emperor placed under house arrest
	1793 Macartney mission to Beijing	**1851–1864** Taiping Rebellion	**1894–1895** Sino-Japanese War	**1900** Boxer Rebellion

Japan			
1853–1854 Perry mission opens trade and diplomatic relations with Japan	**1868–1912** Reign of Emperor Meiji	**1899–1902** Japan abrogates unequal treaties and negotiates alliance with Great Britain	
	1863–1867 Restoration War	**1900** Seiyukai (Constitutional Government Party) founded	

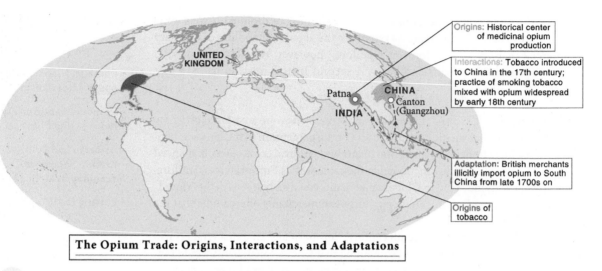

Origins: Historical center of medicinal opium production

Interactions: Tobacco introduced to China in the 17th century; practice of smoking tobacco mixed with opium widespread by early 18th century

Adaptation: British merchants illicitly import opium to South China from late 1700s on

Origins of tobacco

UNITED KINGDOM

Patna

CHINA
Canton (Guangzhou)

INDIA

The Opium Trade: Origins, Interactions, and Adaptations

MAP 24.1 **The Opium Trade: Origins, Interactions, Adaptations.**

map analysis

the foreign trading "factories" in Canton (Gouangzhou), newcomers engaged in the opium trade vied for prestige with older firms involved in legitimate goods.

The push for legitimacy among the opium merchants coincided with an attempt by Westerners to force China to open additional trading ports for legal items. Chinese authorities, however, viewed this Western assertiveness as driven primarily by opium and Christian evangelism.

Far worse, however, were the effects on the ordinary inhabitants of south China as opium usage surged to catastrophic levels. Its addictive properties created a health crisis for tens of thousands, made infinitely worse by the drug's notoriously difficult withdrawal symptoms.

Commissioner Lin Zexu   In the spring of 1839 the Daoguang emperor sent Lin Zexu (1785–1850), a widely respected official, to Canton as an imperial commissioner. Lin, charged with cutting off the opium trade at its source, was given wide-ranging powers to deal with both Chinese and foreign traffickers. In addition to setting up facilities for the recovery of addicts, he demanded that all foreign merchants surrender their opium stocks and sign a pledge that they would not, under penalty of death, deal in the drug anymore.

When the foreign community balked, Lin blockaded the port and withdrew all Chinese personnel from Western firms. The dealers eventually surrendered 20,000 chests of opium, with most also signing the pledge. Following Lin's actions, however, the dealers appealed to the British government for compensation.

In a show of force, the British sent a fleet of warships to Canton to demand reparations for the destroyed opium, pressure the Qing to establish diplomatic relations, and open more ports. When negotiations broke down, a small Chinese squadron sailed out to confront the British men-of-war. The British ships easily scattered the Chinese squadron. Such inauspicious circumstances marked the beginning of the First Opium War (1839–1842) and, with it, a century of foreign intrusion, domination, and ultimately revolution for China.

The Opium Wars and the Treaty Port Era

The hostilities that began in the fall of 1839 between China and Great Britain exposed the growing gap between the military capabilities of industrializing countries and those, like China, whose armed forces had fallen into disuse.

Over the next 2 years, the British attacked and occupied ports along the Chinese coast from Canton to Shanghai at the mouth of the Yangzi River. As the British planned to move north to put pressure on Beijing, Chinese officials opened negotiations in August 1842. The resulting Treaty of Nanjing (Nanking) marked the first of the century's "unequal treaties" that would be imposed throughout East Asia by European powers.

Chinese Opium Smokers. This photograph, taken in the early 1870s, shows the pervasiveness of the opium habit among ordinary Chinese. These men are smoking in the back room of a restaurant, a common practice even in British-controlled Hong Kong.

The Treaty of Nanjing In the Treaty of Nanjing, which ended the First Opium War, the British claimed the island of Hong Kong; levied an indemnity on the Chinese to pay the costs of the war; and forced the Chinese to open the ports of

Steam Power Comes to China. The new technologies of the Industrial Revolution were on painful display in China in 1840 as the British gunboat HMS Nemesis took on provincial warships down the river from Canton. The Nemesis featured an armored hull with a shallow draft put together in detachable sections, steam-powered paddle-wheel propulsion for river fighting, and a large pivot gun to take on shore batteries. Its power and versatility convinced Lin Zexu and a growing number of Chinese officials over the coming decades that China needed, at the very least, the same kinds of "strong ships and effective cannon" if they were to defend their coasts and rivers. By the 1860s the first attempts at such craft were finally under way.

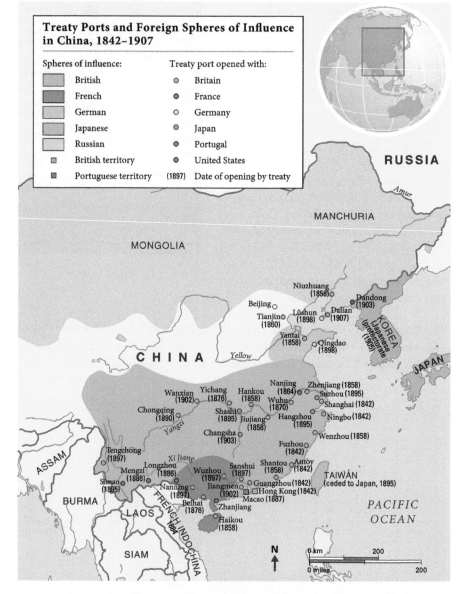

MAP 24.2 **Treaty Ports and Foreign Spheres of Influence in China, 1842–1907.**

Nontariff autonomy: The loss by a country of its right to set its own tariffs.

Shanghai, Ningbo, Fuzhou, and Xiamen (Amoy), in addition to Canton. The British also insisted on **nontariff autonomy:** By treaty the Chinese could now charge no more than a 5 percent tariff on British goods. The British also imposed the policy of **extraterritoriality** in the newly open ports: British subjects who violated Chinese laws would be tried and punished by British consuls.

Extraterritoriality: The immunity of a country's nationals from the laws of their host country.

Similar treaties with France and the United States followed, together with a supplementary treaty with Britain. An important element in these later treaties was the *most-favored nation* clause: Any new concessions granted to one country automatically reverted to those who by treaty were "most-favored nations" (see Map 24.2).

The Taiping Movement, 1851–1864   In addition to the spread of the opium trade to the newly opened ports, long-established trade routes for other items shifted from Guangzhou (Canton) to more convenient outlets. Coastal trade also increased. The economic dislocation that accompanied these changes, along with discontent at the inability of the Qing government to resist foreign demands, made south China particularly volatile. In 1851 the region exploded in rebellion. This largest civil war in world history and its related conflicts would claim as many as 30 million lives.

The catalyst for revolt symbolized the diverse cultural influences penetrating the area. A candidate for the local Confucian examinations, Hong Xiuquan [hung SHI-OO-chwahn] (1813–1864), read some Christian missionary tracts passed on by a colleague. Not long after, he failed the examination for the third time and suffered a nervous breakdown. When he eventually recovered, Hong came to believe in the dreams he had during his illness in which the Christian God had revealed to him that he must now work to bring about the Heavenly Kingdom of Great Peace (*taiping tianguo*) on earth. The movement thus became known as the Taiping Rebellion (sometimes given as "War," "Civil War," or "Revolution") and lasted from 1851 until 1864.

Hong moved into a mountain stronghold and attracted followers from the disillusioned and unemployed, anti-Manchu elements, religious dissidents, and fellow members of south China's Hakka minority. The Hakkas had originally been northerners who migrated south at several points during the turmoil of dynastic changes. They retained their native dialects, did not practice foot binding, often worked marginal farmland, and frequently fortified their villages against attacks by their local southern neighbors. By 1851 Hong and his followers had created a society based on Protestant Christian theology and pre-Confucian Chinese traditions. As a sign that they were no longer loyal to the Qing, the men cut their queues and let the hair grow in on their foreheads, prompting the Qing to refer to them as "the long-haired rebels." The rebels targeted the scholar-gentry in their land seizures and executions, as well as Manchus, Buddhists, Daoists, and other groups they considered heterodox.

By the winter of 1853 the Taipings were narrowly thwarted from driving the Qing from Beijing and were pushed back to central China by imperial forces. For the next decade, however, Hong's movement would remain in control of the Chinese heartland, and the long contest to subdue them would devastate dozens of cities and thousands of towns and villages.

Foreign missionaries and diplomats in China were unsure about the movement's aims. Although Hong talked about instituting Western-style administrative reforms and building a modern industrial base, a powerful Taiping China might throw the new trade arrangements into disarray. Thus, the foreign powers in the end grudgingly elected to continue recognizing the Qing as China's legitimate rulers (see Map 24.3).

MAP 24.3 The Taiping Rebellion, 1851–1864.

Interaction and Adaptation: "Self-Strengthening" and "Western Science and Eastern Ethics"

Most of the important technical innovations taking place in China and Japan during the late eighteenth and most of the nineteenth centuries came from outside East Asia. Confronted by the newly industrialized countries of Europe and America, their possible responses were reaction, reform, and/or revolution. Perhaps most interesting is the middle path of reform taken by both countries in attempting to create a synthesis of Confucian social structures and the best of the new technologies and institutions.

Chinese philosophical concepts tended toward the desire for correlation and the reconciliation of opposites. In this tradition, *ti* and *yong*, or "essence" and "function/application," became the two key terms in the popular self-strengthening formulation *Zhongxue wei ti; Xixue wei yong* ("Chinese studies for the essence; Western studies for the practical application"). Thus, Chinese thinkers were able to acknowledge new foreign technologies using historically and philosophically acceptable terminology. The Japanese were able to justify their own transformation by means of the balanced formula they called "Western science and Eastern ethics."

However, the two sides of the concept were not evenly balanced. As with many Neo-Confucian formulae, the "essence" and "ethics" elements were considered to be primary and the method of implementation—"function"—secondary. Thus, their proponents could argue that their aim was to preserve Confucian society while remaining flexible about the appropriate means of attaining their goals. Opponents, however, argued that the formula could—and eventually would—be reversed: that "function" would eventually degrade the "essence."

The Second Opium War, 1856–1860   At the height of the rebellion in 1856, a new dispute arose between the Qing and the British and French. Britain, France, and the United States all felt by the mid-1850s that the vastly expanded trade in China—and now Japan—called for the opening of still more ports, an end to Qing prohibitions on missionary activity, and diplomatic relations along Western lines. In the wake of an alleged insult to the British flag, hostilities commenced.

The war itself was fought in a localized fashion. In 1858 the Qing court refused a draft treaty. Returning in 1860 with a large expeditionary force, British and French troops advanced to Beijing and drove the emperor from the city. The final treaty stipulated that a dozen ports be opened to foreign trade, that opium be recognized as a legal commodity, that extraterritoriality be expanded, and that foreign embassies be set up in the capital. A newly created Chinese board was to handle Qing foreign relations, and the Chinese were invited to send their own ambassadors abroad.

Self-Strengthening   Although Chinese officials were desperate to roll back the foreign threat and suppress the Taipings, few advocated simply fighting the foreigners. Most felt that over time these new peoples would be assimilated to Chinese

Yet in both China and Japan, one can argue that this has remained a favored approach. The Japanese have made foreign technologies and institutions their own, while retaining Shinto and Buddhist practices alongside social customs still tinged with Neo-Confucianism. Similarly, in China, coupling technological and institutional modernization with an effort to rediscover and preserve what is considered to be the best of traditional Chinese civilization has been the dominant approach. Thus, the present regime pursues a policy of "socialism with Chinese characteristics" in the service of creating what the Communist Party calls "the harmonious society."

Questions

- How were the Chinese and Japanese adaptations to Western innovations similar? How were they different? What do these similarities and differences say about the cultures of these two countries?

- Do you believe that, over the course of time, the "function" of foreign innovations has degraded the "essence" in China and Japan?

Interaction and Adaptation in China and Japan. Weapons on display at the Nanjing Arsenal in 1868 include an early Gatling-type rotary machine gun and a pyramid of round explosive shells (a). An 1890 lithograph of a Japanese seamstress (b) shows the delicate balance between "essence" and "function" that Japan has tried to maintain since the middle of the nineteenth century. The woman is attired in Western dress, and she works a Western-style sewing machine. Has the "function" degraded the "essence" of what she is doing? It is a question that many in Japan still ask today.

norms, like invaders of the past. In the meantime, however, they should be pacified, but not unconditionally.

In order to do this, however, China needed to be able to halt further encroachments by the Western powers. Toward this end, officials advocated a policy called "self-strengthening." During the 1860s, the two most prominent were Li Hongzhang (1823–1901) and his senior colleague Zeng Guofan (1811–1872). Renowned scholars as well as militia leaders, Li and Zeng were also distinguished by the flexibility of their thinking and their growing familiarity with the weapons brought to China by foreign forces. By the end of the rebellion, they had begun to move toward a strategy of what a later slogan called "Chinese studies for the essence; Western studies for practical application."

Toward Revolution: Reform and Reaction to 1900

While China's efforts at self-strengthening seemed promising, signs of their underlying weakness were already emerging. With the ascension of the infant Guangxu emperor in 1874 came the regency of Empress Dowager Cixi. Desperate to preserve Manchu power, Cixi manipulated factions at court and among the high officials to avoid concentration of power in any particular area. Such maneuverings hampered the long-term health of many self-strengthening measures. In addition, the new programs were costly, usually requiring foreign experts, and China's finances were continually strained.

China and Imperialism in Southeast Asia and Korea   By the 1880s foreign tensions exposed more problems. France had been steadily encroaching upon Southeast Asia since the late 1850s and completed its conquest of Vietnam in 1885 (Chapter 27). By the early 1890s rising tensions surrounding the Korean court and intrigues by Japanese and Chinese agents there threatened war. By the fall of 1894, both sides were sending troops and naval forces to Korea, and a full-scale war over the fate of Korea and northeastern Asia was under way.

(a)

(b)

Scenes from the Sino–Japanese War. News accounts of the Sino–Japanese War aroused great interest and an unprecedented wave of nationalism in Japan. They also marked the last extensive use of *ukiyo-e* woodblock printing in the news media, as the technology of reproducing photos in newspapers was introduced to Japan shortly after the conflict. Because few of the artists actually traveled with the troops, the great majority of these works came from reporters' dispatches and the artists' imaginations. In these representative samples from the assault on Pyongyang showing the use of the new technology of the electric searchlight to illuminate an enemy fort (a), the pride in Japan's modernization and the disdain for China's "backwardness" are all too evident. Note the almost demon-like faces and garish uniforms of the Chinese, invariably depicted as being killed or cowering before the Japanese; note, too, the modern, Western uniforms and beards and mustaches of the Japanese (b).

The Sino–Japanese War The war between China and Japan over control of Korea dramatically exposed the problems of China's self-strengthening efforts. While many of the land battles were hotly contested, superior organization and morale enabled the Japanese to drive steadily through Korea. A second force landed in southern Manchuria to secure the territory around the approaches to Beijing, while Japanese naval forces reduced the fortress across from it at Weihaiwei. In spring 1895, Li made his humiliating trip to Shimonoseki and was forced to agree to Japan's terms, as we saw at the beginning of this chapter. The severity of the provisions signaled to the Western powers in East Asia that China was now weak enough to have to acquiesce to massive economic and territorial demands.

image analysis

A "race for concessions" began, in which France demanded economic and territorial rights in south China adjacent to Indochina; Great Britain, in the Yangzi River valley; and Russia and Japan, in Manchuria. A newcomer, Germany, demanded naval bases and rights at Qingdao [ching-DOW] (Tsingtao) on the Shandong Peninsula. China's total dismemberment was avoided in 1899 when John Hay, the US secretary of state, circulated a note with British backing suggesting that all powers maintain an "open door" for all to trade in China.

The Hundred Days of Reform Amid this growing foreign crisis, the aftermath of the war produced a domestic crisis as well. The terms of the Shimonoseki treaty had prompted patriotic demonstrations in Beijing and prompted urgent discussion about reform. A group of younger officials headed by Kang Youwei (1858–1927) petitioned Emperor Guangxu to implement widespread reforms, many modeled on those recently enacted in Japan. Guangxu issued a flurry of edicts from June through September 1898, attempting to revamp China's government and many of its institutions. Resistance to this "hundred days' reform" program, however, was extensive, and centered on the emperor's aunt, the empress dowager. With support from her inner circle at court, she had the young emperor placed under house arrest and rounded up and executed many of Kang's supporters. Kang and his junior colleague, the writer and political theorist Liang Qichao [lee-ahng chee-CHOW] (1873–1929), managed to escape. For the next decade they traveled to overseas Chinese communities attempting to gather support for their Constitutional Monarchy Party.

Dismembering China. The weakness of the Qing during the final years of the nineteenth century prompted the so-called race for concessions among the imperial powers in East Asia. In this French cartoon, China is depicted as a cake around which caricatures of the monarchs and national symbols of the various powers sit with their knives poised to decide who should get the best pieces. A desperate Chinese official—perhaps Li Hongzhang himself—with his long fingernails and flapping gown, looks on helplessly as his empire is carved up.

The Boxer Rebellion and War The turmoil set off by the "race for concessions" was particularly intense in north China, where the ambitions of Russia, Japan, and Germany clashed. The activity of German missionaries on the Shandong Peninsula sparked antiforeign sentiment, increasingly perpetrated by a Chinese group calling itself the Society of the Harmonious Fists. This group was initially anti-Qing as well as anti-foreign, and the foreign community referred to them as the "Boxers."

In the spring of 1900 the the German ambassador was assassinated by one of his Manchu bodyguards. The Germans demanded that the Qing crush the Boxers and suppress all anti-foreign elements, pay a huge indemnity, and erect a statue to their ambassador. In the midst of this crisis, the empress dowager, who had been negotiating in secret with the Boxers, declared war on all the foreign powers in China and openly threw the court's support behind the movement. The result was civil war across northern China.

The foreign governments assembled a multinational relief force led by the Germans and British and largely manned by the Japanese. By August they had fought their way to the capital and chased the imperial court nearly to Xi'an. With Qing power utterly routed, the foreign governments were able to impose the most severe "unequal treaty" yet: They extracted the right to post troops in major Chinese cities, demanded the total suppression of any antiforeign movements, and received such a huge indemnity that China had to borrow money from foreign banks in order to service the interest on the loan.

In Search of Security through Empire: Japan in the Meiji Era

At the close of the nineteenth century, Japan and China faced similar pressures. How, then, was Japan, with only a fraction of China's population and resources, able not only to survive in the face of foreign pressure but join the imperial powers itself?

The Decline of Tokugawa Seclusion   During the eighteenth century, Europeans generally honored Japan's seclusion policies. By the first decades of the nineteenth century, however, the expanded trade with China increased the volume of shipping close to Japanese waters. Moreover, the whaling industry in the northern Pacific brought European and American ships into waters adjacent to Japan.

By the 1840s the pressure to establish relations with the Tokugawa shogunate became even more intense for the Western powers with interests in China. The treaty ports created in the wake of the First Opium War included Shanghai, which was becoming East Asia's chief commercial enclave, and major shipping routes to Shanghai ran directly adjacent to southern Japan. Moreover, the Mexican-American War (1846–1848) (see Chapter 23) brought the Pacific coast of North America under the control of the United States, while the discovery of gold in California made San Francisco the premier port for all American transpacific trade. Plans to open steamship service from San Francisco to Shanghai now threatened to place Japan squarely in the path of maritime traffic.

The Coming of the "Black Ships"   The Tokugawa were well aware of the humiliation of the Qing at the hands of the British in 1842, and as pressure increased on Japan to open its ports, divided counsels plagued the shogunate. While some advocated a military response to any attempt at opening the country, others looking at the situation in China felt that negotiation was the only way for Japan to avoid invasion.

"Proclamation of the Boxers United in Righteousness" (1900)

Visions of the Barbarians. Commodore Matthew C. Perry's expeditions to Japan were thoroughly documented by a number of Japanese artists. Some of the depictions were demonic sketches emphasizing the Americans' outlandish dress and facial hair. Others, like the portrait of Perry above from the series done in 1854 by Hibata Osuke (1813–1870), were truer to life and reflect the aesthetic sensibilities of the *ukiyo-e* tradition. The Japanese calligraphy says "Envoy Perry."

An American fleet of new and powerful warships under the command of Matthew C. Perry arrived in Japan in July 1853. To impress the Japanese with American technology, he brought along a telegraph set and a model railroad, both of which proved immediately popular with the Japanese. When Perry returned in 1854 with even more of the "black ships," as the Japanese dubbed them, the Treaty of Kanagawa was signed, Japan's first with an outside power. Like China, Japan had now entered the treaty port era.

Tokugawa Nariaki, "Memorandum to the Bakufu" (1853)

"Honor the Emperor and Expel the Barbarian!" The treaty with the Americans and the rapid conclusion of treaties with other Western powers reinforced anti-foreignism among many of Japan's warrior elite, while emphasizing the weakness of the Tokugawa. Many samurai felt that dramatic gestures were called for to rouse the country to action. Like the Boxers in China, they attacked foreigners and assassinated Tokugawa officials in an effort to precipitate anti-foreign conflict. By 1863, a movement aimed at driving out the Tokugawa and restoring imperial rule had coalesced. Taking the slogan *Sonno joi* ("Honor the emperor, expel the barbarian") this movement challenged the shogunate and fought a Restoration War, which by the end of 1867 forced the Tokugawa to capitulate. The new regime moved to the Tokugawa capital of Edo and renamed it Tokyo (Eastern Capital).

The new emperor, 15-year-old Mutsuhito, took the reign name of Meiji (Enlightened Rule). As proof that the new regime would adopt progressive measures, in April 1868 the throne issued a "charter oath" renouncing the restrictive measures of the past. A preliminary constitution was also promulgated, which detailed how the new government was to be set up.

Creating a Nation-State While the Tokugawa had created a warrior bureaucracy based on Neo-Confucianism, Japan was still dominated by regional loyalties and fealty to the daimyo of one's feudal domain. The foreign threat and restoration of the emperor provided the opportunity for national unification. Thus, during the 1870s the new government replaced the feudal domains with a centralized provincial structure; the daimyo were replaced by governors, and the samurai were disbanded. In their place, an army modeled after that of Germany was created, and a navy modeled on Great Britain's was established. The new order was reinforced by a national system of compulsory education in which loyalty to the emperor and state was carefully nurtured.

photograph of samurai, 1860s

Government-managed social experimentation flourished. Like the Chinese "self-strengtheners," Japanese senior advisors to the emperor, or *genro* [GEN-roe, with a hard *g*], sought to use new foreign technologies and institutions to strengthen the state against further foreign intrusion. Japan's proclaimed goals of using "Western science and Eastern ethics" in the service of "civilization and enlightenment" were seen as the primary tools in reaching eventual equality with the Western imperial powers and rolling back Japan's unequal treaties.

Creating an Empire Rising tensions between Japan and China over the disposition of Korea ultimately led to the Sino–Japanese War of 1894–1895. The issue was temporarily held in abeyance by the Treaty of Tianjin of 1885, but continuing difficulties arising from the instability of the Korean government kept the region volatile.

Japan's successful showing in the war surprised and alarmed the Western powers in the region. They staged the Triple Intervention, in which Russia, Germany, and France

MAP 24.4 **Japanese Territorial Expansion, 1870–1905.**

forced Japan to return the Liaodong Peninsula to China, only to have the Chinese lease it to Russia the following year. Not surprisingly, this put the Russian empire on a collision course with Japanese aspirations on the Asian mainland. Already in control of Korea, Japan was intensely interested in acquiring concessions in adjacent Manchuria. For Russia, it was vital to build rail links from the Trans-Siberian Railway to their new outposts of Port Arthur and Dairen (Dalian) in Liaodong and to extend the line across Manchuria to Vladivostok on the Pacific. Japan and Russia would shortly fight a war in 1904–05 that would secure Japan's dominant position in northeast Asia and begin a sequence of events that would end in revolution for Russia (see Map 24.4).

Economy and Society in Late Qing China

By 1900, China's treasury was bankrupt; its finances increasingly were controlled by foreign concerns; its export trade was outstripped by European and Japanese competitors; its domestic markets turned to factory-produced foreign commodities; and its land grew less and less capable of sustaining its society.

The Seeds of Modernity and the New Economic Order

The economic policies of late imperial China were increasingly at odds with those of the West. For Chinese thinkers, this was considered sound in both ideological and economic terms. Confucianism held that agriculture was China's primary concern, and that the values of the merchant were in direct opposition to stable agrarian values. As the nineteenth century advanced, the opium trade proved to Confucian officials the correctness of this stance.

Increasing pressure on China to lower its barriers to legitimate trade and the steps taken by those countries exerting the pressure to safeguard their own markets had equally severe long-term effects. The unequal treaties imposed artificially low tariff rates on the empire, making it increasingly difficult to protect its markets; at the same time, trading nations in the West increased tariffs on their own imports.

Self-Strengthening and Economics   Two economic forces had a profound effect on China's later economic development. The first was that in the treaty ports the economic climate created by the Western powers exposed much of China's urban population to modern industrial and commercial society. A class of Chinese people developed who made a living mediating between Westerners and Chinese interests.

1899 map of Tianjin, China

The other force was the popularity of European, Japanese, and American consumer goods. While foreign curiosities had been popular with Chinese elites since the eighteenth century, by the end of the nineteenth century, large foreign concerns, including the Standard Oil Company and the British–American Tobacco Company, had established their products in the empire. With the Qing finally committed to railroad and telegraph construction and modern mining, the seeds of economic modernity had been planted.

Rural Economy and Society   While China's population remained overwhelmingly rural, the old structures of the empire's peasant-based society were slowly crumbling. Landlordism, especially the growing incidence of absentee landlordism, exacerbated these tensions. Living on the edge of poverty in many areas, many peasants saw in the Taiping, the Nian, and assorted local rebellions a way to change their situations. But in many places, poverty increased due to the destruction caused by rebel clashes, and the radical ideologies and ruthlessness of the rebels disillusioned the majority of the peasantry. As a result, by the beginning of the twentieth century, absentee landlordism had become an increasingly acute problem.

Social Trends   While changes were certainly noticeable in the family, the durability of long-standing traditions is probably far more striking. The family endured as the central Chinese institution. Within it, the father continued to be the most powerful figure, and the Confucian ideal of hierarchical relationships between husband and wife, father and son, and elder brother and younger brother remained in force. Daughters, considered a drain on family resources because they would marry outside the family, were educated only to foster the skills the family of their husbands-to-be would consider valuable. The daughters of the wealthy were kept secluded in the home, and most—with the exception of the Manchus and certain minorities like south China's Hakkas—continued the practice of foot binding.

Culture, Arts, and Science

The late Qing period begins with one of China's great literary masterpieces and ends with China's first modern writers pointing toward a vernacular-language "literary renaissance" starting around 1915. Reversing the trend of thousands of years, the most significant Chinese developments in science and technology were those arriving from the West as products of the Industrial Revolution.

The Dream of the Red Chamber   Though the novel was not considered high literature by Chinese scholars during Ming and Qing times, the form proved immensely popular. During the mid-eighteenth century, what many consider to be China's greatest novel, *Hong Lou Meng* (*The Dream of the Red Chamber*), was written by Cao Xueqin [sow shway-CHIN] (ca. 1715–ca. 1764). The novel, which chronicles the decline and fall of a powerful family, has been so closely studied that in China there is an entire field called "red studies" or "redology" (*hong xue*) devoted to examination of the work.

Poetry, Travel Accounts, and Newspapers   China's need to understand new threats as well as opportunities prompted the publication of atlases, gazetteers of foreign lands, and eyewitness travel accounts. The most significant of these were the *Illustrated Gazetteer of the Maritime Countries* of 1844 by Wei Yuan (1794–1856) and the *Record of the World* of 1848 by Xu Jiyu (1795–1873). These accounts, especially Xu's, shaped what Chinese officials knew about the outside world until the first eyewitness accounts of travelers and diplomats arrived in the late 1860s. Officials and diplomats who visited foreign countries were required to keep journals of their experiences for use by the government and/or for publication.

The popular newspaper also emerged in most Chinese cities during this time. For centuries newsletters tracking official doings at the capital had been circulated among the elites. However, the 1860s saw the first popular Chinese-language papers, the most prominent of which was *Shenbao*. Such publications and the growing numbers of journals and popular magazines were vitally important in the transfer of ideas between Chinese and foreigners.

Science and Technology   The most pressing need for China during the early and mid-nineteenth century was military technology. During the period between the two Opium Wars, Chinese officials purchased guns and cannon from European and American manufacturers to bolster their coastal defenses. The self-strengtheners realized that China must begin to manufacture such weapons on its own. Moreover, this would require both infrastructure and such supporting industries as mining, railroads, and telegraphy.

Despite the general animosity directed against them by Chinese officials, missionaries were key players in transfers of science and technology. Protestant missionaries in the nineteenth century directed their efforts at ordinary Chinese, but often did so by attracting them with the new advantages of science. Medical missionaries set up clinics and used their presence in the community to foster conversion. The missionary community also popularized Western science and technology through journals like the *Globe Magazine*. By the latter part of the century, Chinese scholars were studying foreign subjects, going abroad for education, and translating Western works into Chinese.

lithograph from *Puck* magazine satirizing Western missionaries (1895)

Thus, while China had not yet completed its move to the new scientific–industrial society, the momentum had already begun to build among the empire's intellectual leaders.

Zaibatsu and Political Parties: Economy and Society in Meiji Japan

The commercial environment developing through the Tokugawa period was well suited to the nurturing of capitalism and industrialism in the nineteenth century. The law of alternate attendance (see Chapter 21) created a great deal of traffic to and from Edo as daimyo processions made their biannual trips to the capital. This traffic supported all the commercial establishments necessary to maintain the travelers in safety and comfort. The infrastructure of the major roads also required constant improvement, as did the port facilities for coastal shipping and fishing industries. Finally, commercial credit establishments, craft guilds, and large-scale industries had already regularized many of the institutions characteristic of the development of a modern economy.

Commerce and Cartels

Following Perry's visits, the Japanese were quick to go abroad to study the industrially advanced countries of Europe and the United States. Even during the last days of the Tokugawa regime, Japanese entrepreneurs were already experimenting with Western steamships and production techniques.

Cooperation and Capitalism   When the Meiji government began its economic reforms, its overall strategy included two key elements. The first was to make sure that ownership, insofar as possible, would remain in Japanese hands. The second was that Japan would develop its exports to the utmost while attempting to keep imports to a minimum. Japanese entrepreneurship also received an enormous boost from the cashing out of the samurai, as some took to heart the government's injunction that starting economic enterprises was a patriotic duty. Japan's expanding industrial needs meant that by the turn of the century, Japan needed to import much of its raw material.

Families with long-standing connections to capital swiftly moved to unite their enterprises to gain market share. The encouragement of the government and the cooperation of social networks among elites in finance and industry led to the creation of a number of **cartels** called *zaibatsu*. By the end of the nineteenth century, the zaibatsu would control nearly all major Japanese industries.

Cartel: A group of domestic or international businesses that form a group to control or monopolize an industry.

The Transportation and Communications Revolutions   The rapid development of railroads and telegraphs was one of the most stunning transformations of the Meiji era. By the mid-1870s Japan had in place a trunk railroad line along the main coastal road and several branches to major cities in the interior. Similarly, telegraph—and, by the end of the century, telephone—lines were swiftly strung between the major cities and towns, followed by undersea cables to the Asian mainland and North America. By 1895, Japan was estimated to have over 2,000 miles of private and government railroads in operation (see Map 24.5).

Visions of the New Railroads. The marvels of the new systems of railroads and telegraphs springing up in Japan provided practitioners of *ukiyo-e* woodblock art a host of new subjects to depict in the 1870s and 1880s. Here is a view of one of the new stations, Ueno on the Ueno–Nakasendo–Tokyo Railway, with small commuter trains arriving and departing.

The Meiji Constitution and Political Life   While the charter oath and constitution of 1868 were successful, a debate began among the genro concerning the liberalization of representative government in Japan. In 1881 the emperor approved a plan whereby Ito Hirobumi (1841–1909) and several senior colleagues would study the constitutional governments of the United States, Great Britain, France, Germany, and other countries, to see what aspects of them might be suitable for

MAP 24.5 **The Modernization of Japan to 1910.**

Japan's needs. The Meiji Constitution, as it came to be called, was promulgated in 1889 and remained in force until after World War II.

Ito's constitution drew from US, German, and British models. Much of it was also aimed at preserving the traditions of Japan's Confucian society that Ito and the genro most valued. Chief among these was the concept of *kokutai*, the "national polity." In this view, Japan was unique among nations because of its unbroken line of emperors and the singular familial and spiritual relationship between the emperor and his people. There was also a bicameral parliamentary body called the Diet, with an upper House of Peers and a lower House of Representatives. Japan's House of Peers consisted of members of the nobility; the representatives were elected by the people.

As for the people themselves, 15 articles spelled out "the rights and duties of subjects." All of these, however, are qualified by such phrases as "unless provided by law," allowing the government to invoke extraordinary powers during national emergencies.

Political Parties   As constitutional government began to be implemented in the 1890s, the factional debates among senior advisors began to attract followers among the Diet members and their supporters. Two major parties came to the fore by the turn of the century. The Kenseito [KEN-say-toe], or Liberal Party, split into factions at the turn of the century but was later reestablished as the Minseito.

The more powerful party during this time was the Seiyukai, or Constitutional Government Party, founded by Ito and his followers in 1900. The Seiyukai dominated Japanese politics in the era before World War I; after World War II, its adherents coalesced into Japan's present Liberal Democratic Party.

Social Experiments   In addition to creating an industrial base and a constitutional government, Japan's rulers attempted to curb practices in Japan that were believed to offend foreign sensibilities. Bathhouses, for example, were now required to have separate entrances for men and women, and pleasure quarters were restricted in areas near foreign enclaves; meat eating was even encouraged in largely Buddhist Japan. The government attempted to mandate Western dress for men and women, but widespread criticism ultimately forced the government to make the new dress optional.

In the same vein, traditional restrictions on women were altered. Though the home remained their primary domain, women were now seen in public far more often than they had been in the past. Concubines were now accorded the same rights as wives. Courtesans and prostitutes were no longer legally considered servants. More far-reaching, however, was the role of the new education system. With the introduction of compulsory public education, literacy would become nearly universal, and specialized women's education created entire new avenues of employment for women.

This same trend toward emancipation was evident among the rural population. The formal class barriers between peasants and samurai were eliminated, though informal deference to elites continued. During the latter part of the nineteenth century, Japan became the most intensely farmed nation in the world. The result was that although Japan's population increased to 40 million by 1890, it was a net exporter of food until the turn of the century.

colored print showing
Japanese women in
Western dress (1889)

"Civilization and Enlightenment": Science, Culture, and the Arts

While the Tokugawa sought seclusion, they were not cut off entirely from developments in other nations. Of particular importance in this regard was the requirement imposed on the Dutch to report to the Shogun on the state of the world. By the time of Commodore Perry's visit, the accumulated amount of "Dutch learning" was impressive.

Fukuzawa Yukichi, "Good-bye Asia" (1885)

Engaging "Western Science"   Nevertheless, at the time of their initial contact with the Western powers, the Tokugawa were stunned at the degree to which the accelerating technologies of the Industrial Revolution had armed their adversaries. The Japanese were immediately engaged with the notion of the railroad; just as quickly they sought to create oceangoing steamships. By 1860, they had built and manned steamers and insisted that their initial embassy to the United States travel aboard a ship the Japanese had built themselves.

The demand for industrial and military technology encouraged large numbers of Japanese to seek technical education. During the initial stages of the Meiji era, Japanese students studied in Europe and the United States, and the Japanese government and private concerns hired foreign advisors to aid in science and technical training. By the 1880s a university system was offering courses in medicine, physics, chemistry, engineering, and geology. On the whole, however, the bulk of the nation's efforts went into the practical application of science to technology and agriculture.

Culture and the Arts   Japanese intellectuals read works of the Western Enlightenment and followed more recent philosophical and social science developments. Journalism played a dominant role in disseminating information to the public.

As with nearly all the arts in late nineteenth-century Japan, the novel was also influenced by Western examples. The culmination of this trend was *Kokoro*, by Natsume Soseki (1867–1916), published in 1914. Soseki utilizes the wrenching changes in Meiji Japan set against traditional values to create the novel's tension.

More traditional arts such as Noh and kabuki theater and *ukiyo-e* printing survived, but often in a somewhat altered state. Updated kabuki variations now featured contemporary themes. As for *ukiyo-e*, it remained the most popular outlet for depictions of contemporary events until the development of newspaper photography. Especially telling in this regard are *ukiyo-e* artists' interpretations of the Sino–Japanese War.

≫ Putting It All Together

interactive concept map

Scholars of China and Japan have long debated the reasons for the apparent success of Japan and failure of China in their modernizing efforts of the nineteenth century. One school of thought sees the fundamental reasons growing from the respective cultural outlooks of the two countries. China, it is argued, assumed that outsiders would simply be won over to Confucian norms and modes of behavior, because this is what China's historical experience had been for the last 2,000 years. When it became apparent that defensive measures were necessary, it was still assumed that

China's superior culture would win out. Japan, on the other hand, because of its long history of cultural borrowing and its much smaller size, assumed a defensive posture. In addition, the Japanese had the advantage of watching events unfold in China before the danger reached their own shores. This allowed them to act in a more pragmatic fashion to the Western threat.

Some historians, however, disagree with this analysis. They argue instead that the cultural differences between China and Japan were secondary in the face of the foreign threat. According to this school of thought, the primary cause of the radically different outcomes for China and Japan was that China was victimized by foreign imperialism much earlier and much more thoroughly than Japan. Once Japanese modernization efforts were under way, the Japanese won for themselves a breathing spell with which to keep imperialism at bay and ultimately fought their way into the great power club themselves.

Review and Relate

Thinking Through Patterns

Examine the ways historians approach the big questions of this chapter.

The impact of the intrusion of Great Britain, France, the United States, and later Germany and Russia forced both China and Japan into defensive postures. Both countries had sought to keep out foreign influences after an earlier period of exposure to Western traders and missionaries. But the expansion of trade in both legitimate goods and opium and the need of the British for regularization of diplomatic practices pushed Britain and China into a cycle of war and "unequal treaties" under which China was at an increasing disadvantage. Japan, suddenly thrust into international commerce and diplomacy by the young United States, now sought to protect its borders without pushing the Western powers into seizing any of its territory.

>> **What was the impact of Western imperialism on the "regulated societies" of China and Japan?**

China's long history of absorbing and acculturating outside invaders to Confucian norms encouraged its leaders to assume that the Westerners would be no different. Attempts at reform were often undercut by political infighting at court and in the bureaucracy. The Taiping Rebellion further depleted China's strength and resources. As time went on, increasing Western control of China's ports and tariffs, absentee landlordism, and declining agricultural productivity also played a role.

For Japan, after a decade of indecision about how to handle the foreign intrusion, a civil war ended in the dismantling of the shogunate and the unification of the country under Emperor Meiji. Japan embarked upon a reform program aimed at remaking the country along Western lines. The focus and consistency displayed by Meiji and his advisors avoided many of the problems China experienced, and Japan's late Tokugawa

>> **Why did European empire building in Asia have such dramatically different effects on China and Japan?**

economics had predisposed the country toward a smoother transition into scientific–industrial society.

> ≫ **How have historians seen the nature of these outside forces and their influences in East Asia?**

Historians have long debated the relative weight that should be assigned to cultural and material reasons for the differing paths of China and Japan. China's long history as the region's cultural leader, some have argued, made it difficult for the empire to remake itself to face the Western challenge; Japan, on the other hand, has a long history of cultural borrowing and thus found it easier to borrow from the Euro-American world. Some historians have argued that China's earlier experience with imperialism hobbled the modernizing tendencies within the empire and kept it from responding; they argue that Japan had the advantage of being "opened" later and so could respond more effectively. Others have argued that Japan's tradition of military prowess played a role, and still others contend that China's more complete incorporation into the modern "world system" hampered its ability to respond more independently.

Against the Grain

Consider this as a counterpoint to the main patterns examined in this chapter.

Reacting to Modernity

- What factors make people turn to solutions during times of extreme stress that they wouldn't consider otherwise? Can you think of other instances in history where this phenomenon has taken place?

- Are there current movements you can think of that seem to fit this phenomenon? What stresses in their societies do you think are provoking such movements?

One of the enduring patterns of world history has been the complexity of acculturation to innovation from outside. As scientific and industrial society expanded its influence into the old agrarian–urban empires in the nineteenth century, the clashes were particularly fierce, especially in societies (like those of China or Japan) that felt themselves to be culturally superior to the invaders.

Not surprisingly, many people in different parts of the world chose what we might term a "culturally fundamentalist" approach. That is, faced with a threat that seemed insurmountable, they chose to take radical action by harkening back to a time when the virtues that first made their societies great prevailed. In almost every case this involved invented nostalgia and often a charismatic messiah figure. The Taipings and Boxers in China are examples of this phenomenon. In the end, however, all of these movements were ultimately crushed by the modern or modernizing forces arrayed against them. Yet the courage of their stands is often celebrated today—ironically by the representatives of the very societies that they sought to turn back.

🔊))
audio flashcards

Key Terms

Cartel   569   Extraterritoriality   558   Nontariff autonomy   558

For additional resources, please go to
www.oup.com/us/vonsivers.
Please see the Further Resources section at the back of the book
for additional readings and suggested websites.

Adaptation and Resistance

THE OTTOMAN AND RUSSIAN EMPIRES

Serfdom: Legal and cultural institution in which peasants are bound to the land.

O n October 13, 1824, Aleksander Nikitenko, born into **serfdom**, received his freedom from his lord, a landowning count. Nikitenko went on to earn a university degree. He would become a professor of literature at St. Petersburg University, a member of the Academy of Sciences, and a censor in the Ministry of Education.

From the age of 14, Nikitenko kept a diary that provides insights into the role of serfdom in the Russian Empire. He wrote that errant serfs were punished in the form of flogging with birch rods. Nikitenko's lot in life, Russian serfdom, was scarcely different from plantation slavery in the Americas or from untouchability in the Indian caste system. Slavery was also common in the Ottoman Empire, where, though limited to households, it was no less demeaning. The end of serfdom in Russia would not come until 1861 and the end of slavery in the Ottoman Empire not until 1890.

RUSSIAN AND OTTOMAN EMPIRES, 1683–1908

E nlightenment constitutionalism stood against serfdom and slavery, and these institutions were the first of many challenges the world outside western Europe and North America faced from the West in the nineteenth century. The Russian empire had inherited Byzantine Christian civilization, but it had not adopted the New Sciences, the Enlightenment or the Industrial

ABOVE: *Auction of Serfs* (1910), a painting by Klavdiy Vasilievich Lebedev (1852–1916), shows a wealthy Russian family auctioning off its valuables—and its serfs.

Revolution—nor had the Ottoman Empire, heir to both Islamic and Byzantine traditions. It would be the campaigns of Napoleon in the early nineteenth century that introduced these ideas to the Russian and Ottoman Empires.

The Russian and Ottoman empires were enemies, but because both empires became members of the Concert of Europe, their conflict eventually involved the other European powers as well. The partially non-Western identity of the Russian and Ottoman Empires is important to keep in mind. As forcefully as Russia asserted itself in the European Concert in the early years after 1815 and again at the end of the nineteenth century, it was in reality not any more or less "European" than the Muslim Ottoman Empire. Indeed, both empires had far more in common with each other than they did with the evolving nation-states of western Europe. Therefore, we consider them together here as parallel case studies in the overall patterns of constitutionalism, nation-state formation, and the challenge of modernity.

Decentralization and Reforms in the Ottoman Empire

Prior to the Russian–Ottoman rivalry in the 1800s, the traditional enemies of the Ottomans were the Austrian Habsburgs. In the 1700s the Habsburgs were increasingly sidelined by the rise of Russia as a new, Orthodox Christian empire. After consolidating itself in northeast Europe, Russia expanded eastward and southward, clashing with the Muslim Ottomans, conquerors of Constantinople. Soon, Russia became the patron of nationalist movements among the Slavic populations in the European provinces of the Ottoman Empire, and the Ottomans were no match for the combined Russian–southern Slavic aggression. At the end of the Second Balkan War of 1913, the Ottomans had lost nearly the entire European part of their empire to ethnic–nationalist liberation movements and were barely able to hang on to Istanbul (see Map 25.1).

Ottoman Imperialism in the 1600s and 1700s

In the period from 1500 to 1700 the Ottoman Empire was the dominant political power in the Middle East and North Africa. At that time, the main enemy of the Ottomans was the Habsburg Empire. The two powers were fighting each other on dual fronts, the Balkans in the east and North Africa in the western Mediterranean, eventually establishing a more or less stable disengagement. It was during this disengagement period that Russia began its expansion southward at the increasing expense of the Ottomans.

From Conquests to Retreats   At the end of the 1500s, the Ottoman and Habsburg militaries were overextended. Therefore, in 1606 they concluded a peace to gain time for recovery, during which the Ottomans recognized the Habsburgs for the first time as a Christian power. The peace lasted until the end of the 1600s. The Ottoman recovery was based on a shift in emphasis from their cavalry to their Janissary infantry and artillery as the main fighting force (Chapter 16).

In 1683 the Ottomans renewed their competition with the Habsburgs and laid siege to Vienna, the capital of the Austrian Habsburgs. But a Polish relief army allied with the Habsburgs arrived just in time to drive the besiegers into a retreat. The

≫ Which new models did the Ottomans adopt during the nineteenth century to adapt themselves to the Western challenge?

≫ How did the agrarian Ottoman and Russian Empires, both with large landholding ruling classes, respond to the western European industrial challenge during the 1800s?

≫ Why did large, well-established empires like the Russian and the Ottoman Empires struggle with the forces of modernity, while a small, secluded island nation like Japan seemed to adapt so quickly and successfully?

Chapter Outline

- **Decentralization and Reforms in the Ottoman Empire**

- **Westernization, Reforms, and Industrialization in Russia**

- **Putting It All Together**

Life lease: Lifelong tax farm, awarded to a wealthy member of the ruling class, in return for advances to the central imperial treasury on the taxes to be collected from village farmers.

Habsburgs followed up on this retreat by seizing Hungary, Transylvania, and northern Serbia. In the peace of 1699, the Ottomans and Habsburgs finally agreed to recognize each other fully in the territories they possessed.

Renewed Reforms   During the war years of the later 1600s, fiscal shortfalls meant that many Janissaries went unpaid and were forced to earn a living as craftspeople. Reforms were clearly necessary. In the early 1700s, the reformers introduced the institution of the lifetime tax farm, or **life lease**, for agricultural rents from village farmers. The idea was to diminish the temptation for tax farmers to squeeze farmers dry, forcing them to flee from the countryside to the cities. Wealthy and high-ranking courtiers, officers, administrators, and Islamic clerics in Istanbul bought these life leases. Thus, here in the early 1700s was the beginning of a development parallel to similar developments in France and England, with efforts to organize a kind of capital market. As a result of the reforms, in 1720, for the first time in a century and a half, the central budget was balanced again.

Decentralization   The transformation of cavalry-held lands into tax farms started a pattern of political decentralization in the Ottoman Empire. Agents responsible for the collection of taxes withheld increasing amounts from the treasury in Istanbul. By the mid-1700s, these agents were in positions of provincial power as "notables" in the Balkans or "valley lords" in western Anatolia. Starved for funds, the sultan and central administration were no longer able to support a large standing army of infantry and cavalry in the capital.

In 1768–1774 the notables and valley lords played a role not only in financing war against Russia but also in recruiting troops. This war was the first in which the Russian tsars exploited Ottoman decentralization for a systematic expansion southward. When the sultan lost the war, he was at the mercy of these notables and lords in the provinces.

The Western Challenge and Ottoman Responses

Soon after this Ottoman–Russian war, the Ottoman Empire faced the challenge of Western modernity. This adaptation entailed severe territorial losses for the Ottoman Empire. But after initial humiliations, the ruling class was able to develop a pattern of responses to the Western challenge, by reducing the power of the provincial magnates, modernizing the army, introducing constitutional reforms, and transforming its manufacturing sector.

Napoleon's victory at the Battle of the Pyramids, July 1798

External and Internal Blows   During the period 1774–1808, the Ottoman central government suffered a series of humiliations. Russia gained the north coast of the Black Sea and Georgia in the Caucasus. Napoleon invaded Egypt and destroyed the local regime of Ottoman military vassals in 1798. Napoleon's imperialist venture produced a deep shock in the Middle East: For the first time, a Western ruler had penetrated deep into the Ottoman Empire, effectively cutting it in half.

Internally, the lessening of central control in the second half of the 1700s left the provinces virtually independent. Most notables and lords were satisfied with local autonomy, but a few became warlords, engaging in campaigns to become regional leaders. In other cases, especially in Egypt, Syria, and Iraq, *Mamluks*—military slaves from the northern Caucasus whom Ottoman governors had previously employed as auxiliaries in the military—seized power. None of these ambitious leaders, however, renounced allegiance to the sultan, who at least remained a figurehead.

To reclaim power, the sultan and his viziers sought again to reform the empire. In 1792, they proclaimed a "new order," defined by a reorganization of the army with the creation of a new, separate artillery and flintlock musket corps alongside the Janissaries. The ad hoc financing of the new order, however, came to haunt the reformers. During a severe fiscal crisis in 1807, auxiliary Janissaries, refusing to wear new uniforms, assassinated a new-order officer. The revolt of Janissaries as well as religious scholars and students cost the sultan his life and ushered in the dissolution of the new troops. In a counter-revolt, a new sultan came to power in 1808. As a price for his accession, the sultan had to agree to power sharing with the provincial lords.

Renewed Difficulties   The sultan reconstituted another new army and neutralized many notables and valley lords, finally crushing the Janissaries in 1826. But new internal enemies arose in the form of Greek ethnic nationalists, whom the Ottomans would have defeated had it not been for the military intervention of the European powers. As a result, Greece became independent in a war of liberation (1821–1832). Russia, providing support for its fellow Orthodox Christian Greeks, acquired new territories from the Ottomans around the Black Sea, and several Balkan provinces achieved administrative autonomy.

In 1831, the new Ottoman vassal in Egypt, Muhammad Ali (r. 1805–1848), rose in rebellion. After occupying Syria (1831–1840), he would have conquered Istanbul had he not been stopped by Russian, British, and French intervention. Without the diplomacy of Great Britain, which sought to balance the European powers after the end of the Napoleonic empire, the Ottoman Empire would not have survived the 1830s.

Life, Honor, and Property   Ottoman administrators soon realized that only re-centralization would save the empire. In 1839, with a change of sultans, the government issued the Rose Garden Edict, the first of several reform edicts collectively known as **Tanzimat** ("Reorganizations"). In the Rose Garden Edict, the government bound itself to three basic principles: the guarantee of life, honor, and property of all subjects regardless of religion; the replacement of tax farms and life leases with an equitable tax system; and the introduction of a military conscription system, all in accordance with the Sharia, the compendium of Islamic morality and law. The edict avoided a definition of the position of the Christians and Jews in the empire,

Tanzimat: Ottoman reforms inspired by constitutional nationalism in Europe, including the adoption of basic rights, a legal reform, and a land code.

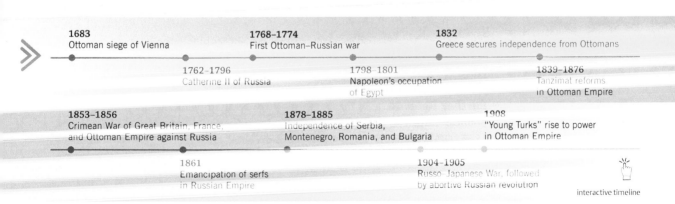

1683	1768–1774	1832
Ottoman siege of Vienna	First Ottoman–Russian war	Greece secures independence from Ottomans

1762–1796	1798–1801	1839–1876
Catherine II of Russia	Napoleon's occupation of Egypt	Tanzimat reforms in Ottoman Empire

1853–1856	1878–1885	1908
Crimean War of Great Britain, France, and Ottoman Empire against Russia	Independence of Serbia, Montenegro, Romania, and Bulgaria	"Young Turks" rise to power in Ottoman Empire

1861	1904–1905
Emancipation of serfs in Russian Empire	Russo-Japanese War, followed by abortive Russian revolution

interactive timeline

The Decline of the Ottoman Empire, 1683–1923

Losses, 1683–99 (Treaty of Karlowitz)	Losses, 1879–1915 (Treaties of London and Bucharest)
Losses, 1700–18 (Treaty of Passarowitz)	Losses, 1916–23 (Treaty of Lausanne)
Losses, 1719–74 (Treaty of Küçük-Kaynarca)	Turkey in 1923
Losses, 1775–1812 (Treaty of Bucharest)	Dependent state
Losses, 1813–29/30 (Treaty of Adrianople)	1913 Date or period of autonomy
Temporary loss to Austria, 1718–39	1832 Date of independence
Losses, 1830–78 (Treaty of Berlin)	

MAP **25.1 The Decline of the Ottoman Empire, 1683–1923.**

offering them the rights of life, honor, and property while maintaining their inequality vis-à-vis Muslims, as proclaimed in Islamic law.

The edict's enumeration of basic human rights was inspired by the American Declaration of Independence and the French Declaration of the Rights of Man. Here, we can see a first adaptation of the Ottoman Empire to the Western challenge: The Ottoman Empire adapted, at least in a partial way, to constitutionalism, the outgrowth of Enlightenment thought.

excerpts from an account of a stay in Paris by an Egyptian cleric (1826–31)

Further Reforms   As these reforms were being implemented, a new European political initiative challenged the Ottoman Empire. Napoleon III (president 1848–1852, emperor 1852–1870), self-declared emperor of France, challenged the Russian tsar's claim to be the protector of the Christian holy places in Palestine, a claim to which the Ottoman sultan had acceded after his defeat in 1774. While the French and Russian diplomats each sought to influence the sultan, the political situation turned increasingly tense. Ottoman diplomats forged a coalition with Great Britain and France. In the Crimean War of 1853–1856 this coalition was victorious against an isolated Russia. It forced Russia in the subsequent peace to recognize the Ottoman Empire's right to full integrity, provided the latter would continue the reforms announced in 1839.

Accordingly, the sultan promulgated the "Fortunate Edict" of 1856, in which he clarified the question of equality left open in the earlier edict: Regardless of religion, all subjects had the right to education, employment, and the administration of justice. Law courts were established for the application of new commercial, maritime, and criminal legal codes, based on European models. Although a system of secular

The Cedid Atlas, the first printed atlas in the Ottoman Empire (1803)

Muhammad Ali. Muhammad Ali transformed Egypt during the first half of the nineteenth century more thoroughly than the Ottoman overlord sultan could in his far-flung empire. He astutely realized that long-staple cotton, bred first in Egypt, could make Egypt a wealthy state in the beginning industrial transformation of the world.

schools, initially for males, was introduced, a lack of funds delayed its construction.

A measure that worked out differently from what was intended was the Land Code of 1858. Theoretically, the code subjected all users of the sultan's land—family farmers as well as landowners—to taxation. But in practice the central administration had no money to appoint tax collectors. It could not do without tax farmers, who still collected what they could get and transmitted to the government as little as they were able to get away with.

Highly uneven forms of landownership thus developed. Overall, tax yields remained low, improving only toward the end of the nineteenth century. The much-needed land reform remained incomplete.

Constitution and War   In the context of nineteenth-century constitutionalism, the Tanzimat decrees appeared like autocratic dictates from above, lacking popular approval. In the 1860s, younger bureaucrats and journalists, meeting in Istanbul and Paris under the name of "Young Ottomans," became advocates for the introduction of a constitution to end the autocracy of the sultan.

The idea of a constitution became reality in the midst of a crisis that embroiled the empire from 1873 to 1878. The crisis began when the Ottoman government defaulted on its foreign loans. In order to service the renegotiated loans, it had to increase taxes. This increase triggered ethnic–nationalist uprisings in Herzegovina, Bosnia, and Bulgaria in the Balkans in 1875 and 1876. The repression of these uprisings resulted in a political crisis, with a palace coup d'état by the Young Ottomans, during which a new sultan, Abdülhamit II (r. 1876–1909), ascended the throne and a constitution was adopted. The Russians exploited the perceived political weakness of the new constitutional Ottoman regime for a new Russo–Ottoman war in support of the Balkan nationalist uprisings.

As Russian troops advanced against a crumbling Ottoman army, the Ottomans held elections for the constitutionally decreed parliament between December 1876 and January 1877. With the invading Russian forces practically at the gates of Istanbul in February 1878, the parliament criticized the government. Irritated, the sultan dismissed the parliament and ruled by decree.

A few months later, at the Congress of Berlin, the sultan had to accept the loss of two-thirds of the empire's European provinces. Montenegro, Serbia, Romania, and Bulgaria gained their independence. Bosnia-Herzegovina and Cyprus, although still Ottoman, received an Austrian administration and a British administration, respectively. Sultan Abdülhamit never reconvened the parliament, and the empire reverted back to autocratic rule.

Autocracy   Sultan Abdülhamit surrounded himself with Tanzimat bureaucrats who did not have the constitutionalist leanings of the Young Ottomans. He had very little financial leeway, since the Public Debt Administration, imposed by the European powers in 1881, collected about one-third of the empire's income to pay for its accumulated foreign debt. Furthermore, the European price depression in the second half of the nineteenth century (1873–1896) was not favorable to foreign investments in the empire except some limited improvements in communications. Once the depression was over, foreign investors enabled the government to build railroads across Anatolia. By the early 1900s, a basic communication infrastructure was in place in the Ottoman Empire.

Given his fiscal limits, the sultan was an active propagandist, burnishing his credentials as the pan-Islamic caliph of Muslims in Eurasia. He sensed that the Balkan events of 1875/1876 and subsequent Congress of Berlin had been a watershed in European politics. The Concert of Europe was being replaced by an imperial rivalry between Germany and Great Britain. France, Austria-Hungary, and Russia played their own imperial roles. Since France and Great Britain, furthermore, carried out their imperialism against the Ottoman Empire, with the conquests of Tunisia in 1881 and Egypt in 1882, respectively, Abdülhamit was particularly affected. His pan-Islamism was therefore an attempt to instill the fear of jihad in European politicians and their publics.

Although most of the Ottoman Balkan provinces had become independent nations by 1878, three ethnic–nationalist movements were still left inside the empire. Abdülhamit brutally repressed them. The first movement consisted of Serb, Bulgarian, Vlach, and Greek nationalists agitating in Macedonia during 1893–1895. Without outside support, none of these feuding groups could impose itself on the province, and Ottoman troops defeated them.

The next were the Armenians, who formed sizable minorities in the six eastern provinces of Anatolia. The sultan armed Kurdish tribal units, which massacred thousands of Anatolian Armenian villagers from 1894 to 1896. Finally, when the Ottomans crushed a pro-Greek revolt in Crete in 1897 and followed up with a full-blown war against Greece, the European Powers decided to step in. They forced the Ottomans to withdraw their forces from the island and settled the Cretan issue with the creation of an autonomous territory under an international force and a Greek high commissioner.

In the later years of his rule, Abdülhamit failed to stem dissatisfaction with the lack of political freedom among the graduates of the elite administrative and military academies. Improved economic conditions after the end of the worldwide recession of 1893 stoked political ambitions, and oppositional circles among Ottoman intellectuals abroad merged with secret junior officer groups in Macedonia and Thrace in 1907. The officers launched a coup d'état in 1908, forcing the sultan to reinstate the constitution of 1878 and, after elections, accept a new parliament.

Ottoman Parliament.
The constitutional reforms (Tanzimat) of the Ottoman Empire culminated in elections for a parliament and two sessions, uniting deputies from a multiplicity of ethnic backgrounds (1876–1878). It met during the Russian–Ottoman War of 1877–1878, which the Ottomans lost. The newly installed Sultan Abdülhamit used the war as an excuse for ending constitutional rule and governing by decree.

image analysis

Decline of the Ottomans   Emboldened by their success, leaders of the coup formed the Committee of Union and Progress (CUP), commonly referred to as the "Young Turks," and in 1909 they forcibly deposed Abdülhamit. The CUP then embarked on a policy of self-strengthening and modernization in order to create a new, Turkish national identity for the Ottoman Empire.

Patterns Up Close | Sunni and Shiite Islam

Like all revealed religions, Islam followed the pattern of splitting into multiple denominations. Revelation is centered on God, whose covenant with humans includes the idea of providence. God's providence is contained in his promise of salvation in the future, on the Day of Judgment. How quickly and under whom this providential future prior to the Judgment unfolds, however, was a major source of conflict among Muslims. This conflict led to the foundation of the two major branches of Islam, Sunnism and Shiism.

During the formative period of Islam in the 800s and 900s, Muslims were deeply divided over the question of providential leadership. Was the leader of the Muslim community until the Day of Judgment a caliph (or representative) of the Prophet Muhammad and descended from the Quraysh, the dominant lineage of Mecca? Sunnis answered this question in the affirmative and regarded the caliphate as an institution guaranteeing the future of Islam until the Judgment in the distant future.

Shiites denied this answer and saw the future of Islam in a community led by the Imam (or leader), who was a descendant of Fatima and Ali, the daughter and cousin of Muhammad, respectively. Until 874, the eldest son in each generation was entitled to lead the Muslims, at which time the last Imam was

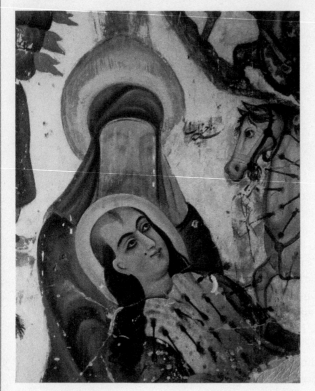

Husayn, Comforting His Dying Son Ali Akbar. In the early stage of the battle of Karbala, the Umayyad soldiers killed Ali Akbar, before Husayn himself was martyred. Processions and performances in remembrance of Karbala during the month of Muharram passed frequently by Shiite shrines which were embellished by local painters with frescoes showing imagined scenes of Karbala. This image, painted in 1905, is from the Imamzadeh Shah Zayd shrine in Isfahan, Iran.

believed to have entered "occultation"—that is, a state of concealment from where he would return as the Mahdi ("rightly guided leader") at the end of time, just before God's Judgment. The Shiite Imam was believed to be sinless and infallible, enabling him to pronounce authoritative interpretations of the Quran and Islamic Tradition. No Sunni caliph ever claimed inspiration, sinlessness, or infallibility.

Just before 900, a conflict broke out among the Shiites over the imminence of the Imam's return. A minority, the Ismailis, believed that the seventh Imam (in the line of descent from Fatima and Ali) would emerge from hiding already in the early 900s. When he indeed emerged at that time, he founded the Ismaili, or Fatimid, Empire in Tunisia, Egypt, and Syria. The majority, the Twelver Shiites, adhered to the belief that it would be the twelfth Imam who would return from occultation at

Unanticipated reactions to what was perceived as a reassertion of Ottoman power in the Balkans threatened to undermine the CUP and to bring down the empire. Austria-Hungary and Bulgaria formally annexed Bosnia-Herzegovina and northern Rumelia, respectively, in 1908. Albania revolted in 1910 and Italy invaded Tripolitania in 1911. In the following year Serbia, Montenegro, Bulgaria, and Greece collaborated in the First Balkan War, forcing Ottoman forces to retreat back toward Istanbul. Fortunately for the CUP, the four victorious Balkan states were unable to a later time. They were the founders of the Buyid dynasty of emirs in Iran and Iraq (934–1055) and, much later, of the Safavid dynasty in Iran (1501–1722). Both dynasties created a body of traditions and legal interpretations which made Twelver Shiism comparable to legalism in Sunni Islam.

The legal school that came to dominate in Twelver Shiism was Usulism. It emerged in the second half of the 1700s and is still dominant in contemporary Iran. It emphasizes the special status of senior legal scholars (ayatollahs ["signs of God"], today about half a dozen in number) who collectively interpret theology and law in an authoritative manner, binding for everyone, even in the absence of the Hidden Imam. Among Sunnis, anyone can acquire learning and practice interpretation, although traditionally theological schools also award diplomas.

In a further interpretation, Ayatollah Ruhollah Khomeini (1902–1989), leader of the Islamic Revolution of Iran in 1979, expanded the religious guardianship of the Shiite clerics (with himself at the head) to include that of political rulership. Accordingly, Iran is a partially elective Islamic theocracy, governed by certified pious Shiites and the Shiite hierarchy of clerics. Sunnis do not have such a hierarchy or clerical establishment.

In the history of Islamic civilization, Shiites have always been a minority; today they account for about 10–20 percent of Muslims worldwide. Even in places where they could live under their own authorities, however, they developed customs that celebrate their minority status, making Shiism a religion of sufferance. Shiites annually reenact the martyrdom of two of Imam Ali's sons, Husayn and Abbas, who perished in 680 at Karbala, Iraq, in an uprising against the Sunni caliph. Participants in these processions often flagellate themselves in their fervor for suffering. Today, the two mausoleums for Husayn and Abbas are important pilgrimage sites for Shiites, together with those of the other nine Imams.

Shiites today are a majority in Iran and pluralities in Iraq and Lebanon, making them important political actors in the Middle East. In present times relations between Sunnis and Shiites are shifting from the relative mutual tolerance of the 1800s and 1900s to increasing tension.

Questions

- Which other revealed religions split into denominations, and over which issues?
- Which questions do rulers face when they declare themselves the returned Imam and Mahdi, as in the case of the founders of the Fatimid Empire in the early tenth century CE and the Safavid Empire in 1501?

agree on the division of the spoils. The Ottomans exploited the disagreements and succeeded in a new peace settlement to push the imperial border westward into Thrace. Nevertheless, the Ottoman Empire had now been driven out of most of Europe, ending more than half a millennium of rule in the Balkans.

Economic Development   While the empire was disintegrating politically, the economic situation improved. The main factor was the end of the depression of

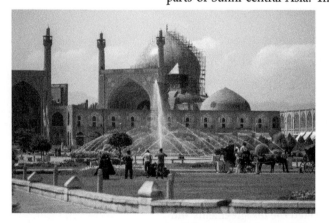

work scenes in the
Ottoman Empire, ca. 1900

1873–1896 and a renewed interest among European investors in creating industrial enterprises in the Middle East, Asia, and South America. When Abdülhamit II was at the peak of his power in the 1890s and early 1900s, investors perceived the Ottoman Empire as sufficiently stable for the creation of industrial enterprises.

The traditional crafts-based textile industry of the Ottoman Empire initially suffered under the invasion of cheap industrially produced English cottons in the period 1820–1850. But a recovery took place in the second half of the 1800s, both in the crafts sector and in a newly mechanized small factory sector of textile manufacturing. This recovery was driven largely by domestic demand and investments. Operating with low wages, domestic small-scale manufacturing was able to hold foreign factory-produced goods at bay.

Throughout the 1800s, the empire was also an exporter of agricultural commodities. But the recovery of domestic textile production demonstrates that the Ottomans did not succumb completely to the British free market system. When foreign investments resumed in the 1890s and early 1900s, there was a base on which industrialization could build.

Iran's Effort to Cope with the Western Challenge

Iran had risen in the 1500s as the Shiite alternative to the Sunni Ottomans. The two dynasties of kings (*shahs*) who ruled Iran, the Safavids (1501–1722) and Qajars (1795–1925), nurtured a hierarchy of Shiite clerics who formed an autonomous religious institution in their state. While the Ottoman sultans controlled their Sunni religious leaders, the Iranian rulers had to respect a balance of power with their Shiite leaders. Therefore, when Iran in the 1800s faced the Western challenges, reformers had to establish an alliance with the Shiite clerics to bring about constitutional reforms.

Safavid and Qajar Kings   The Safavid Empire was a less powerful state than that of the Ottomans. It comprised Shiite Iran, the Caucasus, Sunni Afghanistan, and parts of Sunni central Asia. The Safavid kings could not afford a firearm infantry to match the Janissaries. As a result, the Ottomans kept the Safavid rivalry at a manageable level, especially from the mid-1600s onward.

At this time, the Safavids ruled Iran from their capital of Isfahan in the center of the country. Safavid Iran was a major exporter of silk yarn and clothes, and supplemented its limited agrarian revenues with an international trade in silk.

The Safavids were vulnerable not only to their Ottoman neighbors to the west but also to tribal federations in the Sunni provinces to the east. In 1722, a Pashtun federation in Afghanistan conquered Iran and ended Safavid rule. The Afghanis, however, were unable to establish a stable new regime. Instead, provincial Iranian rulers reunified and even expanded the empire during the 1700s. Stabilization finally occurred in 1796, with the accession of the new Qajar dynasty.

The Qajars had been among the founding Shiite Turkic tribal federation of the Safavids, but they had no Shiite aspirations of their own. Instead, they paid respect

Isfahan, Naqsh-i Jahan Square. At the southeastern end of the square is the majestic Shah (today Imam) Mosque (1611–1629), a major example of the Iranian and Central Asian open courtyard mosque style.

to the clerical hierarchy that had become powerful in the aftermath of the Afghani conquest in the 1700s. The clerics supported themselves through their own independent revenues, and the Qajars were not powerful enough to interfere.

During the 1800s, two developments dominated Iran's historical evolution. First, Iran was subject to oscillating periods of decentralization and recentralization, following the decline or rise of tax revenues from the countryside. Second, the increasingly hierarchical and theologically rigid Shiite clerics were challenged by the popular, theologically less tradition-bound Babi movement. Qajar troops and clerically organized mobs suppressed this movement, which subsequently evolved into the Baha'i faith.

The Qajars also suffered from Russian imperialism. The Russian goal of liberating Constantinople implied the conquest of the central Asian Turkic sultanates as well as the north face of the Caucasus Mountains. Accordingly, Russian armies sought to drive the Qajars from their Caucasus provinces. In response, the Qajar kings embarked on centralizing military and administrative reforms. They hired Russian officers to train a small corps of new troops, the Cossack Brigade. (The tsar, although bent on expanding into the Caucasus, did not want Iran to collapse and cease being a counterweight to the Ottomans.) Swedish advisors trained the police force, and British subjects acquired economic concessions. This foreign influence aroused the ire of the conservative clerical hierarchy, and the kings had to withdraw the concessions.

Perceptive Iranian constitutional nationalists from among the educated younger ruling class founded a tactical alliance toward the end of the 1800s with conservative clerics and merchants. In 1906, this alliance mounted a successful constitutional revolution, imposing parliamentary limits on the Qajar regime. The constitutional–nationalist alliance with the clerics was unstable, and parliamentary rule failed to become a reality. As World War I drew near, Iran reverted to autocratic rule by the shahs.

Westernization, Reforms, and Industrialization in Russia

The Russian Empire that expanded during the 1800s southward at the expense of the Qajar and Ottoman Empires had arisen in 1547 as a tsardom in Moscow, succeeding the Byzantine eastern Christian "caesars" (from which the Russian term "tsar," or "czar," is derived). Given its geographical location at the eastern edge of Europe and outside western Christian civilization, Russia developed along an uneven pattern of relations with western Europe. Western culture became a force in Russian culture only around 1700, when the tsar Peter the Great (r. 1682–1725) became its advocate. The idea of constitutionalism arrived in the wake of the French Revolution and Napoleon's failed invasion of Russia (1812). But it remained weak and was diluted by pan-Slavic ethnic nationalism. Small political groups rose amid the social dislocations that followed the Russian industrialization effort at the end of the nineteenth century, but none was able to take over leadership in the revolution following the defeat at the hands of Japan in 1905. Although this uprising produced a weak Russian parliament, the Duma, the autocratic tsarist regime lasted until World War I.

Russia and Westernization

The states of western Europe were aware of the empire to their east but did not consider it fully European. Tsar Peter the Great began a reform and urbanization process, against considerable resistance from both the ruling class and the population at large, to bring Russia more in line with the western European norms. His legacy was the new capital of St. Petersburg, extensive military reorganization, and attempts to rein in the power of Russia's high nobility. But another legacy was political and cultural resistance to any such measures coming from outside Russia.

The "enlightened despot" Tsarina Catherine II, "the Great" (r. 1762–1796), continued the reform process, but it was slow to take hold. When the constitutionalist revolutions broke out in the United States, France, and Haiti, the Russian Empire was an autocratic, fiscal–military state.

Charter to the Nobility, issued by Catherine II in 1785

Catherine II's Reforms   Catherine the Great was engaged with Enlightenment concepts spreading among the European courts —she exchanged letters with Voltaire and entertained Diderot at St. Petersburg. Her Enlightenment outlook moved Catherine far ahead of the Russian aristocracy, not to mention the small urban educated upper strata, both of which were still much beholden to eastern Christian traditions.

As much an activist as Peter the Great but more subtle, Catherine pushed through a number of major reforms. She strengthened urban development with a provincial reform in 1775 and a town reform in 1785 that allowed local nonaristocratic participation. In a reform of the educational system (1782), the government set up a free, mostly clergy-staffed educational system. But in 1785 she also strengthened the aristocracy with a charter that exempted its members from the poll tax and increased their property rights, including the purchase of serfs. Catherine's legal reform project, however, remained incomplete.

In foreign affairs, Catherine continued the expansionism of Peter the Great. She first undertook the dismemberment of the Kingdom of Poland, accomplished together with Prussia and the Austrian Habsburgs in three stages, from 1772 to 1795. Then, in two wars with the Ottoman Empire (1768–1792), Catherine expanded Russian power over the Tatars, a Turkic-speaking population in Crimea and adjacent northern Black Sea lands. In the first war, Russia gained access to the Black Sea, ending the Tatar–Ottoman alliance and gaining free access for Russian ships to the Mediterranean. In the second war, Russia absorbed the Tatars within its imperial borders, which now advanced to the northern coast of the Black Sea.

Russia in the Early Nineteenth Century

The ideas of the French Revolution first emerged in Russia in the form of the Decembrist Revolt in 1825. But since in the pattern of traditional empire formation the personality of the ruler counted more than the continuity of the administration, the reign of Nicholas I for a generation in mid-1800s Russia checked whatever the Decembrists had set in motion. Nicholas continued his pursuit of an aggressive foreign policy of expansion (see Map 25.2).

Russia and the French Revolution   Catherine's grandson, Alexander I (r. 1801–1825), was educated in Enlightenment ideas. He initially showed inclinations toward constitutionalism, but Napoleon's imperial designs interrupted any idea of implementation.

The Territorial Expansion of the Russian Empire, 1795–1914

☐	Russian Empire, 1795	▨ Russian sphere of influence	◉ Coal mining
☐	Russian acquisitions, 1796–1855	1824 Date of acquisition	◉ Gold mining
☐	Russian acquisitions, 1855–1914	*Kazakhs* People	○ Copper mining

MAP 25.2 **The Territorial Expansion of the Russian Empire, 1795–1914.**

map analysis

Russia emerged as a key power in efforts to undo Napoleon's takeover of Europe. In 1805 it joined Britain and Austria in the Third Coalition against France. After a long war, Russia defeated Napoleon during his disastrous invasion of 1812. At the Congress of Vienna in 1815, Alexander advocated a "holy alliance" of monarchs to be its guarantors. As a result, Napoleon's Duchy of Warsaw became the Kingdom of Poland, with the Russian tsar as its king. In contrast to his monarchical colleagues in Europe, however, Alexander remained open to Enlightenment reforms, initiating the liberation of serfs in Russia's Baltic provinces, pursuing constitutional reform in Finland and Poland, and mapping out a new status for eastern Christianity.

Orthodoxy, Autocracy, and Nationality   When Nicholas I (1825–1855) ascended the throne in 1825, a revolt broke out, led by Russian officers who had been exposed to the ideas of constitutionalism. Known as the Decembrist Revolt, the uprising was quickly suppressed and its leaders were hanged. Despite its relative lack of impact, the revolt represented the first anti-tsarist, constitutional-revolutionary movement and became a harbinger of things to come.

Determined to preclude any future constitutional revolts, in 1833 Nicholas implemented the doctrine known as "official nationality," according to which three concepts would guide the government: *orthodoxy*, reaffirming the adherence to eastern Christianity and rejection of secularist notions; *autocracy*, meaning the absolute authority of the tsar; and *nationality*, or the "spirit" of Russian identity. Nicholas created a secret police agency known as the Third Section, which vigorously suppressed dissidence against the government.

Nicholas joined other conservative European rulers in suppressing constitutional revolts. When a revolt in Poland in 1830 threatened to topple the viceroy, Nicholas abolished the country's autonomy. Then, during the widespread revolutionary constitutional movements across Europe in 1848, Nicholas supported the Austrian emperor in suppressing the Hungarian nationalists.

Nicholas was also determined to continue Russia's drive toward Constantinople (Istanbul). In the Russo–Ottoman War of 1828–1829, Russia helped the Greeks achieve independence. With Russian help, Serbia attained autonomy, while Moldavia and Wallachia—technically still within the Ottoman Empire—became protectorates of Russia. However, when Napoleon III of France in 1853 demanded recognition as protector of the Christians in Palestine under Ottoman rule, Russia did not fare as well. After Nicholas insisted that the Ottomans honor their agreement with the Russian tsars as the actual protectors, the diplomatic wrangling ended in the outbreak of the Crimean War (1853–1856) between Britain, France, and the Ottoman Empire on one side and Russia on the other.

Poor planning, missed opportunities, language barriers, and a lack of coordination between soldiers and officers plagued both sides in the Crimean War.

The Ottomans, still in the initial stages of their military reform, suffered from a weak officer corps and the absence of noncommissioned officers. They would have been defeated, had it not been for allied participation. The Russians did not perform well either, except for their navy, with its superior shells. The Russian army suffered from overextending its battle lines on too many fronts. Thus, for both the Russian and Ottoman Empires, the war was a setback in their effort to meet the challenges of the West. However, their exposure to state-of-the-art military technology and usage would mark reform efforts of both empires in the coming decades.

Hospital Ward, Scutari, Ottoman Empire, 1856. This airy, uncluttered, warm hospital room shows injured and recovering soldiers. Florence Nightingale is depicted in the middle ground, in conversation with an officer.

The Golden Age   During the period 1810–1853, Russia enjoyed an outburst of intellectual and cultural activity considered to be the golden age of Russian culture. Inspired by European romantics, a Russian intelligentsia met in the salons of Moscow and St. Petersburg, where they debated religion, philosophy, and Russian history. Literary journals appeared, which introduced new literary forms as well as new ideas. The first stirrings of reform movements emanated from these circles.

The Great Reforms

The Russian defeat in the Crimean War convinced the newly enthroned Alexander II (r. 1855–1881) of the need for reforms. Russia, so he believed, lost the war because of a technologically inferior army, a lack of infrastructure, and the unwillingness of the serf-owning aristocracy to shift from subsistence to market agriculture. He implemented major reforms, but with many people frustrated, the empire entered a time of social destabilization, balanced somewhat by successes against the Ottoman Empire.

Russian Serfdom The experience of being a serf in Russia varied according to topography, economic status, and the disposition of one's landlord. Settlements were organized into *mirs*, or communes, which oversaw economic and legal affairs. Many Russian peasants lived near the subsistence level. Their economic status, which depended on agriculture, fluctuated because of frequent poor harvests and famines. Organized along patriarchal lines, families were dominated by husbands; misogyny was common. Yet although Russian women were accorded second-class status, they were not without some legal rights.

The Emancipation of Serfs In 1861, Alexander issued the Emancipation Edict, in which peasants were ostensibly freed from their bondage to their villages and their dues and labor services to the Russian landowning aristocracy. However, the edict fell short of liberating the peasantry for three key reasons. First, the decree of emancipation took 2 years to be fully enacted. Second, peasants were not given land titles directly. Finally, serfs had to redeem their new holdings by making annual payments to the state, the proceeds from which were then used to compensate the landowning nobility. Tens of millions of farmers remained mired in poverty-stricken agricultural self-sufficiency.

Starving Russian Peasants.
Severe weather in 1890–1891
resulted in poor harvests, which
in turn led to a period of famine
during the 1890s. Russian
peasants were especially hard
hit by growing hunger and by
the government's policy of
exporting surpluses in order
to boost the Russian economy.
Here, peasants beg food from
a horse-mounted official in
St. Petersburg.

Following Western models, Alexander II enacted further reforms. In 1864 the administration of government at the local level was reorganized by the establishment of regional councils known as *zemstvos*. Each zemstvo was in reality controlled by the local aristocracy, although peasants had a say in their election. Legal reforms were enacted shortly afterward. Then, in 1874, reforms aimed at modernizing the military and bringing it closer to Western standards were introduced. Planned infrastructural reforms, however, remained limited by lack of funds.

Pan-Slavism: Ideology that espoused the brotherhood of all Slavic peoples and gave Russia the mission to aid Slavs in the Balkans suffering from alleged Ottoman misrule.

the Russian menace as portrayed on the cover of a 1909 Muslim magazine

Pan-Slavism and Balkan Affairs   In the 1870s, conservative intellectuals broadened Tsar Nicholas I's earlier concept of the Russian nationality into the ideology of **pan-Slavism**.

Two issues contributed to Russian pan-Slavic engagement in the Balkans. First, during the nineteenth century the Ottomans had been forced to relinquish control of large areas of their empire in the Balkans. Second, the increasingly popular appeal of ethnolinguistic nationalism in Europe strengthened the assertiveness of the Balkan nationalities. In 1875 Bosnia-Herzegovina revolted against the Ottomans, and the rebellion then spread to Bulgaria, Serbia, and Montenegro. Thus, the Balkans became an area of increasing attention for the leading powers, while at the same time resembling a powder keg ready to ignite.

The Russo–Ottoman War   Encouraged by Russian popular support for pan-Slavism and sensing an opportunity to exploit rising anti-Ottoman sentiments among ethnic national movements in the Balkans, the tsar reopened the war front against the Ottomans in July 1877. The pretext was the Ottoman repression of uprisings in Bosnia-Herzegovina and Bulgaria, which had led to a declaration of war by neighboring Montenegro and Serbia in June 1876 and a call for Russian military aid. The Russians invaded, and by December had advanced as far as Rumelia. Serbia, claiming complete independence, and Bulgaria, under Russian tutelage, were now poised to gain control of Istanbul. The other European powers stood by, anxiously waiting to see whether Russia would advance on the Ottoman capital.

In 1878, alarmed over a possible Russian occupation of Istanbul, Austria and Britain persuaded Germany to convene the Congress of Berlin. In order to defuse rising tensions over this "eastern question," the congress decided to amputate from the Ottoman Empire most of its European provinces. Russia agreed to give up its designs on Istanbul in return for maintaining control over lands in the Caucasus Mountains. Serbia, Romania, and Montenegro became independent states. Austria acquired the right to "occupy and administer" the provinces of Bosnia and Herzegovina. There things stood for the rest of the nineteenth century.

Russian Industrialization

Alexander II was assassinated in 1881 by a leftist terrorist organization. The next Romanov tsars reaffirmed autocratic authority and exercised tight political control. These tsarist policies provoked renewed calls for constitutional reforms and generated new movements opposed to the autocracy of the regime. In the 1890s, the country enjoyed a surge in industrialization, aggravating political and social contradictions.

The Reassertion of Tsarist Authority   In the face of demands by constitutionalists and social reformers, Alexander III (r. 1881–1894) unleashed "counter-reforms" in order to shore up autocratic control over the country. These actions turned Russia into a police state; revolutionaries, terrorists, and opponents among the intelligentsia were targeted for intimidation, exile, or even death. Outside Russia, Alexander insisted on a program of *Russification*, or forced assimilation to Russian culture, for Poles, Ukrainians, and the Muslim populations of central Asia.

Nicholas II (r. 1894–1917) followed in his father's footsteps. He felt a special contempt for revolutionary groups and individuals, who increasingly called for the overthrow of the tsarist government. In addition to continuing the repressive policies of his father, Nicholas II distrusted Russian Jews as unpatriotic, and persecuted them in a series of pograms that climaxed in 1903–1906. These pogroms triggered mass emigrations as Russian Jews sought to escape.

Aristocratic Splendor. This oil painting of the coronation of Nicholas II and Alexandra in 1896, by the Danish painter Laurits Regner Tuxen (1853–1927), shows the rich glory of the Eastern Christian Church and the empire in ascendancy in its representation of the couple's iconic art, ermine furs, veiled ladies in waiting, and decorated officers.

Industrialization   Industrial development was as slow in Russia as it was in the Ottoman Empire. Poor transportation infrastructure was a particular obstacle. Railroad construction was difficult, owing to the great distances in the empire that made large capital investments from abroad necessary. Moreover, Russian railroads never adopted the standard gauge of their Western counterparts, necessitating costly and time-consuming changes of equipment at border crossings.

The driving force in Russia's push for industrialization in the 1890s was the minister of finance, Sergei Witte (1849–1915, in office 1892–1903). His "Witte system" included an acceleration of heavy industrial output, the establishment of import tariffs, increased taxes on the peasantry, and conversion to the gold standard in order to stabilize the currency. Witte's crowning achievement was the Trans-Siberian Railroad, built during 1891–1905, connecting Moscow with Vladivostok on the Pacific coast. Witte's objective was not only to make Russia more competitive but also to extend Russia's reach into Siberia with its rich agricultural and mineral resources, while at the same time extending Russia's influence in East Asia.

Industrialism and Society   In the 1890s, British, French, and Belgian capital helped Russia build railroads, mining ventures, iron smelters, and textile factories. This capital was not sufficient, however, to allow Russia access to the latest in Western technology and it continued to lag behind.

excerpts from
Theodor Herzl, *The Jewish State* (1895)

Social adjustments similar to those experienced in industrialized cities in the west occurred in Russian industrial centers. The populations of Moscow and St. Petersburg in the second half of the nineteenth century soared. And, like their western counterparts, industrialized urban centers consisted of overcrowded and unhealthy slums adjacent to factories. Labor conditions in factories and mines were oppressive. Calls for reforms throughout the later nineteenth century led to the formation of protest and socialist groups, all of whom contributed to the increasing pressures that would explode in the 1905 Revolution.

A striking difference between the Russian and western industrial experiences is that, in Russia, the numbers of wealthy factory owners, entrepreneurs, and merchants paled in comparison with the numbers of their counterparts in the West. One reason for the disparity was that many Russian manufacturing plants were controlled by western investors, and those that were not were under the supervision of the Russian government.

The Russo–Japanese War   The dramatic surge in industrialization, in conjunction with imperial ambitions in East Asia, brought Russia into conflict with Japan. In the Sino–Japanese War (1894–1895), Japan occupied Taiwan and the Liaodong Peninsula of Manchuria. Although Japan defeated China and replaced it as the protector of Korea, the European powers forced Japan in the Triple Intervention (1895) to give up the Liadong Peninsula, which was in turn leased to Russia the following year. Determined to continue Russian expansion in East Asia, Witte completed the construction of a railway spur from the Trans-Siberian Railroad through Manchuria to the city of Port Arthur on the southern tip of Liaodong.

The construction of this spur was the final straw for Japan, whose imperial goals were threatened by Russian expansion. In early 1904 Japanese naval forces attacked the Russian fleet moored at Port Arthur. The Russian Baltic fleet, sent for relief, not only arrived too late to prevent the fall of Port Arthur but was destroyed in May 1905 by Japan when it tried to reach Vladivostok. In the peace settlement, Japan gained control of the Liaodong Peninsula and southern Manchuria, as well as increased influence over Korea, which it finally annexed in 1910.

Russian propaganda poster (1904)

The Abortive Russian Revolution of 1905

In addition to Russia's mauling by the Japanese in the war of 1904–1905, other factors in the early 1900s sparked the first revolution against tsarist rule. One of these was a rising discontent among the peasantry. Another was the demand by factory workers for reform of working conditions. Although the government had allowed for the formation of labor unions, their grievances fell on deaf ears. In response, workers in major manufacturing centers across the country mounted protests and strikes.

Revolutionary Parties   Calls for reforms resulted in the creation of new political parties. One of these was the Social Democratic Labor Party, formed in 1898 by Vladimir Ilyich Lenin (1870–1924), a staunch adherent of Marxism (see Chapter 26). This group sought support from workers, whom they urged to overthrow the bourgeois capitalist tsarist government.

During its meeting in London in 1903 the Social Democratic Labor Party developed two competing factions. The more moderate group, the Mensheviks ("minority," though they were actually numerically in the majority), was willing to follow classical Marxism, which allowed for an evolutionary process from capitalism to social revolution and then on to the eventual overthrow of capitalism and tsarist rule. The more radical faction, known as Bolsheviks ("majority"), led by Lenin, was unwilling to wait for the evolutionary process to unfold and instead called for revolution in the near term. Even after the split in the Social Democratic Labor Party, however, the Bolsheviks were still a long way away from the kind of elite "vanguard of the revolution" party Lenin envisaged.

The Revolution of 1905   Amid calls for political and economic reforms during the early 1900s, two concurrent events in 1904 shook the government to its foundations. First, reports of the humiliating defeats during the ongoing Russo–Japanese War began to filter to the home front. Second, on January 22, 1905, 100,000 workers gathered in St. Petersburg to present a petition of grievances to the tsar. Russian troops opened fire, killing over a hundred protestors and wounding hundreds more. The event has been commenorated ever since as "Bloody Sunday," and later regarded by Lenin as "the beginning of the Russian Revolution."

Then, from September to October, workers staged a general strike. Finally forced to make concessions, Nicholas II issued the "October Manifesto," in which he promised to establish a constitutional government, including the creation of a representative assembly, the Duma. During 1905–1907, however, Nicholas repudiated the concessions granted in the manifesto, especially an independent Duma, which remained a rubber-stamp parliament until Nicholas abdicated in 1917. Its momentum sapped, the revolution withered.

The main reason for the failure of the revolution was the absence of a broadly based constitutionalism. Its replacement was small revolutionary parties that lacked popular backing. This failure of constitutionalism made the formation of broader reformist coalitions impossible. The tsarist regime still had enough military resources to wear down the small groups of revolutionaries and demonstrators. Without sympathizers in the army, a determined tsarist regime was impossible to bring down. It was now felt that nothing short of changing the system would be effective.

Vladimir Yegorovich Makovsky (1846–1920), *Death in the Snow* (1905). This dramatic oil painting of the crowd protesting against the tsarist regime during the abortive revolution of 1905 is one of the greatest Russian realist paintings. Makovsky was one of the founders of the Moscow Art School and continued to paint after the Russian Revolution of 1917.

≫ Putting It All Together

Both the Ottoman and Russian Empires faced the initial Western military and constitutional challenges directly on their doorsteps. The Ottoman Empire, as a mature empire struggling to regain its traditional centralism, fought largely defensive wars. Russia, still a young empire, expanded aggressively against the defensive Ottomans and its weaker Asian neighbors (except Japan) but suffered occasional military and diplomatic setbacks.

Interactive concept map

Western constitutional nationalism was another powerful and corrosive pattern. The transformation of kingdoms or colonies into nations in which subjects would become citizens was difficult enough in Europe. In the Ottoman Empire, a wide gap existed between constitutional theory and practice, especially as far as religion was concerned. Russia, plagued by the reluctance of its aristocracy to give up serfdom even after emancipation, left its constitutionalists out in the cold. Sultans, emperors, and kings knew well that none of their constitutions would fully satisfy the demands for liberty, equality, and fraternity.

To complicate matters for both the Ottoman and Russian Empires, in the second half of the 1800s, many members of the rising educated urban middle class deserted constitutionalism and turned to ethnic nationalism (in the Ottoman Empire) or pan-Slavism and Marxism (in the Russian Empire). By contrast, both the Ottoman and Russian Empires met the Western *industrial* challenge without completely surrendering their markets. Once they were able to attract foreign capital for the construction of expensive railroads and factories at the end of the 1800s, they even started on their own paths to industrialization. In spite of wrenching transformations, the two were still empires in control of themselves when World War I broke out. Neither would survive the war. Instead, they would be transformed by the forces that had beset them throughout the nineteenth century.

Review and Relate

Thinking Through Patterns

Examine the ways historians approach the big questions of this chapter.

>> **Which new models did the Ottomans adopt during the nineteenth century to adapt themselves to the Western challenge?**

The traditional model for reform in the Ottoman Empire was based on the Islamic concept of the divinely sanctioned, absolute authority of the sultan: Officials could be appointed or dismissed at will. The later history of the Ottoman Empire is significant in world history because it shows the *adaptation pattern* to the Western challenge— this time, the borrowing of constitutional nationalism and modern military technology from Europe.

>> **How did the agrarian Ottoman and Russian Empires, both with large landholding ruling classes, respond to the western European industrial challenge during the 1800s?**

As agrarian polities with large landowning classes collecting rents from tenant farmers or serfs, the Ottoman and Russian Empires found it difficult to respond to the European industrial challenge. Large foreign investments were necessary for the building of steelworks, factories, and railroads. Given the long economic recession of the last quarter of the 1800s, these investments—coming from France and Germany—went to an expanding Russia, more than the shrinking Ottoman Empire, as the safer bet.

>> **Why did large, well-established empires like the Russian and the Ottoman Empires struggle with the forces of modernity, while a small, secluded island nation like Japan seemed to adapt so quickly and successfully?**

One avenue of inquiry is cultural: How receptive were the Russians and Ottomans—or the Qing, for that matter—to the ideas of the Enlightenment? The short answer must be "Not very." Even the most willing leaders in these empires risked alienating entrenched interests by attempting reforms. The cautious reforms that resulted disrupted traditional routines but left few effective alternatives. In addition, such large multiethnic empires as those of Russia and the Ottomans found it difficult to rally subjects around a distinct "nationality," since they encompassed so many divergent ones. In contrast, the Meiji reformers had the advantage of a unity derived from outside pressures. Moreover, the new regime immediately began creating an ideology of Japaneseness—a form of ethnic nationalism—and institutionalized it in education and national policy. Japan's legacy of cultural borrowing may also have been an advantage, as well as a nascent capitalist system developing in the late Tokugawa era.

Against the Grain

Consider this as a counterpoint to the main patterns examined in this chapter.

Precursor to Lenin

The Emancipation Edict issued in 1861 by Alexander II was touted as making vast improvements in the lives of Russia's peasantry. When it soon became apparent that reform measures fell far short of the mark, radical and even terrorist political factions demanded more far-reaching reforms. In the vanguard was a group of Russian intelligentsia who circulated their ideas in pamphlets and literary journals.

Of these activists, one of the most notable was Nikolai Chernyshevsky (1828–1889), who defied conventional approaches to Russia's problems. As editor of the radical journal *Contemporary*, and inspired by western intellectuals like Hegel, Chernyshevsky wrote critiques of moderate reforms, especially those advocated by liberals and intelligentsia. The only way to resolve the current status quo, according to Chernyshevsky, was through revolution, with the Russian peasantry as driver of meaningful reforms. To this end Chernyshevsky advocated the formation of social collectives, or communes, based on utopian models.

Chernyshevsky's writing resulted in his imprisonment in 1862. During this time he wrote the inflammatory novel *What Is to Be Done?*, frequently referred to as a "handbook of radicalism." In it, Chernyshevsky called for actions and policies informed by socialist ideals, including women's liberation, and programs of social justice. The book inspired radical activists and terrorists during the 1870s and 1880s, and Chernyshevsky was acknowledged as the first revolutionary socialist as well as the forerunner of the 1905 revolution. Lenin was so impressed by Chernyshevsky's novel that he not only referred to it as one of the most influential books he had ever read—including those of Marx—but he also entitled his own manual of revolution *What Is to Be Done?*

- In what ways does Chernyshevsky epitomize radical socialist ideas?
- How does Chernyshevsky compare to earlier contrarians like Thomas Paine and Joseph Sieyès?

Key Terms

Life lease 578	Serfdom 576
Pan-Slavism 592	Tanzimat 579

audio flashcards

For additional resources, please go to
www.oup.com/us/vonsivers.
Please see the Further Resources section at the back of the book for additional readings and suggested websites.

Industrialization and Its Discontents

I n 1845, Mary Paul, age 15, made a life-altering decision. Given her limited prospects in rural Vermont, she decided to head for Massachusetts and a job in the newly expanding textile industry.

In letters she wrote to her widowed father, Bela, Mary reveals that the reason behind her decision was to earn steady wages rather than rely on the uncertainties of farm work. On September 13, 1845, Mary wrote for her father's consent to seek employment in the booming mill town of Lowell, Massachusetts. On November 20, Mary wrote that she had already "found a place in a spinning room and the next morning [she] went to work." She continued, "I like very well have [*sic*] 50cts first payment increasing every payment as I get along in work." Shortly before Christmas, Mary reported that her wages had increased: "Last Tuesday we were paid. In all I had six dollars and sixty cents paid $4.68 for board. With the rest I got me a pair of rubbers and a pair of 50.cts shoes. Next payment I am to have a dollar a week beside my board." She described her daily routine in the mill: "At 5 o'clock in the morning the bell rings for the folks to get up and get breakfast. At half past six it rings for the girls to get up and at seven they are called into the mill. At half past 12 we have dinner are called back again at one and stay till half past seven." Mary concludes,

THE INDUSTRIALIZING
WEST,
1750–1914

ABOVE: Although rather idealized, this illustration depicts the role of women in textile mills, such as this one in Lowell, Massachusetts.

"I think that the factory is the best place for me and if any girl wants employment I advise them to come to Lowell."

Seeing Patterns

》 Where and when did the Industrial Revolution originate?

》 What were some effects of industrialization on Western society? How did social patterns change?

》 In what ways did industrialization contribute to innovations in technology? How did these technological advances contribute to Western imperialism in the late nineteenth century?

》 What new directions in science, philosophy, religion, and the arts did industrialism generate? What kind of responses did it provoke?

Mary Paul's experiences, shared by tens of thousands of her contemporaries, signaled a momentous change in the patterns of American and world history. Like Great Britain and northern Europe, the northeastern United States was in the initial stages of "scientific–industrial society." The agrarian–urban model was giving way to a society based on machine-made goods, large-scale factories, regimented work hours, and wage labor. Moreover, the economies of the industrializing states would increasingly be dominated by capitalism. An ideology of progress, backed by the acceleration of science and technology, constituted the challenge of modernity. That challenge spread through innovations in transportation, communications, and weaponry produced by this Industrial Revolution.

Origins and Growth of Industrialism, 1750–1914

Like the agricultural revolution of the Neolithic age, the Industrial Revolution altered lives around the globe. The process of industrialization originated in Britain in the eighteenth century, spreading next to the European continent and North America in the nineteenth century and subsequently around the globe. The transition from manual labor and natural sources of power to the implementation of mechanical forms of power and machine-driven production resulted in a vast increase in the production of goods, new modes of transportation, and new economic policies and business procedures.

Early Industrialism, 1750–1870

The industrialization of western Europe began in Britain. As with all transformative events in history, however, a number of important questions arise: Why did the industrial movement begin in Britain in the eighteenth century? Was this process "inevitable," as some have claimed, or was it contingent on interactions that we are still struggling to comprehend?

Preconditions   Europe in general and Britain in particular enjoyed two distinct advantages compared to other civilizations: a prosperous and largely independent middle class, and an early scientific revolution.

Three additional factors made Britain especially suitable for launching the industrial movement. First, Britain benefited from reserves of coal and iron ore, combined with overseas colonies and subsequent global trading networks. This provided a foundation for commercial expansion, which in turn created capital to fund new enterprises. Second, a thriving merchant class supported legislation that promoted economic development. Finally, Britain developed a flourishing banking system (Bank of England, founded in 1694) that provided funds to entrepreneurs.

Chapter Outline

- Origins and Growth of Industrialism, 1750–1914

- The Social and Economic Impact of Industrialism, 1750–1914

- Intellectual and Cultural Responses to Industrialism

- Putting It All Together

Cottage industry: Small-scale business or industrial activity carried out in the home by family members.

a spinning mule

Thanks to agricultural improvements, Britain experienced a surge in population, nearly doubling between1600 and 1700. At the same time, a demographic shift in which displaced tenant farmers migrated to towns and cities created greater demand for food and consumer goods. The impact of these changes was especially notable in the textile industry. Although woolen cloth had long been the staple of the British textile industry, new fabrics from Asia, such as silk and cotton, gained in popularity. At first, the demand for finished cloth goods was satisfied by weavers working in the older, domestic cottage industries, a system known as **cottage industry**. Owing to concerns for the woolen industry, Parliament in 1700 and 1720 moved to prohibit the importation of cotton goods from India. But as this legislation led to increased domestic demand for English-made cotton textiles, it soon was apparent that production needed to be sped up.

British Resources   The use of machines was more practical and cost-efficient in Britain than elsewhere for several reasons. Since wages for workers in rural industries were high, the use of labor-saving machinery helped firms be profitable. At the same time, Britain's vast reserves of coal resulted in cheap energy. Moreover, Britain was singularly fortunate in its social and cultural capital. The majority of British inventors had interests in and ties to societies aligned with scientific aspects of the Enlightenment, which served as centers of exchange between scientists, inventors, experimenters, and mechanics.

New Technologies and Sources of Power   These factors produced an explosion of technological innovation in Britain. From 1700 to 1800 over 1,000 inventions were developed, most of which were related to the textile industry. In addition to the steam engine (see "Patterns Up Close"), among the most prominent were the flying shuttle (1733), the spinning jenny (1764), the water frame (1769), and the spinning mule (1779). Each of these devices increased the speed and quality of spinning or weaving. The power loom (1787), which gradually replaced manually operated looms, resulted in hardship for hand weavers, whose livelihoods were now threatened. In desperation, handicrafters of all sorts mounted a campaign to sabotage the use of machines in textile factories (see "Against the Grain").

Even these improvements were not enough, however, to supply both the domestic and colonial markets with textiles. What was needed in order to speed up production was reliable mechanical power to drive the looms. The solution was provided by the development of the steam engine.

The Factory System   The growing dependence on large machinery, the necessity of transporting fuel and raw materials to centers of production, and the need to house many machines under one roof necessitated the construction of large manufacturing buildings. These facilities were initially located near sources of running water in order to provide the power to run mechanical looms. The implementation of steam power to drive machinery allowed entrepreneurs to move factories away from water sources in rural areas to urban settings, where there were large pools of cheap labor and easier access to transportation. These factories drew increasing numbers of workers, which contributed to urban population surges, particularly in the north and Midlands of England. By the 1830s close to 25 percent of Britain's industrial production came from factories (see Map 26.1).

Global Commerce   The application of machines to textile production resulted in Britain's role in the development of intercontinental trade and commerce. Prior to the Industrial Revolution, India and China dominated global trade in textiles. But thanks to its holdings in America and Asia, combined with mercantilist policies, Britain had ready-made markets for the distribution and sale of its goods. Britain also benefited from slave labor in its former colonies, which kept the price of commodities like American cotton low. One result was growing demand among colonial markets for textile products, which stimulated the necessity to step up production. Increased production led to lower prices, making British textiles more competitive in global markets.

Transportation   While steam-powered factories were important to the Industrial Revolution, it was the steam railroad that captivated the public's imagination. Between 1840 and 1870, Great Britain counted a ninefold increase in miles of rail. Railroads improved the shipping of coal and other bulk commodities and enhanced the sale and distribution of manufactures. The railroad itself developed into a self-sustaining industry, employing thousands and spurring further entrepreneurial investment.

the steam engine

The application of steam to ships had far-reaching ramifications. Credit for the first practical steam-powered riverboat goes to the American engineer and inventor Robert Fulton (1765–1815), whose *Clermont*, constructed in 1807, plied the Hudson River in New York. English engineers were quick to copy Fulton's lead; by 1815 there were 10 steamboats hauling coal across the Clyde River in Scotland. During the 1820s and 1830s steamboats were in regular use on Europe's principal rivers. Steamboats opened the Great Lakes and the Ohio and Mississippi Rivers to commerce in the United States. By the 1830s and 1840s the British East India Company used iron-hulled steamers to facilitate maritime trade with its markets in India. Military uses soon followed.

The Spread of Early Industrialism

By the 1830s, in Belgium, northern France, and the northern German states—all of which had coal reserves—conditions had grown more suitable for industrialization. Population increases contributed to higher consumer demand, and urban areas provided pools of available workers for factories. Roads, canals, and railways facilitated the movement of both raw materials to industrial centers and manufactured goods to markets. In addition, governmental involvement enhanced the investment climate, as protective **tariffs** for manufactures and the removal of internal toll restrictions opened up the trading industry.

Tariff: A tax on imported goods, which gives domestic manufactures an advantage.

interactive timeline

1765 James Watt improves the steam engine	1848 Karl Marx and Friedrich Engels publish *The Communist Manifesto*	1869 Opening of the Suez Canal; transcontinental railroad completed in the United States

| 1830 First passenger railroad opened between Liverpool and Manchester | 1859 Charles Darwin publishes *On the Origin of Species by Means of Natural Selection* | 1872 Claude Monet paints *Impression, Sunrise* |

| 1874 Siegfried Marcus perfects the first internal combustion automobile | 1884 Hiram Maxim invents the first fully automatic machine gun | 1901 Guglielmo Marconi sends first transatlantic radio message | 1905 Albert Einstein publishes theory of relativity |

| 1879 Thomas Edison perfects the incandescent light bulb | 1900 Sigmund Freud publishes *The Interpretation of Dreams* | 1903 Wright Brothers achieve first engine-powered sustained flight |

Industrializing Britain in 1850

Industries:

	Textiles
	Copper mining and smelting
	Tin mining and smelting
	Iron extraction and smelting
	Lead mining
	Metalware and cutlery
	Salt, soap, chemicals, and glass manufacture
	Shipbuilding
	Coalfield
	Major port
	Navigable river
	Major railway

MAP **26.1 Industrializing Britain in 1850.**

The United States In 1793, Samuel Slater (1768–1835), a British engineer, established the first water-powered textile factory in America in Rhode Island. By 1825 factories in the American northeast were producing textile goods on mechanically powered looms.

After a brief interruption during the American Civil War, industrialization in America resumed at an accelerated pace. By 1870 America was producing far more spindles of cotton than Great Britain, and its production of iron ingots was swiftly catching up to that of British and European producers. By 1914 the United States had become the world's single largest industrial economy.

In addition to manufacturing, trade and commerce across the American continent were facilitated by the railroads, which took over the carrying trade from the canal networks created in the early nineteenth century. By the conclusion of the Civil War, the US had more miles of rail than the rest of the world combined. In 1869 the first transcontinental railroad was completed with a final golden spike at Promontory Point, Utah.

Later Industrialism, 1871–1914

The next stage of industrialism, often referred to as "the second Industrial Revolution," introduced high-technology innovations that, taken together, altered the course not only of the Industrial Revolution but also of world history. Among the most significant were steel, electricity, and chemicals (see Map 26.2).

MAP 26.2 **The Industrialization of Europe by 1914.**

"The Age of Steam"

The origins of the steam age lie in an environmental crisis. A shortage of wood for fuel and charcoal making in Britain in the early 1700s forced manufacturers to turn to another fuel source: coal. Britain was blessed with vast amounts of coal, but getting to it was difficult because of a high water table. Mineshafts often flooded and had to be abandoned. Early methods of water extraction featured pumps operated by either human or animal power, but these were inefficient, expensive, and limited in power.

The first steam-driven piston engine, based on experimentation with vacuum chambers and condensing steam, came from the French Huguenot Denis Papin (1647–ca. 1712), who spent his later career in England. Thomas Savery (ca. 1650–1715), taking up the idea of condensing steam and vacuum power, built a system of pipes employing the suction produced by this process dubbed the "Miner's Friend." Savery's system was able to extract water from shallow shafts but was useless for the deeper mines of rural Britain.

Although this drawback was partially addressed by Thomas Newcomen (1663–1729), who in 1712 improved the efficiency of Papin's piston-and-cylinder design, the "Newcomen engines" were still slow and energy-inefficient. It remained for James Watt (1736–1819), a Scottish engineer, to create the prototype for fast engines sufficiently efficient and versatile to drive factory machinery. His newly refined model, completed in 1765 and patented in 1769, was five times as efficient as Newcomen's engine and used 75 percent less coal.

Watt introduced a further improved model in 1783 that incorporated more advances. First, by injecting steam into both the top and the bottom of the piston cylinder, its motion was converted to double action, making it more powerful and efficient. Second, through a system of "planetary gearing"—in which the piston

New Materials: Steel   The second Industrial Revolution saw increasing use of steel instead of iron. Refined techniques for making steel had for centuries been the province of skilled craftspeople, but new technical advances now made it possible to produce large quantities of high-grade yet *inexpensive* steel. Subsequent improvements in production in the 1860s and 1870s included the blast furnace and the open-hearth smelting method.

Following the conclusion of the Franco–Prussian war, Germany's annexation of the ore-rich regions of Alsace-Lorraine led to a dramatic increase in industrial production. Germany had had almost no measurable steel production in the 1870s, but by 1914 the country's annual tonnage of steel was more than twice that of Britain. Germany modeled its new industrial facilities on those of its most modern competitors, saving substantial time and investment capital and resulting in newer and more efficient equipment and business methods. Another advantage was Germany's development of sophisticated scientific research capabilities at universities.

Industrialization spread farther afield during the second half of the nineteenth century. Aware of the growing influence of western European industrial powers, both Russia and Japan implemented economic reforms to compete with the West. One factor in Russia's decision to convert from an agrarian to an industrial economy was its defeat by French and British forces in the Crimean War (1853–1856). Following the emancipation of the serfs in 1861, Russia embarked on industrailization. Following the 1853 arrival of Commodore Matthew Perry, which led to the Meiji Constitution in 1868, Japan also adapted its economy to industrialism in order to keep pace with the West.

shaft was connected by a circular gear to the hub of a flywheel—the back-and-forth rhythm of the piston was converted to smooth, rotary motion, suitable for driving machines in factories and mills. Watt's steam engines proved so popular that by 1790 they had replaced all of the Newcomen engines; by 1800, nearly 500 Watt engines were in operation in mines and factories.

Within a few decades, adaptations of this design were being used not just for stationary engines to run machinery but also to move vehicles along tracks—the first railroad engines—and to turn paddle wheels and screw propellers on boats—the first steamships. Both of these innovations enhanced commerce and empire building among the newly industrializing nations. Although societies seeking to protect themselves from outside influence saw the railroad and steamer as forces of chaos, the web of railroad lines grew denser on every inhabited continent, and the continents themselves were connected by shipping lines. Steam may indeed be said to be the power behind the creation of modern global society.

Questions

- How is the innovation of steam power the culmination of a pattern that began with the rise of the New Sciences in western Europe in the sixteenth and seventeenth centuries?

- Does Frederic A. Bartholdi's statement in 1876 that the Corliss steam engine "had the beauty and almost the grace of the human form" reflect a romantic outlook? If so, how?

Corliss Steam Engine. A tribute to the new power of the steam engine was this huge power plant in the Machinery Hall of the American Centennial Exposition in 1876. The Corliss engine pictured here produced over 1,400 horsepower and drove nearly all the machines in the exhibition hall—with the distinct exception of those in the British display. Along with the arm of the Statue of Liberty, also on exhibition there, it became the most recognized symbol of America's first world's fair.

The advantages of steel over iron were that it was lighter, harder, and more durable. Thus, it provided better rails for railroads and, increasingly, girders for the construction of high-rise buildings. The switch from iron to steel construction of ships marked a significant advance in steamship technology during the third quarter of the nineteenth century. By 1900, 95 percent of all commercial ocean liners were being constructed of steel. Steel liners were stronger, faster, and roomier than iron ones—and steel warships proved far more durable in battle.

Chemicals   Advances were also made in the use of chemicals. In 1856 the first synthetic dye was created, which initiated the synthetic dyestuffs industry. New chemical compounds led to the refinement of wood-pulp products, ranging from cheaper paper to artificial silk, known as rayon. The synthesizing of ammonia and its conversion to nitrate for use in fertilizers and explosives were to have far-reaching effects during World War I. The invention of dynamite by the Swedish chemist and engineer Alfred Bernhard Nobel (1833–1896) provided the means to blast through rock formations, resulting in massive excavation projects like the Panama Canal (1914). In yet another chemical advance, Charles Goodyear (1800–1860) invented a process in 1839 that produced vulcanized rubber. Celluloid—the first synthetic plastic—was developed in 1869. Other innovations in chemistry, ranging from pharmaceuticals to soap products, contributed to improved health. By the early part of the twentieth century, these developments had led to a "hygiene revolution" among the industrialized countries.

New Energies: Electricity and the Internal Combustion Engine   The development and application of electricity were greatly advanced after 1850, especially in the generation of electrical power. The first step came with Michael Faraday (1791–1867) patenting the electromagnetic generator in 1861. But large-scale electrical generation would require further innovation before it became a reality. Perhaps the most important devices in this regard were developed by engineer Nikola Tesla (1856–1943). Among Tesla's inventions were the alternating current (AC) and the Tesla Coil (1891) for the more efficient transmission of electricity. In 1888 the introduction of Tesla's "electric induction engine" led to the adoption of electricity-generating power plants throughout industrialized Europe.

Another key source of energy was the internal combustion engine. When oil, or liquid petroleum, was commercially developed in the 1860s and 1870s, it was at first refined into kerosene and used for illumination. A by-product of this process, gasoline, soon revealed its potential as a new fuel source. The first experimental internal combustion engines utilizing the new fuel appeared in the 1860s. They were significantly lighter in weight than steam engines of comparable size and power, and the first practical attempts to use them in powering vehicles came along in the next decade.

The first true automobile was invented by the Austrian mechanic Siegfried Marcus (1831–1898). Marcus developed the carburetor, the magneto ignition system, various gears, the clutch, a steering mechanism, and a braking system. He included all of these inventions in a combustion-engine automobile that he drove in Vienna in 1874.

Internal combustion engines were also applied to early attempts at sustained flight. In 1900 Ferdinand von Zeppelin (1838–1917) constructed a rigid airship—a *dirigible*—consisting of a fabric-covered aluminum frame that was kept aloft by bags filled with hydrogen gas and powered by two 16-horsepower engines. The marriage of the gasoline engine to the glider created the first airplanes. The Wright brothers are usually credited with the first sustained engine-powered flight in Kitty Hawk, North Carolina, in 1903. By 1909, the first flight across the English Channel had been completed; in 1911 the first transcontinental airplane flight across the United States (with many stops) took place. The potential of both the automobile and the airplane were to be starkly revealed within a few years during the Great War.

1901 world map
showing telegraph lines

The Communication Revolution   Although electric telegraph messages were transmitted as early as the 1840s with the advent of the devices and code devised by Samuel F. B. Morse (1791–1872), it was only in the 1860s and 1870s that major continental landmasses were linked by submarine transoceanic cables. By the latter part of the nineteenth century, telegraphic communication was a worldwide phenomenon. The telephone, invented by Alexander Graham Bell (1847–1922) in 1876, made voice communication possible by wire.

Perhaps most revolutionary of all was the advent of wireless communication. The theoretical groundwork for this had been laid in part by Heinrich Rudolf Hertz (1857–1894), who in 1885 discovered that electromagnetic radiation produces unseen waves that emanate through the universe. In the 1890s, Guglielmo Marconi (1874–1937) developed a device using these radio waves generated by electric sparks controlled by a telegraph key to send and receive messages over several miles. By 1903 Marconi had enhanced the power and range of the device enough to send the first transatlantic radio message. The "wireless telegraph" was quickly adopted by ships for reliable communication at sea. Subsequent improvements, such as the development of the vacuum tube amplifier and oscillator, soon resulted in greater range and power, as well as the ability to transmit sound wirelessly.

The Weapons Revolution   The advances in chemistry and explosives, metallurgy, and machine tooling during the second half of the nineteenth century contributed to a vastly enhanced lethality among weapons. Earlier advances from the 1830s to the early 1860s (including the percussion cap, the conical bullet, the revolver, and the rifled musket) provided the base for the development of more sophisticated firearms. **Breech-loading** weapons rapidly came of age with the advent of the brass cartridge. By 1865, manufacturers were marketing repeating rifles, such as the famous Winchester lever-action models. Rifles designed by the German firms of Krupp and Mauser pioneered the bolt-action, magazine, and clip-fed rifles that remained the staple of infantry weapons through two world wars.

Artillery underwent a similar transformation. Breech-loading artillery, made possible by precision machining of breech blocks and the introduction of metallic cartridges for artillery shells, made loading and firing large guns far more efficient. By the early 1880s the invention of the recoil cylinder meant that field artillery could now be anchored, aimed, and fired continuously with enhanced accuracy. Its effectiveness was enhanced further by the new explosives like guncotton, dynamite, and later TNT, for use in its shells. Cordite, or smokeless powder, eliminated much of the battlefield smoke generated by black powder and was three times more powerful as a propellant. Thus, the range and accuracy of small arms and artillery were pushed even further.

By far the most significant—and lethal—advance in weaponry during the later nineteenth century, however, was the invention of the machine gun. Though many quick-firing weapons had been developed during these years—the most famous

Breech-loading: A firearm that is loaded from the rear portion of the barrel, making reloading much more efficient.

Hiram Maxim In this 1888 photo, the proud inventor of the machine gun looks on with self-satisfied pride as Albert Edward, Prince of Wales (the future King Edward VII), experiences for himself the awesome firepower of Maxim's "little daisy of a gun." In 1885 Maxim put on a similar demonstration for Lord Wolseley, commander-in-chief of the British Army. The British Army adopted the gun a year later. The lethal power of the machine gun was first put to use in Africa at the Battle of Omdurman in 1898, where 20,000 Sudanese cavalrymen were employed in a fruitless charge against a line of Maxim guns.

being the Gatling Gun (1861)—the first fully automatic machine gun was conceived by Hiram Maxim (1840–1916), an American inventor.

By the outbreak of World War I, every major army in the world was equipping itself with Maxim's guns. In his memoirs, Maxim notes somewhat ruefully that he was applauded more highly for inventing his "killing machine" than for inventing a steam inhaler for those suffering from bronchitis.

The Social and Economic Impact of Industrialism, 1750–1914

All of these changes in modes of production transformed the daily lives of millions around the globe. Along with new networks of transportation and communication,

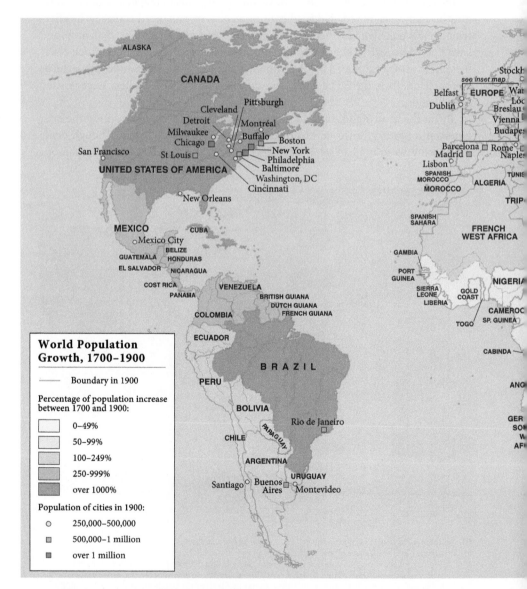

MAP 26.3 **World Population Growth, 1700–1900.**

new materials, and new sources of energy, the industrialized nations underwent significant changes in how they viewed politics, social institutions, and economic relationships.

Demographic Changes

Changes in the demographics of industrialized nations followed the development of new industries. The populations of these countries grew at unprecedented rates and became increasingly urbanized, and Great Britain became the first country to have more urban dwellers than rural inhabitants. This trend would continue among the industrialized nations through the twentieth century.

Population Surge and Urbanization   Between 1700 and 1914, the industrialized nations experienced a population explosion (see Map 26.3). Advances in

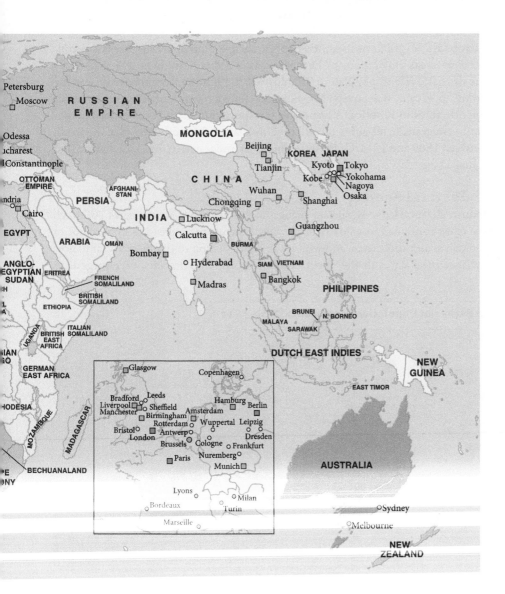

industrial production, the expansion of factories, and improved agriculture during the first Industrial Revolution combined to produce increasing opportunities for jobs as well as more plentiful and nutritious food. In the second Industrial Revolution scientific advances in medicine, along with improved sanitation, contributed to a declining mortality rate. The population of Britain grew from around 9 million in 1700 to around 20 million in 1850. Then from 1871 to 1914, Britain's population soared from 31 million to nearly 50 million. In Germany, the population grew from around 41 million in 1871 to 58 million in 1914.

More revealing than overall population figures is the shift of populations from rural to urban areas. For example, in 1800, around 60 percent of the population of Great Britain lived in rural areas. By 1850, however, about 50 percent of the population lived in cities, including the new industrial and commercial centers of Manchester, Liverpool, Birmingham, and Glasgow. Older capital cities of Europe, such as Paris, Berlin, and St. Petersburg, also saw vast increases in population.

European Migrations   Another social change during the industrial era concerns overseas emigrations of Europeans. While this movement was sparked by the dramatic rise in population in industrialized Europe, another factor was the desire to escape the poverty of underdeveloped regions of Europe for better opportunities in America. Advances in transportation made it easier for Europeans to emigrate. In all, some 60 million Europeans left for other parts of the world between 1800 and 1914. Of these, the majority emigrated to the United States and Canada (see Map 26.4).

Industrial Society

Industrialization led to significant changes in the hierarchy of social ranks. Although the elites continued to enjoy their privileged status, the increasing importance of capitalism and commerce, and with it the accumulation of significant wealth, now enhanced the status of the upper echelons of the middle class, or **bourgeoisie**.

emigrants waiting at the dock in Naples, Italy ca. 1910

Bourgeoisie: Social class that owns and controls the means of production.

MAP 26.4 **European Population Movements, 1750–1914.**

No longer were status and power determined solely by aristocratic birth or privilege. The principal alteration in the social hierarchy, however, was the appearance of a new rank: the working class. The advent of industrialism created the concept of "class consciousness," or growing awareness of social standing determined by occupation and income.

The Upper Classes   At the top of the European social scene were members of the landed aristocracy, sometimes referred to as "old money." They were joined by the new urban elites, known as "noveau riche" (or the "new money" crowd). These urban elites were the extremely rich factory owners, bankers, and merchants who had made personal fortunes from industrial pursuits, who had married into the highest social rank, or whose wealth was not quite at the level of the aristocracy. Together, they constituted only 5 percent of the total population. Although a tiny minority, they managed to control almost 40 percent of Europe's wealth.

The Middle Classes   A notch down from the upper classes were the middle classes, who constituted around 15 percent of Europe's total population. Distinguished from the landed aristocracy above them and from the working classes below, they enjoyed comfortable lifestyles in terms of education, fine homes, and the conspicuous consumption of luxury goods. But the middle classes were themselves divided into an upper and a lower tier by a sense of class consciousness. The former included professionals (lawyers, physicians), high-ranking government officials, and prosperous businessmen and merchants. The latter was comprised of small business owners and shopkeepers, along with skilled workers in factories, mines, and other places.

It was the upper middle class that set the cultural and moral tone for the second half of the nineteenth century. They set themselves apart from those above their social status—and especially from those below it— by emphasizing what they considered their respectability, frugality, and industry.

Paris Street; Rainy Day by Gustave Caillebotte (1877)

The Working Class   Urban factory workers were distinguished by the regulation of their daily routine by the factory time clock and by selling their labor in return for cash wages. In the working class, divisions existed between skilled and unskilled workers, largely determined by their degree of familiarity with industrial machinery and its maintenance.

Working conditions in British textile mills in the early 1800s were deplorable. Without traditional protective guilds or associations, workers were at the mercy of factory owners. The factory clock and the pace of factory machinery determined the day's work, which was repetitive, dirty, and dangerous. Even young children worked in factories. In fact, until the 1840s in Britain, the majority of "hands," or factory workers, were women and children, who, by virtue of their inexperience and expendability, could be paid less than their male counterparts.

Conditions were often even worse in the mines. Children began work in mines most often as "trappers," responsible for opening and shutting ventilation doors in mineshafts. Because of their small size, children were put to work lugging newly dug

Woman and Children Coal Putters, Mid and East Lothian, Scotland ca. 1848. Women and children (some as young as 5 or 6 years old) worked long hours in terrible conditions in underground mines. Here a woman and two children, known as "putters," struggle to push a wagon of coal to the surface. Other children, called "trappers," maintained airflow in the tunnels by opening and closing their doors.

coal along low underground passageways for conveyance to the surface. Girls were especially victimized in underground mines, where they were frequently sexually abused by their supervisors.

Factory Towns   Because industrial cities expanded close to factories and mills, conditions there were as grim as within the factories themselves. The working classes lived in crowded, shoddily built tenements in narrow, dark streets. Clouds of coal smoke blackened buildings, acidified the rain and soil, and caused respiratory ailments. Piles of coal ash, pungent waste materials from coking or from gas works, and outpourings from tanneries and dye works combined with household waste, sewage, and horse manure. Waste disposal was rudimentary, access to clean water was limited, and diseases were rampant in the exploding population.

Adding to the miseries of the inhabitants of factory towns were their wretched living conditions. The working classes lived in crowded, shoddily built tenements in narrow, dark streets. One social activist, Friedrich Engels (1820–1895), the son of a wealthy mill owner and later collaborator with Karl Marx, was determined to call attention to such abysmal conditions.

Critics of Industrialism

It was not long before Engels and other socially conscious observers began to call for reform of working conditions. Efforts to improve these sordid conditions were launched in Great Britain in the 1820s and 1830s and carried over into the 1870s.

Working-Class Tenements in English Industrial Cities. In this engraving, entitled *Over London by Rail*, the celebrated engraver Gustave Doré (1832–1883) depicts the overcrowded and squalid living conditions in working-class tenements during the early years of the Industrial Revolution. Notice the long rows of houses separated by walls and arranged in back-to-back fashion. Notice also the stretched lines for drying clothes, as well as the large number of occupants in each outdoor area.

Socialists   The plight of the working classes inspired many social activists to take up the fight for reform. Henri de Saint-Simon (1760–1825) argued that private property should be more equally distributed—"from each according to his abilities, to each according to his works." Louis Blanc (1811–1882) criticized the capitalist system in his *The Organization of Work* (1839), urging workers to agitate for voting rights and espousing radical ideas like the right to work. He reconfigured Saint-Simon's phrase to read "from each according to his abilities, to each according to his needs." Charles Fourier (1772–1837) advocated the founding of self-sustaining model communities in which jobs were apportioned according to ability and interest, with those doing the most dangerous or unattractive jobs receiving the highest wages.

Robert Owen (1771–1858), a factory owner in the north of England, established a model community in Scotland called New Lanark, where more humane living and working conditions for workers resulted in greater profits. After campaigning for the formation of workers' unions, Owen left for America, where he set up a model socialist community in Indiana called New Harmony, which eventually dissolved amid internal quarrels.

Another reform movement in Britain, **Chartism**, was primarily intent on political reforms. Formed by the London Working Men's Association, its primary goal, among others, was universal male suffrage. Millions of workers signed petitions that were presented to Parliament in 1839 and 1842; these were rejected. Nevertheless, the chartist movement served as a model for future attempts at labor reform.

Karl Marx By far the most famous of the social reformers was Karl Marx (1818–1883). The son of a prosperous German attorney, Marx earned a PhD in philosophy. During a visit to Manchester, where he befriended Friedrich Engels, Marx observed both the miserable lives of factory workers and the inequities of industrialism. From this experience, Marx developed his theory, which he termed "scientific socialism," that all of history involved class struggles. Borrowing the dialectical schema of the German philosopher Georg Wilhelm Friedrich Hegel (1770–1831), Marx replaced its idealism with his own materialist concept based on economic class struggle: *dialectical materialism*. Marx saw revolution as the means by which the industrial working class would topple the capitalist order.

Marx and Engels joined the nascent Communist Party in London. In preparation for a meeting in 1848, the two collaborators wrote *The Communist Manifesto* (1848), propaganda designed to rally support among the working class, or *proletariat*, and to encourage it to rise up and overthrow the capitalist factory owners, or *bourgeoisie*. The *Manifesto* reflects Marx's vision that "the history of all hitherto existing society is the history of class struggle" and that the time had come for the working classes to overthrow the capitalists: "The proletarians have nothing to lose but their chains. They have a world to win. *Working men of all countries, unite!*"

Inquiries and Reforms Critics of industrialism and even some factory owners called for governments to reform working conditions. In 1832 Parliament launched an inquiry into abuses within factories, resulting in the Sadler Report, which pointed out abuses related to child labor. In 1833 the Factory Act was passed, which set a minimum age of 9 for child employees and limited the workday to 8 hours for children between the ages of 9 and 13 and to 12 hours for those aged 13–18. Further reforms in 1847 and 1848 limited women and children to a maximum of 58 hours a week (the Ten Hours Act). Similar inquiries concerning working conditions within mines resulted in the Mines Act of 1842, which forbade the underground employment of all girls and women.

Improved Standards of Living
By the end of the nineteenth century, conditions in factories and mines were substantially better than at the beginning of the century. In addition, wage levels increased across the nineteenth century for industrial workers.

New Jobs for Women As a result of the second Industrial Revolution, many women fared better in terms of employment. In overall terms, women represented around one-third of the workers in later nineteenth-century industrial jobs. But factory work in textile mills was not the only avenue open to women as the industrial era unfolded. Inventions like the typewriter (perfected in the 1870s), the telephone, and calculating machines (in use in the 1890s) required workers to handle other jobs in factories, the majority of which went to single women and widows. As a result, women became particularly prominent in secretarial office jobs. Business firms created countless jobs for secretaries, while department stores opened up jobs for women as clerks.

Chartism: A workers' movement in Britain that sought, in the 1830s and 1840s, to enact the "People's Charter" designed to achieve electoral reform and make Britain the most democratic country in the world.

Testimony of Matthew Crabtree from the Sadler Committee Report (1832) and Andrew Ure, *The Philosophy of Manufactures* (1835)

Caroline Norton, excerpt from *English Laws for Women in the Nineteenth Century* (1854)

Women Working as Telephone Operators. The first telephone exchange appeared in 1879. Women were selected as operators because their voices were considered pleasing to the ear and because they were considered more polite than men.

Women's Suffrage Movement   Although women were afforded new workplace and professional opportunities, they remained in many ways second-class citizens. Women in both the United States and Europe did not begin to gain the right to own property or to sue for divorce until the third quarter of the nineteenth century.

More urgent for many female reformers was the right to vote. Throughout Europe during the late nineteenth and early twentieth centuries, women formed political groups to press for the vote. The most active of these groups was in Britain, where in 1867 the National Society for Women's Suffrage was founded. The most radical of British political feminists was Emmeline Pankhurst (1858–1928), who together with her daughters formed the Women's Social and Political Union in 1903. They and their supporters, known as **suffragettes**, resorted to civil disobedience in order to call attention to their cause.

Political feminists were also active on the Continent. The French League of Women's Rights was founded in the 1870s, and the Union of German Women's Organizations was formed in 1894; in neither country was the right to vote granted women until after World War I. In the United States, after decades of lobbying, women's suffrage was finally granted by constitutional amendment in 1920.

Suffragettes: Women who organized to demand the right to vote. In 1893 New Zealand was the first self-governing country that granted women the right to vote.

Improved Urban Living

Urban living conditions in industrialized nations improved significantly during the late nineteenth and early twentieth centuries. Largely as a result of the application of new technologies, the lives of urban dwellers were improved in the second half of the nineteenth century.

Sanitation and Electricity   Beginning in the 1860s and 1870s large cities in Britain and Europe established public water services and began to construct underground sewage systems to carry waste from houses, outfitted with running water, to locations beyond urban areas. By the latter part of the nineteenth century, gas lamps began to give way to electrical varieties. Thomas Edison (1847–1931) perfected the incandescent light bulb in 1879, making the lighting of homes and business interiors more affordable and practical.

Paris represents a good example of the implementation of these reforms. In the 1850s and 1860s, Napoleon III (r. 1852–1870) appointed the urban planner Georges Haussmann (1809–1891) to begin a massive reconstruction of the city. Haussmann tore down close-packed tenements in order to construct modernized buildings and wide boulevards. Like most cities of the industrialized West, by the turn of the twentieth century, Paris featured lighted and paved streets, public water systems, parks, hospitals, and police. A dramatic symbol of both the newly redesigned city of Paris and the triumph of industry and science during the second Industrial Revolution was the Eiffel Tower, designed by Alexandre Gustave Eiffel (1832–1923) for the Paris Exposition of 1889.

photographs of Paris
by Charles Marville
(1853-1870)

Leisure and Sport   Another advance in urban life was an increase in leisure and sporting activities. The later nineteenth century saw the emergence of sporting organizations and clubs, along with the establishment of rules for play. Games played by professional teams provided recreation for working-class men. In Britain, for example, rules for playing soccer were established in 1863 by the Football Association, and in 1888 the English Football League was established. In the 1870s and 1880s British cricket teams took the game to the colonies, and in 1901 the championship game of the British Football Association (FA)Cup competition drew over 100,000 spectators.

Nor was this trend confined to Britain. In 1896 the first modern Olympic Games took place in Athens, Greece. In 1903 the first Tour de France was run through the French countryside. In 1904 the game of soccer was given international rules. And by the early 1900s, the game of baseball in America had been formalized into two leagues, the National League and the American League.

excerpt from
Thorstein Veblen, *The
Theory of the Leisure
Class* (1899)

Big Business

As urban planning increased toward the end of the nineteenth century, business flourished. As manufacturing, transportation, and financing matured, businessmen became concerned about competition and falling profits. Since governments generally pursued hands-off liberalism in the economy (except for protective tariffs), entrepreneurs sought to establish cartels and monopolies, creating big business enterprises in the process.

Large Firms   As Britain industrialized, it shifted from a closed mercantilist economy to a liberal free-trade policy (see Chapter 22). Britain's competitors, especially Germany and the United States, by contrast, erected high tariff walls in order to help their fledgling industries. After the second wave of steel, chemical, and electrical industrialization, the scale of industrial investments rose exponentially. On domestic markets, governments did not interfere with business organization and practice, except for labor protection in Europe. As a result, big businesses emerged that protected their profit rates through *cartels* (market-sharing agreements) or strove for outright monopolies.

Large firms developed in Germany and the United States, the leaders of the second wave of industrialization. By the 1890s, corporations like the Krupp steel-works in Germany and Standard Oil Company in the United States controlled large shares of their markets. Standard Oil at its height, for example, produced over 90 percent of the country's petroleum. The United States Steel Corporation, founded in 1901 by Andrew Carnegie (1835–1919), dominated the production of American steel.

New Management Styles New technologies that offered more efficient means of production led to significant changes in production processes during the second phase of European industrialism. One example is the implementation of the so-called American System, incorporating the use of interchangeable parts, which greatly enhanced mass production. A related development was the appearance of "continuous-flow production," wherein workers performed specialized tasks at stationary positions along an assembly line. In addition, new "scientific management" tactics were employed in mass-production assembly plants. Since no more than basic skills were required on many assembly lines, labor costs could be kept low. The resulting escalation in the speed of production contributed to an increase in the production of goods for daily consumption and, therefore, in the development of a consumer market at the turn of the twentieth century.

The Assembly Line. The American System of interchangeable parts for muskets of the early nineteenth century had evolved into the assembly line by the early twentieth. Here, Ford Model T automobiles are moved along a conveyor to different stations, where workers assemble them in simple, repetitive steps, resulting in production efficiency and low prices for the cars.

Intellectual and Cultural Responses to Industrialism

The advent of modernity was initially celebrated as an age of progress in science, industry, and the development of a mass culture. Nevertheless, there was a growing sense of unease concerning these advances, especially among intellectuals and artists. Alternative and startlingly innovative modes of cultural expression were upsetting traditional forms. The vibrant but chaotic intellectual and cultural scene in Europe was thus marked by anxiety and uncertainty on the eve of the Great War.

Thomas Carlyle,
"Signs of the Times"
(1829)

Scientific and Intellectual Developments

The latter half of the nineteenth century saw advances in both theoretical and empirical sciences that laid the basis for many of the staples of the twentieth century. Among the most far-reaching were atomic physics and relativity theory, Darwinism and evolution, and the foundations of modern psychology.

New Theories of Matter   Researchers made important discoveries in the 1890s that would have far-reaching consequences in the development of atomic physics and the theories of relativity. In 1892 the Dutch physicist Hendrik Lorentz (1853–1928) demonstrated that the atom contained smaller particles, which he named "corpuscles"; these were later renamed electrons. A few years later, Wilhelm Roentgen (1845–1923) discovered a form of emission he called X-rays. The ability to generate these rays would shortly lead to the development of the X-ray machine. The following year, 1896, saw the first experiments in assessing radioactivity in uranium and radium by Antoine Becquerel (1852–1908) and Marie Curie (1867–1934).

As a result of these experimental findings, theoretical physics advanced new theories on the nature of light and energy. In 1900 Max Planck (1858–1947) proposed that instead of the accepted notion that energy is emitted in steady streams or waves, it is issued in bursts, or what he termed "quanta." This idea, later developed into quantum theory, suggested that matter and energy might be interchangeable. Ernest Rutherford (1871–1937), interested in this interchangeability, demonstrated in 1911 that radioactive atoms release a form of energy in the process of their disintegration. Thus, centuries of speculation about atoms as the building blocks of nature led to experimentally verified theories of subatomic particles.

Albert Einstein   Perhaps the most sensational of the turn-of-the-century scientific theories was the theory of relativity of Albert Einstein (1879–1955). Einstein destroyed the Newtonian notion of a mechanical universe that can be based on the concepts of absolute space and time. He argued that there are no absolutes of time, space, and motion; rather, these are relative to each other and depend on the position of the observer.

Moreover, Einstein demonstrated that Newton was incorrect in thinking that matter and energy were separate entities; they were, in fact, equivalent, and he developed the corresponding mathematical formula. In his equation $E = mc^2$, Einstein theorized that the atom contains an amount of energy equal to its mass multiplied by the square of the speed of light. In other words, relatively small amounts of matter could be converted into massive amounts of energy. This discovery, developed further in the twentieth century, provided the foundation for a better understanding of the forces among subatomic particles and the construction of nuclear weapons.

Charles Darwin The basis of modern theories of evolution was first proposed by Charles Darwin (1809–1882). Darwin's *On the Origin of Species by Means of Natural Selection* (1859) argued that species gradually evolved from lower to higher forms. Further, only those species equipped with the tools to survive in their environments would win out; those without these characteristics would become extinct. The most controversial part of the Darwinian theory of evolution was the notion that characteristics are passed on by means of "natural selection." In other words, there is no intelligence or plan in the universe—only random chance and the process of organisms struggling to survive and reproduce.

Although the *Origin* said nothing about the theory of evolution as applied to humankind—this appeared later in his *The Descent of Man* (1871)—there were those who quickly applied it to society and nations. The English philosopher Herbert Spencer (1820–1903) proposed a theory that came to be called "social Darwinism," which sought to apply ideas of natural selection to races, ethnicities, and peoples. Spencer's ideas were frequently used to support imperial ventures aimed at the conquest and sometimes the "uplift" of non-European or American peoples as well as to justify increasingly virulent nationalism in the years leading to World War I.

Sigmund Freud The best-known of the early psychologists was Sigmund Freud (1856–1939), an Austrian physician. Freud specialized in treating patients suffering from what was then called "hysteria," which he treated using a technique he labeled "psychoanalysis." In *The Interpretation of Dreams* (1900), Freud drew connections between dreams and the unconscious in humans. Freudian psychological theories suggest that humans are in fact irrational creatures, driven by subconscious, and not conscious, urges. Today, although Freud's ideas no longer dominate the field of psychology, his influence still survives in the form of therapeutic counseling and behavior modification.

The Meaning of the New Scientific Discoveries Physics, biology, and psychology—as well as advances in medicine—contributed to the emergence of scientific–industrial society at the end of the nineteenth century. With the arrival of the theories of relativity, Darwinian selection, and the psychological unconscious, however, the transition toward the scientific–industrial age began to provoke deep philosophical and religious confusion.

Charles Darwin as Ape. Darwin's theories about the evolution of humankind aroused enormous scorn. In this scathing 1861 cartoon, Darwin, with the body of a monkey, holds a mirror to a simian-looking creature. The original caption quoted a line from Shakespeare's *Love's Labour's Lost:* "This is the ape of form."

In previous centuries, religious skepticism had never been more convincing than religious faith for most people. The atheism of the Enlightenment and secular concepts such as the Hobbesian embodied mind and the "war of all against all," were considered to be merely unproven speculations. Now, the specter of a meaningless universe inhabited by beings devoid of free will and driven by biological forces over which they have no control seemed to be inescapable. Thus, the new era suggested a disturbing paradox: The same sciences that had eased many burdens of human life had also taken away the sense of purpose that made life worth living. It was left to philosophers, religious leaders, intellectuals, and artists to wrestle with the implications of this central problem of scientific–industrial society.

Toward Modernity in Philosophy and Religion

Despite the achievements of Western industrialized society during the late nineteenth century, detractors—mostly in the intellectual community of western Europe—decried the boastful claims of a "superior" scientific civilization. These voices ridiculed Western bourgeois values and advocated alternative approaches to personal fulfillment.

Friedrich Nietzsche   The most celebrated of these detractors was the German philosopher Friedrich Nietzsche (1844–1900), who railed against the conventions of Western civilization and criticized the perceived decadence of modern culture. One object of derision for Nietzsche was the notion of scientific, rational thought as the best path toward intellectual truth. For Nietzsche, rational thought will not improve either the individual or the welfare of humankind; only recourse to "will" instead of intellect—what Nietzsche called the "will to power"—will suffice. The individual who follows this path will become a "superman" and will lead others toward truth. Another target of Nietzsche's wrath was Christianity, which in his eyes led its believers into a "slave morality"; he infamously declared that "God is dead."

Toward Modernity in Literature and the Arts

The creation of scientific–industrial society—modernity—was a slow and traumatic process. The social realities of the new order were evident in the postromantic period of realism in the arts and literature, and the succeeding decades yielded an even grimmer and more disjointed perspective.

Literature   Literary expression was generally negative toward the "soulless" science and the materialism of the second half of the industrial revolution. Thomas Hardy (1840–1928), for example, in his *Far from the Madding Crowd* (1874) emphasized the despair resulting from the futility of fighting against the grinding forces of modernity. The plays of George Bernard Shaw (1856–1950) reflect the influence of Darwin and Nietzsche, mocking the pretension of urban, bourgeois society. In the mid-1880s two new movements in literature, decadence and symbolism, appeared. The decadents rejected prevailing bourgeois conventions, while the symbolists preferred to revert to a form of the earlier romantic era that emphasized the ideal and the beautiful.

Oscar Wilde, *The Soul of Man under Socialism* (1891)

Modernism in Art   Artistic expression in the period 1871–1914, often collectively labeled "modernism," consisted of a variety of movements skeptical of accepted middle-class conventions and truths. The impressionists, whose style

Wassily Kandinsky, *On the Spiritual Element in Art* (1912)

Modernism in Art. Pablo Picasso's *Les Demoiselles d'Avignon* was unveiled in Paris in 1907. Its distorted and broken forms set in a fractured and flattened space mark a conscious break with the Western artistic tradition. The painting's borrowing from "primitivist" African and ancient Iberian sources, and its forceful and unsettling depiction of *demoiselles*, a euphemism for prostitutes, unsettle the viewer.

image analysis

interactive concept map

dominated from the 1870s until around 1890, took their name from a painting by Claude Monet (1840–1926) entitled *Impression, Sunrise* (1874). By around 1890 the impressionist school had been superseded by a more freewheeling style known as postimpressionism.

The period from 1905 to 1914 saw revolutionary and experimental offshoots of the postimpressionists. Perhaps the best known of these, cubism, is represented in the works of Pablo Picasso (1881–1973). In such works as *Les Demoiselles d'Avignon* (1907), often considered the first of the cubist paintings, Picasso reveals his interest in African masks as an alternative to conventional European motifs.

Modernism in Music Between the 1870s and 1914, musical expression followed two separate tracks: modernism and primitivism. In primitivism, composers abandoned formal structure and convention to express their personal musical perceptions. Modernism was more attuned to cultural developments evolving in other fields during the waning years of the nineteenth century and early years of the twentieth. Some musicians were even more unconventional in their rejection of Western musical conventions. In 1911 the Austrian composer Arnold Schoenberg (1874–1951) published *Theory of Harmony*, in which he announced a new style of musical composition featuring themes reflecting Freudian theories of the unconscious along with the noises and dissonances of engines, machines, and urban life.

❯ Putting It All Together

The dramatic changes associated with the Industrial Revolution had profound implications for both the industrializing countries and the nonindustrialized world. Thanks to new technologies and facilitated by advances in transportation and communication, the period from 1871 to 1914 saw world trade networks and empires dominated by the newly industrialized nations.

The Industrial Revolution began in Britain in the early eighteenth century and eventually spread to Europe and North America during the nineteenth century. Britain began the revolution when it employed steam engines in the production of textiles. The development of the factory system along with more efficient transportation systems expanded British manufacturing. Not everyone benefited, however, from the emergence of the factory system, which led to social unrest and calls for reform.

The second Industrial Revolution in the later nineteenth century expanded the industrial economies of highly industrialized countries beyond Britain, including those of America and Germany. The daily lives of most citizens in industrialized nations were also improved by advances in transportation, communication, and sanitation.

These same advances also contributed to an expansion of European imperialism. The growth of industry and commerce, aided by new technologies and inventions, resulted in a quest among highly industrialized nations for raw materials, cheap labor, and new markets. Moreover, Western industrial nations discovered that new needs required the importation of not only raw materials but also foodstuffs. By the 1880s faster ships powered by steam engines further enabled this expansion, while submarine cables provided for more efficient overseas communications. After 1871, the world's economy was increasingly divided into those who produced the world's manufactured products and those who both supplied the requisite raw materials and made up the growing pool of consumers.

As the basis for many of the patterns of twentieth-century modernity was being laid, World War I and its aftermath would soon reveal the divisions created by modernity and its scientific–technological underpinnings. Yet modern societies would continue their interaction and adaptation with older forms. Today, it is India and China, the successors to the agrarian–urban religious civilizations that resisted the new order most tenaciously, whose economies set the pace for twenty-first-century industrial development. It is to the story of the impact of modernity on these societies and others around the globe that we now turn.

Review and Relate

Thinking Through Patterns

Examine the ways historians approach the big questions of this chapter.

The Industrial Revolution began in Britain in the early eighteenth century. Britain had an earlier political revolution that empowered the merchant classes over the landed aristocracy, a prior agricultural revolution, and abundance of raw materials like coal.

Industrialization resulted in several social changes and adjustments. The capitalist middle classes were enriched and empowered by the growth of industrialism, as were the working classes, which did not exist as a group prior to industrialism. The benefits of industrialism were not evenly distributed across social strata; factory and mine workers were frequently exploited.

With the steam engine, capitalist entrepreneurs were able to substitute mechanical power for natural power and thus to develop the factory system. The factory system spread to the Continent and America as middle-class capitalism eclipsed mercantilism. Further advances contributed to a second Industrial Revolution beginning around 1850 based in steel, chemistry, and electricity.

Progress in industrial technology during the second Industrial Revolution led to practical inventions as well as advances in communication and transportation. These tools facilitated the expansion of Western imperialism in Africa and Asia during the closing years of the nineteenth century

>> **Where and when did the Industrial Revolution originate?**

>> **What were some effects of industrialization on Western society? How did social patterns change?**

>> **In what ways did industrialization contribute to innovations in technology? How did these technological advances** contribute to Western imperialism in the late **nineteenth century?**

> **What new directions in science, philosophy, religion, and the arts did industrialism generate? What kind of responses did it provoke?**

The new society that industrialism was creating spawned new directions in science, philosophy, religion, and the arts. Yet there was also a profound disquiet among scientists, intellectuals, and artists as traditions were abandoned. This disquiet would emerge in the immediate years after World War I.

| Against the Grain

Consider this as a counterpoint to the main patterns examined in this chapter.

The Luddites

- Why did the British government react with such urgency to suppress the Luddite movement?
- How does the Luddite revolt compare with other protest movements against modernity in the later nineteenth century?

Although the mechanization of the textile industry was welcomed by some as providing new opportunities and by others as an indication of technological progress, still others were hardline opponents of the new industrial movement. One group of workers in early-nineteenth-century Britain, known as "Luddites," fiercely opposed the application of machines in the textile industry.

While the term "Luddite" now refers to those who oppose new technologies of any kind, the original Luddites feared the widespread use of new machinery that lowered their wages and threatened their livelihoods. Composed primarily of skilled artisans in the knitting and hosiery trades, Luddites mounted violent protests against the use of mechanical knitting frames and steam-powered looms. Referring to themselves as soldiers in the army of General Ludd, a mythical figure, Luddites began their assaults on the night of November 4, 1811. Breaking into the home of a weaver, they smashed several power looms. During 1812 and 1813 Luddites expanded their assaults, and in a span of 14 months Luddite "armies" smashed and destroyed around 1,000 machines.

The British government dispatched troops to suppress the Luddite movement, and in February of 1812 Parliament passed the Frame Breaking Act, which made attacks on textile machinery punishable by death. This was followed by the trial and hanging of eight Luddites later in the year. After a quick show trial in January of 1813, another 14 Luddites were executed. This effectively ended the movement, although occasional outbreaks of Luddism lingered on.

Even though the Luddite movement was relatively short-lived, it successfully called attention to inequalities inherent in early industrialism. This in turn prompted parliamentary reforms in the 1830s and 1840s, which improved working conditions for workers in factories, mines, and other occupations.

Key Terms

🔊))
audio flashcards

Bourgeoisie   610
Breech-loading   607
Chartism   612

Cottage
industry   600

Suffragettes   614
Tariff   601

For additional resources, please go to
www.oup.com/us/vonsivers.
Please see the Further Resources section at the back of the book
for additional readings and suggested websites.

> Chapter 27 1750–1914

The New Imperialism
in the Nineteenth Century

**THE NEW
IMPERIALISM**

At the end of the Muslim month-long observance of Ramadan in 1827, Hussein (r. 1815–1830), the ruler of the autonomous Ottoman province of Algeria in North Africa, held a celebratory reception for the diplomatic corps of consuls at his palace in the port city of Algiers. When he saw the French consul, Pierre Deval, Hussein publicly accused the consul of defrauding him of a large sum of money owed by France and demanded immediate payment of the debt. To emphasize his demand, Hussein struck Deval with his fan and declared him *persona non grata*, which, in terms of diplomatic protocol, meant that he had to leave the country immediately.

France's restored Bourbon king, Charles X (r. 1824–1830), found this insult to an appointee of the French court intolerable. He dispatched a naval detachment to Algiers in 1828 to demand that Hussein apologize, declare the debt liquidated, and pay reparations for piracy raids of preceding years. When Hussein rejected the demands, the French mounted a blockade of the port. In 1830, a French expeditionary force conquered Algiers, deposed Hussein, and sent him into exile. Less than two decades later, Algeria became a colony of France.

ABOVE: Egypt, Suez Canal. "Flotilla of the Sovereigns" (heads of state) proceeding through the canal on the opening day of November 17, 1869.

The incident illustrates the changing fortunes of those countries that were the beneficiaries of the new forces of modernity—in this case, France—and those that largely were not, like the Ottoman Empire and its territories in Algeria. In this chapter we will study the victims of conquest and occupation in south and Southeast Asia, the Middle East, Africa, and the Pacific Ocean that most clearly make visible the underlying patterns of imperialism and colonialism.

Two new patterns characterized European politics outside western and central Europe in the period 1750–1900. The first pattern was the pursuit of a **new imperialism** by western European countries against the decentralizing Ottoman Empire, under assault by the Russian Empire since the eighteenth century. The Europeans first protected the Ottomans from Russia, only later to help themselves to Ottoman provinces, beginning with the capture of Algeria by France.

The second pattern was a shift from coastal trade forts under chartered companies to the new imperialism of government takeover, territorial conquest, and often **colonialism**. Of course, in the Americas the old trade-fort imperialism had given way to full-fledged Spanish and Portuguese territorial imperialism, followed by conquest and colonialism already in the early1500s, when conquest there proved easier than in more densely settled Africa and Asia. Between 1750 and 1900, the western and central European countries of Great Britain, France, Germany, and Italy competed with each other for the establishment of colonial empires in the Middle East, Africa, Asia, and Pacific Ocean.

The British Colonies of India and Australia

The transition from European trade-fort activities to colonialism in India coincided with the decline of the Mughal dynasty (see Chapter 20). As a result, Britain became a colonial power in the Eastern Hemisphere, with India as its center. Australia and New Zealand began as British settler colonies, the former as a penal colony and the latter against fierce indigenous resistance.

The British East India Company

An important factor in the rise of British power in India was the Seven Years' War, during which fighting took place in Europe, in the Americas, and in India. It was the war in India, along with the political difficulties of the Mughals, that enabled the rise of the British to supremacy on the subcontinent.

The Seven Years' War By the early eighteenth century Britain had established trading posts in provincial cities that would over time be transformed into India's greatest metropolises: Madras (Chennai), Bombay (Mumbai), Calcutta (Kolkata). By 1750 their chief commercial competitors were the French, who were aggressively building up both trade and political power from a base in Pondicherry in southern India.

Seeing Patterns

≫ What new patterns emerged in the transition from trade-fort imperialism to the new imperialism?

≫ How did European colonizers develop their colonies economically, given that they were industrializing themselves at the same time?

≫ What were the experiences of the indigenous people under the new imperialism? How did they adapt to colonialism? How did they resist?

New Imperialism: Conquest by a European country of territories in Africa, Asia, and the Pacific Ocean with the declared goal of the establishment of an empire (European mother country plus overseas colonies).

Colonialism: Establishment of a more or less elaborate administrative system by a European country in the conquered overseas territory, accompanied by economic exploitation. In a number of overseas territories, furthermore, settlers from Europe practiced colonialism by establishing themselves as farmers, planters, and craftsmen.

Chapter Outline

- The British Colonies of India and Australia
- European Imperialism in the Middle East and Africa
- Western Imperialism and Colonialism in Southeast Asia
- Putting It All Together

For the British East India Company, its evolution into a kind of shadow government in the area around Calcutta in Bengal would now bear dividends. The decline of Mughal central power meant that regional leaders were being enlisted as French or British allies. The more powerful sought to use the sepoy (from Persian *sipahi* [see-pa-HEE], "soldier") armies of the European companies as support in their own struggles. Out of this confused political and military situation, the East India Company leader, Robert Clive (1725–1774), won a victory over the Indian French allies at Plassey in 1757 and soon eliminated the French from power on the subcontinent. The East India Company ended up in 1763 as the sole European power of consequence in India, and Clive set about consolidating his position from Calcutta.

Going Native: The Nabobs   The East India Company began to expand its holdings across northern India, extorting funds from local princes. The company men had no interest in reforming Indian institutions. Indeed, many became great admirers of Indian culture. Some went so far as to "go native": They took Indian wives, dressed as Indian princes, and on occasion wielded power as local magnates, or **nabobs** (from Urdu *nawwab* [naw-WAHB], "deputy," "viceroy").

The vast distances separating the company's London directors from operations in India made its local activities virtually autonomous. Its power, organization, and its army influenced local disputes across northern India; its policy of paying low wages while turning a blind eye to employees trading locally for their private benefit led to corruption.

By 1800, British possessions extended across most of northern India (see Map 27.1). This extension prompted a shift in trading from spices to cotton goods—and, increasingly, to raw cotton—as the most lucrative commodity, due to Britain's mechanized textile revolution.

The Perils of Reform   During the nineteenth century, India and China were still the primary economic engines of Eurasia. As the Industrial Revolution developed, however, Britain's share of the world's output increased, while India's declined (see Figure 27.1).

As Britain's share of India's economy grew, the British sought to create markets for their own goods there and to divert Indian exports exclusively into the British domestic market. In addition, officials of the East India Company arbitrated disputes among Indian rulers, taking over their lands as payment for loans, and strong-arming many into becoming wards of the British. Because of this attrition, by the end of the Napoleonic Wars, the Mughal emperor's lands had been reduced to the region immediately surrounding Delhi and Agra.

Perceptions of Empire. The British East India Company's real ascent to power in India began with Robert Clive's victory at Plassey in 1757, the symbolism of which is depicted here. Note the deference with which the assorted Indian princes treat the conqueror (top). Below, the second-from-last Mughal emperor, Akbar Shah II (r. 1806–1837), receives the British resident, ca. 1815. Despite the fact that the British East India Company had extended its sway over much of northern India by this time, the Indian artist depicts the British government official in a pose of supplication to Akbar Shah—in almost a mirror image of the imagined Indian princes in the painting of Clive.

MAP 27.1 **The Expansion of British Power in India, 1756–1805.**

While many in India chafed at company rule, its policy of noninterference with Indian customs and institutions softened the blow of the conquest somewhat. The period following the Napoleonic Wars, however, brought the British government into a more direct role.

Clashes between factory owners and labor and the drive for political reform in Britain during this period found echoes in British policy toward India. From the

Nabob: A person who acquired a large fortune in India during the period of British rule.

1600 Founding of English (later British) East India Company	1757 Battle of Plassey	1788–1840 50,000 British convicts shipped to Australia	interactive timeline
1602 Founding of Dutch East India Company	1763 Opening of British colonialism in India	1830 Dutch introduce cultivation system in Indonesia	

1830–1847 French conquest of Algeria	1857 Great Rebellion, or Sepoy Mutiny, India	1884–1885 Berlin Conference	1899–1913 US conquest of Philippines
1852–1885 French conquest of Vietnam	1882 British expeditionary force occupies Egypt	1893 New Zealand grants women right to vote	

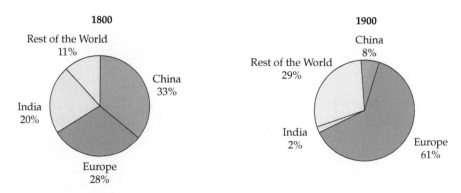

Figure 27.1 Share of World Manufacturing Output, 1800 and 1900.

opening decades of the century, many Protestant missionaries active in mission-based reform in India had also been involved with movements for the abolition of slavery, industrial workers' rights, and electoral reform in Britain. By 1830 these individuals asserted that India should be similarly reformed: better working conditions for the poor, free trade, the abolition of "barbaric" customs, and a vigorous Christian missionary effort.

In addition, the company reformed the tax system into a money-based land fee for greater efficiency of collection. At the same time, new industrial enterprises and transport and communication advances were constructed, benefiting the economy but also disrupting the livelihoods of many. There was a perception on the part of opponents, and even some supporters, that these efforts in both India and England were characterized by arrogance of the English toward Indian society. Perhaps the most famous expression of this was found in the parliamentary reformer and historian Thomas B. Macaulay's 1835 "Minute on Education," where he asserted that "a single shelf of European books is worth more than all the literatures of Asia and Arabia."

India's First War of Independence

Disillusionment with the rapid pace of change and fears that British missionaries were attempting, with government connivance, to Christianize India came to a head among the company's sepoy troops in 1857. With the introduction of the new Enfield rifle, which required its operator to bite the end off a greased paper cartridge full of gunpowder, a rumor started that the grease was cow and pig fat. Since this would violate the dietary restrictions of both Hindus and Muslims, the troops saw this as a plot to leave the followers of both religions ritually unclean and thus open to conversion to Christianity. Though the rumors proved untrue, the revolt became a wholesale rebellion aimed at throwing the British out of India and restoring the Mughal emperor to full power. The perceived insults to Indian religions and culture pushed the troops and their allies to frightful atrocities.

The First War of Independence (as it is commonly referred to in India, along with the Great Rebellion; it is known by the British as the Sepoy Mutiny or Great Mutiny) became a civil war as pro- and anti-British Indian forces clashed. Although the British were ultimately able to reassert control, the occupation of many towns was accompanied by mass executions of suspected rebels and collaborators.

Thomas B. Macaulay, "Minute on Education" (1835), and Ram Mohan Roy, "Letter To Lord Amherst On Education" (1823)

Execution of Indian Rebels. After British troops and loyalist Indian sepoys had restored order in northern India, retribution was unleashed on the rebels. Here, the most spectacular mode of execution is being carried out. Mutineers are tied across the mouths of cannons and blown to pieces while the troops stand in formation and are forced to watch.

image analysis

Direct British Rule

After assuming direct rule (Hindi *raj*, hence the term "Raj" for the colonial government), the British sought to limit their apparatus of civilian administrators while maintaining an army large enough to avoid a repeat of 1857. The Raj functioned by exploiting divisions in Indian society, which prevented the Indians from uniting to challenge British rule.

Creation of the Civil Service   The British government enacted sweeping reforms in 1858. The East India Company was dismantled, and the British government itself took up the task of governing India. An Indian civil service was created for British and Indians alike to administer the subcontinent's affairs. India had now become, it was said, the "jewel in the crown" of the empire (see Map 27.2).

In 1885, Indians first convened the National Congress, the ancestor of India's present Congress Party. The congress's mission was to win greater autonomy for India within the structure of the British Empire and, by the opening decades of the twentieth century, to push for Indian independence.

Divide and Rule   The Indian civil service was intended as a showpiece of British incorruptibility, in contrast to the perception of endemic graft customary among the Indian princes. For officials, the heavy workload demanded a sophisticated understanding of local conditions and sensibilities. The numbers of civil service members increased markedly in the twentieth century as Britain began to implement a gradual devolution to a kind of federated Indian autonomy.

How did such a small government apparatus control such a large country? In many respects it was done by bluff and artifice. The Indian Army of Great Britain

excerpt from Flora Annie Steel and Grace Gardiner, *Complete Indian Housekeeper and Cook* (1888)

MAP 27.2 **The British Empire in India, 1858–1914.**

was small, well trained, but made up mostly of Indians. The British officers and non-commissioned officers included many Scots and Irish, themselves minorities often subject to discrimination at home. British divide-and-rule tactics made large-scale organization across caste, religious, ethnic, and linguistic lines extremely problematic. Most importantly, advances in weaponry during the late nineteenth century—machine guns, rapid-fire artillery, repeating rifles—made any revolt unthinkable.

Though the bureaucracy of British India served to unite the country for administrative purposes, the British secured their rule locally and regionally by divide-and-rule tactics. A key divide they utilized was the obvious one between Hindus and Muslims. British policy had encouraged Muslims to see the British as their protectors, while also often leaning in their favor in disputes with the Hindus. Thus, Muslims often felt they had a stake in the Raj, particularly when the alternative that presented itself was a Hindu-controlled India, should independence from Britain ever come. Other divides exploited differences among the Hindus. For example, in order to undermine the power bases of local Brahmans, lower castes were sometimes given favorable treatment. Different regions might be given preferential treatment as well. The British also exploited the sense of grandeur of the Indian elites with *durbars* (elaborate, formal public celebrations) at the Raj's showpiece capital of New Delhi. Such occasions reinforced traditional notions of deference and hierarchy.

By identifying British rule with India's historic past, it was hoped that the perception of legitimacy would be enhanced. This effort to co-opt local rulers into upholding the British government as the historically destined status quo placed the local rulers in a **subaltern** relationship with their colonial governors. Yet a growing elite of Western-educated Indian leaders began to use the arguments of empire against their occupiers.

The Delhi Durbar, 1911

Subaltern: A person or thing considered subordinate to another.

British Settler Colonies: Australia

British occupation of Australia and New Zealand began with the conquest of small and weak indigenous forager or agrarian populations, followed by the expropriation of indigenous lands and the establishment of settler colonies. In contrast to their modus operandi in India, the British also encouraged large-scale immigration of European settlers to these regions.

White Settlement in Australia   Dutch navigators discovered the western coast of Australia in 1606, but did not pursue any further contacts or trade fort construction. The British navigator James Cook (1728–1779), during one of his many exploratory journeys in the Pacific, landed in 1770 on the Australian east coast and claimed it for Great Britain. After America won its independence in 1783, the British government looked to Australia as the next place to which it could ship convicts. Between 1788 and 1840, some 50,000 British convicts were shipped to the Australian penal colony.

1817 watercolor showing colonists in New South Wales, Australia

Immigration by free British subjects, begun a decade before the end of convict shipments, led to a pastoral and agricultural boom. Settlers pioneered agriculture in south Australia, where rainfall was reliable and provided the population with most of its cereal needs. Sugar and rice cultivation, introduced to the tropical northeast in the 1860s, was performed with indentured labor recruited from Pacific islands. Even during penal colony times, sheep ranching in the east and the exportation of wool developed into a thriving business. The mining of gold and silver began in the east in 1851 and spread to nearly all parts of the continent. Although a colony, commodity-rich Australia sought its wealth through export-led growth.

Mining generated several gold-rush immigration waves, not only from Britain but also from China, as well as internal migrations from mining towns to cities when the gold rushes ended. The indigenous population of Aboriginals, who had inhabited the continent for over 50,000 years (see Chapter 1), shrank during the same time, mostly as a result of diseases but also after confrontations with ranchers intruding on their hunting and gathering lands. As in North America, whites were relentless in taking possession of the continent.

The Difficult Turn of the Century   During the last quarter of the nineteenth century, the economies of the three leading industrial countries of the world—Great Britain, the United States, and Germany—slowed, first with a financial depression

Military Transformations and the New Imperialism

Between 1450 and 1750 firearm-equipped infantries rose to prominence throughout Eurasia. Scholars have debated the significance of the differences among infantries—and military organizations more generally—during this age of empire.

Historians long believed that superior firearms, cannons, and cannon-equipped ships enabled Europeans to achieve imperial conquest and colonization of the Middle East, Africa, and Southeast Asia. However, most scholars now agree that, beginning in the late seventeenth century, it was the flintlock muskets, bayonets, and line drill that distinguished western European infantries from other armies in Asia and Africa and gave Europeans an advantage. These advantages were manifested in the Ottoman–Russian War of 1768–1774 and in Napoleon's invasion of Egypt in 1798.

French Defeat of the Mamluks at the Battle of the Pyramids, 1798. This painting shows the clear advantage of the military innovation of the line drill. The orderly French forces on the right, commanded by officers on horseback, mow down the cavalry charges of the Mamluks.

The Mughals in India and the Qing in China did not have to worry about flintlock, bayonet, and line infantry attacks in the eighteenth century, either from their neighbors or from the faraway Europeans. Like the Ottomans, who continued to maintain large cavalry forces against their nomadic neighbors in the Middle East and central Asia, the Mughals and Qing privileged their cavalries. However, once British East India Company officers elevated indigenous infantry soldiers to the privileged ranks of the sepoy regiments, their efficiency ultimately created such

in the US and Europe in 1873–1879 and later with the worldwide depression, of 1890–1896. Australia had survived the first depression, mainly thanks to continuing gold finds. But in the 1890s, construction as well as banking collapsed, and factories closed. Labor unrest followed; although widespread strikes failed, the newly founded Labor Party (1891) immediately became a major political force. The country adopted labor reforms, an old-age pension, fiscal reforms, and a white-only immigration policy. The discovery of huge gold deposits in western Australia in 1892–1894 helped to redress the economic problems. In 1900, Australia adopted a federal constitution, which made the country the second fully autonomous British "dominion," after Canada (1867).

European Imperialism in the Middle East and Africa

The British in the Middle East during the eighteenth and early nineteenth centuries functioned as merchants, diplomats, or military advisors in an Ottoman Empire with a long tradition of conquering European lands. The situation changed at the end of the eighteenth century when Russia attempted to drive the Ottomans back problems for the company that the British Crown had to take over the governance of India in 1858.

When European innovators introduced workable breech-loading rifles and artillery in the late 1850s, the technological balance shifted decisively toward Europe. The addition of rapid-firing mechanisms in the second half of the 1800s to these improved weapons further cemented Europe's technological superiority.

Thus, in this shift from an initially slight to an eventually pronounced superiority of European arms during this period, the new imperialism and the Industrial Revolution were parallel developments engendered by the same modernity that also saw the rise of constitutionalism and the formation of a new type of polity, the nation-state. Certainly, industrially produced weapons in the later nineteenth century greatly enhanced Europe's ability to dominate much of the Middle East, Africa, and Asia.

Ethiopian Forces Defeating an Italian Army at Adowa, 1896. A hundred years after Napoleon's victory, the tables were turned when an Ethiopian army equipped with repeating rifles, machine guns, and cannon routed an Italian invasion force. In response to the defeat, the *Times* of London complained that "the prestige of European arms as a whole is considerably impaired."

Questions

• Examine the painting showing French forces defeating the Mamluk cavalry. Are the military advantages of the line drill evident? If so, what are they?

• Does the painting of Ethiopian forces defeating an Italian army in 1896 show that indigenous peoples could adapt Western innovations to their own purposes? If so, how?

into Asia, take Istanbul, and convert it back into an eastern Christian capital. The other European powers sought to slow the Russian advances, with Great Britain assuming the lead role in protecting the Ottomans. This policy of containment ultimately failed. Under Russian pressure, Ottoman territory shrank, the Europeans joined Russia in dismembering the Ottoman Empire, and an imperialist competition for carving up other parts of the world ensued.

The Rising Appeal of Imperialism in the West

The Russian Empire sought not only to replace the Ottoman Empire as the dominant eastern European power but also to become the leading Asian power. Its ambition spurred France, Great Britain, Belgium, Germany, and Italy to embark on competitive imperialism in other parts of the world (see Map 27.3).

The Ottoman, Russian, and British Empires   After the failure of Napoleon's imperial schemes in 1815, Great Britain was the undisputed leading empire in the world. On the European continent, Britain worked to restore the monarchies of France, Austria, Prussia, and Russia so that they would balance each other as "great powers" in a **Concert of Europe**. Britain would not tolerate any renewed European imperialism of the kind that Napoleon had pursued.

Concert of Europe: International political system that dominated Europe from 1815 to 1871, which advocated a balance of power among states.

Competitive Imperialism: The World in 1914

Belgian	Dutch	Italian	Portuguese
British	French	Japanese	Russian
Danish	German	Ottoman	Spanish
Independent			

MAP 27.3 **Competitive Imperialism: The World in 1914.**

The Concert of Europe, however, was less successful at curbing the imperial ambitions of its members outside of western Europe. Russia did not hide its goal of throwing the Ottoman Empire (admitted to the Concert in 1856) back into "Asia"—that is, Asia Minor, or Anatolia. Great Britain, although it made itself the protector of the integrity of the Ottoman Empire, could only slow the ambitions of Russia.

The French Conquest of Algeria   The French, unable to embark again on imperialism in Europe, cast their eyes across the Mediterranean to Ottoman North Africa. The conquest of Algeria was the crucial first incidence of a western European power—in this instance France—using a diplomatic incident (see beginning of this chapter) to remove the local rulers. At first, the French stayed on a small coastal strip, encouraging the rise of indigenous leaders to take over from the Ottoman corsairs and Janissaries and share the country with the French. The British discreetly supported Algerian leaders with weapons to be used against the French.

In the end, however, coexistence proved impossible, and the French military undertook an all-out conquest. The civilian colonial administration after 1870 encouraged immigration of French and Spanish farmers as well as French corporate investments in vineyards and citrus plantations on the coast. The indigenous population of Arabs and Berbers, decimated by cholera epidemics in the 1860s, found itself largely relegated to less fertile lands in the interior.

The Great Game: Competition between Great Britain and Russia for conquest or control of Asian countries north of India and south of Russia, principally Afghanistan.

Britain's Containment Policy   Great Britain sought to limit Russian ambitions in central Asia, inaugurating what was called the **Great Game** against Russia in Asia with the first Anglo–Afghan war in 1838. Although Great Britain failed to occupy Afghanistan, it eventually succeeded in turning Afghanistan into a buffer state, keeping Russia away from India. A little later, in 1853–1856, Britain and France teamed up in the Crimean War to stop Russia from renewing its drive for Istanbul. This defeat chastened Russia for the next two decades.

In the second half of the nineteenth century, the Franco–Prussian War destroyed the balance of the European Concert. Germany was now the dominant power in western Europe. Russia exploited the new imbalance in Europe during anti-Ottoman uprisings in the Balkans in 1876, breaking through Ottoman lines of defense and marching within a few miles of Istanbul. However, Great Britain still had enough clout to force Russia into retreating.

British Imperialism in Egypt and Sudan   To prevent a repeat of the Russian invasion, Britain and the Ottomans agreed in 1878 to turn the island of Cyprus over to the British as a protectorate. Thus, in the name of curbing Russian imperialism, Great Britain became an imperial power itself in the Mediterranean.

Winston Churchill's account of the Battle of Omdurman

Instead of watching Russia, however, the commanders of the British navy squadron in Cyprus had to turn their attention to Egypt. This province, the wealthiest part of the Ottoman Empire, had been governed by a dynasty of autonomous rulers since the reign of Muhammad Ali (r. 1805–1848).

Muhammad Ali's successors incurred considerable debts, in part for the French-led construction of the Suez Canal in 1869. Britain took over a large part of the canal shares from the debt-ridden Egyptian ruler in 1875. A year later, Britain and France imposed a joint debt commission that garnished a portion of Egyptian tax revenue. Opposition in Egypt to this foreign interference culminated in 1881 with a revolt in the Egyptian army that endangered the debt repayments.

When British-initiated negotiations between the Ottoman sultan and the leader of the army revolt over the issue of the debt collapsed, interventionists in London, fearing for their bonds and the supply of Egyptian cotton for the British textile industry, gained the upper hand. Overcoming the Egyptian army, a British expeditionary force occupied Egypt in 1882.

The Ottoman sultan acquiesced to the occupation because it was supposed to be only temporary. Costly campaigns by British-led Egyptian troops in Sudan during 1883–1885, however, derailed any early departure plans. Egypt's financial troubles kept the British focused on Egypt. On one hand, the British wanted to put Egyptian finances on a sound footing, but on the other hand, they wanted to avoid responsibility for the country's governance. As a compromise, they proposed a conditional departure, with the right of return at times of internal unrest or external danger. The Ottoman sultan, however, refused to sign this compromise. In the end, Britain stayed for almost 75 years, running Egypt as an undeclared colony for the first 40 years. Without a clear plan, Britain had nonetheless transplanted the pattern of imperialism–colonialism into the Middle East.

Scottish Troops at the Sphinx, 1882. The British occupied Egypt as a means to secure the Suez Canal and guarantee the repayment of Egyptian debts. Subsequent negotiations with the Ottoman sultan for the status of Egypt failed, and the province became an unofficial protectorate of Britain. Although granted internal independence in 1922, Egypt remained in a semicolonial relationship with Britain until 1956.

France's Tunisian Protectorate   Like Algeria and Egypt, Tunisia was an autonomous Ottoman province, ruled by its own dynasty. Fertile northern Tunisia provided limited but fairly reliable tax revenues; annual tax expeditions to the south among the seminomadic sheep and camel tribes served mostly to demonstrate the dynasty's sovereignty.

Tunisian leaders were the first in the Muslim Middle East and North Africa to modernize their military and adopt a constitution (1857). With their more limited revenues, they hit the debt ceiling in 1869, and had to accept a British–French–Italian debt commission for the reorganization of the country's revenues. When the French took over in 1881, anxious to take their share of the Middle East and North Africa in competition with Great Britain, they faced the same task of balancing the budget that the British had in Egypt. Only later did they benefit from the French and Italian settlers they invited to the protectorate to intensify agriculture and transition to colonialism.

The Scramble for Africa

Competitive European imperialism intensified in 1884 as Germany claimed its first protectorates in Africa. German chancellor Otto von Bismarck (in various offices 1862–1890) called a conference in Berlin, which met from late 1884 to early 1885. The conference agenda was how the 14 invited European countries and the United States should "define the conditions under which future territorial annexations in Africa might be recognized." Bismarck's proposed main condition was "effective occupation," with the creation of spheres of influence around the occupied places. The **Scramble for Africa** began (see Map 27.4).

Scramble for Africa: Competition among European powers from 1885 to 1912 to conquer land in Africa and establish colonies.

a British view of the civilizing mission (1902)

Civilizing mission: Belief that Europeans had a duty to extend what they believed were the benefits of European civilization to "backward" peoples.

Explorers, Missionaries, and the Civilizing Mission   Sub-Saharan Africa was still little known by most Europeans in the 1800s. Some explorers had gained access to the interior via trade routes and caravans, long in use by Africans. David Livingstone (1813–1873), a Scottish missionary and opponent of slavery, was among the pioneers who explored much of south central Africa. Livingstone's goals were not only to terminate trafficking in slaves but also to "civilize" Africans by preaching both Christianity and commerce. The generation of explorers after Livingstone was better equipped, led larger expeditions, and composed more precise accounts of their activities. Still, in spite of extensive explorations, at the end of the century, European politicians had only the vaguest idea of the geography of the "dark continent."

European Christian missionaries were at the forefront of the **civilizing mission**, the belief that western Europeans had a duty to extend the benefits of civilization (that is, Western civilization) to the "backward" people they ruled.

In the early 1800s, malaria and yellow fever still confined missionaries to the coasts of Africa, where they trained indigenous missionaries for the conversion of Africans in the interior. When treatment for malaria became available in the middle of the 1800s, missionaries were able to follow their indigenous colleagues into the interior—which led to tensions. While African converts preached the gospel in the spirit of Christian equality, many Western missionaries considered African Christianity to be contaminated by "superstitions" and did not accept Africans as their equals.

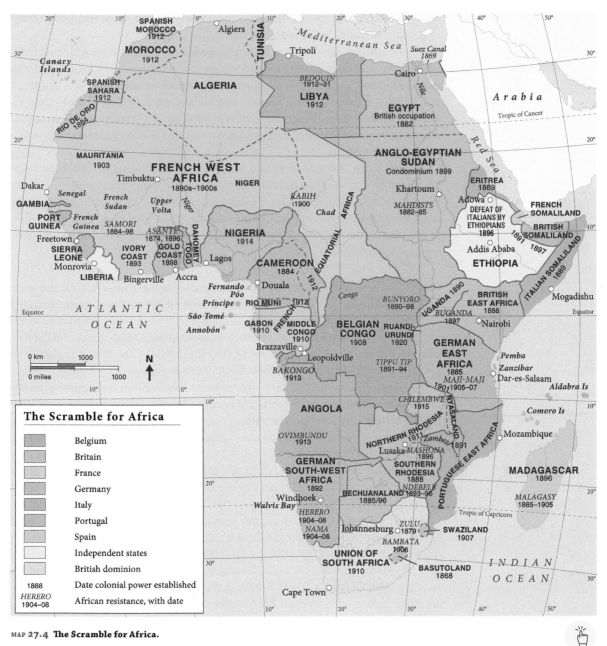

MAP **27.4 The Scramble for Africa.**

map analysis

Conquest and Resistance in West Africa   Conquest and imperialism on the coast of West Africa after 1885 were an outgrowth of the trade-fort system. Ghana, the land of the Ashante kingdom, is a particularly instructive example of the pattern of conquest and resistance. During the time of the Songhay (Chapter 19), the Ashante mined the gold of the Akan fields that caravans carried across the Sahara. When gold declined in importance, the kingdom turned to the Atlantic slave trade. After the 1807 British prohibition of slavery, Ashante merchants switched to commodities (especially palm oil) that were in demand in industrializing Europe. But the Ashante and British traders clashed over the terms of trade in the forts.

Only in 1896, when the British sent regular troops to put down the Ashante, was Ghana finally turned into a protectorate.

French officers after 1850 carried out expeditions into the West African interior for alliances and trade purposes. In 1857 they came into conflict with al-Hajj Umar (ca. 1791–1864), an Islamic reformer in the interior savanna who was building a state in what is today Guinea, Senegal, and Mali. For decades, the French could advance no farther. Once the scramble was on, however, the West African Islamic state was doomed. In 1891, despite Islamist resistance, the French began to carve a new colony in West Africa.

Al-Hajj Umar was one of several West African Muslim religious scholars who became holy warriors (jihadis) seeking to rejuvenate Islam through a return to the Islamic sources. These reformers forcibly converted black traditional spiritualists to Islam. In contrast to earlier Islamic kings and emperors who made little or no effort to proselytize, the jihadists of the 1800s succeeded in making Islam the dominant religion of West Africa.

Conquest and Resistance in East Africa   The new imperialism and colonialism in East Africa were similar to those in West Africa. Here, in the sixteenth century, the Portuguese had established trade forts. When Swahili patricians in the city-states farther north resisted, the Portuguese responded with piracy and the construction of coastal forts in their midst. But the arrival of the Dutch in the 1630s forced the Portuguese to curtail their East African engagement.

An Omani Arab expeditionary force exploited the reduced Portuguese presence in 1698 by conquering the Swahili city-state of Mombasa. Oman seized the opportunity to expand its limited domestic agricultural base on the Arabian Peninsula, developing a plantation system on the coastal islands of East Africa with slaves imported from the African interior. In the 1820s, the Omanis—by now under their separate sultan residing on the island of Zanzibar—became the main exporters of cloves on the world market. Thanks to the Omanis, the Swahili coast was prosperous again.

In 1885 Germany landed on the East African mainland opposite Zanzibar, against the protest of the island's Omani sultan, who had also claimed the nearby region on the mainland. By 1886 the Germans had established their colony of East Africa, comprising what are today Tanzania, Burundi, and Rwanda. In an understanding with Germany, Great Britain declared its sphere of influence over what are today Kenya (also claimed by Zanzibar) and Burundi, and in 1888 chartered a private company to exploit the territory's resources. The company failed and, in order to coordinate its scramble, Britain turned both Zanzibar and the mainland into protectorates (1890 and 1895). The lion's share of land, today's Congo in the center of Africa, went officially in 1885 to King Leopold II (r. 1865-1909) of Belgium. The king had already established a private company several years earlier that explored Congo for its resources under the leadership of Henry Morton Stanley. Thus, the land grab in East Africa proceded in more or less amicable fashion among the European nations.

Atrocities and Genocides   Germany's colonial regime in East Africa was exceedingly brutal. Its administrators decided to grow cotton for its domestic textile industry, using forced labor to keep costs low. When the Maji-Maji rebellion against these labor conditions broke out among the indigenous population, German troops used their superior firepower to systematically kill some 200,000 people, amounting to one-third of the population (1905–1907). In the colony of German Southwest Africa (today's Namibia), occupied in 1884, German settlers displaced the indigenous Herero and Nama in such large numbers that they eventually provoked an uprising. Again, German troops engaged in a massive campaign of genocidal repression, nearly wiping out the Herero and Nama (1904–1907).

North of Namibia, King Leopold II turned his personal colony of the Congo into a forced-labor camp for the production of rubber. Leopold sadistically exploited the native workforce, using beatings and mutilations if collection quotas were not filled. It has been estimated that 10 million Congolese were either killed or starved to death. By the early 1900s, the violence committed in the Congo had become so notorious that the Belgian government ended Leopold II's personal regime and made it a national colony (see "Against the Grain"). As a result, the worst abuses ended, to be replaced by more subtle forms of business privileges, segregation, and racism.

Africa Carved Up   The scramble for Africa was not limited to the major European powers of Great Britain, France, and Germany. Portugal, the first European country in the fifteenth century to have engaged in overseas trade-fort expansion, used the Berlin conference of 1884–1885 to expand its coastal footholds into the territorial colonies of Guinea in West Africa, Angola in Southwest Africa, and Mozambique in Southeast Africa. Subsequently, the country encouraged Portuguese businesses and settlers to take up residence in the colonies. Similarly, Spain acquired the desert territory of Rio de Oro in the northwest in 1884–1885, without, however, investing much beyond a bare-bones administration.

Italy, concentrating on its domestic industrialization, initially entered the scramble modestly, acquiring territory in east African Somalia and Eritrea (1889–1890). Bigger imperialist dreams of conquering Ethiopia in east Africa were stymied, however, by a defeat at the battle of Adowa in 1896 (see "Patterns Up Close"). Thanks to its long tradition as a relatively large, unified kingdom, Ethiopia emerged from the scramble for Africa as the only unconquered state on the continent.

To overcome its humiliation in East Africa, Italy tried its hand at imperialism again in 1911 against the Ottoman province of Tripolitania (today western Libya), just opposite its southern Mediterranean coast. Here, the small Ottoman garrison put up a fierce resistance and surrendered only in 1912. But the outbreak of World War I in July 1914 necessitated the withdrawal of Italian troops. When the Ottoman Empire entered the war in October of that year, a strong indigenous Islamic resistance emerged under the leadership of the Quran teacher Umar Mukhtar (1858–1931). He turned out to be a charismatic and skilled guerrilla leader who had the support from members of the reformist Sanusiyya Brotherhood. He forced the Italians back to a few coastal enclaves and resisted the postwar return of the Italians until 1931, when they captured and hanged him.

By the end of the nineteenth century Great Britain and France had become the dominant colonial powers in Africa. Two strategic obsessions divided them: The influential British imperialist businessman and colonial politician Cecil Rhodes (1853–1902) dreamed of a railroad from the Cape of Good Hope to Cairo; and French imperialist military officers had illusions of conquering a contiguous territory from Senegal in the west to Djibouti on the Red Sea. Troops of both countries

Mark Twain, "King Leopold's Soliloquy" (1905)

met in 1898 at Fashoda on the White Nile in Sudan (today Kodok in South Sudan) and nearly came to blows. Under strong British pressure, the French gave up their dream of a west-east African empire, at the center of which they wished to control the waters of the White Nile. But British colonialists also had to give up their obsession with the Cape-to-Cairo railway for lack of money during the Great Depression (1929–1939).

Subsequently, in the face of Germany's rising power in Europe, France and Britain buried their hatchet in the *Entente Cordiale* of 1904, a treaty of "friendly understanding," one chapter of which stipulated Britain's support for France's goal of beating Germany in its race for a protectorate over the Muslim Sultanate of Morocco in northwest Africa. When France eventually succeeded in occupying Morocco in 1912, the Scramble for Africa ended with all of Africa, except for Ethiopia and Libya, carved up among the European colonial powers. There was a price, however, for France to pay: Germany's defeat in the scramble for Morocco was one of the factors that would contribute to its grievances at the outbreak of World War I in 1914.

Colonial Brutality in the Congo. A young African boy whose hand and foot were severed by sentries after his village failed to meet its rubber quota. The Belgian Congo under King Leopold II employed mass forced labor of the indigenous population to extract rubber from the jungle. As the demand for rubber grew, King Leopold's private army of 16,000 mercenaries was given leave to use any method to coerce the population into meeting quotas, including random killing, mutilation, village burning, starvation, and hostage taking.

Western Imperialism and Colonialism in Southeast Asia

The new imperialism appeared also in Southeast Asia, specifically Indonesia, the Philippines, Vietnam, Cambodia, and Laos. While the new imperialism in Southeast Asia was an outgrowth of the earlier trade-fort presence of Portugal, Spain, and the Netherlands, it also included the return of France to imperial glory.

The Dutch in Indonesia

After liberating themselves from Habsburg–Spanish rule, the Netherlands displaced Portugal from its dominant position as a spice importer to Europe. From 1650 to 1750, the Netherlands was the leading naval power in the world. After 1750, they shifted from the trade of spices in their trade forts in Indonesia to the planting of cash crops on land outside the forts. The aim of the full colonization of Indonesia during the nineteenth century was to profit from European industrial demand for agricultural and mineral commodities.

Portuguese and Dutch Trade Forts
Portuguese sailors arrived in the strategic Strait of Malacca in 1511. They defeated the local sultanate and established a fort in the Malaysian capital, Malacca. Pushing onward to the spice-producing Maluku Islands (known in English as the Moluccas) in eastern Indonesia (between Sulawesi and New Guinea), they established a trade fort in 1522. From there, the Portuguese moved on to China and finally Japan, where they arrived in the mid-1500s. Overall, their role in the Indonesian spice trade remained small, and indigenous Islamic merchants maintained their dominance.

After declaring their independence from Spain in 1581, the northern provinces of the Netherlands formed the Republic of the United Netherlands and pushed for their own overseas network of trade forts. In 1602, the Dutch government chartered the Dutch United East India Company (VOC), which spearheaded the expansion of Dutch possessions in India and Southeast Asia. The company founded Batavia (today Jakarta) in the mid-1600s, with the island of Java as its main Southeast Asian center. The VOC was the largest and wealthiest commercial company in the world during the seventeenth century, with its merchant ships supported by large naval and land forces.

When the Dutch governor of the Netherlands, William of Orange (1650–1702), became king of England after the English Glorious Revolution (see Chapter 17), the Dutch and English overseas trade interests were pooled. Great Britain (as the country was known after England's union with Scotland in 1707) deepened its Indian interests through the British East India Company, and the Dutch VOC pursued their engagements in Indonesia, becoming after 1755 the de facto government on the island of Java over a set of pacified Islamic protectorates.

But governing and maintaining troops was expensive, and VOC employees often paid their expenses out of their own pockets. In the late eighteenth century, the inability of the VOC to shift from spices to commodities, which required investments in plantations and accompanying transportation infrastructures, led in 1799 to the liquidation of the VOC. As the British government would later do in India, the government of the Netherlands stepped in as the ruler of Indonesian possessions that had grown from trade forts into small colonies, surrounded by dependent indigenous principalities as well as independent sultanates.

Dutch Colonialism The Dutch government took the decisive step toward agricultural investments in 1830 when Belgium separated from the Dutch kingdom to form an independent Catholic monarchy. Faced with budgetary constraints and cut off from industrializing Belgium, the Dutch government adopted the **cultivation system** in Indonesia. According to this system, indigenous Indonesian subsistence farmers were forced to either grow government crops on 20 percent of their land or work for 60 days on Dutch plantations. Overnight, the Dutch and collaborating Indonesian ruling classes turned into landowners. They reaped huge profits while Indonesian subsistence farmers suffered. In the course of the nineteenth century, Indonesia became a major—or even the largest—exporter of sugar, tea, coffee, palm oil, coconut products, tropical hardwoods, rubber, quinine, and pepper to the industrial nations.

To keep pace with demand, the Dutch pursued a program of systematic conquest and colonization. They conquered the Indonesian archipelago, finally subduing the most stubborn opponents, the Muslim guerillas of Aceh, in 1903 (see Map 27.5). Conquered lands were turned over to private investors who established plantations. To deflect criticism at home and abroad, the Dutch also introduced reform measures. Severe underfunding, however, kept these reforms largely unimplemented, and it was clear that the profits from colonialism were more important than investments in the welfare of indigenous people.

Cultivation system: Dutch colonial scheme of compulsory labor and planting of crops imposed on indigenous Indonesian self-sufficiency farmers.

Dutch colonists and Indonesians at a rubber plantation in Java (1915)

Spain in the Philippines

In the Philippines, the Spanish built their first trade fort of Manila as a port from which to trade Mexican silver with China for luxury manufactures. Manila suffered from raids by indigenous highlanders in the interior, Islamic rulers from the southern islands, and Dutch interlopers. Imperial conquest had to await the later eighteenth century, and colonization followed in the middle of the nineteenth century with the introduction of sugarcane.

MAP 27.5 **Western Imperialism in Southeast Asia, 1870–1914.**

Galleons and Trade with China   Spain expanded from the Americas farther west in order to prevent Portugal from claiming the lucrative spice islands of Indonesia. A Portuguese explorer in Spanish service, Ferdinand Magellan (ca. 1480–1521), had successfully crossed the sea channels at the southern tip of South America in 1520 and discovered what later became known as the Philippines, in honor of King Phillip II of Spain. It took another half century, however, before Spain could construct a trade fort and small colony. This fort, Manila, became the base for subsequent biannual silver fleets from Mexico. Spanish merchants based in Mexico, from which Manila was administered, benefited from the trade of silver for Chinese silk, porcelain, and lacquerware. Thus, Manila began as a small subcolony of the large Spanish colony of Mexico, or New Spain.

As the Spanish gradually expanded their hold outside Manila on Luzon and Visaya (where the local king had converted to Christianity), they established estates, thus advancing from trade-fort imperialism to the beginnings of territorial expansion. Like the Dutch in Indonesia, the Spanish settlers planted warm-weather cash crops on their estates.

Incipient Colonialism   Indigenous farmers on the Philippine estates were obliged to deliver rents to ensure the food supply for inhabitants of Manila, mostly merchants of Spanish, Chinese, and Japanese origin. Warrior chieftains outside Spanish lands who converted to Catholicism transformed themselves into a Hispanicized landowner class. By the early eighteenth century, the Spanish were able to establish a regular administration for fiscal and juridical matters. The beginnings of colonialism in the Philippines had emerged.

However, fiscal revenue did not yield surpluses, and villagers produced only small quantities of exportable ginger, cinnamon, and gold. Much money had to be invested in defending the Spanish-controlled territory from attacks by independent Filipinos who resisted conquest and conversion. Even more vexing were raids supported by Islamic sultanates that had formed on the southern islands.

Full Colonialism Major reforms instituted by the Spanish in the early 1800s, motivated by the loss of Mexico to independence, resulted in the liberalization of trade and the beginnings of agricultural commodities for export. Ports were opened to ships from all countries, discrimination against Chinese settlements ended, and Spanish administrators and churchmen lost their trade privileges. Foreign entrepreneurs cleared rain forests and exported hardwoods, growing cash crops on the new land. Large-scale rice farms replaced many small-scale village self-sufficiency plots, and thus, commercialization usurped subsistence agriculture.

Resistance by landowners against a reform of the land regime and tax system until the very end of the nineteenth century, however, ensured that Spain did not benefit much from the liberalization of trade. Additionally, Philippine society stratified into a wealthy minority and a large mass of landless rural workers and urban day laborers. This stratification differed from that in the Americas in that there was no real Creole class—that is, a Spanish–Philippine upper stratum of landowners and urban people. Agitation for independence and constitutionalism was largely limited to urban intellectuals. The Philippines remained a colony, producing no revenue and still demanding costly administrative reforms and infrastructural investments, both of which Spain was unable to afford.

The first stirrings of Filipino nationalism, primarily among Hispanicized Filipinos of mixed Spanish and indigenous or Chinese descent, emerged in the second half of the nineteenth century. The principal spokesman was novelist José Rizal (1861–1896). Colonial authorities arrested Rizal and banished him to Hong Kong, but he returned to Manila in 1892, inspiring both overt and underground resistance groups. One of the underground groups, Katipunan, advocated Filipino independence through armed struggle. In 1896 the government executed hundreds of revolutionaries, including Rizal, before firing squads. But it was unable to destroy Katipunan in the provinces, and the two sides agreed in 1897 to a truce that included the end of armed revolt in return for exile of the leadership to Hong Kong.

Philippine–American War Although it appeared that the colonial government had successfully repressed the Filipino revolt, events took a dramatic turn when the Spanish–American War broke out in 1898. The two sides fought their first battle in Manila Bay, where the United States routed a Spanish squadron. An American ship fetched the exiled Filipino rebel Emilio Aguinaldo (1869–1964) from Hong Kong, and he quickly defeated the Spanish and declared independence. Over four centuries of Spanish colonialism in the Pacific had come to an end.

Uncle Sam admonishing his "new students" (1899)

American Soldiers in the Philippines. The US decision to annex the Philippines after the victory of the United States over Spain in 1898 was the first attempt to create an American overseas empire. Resistance was immediate, and a brutal war against Philippine fighters lasted from 1902 until 1913, with isolated outbreaks continuing until Philippine independence in 1946. Here, American troops dig in and fortify an outpost in Luzon.

The United States and Spain made peace at the end of 1898, ignoring the independent Philippine government in their agreement. US forces took possession of Manila in 1899 and defeated the troops of the protesting Filipino government under the elected president, Emilio Aguinaldo. The Filipinos shifted to guerilla war, but US troops captured Aguinaldo in 1901. The United States declared the war over in 1902 but had to fight remnants of the guerillas as well as southern rebels until 1913. Thus, the United States had joined the European contest for imperial and colonial control of the non-Western world.

The French in Vietnam
Indochina, the peninsula on which Vietnam is located, also includes Cambodia, Laos, and Thailand. French imperial and colonial involvement began in 1858. At first focusing on the south of Indochina, France gradually expanded northward, establishing protectorates over the Nguyen royal dynasty, which was the last of a succession of kingdoms that had begun in the third century CE.

French Interests in Vietnam   French efforts in the seventeenth and early eighteenth centuries to sponsor Catholic missions and trading companies had been largely unsuccessful and ended altogether after their defeat in the Seven Years' War. When France renewed these efforts after the French Revolution and Napoleon, it was rebuffed by the Vietnamese kings, who shared Chinese concerns about the Western challenge. Both China and Vietnam adopted a policy of isolationism as their first answer to Western patterns of challenge.

The French, under Napoleon's nephew Napoleon III (r. 1848-1870), were not deterred. Taking as a pretext the torture and execution of French missionaries and Vietnamese converts, the French dispatched a squadron that occupied the sparsely inhabited Mekong River delta in 1858–1862, annexing it as a protectorate.

Conquest and Colonialism   After Napoleon III fell from power, politicians were ambivalent about renewing French overseas imperialism. But a year after pro-imperialists came to power in 1883, the French defeated China in a war for the control of northern Vietnam. In contrast to the thinly settled south, the Red River estuary in the north with the capital of the Vietnamese kingdom, Hanoi, was densely populated. The French conquerors united southern and northern Vietnam into the French colony of Indochina. Two members of the deposed Vietnamese royal dynasty waged a guerilla war against the occupation, but by the early twentieth century the French had captured both and were in full control.

The French government and French entrepreneurs invested substantial sums in the Mekong delta, establishing plantations for the production of coffee, tea, and rubber. Indigenous rice farmers had to deliver 40 percent of their crops to the colonial government. Hanoi was made the seat of the colonial administration in 1902, and the port of Haiphong, downriver from Hanoi, became the main entry point for ships to load agricultural commodities for export. After France added Cambodia and Laos in 1893–1904 to its overseas empire, it derived major financial benefits from the agriculture of its eastern colonies. By the time of World War I, only Siam (today's Thailand) had been able to ward off colonization, mostly as a result of several strong kings deftly playing off French and British efforts at occupation.

Alfred Meynard, reflections on Hanoi (1906)

Early Nationalism   Anti-foreign Vietnamese patriotism was reasserted by Phan Boi Chau (1867–1940), who witnessed the crushing by the French of a protest by Confucian scholars in 1885. Phan Boi Chau's activities inspired anti-tax demonstrations and a provincial uprising in Vietnam in 1908–1909, which the French suppressed harshly. By 1912, a newly formed nationalist grouping favored the expulsion of the French and the formation of a Vietnamese democratic republic.

Putting It All Together

Ever since Vladimir Lenin, the founder of the Soviet Union, declared in 1916 that imperialism was "the highest stage of capitalism," scholars have debated whether or not the capitalist industrialization process in Europe, North America, and Japan needed colonies to sustain its growth. Most recent historians have concluded that imperialism and colonialism were not needed for capitalism to flourish and that all the commodities crucial for industrialization could have been bought from independent countries on the world market. Great Britain, of course, had transformed its activity in India from trade-fort imperialism to territorial imperialism just prior to its industrialization and used Indian cotton as raw material for its textile factories. But this raises the reverse question: Would industrialization have happened had Great Britain not conquered India?

interactive concept map

Perhaps a better approach to the question is to think of trade-fort and territorial imperialism as world-historical patterns of long standing. By contrast, industrialization was a much later phenomenon, appearing around 1800. Thus, old patterns of imperialism persisted during the rise of the new pattern of industrialization. These old patterns were amplified by the new power that industrialization gave the European countries. Therefore, the new imperialism of the nineteenth century, and the colonialism that followed in its wake, can be seen as phenomena in which old patterns continued but were enlarged by new patterns of industrial power.

Review and Relate

Thinking Through Patterns

Examine the ways historians approach the big questions of this chapter.

> **What new patterns emerged in the transition from trade-fort imperialism to the new imperialism?**

During the early modern period, European monarchs commissioned merchant marine companies, such as the British East India Company and the Dutch United East India Company, in order to avoid military expeditions of their own but still receive a share of the profits of trade. The mariner-merchants built coastal forts, granted to them by the local rulers with whom they traded. In the seventeenth and eighteenth centuries, much larger trading companies were formed, and large numbers of mariner-merchants now served in dozens of trade forts overseas. In India and Indonesia, these companies needed their governments in England and the Netherlands to rescue them. In responding, governments became imperialist colonizers.

> **How did European colonizers develop their colonies economically, given that they were industrializing themselves at the same time?**

Great Britain was the pioneer in the development of exportable agricultural and mineral commodities in its colonies for the support of its expanding industries. By the middle of the nineteenth century, other industrializing countries either embarked on imperial conquests or shifted to full colonialism in order to obtain necessary commodities. Because labor for the production of these commodities was scarce, workers were forcibly recruited and paid low wages.

> **What were the experiences of the indigenous people under the new imperialism? How did they adapt to colonialism? How did they resist?**

Many imperial conquests involved campaigns that claimed many indigenous victims. If the colonizers pursued commodity production, the indigenous population was recruited, often forcibly and with low wages. Resistance to European colonialism manifested itself in ethnic nationalism. In Australia and New Zealand and other colonies where European settlement was encouraged, colonial governments or settlers ousted the indigenous population from the most fertile lands, despite fierce resistance.

| Against the Grain

Consider this as a counterpoint to the main patterns examined in this chapter.

An Anti-Imperial Perspective

During the heyday of Western imperialism in the later nineteenth century, many European writers justified the conquest of foreign lands and the exploitation of native peoples by expressing attitudes reflected in social Darwinism. Seen from this perspective, Europeans were pursuing a "civilizing mission," thus exposing "lesser breeds" to the benefits of Christianity and commerce. For proponents of imperialism, it was fitting to pursue a policy of civilizing the "inferior races." Perhaps the best known of these condescending works was Rudyard Kipling's "The White Man's Burden," published in 1899 in response to America's takeover of the Philippines after their victory in the Spanish–American war of 1898.

Many Europeans, however, expressed views contrary to the majority opinion. Among the most outspoken critics of European imperialism was a contemporary of Kipling, the British journalist Edward D. Morel (1873–1924). In 1900, Morel published a series of scathing denunciations that revealed the atrocities of African slave labor on Belgian rubber plantations.

Forced to leave his job, Morel continued his activist campaign by launching a newspaper, the *West African Mail*, in 1903, followed by his foundation of the Congo Reform Association in 1904. By far the most famous of Morel's indictments, however, was *The Black Man's Burden* (1920), a condemnation of the evils of European capitalism and industrialism: "Its destructive effects are . . . permanent. . . . It kills not the body merely, but the soul. It breaks the spirit." For his pacifist activities Morel was sentenced to prison in 1917, but subsequently went on to win a seat in Parliament in 1922. Although he played only a minor role in Parliament, Morel is often considered the father of international activism on behalf of human rights.

- In what ways is Morel a good example of nonconformity with European imperialism in Africa?

- How would you compare Morel's actions with current protest movements around the world?

Key Terms

audio flashcards

Civilizing mission 636	Cultivation system 641	Scramble for Africa 636
Colonialism 625	Nabob 626	Subaltern 631
Concert of Europe 633	New Imperialism 625	The Great Game 634

For additional resources, please go to
www.oup.com/us/vonsivers.
Please see the Further Resources section at the back of the book for additional readings and suggested websites.

PART SIX

From Three Modernities to One

1914–PRESENT

World War I and the Interwar Period

The first great crisis in modern scientific–industrial society was World War I (1914–1918). Although imperialist competition in the Balkans triggered the war, there were even stronger forces at work in the background.

A dramatic effect of the war was that the single nineteenth-century pattern of modernity—constitutionalism, ethnic nationalism, and scientific–industrial society—splintered into three subpatterns, each hostile to the other two: capitalist democracy, socialism–communism, and supremacist nationalism. The open trade regime of the nineteenth century ended, and three self-contained spheres emerged:

- Capitalist democracy (the United States, Britain, France, and parts of Latin America): support for the concepts of freedom, capitalism, and international institutions for maintaining peace;
- Communism–socialism (the Soviet Union): professed support for equality over freedom and a command economy controlled from the top;
- Supremacist nationalism (Italy, Germany, and Japan): contempt for both democracy and communism; celebration of racial supremacy and authoritarian/dictatorial rule, state-controlled economy, and territorial expansion through military conquest.

In the period after World War I, the countries representing these three modernities moved in very different directions:

- Great Britain and France expanded their colonial empires by acquiring new territories taken from the liquidated Ottoman Empire in the Middle East and the Second German Empire in Africa and Asia.

			1919 Versailles Treaty; founding of League of Nations	**1937–1945** World War II in China, the Pacific, and (from 1939) Europe	**1947** Indian and Pakistani independence	
1908 Oil discovered in Middle East	**1914–1918** World War I					**1950–1953** Korean War

1911–1912 Revolution in China; fall of Qing Dynasty	**1917** Bolshevik Revolution in Russia; USSR founded in 1922	**1929–1933** Stock market crash; Great Depression	**1942** Nazi Final Solution against Europe's Jews implemented	**1948** State of Israel founded; first Arab–Israeli War	**1957** USSR launch of Sputnik; decolonizatic begins in Africa

- In Russia, the Communist Party engineered a political takeover, withdrew the empire from the war, and built a communist state: the Union of Soviet Socialist Republics (Soviet Union, or USSR).
- The loser of World War I, Germany, together with Italy and Japan, turned toward supremacist nationalism.

World War II and the Rise of New Nations

World War II was actively planned by the supremacist nationalists. World War I and the Great Depression had ended the global free trade of the nineteenth century. All countries now believed that the future of industry lay in economic "spheres," each of which to be dominated by one *autarkic*—that is, self-sufficient—industrial power. With the victory of the Allies, the United States and Soviet Union emerged after World War II as the leading examples of the two surviving patterns of modernity: capitalist democracy and socialism–communism. The proponents of each of these patterns competed with the other during the Cold War (1945–1991):

- The first, or "hot," phase, 1945–1962: The United States and Soviet Union surrounded themselves with allies in Europe and Asia and fought one another militarily through proxies—that is, smaller allied states. They also sought to align the new nations emerging in the wake of decolonization into their respective camps. The Cold War climaxed with the Cuban Missile Crisis of 1962.
- The second, "cooling" phase, 1962–1991: During this time, the two nuclear powers reduced tensions ("détente"), and agreed to reduce their nuclear arsenals. But their proxy wars continued, in particular in Vietnam and Afghanistan.

Capitalist–Democratic Modernity

Perhaps the most significant event that put the United States on course for eventual victory over the Soviet Union in 1991 was the computer revolution—the third industrial revolution. After fully adapting itself to this revolution, the United States became the unrivaled superpower, deriving its strength from its advanced computer technology, powerful financial services, and unmatched military strength.

Thinking Like a World Historian

>> How are the three patterns that emerged after World War I different adaptations to modernity? Despite their marked differences, what common features do they share?

>> Why, after World War II, was socialism–communism in many ways a more attractive pattern to decolonizing countries than capitalist democracy?

>> Why was the United States better able to adapt to technological innovation than the Soviet Union?

>> How do consumerism and the widespread use of social networking show the emergence of a global culture in the twenty-first century? Can we predict what future patterns will look like?

interactive timeline

| 1958 | 1963 | 1966–1969 | 1979 | 1989–1991 |
| Great Leap Forward in China | Nuclear Test Ban Treaty | Cultural Revolution in China | Shah of Iran overthrown; USSR invades Afghanistan | Collapse of communism in Eastern Europe and Soviet Union |

| | 1962 | 1965–1973 | 1978 | 1985–1989 | 1989 |
| | Cuban Missile Crisis | Vietnam War | "Four Modernizations" in China | Perestroika and glasnost in the USSR | Tiananmen Square demonstrations in China; Berlin Wall breached |

| 1990 | 1990–2000 | 1994 | 2001 | 2008–2011 | 2011 |
| German unification | Civil war and ethnic cleansing in former Yugoslavia | End of apartheid and election of Nelson Mandela as president in South Africa; genocide in Rwanda | Al Qaeda attack on United States | Global financial crisis and economic recession | Arab Spring uprisings; world population reaches 7 billion |

World Wars and Competing Visions of Modernity

or 30 years, Minobe Tatsukichi (1873–1948) had been Japan's leading jurist and constitutional theorist. He had received a noble rank
and occupied an honored place in Japan's House of Peers, the upper chamber of its Diet, or parliament. A self-confident man, he was not accustomed
to having his legal constructs challenged.

But today was different, and only later would Minobe realize what a
dramatic turning point it was. On this February day in 1934, his fellow
peer Baron Takeo Kikuchi publicly denounced Minobe's most famous legal
theory, which posited that the relationship of the emperor to the constitution was one in which the emperor was an organ of the state. More than
a generation of Japanese lawyers and scholars had practiced law
according to Minobe's "organ theory." But now, the baron had accused Minobe of belittling the emperor's role in Japan's unique
kokutai, or "national polity/essence." This concept played a key
role in Japanese supremacist nationalism during the 1930s.

Though Minobe defended his position, the damage had been
done. Following more attacks in the Diet, Minobe resigned from
his position, narrowly escaped being tried for his views, and was nearly

A WORLD AT WAR,
1900–1945

ABOVE: Members of the Chinese People's Liberation Army undergo artillery training.

assassinated in 1936. Already, however, in their drive to "clarify" the meaning of the "national essence," the cabinet had banned Minobe's works from study or circulation. Minobe's experience personalizes a struggle to come to grips with new visions of modernity not only in Japan but in much of the world as well.

Seeing Patterns

≫ Which three patterns of modernity emerged after World War I? How and why did these patterns form?

≫ What were the strengths and flaws of each of the three visions of modernity?

≫ Why did supremacist nationalism disappear in the ashes of World War II?

By the 1930s, the liberal principles of modernity—constitutionalism, capitalism, science, and industry—were severely tested by the Great Depression. In Japan, these values gave way to "supremacist nationalism," similar to the ideologies of fascism in Italy and Nazism in Germany. In Russia, communism represented another new subpattern of modernity. Other nations—Spain, Portugal, and China, for example—struggled with variations of these competing ideologies.

This chapter explores how the conflicts of spreading modernity spawned these new visions and how each fared through two world wars and the largest economic depression in history. We will also see how supremacist nationalism was destroyed by the alliance of communism and capitalist democracy. Their interlude of victory, however, was short-lived. Within a few years the remaining two divisions of modernity renewed the struggle for dominance against each other in the Cold War.

The Great War and Its Aftermath

On July 27, 1914, the last day of peace in Europe for the next four years, the nations on the brink of total war represented different conditions on their way to modernity. Some, like Great Britain, Germany, and France, were, along with the United States, among the world leaders in the development of scientific–industrial society. Others, like Austria-Hungary, the Ottoman Empire, the Balkan nations, Russia, and Japan, were at various stages of industrialization. In terms of political modernity, all of these initial members of what would shortly be known as the Allies and Central powers—with the exception of France—were monarchies, though a number had become modified with the addition of constitutions and legislative assemblies. The larger powers were also imperial powers that had reduced much of Asia and Africa to the status of colonies. Over the next 4 years, this picture would change completely.

Total War. By 1918, large swaths of northern France and Belgium resembled moonscapes from 4 years of destruction and carnage. One of the unluckiest places was the Belgian city of Ypres, which suffered three battles and was all but completely obliterated by war's end.

A Savage War and a Flawed Peace

Imperial competition, tempered by the need for a balance of power among the major states, dominated Europe during the century following the Napoleonic Wars. This intersected with two trends of nineteenth-century modernity: the political patterns of constitutionalism and ethnic nationalism, and the pattern of industrialization.

Chapter Outline

• The Great War and Its Aftermath

• New Variations on Modernity: The Soviet Union and Communism

• New Variations on Modernity: Supremacist Nationalism in Italy, Germany, and Japan

• Putting It All Together

The rise of the new imperialism in the nineteenth century disrupted the efforts of statesmen to adjust the balance of power to ever-shifting political conditions.

Empires and Nations in the Balkans   German aspirations for expansion into eastern Europe constituted one reason for its support of Austria against Serbia in 1914. For its part, France had sought revenge for Germany's annexing of Alsace and Lorraine in 1871. In the first decade of the twentieth century, however, the key to the preservation of peace in Europe was seen as maintaining the balance among the three empires that met in the Balkans.

The shrinking Ottoman Empire, beset by continuing demands from ethnic-nationalist minorities for independence, struggled to survive. The expanding Russian Empire, despite having suffered a defeat at the hands of Japan and an abortive revolution in 1904–1905, was rapidly recovering its military strength. And the Habsburg Empire of Austria-Hungary opposed Russian expansionism but also sought to benefit from Ottoman weakness. Germany had replaced Great Britain as the protector of the Ottomans and assisted the latter in strengthening their army. Though it had taken Mediterranean territories from the Ottomans, Britain still had a stake in preserving the rest of the Ottoman Empire, as did the other powers, all of whom feared a territorial scramble if the Ottoman Empire collapsed. Hence, there was a rough community of interest aimed at strengthening the Ottoman Empire, whose leaders were seeking to improve their military posture.

One unresolved ethnic-nationalist issue was Bosnia-Herzegovina. After the Balkan war of 1878, Austria-Hungary had become the territory's administrator—but not sovereign—as a compromise with the Ottomans, who were unable to keep Serbs, Croats, and Muslims apart. When Russia renewed its support for Serb ethnic nationalism in the Balkans after 1905, Austria-Hungary assumed sovereignty of Bosnia-Herzegovina in a protective move in 1908. Russia, committed to the policy of pan-Slavism, reacted to Austria-Hungary's move by stirring up Serb nationalists in Bosnia-Herzegovina who sought to join their province to the neighboring Kingdom of Serbia. On June 28, 1914, members of a Bosnian Serb nationalist group assassinated the Austrian heir to the throne, Franz Ferdinand, and his wife in the Bosnian city of Sarajevo. This assassination began the slide of Europe into World War I.

The Early Course of the War   This war was comprehensive from the start: **total war**. The combatants relied on precise timing and speedy mobilization of their forces. For example, in order to avoid a two-front war, Germany, with its allies Austria-Hungary and, later, the Ottoman Empire (the Central powers), had to defeat France before Russia's massive army was fully mobilized (France, Russia, and Great Britain formed the Allied powers.). The German Schlieffen Plan therefore called for a massive assault on northern France through Belgium, while trapping and isolating the French armies seeking to invade Alsace and Lorraine.

The German plan ultimately failed after the French–British victory in the first Battle of the Marne in September 1914, a more rapid Russian mobilization than expected, and a poor showing by the Austrians against Russia. After months of fighting along the lines of the initial German advance into France, the Germans and the French and British dug in. By 1915 the two sides were forced into trench warfare in northeastern France and Belgium and an initially inconclusive war in the east against Russia.

Total war: A type of warfare in which all the resources of the nation—including all or most of the civilian population—are marshaled for the war effort. As total war unfolded, all segments of society were increasingly seen as legitimate targets for the combatants.

The Germans were able to halt the Russian advances in mid-1916 and to begin inflicting heavy losses on their troops. For its part, the Ottoman Empire suffered a crushing Russian invasion in the Caucasus, prompting it to massacre its Armenian minority, which was alleged to have helped in the invasion. This planned genocidal massacre, which may have killed 1 million Armenians, still requires a full accounting today.

As the war dragged on, both camps sought to recruit new countries to their sides. Italy, Greece, and Romania entered on the Allied side with the hope of gaining territory from Austria-Hungary and the Ottomans; Bulgaria joined the Central powers in the service of its own territorial ambitions. Japan declared war on Germany in 1914 as part of a previous alliance with Britain but used its occupation of German colonies in the Pacific and concessions in China as a step toward expanding its own empire. The Allies also recruited volunteers from their dominions and colonies. With the entrance of China in 1917 and the pivotal entrance of the United States that same year, the war now involved every major state in the world.

images of
trench warfare

The Turning Point: 1917   In March 1917, the toll of the war contributed to the collapse of tsarist Russia. The February Revolution (actually in March, so called because it took place during February in the old-style Julian calendar still in use in Russia) forced Tsar Nicholas II to abdicate and created a provisional government. The new social-democratic government committed itself to carrying on the war, which grew even more unpopular. The communist Bolshevik Party of Vladimir Lenin (1870–1924) campaigned against continuing the war and in early November (October in the Julian calendar), armed workers, sailors, and soldiers launched a takeover of the government in the capital of Petrograd (as St. Petersburg had been renamed).

After seizing power, the Bolsheviks began negotiations with the Germans, which resulted in the disastrous Treaty of Brest-Litovsk in March 1918. Roughly one-third of the Russian Empire's population, territory, and resources were handed over to the Germans in return for Russia's withdrawal from the war. The Germans had now come close to achieving their secret war goal: the creation of *Lebensraum* (living space) for Germany in the industrialized European part of Russia.

The United States had declared neutrality at the outset of the war, but the course of the war had shifted US opinion toward the Allied side. The German torpedoing and sinking of the British liner *Lusitania* on May 7, 1915, which cost the lives of more than 100 Americans, brought the United States to the brink of war. Germany discontinued unrestricted submarine warfare but, in early 1917, resumed it in a bid to isolate Great Britain. Wilson asked Congress to declare war, which it did on April 6, 1917.

interactive timeline

| 1908 Oil discovered in the Middle East | 1914–1918 World War I | 1917 Britain promises Jews a homeland in Palestine | 1917 Bolshevik Revolution | 1922 Mussolini's March on Rome |

1911–1912 Revolution in China; fall of Qing Dynasty   1915–1916 Britain promises Arabs a kingdom in the middle east   1915–1916 Massacre of Armenians in Ottoman Empire   1919 Versailles Treaty; League of Nations   1929 Stock market crash; Great Depression begins

1931 Japanese annexation of Manchuria   1932–1945 New Deal in United States   1936–1939 Spanish Civil War   1937 Rape of Nanjing   1942 Hitler implements the Final Solution: genocide of European Jews

1929–1932 Collectivization of agriculture in Soviet Union   1933 Hitler becomes chancellor in Germany   1937–1945 World War II in China and the Pacific   1939–1945 World War II in Europe, the Mediterranean, and North Africa

Woodrow Wilson, "Address on the Fourteen Points for Peace" (1918)

The entrance of the United States added the critical resources needed by the Allies to ultimately win the war. Wilson's war aims (the Fourteen Points) called for freedom of the seas, the rights of neutral powers, self-determination for all peoples, and peace "without annexations or indemnities." These new causes not only represented American goals but now were presented as the Allies' war aims as well.

In early 1918, American troops began to land in France in appreciable numbers. This coincided with a spring offensive mounted by Germany. The new American troops in France gave the Allies the advantage they needed to stop the German effort, which soon collapsed. Faced with these new conditions and reeling from the Allies' September counteroffensive, which now threatened to advance into Germany, the Germans agreed to an armistice on November 11, 1918.

The Versailles Peace   The toll of the war was staggering. About 20 million soldiers and civilians were dead, and 21 million were wounded. Many more millions perished in a global influenza pandemic, abetted by the transportation of goods and soldiers at war's end. The settlement was signed at Versailles on June 28, 1919—the fifth anniversary of the assassination of Franz Ferdinand.

The German, Austro-Hungarian, and Ottoman Empires were all dismantled, and new nation-states were created. Germany lost its overseas colonies, Alsace-Lorraine, and West Prussia. The Allies declared Germany responsible for the war and subjected it to military restrictions and reparation payments. France acquired temporary custody of the German Saar province with its coal reserves and steel factories as a guarantee for the payment of war reparations. While historians long considered the Allied-imposed reparations excessive, recent research has concluded that Germany, which was not destroyed by war, had the industrial-financial capacity to pay.

League of Nations: An international body of 58 states, created as part of the Versailles Treaty and functioning between 1919 and 1946, that sought to ensure world peace.

A new supranational **League of Nations** was entrusted with the maintenance of peace. But since one of its clauses required collective military action in case of aggression, the US Senate refused ratification, rejecting this infringement on American sovereignty. Altogether, the Versailles peace was deeply flawed. Instead of binding Germany into a common western European framework, the Allies actually encouraged it to go it alone by flanking it in the east with weak countries that could be dominated in the future (see Map 28.1).

America First: The Beginnings of a Consumer Culture and the Great Depression

The United States emerged from the war as the strongest among the Allied democracies. It had turned from a debtor country into a creditor country; a majority of Americans now lived in nonrural environments; and the war economy shifted relatively easily into a sustained peacetime expansion.

John Maynard Keynes, excerpts from *The Economic Consequences of the Peace* (1919)

Modernity Unfolding in the United States   Increased mechanization in many industries spurred the economic expansion. Americans aspired to move from countryside to city and to own a house, car, and appliances. During the Roaring Twenties, as the 1920s came to be called, Americans wanted to be entertained. A flourishing of popular culture accompanied the rising urban prosperity. The film industry of Hollywood and a recording industry came into being, churning out "hits," as their popular products came to be called, for the entertainment of the new consumers. And the rapid development of the radio now allowed news and entertainment to enter every household that could afford a set.

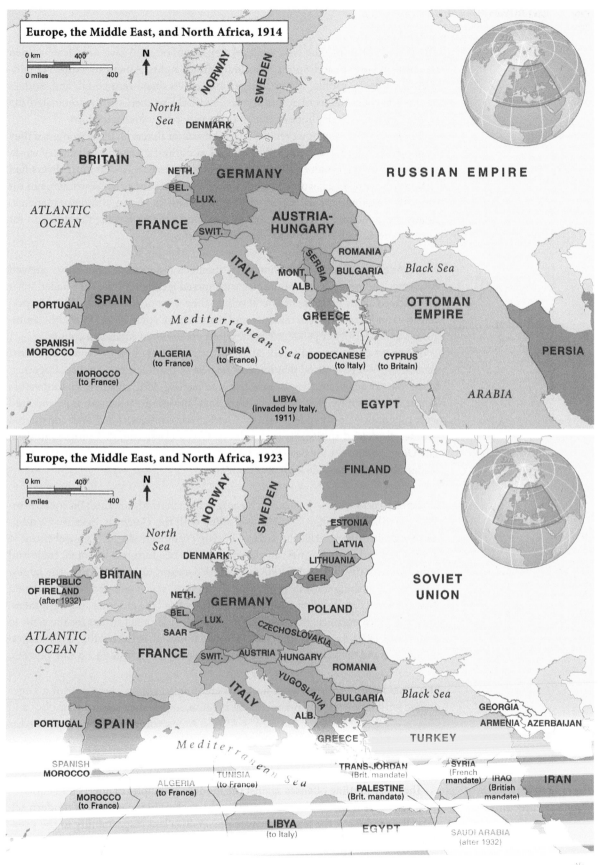

Europe, the Middle East, and North Africa, 1914

0 km 400
0 miles 400
N

NORWAY
SWEDEN
North Sea
DENMARK
BRITAIN
NETH.
BEL.
LUX.
GERMANY
ATLANTIC OCEAN
FRANCE
SWIT.
AUSTRIA-HUNGARY
ITALY
MONT.
SERBIA
ALB.
ROMANIA
BULGARIA
GREECE
RUSSIAN EMPIRE
Black Sea
OTTOMAN EMPIRE
PORTUGAL
SPAIN
Mediterranean Sea
DODECANESE (to Italy)
CYPRUS (to Britain)
PERSIA
SPANISH MOROCCO
ALGERIA (to France)
TUNISIA (to France)
MOROCCO (to France)
LIBYA (invaded by Italy, 1911)
EGYPT
ARABIA

Europe, the Middle East, and North Africa, 1923

0 km 400
0 miles 400
N

NORWAY
SWEDEN
FINLAND
North Sea
DENMARK
ESTONIA
LATVIA
LITHUANIA
REPUBLIC OF IRELAND (after 1932)
BRITAIN
NETH.
BEL.
LUX.
GER.
GERMANY
SAAR
POLAND
SOVIET UNION
ATLANTIC OCEAN
FRANCE
SWIT.
AUSTRIA
CZECHOSLOVAKIA
HUNGARY
ROMANIA
ITALY
YUGOSLAVIA
BULGARIA
Black Sea
ALB.
GEORGIA
ARMENIA
AZERBAIJAN
PORTUGAL
SPAIN
GREECE
TURKEY
Mediterranean Sea
SPANISH MOROCCO
ALGERIA (to France)
TUNISIA (to France)
TRANS-JORDAN (Brit. mandate)
SYRIA (French mandate)
IRAQ (British mandate)
IRAN
MOROCCO (to France)
PALESTINE (Brit. mandate)
LIBYA (to Italy)
EGYPT
SAUDI ARABIA (after 1932)

MAP 28.1 Europe, the Middle East, and North America in 1914 and 1923.

map analysis

The New Woman   The Nineteenth Amendment of 1920 gave American women the right to vote. In addition to winning political rights, American women heightened their social profile. Many colleges and universities went co-ed, and women became teachers, secretaries, and nurses. Similarly, women swiftly dominated the new occupation of telephone operator as the new century advanced.

For people of color, however, the situation was far different. Black women, if they were not agricultural laborers, often worked as domestic servants or laundry workers in the growing urban economy. In larger segregated areas with more diversified economies, some black women found similar kinds of jobs as white women, but for the most part, their opportunities were far more limited. Hence, although emancipation was expanding for white women, it remained gendered, while the situation for black women continued to be hampered by racism.

High Artistic Creativity   American intellectuals, writers, and artists viewed consumer and pop culture modernity with mixed feelings. While they hailed what they viewed as the progress of liberal values, they were uneasy about what they perceived as an increasing superficiality and materialism. After World War I, the ambiguities of modernity engendered tremendous creativity in American culture.

Langston Hughes, "The Negro Artist and the Racial Mountain" (1926)

A cohort of artists and intellectuals viewed themselves as belonging to a "lost generation,"—a generation that had lost its best years of life, or even life altogether, to the war. The Harlem Renaissance featured leading African American innovators in jazz and literature (see "Patterns Up Close"). Modernist writers experimented with the inner emotional tensions of a "stream of consciousness" style, or offered counter-models of spirituality, naturalness, Greek classicism, or Chinese monism. The United States set the pace for mass culture, providing many of the literary tools readers needed to grapple with modernity.

Business and Labor   Just as much energy characterized American business. Presidents Harding, Coolidge, and Hoover, along with the Congress, exercised a minimum of political control, illustrated by Harding's campaign slogan "Less government in business and more business in government." While business boomed, trade and industrial unions stagnated. The American Federation of Labor (AFL), the largest trade union pushing for improved labor conditions, was hampered by the fact that its members were unskilled workers of many diverse backgrounds and were therefore difficult to organize. Business easily quashed widespread strikes for the right to unionize in 1919. An anti-immigration hysteria followed, with laws that cut immigration by half and the famous murder trial of immigrant anarchists Sacco and Vanzetti.

The Backlash   Anti-foreigner and anti-communist hysteria was part of a larger unease with modernity. Fundamentalist religion, intolerance toward Catholics and Jews, and fear and violence directed at African Americans rose visibly. The Ku Klux Klan was at the center of repeated waves of lynchings in the South and attempts to control the local politics of many states. The Klan remained a powerful force in the South and Midwest until World War II.

Eugenics: The discredited idea of the hereditary breeding of better human beings by genetic control.

The most startling offenses against the modern principles of liberty and equality, however, came from ideologues wrapping themselves in the mantle of modern science. Researchers at the leading private universities lent respectability to the pseudoscience of **eugenics**, conceptualizing an ideal of a "Nordic" race. Foundations

Lynching. Outside the South, Indiana was the state that experienced the greatest surge in racial tensions in the period immediately after World War I. In 1925, the governor and half the state assembly were members of the Ku Klux Klan, as were about 30 percent of the state's white population. In this photo from August 1930, a crowd gathers to gawk at Tom Shipp and Abram Smith, two African American men who were lynched by a mob in Marion, Indiana, for allegedly committing robbery and rape.

such as the Carnegie Endowment and businessmen such as Henry Ford financed research on how to prevent the reproduction of genetically "inferior" races. California and other states passed laws that allowed for the sterilization of thousands of women. Ironically, some of the practices that would inspire Hitler and the Nazis were already in place during the 1920s in the United States and actually regarded by some as progressive.

The Great Depression   By 1929, saturation of the market for consumer goods behind high tariff walls led to falling profit rates in businesses. Many of the wealthy had begun to shift their money from investments in manufacturing to speculation on the stock market. In addition, ordinary investors participated in the stock market, many buying shares on high margins As long as the market boomed, investors made money, but if stocks went down, investors could be bankrupted as their margins were called in.

By the late 1920s, a slowdown in production shifted attention to unsustainable debt levels. Farmers were deep in debt, having borrowed to mechanize while speculating wrongly on a continuation of high prices for commodities. In October 1929, the speculators panicked, selling their stock for pennies on the dollar. The panic rippled through both the finance and manufacturing sectors. As banks began calling in loans at home and abroad, the panic became a worldwide crisis: the **Great Depression** of 1929–1933. Harrowing levels of unemployment and poverty put the American system of capitalist democratic modernity to a severe test.

Americans largely blamed their president, Herbert Hoover (in office 1929–1933), for failing to manage the crisis, and in 1932 they elected Franklin D. Roosevelt (in

Great Depression: The global economic crisis that followed the crash of the New York Stock Exchange on October 29, 1929, and resulted in massive unemployment and economic misery worldwide.

Patterns Up Close | The Harlem Renaissance and the African Diaspora

Langston Hughes. The noted poet and writer Langston Hughes first emerged on the literary scene during the Harlem Renaissance and went on to influence the shaping of African and African American literary identity for decades afterwards.

The modern period saw some of the largest migrations in human history. Such "diasporas"—a term originally used to describe the scattering of the Jews around Europe, the Middle East, and North Africa—not only threw those affected into new and sometimes hostile environments but over time also created complex cultural conditions in which new generations forged their identities. In the case of African Americans in the 1920s, a new and vital cultural touchstone was the Harlem Renaissance.

Growing—though still limited—educational opportunities, an increase in urbanization stemming from the "Great Migration" of rural southern African Americans seeking work in northern factory cities during World War I, and a new political assertiveness all contributed to a cultural explosion. As the largest African American enclave in America's largest city, New York, Harlem became the most vital black cultural center. Jazz and its offshoots came to dominate popular tastes; young people of all ethnicities sought to take up the latest dances from "uptown"; and writers such as Claude McKay (1889–1948), Langston Hughes (1902–1967), James Weldon Johnson (1871–1938), Zora Neale Hurston (1891–1960), and many others achieved national and international recognition.

office 1933–1945). Hoover's approach had been one that previous administrations had turned to in times of economic crisis: cut government spending, raise tariffs to protect US industries, and let market forces correct themselves. But such measures now only made things worse, while the record high Smoot-Hawley Tariff of 1930 encouraged retaliatory tariffs in other countries and discouraged world commerce, thus contributing to a worldwide economic collapse.

Under Roosevelt's prodding, Congress enacted what he called the "New Deal," in which the government engaged in deficit spending to help the unemployed and revive business and agriculture. One showpiece of the New Deal was the Tennessee Valley Authority, a government-owned corporation for the economic development of large parts of the southeastern United States particularly hard hit by the Depression. In addition, a social safety net was created, including unemployment benefits and the Social Security Act. Finally, the Securities and Exchange Commission (SEC) was created in 1934 to enforce regulations governing the stock market in order to prevent practices that had led to the collapse of 1929.

In 1937, however, a Congress frightened by the deficit slackened efforts to reduce unemployment, while the Supreme Court declared several of the New Deal

Though relatively few writers (among them Langston Hughes) actually visited Africa, its resonance was powerful. To be African in this sense was to be beyond the history of slavery and oppression and to be part of a larger and richer collective history extending to the first human beings. This solidarity was expressed in the Pan-African movement of which the educator, activist, and cofounder of the NAACP, W. E. B. DuBois (1868–1963) was a prominent popularizer. During the 1920s the most popular mass movement among African Americans was the Universal Negro Improvement Association led by Jamaican Marcus Garvey (1887–1940), which sought to help those of the African diaspora repatriate to the continent with a view to creating a prosperous Africa for the Africans.

For its part, the Harlem Renaissance also had a profound effect on people of African descent in places far removed from the United States. African expatriates in Paris in the 1930s championed a cultural movement called Négritude, which called for a new pride in African history, culture, and "blackness" itself. Influenced by such writers as Aimé Césaire (1913–2008) and Léopold Senghor (1906–2001), the movement was powerfully influential in French-speaking Africa. Senghor himself became Senegal's first president and served for two decades.

Questions

- What were some of the factors that led to the Harlem Renaissance emerging in the 1920s, instead of some other time?

- Why were the questions these writers raised about identity so important to them? Why was this especially so in the new "modern" age?

programs unconstitutional. The result was a new slump, from which the economy finally recovered only with America's entry into World War II.

Great Britain and France: Slow Recovery and Troubled Empires

In the aftermath of World War I, Britain and France suffered severely. A lack of finances hampered the recovery, as did the enormous debt both countries took on during the war. Conservative politicians relinquished the state capitalism of the war period and returned to politics favorable to private investors. Although socialist politicians gained in importance, they did not succeed in improving working-class conditions or the safety net. The demands of the League of Nations mandate system, whereby the colonies were to be prepared for future independence, were not pursued vigorously by either France or Britain.

Weak British Recovery   As Britain's economy shifted from state control during the war back to market capitalism and industry, it was also dependent on world trade. Unfortunately, world trade declined dramatically after the war. In addition,

Britain owed a war debt of $4.3 billion to the United States. Since much of Britain's ability to repay these debts rested upon Germany's ability to pay its reparations, the entire European economic system remained fragile throughout the 1920s.

With the restructuring of Germany's debts in 1924, some stability finally came to the international capital markets. Still, close to half of the annual British budgets in the interwar period went to paying off the war debt. In this situation, industrial investments were low and unemployment was high. In addition, business lowered wages, causing labor to respond with a massive general strike in 1926.

The dominant conservatives in the government could not bring themselves in the 1930s to accept deficit spending. At a minimum, however, they went off the gold standard and devalued the currency to make exports competitive again. World trade had declined; but by lowering tariffs within the empire, Britain created the equivalent of the **autarky** that Nazi Germany and militaristic Japan were dreaming of with their planned conquests. A semblance of prosperity returned to the country in the 1930s.

Autarky: The condition of economic independence and self-sufficiency as state policy.

France: Moderate Recovery   France suffered devastating human losses and destruction of property during the war. Alsace-Lorraine, the most important industrial region and the territory that France desperately wanted to recover from the Germans, was now a wasteland. The war had been fought with war materiel borrowed from the United States and Great Britain, to be paid for after the war. The money for the reconstruction of industry and housing came from increased taxes, German reparations, and taxes from German provinces occupied after the war. But reconstruction could be completed only in 1926–1929, when taxes were once more increased and Germany finally made full reparation payments.

French governments were dependent on coalitions among parties, and labor was more often than not represented. France did not suffer a traumatic general strike as Britain did, and even though it returned to the gold standard (1928–1936), it wisely avoided the prewar parity, thereby making the low wages for its workers a bit more bearable.

Thanks to its successful reconstruction, France weathered the Depression until 1931. Even then, conservative politicians found the idea of deficit spending as a way to get out of the Depression too counterintuitive. Instead, like the Hoover administration in America, they slashed government spending and refused to devalue the currency. By 1933–1934, unrest in the population and rapidly changing governments made supremacist nationalism an attractive model, especially for business, which was afraid of labor strife. When fascist–communist street fighting broke out in Paris, the Communist Party initiated the formation of a Popular Front coalition with the Socialist Party and others (1936–1938). Although this coalition checked supremacist nationalism, it was too short-lived to allow the centrist middle-class core to broaden, with disastrous consequences for France's ability to resist Hitler in World War II.

Colonies and Mandates   After World War I, the British Empire grew by 2 million square miles to 14 million, or one-quarter of the earth's surface, encompassing one-quarter of the world's population. The French Empire at the same time measured 5 million square miles, with a population of 113 million. Although the wisdom of maintaining expensive empires was debated in the interwar period, conservatives

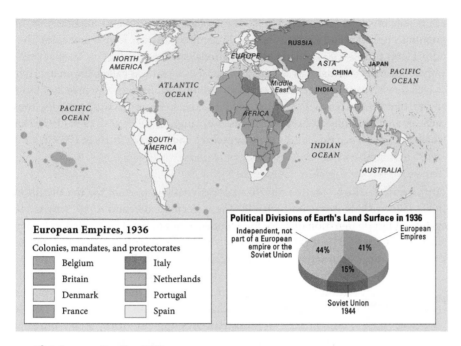

MAP 28.2 **European Empires, 1936.**

clung to the prestige that square mileage was presumed to bestow on its holders. Defense of these empires dominated the policies of Britain and France toward their dependencies and mandates during the interwar period (see Map 28.2).

The most important area, strategically, for both the British and the French after World War I was the Middle East. Under the postwar peace terms, the British and French had received the Arab provinces of the former Ottoman Empire (other than Egypt and Sudan, acquired already in 1881) as **mandates**—that is, as territories to be prepared for independence. Because of the discovery of oil in southwestern Iran, however, neither Britain nor France was in a hurry to guide its mandates to independent nationhood.

Mandates: Quasi-colonies created by the League of Nations, which mandated key territories of the defunct Ottoman Empire to Britain and France.

Twice-Promised Lands   Arab leaders were strongly opposed to the British and French mandates. A British agent, T. E. Lawrence (1888–1935), the famous "Lawrence of Arabia," helped the members of a prominent family, the Hashemites from Mecca in western Arabia, to assume leadership of the Arabs for a promised national kingdom in Syria and Palestine in the so-called McMahon–Hussein correspondence of 1915–1916.

Since the British, seeking Jewish support for World War I, also promised the Jews a "national home" in Palestine in the Balfour Declaration of 1917, Arab nationalism was stymied even before it could unfold. The British moved the Hashemites into their mandates of Iraq and Transjordan in 1921, in accordance with the Sykes–Picot agreement (1916) concerning the imperial division of the Middle East between the Allies. As Iraq was divided by majority Shiites and minority Sunnis, the British inaugurated a policy of divide and rule in this Middle Eastern mandate.

In Palestine, the contradiction between the promises to Arabs and Jews during the war forced Britain to build a direct administration under a high commissioner.

The Balfour
Declaration (1917)

Zionism: The belief, based on the writings of Theodor Herzl, that European Jews—and by extension all Jews everywhere—were entitled to a national homeland corresponding to the territory of ancient Israel. It grew into a form of ethno-religious nationalism and ultimately led to the formation of the state of Israel in 1948.

Many religious Jews had arrived in Palestine as refugees from anti-Semitic riots, or pogroms, in Russia and Eastern Europe. When the Austrian Jewish journalist Theodor Herzl (1860–1904) made ethnic nationalism the ideology of secular Jews, early pioneers of **Zionism**, as secular Jewish nationalism was called, began to arrive as well. Jewish settlers purchased land from willing Palestinian absentee landlords and evicted the landlords' Palestinian tenant farmers. These evictions were the root cause of two Palestinian–Arab nationalist uprisings, in 1929 and 1936–1939, for which the British had no real answer except force and belated efforts in 1939 to limit Jewish immigration.

Egypt and Turkey   As the Suez Canal was vitally important for the British in India, relinquishing it was unthinkable. They rejected a demand in 1919 by a delegation of Egyptian nationalists for independence out of hand and exiled its leader, Saad Zaghlul (ca. 1859–1927). After deadly riots, the British relented and invited Zaghlul to peace negotiations. But the independence the British granted in 1923 withheld both military defense and control of the Suez Canal from Egypt. A year later, Zaghlul and the Wafd Party won the first independent elections. The Egyptian ruling class was largely uninterested in industrial development. Thus, at the onset of World War II, Egypt still depended on agricultural production and exports, while its strategic position was absolutely vital to the British Empire.

The severe punishment of the Ottoman Empire by the Allies provoked the rise of grassroots resistance groups in Anatolia. These groups merged under the leadership of General Mustafa Kemal "Atatürk" ("Father of the Turks," 1881–1938) into a national liberation movement that drove out the Greeks from western Anatolia, occupied one-half of Armenia, and ended the Ottoman sultanate/caliphate (1921–1924). Atatürk, who had earned renown during World War I for his defense of Gallipoli against the British, was the driving force behind the creation of a modern, secular Turkey that could stand up against the European powers.

Although authoritarian, Atatürk kept the new Turkish parliament open to pluralism. Parliament adopted the French model of separation of state and religion, European family law, the Latin alphabet, the Western calendar, metric weights and measures, modern clothing, and women's suffrage. During the Depression, Atatürk's economic advisors launched *étatism*, the Turkish version of deficit spending. Both modernism and étatism showed only modest successes by 1939, and the rural masses in Anatolia remained mired in small-scale self-sufficiency farming and religious tradition. But the foundation was laid in Turkey for both a Westernized ruling class and an urbanized middle class.

Secularizing Turkey. Atatürk was a committed educational reformer who sought to create a "public culture." He was advised by the famous American philosopher of education John Dewey (1859–1952). Here, in 1928, dressed in a Western-style suit and necktie, he gives a lesson on the new Turkish alphabet, a variant of the Latin alphabet, whose use was mandated throughout the republic.

Indian Demands for Independence   In India in April 1919, frustrated by a British crackdown on political protest, a crowd gathered in the Sikhs' sacred city of Amritsar. The protesters were slaughtered by an elite unit of Gurkha troops. As the international furor over this "Amritsar Massacre" raged, the British offered token reforms to the Indian Legislative Assembly. The Indian National Congress was infuriated by this minimal improvement and called for full self-rule (Hindi *swaraj*), urging nonviolent noncooperation.

Inevitably, civil disturbances accompanied the Congress's push for self-rule. Mohandas Gandhi (1869–1948), the most prominent advocate of nonviolence, suspended the push in 1921. Party leaders exited the cities and, with the help of party workers, preached nonviolent civil disobedience in the countryside. It was during this time that the National Congress transformed itself from a small Westernized elite into a mass party.

In 1929, the new Labour government in Britain explored the possibility of giving India dominion status, but there was strong opposition from the other parties. When Labour could not deliver, Gandhi demanded complete independence and, on March 12, 1930, embarked on the 24-day Salt March to the sea with his followers to pan salt, which the government had refused to free from taxation. Disturbances accompanied the marches, and in a massive crackdown, the British government succeeded in repressing the National Congress.

The British government in 1935 passed the Government of India Act, which devolved all political functions except defense and foreign affairs to India. The members of the National Congress were unhappy, however, because of the decentralized structure of the reformed Indian government and particularly because the act recognized the Muslim League of Muhammad Ali Jinnah (1876–1948), not the Congress, as the representative of the Muslims. As in Egypt and Iraq, there was a profound reluctance by the Western powers to relinquish colonialism.

Swaraj: Literally, "self-rule" [*swah-RAHJ*]. Gandhi interpreted this term as meaning "direct democracy," while the Congress Party identified it with complete independence from Great Britain.

Latin America: Independent Democracies and Authoritarian Regimes

Latin America remained faithful to its constitutionalist heritage throughout the nineteenth century, though with a preference for authoritarian rule. A pattern of elite rule had evolved in which large estate owners controlled the politics of their countries and, through the military, kept rural black and indigenous peoples, as well as the mixed urban populations, in check. Politicians in some countries realized the voting potential of the urban populations after World War I and pursued a new type of autocratic politics, called populism, in conjunction with industrialization. Estate-owner politics and populism, together with industrialization programs, characterized Latin America during the interwar period.

Gandhi Leading the Salt March. Perhaps the most famous act of civil disobedience in Gandhi's career was the Salt March in 1930 to protest the British salt monopoly in India. It was a perfect embodiment of Gandhi's belief in nonviolent resistance, which he called *satyagraha*, "soul-" or "truth-force." Though it failed to win major concessions from the British, it focused worldwide attention on the Indian independence movements.

The Years of Depression In Mexico, rapid urbanization continued during the interwar period. Immigration from overseas as well as rural–urban migration fueled this process. In 1929 the new Institutional Revolutionary Party (Partido Revolucionario Institucional, PRI) brought the revolution of 1910–1917 to an end. A now strong government moved to complete land distribution to poor farmers, expand education, and begin social legislation. The PRI weathered the Depression with some difficulty, but thanks to increased state control of economic investments, it maintained its footing until European and East Asian war preparations increased demand for commodities.

The South American countries with the largest internal markets, such as Argentina and Brazil, rode out the Depression more successfully than others. Nevertheless, overall the impact was substantial, with a reduction of commodity exports by over 50 percent. The Depression resulted in urban unrest, especially in countries with newly expanded mines or oil wells, such as Chile, Peru, and Venezuela, or expanded administrative bureaucracies, such as Brazil.

An important shift away from landed oligarchies, however, began to appear among the ruling classes. A new generation of military officers, with urban backgrounds and no ties to the traditional oligarchy, appeared. They offered populist authoritarian programs that mixed elements from the prevailing European ideologies.

New Variations on Modernity: The Soviet Union and Communism

Communism was the second pattern of modernity that arose out of the ashes of World War I. Following their coup in November 1917, the Bolsheviks under Lenin triumphed in a debilitating civil war and established the Union of Soviet Socialist Republics. Lenin's successor, Joseph Stalin (1879–1953), built the Communist Party into a powerful apparatus that shifted resources from agriculture into industry and dealt ruthlessly with opposition. By World War II, the Soviet Union had joined the ranks of the industrialized powers.

The Communist Party and Regime in the Soviet Union

Karl Marx, the founder of communism, did not think that the Russian Empire would be ready for a communist revolution for a long time to come. It was the achievement of Vladimir Lenin to adapt Marxism to his circumstances. For him, the party was not the mass movement envisioned by Marx but rather the disciplined, armed vanguard that ruled with monopoly power and instilled the ideology of communism in an expanding working class after the revolution.

The Bolshevik Regime   Lenin was from a middle-class family; his father had been given a patent of nobility, and Lenin himself had a degree in law. The execution of his brother by the tsarist government for alleged complicity in the assassination of Tsar Alexander II (1881) imbued him with hatred for Russian autocracy.

The fall of the tsar's government in the spring of 1917 allowed Lenin and his fellow Bolsheviks to return from political exile. These included Leon Trotsky (1879–1940), the son of an affluent Ukrainian Jewish family, and Joseph Stalin, the son of an impoverished Georgian cobbler. By the summer of 1917, the Bolsheviks were mounting massive demonstrations. The collapse of a disastrous Russian summer offensive emboldened the Bolsheviks, who controlled the Petrograd Soviet (council of workers and soldiers that helped maintain order as the nation struggled to create a constitution), to make a bid for power. In early November 1917, the Bolsheviks staged a successful coup d'état in Petrograd.

Bolshevik propaganda painting (1920)

Civil War and Reconstruction   The takeover of Russia by a radical minority unleashed a storm of competing factions. For the Bolsheviks, the first necessity was building an army. From his armored train, flying the new "hammer and sickle" red flag, Trotsky rallied his "Red" forces against the more numerous but disunited "White" armies. From 1918 to 1921, Georgia, Armenia, Azerbaijan and the Ukraine were each forced back into the new Bolshevik state.

The price for communist victory in the civil war was a complete collapse of the economy, amid a coincidental harvest failure. Lenin's policy of "war communism" sent the Red Army into the countryside to requisition food, often with brutality. Peasants fought back, and by 1922 a second civil war threatened. Only then did Lenin relent by inaugurating the temporary New Economic Policy (NEP), with a mixture of private and state investment in factories and small-scale food marketing by peasants. By 1928, a successful NEP had helped the Soviet Union to return to prewar levels of industrial production.

The Collectivization of Agriculture and Industrialization

Lenin died in 1924. His successor, Joseph Stalin, took his place as the general secretary of the Communist Party. Stalin fought for six years against potential and imagined rivals, a struggle that left him deeply suspicious. His chief victim was Trotsky, whom he forced into exile and ultimately had assassinated in Mexico in 1940.

"Liquidation of the Kulaks as a Class"   Stalin decided that industrialization through the NEP was advancing too slowly. Funds to finance industrialization came from the sale of grain on the world market, but farmers had lost all trust in the communist regime after the forcible requisitions during the civil war, and hoarded their grain. In November 1929, the party decreed the collectivization of agriculture as the necessary step for an accelerated industrialization. Over the next two years, 3–5 percent of the "wealthiest" farmers on grain-producing lands, called *kulaks* (Russian for "fist," indicating the tightfistedness of wealthier farmers vis-à-vis poor indebted ones), were "liquidated"—selected for execution, removal to labor camps, or resettlement on inferior soils. Their properties were confiscated, and the remaining peasants were regrouped as employees either of state farms or of poorer collective farms. Between 6 and 14 million farmers were forcibly removed, with the majority killed outright or worked and starved to death.

Stalinism   The impact on agriculture was devastating. Production plummeted; food requisitions were resumed; bread was rationed; and wages sank. This one-time transfer of confiscated wealth from the kulaks to industry was substantial. Income from accelerated oil exports and renewed grain exports from state farms in the 1930s was poured into factory construction. By 1939, industrialization had been accomplished, though at an unparalleled human cost.

Joseph Stalin, "On the Tasks of Workers In the Economy" (1931)

The industrial and urban modernity that the Soviet Union reached was one of enforced solidarity without private enterprises and markets. The communist prestige objects were huge plant complexes producing industrial basics. Little investment was left over for consumer goods and household articles, and people had to make do with shoddy goods, delivered irregularly to government outlets and requiring patient waiting in long lines.

The disaster of collectivization made Stalin even more concerned about potential resistance. Regular party and army purges decimated the top echelons of the communist ruling apparatus. Considering the enormity of Stalin's policies, scholars have since wondered about the viability of this communist–socialist attempt at accelerated modernity.

New Variations on Modernity: Supremacist Nationalism in Italy, Germany, and Japan

The third vision of modernity was an ideology of supremacist nationalism. Fascism became a persuasive alternative to democracy and communism in Italy after World War I. The much more brutal German Nazi and Japanese militarist ideologies became acceptable only after the Depression appeared to reveal capitalist democracy to be incapable of weathering the crisis.

"Comrade, Come Join Us at the Collective Farm!" This is the call with which the woman on this wildly optimistic poster of 1930 is seen. In reality, Russian peasants experienced the collectivization program of 1929–1940 as a second serfdom, especially in the Ukraine, where private rather than collective village farming was widespread. They resisted it both passively and actively, through arson, theft, and especially the slaughtering of livestock.

Corporate state: Sometimes called an "organic state"; based on a philosophy of government that sees all sectors of society contributing in a systematic, orderly, and hierarchical fashion to the health of the state, the way that the parts of the body do to a human being.

From Fascism in Italy to Nazism in the Third Reich

Benito Mussolini (1883–1945) worked as a journalist at various socialist newspapers. His support for the war as an instrument of radical change brought him into conflict with the majority of socialists, who opposed the war. Disillusioned with Marxism, he founded the Italian Combat Squad. War veterans, dressed in black shirts and organized in paramilitary units, broke up communist rallies and strikes. The symbol of the movement was the *fasces* [FAS-sees]—derived from the old Roman emblem of solidarity in the form of a bundle of sticks and an ax, tied with a ribbon.

With their street brawls, the fascist "Blackshirts" contributed to the impression of a breakdown of law and order, which the democratic government could not control. Anti-communism thus was accompanied by denunciations of democracy as incapable of decisive action. Although Mussolini's party was still behind other parties in the parliament, he demanded the premiership by threatening a march on Rome by 10,000 Blackshirts. This turned into a victory parade, with the king acquiescing to the fascists.

In 1923 Mussolini led his coalition government in the passing of a law that gave two-thirds of the seats in parliament to the party that garnered the most votes. A year later, Il Duce ("the Leader"), as he now styled himself, won his two-thirds and began to implement his fascist **corporate state**.

By 1926, elections were abolished, the press was censored, and the secret police monitored the population. Fascist party officials, provincial governorships, and mayors were appointed from above, and labor unions were closed down. In the Ministry of Corporations, industrialists and bureaucrats representing labor, met and sharply curtailed wages and labor regulations. Catholicism was made the Italian state religion in return for full support by the Vatican for the fascists.

Depression and Conquests   Italy weathered the Depression through deficit spending and state investments. In 1933, Mussolini formed the Industrial Reconstruction Institute, which took over the industrial and commercial holdings of the banks that had failed earlier. This institute was crucial in efforts to revive the Italian industrial sector. Only in the mid-1930s did the urban population, concentrated mostly in the north, come to outnumber its rural counterpart. The fascists had no solution for southern Italy, a region that remained overwhelmingly rural and poor.

Italy's military industry allowed Mussolini to proclaim a policy of autarky with the help of overseas territories. First, the conquest of formerly Ottoman Libya (see Chapter 27) was brutally completed in 1931. The other major colony was Ethiopia, conquered by Italy in 1935–1936 and merged with Italian Eritrea and Somalia into Italian East Africa. Eager to avenge Italy's defeat by the Ethiopians forty years before, Mussolini's forces crushed Ethiopian resistance and then pacified the new colony with the settlement of 200,000 Italians.

The Ethiopian conquest prompted protests by the League of Nations. Although these were ineffective, Mussolini felt sufficiently isolated that he sought closer relations with Adolf Hitler and the Nazis, whom he found to be a counterweight against international isolation. An increasingly close cooperation began between the two dictators, who formed the nucleus of the Axis powers, joined in 1941 by Japan.

The Founding of the Weimar Republic   In September 1918, the German Supreme Army Command (OHL) concluded that Germany had lost World War I. Soon after, unrest broke out in the military and among workers. Alarmed civilian politicians in Berlin struggled to bring about a peaceful transition from empire to republic. When the emperor eventually abdicated, his last chancellor appointed Friedrich Ebert (1871–1925), a prominent member of the German Social Democratic Party, on November 9, 1918, as his successor. In secret contacts Wilhelm Groener of the OHL offered Ebert armed support, and in the following months the two cooperated in crushing the communist workers' councils.

The first test for the new republic (founded in nearby Weimar) came in the summer of 1919, when the Allies presented their peace settlement. The French would have liked to have Germany divided into individual states again, as it was before 1871. The British and the Americans, however, were opposed to such a drastic settlement. Germany was let off with what historians now see in retrospect as relatively moderate reparations for civilian casualties, along with the loss of two western provinces, although it was also forced to accept responsibility for beginning the war. The compromise satisfied no one. France's security remained uncertain, German conservatives and nationalists screamed defiance, and the democrats of Weimar who accepted the settlement were embittered by its consequence: inflation.

Asked to begin the payments immediately, Germany was unable to correct the general inflation when pent-up consumer demand had exploded with the onset of peace. The German mark quickly became virtually worthless, and Germany had to suspend payments. France and Belgium responded by occupying the industrial Ruhr province in 1923. German workers in the Ruhr retaliated with passive resistance, and a deadlock was the result.

Play Money. German children in 1923 playing with bundles of money in the streets. Hyperinflation had made money in the early Weimar Republic worthless: At the height of the inflation, in November 1923, $0.24 US was worth 1 trillion "paper marks." To overcome the hyperinflation, the German Central Bank cut the "trillions" off the mark and created the "reichsmark." This currency was tied again to the gold standard and was in circulation until 1948.

Faced with this crisis, the new Weimar Republic made peace with the French by recognizing the new borders. Recognizing, too, the dire financial implications of an economically crippled Germany, the American-crafted Dawes Plan of 1924 had US banks advance credits to European banks to refinance the resumed German reparation payments, significantly reduced by the plan. France and Belgium withdrew from the Ruhr, inflation was curtailed, and the currency stabilized. The newly solvent Weimar Republic then flourished during the rest of the decade.

The Rise of the Nazis This effloresence wilted in the months after the US stock market crash of 1929. American banks, desperate for cash, began to recall their loans made to Europe. European banks began to fail, and as world trade shrank, exporting nations like Germany were hit particularly hard. Unemployment soared to 30 percent of the workforce. The number of people voting for extremist opponents of democracy—communists and supremacist nationalists—rose to more than half of the electorate by July 1932, and the National Socialist German Workers' Party (NSDAP, or Nazi Party) became the largest party in parliament.

The Nazi leader, Adolf Hitler (1889–1945), had led a failed uprising in 1923 and done time for it in prison. In *Mein Kampf* (*My Struggle*), published in 1925, he advocated ridding Germany of its Jews, whom he blamed for World War I, and communists, whom he blamed for the Central powers losing the war. He further supported the German conquest of a "living space" (*Lebensraum*) in Russia and Eastern Europe for the "superior" "Aryan" (German) race, with the "inferior" Slavs reduced to forced labor. No one who followed politics in Germany during the 1920s could be in doubt about Hitler's unrestrained and violent supremacist nationalism. Throughout the decade, however, he remained marginalized.

The Nazis in Power When the Nazis won a plurality in parliament in 1932, Hitler demanded the chancellorship. President Paul von Hindenburg (in office 1925–1934) nominated Hitler to the post on January 30, 1933, in an effort to neutralize Nazism and keep Hitler under control. Hitler, however, wasted no time in escaping all restraints.

Following a fire in the Reichstag (German parliament) building in February 1933, which Hitler blamed on the communists, the president allowed his new chancellor the right to declare martial law for a limited time. Two months later, the Nazi Party in parliament passed the Enabling Act with the votes of the mostly Catholic Centrist Party; its leaders calculated that they could control Hitler and also reach a much-desired agreement between the Vatican and Germany parallel to the one of Mussolini. According to the constitution, Hitler now had the power to rule by emergency decree for 4 years.

Taking their cue from Mussolini's policies, the Nazis abolished the federalist structure of the Weimar Republic, purged the civil service of Jews, closed down all parties except the NSDAP, enacted censorship laws, and sent communists to newly constructed concentration camps. Other inmates of these camps were Roma

(Gypsies), homosexuals, and religious minorities. In order to gain the support of Germany's professional army, Hitler replaced his *Sturmabteilung* (SA) militias with the *Schutzstaffel* (SS). A new secret police force (abbreviated *Gestapo*) established a pervasive surveillance system in what was now called the Third Empire, following that of the Holy Roman Empire and Germany after its unification in 1871.

Hitler gained enthusiastic support among the population. Aided by a recovery of the economy, within a year of coming to power he lowered unemployment to 10 percent. Economists advised him to reduce unemployment through deficit spending and build a mixed economy of state-subsidized private industrial cartels. Hitler denounced the "decadence" of modern art and pushed his planners to create monumental buildings in older neoclassical or contemporary Art Deco styles. In his appeal to their patriotic and economic aspirations, Hitler made himself a genuinely popular leader (*Führer*) among the great majority of Germans.

German rearmament became public knowledge after 1935 with the introduction of the draft and the repudiation of the peace settlement cap on troop numbers. France, realizing the danger this rearmament signified for its security, signed a treaty of mutual military assistance with the Soviet Union, which Hitler took as a pretext for the remilitarization of the Rhineland (one of the German provinces temporarily occupied by France after World War I) in 1936.

This first step of German military assertion was followed with unofficial support for General Francisco Franco (1892–1975), who rose against the legitimate republican government in the Spanish Civil War (1936–1939), and the incorporation of Austria into Nazi Germany in 1938. Now alarmed at Germany's appetite for expansion and committed by treaty to defend the Eastern European states created after the war, the heads of state of Britain and France met with Hitler and Mussolini in Munich in the summer of 1938 to hammer out a general agreement on German and Italian territorial claims. The British prime minister, Neville Chamberlain (in office 1937–1940), claimed that this appeasement of Germany, the "Munich Agreement," promised "peace in our time." Hitler went to war, however, in little more than a year.

World War II in Poland and France   In 1939 Hitler decided that the German armed forces were ready to begin the quest for *Lebensraum* in Eastern Europe (see Chapter 27). Because Poland needed to be taken first, Stalin had to be convinced that it was in the best interests of the Soviet Union and Germany to share in the division of Eastern Europe. Stalin, who needed time to rebuild his army after his purges, found the idea of a Russian-dominated Polish buffer against Germany appealing. Accordingly, the two signed a nonaggression pact on August 23, 1939, and German troops invaded Poland on September 1, triggering declarations of war by Poland's allies Britain and France 2 days later. World War II had begun in Europe.

Having removed the two-front problem that had plagued Germany in World War I, Hitler had to eliminate Britain and France before turning to the next phase in the east. This he did by attacking France on May 10, 1940. The German army in Poland had pioneered a new kind of warfare: *Blitzkrieg*, or "lightning war," which turned warfare from the stagnant defensive posture of World War I into a fast, highly mobile conflict. The French, bled dry of manpower in the previous war, had since relied on the fixed defenses of their Maginot Line. Now, the German troops simply went around these fortifications. After breaking through the Ardennes Forest in southern Belgium, to the great surprise of the French and British, the German troops turned

Adolf Hitler, speech in Danzig after the invasion of Poland (September 1939)

northward, driving the Allies toward the Atlantic coast. The encircled French and British troops escaped across the English Channel to Britain as the Germans regrouped for their final thrust.

France surrendered and agreed to an armistice. Hitler divided the country into a German-occupied part, consisting of Paris and the Atlantic coast, and a smaller unoccupied territory under German control, with its capital in Vichy. The German attempt of an invasion of Britain failed when their air force, having suffered more losses than anticipated in the invasion of France, was unable to deliver the final blow. During the period of the worst air raids, the Conservative politician Winston Churchill (in office 1940–1945) replaced Neville Chamberlain as prime minister. Churchill's unbending will during the aerial Battle of Britain proved to be a turning point in rallying the Allied cause.

The Eastern Front   Hitler launched an invasion of the Soviet Union on June 22, 1941, to the surprise of an unprepared Stalin. Although the Soviet forces were initially severely beaten, they did not disintegrate, thanks in part to a force of superior T-34 tanks that were four times more numerous than the Germans expected. Neither side made much progress until the Soviets succeeded in trapping a large force of Germans in Stalingrad. The Soviet victory on February 2, 1943, became the turning point in the European war. Thereafter, it was an almost relentless and increasingly desperate retreat for the Germans, particularly after the western Allies invaded the European continent in Italy and France.

Mass Murder   As Hitler's *Mein Kampf* foretold, the war in the east became an ideological war of annihilation: Either the supremacist or the communist vision of modernity would prevail. The Soviets began in 1940 with the massacre of nearly 22,000 Polish prisoners of war and the subsequent condemnation of hundreds of thousands of Eastern Europeans to death in labor camps. The German SS and army, driven by their racism against Slavs, murdered soldiers and civilians alike, and German businesses worked their Slavic slave laborers to death.

Final Solution: German supremacist-nationalist plan formulated in 1942 by Adolf Hitler and leading Nazis to annihilate Jews through factory-style mass extermination in concentration camps, resulting in the death of about 6 million Jews, or roughly two-thirds of European Jewry.

The so-called **Final Solution,** the genocide of the European Jews, was the horrendous culmination of this struggle. After Poland and the western Soviet Union were conquered, the number of Jews under German authority increased by several million. The Final Solution, set in motion in January 1942, entailed transporting Jews to extermination camps to be murdered. In its technological sophistication in creating a kind of assembly line of death and the calm, bureaucratic efficiency with which its operators went about their business, the Holocaust marks a milestone in twentieth-century inhumanity.

The Turn of the Tide in the West   The first counteroffensives of the Allies in the west after their defeat in 1940 came in November 1942. After fighting a desperate rearguard action, British forces in Egypt and American forces landing in occupied French North Africa launched a combined offensive, driving German forces to capitulate 6 months later. But it took another 2.5 years to grind down the forces of the Axis powers. Here, advantages in manpower as well as the industrial capacity of the United States proved to be the determining factors. Finally, the natural barriers of the Atlantic and Pacific Oceans and American naval power protected America against invasion, while the lack of a long-range strategic bombing force prevented Axis air attacks on North America.

Starting in 1943, the US Army Air Force and Britain's Royal Air Force began around-the-clock bombing of military and civilian targets in Germany. Despite heavy Allied losses in planes and men, by war's end there was scarcely a German city or industrial center that had not been reduced to rubble by air attack. With the landing of troops in Sicily in July 1943, on the Italian Peninsula in early September, and in Normandy in June 1944, along with the steady advance of Soviet forces in the east, the eventual unconditional German surrender on May 8, 1945 (VE, or "Victory in Europe" Day) was inevitable (see Map 28.3).

Japan's "Greater East Asia Co-Prosperity Sphere" and China's Struggle for Unity

The Japanese ruling class that implemented the Meiji industrialization consisted of lower-ranking samurai "oligarchs." After World War I, this generation retired, and for the first time, commoners entered politics. They formed two unstable conservative party coalitions, representing small-business and landowner interests, respectively, but were financed by big-business cartels, the *zaibatsus* (see Chapter 24). By the mid-1920s Japan's interwar liberalizing era had reached a high point. Thereafter, however, the military increased its power and ended the liberalizing era.

Genocide. The specters of the Holocaust that haunt us usually involve the infamous extermination camps—Auschwitz, Treblinka, Majdanek, Sobibor—but millions of Jews and other "undesirables"—Slavs, Gypsies (Roma), and homosexuals—were shot, such as this man calmly waiting for the bullet to penetrate his brain while SS executioners look on.

image analysis

Liberalism and Military Assertion   In the midst of the middle-class ferment of "Taisho Democracy," as Japan's politics during the reign of Emperor Taisho (r. 1912–1926) was known, the government not only broadened suffrage but also enacted the first of many security laws. Worried about communist influence, the Peace Preservation Law of 1925 drew a line against frequent labor strikes and general leftist agitation. Anyone violating the "national essence" (*kokutai*) in thought or action could be arrested. A branch of the secret services, the *Tokko*, made some 70,000 mostly arbitrary arrests between 1925 and 1945. The law was the turning point when Western-inspired liberalism began to swing toward militarism.

Military officers of modest rural origin were unable or unwilling to comprehend the democracy, cultural transformation, and labor strikes of the 1920s. Supremacist nationalism, especially the absolutism of the emperor and the right of junior officers to refuse to execute parliamentary laws, were decisive for actions through which the military achieved dominance over parliament in the 1930s.

Militaristic Expansion   The early 1930s saw the end of a period of diplomacy by which Japan sought to consolidate its gains in international prestige. The growth of the power of the Chinese Nationalist Party (Guomindang, GMD) altered the fragile balance of power among the contending warlord regimes that Japan had exploited in order to expand its influence. The junior officers who chafed at the liberalization of Japan and hearkened back to samurai values increasingly found opportunity in the colonial armies of Manchuria.

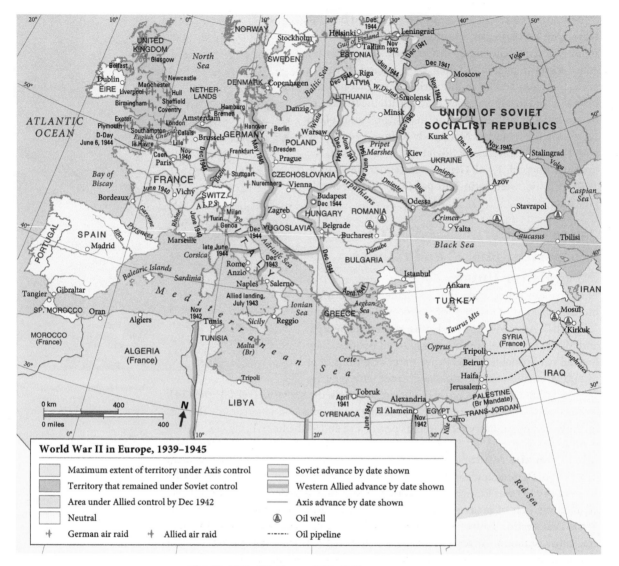

MAP **28.3 World War II in Europe, 1939–1945.**

The first step in this new direction was taken in 1928 when the Japanese Kwantung Army (Japan's force in Manchuria) blew up the train of the Chinese warlord Zhang Zuolin because of his leanings toward the GMD. This was followed by the Mukden Incident of 1931, in which the Japanese military engineered another railroad bombing, which was blamed on local warlords and used as the pretext for the annexation of Manchuria. Politicians in Tokyo, cowed by the aggressiveness of supremacist nationalist ideologues, acquiesced. By way of making it a puppet state, they installed the last Manchu Qing Chinese emperor, (Henry) Pu-Yi (r. 1908–1912; 1932–1945), who had been deposed as a six-year-old boy in the Chinese Republican Revolution of 1911–1912. Over the next several years, the Japanese army in Manchuria moved into northern China. In July 1937, after a clash between Chinese and Japanese forces near the Marco Polo Bridge outside Beijing, Japan launched an invasion of China.

The Republican Revolution in China   The Qing dynasty had failed to develop a sustained effort at reform in response to the Western challenge during the 1800s. Following the Boxer Rebellion in 1900, radical groups, aided by overseas Chinese, began to work for the overthrow of the Qing. The most important figure among these groups was Sun Yat-sen (1866–1925), with his Revolutionary Alliance of 1905.

On October 10, 1911, an explosion in a Wuhan barracks signaled a takeover of the base. The movement quickly spread, and by the end of the year three groups of Qing opponents—provincial warlords, scholar-gentry, and nationalists—staged uprisings that reduced the Qing to a small territory in the north. The Qing commander, Yuan Shikai (1859–1916), struck a deal with the insurgents whereby he came over to them in return for the presidency of the new republic, formed upon the abdication of the Qing in February 1912. Sun was thus elbowed aside by the revolution he had done so much to begin. With Yuan's death in 1916, the remaining warlords feuded with each other for control of the country.

Reemergence of Nationalism   Sun Yat-sen, however, remained an inspirational figure for Chinese nationalists, even though he was exiled in the Western treaty port of Guangzhou (Canton). Meanwhile, the decision announced on May 4, 1919, by the Allies at Versailles to allow Japan to keep the German territory in China it had seized at the beginning of the war set off mass demonstrations and a boycott of foreign businesses. This May Fourth Movement, as it came to be called, is often cited as the modern beginning of Chinese nationalism. Shortly thereafter, inspired by the Bolshevik Revolution in Russia, the Chinese Communist Party (CCP) was founded (1921).

By 1923, Sun's Nationalist Party was being reorganized and supplied with Soviet help through the Third Communist International (Comintern), in return for which the party agreed to allow members of the CCP to join with it to form what became known as the First United Front (1924–1927). Sun died in 1925, and a year later Chiang K'ai-shek (1887–1975) ascended to the leadership of the army. Chiang was a military officer trained in the Nationalist Party academy and in Moscow. The most pressing objective in 1926 was the unification of China. The two parties mobilized an army, and the so-called Northern Expedition of 1926–1927 successfully brought about the unification of southern China as far north as the Yangzi River.

In the middle of the campaign, however, the bonds between the GMD and the CCP ruptured. The socialist wing of the GMD and the CCP had taken the important industrial centers of Wuhan and Shanghai in the Yangtze Delta from warlords, setting the stage for a showdown with the nationalist wing. Chiang had grown suspicious of Comintern and CCP motives and thus launched a preemptive purge of communists in nationalist-held areas.

Though much of the leftist opposition was eliminated, a remnant under Mao Zedong (1893–1976) fled to the remote province of Jiangxi to regroup and create their own socialist state. Mao, an inspiring rural organizer, set about developing his ideas of Marxist revolution with the heretical idea of having peasants in the vanguard. By the early 1930s Mao's Chinese communists had developed this variant of rural communism, which Marx and Lenin had found impossible to envisage. Mao replaced the capitalists with the landlords as the class enemy and promised a much-needed land reform to the peasants. Moreover, the peasants would be the leading participants in the "People's War"—a three-stage guerilla conflict involving the entire populace.

📄

Mao Zedong,
"Fighting for
Perpetual Peace"
(1938)

Believing the communist threat to be effectively eliminated, Chiang resumed his Northern Expedition in 1928, subjugating Beijing but failing to eliminate the strongest northern warlords. Nevertheless, China was now at least nominally unified, with the capital in Nanjing, the National Party Congress functioning as a parliament, and Chiang as president. Chiang made substantial progress with railroad and road construction as well as cotton and silk textile exports. Thanks to the silver standard of its money, rather than the fatal gold standard of many other countries, the financial consequences of the Depression of 1929–1933 remained relatively mild. Chiang made little headway, however, with land reform. Furthermore, the volatile relations with the remaining warlords made the government vulnerable to border violence and corruption. Hovering above all after 1931 was the Japanese annexation of Manchuria and encroachment on northern China.

The Long March and the Rape of Nanjing   In the early 1930s, Chiang was aware of the need to completely eliminate his internal opponents. He resolved to eliminate the remaining threat from Mao's "Jiangxi Soviet" by mounting "bandit extermination" campaigns from 1931 to 1934. Each campaign, however, was defeated by Mao's growing People's Liberation Army. With the help of German advisors, Chiang turned to encircling the CCP areas to limit the mobility of his opponents. By the fall of 1934 he had tightened the noose around the communists and almost succeeded in destroying their army.

But Mao and about 100,000 soldiers broke out in October 1934, thanks to the inaction of a treacherous warlord allied with Chiang K'ai-shek. Once free, the majority of the Red Army embarked on a Long March of 6,000 miles, from the south through the far west and then northeast toward Beijing. Along the way harassment by nationalist troops, warlords, and local people as well as other hardships decimated the marchers. In the fall of 1935 some 10,000 communists eventually straggled into Yan'an (Yenan), out of Chiang's reach.

The communists had seized upon Japan's aggression as a valuable propaganda tool and declared war against Japan in 1932. Chiang's obsession with eliminating his internal enemies increasingly made him subject to criticism of appeasement toward Japan. In 1936, a group of dissident nationalist generals arrested Chiang and brought him to CCP headquarters at Yan'an. After weeks of negotiations, Chiang was released as the leader of a China now brought together under a Second United Front, this time against Japan.

Seeing their prospects for gradual encroachment quickly fading, Japan seized on the so-called Marco Polo Bridge Incident in July 1937 and launched an all-out assault on China. Though Chinese resistance was stiff in the opening months, the Japanese were able to use their superior mobility and airpower to flank the Chinese forces and take the capital of Nanjing (Nanking) by December 1937.

Realizing the need to defeat China as quickly as possible, the Japanese military subjected the capital to the first major atrocity of World War II: the "Rape of Nanjing." It is estimated that between 200,000 and 300,000 people were slaughtered in deliberately gruesome ways. Rape was systematically used as a means of terror and subjugation.

The direct message of this brutality was that other Chinese cities could expect similar treatment if surrender was not swiftly forthcoming. However, the destruction only stiffened the will to resist of the Chinese. Continually harassed as they retreated from Nanjing, the Chinese adopted the strategy of trading space for time to regroup. In an epic mass migration, Chinese soldiers and civilians moved to the region around the remote city of Chongqing (Chungking), which became the wartime capital of China until 1945. Thereafter, both nationalists and communists used the vast interior as a base for hit-and-run tactics, effectively limiting Japan to the northeast and coastal urban centers but remaining incapable of mounting large offensives themselves.

World War II in the Pacific   While Japan had used its control of Manchuria, Korea, and Taiwan in its quest for autarky and economic stability in the 1930s, it portrayed its imperial bid in the Pacific as the construction of a "Greater East Asia Co-Prosperity Sphere." This expansion was considered essential because raw materials were still imported from the United States and the Dutch and British possessions in Southeast Asia. After Hitler defeated the Netherlands and France in 1940, the opportunity arrived for the Japanese to remove the United States from the Pacific. Moreover, the stalemate in China was increasingly bleeding Japan of resources, while mounting tensions with the United States over China were already resulting in economic sanctions.

Accordingly, in the summer of 1941, the Japanese government decided on extending the empire into the Dutch East Indies and Southeast Asia, even if this meant war with the United States. Under the premiership of General Tojo Hideki (in office 1941–1944), Japan attacked Pearl Harbor in Hawaii, the Philippines, and Dutch and British territories on December 7–8, 1941. Within a few months, the Japanese completed the occupation of all the important Southeast Asian and Pacific territories they had sought (see Map 28.4).

However, within 6 months, in the naval and air battle around Midway Atoll in June 1942, American forces gained the initiative. The Japanese now exploited the populations of their new territories in extracting their raw materials with increasing urgency. Using an "island hopping" strategy of bypassing Japanese strongholds, American forces came within bombing range of the Japanese home islands by late 1944. Starting in March 1945, they subjected Japan to devastating firebomb attacks. Finally, President Harry S Truman (in office 1945–1953) had two experimental atomic bombs dropped on Hiroshima and Nagasaki (August 6 and 9, 1945). With the Soviets declaring war against Japan on August 8 and advancing into Manchuria, the Japanese were finally convinced that the war was lost. They surrendered on August 14, 1945.

≫ Putting It All Together

The patterns of constitutionalism and industrialization in the late eighteenth and early nineteenth centuries were most visible in Great Britain, the United States, and France. Subsequently, two further patterns complicated the evolution of nations engaging in the pursuit of modernity: ethnic nationalism and the rise of the industrial working class. All of these patterns collided in World War I. After the war, they recombined into the three ideologies of modernity analyzed in this chapter: capitalist democracy, communism, and supremacist nationalism.

interactive
concept map

MAP 28.4 **World War II in the Pacific, 1937–1945.**

For the most part, only democracy and communism are considered to be genuine ideologies of modernity, in the sense of being based on relatively coherent programs. More recent historians, however, argue that supremacist nationalism was a genuine variety of modernity as well. The adherents of the three modernities bitterly denounced each other. All three considered themselves to be genuinely "progressive" or modern.

It may be difficult to understand how anyone could be an ardent ethnic nationalist, have little faith in constitutional liberties, find the conquest of a large and completely self-sufficient empire perfectly logical, and think of all this as the ideal of a future modernity. Yet, as we have seen so often, innovations frequently cause their opposition to take new and often unexpected forms. The "modern" notion of ethnic nationalism thus created ways of opposing other modern innovations such as constitutionalism and industrialism by insisting on a purer, more mystical bond for the modern nation-state that, ironically, harkened back to a simpler, reimagined past. But Mussolini, Hitler, and the Japanese generals all aspired to the same scientific–industrial future as Roosevelt, Churchill, Stalin, Chiang K'ai-shek, and Mao Zedong.

Review and Relate

| Thinking Through Patterns

Examine the ways historians approach the big questions of this chapter.

Ethnic nationalism was difficult to accommodate in the nineteenth century, which began with the more inclusive constitutionalism of Great Britain, the United States, and France. New nations like Italy, Germany, and Japan, formed on the basis of ethnic nationalisms, were not necessarily inspired by the ideals of equality embodied in constitutional nation-states. After World War I, Germany, Italy, and Japan elevated their ethnic nationalism into supremacist nationalism and adopted imperialism, all under the banner of modernity. In Russia, communists used the turmoil of World War I to turn a constitutionally as well as industrially underdeveloped empire into a communist, one-party industrial empire. The United States, Britain, and France, each based on variations of constitutionalism, industry, and smaller or larger empires, became advocates of a capitalist democratic modernity.

> » **Which three patterns of modernity emerged after World War I? How and why did these patterns form?**

Capitalist democracy was a modernity that upheld free enterprise, the market, and consumerism. It suffered a major setback in the Depression and had to be reined in through tightened political controls. It also withheld freedom and equality from minorities and the colonized. Communism succeeded in industrializing an underdeveloped empire and providing the bare necessities for modern life; it did so with untold human sacrifices. Supremacist nationalism was attractive to nationalists who were not workers and therefore afraid of communism. Supremacist nationalists held democracies in disdain because they considered constitutions meaningless.

> » **What were the strengths and flaws of each of the three visions of modernity?**

Supremacist nationalism was a modernity that failed because the conquest of new, self-sufficient empires proved to be impossible. The advocates of democratic capitalist and communist modernity—most notably the United States, Great Britain, France, and the Soviet Union—were dangerously threatened by Germany, Italy, and Japan and came together to destroy these supremacist-nationalist countries.

> » **Why did supremacist nationalism disappear after World War II?**

| Against the Grain

Consider this as a counterpoint to the main patterns examined in this chapter.

Righteous among the Nations

Thousands of men and women defied the Nazi regime (1932–1945) and saved Jews from arrest, deportation, and the gas chamber. Their acts of defiance are proof that ordinary citizens in Germany and the countries conquered by Germany during

- Faced with a situation similar to that of Irena Sendler, what would you do?

- Can you think of other twentieth-century mass atrocities in which people like Irena Sendler desperately tired to save innocent lives?

World War II did not all cower before the Gestapo, nor did they all attempt to claim helplessness or ignorance regarding what was happening around them. Although many of the saviors were martyred at the hands of Nazi authorities, they acted as they did because they considered it their human calling.

Thousands of the saviors of Jews were Poles, Dutch, French, Ukrainians, and Belgians, all under German occupation during the war. By contrast, only 563 and 525 Italians and Germans, respectively, have been recognized as helping Jews to survive. The contrast in numbers illustrates the feelings of hatred among many in the conquered territories for the Germans on one hand and the pervasiveness of the supremacist-nationalist fascist and Nazi ideologies in the populations of Italy and Germany on the other. Even if it had not been as difficult to help Jews in Nazi Germany as many Germans pretended after the war, their anti-Semitism prevented them from feeling any pangs of conscience.

Today, Israel recognizes 24,811 saviors of Jews as "Righteous among the Nations" and honors them in the Yad Vashem Holocaust memorial museum in Jerusalem. One of them, Irena Sendler (1910–2008), was a health worker, the daughter of a Polish physician who treated Jewish patients. When the Germans invaded she was an administrator for the Warsaw Social Welfare Department. During the time of the Warsaw Ghetto (1940–1943), she smuggled some 2,500 Jewish children out of the country, hiding them under loads of goods, in potato sacks or even in coffins. She provided them with false identities and had them taken to hiding places with Christian families. When the Nazis finally discovered her activities in 1943, they arrested and tortured her. But after members of the Polish resistance succeeded in bribing her would-be executioners, Sandler escaped and went into hiding until the end of the war. Yad Vashem honored Irena Sendler in 1965 as a righteous person and planted a tree in her name at the entrance of the Avenue of the Righteous among Nations.

Key Terms

Autarky 660
Corporate state 666
Eugenics 656
Final Solution 670

Great Depression 657
Mandates 661
League of Nations 654
Swaraj 663

Total war 652
Zionism 662

◁))
audio flashcards

For additional resources, please go to
www.oup.com/us/vonsivers.
Please see the Further Resources section at the back of the book for additional readings and suggested websites.

Reconstruction, Cold War, and Decolonization

The 1960 election of the world's first female prime minister, Sirimavo Bandaranaike (1916–2000), of what was then called Ceylon (renamed Sri Lanka in 1972), seemed symbolic of a new pattern, one in which the emerging nonaligned nations would set the pace of innovation.

Bandaranaike believed in her country as an independent nation beholden to neither West nor East. As a socialist, she continued the nationalization of the banking, insurance, and petroleum sectors; ordered the state to take over all Catholic schools; and joined the Non-Aligned Movement in 1961. The movement sought to bring India, Egypt, Yugoslavia, Indonesia, and other states together as a bloc to retain their independence from the Cold War superpowers—the United States and the Soviet Union—and their allies. Her commitment to a Sinhalese-only language policy, however, aroused resistance from the Tamil minority in the north. Only 2 years into Bandaranaike's tenure, the country was gripped by a Tamil civil disobedience campaign, and Ceylon entered a time of political turbulence. Ultimately, anti-Tamil discrimination led to the brutal Tamil Tiger liberation war (1976–2009). Bandaranaike's legacy, therefore, is

THE COLD WAR AND DECOLONIZATION

ABOVE: Voters line up to cast their ballots in Ceylon (now Sri Lanka) on March 22, 1960. Sirimavo Bandaranaike was elected the world's first woman prime minister.

≫ Why did the pattern of unfolding modernity, which offered three choices after World War I, shrink to just capitalist democracy and socialism–communism in 1945? How did each of these two patterns evolve between 1945 and 1962?

≫ What are the cultural premises of modernity?

≫ How did the newly independent countries of the Middle East, Asia, and Africa adapt to the divided world of the Cold War?

United Nations: Successor of the League of Nations, founded in 1945 and today comprising about 200 countries, with a Secretary General, a General Assembly meeting annually, and a standing Security Council composed of permanent members (United States, China, Russia, the United Kingdom, and France) as well as five rotating temporary members.

Cold War: Ideological struggle between the United States and its allies, and the Soviet Union and its allies that lasted from 1945 to 1989.

mixed: On one hand she was a paradigmatic first-generation non-Western nationalist leader; but on the other, her failure to balance constitutional and ethnic principles led inevitably to civil war.

Like her fellow female prime ministers Benazir Bhutto in Pakistan and Indira Gandhi in India and first-generation nonaligned leaders like Jawaharlal Nehru of India, Sukarno of Indonesia, and Gamal Abdel Nasser of Egypt, Bandaranaike contended with ethnic and religious conflict, superpower pressure, and nation building in an increasingly competitive economic arena. The actions of these nonaligned nations were influenced by two main elements in the unfolding pattern of scientific–industrial modernity: the Cold War and decolonization.

Superpower Confrontation: Capitalist Democracy and Communism

World War II was the most destructive war in human history. The total loss of life is estimated at over 50 million, more than twice as many as in World War I. Most ominous was the use of the first atomic weapons. Yet in the aftermath, the foundations of a new world organization to replace the old League of Nations—the **United Nations (UN)**—were being laid. Within a few years, the world's remaining patterns of modernity—capitalism–democracy and socialism–communism—would reemerge from the ruins stronger than ever.

The Cold War Era, 1945–1962

As the world rebuilt, the United States and the Soviet Union promoted their contrasting visions of modernity—capitalist–democratic and communist. While each on occasion engaged in brinkmanship, both sought to avoid direct confrontation. Instead, they pursued their aims of expansion and consolidation in a conflict dubbed the "Cold War" through ideological struggle and proxy states. During the first phase of the early Cold War (1945–1956), the Soviet Union continued to pursue Stalin's prewar policy of "socialism in one country," which now included Eastern Europe. During the second phase (1956–1962), Stalin's successor, Nikita Khrushchev (1894–1971, in office 1953–1964), reformulated the policy to include spreading aid and influence to new nationalist regimes in Asia and Africa that had won their independence from Western colonialism (see Map 29.1).

Cold War Origins While it may not be possible to establish an exact event marking the beginning of the **Cold War**, we can point to certain mileposts in its development. Tensions between the United States and the Soviet Union began to emerge as early as the Bolshevik Revolution (1917), when concerns mounted in the West regarding communist expansion. Uneasiness about Joseph Stalin's policies in the 1930s delayed American recognition of the Soviet government until 1933.

Another milepost came in the spring of 1945, when the Soviet Red Army occupied German-held territories in Eastern Europe and communist guerillas advanced in the Balkans. In a secret deal between British prime minister Churchill and Soviet leader Stalin in May 1944, Greece became part of the British sphere, in return for

Destruction and Despair in the Nuclear Age. World War II was the most destructive human conflict in history, far exceeding the damage of what had only a short time before been considered to be "the war to end all wars"—World War I. Nowhere was the damage more complete than in Japan, where an aerial campaign of firebombing Japanese cities by American B-29s had destroyed nearly every major Japanese center. The Japanese cities of Hiroshima and Nagasaki were bombed in August 1945 in the first—and, to date, last—use of nuclear weapons in warfare. Here, a mother and child who survived the nuclear destruction of Hiroshima sit amid the utter devastation of their city in December 1945.

Chapter Outline

- **Superpower Confrontation: Capitalist Democracy and Communism**

- **Populism and Industrialization in Latin America**

- **The End of Colonialism and the Rise of New Nations**

- **Putting It All Together**

Romania and Bulgaria being apportioned to the Soviets for occupation at war's end. As early as March 1946, however, citing growing tensions between the former allies, Churchill warned in a speech at Westminster College in Fulton, Missouri, of an "iron curtain" descending across Europe "from Stettin in the Baltic to Trieste in the Adriatic."

When it became increasingly clear that Stalin was determined to maintain a communist presence in Eastern Europe, the United States formulated a policy known as **containment** to thwart Soviet expansion. The proposed policy served as the foundation for the administration's effort to confront communist expansion.

Confrontations, 1947–1949 The apportionment of spheres of interest in the Balkans did not work out well. In Yugoslavia, Josip Broz Tito (1892–1980) took over the government in November 1945 with the help of Soviet advisors. He then provided Greek communists with aid to overthrow the royal government that had returned to rule with British support in 1946. The United States stepped in with supplies for the Greek government in 1947. Under the **Truman Doctrine**, the United States announced its support of all "free peoples who are resisting attempted subjugation by armed minorities or by outside pressures."

A 2-year proxy civil war in Greece ended in a split between Tito and Stalin. In 1948, Tito claimed his right to regional communism, against Stalin's insistence on unity in the Communist Bloc. Although Stalin had never supported the Greek communists directly, a surprising majority of them opted for Stalin. Tito withdrew his support for the pro-Stalin Greek communists, and the bid for communism in Greece collapsed in 1949.

In keeping with his doctrine, Truman announced the **Marshall Plan** of aid to Europe, for the recovery of the continent from the ruins of the war. Stalin rejected American aid and forbade Hungary, Czechoslovakia, and Poland to ask for it. In addition to the political reasons behind Stalin's injunction, the Marshall Plan's requirement

Containment: US foreign policy doctrine formulated in 1946 to limit, as much as possible, the spread of communism.

Truman Doctrine: Policy formulated in 1947, initially to outline steps directed at preventing Greece and Turkey from becoming communist, primarily through military and economic aid.

Marshall Plan: Financial program of $13 billion to support the reconstruction of the economies of 17 European countries during 1948–1952, with most of the aid going to France, Germany, Italy, and the Netherlands.

The Cold War, 1947–1991

Countries in North Atlantic Treaty Organization (NATO) (1949–)

Countries ruled by communist regimes for all or part of Cold War

Nonaligned countries, 1961

Country with nuclear capability by 1987

Direct military action by USSR and/or allies

Direct military action by US and/or allies

Economic and political intervention by USSR and/or allies

Economic and political intervention by US and/or allies

Iron Curtain

MAP 29.1 **The Cold War, 1947–1991.**

of free markets and convertible currencies contradicted the communist ideology of a central command economy. Stalin instead engineered communist governments in Eastern Europe and the Balkans, transforming them into the Communist Bloc and integrating their economies with that of the Soviet Union. This was formalized in 1949 as the Council for Mutual Economic Assistance (COMECON).

The success of the American Marshall Plan further irritated Stalin because it made the Western sectors of Germany and Berlin magnets for Eastern Europeans fleeing to the West. In 1948, therefore, the Soviets took the provocative step of setting up a highway and rail blockade of food and supplies to Berlin. The United States and Britain responded with the "Berlin Airlift," a demonstration of technological prowess as well as humanitarian compassion. For nearly a year, food, fuel, and other supplies required by this large city were flown in until Stalin finally gave up the blockade.

So far, the Cold War in Europe had been confined to diplomatic maneuvering between Washington and Moscow. However, the confrontation soon assumed military dimensions, as the Soviets accelerated their efforts to build a nuclear bomb. In 1949, they detonated their first device 4 years earlier than anticipated. Now, with its advantage in nuclear weapons eliminated and concern increasing over the possibility of a communist takeover in Western Europe, the United States formed a defensive alliance known as the North Atlantic Treaty Organization (NATO) in 1949. In response, the Soviet Union later formed the Warsaw Pact in 1955 among the states of the Eastern Bloc.

George F. Kennan, "The Sources of Soviet Conduct" (1947), and Nikolai Novikov, "On Postwar American Policy" (1946)

The Central Intelligence Agency   In addition to military and diplomatic initiatives to contain the spread of communism, the United States used alternative means to overthrow left-leaning and socialist movements and governments around the globe. For these purposes the government relied primarily on the Central Intelligence Agency (CIA), an offshoot of the Office of Strategic Services (OSS) developed during World War II. To carry out its mission the CIA employed a variety of covert operations including spy missions, electronic eavesdropping, photographs obtained by high-flying aircraft, and even outright assassination plots. CIA involvement in regime changes spanned the globe.

Hot War in Korea   In June 1950, the Cold War turned hot as North Korean communist troops invaded South Korea in an attempt at forcible unification. South Korean troops fought a desperate rearguard action at the southern end of the peninsula. Under US pressure and despite a Soviet boycott, the UN Security Council

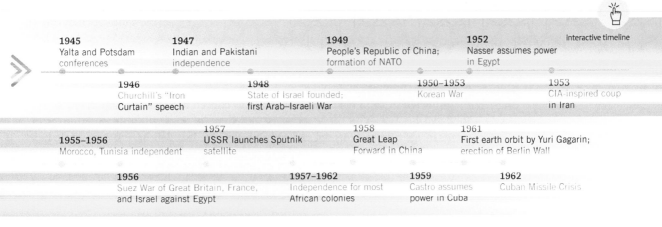

interactive timeline

| 1945 | 1947 | 1949 | 1952 |
| Yalta and Potsdam conferences | Indian and Pakistani independence | People's Republic of China; formation of NATO | Nasser assumes power in Egypt |

| 1946 | 1948 | 1950–1953 | 1953 |
| Churchill's "Iron Curtain" speech | State of Israel founded; first Arab–Israeli War | Korean War | CIA-inspired coup in Iran |

| 1955–1956 | 1957 | 1958 | 1961 |
| Morocco, Tunisia independent | USSR launches Sputnik satellite | Great Leap Forward in China | First earth orbit by Yuri Gagarin; erection of Berlin Wall |

| 1956 | 1957–1962 | 1959 | 1962 |
| Suez War of Great Britain, France, and Israel against Egypt | Independence for most African colonies | Castro assumes power in Cuba | Cuban Missile Crisis |

branded North Korea as the aggressor, entitling South Korea to UN intervention. By October US troops, augmented by troops from a number of UN members, had fought their way into North Korea, occupied the capital (Pyongyang), and advanced to the Chinese border.

In the meantime, the United States had sent a fleet to the remnant of the Chinese nationalists who had formed the Republic of China on the southern island of Taiwan, to protect it from a threatened invasion by a newly communist China. Thwarted in the south at Taiwan, Mao Zedong seemingly took the pronouncements of General Douglas MacArthur, the commander of the UN forces in Korea, about raiding Chinese supply bases on the North Korean border seriously. Stalin, on the other hand, opposed escalation and gave Mao only token support.

In October 1950, however, communist Chinese troops launched a massive surprise offensive into the peninsula, pushing the UN forces back deep into South Korea. Unwilling to expand the war further or use nuclear weapons, the new Eisenhower administration and the North Koreans agreed to an armistice in 1953. The armistice has endured since that date. No official peace treaty was ever signed, and the border between the two Koreas remains a volatile flashpoint.

McCarthyism in the United States   The war in Korea had a troubling domestic impact in the increasingly anti-communist United States. Joseph McCarthy (1908–1957), a Republican senator from Wisconsin, sensationally announced in 1950 that he had a list of members of the Communist Party employed by the State Department. Though he never produced the list, his smear tactics, together with the House Un-American Activities Committee, ruined the careers of hundreds of government employees, celebrities, and private persons. After 4 years of anti-communist hysteria, enough voices of reason arose in the Senate to censure McCarthy. The legacy of bitterness engendered by the "McCarthy era" generated abundant political accusations on both sides.

Joseph McCarthy, speech in Wheeling, West Virginia (1950)

Revolt in East Germany   The death of Stalin in April 1953 was profoundly unsettling for the governments of the Eastern Bloc, especially in the German Democratic Republic (East Germany). The East German government, nervous about defections to the Federal Republic (West Germany), had sealed off the border with fences and watchtowers. But Berlin—divided into East and West sectors—was still a gaping hole. The population was seething over rising production quotas, shortages resulting from the shipment of industrial goods to the Soviet Union (in the name of reparations), and the beginnings of a West German economic boom in which it could not share.

In June 1953, a strike among East Berlin workers quickly grew into a general uprising. East German police and Soviet troops, stunned at first, quickly moved to suppress the revolt. The Politburo (the Communist Party's Central Committee Political Bureau) in Moscow refused any concessions, and the German Stalinist government obediently complied.

In the fall of 1953 Nikita Khrushchev was chosen to succeed Stalin. As he consolidated his power as party secretary and premier, he made substantial investments in agriculture, housing, and consumer goods. In a February 1956 speech, he denounced Stalin's "excesses" during collectivization and the purges of the 1930s. In the Communist Bloc Khrushchev replaced Stalinists with new faces willing to improve general living conditions. To balance the new flexibility within the Soviet Bloc, Khrushchev maintained toughness toward the West. He alarmed leaders of the West when he announced a new policy that supported anticolonial nationalist independence movements around the globe even if the movements were not communist.

Khruschev on Stalin's crimes (1956)

Revolt in Poland and Hungary Khrushchev's reforms awakened hopes for change in Eastern Europe. In Poland, where collectivization and the command economy had progressed slowly and the Catholic Church could not be intimidated, Khrushchev's speech resulted in worker unrest. Nationalist reformists gained the upper hand over Stalinists in the Polish Politburo, and Khrushchev realized that he had to avoid another Tito-style secession at all costs. After a few tense days in mid-October, Poland received limited autonomy.

In Hungary, the Politburo was similarly divided between reformers and Stalinists. People in Budapest and other cities, inspired by events in Poland, took to the streets. The Politburo lost control, and the man appointed to lead the country to a national communist solution similar to that of Poland, Imre Nagy [noj] (1896–1958), announced a multiparty system and the withdrawal of Hungary from the Warsaw Pact. This was too much for Khrushchev, who unleashed the Soviet troops stationed in Hungary to repress what had become a grassroots revolution. Aware that the British, French, and Americans were preoccupied with the Suez Crisis (see below), the Soviets crushed the uprising in November 1956. Nagy was arrested, and in 1958 he was executed by the new pro-Moscow government.

Unrest in the Soviet Bloc. In the Hungarian uprising from October to November 1956, some 2,500 Hungarians and 700 Soviet troops were killed, while 200,000 fled to neighboring Austria and elsewhere in the West. Here, a young boy and older man watch while a Soviet tank rumbles through an intersection with barricades set up by Hungarian "freedom fighters."

The Atomic Age

ICBMs and Sputniks   Advances in weapons technologies, including missiles and space flight, put a powerful military punch behind Soviet repression. In 1957 the Soviet Union developed the world's first intercontinental ballistic missile (ICBM), with a range capable of reaching America's East Coast. In the same year, the Soviet Union launched the world's first orbiting satellite, named Sputnik, into space. Then, in 1961, Russian scientists sent the world's first cosmonaut, Yuri Gagarin (1934–1968), into space.

As the implications of nuclear weapons descending from space with no practicable defense against them began to set in, Americans became frightened. Politicians goaded Congress into accelerating the US missile and space program even at the risk of reheating the Cold War with the Soviet Union. Thus, in 1958 the United States successfully launched its first satellite, Explorer 1, and the following year its first ICBM, the Atlas. The space and missile races were now fully under way.

Communism in Cuba   In 1959, Fidel Castro (1926–2016), a nationalist guerilla fighter opposed to the influence of American companies over a government generally perceived as corrupt, seized power in Cuba. About 6 months after the coup, Cuba was the new symbol of the Khrushchev government's openness toward national liberation movements. The Soviet Union lavished huge sums on the development of the island's economy. Khrushchev's instincts were proven right when Castro openly embraced communism in 1960.

To counter Khrushchev's overtures to national liberation movements, President Eisenhower and the head of the CIA (the successor intelligence office to the wartime OSS), Allen Dulles (1893–1969), secretly supported and trained anticommunist dissidents in the Middle East, Africa, and Latin America. In the case

Aiming for the Stars. As this commemorative postcard reveals, the connection between the technological achievement of Sputnik and Russian popular interest in space travel was strong. The legend reads in Russian: "4 October, the USSR launched Earth's first artificial satellite; 3 November, the USSR launched Earth's second artificial satellite."

of Latin America, a group of Cuban anti-communists trained in Guatemala for an invasion and overthrow of Castro in Cuba. President John F. Kennedy (in office 1961–1963) inherited the initiative and sanctioned an invasion of Cuba by seemingly independent freedom fighters with no direct US military support. The so-called Bay of Pigs invasion in April 1961 (named for the small bay in southern Cuba where the anti-communist invasion began) was easily defeated by Castro's forces, to the great embarrassment of Kennedy.

The Berlin Wall   East Germany, which retained its Stalinist leadership, pressured Khrushchev in 1961 to close the last opening in Berlin through which its citizens could escape to West Germany. Between 1953 and 1961, nearly one-fifth of the East German population had defected. The East German Stalinists, allied with a few remaining Stalinists in the Politburo, prevailed over Khrushchev's opposition and built the Berlin Wall in 1961, effectively turning the German Democratic Republic into a prison.

Postwar Eastern Europe   The Eastern (or Soviet) Bloc included Albania, Bulgaria, Czechoslovakia, East Germany, Hungary, Poland, Romania, and Yugoslavia. Adherence to official Soviet policies was rigidly controlled by state centralization administered ultimately by the Communist Party in Moscow, enforced at the local level by Party committees. Coercion was enforced through a network of secret police, the KGB, and concentration camps in the Russian gulag system. Although throughout the Stalinist era (1945–1953) and post-Stalinist period (1953–1968) industrialization was increased, shortages and even rationing of consumer goods were common. Employment opportunities were not on a par with those created by the Western economic postwar recovery, and although some women joined the workforce, their principal responsibilities still lay within the home. State-sponsored educational programs stressed Soviet propaganda and the sciences. The media were monitored, cultural and religious expression was censored, and Western culture was condemned. Even so, some aspects of Western culture found their way around the censors.

The first direct confrontation between the Soviet Union and the United States occurred in October 1962, when US spy planes discovered the presence of missile launching pads as well as missiles in Cuba. President Kennedy demanded their immediate destruction and then followed up with a naval blockade of the island to prevent the arrival of Russian missiles. In defiance, Khrushchev dispatched Russian ships to Cuba; when it was discovered that they were bearing more missiles, President Kennedy demanded that Khrushchev recall the ships. The world held its breath as the ships headed for Cuba, with the possibility of a nuclear exchange between the world's superpowers (see Map 29.2).

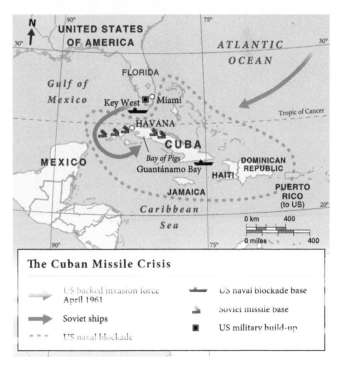

The Cuban Missile Crisis

US backed invasion force April 1961

Soviet ships

US naval blockade

US naval blockade base

Soviet missile base

US military build-up

MAP 29.2 **The Cuban Missile Crisis.**

In the end, Khrushchev recalled the ships at the last minute, while Kennedy agreed to remove American missiles from Turkey. Kennedy and Khrushchev signed the Nuclear Test Ban Treaty in 1963, an agreement banning the aboveground testing of nuclear weapons. The treaty also sought to prevent the spread of these technologies to other countries.

Modernism: Any of various movements in philosophy and the arts characterized by a deliberate break with classical or traditional forms of thought or expression.

Existentialism: A form of thought built on the premise that modern scientific–industrial society is without intrinsic meaning unless an answer to the question of what constitutes authentic existence is found.

Society and Culture in Postwar North America, Europe, and Japan

In the years after World War II, veterans pursued civilian lives of normalcy and comfort. Intellectuals and artists cast a critical eye on modern culture, as the previous generation had after World War I. Among the emerging nations, artists and intellectuals forged new paths, often combining indigenous culture and socialist and democratic ideas.

Mass Consumption Culture   American soldiers returned to civilian life and started families, launching the so-called baby-boomer generation (1945–1961). The growing population triggered increased consumer demand for basics as well as consumer durables that increased the comfort of living, such as appliances, televisions, and cars. In the United States, the GI Bill supported university studies for veterans that led to better-paying jobs. Americans increasingly took on debt to move into their middle-class lives, while Europeans tended to save first before purchasing consumer goods.

In the idealized family of the 1950s and early 1960s, gender roles and spatial segregation—in which men tended to commute to work while women ran the households—were highly structured, corresponding to the yearning of the middle classes for order after the years of economic depression and war. In Europe and Japan, similar changes in consumer culture took place.

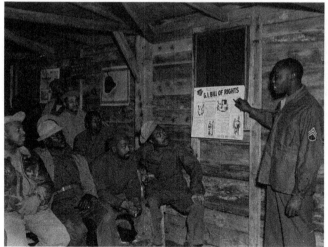

The GI Bill for African Americans. Staff Sergeant Herbert Ellison explains the GI Bill to members of his company. The bill, enacted in 1944, provided soldiers returning from the war with support for training and education as well as subsidized home loans. Some 7.8 million veterans benefited from the training and education it provided.

Artistic Culture   Enlightenment ideas of materialism and the social contract continued to dominate the Anglo-American cultural sphere and also became dominant in the European arts. They were reflected in new forms of **modernism** in thought, writing, theater, painting, music, and film, such as neorealism, **existentialism**, abstract expressionism (see the images on p. 689), and serialism. After two world wars, intellectuals and artists remained strongly committed to modernism, yet were much more sensitive to its contradictions.

Thinkers and artists reflecting on modernity versus tradition provided for rich artistic post–World War II cultures in Western countries. As culture-specific as many artists were, by not merely dwelling on the inevitability of modernity but rather confronting it with their inherited premodern traditions, they created works that could be understood across cultures.

Abstract Expressionism. (*a*) Hans Hofmann (1880–1966), *Delight*, 1947. (*b*) Willem de Kooning (1904–1997), *Montauk Highway*, 1958. Abstract expressionism was a New York–centered artistic movement that combined the strong colors of World War I German expressionism with the abstract art pioneered by the Russian-born Wassily Kandinsky and the artists of the Bauhaus school. Before and during the Nazi period, many European artists had flocked to New York, including Hofmann and de Kooning. The movement caught the public eye when Jackson Pollock, following the surrealists, made the creation of a work of art— the process of painting a large canvas on the floor through the dripping of paint—an art in itself.

Populism and Industrialization in Latin America

Western political and cultural modernity was also a part of the Latin American experience. But the region's Amerindians and blacks participated only marginally, as many were mired in rural subsistence. Since these populations increased rapidly after World War II, Latin America began to resemble Asia and Africa, which also had massive rural populations, small middle classes, and limited industrial sectors. Populist leaders relying on the urban poor thus sought to steer their countries toward industrialization.

Slow Social Change

Latin America had stayed out of World War II. The postwar aftermath therefore neither disrupted established patterns nor offered new opportunities to its patterns of social and economic development. The region had suffered from the disappearance of commodity export markets during the Depression of the 1930s, and politicians realized that import-substitution industrialization, replacing imported manufactures with domestically produced ones, had to be adopted with greater energy. However, landowners opposed industrialization and the great majority of rural and urban Latin Americans were too poor to become consumers.

Rural and Urban Society   Prior to 1945, the rural population still composed about two-thirds of the total population. But during 1945–1962, the pace

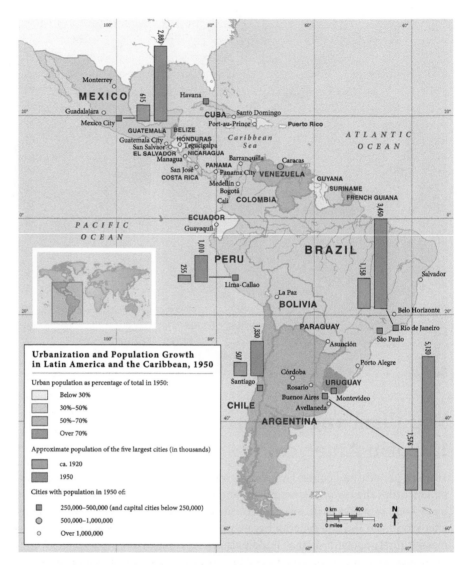

MAP **29.3** **Urbanization and Population Growth in Latin America and the Caribbean, ca. 1950.**

Gabriel Capote
Pacheco, a popular
perspective on life in
revolutionary Cuba
(1969)

of urbanization picked up, with the proportions nearly reversing (see Map 29.3). While overall population growth during this period accelerated, poverty rates remained the same or even increased, making Latin America the world region with the greatest income disparities. Cuba's land reform (1959) and the threat of local peasant revolutions made the issue of land reform urgent, and agrarian reforms picked up in the 1960s.

Much of the landless population migrated to the cities, settling in sprawling shantytowns with no urban services. While some migrants found employment in the expanding industrial sector, more worked in the so-called informal sector, a new phenomenon of peddling, repairing, and recycling. In contrast to the villages, rural–urban migrants had some access to the health and education benefits that populist politicians introduced. The industrial labor force grew to about one-quarter of the total labor force, a rate that reflected the hesitant attitude of politicians toward industrialization in view of rebounding commodity exports in the 1960s.

At the end of World War II, industrialism was still confined mainly to food processing and textile manufacturing. In the later 1940s and early 1950s, the larger Latin American countries moved to capital goods and consumer durables. As a result, expanded production of manufactures reduced dependence on foreign imports. Unfortunately, limited private capital was available on the domestic market for risky industrialization ventures, requiring the state to allocate the necessary funds. Smaller countries that overextended themselves with industrial import substitution had to return in the early 1950s to prioritizing commodity exports.

Populist-Guided Democracy

During the period 1945–1962, democracy and communism were the main political and ideological choices. The attraction of democracy in its constitutional North American and European forms in Latin America, however, was limited, since the United States, in the grip of the Cold War, was primarily interested in the professed loyalty of autocratic rulers in its Latin American backyard. Communism was initially also of limited appeal, and flourished only once Khrushchev supported national liberation movements, as in Cuba. **Populism** was an intermediate form of governance that found strong support in Latin America from 1945–1962.

The Populist Wave   Democracy in Latin America was represented by Venezuela (1958), Colombia (1953–1964), and Costa Rica (1953). Democratic politicians, however, were unable to put Venezuela's oil to productive use or bring about land reform in Colombia, resulting in the formation of a communist guerilla underground in the latter country in 1964. Eight Latin American countries had populist regimes from the mid-1940s onward: Guatemala (1944–1954), Argentina (1946–1955), Brazil (1946–1954), Venezuela (1945–1948), Peru (1945–1948), Chile (1946–1952), Costa Rica (1948–1953), and Ecuador (1948–1961).

Peronism is the best-known example of the populist interlude in Latin America. Colonel Juan Perón (1895–1974) was a member of a group of officers who staged a coup in 1943 against the traditional landowners and their conservative military allies. As minister of labor, Perón entered into an alliance with labor unions and improved wages, set a minimum wage, and increased pensions. At a fundraiser after an earthquake, Perón met Eva Duarte (1919–1952), a popular movie actress. They were married and became the symbols of Peronism. In elections in 1946, at the head of a fractious coalition of nationalists, socialists, and communists, Perón gained a legitimate mandate as president.

After the elections he started a 5-year plan of nationalization and industrialization—the characteristic state socialism pursued also in Asia and Africa. A year later, construction of plants for the production of primary and intermediate industrial goods got under way. During Perón's tenure, the economy expanded by 40 percent.

The factories, however, had to be equipped with imported machinery. Initially, Perón paid for these imports with reserves accumulated from commodity exports during World War II. But soon the costs exceeded the internal reserves and revenues of Argentina, leading to inflation and strikes. Plagued by chronic deficits and unable to pay its foreign debts, the Perón government was overthrown by a conservative-led coup in 1955.

Populism: Type of governance in which rulers seek support directly from the population, through organizing mass rallies, manipulating elections, and intimidating or bypassing representative bodies.

Peronism: Argentinian political movement that aims to mediate tensions between the classes of society, with the state responsible for negotiating compromise in conflicts between business and workers.

CIA assessment of Communist threat to US Interests In Guatemala (1952)

The End of Colonialism and the Rise of New Nations

Like Latin America, Asia and Africa also experienced rapid population growth and urbanization in the period 1945–1962. But in contrast to the politically independent American continent, colonialism was still dominant in Asia and Africa. The governments of Great Britain and France had no inclination to relinquish their empires, but both were too exhausted to hold them completely. Thus, in a first wave after the end of war, a few independence movements succeeded. A major shift in attitudes toward colonialism had to take place, however, before Britain and France were willing to loosen their grip in Africa.

"China Has Stood Up"

After World War II, China was still fundamentally a peasant-based economy with scant industrial resources. Mao's reinterpretation of Marxism opened up fresh possibilities of development, leading eventually to an abortive attempt at decentralized village industrialization. During the Stalin years, China depended on Soviet material aid and advisors. Under Khrushchev, estrangement set in, culminating in the Soviet Union's withdrawal of all advisors from China in 1960.

Mao Zedong, address on the eve of the founding of the People's Republic of China (1949)

Victory of the Communists   China emerged from World War II severely battered. Moreover, the wartime alliance between the communists under Mao Zedong and the nationalists under Chiang K'ai-shek unraveled in the ensuing civil war. The communists, entrenched in the countryside, were at a strategic advantage in China's rural society. Despite the nationalists' material superiority, resulting partly from American support, the communists systematically strangled the cities, causing hyperinflation in Shanghai and other urban centers in 1947.

By 1948 the size of the two armies had reached parity, but Mao's People's Liberation Army had popular momentum, and the United States cut back on its aid to Chiang. By 1949, Chiang had fled to Taiwan, Mao's forces took Beijing, and the new People's Republic of China began implementing the Maoist vision of the communist pattern of collectivist modernity. For millions of Chinese, Mao's pronouncement that "China has stood up" against imperialism was a source of enormous pride.

Land Reform   During the 1950s, a central aspect of Maoism was that Chinese peasants were the only reliable resource. With China lacking an industrial and transportation base, the early Maoist years were marked by repeated mass mobilization campaigns, the most important of which was the national effort at land reform. Party cadres expropriated rural land, dividing it among the local peasants. Landlords who resisted were punished and sometimes executed by local "people's tribunals." By some estimates, land reform between 1950 and 1955 took as many as 2 million lives. As hoped for, however, peasant landownership caused agricultural productivity to increase.

When party leaders decided to take the next step toward socialized agriculture, Mao sought to avoid the chaos of Soviet collectivization of agriculture in 1930–1932. The party leadership felt that by going slowly they could greatly ease the transition. Thus, in 1953 peasants were encouraged to form "agricultural producers' cooperatives" in which villages would share resources. Those who joined were given incentives. By 1956, agricultural production was registering impressive gains.

"Let a Hundred Flowers Bloom" By 1957, Mao was ready to evaluate the commitment of the nation's intellectuals. Adopting a slogan from China's late Zhou period, "Let a hundred flowers bloom, let a hundred schools of thought contend," the party invited intellectuals to submit public criticism of the party's record, assuring the intellectuals that offering their critique was patriotic.

But in mid-1957, when some critics suggested forming an opposition party, Mao acted swiftly. The "Hundred Flowers" campaign was terminated and the "Anti-Rightist" campaign was launched. Calls for an opposition party were denounced as opposed to the "correct" left-wing thinking of the monopoly Communist Party. Those accused of rightism were subjected to "reeducation." In addition to being imprisoned, many intellectuals were sentenced to "reform through labor" in remote peasant villages.

The Great Leap Forward Mao, growing impatient with the pace of Chinese agricultural collectivization, prodded the Communist Party into its most colossal mass mobilization project yet: the **Great Leap Forward** (1958–1961). The entire population of the country was to be pushed into a campaign to communalize agriculture into self-sustaining units that would function like factories in the fields. Men and women would work and live on enormous collective farms. Peasants were to surrender all their iron implements to be melted down and made into steel to build the new infrastructure of these communes. The most recognizable symbol of the campaign was the backyard steel furnace, which commune members were to build and run for their own needs. Technical problems were to be solved by the "wisdom of the masses" through "red" (revolutionary) thinking as opposed to those who emphasized technical skills ("experts").

Great Leap Forward: Mobilization project led by Mao Zedong that aimed to rapidly transform China from an agrarian economy into a socialist society through rapid industrialization and collectivization.

Predictably, the Great Leap was the most catastrophic policy failure in the history of the People's Republic. Peasants began to actively resist the seizure of their land and implements. So many were forced into building the communal structures and making unuseable steel that by 1959 agricultural production in China had plummeted and the country experienced its worst famine in modern times. By 1962 an estimated 30 million people had died.

During 1959 conditions in China became so bleak that Mao stepped down from his party chairmanship in favor of "expert" Liu Shaoqi (1898–1969) and retreated into semiretirement. Liu, along with Deng Xiaoping (1904–1997), moved to rebuild the shattered economy and political structures. They had to do so without Soviet help, however: For the Soviet leader Nikita Khrushchev, Mao's Great Leap Forward was the kind of relapse into the Stalinism that he sought to leave behind. In 1960 the Soviets withdrew their aid and technical personnel in what became known as the "Sino-Soviet Split." The return to something like normalcy in the wake of Mao's mass mobilization campaigns was such a relief in China, however, that even without Soviet aid the country achieved impressive gains in the technical, health, and education sectors.

Decolonization, Israel, and Arab Nationalism in the Middle East

After World War II, independence movements arose in the Middle East and North Africa against the British and French colonial regimes. Here, countries achieved their independence in two waves, the first following World War II and the second during 1956–1970 (see Map 29.4). The first wave was the result of local pressures, while the second wave had to await the realization of the British and French governments that

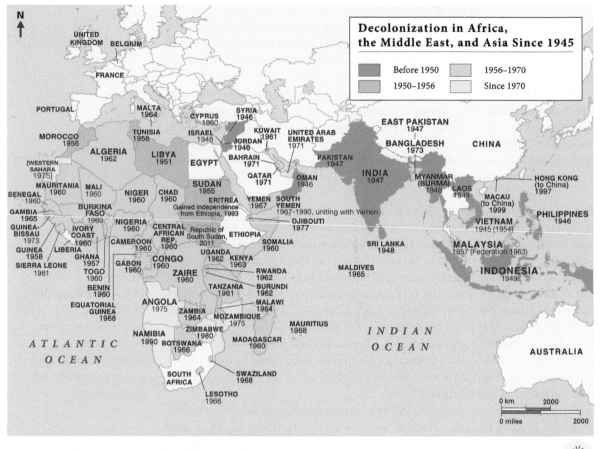

MAP **29.4** **Decolonization in Africa, the Middle East, and Asia since 1945.**

map analysis

they could no longer maintain their empires in a world dominated by the United States and the Soviet Union.

Palestine and Israel   As World War II ended, Britain found itself in a tight spot in Palestine. After the suppression of the uprising of 1936–1939, Zionist guerilla action protesting the restrictions on Jewish immigration and land acquisitions had begun in the middle of the war. Sooner or later some form of transition to self-rule had to be offered, but British leaders were determined to hold on to the empire's strategic interests (oil and the Suez Canal), especially once the Cold War began.

But unable to overcome the Palestinian–Zionist impasse, in February 1947 Britain turned the question of Palestinian independence over to the United Nations. Accordingly, the United Nations adopted a partition plan worked out with American assistance in November, and Israel declared its independence on May 14, 1948 (see Map 29.5).

The Soviet Union backed up its Cold War–motivated support for Israel by releasing 200,000 Jewish emigrants from the Soviet Bloc and having Czechoslovakia deliver weapons to Israel. Israel was victorious against the Arab armies that invaded from surrounding countries, which were unable to obtain weapons as the result of British and American embargoes. Only Jordan was partly successful, conquering the West Bank and the Old City of Jerusalem. Between November 1947 and the end of fighting in January 1949, some three-quarters of a million Palestinians were either forced from their villages or fled, leaving only 150,000 in an Israeli territory now substantially larger than that of the original partition plan.

In response, the Arab countries expelled about half a million Jews from their countries during the next decade. In the end, the Soviet Union's Cold War tactics were a miscalculation: Israel became a staunch Western ally. But the Western camp did not fare much better: Liberal, landowning Arab nationalists were replaced by military hard-liners of refugee background determined to end Western colonialism—which now, in their eyes, included the state of Israel.

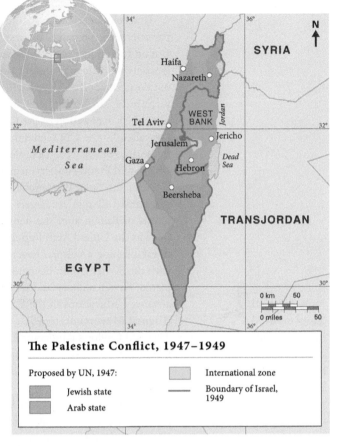

The Palestine Conflict, 1947–1949

Proposed by UN, 1947:
- Jewish state
- Arab state
- International zone
— Boundary of Israel, 1949

MAP 29.5 **The Palestine Conflict, 1947–1949.**

The Officer Coup in Egypt   One Egyptian officer in the war against Israel was Colonel Gamal Abdel Nasser (1918–1970), the eldest son of a postal clerk from southern Egypt. He was bitter toward the Egyptian royalty and the landowners who supported them; neither had done much to support the country in the 1947–1949 war. In the middle of a declining internal security situation, the secret "Free Officers," with Nasser at the center, assumed power in a coup in July 1952. They closed down parliament and sent the king into exile. The coup was bloodless, and there was little reaction in the streets.

To break the power of the landowners, the Free Officers in 1952 initiated land reform that eventually eliminated large estates. A rival for power was the Muslim Brotherhood, a militant organization founded in 1928 by the preacher Hasan al-Banna (1906–1949), who advocated the establishment of an Islamic regime. Accusing the Brotherhood of an assassination attempt, Nasser outlawed it in 1954. In a plebiscite in 1956, Nasser made himself president.

Once in power, Nasser espoused the Arab nationalist cause. Palestinian Arab "freedom fighters" raided Israel from refugee camps in the Arab countries, which provoked Israeli reprisals. After the first raid and reprisal involving Egypt in February 1955, Nasser realized that the Egyptian military needed urgent improvements. Khrushchev, as part of his strategy of supporting anticolonial nationalists, stepped up. After its failure in Israel, the Soviet Union was in the Middle Eastern Cold War struggle again.

Nasser also planned infrastructural improvements, and asked the World Bank for a loan to finance the Aswan High Dam. Initially, the United States and Britain, the main underwriters of the World Bank, were in support. But they withdrew this support in spring 1956 when Nasser pressured Jordan into dismissing the British commander of its troops, the Arab Legion. Nasser responded with the nationalization of the Suez Canal and closure of the Strait of Tiran (used by Israel for Indian Ocean shipping) in July 1956. Without the necessary loans, Nasser had to suspend construction of the High Dam.

Gamal Abdel Nasser, *The Philosophy of the Revolution* (1952)

Israel considered the closure of the Strait of Tiran an act of war and, with French participation, prepared for a campaign to reopen the straits. France persuaded Britain to join in a plan that would be initiated with an attack on Egypt by Israel. If Nasser would close the Suez Canal, France and Britain would occupy it, reestablishing Western control. The plan unraveled badly when Israel ended its canal campaign victoriously on November 2, but the British and French troops were unable to complete their occupation of the Canal Zone before November 4, the day of the ceasefire called by the UN General Assembly and the United States. Although defeated militarily, Nasser scored a diplomatic victory, effectively ending the last remnants of British and French imperialism in the Middle East.

After the Suez War, monarchical regimes in Arabia were on the defensive and maintained themselves largely due to the United States, heir to the strategic oil interests of Britain after the demise of the latter's empire. Although unification with Syria as the United Arab Republic (1958–1961) did not work out, Egypt succeeded in establishing a cultural hegemony from North Africa to Yemen. The relationship with the Soviet Union deepened: Thanks to the Soviets, the Aswan Dam was completed, Soviet military and technical support grew, and Egyptian students received advanced educations in the Eastern Bloc. In 1961, the regime cofounded the **Non-Aligned Movement**, together with Indonesia's Sukarno, India's Nehru, Yugoslavia's Tito, and Ceylon's Bandaranaike. In the same year, Nasser announced his first 5-year plan, which embraced industrial modernity but under the aegis of state investments similar to what Stalin had pioneered in 1930. Nasser called this "Arab socialism."

Decolonization and Cold War in Asia

Nationalist forces arose also in South and Southeast Asia as a consequence of World War II. The war had diminished or destroyed the colonial holdings of Great Britain, France, the Netherlands, and Japan in Asia. In several colonies, independence movements established nationalist governments or fought against the attempted reimposition of European rule. In quick succession, India and Pakistan (1947), Burma (1948), Malaysia (1957), Ceylon (1948), Indonesia (1949), and Vietnam (1954) achieved independence from the British and French.

Independence and Partition on the Subcontinent   India, Pakistan, and Bangladesh illustrate the difficulties of colonial populations just prior to and during the achievement of independence. In 1943, the British Raj requisitioned so much grain from northeastern India to fight the Japanese in Burma, without reallocating available food stocks from elsewhere in India, that the ensuing "Bengal Famine" ravaged some 3 million victims. During World War II, the all-volunteer Indian troops of some 2.5 million soldiers contributed heavily to the Allied victory, mourning some 90,000 deaths at war's end. In view of these sacrifices, the Indian nationalists renewed their "Quit India" protests of 1942 and demanded full independence at the end of World War II. Gandhi, Nehru, and the majority of the Indian National Congress envisaged an Indian nation on the entire subcontinent in which a constitution, patterned after that of Britain, would trump any ethnic, linguistic, and/or religious identities.

The Muslim minority, however, had drifted increasingly toward religious nationalism since the 1930s, and demanded a separate state for themselves in regions where they formed a majority. There was also a small minority of Hindu religious

Non-Aligned Movement: An international, anticolonialist movement of state leaders that promoted the interests of countries not aligned with the superpowers.

Competing visions of India: writings of Nehru, Gandhi, and Jinnah (1940–1945)

nationalists who advocated independence under the banner of "Hindu-ness" (hindutva). To the dismay of the Indian National Congress, the British negotiators listened to the Islamic religious nationalists and prevailed on Gandhi and Nehru to accept independence with partition.

When, on August 15, 1947, the two nations of India and Pakistan became independent, the jubilation of freedom was immediately mixed with the horrors of a massive population exchange. Desperate to save themselves from their Hindu and Muslim neighbors, millions of people fled from their homes to reach their new respective countries. More than 300,000 Indians died in the accompanying communal violence. Gandhi himself fell victim 5 months later to an assassin from the hindutva religious-nationalist minority.

While India settled into federal parliamentary democracy, Pakistan's regime became authoritarian. From the start, it was clear that religious nationalism was insufficient to define the identity of Pakistanis. The capital, Islamabad, was in the west, and Urdu became the national language, relegating Bengali in the east to secondary status (to the dismay of its speakers, who seceded in a civil war and formed the nation of Bangladesh in 1971).

A decade into independence, a military officer, Field Marshal Ayub Khan (1907–1974) from the Pashtun ethnic minority in Waziristan on the western border, assumed power in a bloodless coup. Subsequently, in 1962, he imposed a new constitution. The constitution's definition of Islam as a national identity and its relationship to subsidiary ethnic and linguistic identities in the country, however, were so contentious that they remained unresolved.

Given the role of Islam as the religious–nationalist foundation principle, Pakistan was in conflict with India over Kashmir, a province lying in the north between India and Pakistan. In 1947, its Hindu prince hesitated to join Pakistan, while its majority Muslim population demanded incorporation. In the ensuing first war between India and Pakistan, India conquered most of the province, but Kashmiri Muslims remained restive. As in many postcolonial territorial disputes, clashes between constitutionalists and ethnic–religious nationalists became irresolvable.

Independent India India's first prime minister, Jawaharlal Nehru (in office 1947–1964), worked to tie the subcontinent's disparate constituencies together into a united government. Local princes now had to surrender their realms to the national government, and the array of castes and systemic social inequalities also posed a powerful obstacle to unity. In the end, the British parliamentary and court systems were adopted and the old civil service was retained, while the economy of the new government would officially be a modified, nonrevolutionary kind of socialism. Nehru's admiration for Soviet successes persuaded him to adopt the 5-year-plan system of development, and India's first 5-year plan (1951–1955) was similarly geared toward raising agricultural productivity as a precondition for industrial development.

The most formidable problem was poverty. Though the cities were rapidly expanding, India was still fundamentally rural. The strains upon the land and reliance on the monsoon cycle meant a constant risk of famine. In the 1950s, India launched a family planning program, but cooperation from villagers was difficult to achieve as long as urbanization and industrialization were in their initial stages. For poor families, children were important laborers as soon as they were old enough to work.

a perspective on life in rural India: excerpt from Kamala Markandaya, *Nectar in a Sieve* (1954)

Bandung and the Origins of the Non-Aligned Movement (NAM)

One of the most momentous events of the post–World War II period was the dismantling of the colonial empires of the Western powers and Japan and the emergence from them of new nation-states. While nationalist movements in these empires had long predated the war, the complete defeat of Japan accompanied by the exhaustion of Great Britain, France, and the Netherlands and the emergence of the Cold War proved powerful catalysts for independence—as had Allied propaganda during the war and the newly created United Nations after 1945.

As these new nations arrived on the scene, they faced unprecedented problems, including poverty, developmental gaps, and ethnic and religious conflicts. Looming over all of these emerging nations was the intensifying struggle during the Cold War between the United States and its allies in the capitalist camp and the Soviet Union and the Communist Bloc. As a result, many leaders of these new nations saw themselves as natural colleagues. They shared a common colonial experience, and many had also been fighters for national independence. Now, they also had to contend with both Cold War rivals attempting to enlist their support. Thus, led by the dynamic Indonesian president Sukarno and India's Prime Minister Nehru, Indonesia, India, Burma (Myanmar), Pakistan, and Ceylon (Sri Lanka) convened a conference in April 1955 attended by 25 countries at the Indonesian town of Bandung.

Although the Bandung Conference established the base on which the Non-Aligned Movement was founded, politics proved a corrosive force in its interactions. Delegates agreed on the principle of Afro-Asian solidarity and cooperation, and were unanimous in their opposition to colonialism by any country. They were much less agreed, however, on exactly what constituted colonialism: Some equated the Soviet position in Eastern Europe with colonialism and worried about China's emergent predominance in East Asia. Others, friendlier toward Marxist developmental approaches and eager for aid from socialist countries, dismissed such ideas as Western propaganda. The United States refused to attend, at least in part because of its policy of not recognizing the People's Republic, though American congressman Adam Clayton Powell and the writer Richard Wright—both African American—did attend in

Political and Economic Nonalignment Nehru and the Congress Party argued that the pressing rural poverty could be overcome only through rapid industrialization undertaken by the state and its financial power. A hybrid regime of capitalist–democratic constitutionalism with private property and guided "socialist" state investments emerged, which was officially aligned with neither the West nor the East. This nonalignment became the official policy of India and under its initiative also the founding principle of the Non-Aligned Movement, formally inaugurated in 1961 (see "Patterns Up Close"). The Non-Aligned Movement, still in existence today, sought to maintain neutrality in the Cold War and was successful in maintaining its own course independent from the Western and Soviet Blocs.

unofficial capacities. In the end, the conference unanimously adopted a 10-point declaration of "world peace and cooperation," very much in keeping with the tenets of the UN Charter.

Though regional rivalries and competing political aims, as well as the circumstances of the Cold War, never allowed the development of the kind of solidarity championed at Bandung, successive conferences in Cairo and Belgrade led to the official creation of the Non-Aligned Movement in 1961. The movement marked the maturation of an important pattern that helped to regulate the behavior of the Cold War players. The search for a third way beyond capitalism and Soviet communism spurred economic and developmental experimentation and encouraged both Cold War camps to woo nonaligned members into their respective ideological orbits. New nations seeing security in a coalition opposed to superpower domination made the movement a genuine power of its own.

The pattern of resistance to superpower dominance continues today, decades after the end of the Cold War. The Non-Aligned Movement still casts itself as the champion of the developing "global south" in opposition to the economic power of the wealthy "north." Accordingly, it pushes the United Nations toward greater attention to the inequalities in the world economic order. Although the NAM boasts a membership of 120 countries and 17 observer nations, at present it is increasingly fighting for relevance. The Tehran summit of 2012 was attended by more than 30 heads of state; but the Venezuela summit of 2016 assembled only 12, with the notable absence of Norendra Modi, Prime Minister of India. Muhammadu Buhari, President of Nigeria was in attendance but demanded a restructuring of NAM. Since he did not submit any details, however, the future of the movement remains uncertain.

Bandung Conference. (L-R) Dr. Ali Sastroamidjojo (Premier of Indonesia), Sir John Kotelawala (Premier of Sri Lanka), Chaudry Mohammed Ali (Premier of Pakistan) Jawaharlal Nehru (Premier of India), and U Nu (Premier of Burma, today Myanmar) at the Bandung Conference, April 1, 1955.

Questions

- How does the Non-Aligned Movement reflect the pattern of postwar developments regarding the trend toward anticolonialism?

- Will the revival of the Russia-United States rivalry allow NAM to regain relevance? If yes, how?

Indian state socialism began with the state's second 5-year plan (1956–1961), which focused on state investments in heavy industry. Planners hoped that private Indian investors would buy the heavy industrial goods to construct housing and build factories for the production of basic consumer goods. The giant domestic market of India was to become fully self-sufficient and independent of imports.

Though begun with much hope at a time of prosperity, the second plan failed to reach its goals. The government debt grew astronomically. Tax collection was notoriously difficult and unproductive, and chronic budget deficits drove up inflation. Bad monsoon seasons caused food shortages. In democratic India it was not possible to use the draconian dictatorial powers that Stalin had employed.

The Strains of Nonalignment. India's determined stance to navigate its own course between the superpowers was a difficult one, especially during the height of the Cold War. Here, however, a degree of diplomatic warmth appears to pervade the proceedings in Geneva, Switzerland, as the foreign minister of the People's Republic of China, Chen Yi (left), toasts his Indian colleague, defense minister V. K. Krishna Menon (right), and the Soviet foreign minister, Andrei Gromyko (center background), smiles at them both. The date of this conference, however, formally convened to discuss issues between the Soviet and American sides over influence in the Southeast Asian nation of Laos in July 1962, also coincided with rising border tensions between India and China. This photo was specifically released to show that both sides were still on friendly terms. Within a few months, however, they were shooting at each other.

Ho Chi Minh,
The Vietnamese
Declaration of
Independence (1945)

Southeast Asia   In contrast to the British in India, the French under Charles de Gaulle (1890–1970) in 1944–1946 were determined to reconstitute their empire. De Gaulle found it inconceivable that the new postwar Fourth Republic would be anything less than the imperially glorious Third Republic. However, French military efforts to hold on to Lebanon and Syria failed against discreet British support for independence and the unilateral establishment of national governments by the Lebanese and Syrians in 1943–1944. After these losses, the French were determined not to lose more colonies.

Unfortunately for the French, however, when they returned to Indochina (composed of Vietnam, Laos, and Cambodia) in the fall of 1945, the prewar communist independence movement had already taken over. With covert American assistance, the communist Vietminh had fought the Japanese occupiers in a guerilla war, and on September 2, 1945, the day of Japan's surrender to the United States, Ho Chi Minh, the leader, declared Vietnamese independence.

Following a stalemate in negotiations between Ho and the French, the Vietminh relaunched their guerilla war. Because of the rapid escalation of the Cold War, the French persuaded the American administration that a Vietminh victory meant an expansion of communism. By the early 1950s, the United States was providing much of the funding, and the French and allied Vietnamese troops did the actual fighting. In May 1954, however, the Vietminh defeated the French decisively at Dien Bien Phu. During negotiations later that year, the French surrender resulted in a division of Vietnam into north and south, pending national elections, and the creation of the new nations of Laos and Cambodia.

The elections, however, never took place. Instead President Ngo Dinh Diem [NO deen jem] (in office 1955–1963), a politician who envisioned a republican Vietnam but had a limited power base, emerged in the south. President Dwight D. Eisenhower (in office 1953–1961) initially took a dim view of Diem's staying power. But when Diem was able in 1955 to eliminate his strongest opponents and legitimize his rule through a (fraudulent) plebiscite, the United States renewed its aid for Vietnam previously given to France. Sharing Diem's vision of nation building, the US granted the Vietnamese president more than $2 billion in military and economic aid during 1955–1961. As a result of this aid, Diem's military was able by 1957 to drive the South Vietnamese communist guerillas, the Vietcong, into the mountains. The unification of the South Vietnamese population appeared to be making progress. John F. Kennedy, who had a high regard for Diem, continued the aid and increased the US troop strength to 16,000. But in 1959–1960, after Ho Chi Minh had gained the support of both the Soviet Union and China (by now fierce rivals, see above, p. 693), the Vietcong rebuilt their insurgency in South Vietnam. President Kennedy was increasingly forced to subordinate nation-building in South Vietnam to less lofty Cold War considerations. The Diem government, beset by major Vietcong gains, eventually hastened its own demise when it alienated the Buddhist majority of South Vietnam in May-August 1963 by having its special armed forces and combat police suppress unarmed protests and raid several temples. But it took several months of plotting and counter-plotting in Saigon before Kennedy decided to drop Diem and support a generals' coup on November 1–2. Once the generals were firmly in power, in the name of the Cold War the United States committed itself fully to the war against the Vietcong, with half a million troops by1967.

Vo Nguyen Giap, "The People's War" (1961)

Decolonization and Cold War in Africa

On November 1, 1954, the French faced a declaration of a war for independence by the Algerian Front of National Liberation. Algeria, a French colony of 10 million Muslim Arabs and Berbers, had a European settler population of nearly 1 million. France hung on to Algeria and was even able to largely repress the liberation war by the later 1950s. But in the long run, Algerian independence (in 1962) could not be prevented. France's colonial interests were too costly to be maintained, and the United States took over the West's strategic interests in the world.

While some European governments began to liquidate their African empires, beginning in 1957, Portugal and Spain (governed by national-supremacist dictators) maintained their colonies of Angola, Mozambique, and Rio de Oro. South Africa introduced its apartheid regime (1948–1994), designed to segregate the white ruling class from the black majority. As the British, French, and Belgians decolonized, however, they ensured that the newly independent African countries would remain their loyal subalterns. For them, African independence would be an exchange for support in the Cold War and continued economic dependence.

The Legacy of Colonialism   Between 1918 and 1957, vast changes had occurred in sub-Saharan Africa. The population had more than doubled; urbanization was accelerating; economies were relying too heavily on commodity exports; and an emerging middle class was becoming restless. Heavy investments were required in mining and agriculture as well as in social services. Faced with this financial burden, most of the colonial powers decided to grant independence rather than divert investments badly needed at home.

Ghana, the African Pioneer   Once Britain had decided to decolonize, the governmental strategy toward African independence was to support nationalist groups that adopted British-inspired constitutions, guaranteed existing British economic interests, and abided by the rules of the British Commonwealth of Nations. The first to fit these criteria was Ghana in 1957. Its leader, Kwame Nkrumah (1909–1972), son of an Ashante goldsmith, held a master's degree in education from the University of Pennsylvania and appeared to be a sound choice.

Ghana was the pioneer of sub-Saharan independence and development. It had a healthy economy, and its middle class was perhaps the most vital of any African colony. Nkrumah was an activist for African independence and a leading advocate of pan-African unity. Although he had been jailed during the 1950s for his activism, the British nevertheless realized that Nkrumah wielded genuine authority among a majority of politically inexperienced Ghanaians.

Only 2 years into his rule, however, Nkrumah discarded the independence constitution. Exploiting ethnic tensions among Ashante groups, where an emerging opposition to his rule was concentrated, he promulgated a new republican constitution, removing the country from the British Commonwealth. A year later, he turned to socialist state planning.

The construction of a hydroelectric dam on the Volta River, begun in 1961, was supposed to be the starting point of a heavy industrialization program. But the country soon ran into financing problems, since prices for cocoa, the main export commodity, were declining and large foreign loans were required to continue the program. On the political front, Nkrumah in 1964 amended the constitution again, making Ghana a one-party state with Nkrumah himself as leader for life. An unmanageable foreign debt eventually stalled development, and an army coup, supported by the CIA, ousted Nkrumah in 1966.

Resistance to Independence in Kenya   In Kenya, decolonization was not achieved as easily as in Ghana. Efforts to terminate British colonialism were advanced by Jomo Kenyatta (1894–1978), who founded the Kenya African National Union. Kenyatta's movement was met with resistance by British settlers who were reluctant to relinquish control of their economic and political interests. In the face of British opposition, the African nationalists formed the Mau Mau movement, which resorted to terrorist attacks on British estates. Finally, independence was granted Kenya in 1963, and in the following year Kenyatta was named as the first president of the newly created republic.

The Struggle for the Congo's Independence   The Belgian Congo, like Vietnam, became a battleground of the Cold War. The Belgian Congo had been under the authority of the Belgian government since the beginning of the twentieth century, when it took over from the king (see Chapter 27). During the interwar period, concession companies invested in mining, especially in the southern and central provinces of Katanga and Kisaï. Little money went into human development

Kwame Kkrumah on socialisam for Ghana (1964)

Jomo Kenyatta, excerpt from *Facing Mount Kenya* (1937)

until after World War II. The urban and mine workforce expanded considerably, but no commercial or professional middle classes existed.

Serious demands for independence arose in the Congo only after Ghana became independent in 1957. Groups of nationalists, some advocating a federation and others a centralized state, competed with each other. The urban and mine worker–based National Congolese Movement (*Mouvement National Congolais*, MNC), founded in 1958 by Patrice Lumumba (1925–1961), was the most popular group, favoring a centralized constitutional nationalism that transcended ethnicity, language, and religion. After riots in 1959 and the arrest of Lumumba, Belgian authorities decided to act quickly: They needed compliant nationalists who would continue existing economic arrangements. A Brussels conference with all nationalists—including Lumumba, freed from prison—decided to hold local and national elections in early 1960. To the dismay of Belgium, the centralists, led by Lumumba, won. On June 30, 1960, the Congo became independent, with Lumumba as prime minister and the federalist Joseph Kasa-Vubu (ca. 1910–1969) from the province of Katanga as president.

Lumumba's first political act was the announcement of a general pay raise for state employees, which the Belgian army commander undermined by spreading a rumor that the Congolese foot soldiers would be left out. Outraged, the soldiers mutinied, and amid a general breakdown of public order, Katanga declared its independence. Lumumba fired the Belgian officers, but to restore order he turned to the United Nations. Order was indeed restored by the United Nations, although Belgium made sure that Katanga did not rejoin the Congo. To force Katanga, Lumumba turned for support to the Soviet Union. The Cold War had arrived in Africa.

At that time, the Belgian and American governments were convinced that Lumumba was another Castro in the making, a nationalist who would soon become a communist, influenced by Khrushchev. In the Cold War, the fierce but inexperienced Lumumba was given no chance by the Belgian and American governments acting with mutual consultation. At all costs, the Congo had to remain in the Western camp as a strategic, mineral-rich linchpin in central Africa.

Kasa-Vubu and Lumumba dismissed each other from the government on September 5, giving the new Congolese army chief, Mobutu Sese Seko (1930–1997), the opportunity to seize power on September 14. Mobutu was a member of the MNC whom Lumumba had appointed as army chief, even though it was general knowledge that he was in the pay of the Belgians and the CIA. (Mobutu went on to become the dictator of the Congo, renamed Zaire, and was a close ally of the United States during the period he held power, 1965–1996.) He promptly had Lumumba arrested. Eventually, Belgian agents took Lumumba to Katanga, where they executed him on January 17, 1961.

During the 1960s, some 35 sub-Saharan colonies achieved their independence through a mostly peaceful transfer of power from their British, French, Belgian, Italian, and Spanish colonial masters. Only Portugal dragged its feet, holding on to its large settler colonies until its own "Carnation Revolution" of 1974 that ended the authoritarian Salazar regime established in 1933. The majority of the newly independent states fell under the sway of authoritarian rulers paying scant attention to their constitutions and favoring their ethnic relatives over the myriads of other ethnic groups. The tension between constitutionalism and ethnicity continues to be a major factor in African politics today.

cartoon depicting Lumumba as mouthpiece of the Soviets

❯ Putting It All Together

interactive
concept map

Frantz Fanon, *The Wretched of the Earth* (1961)

Rapid, breathtaking change characterized the pattern of modernity in the middle of the twentieth century as an intense Cold War competition between the proponents of the ideologies of capitalist democracy and communism unfolded. Imperialism and colonialism collapsed, and nearly 200 nations came to share the globe in the United Nations. Compared to the slow pace of change in the agrarian–urban period of world history, the speed of development during just 145 years of scientific–industrial modernity was dizzying.

Perhaps the most noteworthy events characterizing the early and intense Cold War between capitalist democracy and communism in 1945–1962 was the sad fate of many countries as they emerged into independence or as they struggled to accommodate themselves in the Western camp, the Eastern Bloc, or the Non-Aligned Movement. As we have seen, US and Soviet leaders were ruthless wherever they perceived communist or capitalist influence in their ranks. But even when new nations pursued a policy of nonalignment, there were subtler ways through which both West and East could apply financial pressures with devastating consequences: Egypt lost its finances for the Aswan Dam, and China lost its Soviet advisors during the Great Leap Forward.

Not that capitalist democracy and communism were on the same plane: The former provided greater political participation than the latter, which paid only lip service to its notions of equality, as became obvious in 1989–1991, when it collapsed. But the period of the early, active Cold War and decolonization from 1945 to 1962 was far less brutal than the preceding interwar period.

Review and Relate

| Thinking Through Patterns

Examine the ways historians approach the big questions of this chapter.

> ❯ Why did the pattern of unfolding modernity, which offered three choices after World War I, shrink to just capitalist democracy and socialism–communism in 1945? How did each of these two patterns evolve between 1945 and 1962?

The pattern of modernity evolved in the nineteenth century with four major ingredients: constitutional nationalism, ethnic–linguistic–religious nationalism, industrialism, and communism. However, traditional institutions such as monarchies and empires from times prior to 1800 continued to flourish. World War I wiped out most monarchies, but capitalist democracy continued, communism came into its own in the Soviet Union, imperialism and colonialism survived, and supremacist nationalism attracted those who found democracy and communism wanting. World War II eliminated supremacist nationalism and, eventually, also imperialism and colonialism. The remaining choices of capitalist democracy and communism were divided between two power blocs, which during the early Cold War period of 1945–1962 shared the world almost evenly.

Modernity's roots are in the New Sciences of the 1600s, with its assumptions of materialism and the social contract. It evolved into scientific–industrial modernity, with profound cultural consequences. Successive waves of increasingly modern artistic movements were insufficient to address the basic materialist flaw of modernity, which in each generation gave rise to the question of the meaning of it all.

>> What are the cultural premises of modernity?

After 1945 the number of nations on earth rose to the total of 196 today. The new nations, emerging from colonialism, were largely agrarian, putting industrialism beyond reach. With great hope, the ruling elites in many new nations embraced a mixed capitalist–democratic and socialist regime, with heavy state investments in basic industries. However, in contrast to Stalin, who introduced these types of investments under the label of state-guided socialism, none of the elites in the new nations had the will to collect the money for these investments from their rural population. Instead, they borrowed heavily from the capitalist–democratic countries. True independence remained elusive.

>> How did the newly independent countries of the Middle East, Asia, and Africa adapt to the divided world of the Cold War?

Against the Grain

Consider this as a counterpoint to the main patterns examined in this chapter.

Postwar Counterculture

Postwar Europe and North America during the 1950s embarked on programs of reconstruction, reflecting a yearning for normalcy following years of hardship. Central to this agenda was a mood of traditionalism. In America, however, fear of socialism and communism amid Cold War tensions generated a new element of suspicion. Crackdowns on groups by the House Un-American Activities Committee promoted a prevailing trend toward conformity with traditional Western values.

Not everyone fell in line with this trend. The early 1950s witnessed the emergence of a countercultural movement known as the "Beat Generation," initiated by a group of writers and students affiliated with Columbia University. Finding prevailing conformity stultifying, Jack Kerouac, Allen Ginsberg, William Burroughs, and others sought new avenues of nonconformist expression, including experimentation with drugs, alternative sexuality, and a fascination with Eastern religions—especially Buddhism—and music. Ginsberg's *Howl and Other Poems* (1956), an indictment of traditional norms, represents the earliest expression of the Beat ethic. *Howl* was followed by Kerouac's *On the Road* (1957); drawn from a series of road trips around America, the work expresses the emptiness of current culture.

Beats roamed the globe in quest of non-Western intellectual inspiration. In turn, Beat culture transcended American borders, and was assimilated into countercultural

• What did the Beat Generation find so offensive and alienating about America during the postwar era of the 1950s?

• How does the Beat countercultural movement following World War II compare with expressions of the Lost Generation in the aftermath of World War I?

movements in Europe and Asia. Among the more telling instances of Beat influence abroad was John Lennon's meeting with a Beat poet in 1960, which resulted in his changing the spelling of the name of the famous rock group from "Beetles" to "Beatles."

The Beat Generation nurtured later countercultures, including the hippies of the 1960s. Whereas the Beats simply explored alternative lifestyles, later exemplars were more motivated by, and interested in, political expressions. Their reach even extended to musical expressions of the 1960s; Bob Dylan, Jim Morrison, and the Beatles are among their many devotees.

Key Terms

audio flashcards

Cold War 680	Marshall Plan 681	Populism 691
Containment 681	Modernism 688	Truman Doctrine 681
Existentialism 688	Non-Aligned Movement 696	United Nations 680
Great Leap Forward 693	Peronism 691	

For additional resources, please go to
www.oup.com/us/vonsivers.
Please see the Further Resources section at the back of the book
for additional readings and suggested websites.

> Chapter 30   1963–1991

The End of the Cold War, Western Social Transformation, and the Developing World

A s the helicopter approached, the fighter on the ground recognized it immediately: *Shaitan Arba*, "Satan's Chariot," the Soviet MI-5 "Hind," a heavily armed and armored gunship that had proven largely impervious to the rifle and small arms fire of the fighter and his *mujahideen* Afghan warriors. In this fight in the Afghan high country, the Soviets, it appeared, had acquired a technological edge as they sought to eliminate resistance to the client regime they had installed in the capital of Kabul in 1979.

But just before the soldier took cover, the helicopter exploded in a fireball. A vapor trail marked a spot from where it appeared a rocket had been fired. A group of men shouted, "God is great!" as they cheered their victory.

The weapon that had downed the helicopter was a new American "Stinger" shoulder-fired missile, which the United States was clandestinely supplying to the Afghan Muslim fighters attempting to expel the Soviet occupying forces. The Stinger neutralized the Soviet advantage

THE WORLD, 1963–1991

ABOVE: **Afghan Mujahideen soldiers, battling the Soviet invasion, celebrate the downing of a Russian helicopter in January 1980.**

Seeing Patterns

≫ How did the political landscape of the Cold War change from 1963 to 1991?

≫ Why did such radically different lifestyles emerge in the United States and the West during the 1960s and 1970s? What is their legacy today?

≫ Why did some nations that had emerged from colonialism and war make great strides in their development while others seemed to stagnate?

in airpower and enabled the mujahideen to push the Soviets out of Afghanistan in this last contest of the Cold War. In fact, the immense cost of the Soviet–Afghan War, combined with the price of trying to match the American effort to create a missile defense system against intercontinental ballistic missiles (ICBMs), contributed to the collapse of the Soviet economy by the end of the 1980s and led to the end of the Eastern Bloc and the Soviet Union itself. The West and its version of modernity—capitalist democracy—had won both the physical and ideological contests of the Cold War.

Although the end result of the Cold War was an apparent victory for democracy and capitalism, the contest in the developing world was still active. From the triumph of Muslim resistance in Afghanistan would emerge a new global movement of resistance to the secular West and democratic capitalism: al-Qaeda and its affiliates.

The Climax of the Cold War

The Cold War continued into the 1980s, when the power of the Soviet Union began to ebb. During the 1960s, despite the enactment of the Nuclear Test Ban Treaty, the United States and the Soviet Union remained bitter ideological enemies. Moreover, both sides continued to upgrade and expand their nuclear arsenals. Despite this continuing hostility, the late 1960s and early 1970s also witnessed the era of détente: a downplaying of overt aggression and the pursuit of competition through diplomatic, social, and cultural means. In the end, the Soviet Union's resources were simply not sufficient to outlast those of the West in the struggle.

The Soviet Superpower in Slow Decline

In 1963, only a few months after the Cuban Missile Crisis, it appeared that the Soviet Union was an adversary more or less equal to the United States. Yet in less than 30 years, the Soviet Union would fall apart. What set this course of events in motion?

From the Brink of War to Détente   The initial success of Nikita S. Khrushchev in rolling back some of the worst abuses of Stalinism had been overshadowed by three failures during the early 1960s. The first was the Sino–Soviet split of 1960, which became a complete break. Second, Khrushchev's building of the Berlin Wall had been a propaganda failure. But Khrushchev's key blunder had been in appearing to back down during the Cuban Missile Crisis in October 1962, which meant the dismantling of Soviet bases in Cuba. Though the United States also agreed to dismantle its own medium-range missiles in Turkey, the Soviet Politburo ousted Khrushchev, who resigned in October 1964.

The years of Leonid Brezhnev (in office 1964–1982) were marked by actions demonstrating just how shaken the Soviet Union and United States had been by the Cuban Missile Crisis. One way that this danger had been partially defused was by the Nuclear Test Ban Treaty, signed in October 1963. Nonnuclear nations were discouraged from developing their own weapons in subsequent "nonproliferation" treaties. Additional safeguards were built into the detection and early warning systems

Federal Civil Defense Administration pamphlet, "Facts about Fallout" (1955)

Détente. In the wake of the Arab–Israeli War, President Lyndon B. Johnson (in office 1963–1969) and Soviet Minister of Foreign Affairs Andrei Gromyko (in office 1957–1985) met in the beginning of June 1967, at Glassboro State College (now Rowan University) in New Jersey. The talks centered on the US position in Vietnam and the possibility of opening talks on lessening nuclear tensions. Here, President Johnson and Premier Gromyko are engaged in a frank discussion.

Chapter Outline

• **The Climax of the Cold War**

• **Transforming the West**

• **From "Underdeveloped" to "Developing" World, 1963–1991**

• **Putting It All Together**

both sides used as part of missile defense. Finally, a direct telephone link between the White House and the Kremlin was created, so that American and Soviet leaders could alert each other if an accident or false attack signal was in progress. Nonetheless, the mood of the 1960s remained one of nuclear tension on both sides.

By the late 1960s, the United States and the Soviet Union had entered into a period often referred to by historians as "détente," from the French term for "release of tension." However, for the Soviets, tensions were mounting with the People's Republic of China over borders along the Amur River and the chaos of the Cultural Revolution. At several points, military engagements took place, and at least once, the Americans were approached by the Soviets about the possibility of a preemptive nuclear strike against China.

The era of détente ended in the fall of 1973 with the Egyptian and Syrian surprise attack on Israel, which sparked the largest Arab–Israeli conflict to date. The Soviets actively supported the boycott by the largely Arab Organization of the Petroleum Exporting Countries (OPEC) of oil shipments to the United States during the mid-1970s and resumed support for North Vietnam's final drive to conquer South Vietnam after the American withdrawal in 1973.

Prague Spring in Czechoslovakia and Solidarity in Poland   The Brezhnev years were marked by increasing dissent, both in the Soviet Union and in its Eastern European client states (see Map 30.1). In Hungary, for example, government efforts to stifle dissent threatened to stir up nationalistic feelings. One result was what came to be called "goulash communism": a relatively relaxed attitude toward criticism of the regime, the introduction of limited market reforms, some attention to consumer demands, and limited trade with the West.

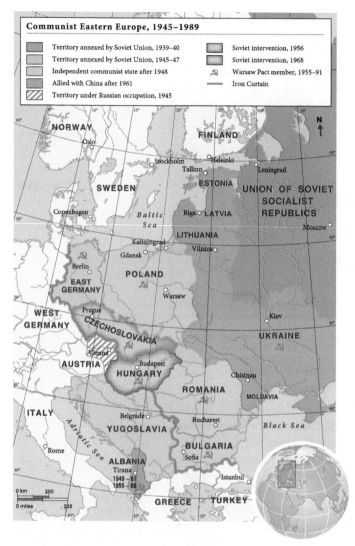

Communist Eastern Europe, 1945–1989

■ Territory annexed by Soviet Union, 1939–40		■ Soviet intervention, 1956	
■ Territory annexed by Soviet Union, 1945–47		■ Soviet intervention, 1968	
■ Independent communist state after 1948		⚔ Warsaw Pact member, 1955–91	
■ Allied with China after 1961		— Iron Curtain	
▨ Territory under Russian occupation, 1945			

MAP 30.1 **Communist Eastern Europe, 1945–1989.**

In 1968, dissent took a more direct course in Czechoslovakia, in what came to be called the "Prague Spring." With the rise to power of Alexander Dubček (in office 1968–1969) in January 1968, there were calls for a new decentralized administrative structure, relaxation of censorship, and opposition political parties. Brezhnev's government, however, entered into negotiations in order to bring the country back into line. By August, as the push for reform became more persistent, the Soviets sent Warsaw Pact forces into Czechoslovakia, where they ousted Dubček, installed Gustáv Husák (1913–1991), and dismantled the reforms. The Soviet move demonstrated the "Brezhnev Doctrine"—the right of the Soviets and the Warsaw Pact to forcibly restrain any member country attempting to abandon their alliance with the Soviet Union.

With the shadow cast by the Brezhnev Doctrine, dissent went underground. In 1980, however, it reemerged in Poland with a strike by electrical workers at the Lenin Shipyard in Gdansk. A new labor union called "Solidarity," led by an electrician named Lech Wałęsa (b. 1943), called for an end to censorship, the lifting of economic restrictions, and the right of workers to organize outside of the Communist Party. Despite arrests, by the end of 1980, 80 percent of Poland's workers had joined the movement.

The Polish government declared martial law in an attempt to stave off a Soviet invocation of the Brezhnev Doctrine, but the installation of Mikhail Gorbachev as the new Soviet leader in 1985 and his liberalizing policies of *glasnost* and *perestroika* ensured the future of Solidarity as a political movement. Wałęsa was elected president of Poland, and served from 1991 to 1995.

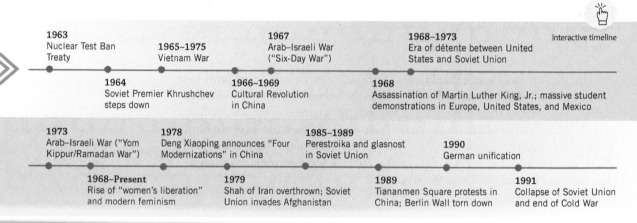

1963 Nuclear Test Ban Treaty	1965–1975 Vietnam War	1967 Arab–Israeli War ("Six-Day War")	1968–1973 Era of détente between United States and Soviet Union	Interactive timeline
	1964 Soviet Premier Khrushchev steps down	1966–1969 Cultural Revolution in China	1968 Assassination of Martin Luther King, Jr.; massive student demonstrations in Europe, United States, and Mexico	

1973 Arab–Israeli War ("Yom Kippur/Ramadan War")	1978 Deng Xiaoping announces "Four Modernizations" in China	1985–1989 Perestroika and glasnost in Soviet Union	1990 German unification	
	1968–Present Rise of "women's liberation" and modern feminism	1979 Shah of Iran overthrown; Soviet Union invades Afghanistan	1989 Tiananmen Square protests in China; Berlin Wall torn down	1991 Collapse of Soviet Union and end of Cold War

The 1980s: Afghanistan and "Star Wars"   Despite the tensions following the collapse of détente and the Brezhnev Doctrine, progress on strategic arms limitation was achieved between the superpowers. During the SALT II talks from 1977 to 1979, a historic agreement was reached in 1979 that would, for the first time, require the United States and the Soviet Union to limit certain types of nuclear weapons and begin a process of actually reducing them—a process that would later be known as START (Strategic Arms Reduction Talks/Treaty).

Much of the sense of progress achieved by this breakthrough was checked, however, by the Soviet invasion of Afghanistan in December 1979. Fearful of a weak, nominally communist Afghan government on its flank, adjacent to pro-American Pakistan and a China that appeared to have shifted toward the United States, the Soviets launched a coup in Afghanistan and installed a communist leader with a massive military force to back him up. The Soviets were immediately subjected to international condemnation.

The new administration of President Ronald Reagan (in office 1981–1989) in the United States sought a more assertive policy toward the Soviet Union. At the same time, technological breakthroughs in computers and satellite communications made it theoretically possible for the United States to create an antiballistic missile system in space. Such a system was in violation of the antiballistic missile provisions of the 1969 SALT I accords, but its advantages appeared overwhelming to American defense planners. Thus, over Soviet protests, the United States began to develop its Strategic Defense Initiative (SDI), nicknamed "Star Wars" after the popular movie of the same name.

From the mid-1980s, both superpowers thus undertook an enormously expensive strategic arms development race. For the Soviets, however, the drain of this new arms race, combined with the increasingly costly war in Afghanistan, was unsustainable.

Glasnost and Perestroika   The death of Leonid Brezhnev in 1982 ushered in two short-lived successors before Mikhail Gorbachev (b. 1931) took office as general secretary in the Politburo in 1985. Faced with growing dissent in Eastern Bloc countries, an increasingly inefficient economy, the endless war in Afghanistan, and now the arms race with the United States, Gorbachev called for large-scale structural reforms.

Up until the 1980s, the Soviet economy had functioned as a giant economic command pyramid. An army of ministerial bureaucrats oversaw every detail of the production and distribution process, but both workers and managers had every incentive to overreport production figures and to manufacture shoddy consumer goods as cheaply as possible. Periodic shortages were the inevitable result.

By the mid-1980s, Soviet planners realized that their command system was delivering diminishing returns. Several factors were responsible for the decline: fewer people were working in factories and more people were in the service sector; a lack of investment in new technologies meant that factories were becoming less productive; and the percentage of people over 60 years of age had doubled between World War II and the mid-1980s, requiring the labor force to support more and more retirees.

Lech Wałęsa and Solidarity. The strike at the Gdansk shipyard in Poland brought to the fore an obscure electrician but able leader named Lech Wałęsa [vɔ-WEN-sɑ]. He was one of the founders of the trade union *Solidarność* [soh-lee-DAR-noshtsh] (Solidarity), which ultimately succeeded in toppling Poland's communist government. Wałęsa went on to win the Nobel Peace Prize and served as president of Poland 1990–1995.

Perestroika:
"Restructuring" of the Soviet bureaucracy and economic structure in an attempt to make it more efficient and responsive to market demand.

Glasnost: "Openness"; an attempt to loosen restrictions on media in the Soviet Union with an aim at more accurate reporting of events and the creation of "socialist pluralism."

Vaclav Havel, "The Power of the Powerless" (1979)

Two years after becoming secretary of the Politburo in 1985, Gorbachev launched two economic and political programs, "restructuring" (**perestroika**) and "openness" (**glasnost**), which were intended to revitalize communism. Restructuring entailed the partial dismantling of the command economy. Freed somewhat from the planners' oversight, managers could sell part of what their factories produced on the market, instead of delivering everything to the state. Citizens were free to establish "cooperatives," the communist euphemism for private business enterprises. Gorbachev promoted the new mixed command and market economy as a "socialist" or "regulated" system.

In practice, perestroika did not work out as intended. Market production rose to a meager 5 percent of total production, and many managers were stuck with the manufacture of unprofitable goods. Consumers still complained about shortages. Some who established small businesses charged outrageous prices and evaded payment of taxes. Practical support structures for the co-ops were lacking. Gorbachev's measures, therefore, inadvertently encouraged the rise of wild "carpetbagger" capitalism.

Gorbachev also introduced political "openness," or glasnost. The catalyst for glasnost was the nuclear accident at Chernobyl in the Ukraine in April 1986, about which reporting in the media was remarkably frank. However, while Gorbachev's glasnost was supposed to produce a "socialist pluralism," the unintended result was a more individualist pluralism, reducing communism to just one of many competing ideologies.

Transformations in the Soviet Bloc The countries of the Soviet Bloc had borrowed heavily from the West in the 1970s and early 1980s for oil imports and industrial renewal. Others borrowed to build oil and gas pipelines from Russia via their territories to Western Europe. But the oil price collapse of 1985–1986 forced all Soviet Bloc countries to reschedule their debts and cut their budgets. Protests against these cuts in 1989 and 1990 in Poland, Hungary, and Czechoslovakia were accompanied by demands for power sharing.

Yielding to pressure, in 1989 the Communist Party in Poland permitted the first free elections in over 40 years, in which Solidarity won a landslide victory. When no reprisals from Moscow were forthcoming, Lech Wałęsa was elected Poland's president in 1990. In Czechoslovakia, demonstrations toppled the ruling communist regime of President Husák in 1989 without bloodshed (the so-called Velvet Revolution). In its place, a coalition government consisting of the Party and members of the noncommunist Civic Forum was established, and in 1990 Vaclav Havel (1936–2011), a writer and dissident, was named president.

In the German Democratic Republic (GDR, East Germany), a particularly dramatic shift occurred. Massive demonstrations led to the fall first of the communist government and then of the Berlin Wall on the night of November 9, 1989. A year later, with Gorbachev's blessing, the two Germanys united, ending nearly a half century of division.

Communist governments now fell in other Soviet Bloc countries, as well (see Map 30.2). The governments of the Baltic states of Estonia, Latvia, and Lithuania, as well as that of Bulgaria, gave way to democracy. Albania followed suit in 1992. The only exception was Romania, where Nicolae Ceauşescu (in office 1974–1989) had built a strong personality cult. Following a mass demonstration in Bucharest

The Fall of Communism in Eastern Europe and the Soviet Union

Former republics of the Soviet Union gaining independence in 1991	Independence from Soviet Union declared 1991; at war with Russia, 1994–2000	—— Boundary of the former Soviet Union to 1991
Boundary of Russian Federation after December 1991	Former Warsaw Pact country holding free elections, 1990–1992	♨ Violent ethnic conflicts

MAP 30.2 **The Fall of Communism in Eastern Europe and the Soviet Union.**

map analysis

in November 1989, portions of the army defected and arrested Ceaușescu and his wife, Elena. Army elements assembled a tribunal, sentenced the two to death, and executed them on December 25, 1989. Subsequently, the army and the Communist Party reconciled, and the country returned to a dictatorship. It was not until 1996 that Romania adopted a democratic system.

In 1990, most of the 15 states making up the Soviet Union declared their sovereignty or independence. Gorbachev agreed with the state presidents to a new federal union treaty for the Soviet Union in spring 1991. This treaty triggered an abortive plot by eight communist hardliners who briefly succeeded in arresting

Two views of why the Cold War ended: Stephen Sestanovich, "Did the West Undo the East?" (1993), and Wade Huntley, "Who Won the Cold War?" (1993)

Gorbachev. In a tense showdown with troops sent to occupy the Russian parliament, a crowd of Muscovites forced the hardliners to relent. Officially, the Soviet Union ended on Christmas Day, 1991, replaced by the Commonwealth of Independent States.

Transforming the West

While North America and Western Europe enjoyed growth and social change from the late 1940s through the early 1960s, the period from 1963 through the early 1970s was particularly dynamic. Social movements involving peaceful protests and civil disobedience rose in prominence. Other movements, however, advocated violent confrontation.

Civil Rights Movements

The massive mobilization of Americans during World War II accelerated civil rights efforts. Recognition of African American participation in the armed forces, along with repugnance toward Nazi racial policies, made segregation in the military increasingly untenable. In 1947, therefore, President Truman desegregated the American armed forces. In 1954, the Supreme Court reversed its earlier stand on segregation in education in the *Brown v. Board of Education* ruling. Overturning the 1896 *Plessy v. Ferguson* decision that "separate but equal" facilities were constitutional, the court now ruled that the separate facilities were by definition not equal. This met with resistance in many communities; in 1957, President Dwight D. Eisenhower (in office 1953–1961) was compelled to deploy US Army troops to Little Rock, Arkansas, to enforce the ruling. Still, by the early 1960s there was a dramatic movement under way for civil rights and equal treatment for African Americans in the American south.

Lyndon Johnson on the Great Society: commencement address at the University of Michigan (1964)

The Civil Rights Struggle. The career of the charismatic minister Dr. Martin Luther King, Jr., was launched during the 1955 Montgomery, Alabama, bus boycott. By the early 1960s he had emerged as America's preeminent civil rights leader. Here, he is shown at the peak of his influence, delivering his famous "I Have a Dream" speech on the Mall in Washington, DC, in August 1963.

The Postwar Drive for Civil Rights The movement for desegregation was prompted by international conditions, as well. Postwar anti-colonialism, particularly in Africa, had a powerful influence on the American civil rights movement. The Cold War also played a role, as Soviet propaganda had exploited the discrepancies between American claims of equality and its treatment of African Americans. Guaranteeing civil rights would render that Soviet argument obsolete.

Finally, when participants in civil rights marches were attacked in some cities in the early 1960s, President John F. Kennedy reacted by sponsoring civil rights legislation.

After Kennedy was assassinated in 1963, his successor, Lyndon B. Johnson, secured the passage of the Civil Rights Act of 1964, followed by the 1965 Voting Rights Act. With legal remedies now in place for past discrimination, civil rights leaders increasingly turned their attention to economic and social justice.

Civil Rights for Native Americans Native American activists in the 1960s and 1970s also campaigned to rectify previous abuses, including past treaty violations. The American Indian Movement (AIM) initiated actions in 1968 to end police mistreatment and harassment and advocate for better housing and other issues. In 1973 armed AIM members laid siege to Wounded Knee, South Dakota, to commemorate the massacre of hundreds of Native Americans there in 1890. After a standoff with federal troops, several AIM leaders were charged with violations of federal laws; a negotiated settlement was finally reached when these charges were dismissed. The end result, however, was improved conditions for Native Americans.

Women's Rights and the Sexual Revolution   While the suffragist movement during World War I had led to voting rights for women in both Great Britain and the United States, the more sweeping social changes brought on by World War II and the Cold War advanced the movement for equality in gender relations further. European and American women demanded an end to restrictions placed upon their reproductive and sexual freedoms. Laws prohibiting contraception and abortion were overturned in several Western countries during the 1960s and 1970s, and the 1973 US Supreme Court decision *Roe v. Wade* protected a woman's right to have an abortion. By the late 1960s, the "women's liberation" movement worked toward equal pay for equal work and more social freedom for women to pursue careers outside the home.

National Organization of Women, statement on rights for American women (1966); Pope Paul VI, *Humanae Vitae* (1968)

Gay Rights Movement   Gay and lesbian Americans also fought for their civil rights during this era. The so-called Stonewall Riot is considered the flashpoint of the contemporary gay rights movement. On the night of June 28, 1969, New York City police raided the Stonewall Inn, a gay bar in Greenwich Village. Patrons fought back, shouting "Gay power!" Gay activists and protesters converged on the scene in subsequent days, demanding an end to discrimination against gays and lesbians.

interview with members of the Gay Liberation Front (1970)

In the months that followed gay and lesbian activists launched the Gay Liberation Front (GLF), and the movement spread around the globe. In subsequent years, greater social and legal equality for LGBT (Lesbian, Gay, Bisexual, Transgender) people, including same-sex marriages, has emerged.

The Global Youth Movement   A new global generation, known as "baby boomers" (those born during the postwar "baby boom" between 1945 and 1964), emerged during the postwar era. United by common bonds expressed in terms of dress, pop music, and shared ideologies, this new generation repudiated the rigidity of their parents by growing their hair long, wearing jeans, T-shirts, and "workers'" clothing; dabbling in Asian philosophies; taking drugs; and engaging in sexual experimentation.

The early center for this "hippie" movement was San Francisco, in which 1967 was proclaimed the "summer of love." Musical groups espousing hippie values— often crudely summed up as "sex, drugs, and rock and roll"—dominated much of the popular music scene during this time. Perhaps the peak of this movement came in August 1969, when the Woodstock Festival in New York State drew an estimated 300,000–500,000 attendees. Though the hippie movement as a force for liberation from confining mainstream values had largely spent itself by the early 1970s, its influence in fashion, sexual attitudes, music, and drug use continues to some extent even today.

From Women's Liberation to Feminism

The 1960s and 1970s are considered to mark the beginning of "second-wave feminism," a renewal of the push that crested with "first-wave" feminism's achievement of suffrage (see Map 30.3). During this period, women seeking change had the examples of the African American civil rights and anti-war movements on which to draw.

By the mid-1960s American women were becoming dissatisfied with what they perceived as the latent *sexism* of other progressive organizations. In response, they founded the National Organization for Women (NOW) in 1966. The term "women's liberation" began to appear. At first, leaders of the movement agitated for equity in the workplace, women's studies in higher education, and less gendered forms of address (like "Ms."). Previously personal matters, such as birth control and abortion, became political issues as well.

By the 1990s, feminist concerns became part of the political landscape of

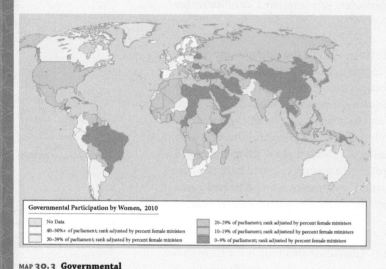

Governmental Participation by Women, 2010

No Data	20–29% of parliament; rank adjusted by percent female ministers
40–50%+ of parliament; rank adjusted by percent female ministers	10–19% of parliament; rank adjusted by percent female ministers
30–39% of parliament; rank adjusted by percent female ministers	0–9% of parliament; rank adjusted by percent female ministers

MAP 30.3 **Governmental Participation by Women.**

Students recall the Mexican Student Movement of 1968

Student Demonstrations in the 1960s   In protest against what they perceived as the excessive materialism, conformism, and sexual prudishness of the previous generation, student activists in the 1960s and 1970s held protests in the United States, Japan, and European and South American countries. Even developing countries like Cuba and China, as well as Eastern Bloc countries, experienced similar protests. In each instance, student activists shared similar ideologies and goals.

For many of the thousands of idealistic students who had taken part in civil rights demonstrations in the early 1960s, the anti-war movement seemed to be a natural transition. By 1965, the American military effort in Vietnam sparked protests against the war. This was particularly true for young people of draft age. The anti-war movement became more mainstream over the next several years.

In 1968, the assassinations of civil rights leader Martin Luther King, Jr. and the anti-war presidential candidate Robert Kennedy increased tensions. Student demonstrations now shook much of the Western world. The most serious of these took place in Paris, where students at the University of Paris took to the streets in a rebel movement that spread beyond the students to the labor sector and eventually brought down the French government. Many around the world now called for revolutionary violence directed against governments and programs funded by the military.

In Italy and West Germany, violent revolutionary organizations such as the Red Brigades and the Baader-Meinhof Gang emerged. With the end of American many countries. "Feminism" encompasses such causes as equal pay in the workplace, reproductive rights, greater sexual freedom, and the elimination of discrimination on the basis of gender. Greater attention is now paid to the problem of the "feminization of poverty" in the developing world, and female poverty is understood to be linked with the patriarchy embedded in long-standing cultural practices.

Cross-cultural interactions have enhanced worldwide movements to advance women's rights. In 1977 the UN General Assembly declared the first annual International Women's Day. Feminist authors and activists found audiences in countries around the world—among them, Ding Ling in China, Huda Shaarawi and Nawal El-Saadawi in Egypt, Madhu Kishwar in India, and Fatima Mernissi in Morocco. As an indication of women's increasing importance in global politics, many countries have had female prime ministers and presidents.

Women's Liberation in India. Members of the National Federation of Dalit Women demonstrate in support of rights for women of the dalit ("untouchables") caste in New Delhi, India, in 2008. While discrimination against dalit is proscribed by law in India, bias against dalit women is still widespread.

Questions

- How does the women's liberation movement demonstrate many of the characteristics of evolving modernity?

- Why does feminism promise to be the great emancipation movement of the twenty-first century?

involvement in Vietnam and the draft in the early 1970s, however, these groups either disbanded, went fully underground, or were dismantled by the authorities.

Economy and Politics in the 1970s and 1980s   A sudden economic downturn in the early 1970s initiated a prolonged period of economic stagnation. One cause was the ramping down of the Vietnam War effort, which had driven the US defense industry. Another cause stemmed from renewed hostilities between the Arabs and Israelis in 1973. In retaliation for American support of Israel in the so-called Yom Kippur or Ramadan War of this year (see p. 709), the newly formed OPEC, led by Arab states, dramatically increased the price of oil for export to America. The consequences of these economic downturns were at first inflation and then, by the late 1970s, **stagflation**. The emergence of developing economies in Asia and South America also began to lure American manufacturers to relocate to these countries in order to take advantage of lower labor costs.

These economic circumstances caused corresponding realignments in politics in the 1970s and 1980s. In some Western countries, the trend shifted toward the adoption of more conservative policies, most notably those of the American president Ronald Reagan and Britain's prime minister Margaret Thatcher (in office 1979–1990). Both leaders orchestrated cutbacks in governmental spending for social services and welfare programs, and in both countries industrial strikes and the power of labor unions were restricted and the nationalization of major industries was replaced by privatization.

Stagflation: Increased prices and record high interest rates but a stagnant economy overall.

From "Underdeveloped" to "Developing" World, 1963–1991

From the 1960s through the 1980s, the drive for economic development, national prestige, and national power continued to grow among newly independent nations. The period also marked the height of the contest among the nonaligned nations for preeminence between the two competing modernisms: market capitalism with democratic governments and variants of communism. Although many countries remained in dire poverty, the period also witnessed many more moving from the category of "underdeveloped" to the more optimistic one of "developing."

While the prosperity of the West in this period impressed leaders in the developing world, many, if not most, continued to question whether capitalism was appropriate for their nations as an economic system. The examples of the Soviet Union and China, and implicitly the Communist Bloc countries, appeared to show that formerly poor countries could quickly become rich and powerful—even to the point of being superpowers. Moreover, Marxist theorists argued that underdevelopment was *caused* by capitalism and imperialism.

China: Cultural Revolution to Four Modernizations

The People's Republic of China experienced wrenching policy changes during the period 1963–1991. The death of Mao in 1976, for example, ushered in a complete reversal of economic course. In 1978, the new Chinese leader Deng Xiaoping called for opening the country and creating a market economy—that is, introducing capitalism. To this day, China's economic policy is officially called "socialism with Chinese characteristics."

China's "Thermidorean Reaction," 1960–1966   The turbulence of the first round of the Maoist years calmed under the leadership of Liu Shaoqi. Some scholars, seeing in this retreat from radicalism a movement akin to France's end of the Reign of Terror during the month of "Thermidor" in 1794, have dubbed the Liu Shaoqi period as China's "Thermidorean Reaction." The decade began, however, with the Sino–Soviet split, in which mutual distrust between Mao and Khruschev led to a withdrawal of Soviet aid in 1960.

In the early 1960s, China made important technological advances with military implications: the detonation of China's first nuclear device in October 1964, the testing of a thermonuclear (hydrogen) device in 1966, and advances in missile technology that led to the first Chinese satellites. In addition, Liu's regime engaged in a more assertive policy of border rectification. This kind of display of force would be seen later in China's attack on Vietnam in 1979.

The Cultural Revolution   As China's Communist Party and government assumed a more Soviet-style approach, Mao Zedong grew uneasy about the party's seeming lack of interest in pushing the revolution toward a pure communism. Mao's position of politics taking command was in direct opposition to the increasingly technocratic stance he saw in Liu Shaoqi's policies. Mao plotted his comeback, publishing his famous "little red book," *Quotations from Chairman Mao Zedong*, in 1964.

Cultural Revolution
poster (1967)

His ideological ally Lin Biao, vice premier and head of the People's Liberation Army (in office 1954–1971), made it required reading for the troops and helped Mao establish a power base.

In the spring of 1966, Mao called on the nation's youth to rededicate themselves to "continuous revolution." He announced the Great Proletarian **Cultural Revolution**, the purpose of which was to stamp out the last vestiges of "bourgeois" and "feudal" Chinese society. Students formed squads of Red Guards and attacked their teachers, bosses, and elders. By August, millions of Red Guards converged on Beijing, where Mao addressed them in Tiananmen Square.

From 1966 until 1969, when the Cultural Revolution was officially declared over, millions of people were persecuted or murdered by Red Guards and their allies. China's official ideology was now listed as "Marxism–Leninism–Mao Zedong Thought." By 1968 the country was in complete chaos as pro– and anti–Cultural Revolution factions battled each other. It was chiefly to end this civil war that in the following year Mao declared the Cultural Revolution over.

Cultural Revolution: Socio-political movement (1966–1976) set in motion by Mao Zedong that purged remnants of capitalist and traditional elements from Chinese society and reimposed Maoist thought as the dominant ideology within the Communist Party.

"To Get Rich Is Glorious": China's Four Modernizations   Despite the Sino–Soviet split, the People's Republic had maintained a strong anti-American posture. This was matched by American Cold War antipathy toward "Red China" as a linchpin of the Communist Bloc. By the early 1970s, however, with Soviet–Chinese tensions still high, President Richard Nixon made a bold visit to the People's Republic, which resulted in the Shanghai Communiqué of 1972. In this document, the United States and the People's Republic of China announced plans to initiate formal diplomatic and cultural relations; the United States pledged to no longer block the People's Republic's bid for a seat in the United Nations; and the United States agreed to downgrade its diplomatic presence in Taiwan.

The death of Mao Zedong in September 1976 led to a repudiation of the Cultural Revolution and an entirely different direction in strategy for China. Deng Xiaoping ([Deng shiao PING]; in office 1978–1992) emerged in 1978 as the new leader. The pragmatic Deng implemented the fundamental policies that remain in force in China: the Four Modernizations.

Deng Xiaoping on reforming socialism (1979)

Deng's strategy relied on upgrading the quality of agriculture, industry, science, technology, and the military. China would pursue a new "open-door" policy with regard to foreign expertise from the West; it would allow its own students to study abroad; and it would allow the market forces of capitalism to encourage innovation in all sectors of the economy. China's new motto became "To get rich is glorious!"

The "responsibility system," as it was called, was introduced in a special economic zone set up in south China at Shenzhen. The experiments in capitalism would then be expanded to the country at large once any flaws had been corrected. Peasants were among the first beneficiaries as the communes were disbanded, individual plots assigned, and market incentives introduced. By the mid-1980s, China was rapidly approaching self-sufficiency in food production; by the 1990s, it would register surpluses. With the privatization and modernization of Chinese industry, the 1990's saw the People's Republic's GDP register annual double-digit rises. By 2010 it surpassed Japan as the second-largest economy in the world, after the United States.

Tiananmen Square Demonstrations. At their peak in May 1989, the demonstrations by students seeking greater government accountability and a more open political system were joined by workers and people from all walks of life. This memorable image of the suppression of the demonstration shows a lone figure, known to the world afterward only as "Tank Man," confronting a Chinese armored column. The driver of the tank tried to get around the man and eventually stopped, together with the other tanks. At that point, demonstrators pulled the man back to safety. His subsequent fate remains unknown. Both images were widely broadcast throughout the world.

Another, more controversial, innovation was the "one-child" policy. Population pressures were a powerful brake on China's development. Thus, a policy was inaugurated in 1979 mandating that most families were to have only one child. Despite the problems in enforcing such a policy, and its severe cultural impact on the male-centered traditional Chinese family structure, China's population has remained remarkably stable since the 1980s at around 1.3–1.5 billion. The policy has, however, abetted problems of selective female abortion, the giving up of girl babies for adoption, and even female infanticide. There is also a significant gender imbalance: China currently has 117 male births for every 100 female births. Because of this imbalance and the fear that a reduced working population will not be able to support the expanding number of retirees, the one-child policy was effectively discontinued in 2015.

Tiananmen Square Massacre   Pro-democracy protests began taking place in Beijing following the death of the popular moderate leader Hu Yaobang in 1989. The gatherings grew as the seventieth anniversary of the May Fourth nationalist movement grew closer. The Politburo debated how to deal with the protests. When they prepared a declaration of martial law, a number of high-ranking army officers expressed doubts: They argued that the People's Army could not possibly shoot its own people. The most prominent figure refusing any order to shoot was Major General Xu Qinxian [shoo chin-SHEE-YAN], according to new documents publicized by the *New York Times* in June 2014 at the occasion of the twenty-fifth anniversary of the Tiananmen Massacre. But the Politburo prevailed, and during June 2–4, soldiers crushed what to many among the leaders seemed to be an incipient rebellion. To this day, the number of killed is unknown. General Xu was court-martialed and imprisoned for four years, living thereafter in a military sanatorium in northern China.

Vietnam and Cambodia: War and Communist Rule
In a US-supported coup in Vietnam, a group of generals overthrew President Ngo Dinh Diem shortly after the climax of the Cold War, the Cuban Missile Crisis, in November 1963. Neither the generals nor the new constitutional government under the now civilian President Nguyen Van Thieu (in office 1965–1975), however, were able to stem the advances of the Communist Vietcong that had begun in 1959–1960 under the direction of the North Vietnamese communists. In spite of massive American support until 1973, the Thieu government, plagued by accusations of corruption, failed to gain popular support and eventually fell to the communists in 1975.

The American War in Vietnam   In the summer of 1964, a US-supported South Vietnamese naval raid on two North Vietnamese islands provoked a North Vietnamese retaliation with torpedo boats against American ships in the Gulf of Tonkin. (Documents declassified in 2005–2006 reveal that there was indeed such a retaliation but that a reported massive follow-up two days later never took place.)

The American Secretary of Defense, Robert McNamara (in office 1961–1968), failing to reveal the US-supported raid and asserting the truth of the North Vietnamese follow-up attack, persuaded President Johnson to ask and receive from Congress the so-called Gulf of Tonkin Resolution. This resolution empowered Johnson to conduct full conventional warfare in Southeast Asia, including against North Vietnam.

Accordingly, by 1965 tens of thousands of American combat troops had been sent to support the South Vietnamese against the Vietcong. But the US action was plagued by murky goals and the impatience of a domestic American public hoping for quick, decisive results. Was this war a necessary part of the Cold War—pushing back against Soviet Communism—or was it a war against a Southeast Asian communist national liberation movement? Should young Americans, at that time subject to the draft, serve in this war? The task of "winning the hearts and minds of the people" of South Vietnam against the Vietcong, in addition, was tortuous at best and hampered by the increasing presence of the foreign US military, which reached a high of over a half-million troops by 1967 (see Map 30.4).

In February 1968, on the Vietnamese lunar new year (*Tet*), the Vietcong, supported by North Vietnamese forces, attacked the South Vietnamese capital of Saigon and other cities. American and South Vietnamese forces counterattacked, destroying the Vietcong as an effective fighting force. In the US, however, the magnitude of the Tet Offensive, as it came to be called, was seen as evidence that US strategy had not been effective and was thus considered by many as an American defeat. In the wake of massive protests against the war, President Johnson announced he would not seek reelection, and the way

MAP 30.4 **The Vietnam War.**

The Arab–Israeli War of June 1967. The stunning victory of Israel over the combined armies of Syria and Egypt generated admiration in the West and consternation in the Arab world and the Soviet Bloc. The Israelis' preemptive use of air power against Egyptian and Syrian air forces and tank and troop concentrations and their expert use of armor proved the deciding factors in the conflict. Here, Egyptian prisoners (in white underclothes in the truck to the right) are being transferred to holding camps (*top*). The war also led to a dramatic rise in the popularity of the Palestinian cause in the Arab and communist spheres. Here, Yasir Arafat marches with members of Fatah in 1970 (*bottom*).

image analysis

was clear for the United States to begin negotiations to end the war by political means. With the election of Richard Nixon in 1968, a combination of massive bombings of North Vietnam and Cambodian supply lines for North Vietnamese forces and peace talks in Paris eventually brought America's role in the war to an end. Though South Vietnam survived the peace treaty in 1973, the American withdrawal spelled its demise within 2 years. The country was now finally united under Communism.

The Khmer Rouge   Much of Vietnam, Cambodia, and Laos lay devastated from fighting and bombing. Over the next 2 years a Cambodian revolutionary group, the Khmer Rouge ("Red Khmers," that is, the Communists in the dominant ethnic group of Khmers), launched a radical program of urban depopulation, forced labor, and mass killing against religious and political opponents. Perhaps one-third of the country's population (equal to 1.3 million dead) was killed as a result. The genocidal ideas and practices of the Khmer Rouge leader, Pol Pot (1925–1998), were so radical and brutal that in 1977 Vietnam invaded the state and initiated his overthrow in favor of a more moderate and pliable candidate. In response, China invaded Vietnam in 1979 but was soon repulsed by Vietnamese forces—an invasion that was the last and least successful of the many Chinese attempts launched over two millennia.

The Middle East

One of the most troubled areas of the world during the twentieth century was the Middle East. Since 1945, the area encompassing the Arabian Peninsula, Iran, Iraq, and the eastern shores of the Mediterranean has seen a number of major wars and minor conflicts, as well as attacks directed against the religious symbols of Judaism, Christianity, and Islam.

Israeli and Arab Conflict   By far the most contentious issue in the Middle East has been the presence of the Jewish state of Israel. During the 1950s and 1960s, Israel was largely seen in the West as fighting democracy's battles against authoritarian Arab states supported by the Soviet Union. Immigrants in the postwar decades helped the new state to build an efficient agriculture—often through the socialist device of the communal farm, or *kibbutz*—and a sophisticated manufacturing sector. West German reparations, compensating for Jewish losses during the Third Reich, helped financially. Mandatory military service and American support also contributed to the creation of superior armed forces.

The "Six-Day War" For the Palestinian Arabs and their allies, the rise of Israel was "the disaster." Hundreds of thousands displaced since 1948 awaited decades to return. In the Cold War climate, the Arab states viewed Israel as a new Western imperial outpost in what was rightfully Arab territory. Consequently, attempts at Arab unity were premised on war with Israel. While Arab nationalism was largely secular, and often socialist-leaning with Soviet support, Muslim fundamentalist groups such as Egypt's Muslim Brotherhood gained adherents, despite government repression.

In 1964, Yasir Arafat (1929–2004) formed the Palestine Liberation Organization (PLO), whose militant wing, Fatah, began a guerilla war against Israel. Matters came to a head on May 22, 1967, when Egypt closed the Gulf of Aqaba to Israeli shipping, preventing the importation of oil. President Gamal Abdel Nasser (in office 1956–1970) relied on faulty Soviet secret service information of an Israeli mobilization. Following an Egyptian military buildup along the Sinai border and the expulsion of UN forces there, Iraq sent troops to Jordan at its invitation, and local Muslim leaders began to call for holy war against Israel. On June 5 the Israelis launched an air assault to neutralize the Egyptian and Syrian air forces. With an overwhelming advantage in numbers and quality of aircraft, Israel took out the Arab armor and ground troops. The Six-Day War, as it came to be called, enlarged the state of Israel by conquering the West Bank, the Golan Heights, and the Gaza Strip and Sinai Peninsula—territories belonging to Jordan, Syria, and Egypt, respectively. To many observers in the Middle East, it appeared that Israel was now a state bent on expansion.

The Arab-Israeli Wars of 1967 and 1973

▓ Israel, before 1967 war	▨ Territory occupied by Israel, Oct 1973
☐ Territory occupied by Israel, June 1967	▨ Territory occupied by Egypt, Oct 1973

MAP 30.5 **The Arab–Israeli Wars, 1967 and 1973.**

The Yom Kippur/Ramadan War In early October 1973, Egypt, Syria, and a coalition of Arab states launched a massive attack during the Jewish holy day of Yom Kippur, which in 1973 coincided with the Muslim holy month of Ramadan. This time, with Israel, the United States, and the Soviet Union caught unawares, Egyptian tanks crossed the Suez Canal and attacked Israel (see Map 30.5). After initially conceding ground, Israeli forces managed to ultimately defeat the combined Arab armies once again.

A cease-fire was brokered by the United Nations, but the intensity of the fighting and the resupply efforts by the United States and Soviet Union moved both superpowers dangerously close to direct confrontation. For their part, the Arab oil producers and Iran launched an oil embargo against the United States. Stringent measures

National Charter of the Palestinian Liberation Organization (1968), Likud Party platform, Israel (1977)

and sharply higher gasoline prices drove home to Americans how dependent they had become on foreign oil, and encouraged new interests in alternative forms of energy.

For Egypt, the defeat resulted in a transformation of its hitherto futile policy toward Israel. President Anwar el-Sadat (in office 1970–1981) took the initiative in undertaking peace talks by visiting Israel in 1977. In 1979, with the backing of the American president Jimmy Carter, Egypt and Israel signed the first treaty between an Arab country and the Jewish state. Egypt and Jordan are the only Arab states to date to maintain diplomatic and cultural relations with Israel. Syria remained hostile, while the PLO continued its efforts from Jordan. Profound resentment of Sadat for signing the treaty festered among many Egyptians. Despite some concessions to increasingly vocal fundamentalist Muslim groups, Sadat was assassinated in 1981.

The Lebanese Civil War   This war of 1975–1989 had it roots in the transfer of the PLO's power base from Jordan to Lebanon in the aftermath of the 1967 war. Jordan's stability was built on a precarious balance between the Palestinian refugees of 1948 and the indigenous Jordanian Arab population. After Jordan lost the West Bank to Israel, Arafat moved the PLO to the east bank and intended to build up a state within the state of Jordan from which to continue to attack Israel. But in the "Black September" of 1970, the Jordanian army expelled the PLO to protect the integrity of its state.

After transferring to Lebanon, the PLO upset the precarious balance among the different religious and political factions of this Arab country. The Maronites (eastern Christians in communion with Catholicsm) were politically dominant, though numerically inferior to the Muslims, who were divided into a Shiite majority and a Sunni minority. By taking over command in the Palestinian refugee camps (12 percent of Lebanon's population), Arafat again built a Palestinian state, this time within the state of Lebanon, from which the PLO and other Palestinian groups launched attacks on Israel. The Maronites, taking a dim view of the growing strength of the PLO, expanded their paramilitary militias, which existed parallel to the national army. Since the government refused to have the national army intervene in the Christian–PLO conflict in favor of one or the other side, the Christian militias took matters into their own hands in April 1975. In a number of clashes, they inflicted severe losses on the PLO and allied Muslims. The army dissolved and its constituent elements joined the various militias. The Christian-PLO confrontation evolved into a general Christian–Muslim civil war, which the Christians were losing.

Syria entered the war in 1976 and Israel in 1982, complicating the civil war further. On one hand, Syria ended the worst fighting, but on the other, its entry on the Christian side meant that the sectarian lines were frozen, with each group establishing its predominance in a part of the country. The PLO, for its part, became the dominant faction in the Shiite south, from where it launched raids into Israeli territory. Israel responded first with the erection of a security zone in southern Lebanon in 1976 and then, in 1982, with a three-month invasion of the country, in order to drive the PLO from Lebanon. The PLO was forced to relocate to Tunisia, far from Israel. Syria remained the dominant power in Lebanon, but in the face of its unrestrained manipulation of Lebanese politics, which included disappearances and assassinations, the Arab League eventually stepped in and in 1989 brokered the so-called Taif Agreement, which established an uneasy peace. In 2005 the UN eventually forced Syria to withdraw, but Lebanon found it difficult to return a unified government back to power.

The Iranian Islamic Revolution Massive urban demonstrations drove Shah Muhammad Reza Pahlavi (r. 1941–1979) into exile in November–December 1979. Moderately Islamist opposition leaders took over the government but were soon outmaneuvered by Ayatollah Ruhollah Khomeini (1902–1989), who returned triumphantly from his French exile on February 1, 1980. Using a small book entitled *The Islamic Government*, published in 1970, as his blueprint, Khomeini proclaimed an Islamic revolution in the country and systematically revamped all Iranian institutions according to this blueprint. For the execution of the revolution, he relied on a half-dozen militant and paramilitary groups that bypassed the Iranian army with its many royal sympathizers.

poster showing the overthrow of the Shah (1980)

The overthrow of the Pahlavi monarchy was possible because the shah, an indecisive but at times also ambitious ruler, lost his nerve in the course of urban demonstrations in 1978. He had introduced the so-called White Revolution in 1964 with which he wanted to bring about an agrarian reform and industrial revolution that would propel Iran within a short time into the ranks of the industrial powers. While in principle such a revolution made sense, the shah was not ruthless enough—nor could he count on enough dedicated supporters—to see his White Revolution to its end. Among the losers in the White Revolution was the Shiite clergy, which had to give up a great deal of the agricultural property associated with the shrines and seminaries—hence Khomeini's bitter opposition and exile beginning in 1964.

The Islamic Republic created by Khomeini is a theocracy ruled by the Quran and the Islamic Tradition as defined by Shiite Islamic religious scholars and additionaly defined by Khomeini as ruled by Iran's Shiite clergy. Accordingly, Iranian women have to follow a dress code, men and women are gender-segregated, and candidates for office are vetted for their faith. This utopian return to a premodern Islamic past is modernized by a constitution that allows for elections and a parliament under a president. But ultimate authority lies with a "Spiritual Guide," who is selected from among about half-a-dozen ayatollahs at the top of the clergy. Until the return of the Twelfth Imam at the end of time (see Chapter 10), the Spiritual Guide rules on both spiritual and worldly matters.

While the Iranian revolution was still unfolding, the president of neighboring Iraq, Saddam Hussein (in office 1979–2003) decided in September 1980 to invade the fledgling theocracy and occupy the oil-rich province of Khuzistan. But after some initial successes, his army got bogged down, and a ferocious war of position ensued, in which the initially militarily inferior Iranians sent wave after wave of young men into the artillery fire of the Iraqis. Khomeini sought to salvage the Shiite revolutionary fervor by having one of his militant groups, the "Muslim Student Followers of the Imam's Line," take 52 US embassy personnel hostage, in retaliation for the US granting the Shah medical asylum. The hostage crisis, lasting 444 days, was eventually resolved by President Jimmy Carter in January 1981, and the Iran–Iraq War was eventually settled with UN intervention in 1988, largely in favor of Iran.

Ayatollah Ruhollah Khomeini, "Message to the Pilgrims" (1980)

Africa: From Independence to Development

During the period 1963–1991, the main struggles in Africa moved from ones mainly concerned with completing the pattern of decolonization and independence to ones involving development. As in other parts of the postcolonial world, vigorous internal debates were conducted about strategies for economic development. But in nearly all cases, the economies of the newly independent states were problematic. In most cases they were tied to their former colonial regimes by means of the same raw materials that had been exploited under colonialism. Moreover, they were competing in the markets for these products with other former colonies.

Catholic relief organization poster illustrating the crisis in Biafra (1968)

Nigeria: Civil War and Troubled Legacies   Nigeria's independence had a promising start; it entered the postcolonial era as a republic with a British parliamentary system, Commonwealth membership, and a federal-style constitution. Like many African former colonies, however, Nigeria was also saddled with ethnic and religious conflicts as a legacy of the colonial divisions of the continent. Thus, its growing pains were marked by clashes between its established system of constitutionalism and the desires of its major constituent groups for their own nation-states.

The three major antagonistic groups, the Hausa, Igbo, and Yoruba, were divided by history, culture, religion, and language. The largest, the Hausa, were Muslims from the northern region. The Igbo, living mostly in the eastern region where valuable oil deposits had been recently discovered, were predominantly Christian or African-spiritual. The Yoruba in the west, who controlled most of the national offices, were predominantly Muslim, although there were also Christian Yoruba.

Starting in 1966, under strongman Yakubu Gowon (in office 1966–1975), the central government had authorized raids to bring Igbo areas under greater control. In 1967, the eastern Igbo region declared itself independent as the state of Biafra. What followed was perhaps the bloodiest civil war of the era. More than 1 million Biafrans died before Biafra surrendered in early 1970. From then until 1991, Nigeria was ruled by a series of military strongmen. By 1991, the future that had seemed so promising in 1960 seemed impossible.

Zimbabwe: The Revolution Continued   Some of the former European colonies in Africa came to independence with substantial populations of white settlers who were opposed to independence. When it came, they sought guarantees from the new governments against expropriation of land, discrimination, and reprisals. In 1964 the old colony of Northern Rhodesia gained independence as Zambia. Threatened by the independence of nearby black African nations and confident of support from apartheid-based South Africa, the white leaders of the territory that had been Southern Rhodesia but now called itself simply "Rhodesia" declared unilateral independence in 1965 and set up a government under Ian Smith (in office 1965–1970). Distressed at this move, Britain refused to recognize the new government and expelled Rhodesia from the Commonwealth. Few countries outside of South Africa recognized the regime, which now faced a guerilla movement from within.

Two rival groups, the Zimbabwe African National Union (ZANU) under Robert Mugabe (b. 1924) and the Zimbabwe African People's Union (ZAPU) led by Joshua Nkomo (1917–1999), struggled to bring Smith's regime down and create a majority-rule state. The war lasted throughout the 1960s and 1970s, until Mugabe and ZANU finally triumphed and created a new state called Zimbabwe in 1980. Mugabe's regime pledged fairness to the remaining white settlers and set about creating a socialist state. By the 1990s, however, vigilante seizures of white lands by "revolutionary veterans" became a regular occurrence. By the early 2000s, the chaotic agricultural sector combined with repression of opposition to ZANU one-party rule had plunged the country into a serious economic crisis.

South Africa: From Apartheid to "Rainbow Nation"   South Africa, the richest of the continent's countries, also had the most complex and restrictive racial relations. By the nineteenth century, the Dutch-descended Boers had moved inland, pushing out the local people. The expansion of Zulu power forced the British rulers and Dutch settlers into protracted Zulu wars that by 1879 broke the last black polity

map showing segregated black "homelands" in South Africa (1973)

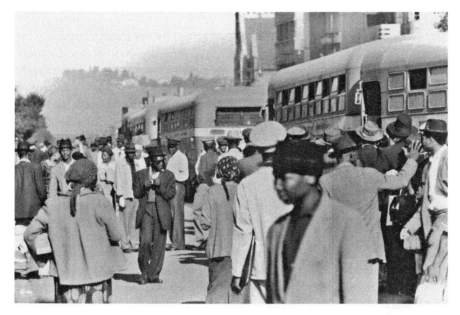

Black Commuters in South Africa. The regime of apartheid (the strict separation of the races) that had been inaugurated by the white minority government in South Africa in 1948 obliged all black citizens, such as these workers congregating in a Johannesburg train station in the late 1950s, to carry "passbooks" that specified what areas they were permitted to enter. Resentment at the passbook requirement prompted mass demonstrations that resulted in the Sharpeville Massacre of March 21, 1960, which in turn sparked widespread protests against the apartheid system.

in the region. By the end of the nineteenth century, the discovery of vast mineral wealth led to both the expansion of the colony's holdings and an influx of immigrants, including Chinese and Indians.

After 1910, immigration restrictions on Asians went into effect along with laws governing relations between whites and Africans. This trend culminated in the institution of **apartheid** (Afrikaans, "apartness") in 1948. Black South Africans were relegated to a legal second-class status.

Through the 1950s, South Africa faced international criticism for its policies. Moreover, as newly independent black majority countries completed the pattern of decolonization, the white government felt itself increasingly besieged. It pointed out that a few of these emerging states were Marxist and thus claimed that it was fighting against the expansion of the Soviet Bloc in Africa. Nonetheless, South Africa withdrew from the British Commonwealth in 1961, and a number of black political organizations—most prominently the African National Congress (ANC)—campaigned for the dismantling of apartheid.

By the 1980s it was clear that events would eventually force the dismantling of apartheid. International boycotts of South Africa had gained momentum, and the ANC, through a political and guerilla campaign, was making gradual gains. Finally, amid the collapse of communism in the Soviet Bloc, the newly elected president, Frederik Willem de Klerk (b. 1936), began reforms aimed ultimately at dismantling apartheid. The ANC was legalized and became South Africa's largest political party; its leader, Nelson Mandela (1918–2013), who had been imprisoned for nearly three decades, was released; in 1991 all apartheid laws were repealed; and finally, in 1992 white voters amended the constitution to mandate racial equality among all citizens. By 1994, the first multiracial elections were held, and Mandela became president of the new South Africa.

Apartheid: System of social and legal segregation by race enforced by the government of South Africa from 1948 until 1994.

Steve Biko "Black Consciousness and the Quest for a True Humanity" (1973)

Che Guevara, "Message to the Tricontinental" (1967)

Latin America: Proxy Wars

The 1960s in Latin American politics were marked by the forces contending for dominance against the backdrop of the Cold War. Here, however, because the countries in question had long since achieved their independence, the issues were largely ideological and economic, and centered around revolutionary politics.

By the 1970s, dissatisfaction with the authoritarian regimes of the region, particularly in Central America, resulted in revolutionary efforts, the most notable being in Nicaragua and El Salvador. Since the mid-1930s, the United States had supported the family of the authoritarian Nicaraguan strongman Anastasio Somoza García (collectively in office from 1936 to 1979). From the early 1960s a guerilla insurgency called the Sandinista National Liberation Front (FSLN) had sought to overthrow the Somozas and mount a socialist land-reform scheme. The Somoza regime fell in 1979, and Daniel Ortega (in office 1979–1990; 2007–) took the head of a new Sandinista government.

The socialist direction of the new regime prompted the American administration to cut off aid to Nicaragua, begin a covert operation to destabilize Ortega through the funding and arming of opposition groups known collectively as the Contras, and end trade with the regime. With US support increasing and aid from Cuba and the Soviet Bloc fading in the late 1980s, the two sides agreed to elections in 1990. These resulted in the presidency of the conservative Violeta Barrios de Chamorro (in office 1990–1997).

In similar fashion, guerilla groups in El Salvador fought US-backed government forces in a bloody conflict throughout the 1980s, until elections were finally held in 1992. By the early 1990s, however, the two sides, as in Nicaragua, had resolved to work within the new political system.

The commitment of the United States to opposing any groups espousing Marxist or communist beliefs in Latin America also revealed itself in covert policy toward governments recognized as legitimate. One such action was directed at Chilean President Salvador Allende (in office 1970–1973) in 1973. Allende had led a political coalition to a plurality win in 1970. Many of his policies met opposition within Chile, while his ideology and nationalization of American interests in Chile's mines pushed the Nixon administration to back his opposition.

With CIA help, Allende was overthrown, and the repressive regime of General Augusto Pinochet (in office 1973–1990) installed. Determined to suppress leftist groups, Pinochet launched Operation Colombo in 1975, resulting in the disappearance of activists and others perceived as threats to the government's plan to restore a capitalist economy. Throughout Pinochet's 16 years in power, his rule remained repressive, but Chile also became economically vibrant and began to move toward a more democratic government. In 1998 Pinochet was arrested in London on charges of human rights violations and torture. After a court battle, he was ultimately released and returned to Chile, where he died in 2006.

"The Dirty War" and the "Disappeared" One of the most tragic and internationally condemned episodes of this period was the "Dirty War" initiated by the military junta that overthrew the authoritarian regime of the Peróns (Juan and his third wife, Isabel) in Argentina. During the brutal regime of this junta, tens of thousands of real and alleged leftist Argentinians were kidnapped, imprisoned, and killed. These victims became known as the "disappeared." Their fate was poignantly brought to light by the Mothers of Plaza de Mayo, a group of women who kept vigil for lost friends and relatives in that plaza in Buenos Aires during 1977–2006.

In 1983, having provoked and lost the Falklands War with Great Britain, the junta stepped down, elections were held, and a National Commission on the Disappearance of Persons (CONADEP) was established in December. The progress of the commission and its findings of torture, killing, and indefinite incarceration caused an international sensation. Today, most of the surviving military and political leaders held responsible are in prison or have already served lengthy terms.

photos of the
Mothers of Plaza de
Mayo

The Brazilian Economic Miracle   Brazil experienced a right-wing military coup and regime during almost the same time (1964–1985) as Argentina. The military came to power during a period of import substitution industrialization, when the government made far-reaching plans for the nationalization of businesses and agrarian reform, both considered by the military to be communist-inspired. As in Argentina, the military hunted down dissidents, whether they were professed communists or not, and tortured them in prison. Small leftist guerilla movements operated in a few urban centers as well as in the rain forest, but their numbers were too small to withstand determined government action to wipe them out. Brazil coordinated its anti-leftist measures closely with the other southern cone countries, including Argentina.

The military leaders were astute enough to entrust the Brazilian economy to technocrats who continued the policy of import substitution. Easy foreign loans allowed for further investments in basic industries, infrastructure, nuclear research, and oil exploration. The results of the import substitution policy were impressive: Society became mostly urban (67 percent) and industrial exports grew from 20 percent in 1968 to 57 percent in 1979. The two massive oil price increases of 1973 and 1979, however, threw Brazil's foreign-debt-heavy economy into a deep crisis, severely damaging the popularity of the military regime. After years of economic crisis, the officers resigned themselves to retreating from politics and initiating a transition toward democracy with elections in 1985 and an amended constitution in 1988.

≫ Putting It All Together

During the years 1962 to 1991, the Cold War contest between capitalist democracy and various types of communism–socialism reached its climax. In the end, the wealth and power of the West, particularly the United States, ultimately wore the Soviet Bloc down. Along the way, China abruptly changed from extreme radical leftist programs during its Cultural Revolution to a capitalist style of market economics by 1991. Many other countries were now looking for some mixture of the two systems or a third way between the two. As the period drew to a close, it was, ironically, the two iconic communist regimes, the Soviet Union and the People's Republic of China, that were pioneering the way *out* of Marxist socialism. The Chinese sought to do this by retaining a powerful authoritarian government while embracing market economics. The former Soviet Union adopted democratic political values and guardedly introduced capitalism.

The next two decades, however, saw the emergence of new and unanticipated challenges to the domination of the capitalist–democratic order. For many, its secular character was evidence that the evolving culture of this version of modernity

interactive concept
map

Review and Relate

| Thinking Through Patterns

Examine the ways historians approach the big questions of this chapter.

≫ **How did the political landscape of the Cold War change from 1963 to 1991?**

Perhaps the biggest changes came in the 1980s. Though the United States had been defeated in Vietnam and was facing a recession at home, it still was the world's largest economy and could weather a protracted arms race. The Soviet Union was far more economically fragile—which ultimately made it ideologically fragile as well. The strains of Polish dissent, the Afghan War, and a renewed arms race with the United States wore the Soviet state down.

≫ **Why did such radically different lifestyles emerge in the United States and the West during the 1960s and 1970s? What is their legacy today?**

The prosperity of the United States and the West allowed younger people to experiment with new ideas of living and indulge their desires for new experiences. The idealism of the era also played a role, as did the threats of the military draft and nuclear war. The materialism of the age repelled many and made them long for a simpler existence.

≫ **Why did some nations that had emerged from colonialism and war make great strides in their development while others seemed to stagnate?**

The nations that prospered had already achieved self-sufficiency in agriculture, had a transportation and communications infrastructure, and maximized their labor force. China, under Deng Xiaoping, followed a modified version of this strategy and was already growing at record levels by 1991. In the following decades, nearly all Asian countries would follow suit, with India moving into the top ranks of development and growth. Many Latin American countries—in particular, Brazil—also made great strides.

In all cases, culture and ideology played a powerful role in encouraging citizens to believe that progress was possible. Peace and stability also played an important role. The many internal conflicts that plagued Latin America and Africa held back development during this period.

| Against the Grain

The African National Congress

Consider this as a counterpoint to the main patterns examined in this chapter.

In the early 1900s, the Union of South Africa adopted laws that formed the backbone of what in 1948 was to become apartheid, an official program of racial segregation. According to these laws, blacks were to be removed to reservations and trust lands, called "Bantustans," in the less-fertile eastern part of the country.

In protest against segregation and demanding equal rights, in 1912 a few black professionals organized what was to become the African National Congress (ANC). Their demands set the beginnings of the pattern of decolonization in the twentieth century. It required another generation, however, and the leadership of the law partners Oliver Thambo (1917–1993) and Nelson Mandela (1918–2013), before the ANC was able to become a mass movement. Thambo and Mandela formulated demands for land distribution, labor organization, and mass education.

After the Afrikaner nationalists came to power in 1948 and established outright apartheid, black South Africans were increasingly driven to join the ANC. During the 1950s, the government introduced race-marked passports, outlawed interracial marriages and sexual relations, demolished black shantytowns, resettled blacks, banned communism, and decreed segregated parks, beaches, buses, hospitals, schools, and universities. Determined to enforce apartheid, the government built up a massive bureaucracy, including an effective secret service.

Even though the events of the 1950s made the ANC a true representative of South African blacks, it held fast to its original program of multiracial and ideologically varied integration. Its mass protests and acts of sabotage through a newly created armed wing in 1961–1964 were met by the government with brutal repression. In the so-called Rivonia trial, the arrested ANC leadership, including Mandela, was condemned to imprisonment on Robben Island.

Courageous protests by student and labor organizations, churches, and white liberals continued, as did government brutality in response. The ANC, driven underground, also operated from abroad, where it helped in the creation, by the 1980s, of a coalition of Western states and organizations that sought to force South Africa to abolish apartheid. Ultimately, the ANC prevailed because of the collapse of the Soviet Bloc in 1989–1991; the apartheid regime could no longer claim that it was the final bulwark against world communism. In 1994, South Africa became a black-governed nation under the rule of the ANC.

- How does the ANC's support for racial integration, and its acceptance of differing political views, contrast with other nationalist and liberation movements from this period?

- Compare and contrast South African apartheid and segregation in the United States between 1918 and 1964. What are the similarities? What are the differences?

Nelson Mandela, Rivonia trial statement (1964)

Key Terms

audio flashcards

Apartheid 727	Glasnost 712	Stagflation 717
Cultural Revolution 719	Perestroika 712	

For additional resources, please go to
www.oup.com/us/vonsivers.
Please see the Further Resources section at the back of the book for additional readings and suggested websites.

A Fragile Capitalist-Democratic World Order

During the months of winter and spring of 2010–2011, crowds across the Arab world gathered to remonstrate with authoritarian governments over a wide range of issues. The governments challenged by these movements had long been propped up by brutal security services. Further, even if rulers pretended to have liberalized the economies of their countries, instead "crony capitalism" benefited their relatives and followers. Chronic unemployment left both the poor and the middle classes in despair over their future. While some unemployed youth had found solace in an Islamism whose preachers promised the solution for all ills, these preachers were no less able than the rulers to improve the daily lives of the people.

By mid-spring 2011 the massive protests had toppled the governments of Tunisia and Egypt. Syria and Bahrain sought to suppress the democracy movements, while in Libya, Yemen, and Syria, civil wars tore the populations apart. Remarkably, in conservative and male-dominated Yemen, the movement was led by a woman.   Tawakkol Karman, 32, the leader of Women Journalists Without Chains, harangued mostly male crowds with calls for revolution. "We are in need of heroes," said one Yemeni observer. "She manages to do what

Population increase, 1950–2010
Country where population increased by:
- ☐ 0–100%   ☐ 200–300%
- ☐ 100–200%   ☐ over 300%

ABOVE: Traumatized inhabitants lining up for humanitarian aid in the besieged eastern part of Aleppo, Syria, 2016, just prior to its fall.

most men cannot do in a society that is highly prejudiced against women." The Norwegian Nobel Committee made Tawakkol Karman the co-winner of the Peace Prize in 2013.

Unfortunately, the Yemeni political process did not stabilize. The country slid into a civil war after 2012, in which the Shiite minority of the Houthis sought to dominate the Sunni majority. The civil war turned into a proxy war between Shiite Iran and Sunni Saudi Arabia, the two dominant Middle Eastern powers. Unhappily, the civil war pushed Tawakkol Karman and her hope for a democratic Yemen completely to the sidelines.

A chieving modernity through urbanization, science, industrialization, the accumulation of capital, and grassroots participation in political pluralism has become close to a universal goal in the world. The story of how this pattern of modernity has grown to become nearly universal is the focus of this chapter.

Capitalist Democracy: The Dominant Pattern of Modernity

With the demise of communism, the struggle among the three ideologies of modernity that had characterized much of the twentieth century was now over. Some viewers argued that modernity had ended and we were at the beginning of a new age of **postmodernism** and **postcolonialism**. Less triumphant observers realized that democracy would not spread as long as countries remained poor and stuck in inherited forms of authoritarianism or even autocracy.

A Decade of Global Expansion: The United States and the World in the 1990s

In the aftermath of the collapse of communism, the United States was the most economically and politically powerful country on earth. Two characteristics made the United States the sole superpower. First, the US dollar functioned as the currency for all oil sales and purchases. Second, with its giant consumer economy, the United States functioned as the world's favored destination for manufactured goods. The leverage the United States gained from these two economic functions was bolstered by its possession of overwhelming military force.

A Hierarchy of Nations   During the 1990s, the sovereign countries of the world formed a three-tier hierarchy. At the top of the first tier was the United States. Below the United States, the fully industrialized democracies in Europe, North America, Japan, and Australia occupied the rest of the first tier. In the course of the 1990s, four "newly industrialized countries" joined this tier: Taiwan, South Korea, Hong Kong, and Singapore. Since the early 2000s, the so-called BRIC countries—Brazil, Russia, India, and China—as well as Turkey and Mexico, were added. In 2010 China surpassed Japan to have the second largest economy by nominal GDP (Gross Domestic Product).

Seeing Patterns

> How did the United States demonstrate its dominant economic position toward the end of the twentieth century? How did it accelerate the pattern of globalization?

> What made capitalist democracy so attractive toward the end of the twentieth century that it became a generic model for many countries around the world to strive for?

> Which policies did China and India pursue so that they became the fastest-industrializing countries in the early twenty-first century?

> How have information technology and social networking altered cultural, political, and economic interactions around the world?

> What is global warming, and why is it a source of grave concern for the future?

Postmodernism and postcolonialism: Cultural movement influential across the world from ca. 1970 to 2010 which centers on "critical theory," according to which reality is constructed through discourse and the will to power determines society's institutions.

Chapter Outline

• **Capitalist Democracy: The Dominant Pattern of Modernity**

• **The Environmental Limits of Modernity**

• **Putting It All Together**

In the second tier of the world hierarchy were "middle-income countries," according to the United Nations' definition. They were either industrializing states in the Middle East, south Asia, East Asia, and Latin America or reindustrializing states in the former Communist Bloc. In the broad bottom tier were countries defined as "low-income" or "poor," located for the most part in sub-Saharan Africa and Southeast Asia (see Map 31.1).

In 2000, about one-fifth of the world's population of 6 billion lived in fully industrialized countries, two-thirds in middle-income countries, and 15 percent in poor countries. Only two centuries after the beginnings of capitalist modernity, 90 percent of the world population was more or less integrated into the pattern characterized by market exchange and consumerism.

The Dollar Regime The United States stood at the top of the world hierarchy, thanks largely to the power of its financial system. The beginnings of this system date to the years following 1971 when President Richard Nixon took the dollar off the gold standard. Two years later, Nixon persuaded the Middle East–dominated Organization of the Petroleum Exporting Countries (OPEC) to accept only dollars as payment for oil. OPEC, anxious to remain in the good graces of the United States as its largest buyer, agreed. As a result of the Nixon–OPEC deal, the dollar replaced gold as the acknowledged international standard of exchange.

Under the **dollar regime**, all oil-importing countries, except the United States, had to manage two currencies. One,

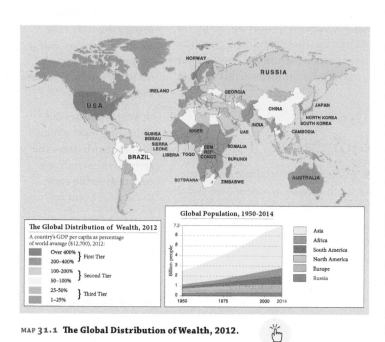

MAP 31.1 **The Global Distribution of Wealth, 2012.**

map analysis

interactive timeline

1975
Greenhouse gases
310 ppm

1990–2000
Civil war and ethnic cleansing
in former Yugoslavia

1994
End of apartheid and election of Nelson
Mandela as president in South Africa; Hutu
genocide against Tutsis in Rwanda

2002
US military budget
reaches $400 billion

1989–1991
Collapse of communism
in Soviet Bloc

1992
US invasion
of Kuwait

2001
Al-Qaeda attack on United States;
US invasion of Afghanistan

2003
US invasion of Iraq,
Darfur crisis

2008
Global financial
crisis and economic
recession

2011
Arab Spring; world population
reaches 7 billion; greenhouse
gases 380 ppm

2014
ISIS jihadist movement in Iraq and
Syria; political unrest in Ukraine,
Russia annexes Crimea; war between
Israel and Hamas

2016
Great Britain votes to leave
European Union; failed coup
in Turkey; Paris Global Climate
Agreement ratified

2010
Number of cell phones
reaches 5 billion worldwide

2013
Military coup d'état in Egypt; Edward
Snowden reveals secret documents on
the extent of US spying efforts

2015
Saudi Arabian military intervention in Yemen;
Russian intervention in Syria; US–Iranian nuclear
agreement; massive refugee crisis in Europe

denominated in dollars, was for energy purchases; the other, in domestic currencies, was for the internal market of oil consumption. There were repeated grumblings among the non–oil producers of the world, both developed and developing, about being cheated by the dollar regime. But the US–OPEC deal endured, backed up by a gigantic American financial system that emerged as a result of the dollar regime.

Dollar regime: A system maintained by the United States whereby dollars are the sole currency in which the price of oil and most other commodities and goods in the world are denominated; the regime forces most countries to maintain two currencies, with consequent financial constraints.

The United States as an Import Sinkhole   The United States became the country to which everyone wanted to export. Building this relationship was particularly important in East Asia. During the Cold War, the United States had encouraged import substitution industrialization in Korea, Taiwan, Hong Kong, Thailand, and Southeast Asian countries. By becoming prosperous, so it was assumed, these countries would be less susceptible to communism. By the 1990s, the industrialization process reached levels where the United States began to pressure the Asian Tigers to reduce import substitution protectionism and replace it with free trade. In return for the United States buying their industrial goods, the countries of East Asia agreed to give free access to American financial institutions.

After communism collapsed, China, pushing its own import substitution industrialization, began to export cheap industrial goods to the United States, as well. In the 1990s, these goods undercut those produced by the Asian Tigers, and the United States became an even deeper "sinkhole," this time for products made in the People's Republic of China. The United States in effect underwrote China's industrialization, binding the country's economic interests closely to its own financial interests within the dollar regime (see Map 31.2).

US Technological Renewal and Globalization   Electronics was one of those periodic new technologies with which capitalism, always threatened by falling profit

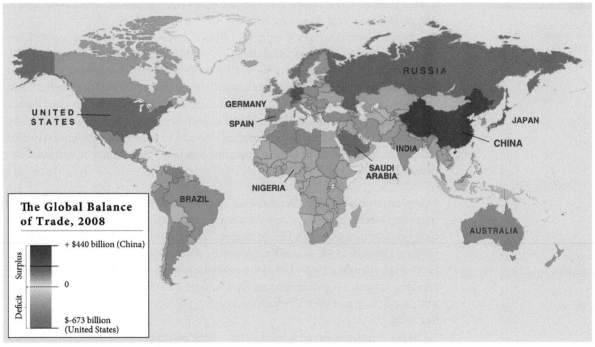

The Global Balance of Trade, 2008

+ $440 billion (China)

Surplus

0

Deficit

$-673 billion (United States)

MAP 31.2 **The Global Balance of Trade, 2008.**

Information technology: The array of computers, information, electronic services, entertainment, and storage available to business and consumers, with information increasingly stored in the "cloud"—that is, online storage centers rather than individual computer hard drives.

Globalization: The ongoing process of integrating the norms of market economies throughout the world and binding the economies of the world into a single uniform system.

Robert Reich, excerpt from *The Work of Nations* (1991)

rates in maturing industries, became more profitable again. An entirely new branch of industry, **information technology (IT)**, put cell phones, online delivery of music and entertainment, and a host of other services into the hands of consumers.

During the 1990s, America became the leader in the "high-tech industry" of electronics, biotechnology, and pharmacology. Worldwide, the volume of trade goods doubled and the volume of capital flows quadrupled.

The only blemishes in the **globalization** process, from an American perspective, were continued protectionism and low consumption in many Asian countries. The closest economic advisors of President Bill Clinton (in office 1993–2001) were bankers and investors who had greatly expanded the size and influence of the financial services sector. The US globalization offensive in the 1990s was thus in large part an effort to open protected foreign markets to American financial institutions.

The dollar- and import-sinkhole regimes attracted critics from the entire political spectrum. Conservative critics were appalled that the United States no longer adhered to the gold standard. They further bemoaned the disappearance of the traditional manufacturing sector and its replacement by financial institutions and Internet start-ups that produced nothing tangible. Progressive critics accused the United States of using its arrangements with OPEC and the East Asian countries to exclude poorer countries. In their opinion, the United States upheld an imperialist capitalist system that limited wealth to a minority and refused to share it with the have-nots.

US Military Dominance   By the year 2002, the US military budget had risen to $400 billion. This astronomical sum was considerably smaller than during the Cold War but still larger than the defense budgets of the next eight countries combined. On the basis of this military machine, President Bill Clinton operated from a position of de facto world dominance.

His successor, President George W. Bush (in office 2001–2009), articulated this dominance eventually in a formal doctrine, the National Security Strategy of 2002. American might was highly visible in all parts of the world, generating resentment among those for whom the combined economic–military power of the United States amounted to a new kind of world dominance. After 2009, however, President Barack Obama (in office 2009–2017) sought to reduce the American military posture by withdrawing troops from Iraq and Afghanistan and reducing the now-unsustainable military budget. In spite of these reductions, American predominance remained undiminished (see Map 31.3).

Intervention in Iraq   The national security strategy sought to prevent countries from establishing dominance in a region and to destroy terrorist organizations bent on destruction in the United States. The first policy was enacted after Iraq's Saddam Hussein (1937–2006) occupied Kuwait (1990–1991). President George H. W. Bush (in office 1989–1993) intervened when it became clear that Hussein, by invading Kuwait, sought dominance over Middle Eastern oil exports. At the head of a coalition force and with UN backing in 1992, US troops drove the Iraqi occupiers from Kuwait.

In the following decade, the United States and the United Nations subjected Iraq to a stringent military inspection regime to end Saddam Hussein's efforts to acquire nuclear and chemical weapons. The inspectors were successful in destroying these weapons, but Hussein, anxious to project his power among the Arabs, did his best to pretend that he still possessed them. This pretense touched off an intense debate among the members of the UN Security Council. In the end, in March 2003, President George W. Bush ordered a preemptive invasion without Security Council backing, arguing that Iraq had once more become a regional threat. To the surprise of many, Saddam Hussein's regime put up little resistance and fell after just 3 weeks to the US armed forces. Afterward, no weapons of mass destruction were discovered.

Intervention in Afghanistan The second US principle announced in President George W. Bush's national security strategy was a response to the rise of Islamic terrorism. In 1992, al-Qaeda ("the Base") under the leadership of Osama bin Laden (1957–2011) had emerged as the principal international terrorist organization.

Al-Qaeda's campaign of terrorism climaxed on September 11, 2001, when suicide commandos hijacked four commercial airliners and crashed them into the World Trade Center's Twin Towers in New York City, the Pentagon outside Washington, DC, and a field near Shanksville, Pennsylvania. Nearly 3,000 people died in the disasters. In response, US troops invaded Afghanistan on October 7, 2001, in an effort to eliminate bin Laden, who was protected by the Islamist Taliban regime in power. They destroyed the regime and drove the al-Qaeda terrorists to western Pakistan. It took another decade for the United States to track down and assassinate bin Laden (May 2011), and even then, it failed to come to grips with the resurgent Taliban terrorists in its ongoing war in Afghanistan. In the course of 2017, this resurgence made considerable progress, ineffectively dealt with by the fledgling Afghan army and a residual US military.

The United Nations and Regional Peace During the 1990s and early 2000s, the United Nations fulfilled vital, if not always successful, peace missions in regional conflicts. A tragic failure in this regard was the Rwandan civil war of 1994, in which peacekeeping troops serving under UN auspices stood by as the Hutu ethnic majority massacred the Tutsi ethnic minority.

On the other hand, despite the bloodshed on both sides, the crisis in the Sudan saw the United Nations fare somewhat better. Two civil wars raged—one between Arab Muslims in northern Sudan and Christian and African-spiritual populations in southern Sudan (1983–2005), and the other within the non-Arab Muslim region of Darfur in western Sudan (2003–present). After UN mediation, the two sides in the first conflict agreed to the secession of South Sudan as an independent country in 2011. The Darfur conflict continued to smolder, with the United Nations pursuing criminal charges against the president of Sudan and an African Union force seeking to protect the refugees from Arab-inspired attacks. Unfortunately, after two years of independence in South Sudan, the power struggle between two leading politicians degenerated into a savage ethnic civil war.

Day of Infamy. Smoke billowing from the south tower of the World Trade Center in New York City on September 11, 2001. The north tower had already collapsed. Nearly 2,600 people died in the inferno, in which the heat of the exploding commercial airplanes in the interior of the high rises melted the steel girders supporting the buildings.

MAP 31.3 **US Security Commitments since 1945.**

American Finances Go Global: Crisis and Recovery   The world economy dominated by the dollar regime expanded during the late 1900s and early 2000s. In the so-called Washington Consensus (1989–2002), Western economists and foreign aid officers preached the motto "Stabilize, Privatize, and Liberalize" to emerging nations. To receive investments, foreign aid, or emergency loans to overcome recurrent economic crises, recipient countries had to submit to stringent rules concerning balanced budgets, the privatization of state firms, and the opening of protected branches of the economy.

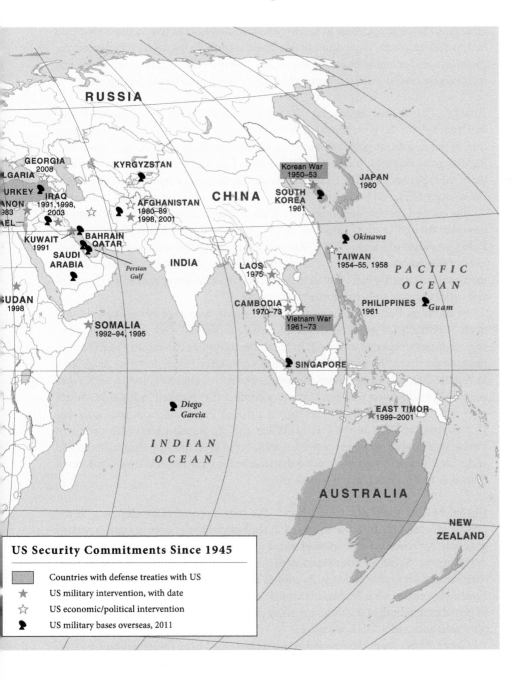

US Security Commitments Since 1945

▢	Countries with defense treaties with US
★	US military intervention, with date
☆	US economic/political intervention
♟	US military bases overseas, 2011

Spurred by the Consensus in the 1990s, private US investors had nearly tripled the value of their assets abroad. The now more accessible financial systems in many newly industrialized and developing countries, however, often could not respond adequately. A series of financial crises gripped Mexico and most Southeast Asian countries. Here, either the state finances were in disarray (Mexico) or overcommitted banks with non-performing portfolios (Southeast Asia) proved so vulnerable that the US Congress or the International Monetary Fund (IMF) had to step in with loans. (The IMF is an international bank, with the US government as the largest shareholder, that provides emergency loans to countries in sudden financial distress.) In return, these countries had to tighten credit, close unprofitable banks and factories, tolerate higher unemployment, and promote increased exporting. Newly industrialized South Korea was relatively successful with its reforms and quickly cranked up its exports again.

Russia's Crisis and Recovery   Russia defaulted in 1998 on its internal bonds and from 1999 to 2001 on several of its external loans. These defaults were a culmination of the disastrous postcommunist economic free fall. In the decade after 1991, Russia's gross domestic product (GDP) dropped by nearly half, a decline far worse than that experienced by the United States during the Great Depression of the 1930s. Fortunately, higher oil prices after 2001 eased the debt situation of Russia somewhat.

The oil and gas revenues from state firms available directly to the government, however, strengthened its autocratic tendencies. The former KGB officer Vladimir Putin, president of Russia 2000–2008 and again after 2012, was the principal engineer of this autocracy. Given the small size of the private sector in the early 2000s, the country was still years away from subjecting its state enterprises to market rules and creating a comprehensive market economy.

In addition, Putin sharply curtailed civil rights, restricted press freedom, and made it difficult for non-governmental organizations (NGOs) and human rights organizations to operate in Russia. In his desire to restore the country to its former imperial greatness, he promoted an agenda of Russian hegemony over neighbors. In August 2008, Putin provoked the former Soviet republic of Georgia, which was on track for admission into NATO, into a conflict that resulted in Russian control over one-fifth of its territory. The biggest prize in Putin's imperial land grab was Crimea, part of Ukraine since 1954. When the pro-Russian Ukrainian president Viktor Yanukovych was overthrown in 2014, Putin used this opportunity to invade and seize Crimea. A separatist, pro-Russian rebellion in eastern Ukraine continued thereafter to tie down Ukraine's weak army.

A portrait of three families in three worlds (1993–1994)

Globalization and Poor Countries   The mixed record of development in the middle-income countries was mirrored in the bottom tier of poor countries, whose governments relied on the export of mineral or agricultural commodities to finance development. Some 50 poor states depended on three or fewer commodities for over half of their export earnings. As a result of overproduction on the world market, commodity prices were depressed through most of the 1990s. The price depression imposed severe budget cutbacks on many poor countries, with consequent unemployment and middle-class shrinkage.

Generally, however, the developing world benefited from the globalization of the 1990s. Poverty declined up until the recession of 2008, although this decline was unevenly distributed. The number of people in absolute poverty actually increased in sub-Saharan Africa, Southeast Asia (except Vietnam), Russia and central Asia, and Latin America. Thus, while globalization benefited an absolute majority of humans, its uneven geographical distribution made the benefits look substantially smaller in many regions.

Two Communist Holdouts: China and Vietnam

Communism or socialism as an official ideology survived in North Korea, China, Vietnam, North Korea, and Cuba. China and Vietnam opened their command economies to the market but maintained many large state firms and single-party control. In both cases, the parties remained communist in name but became in fact ordinary autocracies presiding over capitalist economies.

The Chinese Economic Boom After 1989, the new Chinese middle class, benefiting from the economic reforms of the Open Door and Four Modernizations, had to accommodate itself to a monopoly party that was communist in name but autocratic in practice. Socially conservative migrants from the provinces to the cities found unskilled jobs in the early 1980s. They acquired skills and earned enough to send their children to school. From around 2005, the children, now with college degrees, took jobs as managers, technicians, professionals, and entrepreneurs in state companies, private firms, and Chinese branches of foreign firms. They began to flex their muscles as consumers.

To keep the middle class from demanding political participation outside the Communist Party, the government pursued accelerated annual GDP growth. Instead of spending its earnings, however, the middle class saved at rates double those in Japan or Europe prior to the recession of 2008–2011. The only partially subsidized new health care and education systems consumed many of those savings. In addition, urban real estate and rental apartments became increasingly unaffordable in many Chinese cities during the early 2000s.

Under the slogan of the "harmonious society"—in which all segments of the populace worked together with no toleration for "disruptive elements"—the government and party staked its continued legitimacy to ongoing economic progress. For how long this progress can be maintained is unclear: The economic growth rate—about 6.7 percent in 2015–2016—was still strong in comparison to that of Europe and the US, but the legitimacy of the Communist Party was increasingly called into question by a middle class opposed to corruption and less afraid of censorship.

Vietnam Taking Off With double-digit growth rates in the 1990s, Vietnam outpaced other poor Asian neighbors, such as Cambodia and Bangladesh, by diversifying its manufacturing sector. Companies in Hong Kong, Taiwan, and Korea, showed a strong preference for investment in Vietnam, because it had a high literacy rate and a low wage rate. A major new export sector from the later 1990s onward was aquaculture—the farming of shrimp, catfish, and tilapia. Vietnam moved in 2010 from the poor to the intermediate countries on the world list of nations.

Pluralist Democracy under Strain

In the first and early second decade of the 2000s, there was a palpable swing toward pessimism in the West. Two recessions, the demise of the Washington Consensus,

Two Views of China. Despite attempts to regulate its rate, China's economic acceleration continued at a torrid pace. In 2010, its GDP surpassed that of Japan to become second only to that of the United States. The new prosperity created startling contrasts and a growing diversity of lifestyles in the People's Republic. In the image above, young Chinese hipsters sport T-shirts harkening back with deliberate irony to revolutionary leaders—China's Mao Zedong and Cuba's Che Guevara. In the lower panel, China's contemporary leadership—smartly decked out in Western suits and "power ties"—strive to steer the country toward continued growth as the means to preserve the ascendancy of the Chinese Communist Party.

and the problematic postwar settlements in Afghanistan and Iraq demonstrated the limits of US power. Syria fared even worse, with a continuing civil war that killed 400,000 and forced 3 million to flee abroad by the end of 2016. Peace continued to elude the Palestinians, and Turkey lost its political and economic stability after the renewal of terrorism by Kurdish militants and a failed military coup. The only ray of hope in this region was the US–Iran agreement of 2016, according to which Iran would not build a nuclear bomb during the next 15 years.

The future in the other parts of the world looked a bit less grim. China and India, with robust economic growth rates, expanded their educated and entrepreneurial middle classes. Africa and Latin America, except for Venezuela, benefiting from the demand for oil and minerals in China and India, experienced similarly strong growth. But by the second decade of the 2000s, all world regions were struggling to overcome the effects of the recession of 2008–2011.

Unease in the West   Two recessions in the first decade of the 2000s in the United States sapped enthusiasm about the future of modernity. The first recession, of 2001–2003, was the so-called dot-com crisis, which had its origins in uncontrolled speculation about the expansion of the Internet. The second—much more severe—recession of 2008–2011 began with the collapse of the housing market, a result of the overly risky granting of real-estate mortgages to buyers with insufficient funds. The mortgage crisis snowballed into a general credit crisis, reducing consumer demand. Manufacturers became insolvent, and mass unemployment deepened the recession. The unemployment rate reached 9.6 percent in 2010, compared to half that rate in 2000–2008.

The crisis of 2001–2003 hit the African American and Hispanic working class particularly hard; in the following recession of 2008–2011, many white workers lost their jobs. By contrast, a majority of employees in the financial sector and the information technology industry, as well as the upper management of large corporations, survived the recession relatively unscathed. The American public became increasingly aware of the gap that separated the top one percent of income earners and asset owners from the middle and working classes, whose incomes stagnated.

In addition to the unease about economic inequalities, unhappiness about political and social issues grew, especially among white, working class, older, and evangelical voters. The Tea Party movement (TEA as an acronym for "Taxed Enough Already") of 2009 introduced radically populist anti-establishment and anti-foreigner agendas into the political debate. This movement opted to work inside the Republican Party, pushing the party to the right and polarizing American politics.

At first, the presidential campaign of Barack Obama (in office 2009–2017), the first African American president, gave many Americans a boost of optimism to emerge from the recession. The president's deficit spending helped to steady the economy, and the nation finally drew even with the other industrialized countries by making health care insurance available to all citizens through the Affordable Care Act (ACA). But Tea Party activists and conservatives unleashed a storm of criticism over the ACA (passed without Republican votes and derided as "Obamacare"), unemployment, government spending, illegal immigration, abortion, and questioned the reality of climate change.

In midterm elections, the Republicans regained the House (2010) and Senate (2014). The Republican majority brought the country twice (2011 and 2013) to a standstill over the national debt ceiling and the ACA. Last-minute compromises patched differences over, but the relationship between President Obama (re-elected 2012) and the Democrats on one side and the Republican Party (more and more beholden to its hardline populists) on the other became embittered.

Out of this stalemate came the unlikely nomination of real-estate developer and reality-television show host Donald Trump (b. 1946) as the Republican candidate for president in the 2016 election. Trump advocated building a wall along the US–Mexican border to curtail illegal immigration, abandoning a number of existing and proposed international trade agreements, and "bringing back" American manufacturing jobs. His brash persona and often coarse speech appealed to many voters who considered him "authentic" and who felt the "system" was rigged against them. Yet he also alienated many women, who considered him sexist, and the vast majority of people of color. He actively courted the National Rifle Association and various pro-life/anti-abortion groups, as well as the so-called "Alt-Right," whose supporters include white supremacists, anti-immigration activists, and anti-government militias. For them, the Democratic nominee—former First Lady, US senator, and Secretary of State Hillary Clinton (b. 1947)—personified the globalizing elites who had abandoned them. In one of the most hard-fought campaigns in American history, Ms. Clinton won the popular vote, but Mr. Trump won the electoral college and thereby the presidency. His election, closely following the United Kingdom's decision to leave the European Union (called "Brexit") and strong nationalist, isolationist, anti-globalization movements in France and other European countries, appears to signal a major retreat from post–Cold War internationalist political, economic, and diplomatic trends.

inaugural address of President Donald Trump, January 20, 2017

Europe saw a similar trend of rising income disparities, although this was mitigated by a stronger manufacturing sector (around 20 percent of GDP versus 11 percent in the United States in 2010) and a more generous social safety net. But the costs of this net seriously imperiled the future not only of Greece, Portugal, Spain, and Ireland (all of which fell into near-bankruptcy during the recession of 2008–2011), but also of the European Union itself. Questions arose whether the euro, which had been launched with great fanfare in 1999, could be maintained as the common currency.

Since the unemployed were entitled to long-term support in most European countries, the angry populist debate was more muted during the early stages of the recession. But the rigorous policy of budget-cutting and public savings in the countries of the European Union, largely imposed by Germany, slowed the recovery to a crawl in 2011. After several years of political and economic immobility in the European Union (EU), elections in Hungary (2014) and Poland (2015) brought nationalist parties to power that voiced frustration with the bureaucratic policies of the EU.

In the summer of 2015, a flood of refugees from Syria inundated Turkey and the Balkans and swept some 890,000 men, women and children into Germany and smaller numbers as far as Scandinavia. Initially, given the revulsion against the Assad regime's atrocities in Syria, the foreigners were received with open arms—but then the inevitable backlash set in. Populist anti-foreign activists organized themselves nearly everywhere and in Great Britain even won a referendum in the summer of 2016 for the country to leave the European Union. As in the United States, optimism about the future of the international order and democratic pluralism was at low ebb in the second decade of the twenty-first century.

anti-immigrant posters in Europe, 2008–2013

A Bloody Civil War in Yugoslavia   Like Russia and the other former Soviet republics, Eastern Europe and the Balkans went through an economic collapse and political restructuring during the 1990s. This collapse and restructuring was mostly peaceful except in Yugoslavia, where a civil war raged from 1990 to 1995. Until the 1980s, communism was the main ideology in Yugoslavia, through which the country's ethnic nationalisms of the Orthodox Christian Serbs, Catholic Croats, Muslim Bosnians, Catholic Slovenes, and mostly Muslim Kosovar Albanians were subsumed under a federal constitution granting these ethnic groups a degree of autonomy. The main enforcer of communist unity was President Josip Tito (1892–1980), a Croat. After Tito's death, however, the Serb president Slobodan Milošević (1941–2006) exploited the demographic superiority of his ethnic community for the establishment of political dominance while retaining communism.

Yugoslavia had borrowed heavily from Western countries to keep its industries from collapsing during the oil price slump of 1985–1986. At the end of the 1980s, it was practically bankrupt. This disappointment exploded in 1990 into religious-nationalist hatred, led by the smaller ethnic groups against Serbs in their territories. The Serb supremacist-nationalist backlash, with an effort to "cleanse" minorities from "greater Serbian" territory, was no less explosive. It took more than a decade for the European Union and the United States to stop the Orthodox Serbs from murdering Muslim Bosnians and Albanians and to enforce a semblance of peace in the Balkans.

Since then, the five successor states of Yugoslavia have struggled to adapt to capitalism and democracy. Serb supremacist nationalism survived the longest and only gradually began to subside when the democratically elected pro-European government decided to arrest the main perpetrators of ethnic cleansing. With these arrests and much relief, the Serbian government opened the way toward joining the European Union.

The Middle East: Paralysis, Liberation, and Islamism   The momentum generated after the collapse of communism largely dissipated in the Middle East and North Africa during the early 2000s. With the exception of Turkey, a pall of economic and political paralysis hung over the region. The republics in the 1990s and early 2000s (e.g., Egypt, Syria, Algeria, Tunisia, and Yemen) inched toward privatization of state-run businesses but not at all toward democratization. Monarchies (Saudi Arabia, Jordan, Oman, and the Gulf sheikhdoms) encouraged private investment but were extremely cautious, if not altogether hostile, toward democratic reforms. The "rejection front" of autocratic regimes in Iran and Syria, as well as the guerilla terrorist organizations Hezbollah in southern Lebanon and Hamas in the Gaza Strip, rejected the Washington Consensus and globalization out of hand. Syria did, however, cautiously open its state-controlled economy to privatization in the early 2000s.

Islamism: Religious-nationalist ideology in which the reformed Sunni or Shiite Islam of the twentieth century is used to define all institutions of the state and society.

Fear of **Islamism** accounted for the immobility of "republican autocrats" as well as monarchs. While Islam was less visible in the region in the twentieth century when the political elites consisted of secular liberals and nationalists, it had not receded at all from the villages and poor city quarters, where it remained as vital as ever.

The rise of Islamism lay in the acceleration of rural–urban migration in the Middle East in the late 1990s and early 2000s. When Middle Eastern and North African governments built the first large state-run manufacturing plants in their cities in the 1960s, the workers were largely peasants who encountered militant preachers for the first time in the cities. These preachers represented a reformed, standardized, urban Sunni Islam. The children of these workers learned a standardized Islam in the schools, intended to buttress Arab nationalism, in which the Prophet Muhammad was the first nationalist. Standard Islam and militant urban Islamism gradually produced offshoots of Islamist terrorism, such as al-Qaeda, the Taliban, and the Salafists.

In the 1990s and early 2000s Middle Eastern governments essentially barricaded themselves behind their secret services and armies against the onslaughts of these Islamists. Under the threat of Islamist terrorism, Middle Eastern and North African governments found it impossible to pursue bold new initiatives of the kind that China or India advanced.

The Growth of Hezbollah   One area where Islamists achieved a breakthrough was in Lebanon. Hezbollah ("Party of God"), an Islamist guerilla organization recruiting from among the Shiite majority of Lebanese Muslims, waged an underground war against Israel. It succeeded in driving Israel from southern Lebanon in 2000, after an 18-year occupation that had begun with Israel expelling the Palestine Liberation Organization (PLO) from the country (see Chapter 30). By the second decade of the 2000s, Hezbollah had evolved into the most formidable enemy of Israel.

In 2013, Hezbollah even grew into the role of a regional, quasi-state actor. Not only did it come to dominate the Lebanese administration after the end of the civil war in 1989, it became a decisive force strengthening Syrian President Bashar al-Assad (b. 1965) in his civil war against his Arab Spring challengers. Increasingly, Sunni terrorist groups were elbowing the challengers aside, seeking to turn the Syrian civil war into a sectarian conflict. Hezbollah and its patron, Iran, were determined to assert the role of Shiism in the contemporary Middle East.

Israel and Gaza   In 1994, Israel was officially at peace with two Arab neighbors, Egypt and Jordan. But it continued to face a hostile Arab Middle East in general and restless Palestinians in the occupied territories on the West Bank and in Gaza, in particular. To protect its citizens from guerilla attacks, the Israeli government built a border fence in 2002–2013 inside the entire length of the occupied West Bank. In a parallel move, it withdrew from the fenced-in Gaza Strip in 2005. Suicide attacks were fewer, but cross-border rocket attacks from Gaza increased.

After 2006, Israel slid into an even worse trap. In the first-ever Palestinian elections, the victory in Gaza went to the Islamic guerilla organization Hamas, founded in 1988, over the older, secular, ethnic-nationalist PLO. The PLO refused to recognize the elections, and a civil war broke out in which Hamas was victorious, forcing the PLO to retreat to the West Bank. Israel imposed a complete embargo on Hamas-ruled Gaza in an attempt to bring the organization down.

For those in Israel who wished to renew the peace process, the PLO–Hamas split was a disaster, since it threw the entire idea of a two-state solution into doubt. Hamas deepened this doubt in the following years by launching rockets against Israel. In retaliation, Israel invaded Gaza in December–January 2008–2009, causing unmitigated misery for the Palestinian population of Gaza, but was not able to defeat Hamas. Efforts at healing the split between PLO and Hamas produced no results. Likewise, the hostility between Israel and Hamas continued unabated.

Sayyid Qutb, excerpt
from *Milestones*
(1964)

Israel's Predicament and Iranian Ambitions   The failure of the Lebanon invasion in 2009 brought a conservative government into power in Israel. The government renewed Israeli settlement construction in the West Bank while tightening the embargo on Gaza. But neither building more Jewish settlements in the West Bank nor punishing Israel's neighbors Hezbollah and Hamas with invasions and/or embargoes brought the country closer to peace. The formation of a PLO–Hamas unity government of technocrats in 2014 was greeted by Israel with further settlement plans. Israel's long dominance over its neighbors appeared to have reached its limits.

Hezbollah and Hamas used Iranian-supplied rockets against Israel. Iran, a leader of the rejectionist front against Israel, had experienced a "pragmatic" period of reform after the death of its spiritual guide, Ruhollah Khomeini, in 1989. But the reformers were timid, and the still-powerful clerics systematically undermined attempts at democratic and cultural reforms.

Any remaining hopes for reform were dashed when Mahmoud Ahmadinejad (b. 1956) was elected president. He renewed the anti-Western crusade and adopted a policy of populism. Under his leadership, the Revolutionary Guard became not only the most effective military organization but also a huge patronage machine.

The precipitous decline of revenues from oil exports during the recession of 2008–2011, however, seriously reduced Ahmadinejad's populist appeal. Hence, he needed the Revolutionary Guard commanders to falsify the elections of 2009 to stay in power. Suspected Iranian ambitions for acquiring a nuclear bomb, coupled with North Korea's already existing nuclear arsenal, created global concerns about the possibility of nuclear war by "rogue" nations. Put under a severe economic sanctions regime by the United Nations, Iran elected a less populist and more pragmatic president, Hasan Rouhani (b. 1948), in 2013 (reelected 2017), with a mandate to improve the stagnating economy. After two years of negotiations with the United States, the UN Security Council nations, and Germany, Iran agreed in 2015 to sign a nuclear deal in which it gave up on building nuclear bombs for 15 years, in return for an end to the sanctions.

The Ascent of Turkey   Turkey largely escaped Islamist militancy to become one of the most dynamic newly industrialized countries in the world. In contrast to other regimes in the Middle East, Turkish Muslims enjoyed a well-established and functioning multiparty system. A right-of-center party with a strong contingent of Islamists in 1983 not only captured the premiership of the country but simultaneously implemented new initiatives of economic privatization and industrial export orientation. Benefiting from these initiatives, a middle class of socially conservative but economically liberal businesspeople arose.

In a second wave of Islamist middle-class expansion after 2003, under Prime Minister Recep Tayyip Erdoğan [RE-jep TAY-ip ER-dow-ahn] (b. 1954), Turkey's GDP grew to become the world's fifteenth largest. Elections in June 2011 enabled Erdoğan's party, the AKP, to garner slightly more than half of the vote. On the basis of this vote, it enacted constitutional reforms that rescinded the military's power in politics. The party's electoral strength, however, misled Erdoğan into believing that he could on occasion ignore the democratic process, as in 2013 when he took unilateral action to suppress popular demonstrations in Istanbul and in 2014 when he ignored a court injunction to stop constructing his massive new government palace.

Hezbollah iconography (2010)

Recep Erdoğan on Turkey's place in world affairs (2004)

The palace was being built in anticipation of Erdoğan's elevation from the premiership to the presidency in an election in 2014.

After the election, Erdoğan sought to change the president's ceremonial office into an executive one, similar to that of Iran, with a vision to transform Turkey from a secular into an Islamic republic. Although two parliamentary elections in 2015 denied his party the supermajority necessary for this constitutional change, he made himself into an executive president anyway. In both elections, for the first time in the Republic's history, a Kurdish party won seats in parliament. But the arrival of this party in parliament meant not only that the AKP stood in the way for the AKP's efforts at changing the constitution but also resulted in the end of a truce with the Kurdish guerilla organization PKK. The renewed Kurdish guerilla war in southeastern Turkey weighed heavily on Turkish resources, as did 2.7 million refugees from the civil war in Syria.

The mounting problems for Turkey climaxed with a military coup attempt in July 2016. Military units occupied key state institutions in the night of July 15–16, killing 265 citizens in the process, but failed to coordinate their actions among themselves. Erdoğan was able to evade arrest and call for the citizenry to stage mass rallies the next day. In the face of these rallies, the coup collapsed and in waves of unprecedented retaliatory purges, the government dismissed 45,000 military officials, police officers, judges, governors, civil servants, university administrators, and professors from their positions. It declared the Gülen religious and educational movement to be responsible for the coup attempt and demanded the extradition of its founder, Fethullah Gülen (b. 1941), from his self-imposed exile in the United States. Until about 2011, Gülen had been an ally of Erdoğan, but their alliance broke down over different visions of the kind of Islamic state each was aspiring to. As the dust began to settle at the end of 2016, President Erdoğan was the undisputed autocrat in a by now nearly constitutionally hollowed-out republic.

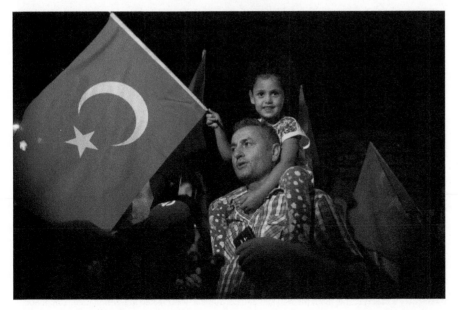

Turkish Citizen with His Daughter. A Turkish father and daughter during mass demonstrations in support of Turkish President Recep Erdoğan after the failed military Coup of July 15, 2016. A referendum in April 2017 gave the presidency sweeping new executive powers, allowing Erdogan to consolidate his position.

The Arab Spring of 2011   Prior to the failed coup of July 2016, Turkey was the most frequently cited model for the compatibility of Islam and democracy in the Middle East. In spring 2011 Tunisia and Egypt, however, each underwent constitutional revolutions, which demonstrated that democracy could sprout in Arab countries as well. On December 17, 2010, 26-year-old Mohamed Bouazizi set himself ablaze in an act of despair brought about by the humiliations he had suffered at the hands of a Tunisian policewoman and thereby unleashed massive demands for democracy across the Middle East.

Bouazizi's death touched off the mostly peaceful democratic revolutions dubbed the "Arab Spring." Beginning in Tunisia, they spread into Egypt, Libya, Bahrain, Yemen, and Syria in the course of early 2011. In Tunisia and Egypt they ousted longtime and aging autocrats. After months of fighting, Libya's Muammar el-Qaddafi (r. 1969–2011) was toppled in September 2011 and killed a month later. Autocratic rulers in other Arab countries held on with unrestrained brutality. The demonstrators—for the most part young, urban, and Internet-savvy—documented the events online and revealed police violence for the world to see. As these revolutions developed, however, they raised the question of how closely the young demonstrators were integrated into the rest of the population, which included urban and rural traditional Muslims as well as Islamists.

Unfortunately, the Arab Spring activists could not translate their newfound power into electoral victories. In both Tunisia and Egypt, elections brought Islamist parties to power. These parties sought to Islamize Tunisia and Egypt, even though they had not participated much in the Arab Spring demonstrations. Renewed mass demonstrations in 2013, this time against the Islamization measures, became

interviews with young Egyptians who demonstrated in Tahrir Square (2011)

image analysis

Democracy's Martyr. This monument in Sidi Bouzid, Tunisia, was erected in December 2011 in honor of Mohamed Bouazizi, a street vendor selling fruits and vegetables. After months of harassment by the police, he set himself afire in despair on December 17, 2010. His example galvanized young, educated, and social network-savvy Tunisians into their peaceful "Arab Spring" revolution during December 2010–January 2011, which culminated with the resignation of the Tunisian president.

unmanageable, and in Egypt the military stepped in. In a coup d'état, the military ended both the tenure of President Muhammad Morsi (r. 2012–2013) and the Arab Spring. In Tunisia, the political process also broke down in 2013, but the opponents sought to resolve the breakdown through negotiations.

The Egyptian military deepened its rule in 2014 through the adoption of a new constitution and the election of a new president, Abdel Fattah Sisi (b. 1954), even though only a minority of the citizens voted on both occasions. In Tunisia, by contrast, the Islamist party won the constituent assembly election of 2011. After the adoption of a new constitution and presidential and parliamentary elections in 2014, a secularist-led coalition of parties took over the government in a peaceful changing of the guard. A deteriorating security situation after major terrorist attacks during 2015–2016, however, prompted the parliament to form a more broadly based—though still secularist-led—government coalition. The mandate of this government was the re-establishment of security, the provison of jobs, and the curbing of corruption.

In Syria, the hopes for an Arab Spring were dashed almost immediately. The first pro-democracy protests began in March 2011, but the president, Bashar al-Assad, brutally suppressed them. By early June, the protests turned into an armed rebellion. Assad was the heir of the secular Arab-socialist regime of the Baath Party, in which members of the Shiite sect of the Alawites held the key army and secret service positions. Baath bureaucrats pursued a policy of state capitalism as late as 1991, when first concessions to economic liberalization were finally granted.

Bashar al-Assad on the civil war in Syria (2013)

Although a large majority of Sunni Arabs, Sunni Kurds, and Christian Arabs benefited from the Baath's policies, income disparities grew during the period of economic liberalization in the 1990s and early 2000s. Although Syria was led by a young president, it did not differ much from the old-men regimes of Tunisia and Egypt in early 2011.

During the summer of 2011, the Arab Spring uprising became a civil war. The rebels were joined in 2012 by Sunni jihadists with battle experience from Afghanistan, Iraq, Yemen, and the Russian Caucasus. At the same time, Assad released Islamists from his own prisons to the rebels in order to discourage the United States and Europe from arming the secular wing of the opposition, for fear of their weapons falling into the hands of the jihadists. The brutality with which Assad battled his opponents caused a mass exodus of refugees to neighboring countries. Until the end of 2013 Assad was on the defensive, but thanks to unwavering support from Russia and Iran, as well as soldiers from Iran and the Lebanese Hezbollah, he regained the initiative.

In the northeast, Assad discreetly gave some of the most radical jihadists free rein. The organization "Islamic State in Iraq and al-Sham" [historical Syria], or ISIS, took advantage of the opportunity. Aiming for the reconstruction of the seventh-century caliphate allegedly based on the pristine Islam of the Quran and Sunna, ISIS developed forms of brutality that alienated it from the other anti-Assad jihadist groups in northern Syria. Led by the former Iraqi al-Qaeda operative Abu Bakr al-Baghdadi (b. 1971), ISIS built a state in northeastern Syria.

In early 2014, ISIS units crossed into Iraq. The troops of the Iraqi government fled with hardly a shot fired. The result of this unexpected turn of events was not only the de facto division of Iraq into a triad of Kurdish, Sunni, and Shiite polities but also the evaporation of the minimal achievements of the US war in Iraq during 2003–2011. An intensive US air campaign during 2015–2016, with support from

the caliphate, as portrayed in an ISIS map

Kurdish fighters on the ground, weakened ISIS and reduced its territory by nearly half, but suspected donors in the Persian Gulf and Saudi Arabia were still keeping it functional.

The New Middle Class in India   During the 1990s and early 2000s, India saw the rise of a religiously conservative Hindu middle class of shopkeepers, traders, merchants, and small manufacturers. The secular Congress Party enjoyed the trust of the new middle class. But an economic slowdown in 2013 and the perception of bureaucratic immobility and corruption returned the religiously oriented Bharatiya Janata Party to power in the 2014 elections.

The rapid expansion of Indian urban centers contributed to the decline of the traditional caste divisions in Hinduism. Since a person's ancestry could be hidden in the cities, even the untouchable caste (*dalit*) began to enter the new middle class. Widespread protests in 2006 and again in 2016, however, indicate continuing tensions among the castes.

The success of the middle class in India must be measured against conditions in the countryside, much of which is still largely outside the market economy. In the 1990s, an overwhelming majority of villagers continued to live in extreme poverty (less than $1.25 per day), existing completely outside the market circuit and depending on handouts. This majority declined in the first decade of the 2000s, perhaps by one-quarter, helped by a sinking birthrate. A major factor in the persistence of poverty was an incomplete land reform. Landlordism and tenancy continued to encompass nearly half of the rural population. As a major voting bloc in the Congress Party, the landlords were successful in resisting further land reform.

Driving Toward Prosperity. The Bajaj scooter was the early status symbol of the emerging Indian middle class. On account of their size, the Indian and Chinese middle classes, numbering in the hundreds of millions, are powerful groups, representing a huge reservoir of ever-more-demanding consumers. This picture is from 2010, when the Indian middle class had come of age.

African Transformations   The half-decade between the oil price slump and the debt crisis (1985), and the disappearance of Communism (1991) was challenging for sub-Saharan Africa. The continent's GDP in the early 1990s was down by almost half from what it had been in 1975, when all main social and economic indicators had been at their peak. Many countries now expended more hard currency on their debt services than on education. With a doubling of the population at the absolute poverty level, sub-Saharan Africa became by far the poorest region in the world.

street scene, Lagos,
Nigeria (2006)

During this time, the urban population of sub-Saharan Africa increased to almost one-third of the total population. The urbanization process was an important factor for the political consequences of the crisis: Students, civil servants, and journalists demanded political reforms. Up until the early 1990s, almost everywhere state structures were patronage hierarchies: The civilian or military rulers provided cushy government jobs for the ethnic groups from which they hailed. Urban dwellers, however, were less tied to ethnicity and more committed to constitutionalism. They felt little sympathy for autocratic rulers and their kin who were running the states into financial ruin and pushed for democratic reforms in the late 1990s and early 2000s.

This push for reforms had mixed results. Incumbents still won elections more often than not, and honest elections were rare. Yet some regime changes were truly thrilling, notably the end of apartheid and the election of Nelson Mandela (1918–2013, president 1994–1999) in the Republic of South Africa; four cycles (2004–2016) of clean multiparty elections in Ghana; the first election of a female African president, the Harvard-trained economist Ellen Johnson Sirleaf (b. 1938, elected 2006 and

Freedom, Justice, and Dignity. The end of apartheid in 1994 and the election of Nelson Mandela (1918–2013), seen here visiting his former prison cell, was an inspiring event in Africa and the rest of the world. South Africa is the richest and most industrialized country of Africa, with large mineral and agricultural resources. Nearly 80 percent of the population is black, speaking its own languages, including isiZulu and isiXhosa. But Afrikaans (a Dutch-originated language) remained the dominant media language, with English being only the fifth most spoken language. In spite of South Africa's relative wealth, years of apartheid have resulted in vast income disparities.

Social Networking

The movements of the Arab Spring were organized and carried out by means of social networking sites (SNSs) like Twitter, Facebook, and YouTube, supported by cell phones and other modern communication technologies. But what are the origins of these devices, and how have they developed into such important tools of political and social revolution?

SNSs can be traced back to the origins of the Internet and the World Wide Web. The Internet is a product of the Cold War. In 1969 the US government initiated the Advanced Research Projects Agency (ARPA), which created a system linking computers at major universities into a network that allowed them to share information. This fledgling Internet expanded during the 1990s into a global computer network. The World Wide Web was conceived in 1989 and launched two years later as a part of the Internet.

SNSs sprang up in the 1990s when it was recognized that the Internet allowed social groups to communicate with each other and to share

The Face of Revolution. Perhaps the most novel aspect of the ongoing "Arab Spring" has been the widespread use of social media in recruiting, organizing, and popularizing the efforts of activists in various countries. The inventiveness of the participants in avoiding government scrutiny and bypassing restrictions on SNSs has become legendary. Here a Syrian man logs into his Facebook account "legally" for perhaps the first time in February, 2011.

map of the Internet (2003)

reelected 2011) in Liberia; and the relatively clean Nigerian presidential elections of 2007, 2011, and 2015.

Setbacks in 2012 and 2013, however, with coups d'état and armed revolts in Guinea Bissau, Mali, the Central African Republic, and South Sudan, were stark reminders that African democratization is still fragile.

Islamism was also a factor in a bloody conflict in Nigeria. In Northern Nigeria, the government proved to be completely incompetent against the Islamist movement Boko Haram ("Western education is sin"). Founded in 2002, this jihadist organization intent on introducing Sharia law staged daring raids, culminating in 2014 with the abduction of over 276 Christian schoolgirls (82 released in May 2017, in exchange for 5 Boko Haram leaders). African as well as foreign observers noted the rise in sectarian conflicts on the continent with growing concern.

The African economy picked up in the early 2000s, mostly because of rising commodity prices. The main oil exporters benefited from higher oil prices, as did the mining countries. Agricultural products also regained significance in the early 2000s. The global recessions of 2001 and 2008 did not have a major impact, largely because of the arrival of China on the scene as a major buyer and investor. Optimism about a sustained recovery and modernity within reach was clearly visible on the continent, even if tempered by continuing ethnic and sectarian conflicts.

information. By the 2000s, social networking sites revolutionized the nature of communication.

An early example of the power of SNSs to effect change was the so-called Twitter Revolution in Iran in 2009, during which anti-government activists used SNSs in an ultimately futile effort to overthrow the Iranian regime. Following the success of the Tunisian revolution, however, an even more spectacular display of the power of SNSs erupted in Egypt on January 25, 2011, when thousands of protesters took to the streets to demand the ouster of the authoritarian president Hosni Mubarak. This "Facebook Revolution" was launched by the April 6 Youth Movement, a Facebook group composed of social and political activists.

For all their success in facilitating uprisings against authoritarian governments, however, SNSs are used with equal effectiveness by terrorist groups. Al-Qaeda and the Taliban take advantage of Facebook and Twitter to broadcast their calls for global *jihad*. Moreover, SNSs serve as effective recruitment tools. How ironic that Internet websites originally intended for exchanges among friends have been transformed into tools to spread revolution, violence, and terrorism.

Questions

- How do SNSs show how an innovation can be adapted for purposes wholly different from the original purposes for which they were intended?

- Do you believe SNSs have allowed young people around the world to make their wishes and aspirations more powerfully felt? If so, what does this say about the connection between technology and youth?

Latin American Expansion   Elections after the financial meltdowns of the 1990s produced more fiscally restrained, socially engaged governments in the large Latin American countries during the early 2000s. Democratic transitions in Mexico, Brazil, Argentina, and Chile demonstrated that the unhappy years of military dictatorships in the 1980s had been left behind. In Mexico the long rule of the Institutional Revolutionary Party (PRI) was interrupted from 2000 to 2012, with an orderly transition to less socially engaged Christian Democratic presidents. Only in 2012 did a markedly rejuvenated PRI return to power. It continued the pattern of economic liberalization begun at the beginning of the century.

Two extraconstitutional events in smaller Latin American countries, however, demonstrated that authoritarian temptations still survived. The first was an abortive uprising in 2002 of army units in Paraguay, allegedly instigated by a former commander outside the country who was wanted for an earlier coup attempt. The second, in Honduras in 2009, was the forcible removal of the president, who intended to hold a referendum on his plan for reelection, even though it had been forbidden by the Honduran constitutional court.

In Colombia, a Marxist guerilla war of more than half a century came to an end with a truce in 2016; but in a referendum, the voters rejected the government's proposed peace agreement. They expressed deep concern over the high degree of immunity the government accorded to the guerillas. After renewed negotiations, parliament passed the agreement. In neighboring Venezuela, President Hugo Chávez (in office 2002–2013), a former officer from a working-class background, used the country's vast oil revenues to construct an ambitious state-socialist system. After his death, however, when the world oil price slump of 2014–2016 deprived the government of revenue, state socialism fell apart, with the population being unable to buy even the most basic staples. Nevertheless, authoritarianism continued to survive in Venezuela, as it did in Bolivia and Nicaragua, as well.

Industrialization, largely through foreign investments but increasingly also through internal financing, stimulated state-run firms to become competitive and even to privatize in several large Latin American countries. In some cases, Latin American countries have become world competitors. All four large economies—Brazil, Mexico, Argentina, and Chile—exported more manufactured goods than commodities by 2008. These countries clearly displayed the features of scientific–industrial modernity by the second decade of the 2000s, even though corruption (in Brazil and Mexico) and foreign debt woes (in Argentina), as well as a highly unequal income distribution still weigh heavily on economic and social development.

The Environmental Limits of Modernity

Systems of capitalism, consumerism, and democracy embodied by the United States, Canada, Western Europe, and Australia have increasingly become the ones to emulate. All new nations in the world are either industrializing or seeking to do so. The principal obstacle for these nations is the debilitating poverty of the great majority of their inhabitants, who are still mired in either subsistence farming or marginal work in the cities. The poorest are unskilled and uneducated and still view large families as a necessity. Improved public health care is helping to lengthen life spans for the poorest people, but the combination of modern medicine and the desire for large families has caused a startling increase in the world population.

Sustainability and Global Warming   In 1800, there was only one country (Great Britain) embarking on industrialization; today, about two-thirds of the 196 independent countries of the world are either industrialized or on the way toward full industrialization. We are beginning to grasp the environmental consequences of this move to scientific–industrial modernity. Between the start of the industrial revolution and the last quarter of the twentieth century, the carbon footprint of these countries had risen from 280 parts per million (ppm) of atmospheric carbon dioxide and other chemical compounds—commonly called "greenhouse gases"—to 330 ppm. Between 1975 and 2010 the concentration of greenhouse gases in the atmosphere climbed to 380 ppm, and in September 2016, it reached the record of 400 ppm for an entire month. According to climate scientists, this milestone means that the atmosphere can never be restored to the "safe" level of ca. 350 ppm.

While there has been considerable debate on the nature and degree of global warming—whether it is a natural cyclical phenomenon or human-produced or even if it exists at all—there is a general scientific consensus that greenhouse gases are the main contributors to temperature increases on earth. Scientists generally assume that at current rates of greenhouse gas production, the earth will reach a "tipping point" of 450 ppm, with irreversible consequences for the planet's climate, before the middle of this century.

J. R. McNeill, excerpt from *Something New Under the Sun: An Environmental History of the Twentieth Century* (2000)

A Smoggy Future. China, the world's worst emitter of greenhouse gases, has large numbers of coal-fed power plants and factories that continue to belch out carbon dioxide as well as toxic substances into the air, with little scrubbing or other devices to clean the emissions before they reach the atmosphere. Here, a power plant on the outskirts of Linfen in Shanxi Province southwest of Beijing fouls the environment in 2009. China's latest Five-Year Plan (2016) calls for stringent efforts to cut back air pollution by 2021, though whether these goals are feasible is the subject of considerable debate.

What will happen when this tipping point is reached? If projections hold true, the polar ice caps and high mountain glaciers will melt completely. Ocean levels, rising from the melted ice, will submerge islands and make inroads on the coasts of all continents. Widespread droughts and violent storms will erode by wind and flood what had been fertile land. Forests, already reduced from timber harvesting and agricultural expansion, may well be wiped out, removing the most important agents for cleaning the atmosphere of greenhouse gases. Pollution and overfishing will leave little of the world's marine life. Biodiversity will be dramatically reduced. The consequence of these grim developments will likely be a severe reduction of the earth's arable land and fisheries needed for the production of food.

The ultimate outcome of this prospective climate transformation will be much worse for the new countries than for the older ones that industrialized early and have the resources to adjust. The irony of such projections, therefore, is that the nations that viewed their adaptation to modernity as their salvation may well find themselves among the first to be doomed.

Scientific and Political Debate   There is a consensus among scientists that the warming trend in the world from greenhouse gases is real. Very few scientists still hold a skeptical view. Vocal minorities still vociferously denounce climate warming as a hoax or conspiracy. So far, political responses have been tepid and largely divided.

By 2013, nine UN conferences had been convened since the 1997 Kyoto Protocol that established benchmarks for the reduction of greenhouse gases in the European Union and 38 industrialized countries. But only the European Union was on track to meet its provision, mandating an annual reduction of 5.2 percent. The

shrinking sea ice in the Arctic, 1984 and 2012

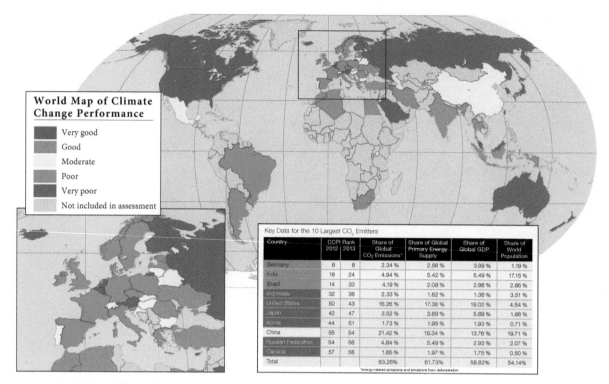

World Map of Climate Change Performance

- Very good
- Good
- Moderate
- Poor
- Very poor
- Not included in assessment

Key Data for the 10 Largest CO$_2$ Emitters

Country	CCPI Rank 2012	2013	Share of Global CO$_2$ Emissions*	Share of Global Primary Energy Supply	Share of Global GDP	Share of World Population
Germany	6	8	2.34 %	2.56 %	3.99 %	1.19 %
India	18	24	4.94 %	5.42 %	5.49 %	17.15 %
Brazil	14	33	4.19 %	2.08 %	2.86 %	2.85 %
Indonesia	32	36	2.33 %	1.62 %	1.36 %	3.51 %
United States	50	43	16.26 %	17.36 %	19.02 %	4.54 %
Japan	42	47	3.52 %	3.89 %	5.89 %	1.86 %
Korea	44	51	1.73 %	1.95 %	1.93 %	0.71 %
China	55	54	21.42 %	19.34 %	13.76 %	19.71 %
Russian Federation	54	56	4.84 %	5.49 %	2.93 %	2.07 %
Canada	57	58	1.65 %	1.97 %	1.75 %	0.50 %
Total			63.26%	61.73%	58.82%	54.14%

*energy-related emissions and emissions from deforestation

MAP **31.4 World Map of Climate Change Performance.**

remaining countries were substantially off the mark. The 2013 Warsaw conference saw bitter conflicts over the inclusion of newly industrialized countries into the Kyoto Protocol and financial compensation demanded by developing countries for damages suffered from extreme weather. As agreed upon in Warsaw and the Paris conference of 2015, governments are now supposed to formulate new targets for greenhouse gas emission curbs to begin in 2020.

At present, the consensus is that if the European 5.2 percent reduction rate were to continue after 2013 and everyone would sign on to this rate, the temperature by the middle of the twenty-first century would be 0.2 degree Fahrenheit below the current average temperature. But President Trump's decision in 2017 to withdraw from the Paris Agreement might instead lead to an increase of 3–4 degrees Fahrenheit, enough to make climate change irreversible—unless collective efforts can still be maintained.

≫ Putting It All Together

The first decade of the twenty-first century witnessed the final transformation of the world from the agrarian–urban pattern of life to a new scientific–industrial pattern. Everywhere in the world, people have been adapting to a new role as individuals with well-defined "human rights," who aspire to be educated, find fulfilling jobs, become consumers, and achieve a materially secure life—in short, they are becoming *modern*.

interactive concept map

The twentieth century also saw the original pattern of modernity split into three. The first modernity sought to create competitive, capitalist, democratic societies; the second modernity sought equality in socialist–communist societies; and in the third modernity supremacist-nationalist societies sought to impose the will of allegedly superior races or ethnic groups through conquest (if not complete elimination) of "inferior" ones. Tremendous destruction accompanied the struggle among the proponents of these visions of modernity, and capitalist democracy was the form that ultimately survived.

With regard to the future of the environment, the devil's bargain of materialism that accompanied the evolution of modernity continues to haunt us: On one hand, it gave us the expectation of a decent existence in material security; on the other hand, the means of achieving that security through exploitation of the earth's material resources has given us the nightmare prospect of an irreversibly damaged planet.

Review and Relate

| Thinking Through Patterns

Examine the ways historians approach the big questions of this chapter.

The United States demonstrated its dominant economic position through the dollar regime and by becoming the sinkhole for industrial exports from developing countries. In compensation for the latter, it expanded the reach of its financial system worldwide. The result was the globalization of the world economy.

» How did the United States demonstrate its dominant economic position toward the end of the twentieth century? How did it accelerate the pattern of globalization?

Capitalist democracy became the universal model of modernity in part because growing middle classes in cities demanded liberalized markets where they could develop personal initiative and accumulate capital. Socially conservative new middle classes empowered successful industrialization processes throughout Asia, Latin America, and Africa.

» What made capitalist democracy so attractive toward the end of the twentieth century that it became a generic model for many countries around the world to strive for?

China and India accelerated their industrialization by encouraging the expansion of their middle classes as the engines of investment and innovation. China, however, did not allow the development of a multiparty system, fearing the chaos of popular agitation. India, by contrast, possessed constitutional traditions that included constraints against populism and allowed for peaceful democratic competition.

» Which policies did China and India pursue so that they became the fastest-industrializing countries in the early twenty-first century?

The communications revolution has reshaped the way humans interact with each other. Because of this connectedness, politics, culture, and economic activity now mutate more rapidly—and with more volatility—than ever before.

» How have information technology and

social networking altered cultural, political, and economic interactions around the world?

❯ **What is global warming, and why is it a source of grave concern for the future?**

Global warming is caused by carbon dioxide and other gases that accumulate in the upper atmosphere and trap the sun's heat in the lower atmosphere. Warming and cooling trends have occurred periodically since the end of the last ice age, and for a long time scientists labored to distinguish clearly between a temporary trend toward warmer temperatures and a permanent, greenhouse gas–caused trend that will permanently alter nature. Today, there is an overwhelming scientific consensus concerning the reality of global warming. But politicians and the general public are not yet entirely convinced that the efforts reached with the Paris Agreement of 2015 should be translated into serious action.

| **Against the Grain**

Consider this as a counterpoint to the main patterns examined in this chapter.

North Korea: Lone Holdout against the World

- Which factors explain the spectacular agricultural collapse in North Korea during the 1990s?
- Why is North Korea so steadfastly devoted to its military program? Why is this military program so worrisome for the world?

In the second decade of the 2000s, North Korea was among the few countries that remained committed to socialism. Although it formally abandoned the ideologies of Marxism-Leninism and communism in its constitutions of 1972 and 2009, respectively, as unfulfillable, it retained its commitment to socialism, self-sufficiency, isolation, and militarism.

The disappearance of Soviet Bloc aid in 1991, in combination with harvest failures during the 1990s, led to mass starvation on a scale similar to famines earlier in the century in the Soviet Union and China. Chinese, South Korean, and international food aid brought only minimal relief. The constitutional principle of food self-sufficiency was a cruel joke.

In 2002 the regime enacted the first small steps of economic reform, recognizing the existence of an informal sector of private garden plots, mechanical workshops, and neighborhood markets. An economic free zone with South Korean factories was established near the border, and some foreign investment was allowed. Collective farmers were entitled to their own produce, in return for a steep 15 percent "rent" on their state-owned lands. After Kim Jong-un's succession to his father's position of supreme leader in 2013, reforms accelerated, and North Korean businesses began to export cheap consumer products.

But sanctions imposed after the country's nuclear tests in 2006 significantly slowed its small arms and missile exports to developing countries, which had provided revenue for keeping the regime and its outsized military program in power. Yet it continued doggedly with its nuclear and missile testing programs in 2015–2017, evidently still pursuing the elusive dream of a limited nuclear war in Korea leading to its reunification with South Korea. With the country ranking lowest in the democracy index, and no. 29 in military expenditures among the 196 nations in the world, North Korea is the most extreme example of a nation going against the grain of the twenty-first century.

Key Terms

audio flashcards

Dollar regime 734	Information technology 736	Postmodernism and
Globalization 736	Islamism 744	postcolonialism 733

For additional resources, please go to
www.oup.com/us/vonsivers.
Please see the Further Resources section at the back of the book for additional readings and suggested websites.

Further Resources

Chapter 1

Burroughs, William J. *Climate Change in Prehistory: The End of the Reign of Chaos*. Cambridge: Cambridge University Press, 2005. Very well-researched and up-to-date discussion of climate and human evolution.

Finlayson, Clive. *The Humans Who Went Extinct: Why Neanderthals Died Out and We Survived*. Oxford and New York: Oxford University Press, 2010. A comprehensive history of human evolution in the context of geological and climatic changes, by the excavator of the last Neanderthal traces in Europe.

Flood, Josephine. *Archaeology of the Dreamtime: The Story of Prehistoric Australia and Its People*. New Haven, CT.: Yale University Press, 1989. Overview of the Australian archaeological record; short on discussion of Aboriginal Dreamtime and myths.

Johanson, Donald, and Kate Wong. *Lucy: The Quest for Human Origins*. New York: Three Rivers, 2009.

Lawson, Andrew J. *Painted Caves: Palaeololithic Rock Art in Western Europe*. Oxford and New York: Oxford University Press, 2012. Presents an extensive overview ("gazetteer") of the various sites and analyzes the rock art phenomenon in great detail.

McBrearty, Sally, and Allison S. Brooks. "The Revolution that Wasn't: A New Interpretation of the Origin of Modern Human Behavior." *Journal of Human Evolution* 39 (2000): 453–463. Crucial, pioneering article in which the authors grounded anatomically and intellectually modern *H. sapiens* in Africa.

Pääbo, Svante. *Neanderthal Man: In Search of the Lost Genomes*. New York: Basic Books, 2014. Pääbo is the first palaeogeneticist to sequence the full genome of a Neanderthal fossil as well as that of a new species of hominin, Dinoseva, discovered in Siberia in 2010.

Pauketat, Timothy, ed. *The Oxford North American Handbook of Archaeology*. Oxford and New York: Oxford University Press, 2012. Very detailed coverage of Paleo-Indian migrations and settlements. Needs to be supplemented with the March 2014 article in *Science* by Dennis O'Rourke, John Hoffecker, and Scott Elias on humans being trapped for 10,000 years on the habitable south coast of Beringia.

Tattersall, Ian. *Masters of the Planet: The Search for Human Origins*. New York: Palgrave Macmillan, 2012. A scholarly well-founded overview for the general reader, by one of the leading senior paleoanthropologists.

WEBSITES

Bradshaw Foundation, http://www.bradshawfoundation.com/. The Bradshaw Foundation has a large website on human evolution and rock art, with many images, and a link to Stephen Oppenheimer's website Journey of Mankind: The Peopling of the World, an important overview of *Homo sapiens'* migrations.

Institute of Human Origins, Arizona State University, http://iho.asu.edu/. Arizona State University's Institute of Human Origins runs the popular but scholarly well-founded website Becoming Human (http://www.becominghuman.org/).

Chapter 2

Alcock, Susan E., John Bodel, and Richard J. A. Talbert, eds. *Highways, Byways, and Road Systems in the Pre-Modern World*. Chichester: John Wiley & Sons, 2012. Fascinating global survey of methods of transport and communication.

Assmann, Jan. *The Search for God in Ancient Egypt*. Ithaca, N.Y.: Cornell University Press, 2001. Reflective investigation of the dimensions of Egyptian polytheism by a leading Egyptologist.

Bottéro, Jean. *Mesopotamia: Writing, Reasoning, and the Gods*. Chicago: University of Chicago Press, 1992. Classic intellectual history of ancient Mesopotamia.

Drews, Robert. *The End of the Bronze Age: Changes in Warfare and the Catastrophe ca. 1200 B.C.* Princeton, N.J.: Princeton University Press, 1993. Closely argued essay on the destruction of Mycenaean culture and its consequences for the eastern Mediterranean.

Finkelstein, Israel. *The Archaeology of the Israelite Settlement*. Jerusalem: Israel Exploration Society, 1988. Authoritative presentation of the archaeology of the earliest period of Israelite social formation.

Kramer, Samuel Noah. *The Sumerians: Their History, Culture, and Character*. Chicago: University of Chicago Press, 2010. An expanded version of Kramer's earlier work, *History Begins at Sumer* (1988), this is a fascinating presentation of the many "firsts" originating in the world's earliest urban civilization, written by a leading Sumerologist.

Mithen, Steven. *After the Ice: A Global Human History, 20,000–5000 B.C.* Cambridge, Mass.: Harvard University Press, 2003. Engagingly written story of humans settling, becoming farmers, and founding villages and towns, as seen through the eyes of a modern time traveler.

Podany, Amanda H. *The Ancient Near East: A Very Short Introduction*. Oxford and New York: Oxford University Press, 2014. Readable survey of the origin and development of Near Eastern civilizations.

Van de Mieroop, Marc. *The Ancient Mesopotamian City*. Oxford: Clarendon, 1997. Full examination of Mesopotamian urban institutions, including city assemblies.

WEBSITES

British Museum. Ancient Egypt, http://www.ancientegypt.co.uk/menu.html. Pictorial introduction, with short texts.

Livius.org. "Mesopotamia," http://www.livius.org/babylonia.html. A large collection of translated texts and references to philological articles, with portals on Mesopotamia, Egypt, Anatolia, and Greece.

Oriental Institute, University of Chicago. Ancient Mesopotamia, http://mesopotamia.lib.uchicago.edu/. A user-friendly portal to the world-renowned Mesopotamia collection of the Oriental Institute.

Chapter 3

Bryant, Edwin. *The Quest for the Origins of Vedic Culture: The Indo-Aryan Migration Debate*. Oxford and New York: Oxford University Press, 2001. A scholarly yet readable attempt to address the linguistic and archaeological evidence surrounding the thesis of Aryan migration versus the more recent theory of indigenous Vedic development.

Embree, Ainslee T., ed. *Sources of Indian Tradition*, vol. 1, 2nd ed. New York: Columbia University Press, 1988. Though the language is dated in places, this is still the most comprehensive sourcebook of Indian thought available. Recent additions on women and gender make it even more so. Sophisticated yet readable introductions, glosses, and commentary.

Eraly, Abraham. *Gem in the Lotus: The Seeding of Indian Civilization*. London: Weidenfeld & Nicholson, 2004. Readable, comprehensive survey of recent scholarship from prehistory to the reign of Ashoka during the Mauryan dynasty of the fourth and third centuries BCE. Emphasis on transitional period of sixth-century religious innovations, particularly Buddhism.

Kenoyer, Jonathan Mark. *Ancient Cities of the Indus Valley Civilization*. Oxford and New York: Oxford University Press, 1998. Comprehensive work by team leader of Harappan Research Project. Particularly good on Lothal.

Klostermaier, Klaus. *A Survey of Hinduism*, 3rd ed. Albany, NY: SUNY Press, 2007. Comprehensive thematic treatment of major themes of Hinduism from the Vedas to Hinduism's relationship to modern science.

Possehl, Gregory L., ed. *Harappan Civilization: A Recent Perspective*, 2nd ed. New Delhi: Oxford University Press, 1993. Sound and extensive treatment of recent work and issues in Indus valley archaeology by one of the leading on-site researchers and a former student of Fairservis. Used to best advantage by experienced students.

Singh, Upinder. *A History of Ancient and Early Medieval India: From the Stone Age to the 12th Century*. New Delhi: Pearson, 2008. Sweeping text by a longtime instructor of Indian history at the University of Delhi. Suitable for undergraduates and current on the latest debates on ancient origins.

Trautmann, Thomas. *India: Brief History of a Civilization*. Oxford and New York: Oxford University Press, 2011. A succinct and lucid account of 4,000 years of Indian history, with particular emphasis on early developments.

Wolpert, Stanley. *A New History of India*, 5th ed. Oxford and New York: Oxford University Press, 2004. Another extremely useful, readable, one-volume history from Neolithic times to the present. Excellent first work for serious students.

WEBSITES

Columbia University Libraries. South and Southeast Asian Studies, www.columbia.edu/cu/lweb/indiv/southasia/cuvl/history.html. Run by Columbia University, this site contains links to "WWW.Virtual Library: Indian History"; "Regnal Chronologies"; "Internet Indian History Sourcebook"; and "Medical History of British India."

Harappa, http://www.harappa.com. Contains a wealth of images of artifacts and other archaeological treasures from the Indus Valley.

Chapter 4

Chang, Kwang-chih. *The Archaeology of Ancient China*, 4th ed. New Haven, CT.: Yale University Press, 1986. Sophisticated treatment of archaeology of Shang China. Prime exponent of the view of overlapping periods and territories for the Sandai period. Erudite, yet accessible for experienced students.

Ebrey, Patricia Buckley, ed. *Chinese Civilization: A Sourcebook*, 2nd ed. New York: Free Press, 1993. Wonderful supplement to the preceding volume. Some different classical sources and considerable material on women and social history. Time frame of this work extends to the modern era.

Keightly, David N., ed. *The Origins of Chinese Civilization*. Berkeley and Los Angeles: University of California Press, 1983. Symposium volume on a variety of Sandai topics by leading scholars. Some exposure to early Chinese history and archaeology is necessary in order to best appreciate these essays.

Linduff, Katheryn M., and Yan Sun, eds. *Gender and Chinese Archaeology*. Walnut Creek, CA: Altamira, 2004. Reexamines the role of gender in ancient China in the context of a critique of the general lack of gendered research in archaeology as a whole.

Liu, Xiang. *Exemplary Women of Early China: The Lienu zhuan of Liu Xiang*. Edited and translated by Anne Behnke Kinney. New York: Columbia University Press, 2014. One of the few accounts we have of the lives of women during the Three Dynasties period; covers 120 short biographies of Zhou women.

Lowe, Michael, and Edward L. Shaughnessy, eds. *The Cambridge History of Ancient China: From the Origins of Civilization to 221 B.C.* Cambridge, UK: Cambridge University Press, 1999. The opening volume of the Cambridge History of China series, this is the most complete multiessay collection on all aspects of recent Chinese ancient historical and archaeological work. The place to start for the serious student contemplating in-depth research.

Thorp, Robert L. *China in the Early Bronze Age: Shang Civilization*. Philadelphia: University of Pennsylvania Press, 2006. Comprehensive yet accessible survey of recent archaeological work on the period 2070–1046 BCE, including traditional Xia and Shang periods under the heading of China's "bronze age."

Wang, Aihe. *Cosmology and Political Culture in Early China*. Cambridge: Cambridge University Press, 2000. Part of the Cambridge Studies in Chinese History, Literature, and Institutions series. Wang argues that control of *cosmology*—how the world and universe operate—was a vital key to the wielding of power by the Shang and Zhou rulers. Recommended for serious students.

Wang, Robin. *Images of Women in Chinese Thought and Culture: Writings from the Pre-Qin Period Through the Song Dynasty*. Indianapolis, IN: Hackett Publishing, 2003. Excerpts from classical and more obscure texts on the role and treatment of women in early China. A large and useful section on pre-Confucian texts.

Watson, Burton, trans. *The Tso Chuan: Selections from China's Oldest Narrative History*. New York: Columbia University Press, 1989. Elegant translation by one of the most prolific of scholars working today. Excellent introduction to Zhou period and politics. Appropriate for beginning students, though more useful for those with some prior introduction to the period.

WEBSITES

http://lucian.uchicago.edu/blogs/earlychina/ssec/. This is the site of the journal *Early China*, published by the Society for the Study of Early China.

British Museum. Ancient China, http://www.ancientchina.co.uk. This site provides access to the British Museum's ancient Chinese collections and is highly useful for students seeking illustrations of assorted artifacts in a user-friendly environment.

Chapter 5

The Americas

Bellwood, Peter. *First Migrants: Ancient Migration in Global Perspective.* Chichester, UK: John Wiley & Sons, 2013. An intriguing study of prehistoric migration and its role in shaping the emergence of civilization.

Benson, Sonia, and Deborah J. Baker. *Early Civilizations in the Americas Reference Library,* 3 vols. Farmington Hills, MI: Gale UXL, 2009. Extensive three-volume encyclopedia available as a download or in hard copy. Contains an almanac of historical information and one of biographies and primary sources. Recommended for beginning and experienced students.

Bruhns, Karen Olsen, and Karen E. Stothert. *Women in Ancient America.* Norman: University of Oklahoma Press, 1999. A comprehensive account of women's roles in daily life, religion, politics, and war in foraging and farming as well as urban societies in the Americas.

Fiedel, Stuart J. *Prehistory of the Americas,* 2nd ed. Cambridge, UK: Cambridge University Press, 1992. Accessible, detailed survey of the archaeology of the Americas by a leading American scholar.

Solis, Ruth Shady, Haas, Jonathan, and Creamer, Winifred. "Dating Caral, a Preceramic Site in the Supe Valley on the Central Coast of Peru," *Science* 292:5517(2001): 723-726. Path-breaking early report of early scientific work on Caral Supe and the oldest American cities.

Thomas, David Hurst. *Exploring Native North America.* Oxford and New York: Oxford University Press, 2000. Selected chapters are useful on the major early North American sites, particularly Adena and Hopewell.

Trigger, Bruce G., Wilcomb E. Washburn, Richard E. W. Adams, Murdo J. MacLeod, Frank Salomon, and Stuart B. Schwartz, eds. *Cambridge History of the Native Peoples of the Americas,* 3 vols. Cambridge, UK: Cambridge University Press, 1996–2000. As with all of the Cambridge histories, this is a highly useful set for beginner and accomplished scholar alike. Useful bibliographies with the article entries.

von Hagen, Adriana, and Craig Morris. *The Cities of the Ancient Andes.* New York: Thames & Hudson, 1999. While more geared to later periods, still a useful overview, with illustrations, by specialists on Andean cultures.

Oceania

Carson, Mike T., *First Settlement of Remote Oceania: Earliest Sites in the Mariana Islands.* Heidelberg: Springer-Verlag, 2014. Study based on new archaeological research by a specialist on Pacific research.

Kirch, Patrick V. *The Lapita Peoples: Ancestors of the Oceanic World.* Cambridge, MA: Blackwell, 1997. Basic introduction by one of the pioneers of Polynesian research.

Matsuda, Matt K.. *Pacific Worlds: A History of Seas, Peoples, and Cultures.* Cambridge, UK: Cambridge University Press, 2012. General history of the Pacific with an emphasis on the early modern period.

Vlchek, Andre. *Oceania: Neocolonialism, Nukes and Bones.* Auckland, New Zealand: Atuanui, 2013. Analysis and discussion of the harmful effects of colonialism and neocolonialism on the development of Oceania.

WEBSITES

Foundation for the Advancement of Mesoamerican Studies (FAMSI), http://www.famsi.org/. Home page for the foundation, which has recently begun collaboration with the Los Angeles County Museum of Art and runs a wide range of scholarly, funding, and educational outreach programs aimed at advancing studies of Mesoamerica.

http://www.britannica.com/EBchecked/topic/468832/Polynesian-culture. Good link leading to an 8,000-word essay on leading topics concerning Polynesia and Oceania. In order to access the complete essay the reader must apply for a free trial of the online *Encyclopedia Britannica.*

Chapter 6

Sub-Saharan Africa

Chami, Félix. *The Unity of African Ancient History: 3000 BC to 500 AD.* Dar es Salaam: E&D, 2006. General overview by one of the leading archaeologists of East Africa.

McIntosh, Roderick J. *Ancient Middle Niger: Urbanism and the Self-Organizing Landscape.* Cambridge, UK: Cambridge University Press, 2005. Important revisionist work on the origins of urbanism and kingship in West Africa.

Mitchell, Peter, and Paul Lane. *The Oxford Handbook of African Archaeology.* Oxford: Oxford University Press, 2013. A total of 70 essays by specialists on all aspects of human culture in Africa, with an emphasis on foragers, agriculturalists, and early urbanists.

Vansina, Jan. *Paths in the Rainforests: Toward a History of Political Tradition in Equatorial Africa.* Madison: University of Wisconsin Press, 1990. Magisterial presentation of the Bantu dispersal and village life in the rain forest.

Mesoamerica and the Andes

Aveni, Anthony F. *Skywatchers,* rev. ed. Austin: University of Texas Press, 2001. Classic study on astronomy and calendars of pre-Columbian Americans, including a discussion of the Nazca lines.

Braswell, Geoffrey E., ed. *The Ancient Maya of Mexico: Reinterpreting the Past of the Northern Lowlands.* Milton Park, UK, and New York: Routledge, 2014. Contains articles on the origins of the ballgame and the Mayan "collapse."

Evans, Susan Tobey. *Ancient Mexico and Central America: Archaeology and Culture History.* London: Thames & Hudson, 2004. Densely but clearly written and detailed, with many sidebars on special topics.

Grube, Nikolai, ed. *Maya: Divine Kings of the Rain Forest.* Cologne, Germany: Könemann, 2001. Lavishly illustrated book with short contributions by many hands.

Schele, Linda, and David Freidel. *A Forest of Kings: The Untold Story of the Ancient Maya.* New York: Quill-William Morrow, 1990. Classic study summarizing the results of the decipherment of Maya glyphs, by two pioneers.

Stuart, David. *The Order of Days: Unlocking the Secrets of the Ancient Maya.* New York: Three Rivers Press, 2011. Magisterial summary of our current knowledge of Maya culture.

WEBSITES

Museum of Native American History. http://www.monah.us/precolumbian: Basic but fairly comprehensive website on pre-Columbian peoples and civilizations.

Stanford University Libraries. Africa South of the Sahara, http://www-sul.stanford.edu/depts/ssrg/africa/history.html. A large, resource-filled website based at Stanford University.

Chapter 7

Boatwright, Mary, Daniel J. Gargola, and Richard J. A. Talbert. *The Romans: From Village to Empire.* New York: Oxford University Press, 2004. Clearly written, comprehensive introduction to Roman history.

Boyce, Mary. *A History of Zoroastrianism.* Vol. 1, *The Early Period,* rev. ed. Handbuch der Orientalistik. Leiden, the Netherlands: E. J. Brill, 1989. Standard work by the leading scholar on the subject.

Briant, Pierre. *From Cyrus to Alexander: A History of the Persian Empire.* Winona Lake, IN: Eisenbrauns, 2000. Monumental work; the most detailed and authoritative study of the topic to date.

Cameron, Averil. *The Mediterranean World in Late Antiquity, AD 395–600.* London: Routledge, 1993. New perspective on the strengths and weaknesses of the late Roman empire.

Dignas, Beate, and Engelbert Winter. *Rome and Persia in Late Antiquity: Neighbours and Rivals.* Cambridge, UK: Cambridge University Press, 2007. Detailed historical investigation of the rivalry between Rome and Persia.

Freeman, Phillip. *Alexander the Great.* New York: Simon & Schuster, 2011. Illuminating study of Alexander the Great intended for a general audience.

Hubbard, Thomas K., ed. *A Companion to Greek and Roman Sexualities.* Chichester, UK: John Wiley & Sons, 2014. Far-ranging and informative collection of essays on all aspects of sexuality in ancient Greece and Rome.

Lehoux, Daryn. *What Did the Romans Know? An Inquiry into Science and Worldmaking.* Chicago: University of Chicago Press, 2012. Sophisticated analysis of Roman science in both its derivative and unique aspects.

Mathisen, Ralph. *Ancient Mediterranean Civilizations: From Prehistory to 640 CE,* 2nd ed. Oxford and New York: Oxford University Press, 2014. Revised overview with special emphasis on ethnicity, gender, and slavery.

Shaked, Shaul. *Dualism in Transformation: Varieties of Religion in Sasanian Iran.* London: School of Oriental and African Studies, 1994. Short history of the different religions in Sasanid Persia.

Smith, Mark S. *The Early History of God: Yahweh and the Other Deities in Ancient Israel.* San Francisco: Harper & Row, 1990. Very readable introduction to the problem of early monotheism among Israelites.

WEBSITES

British Museum. Ancient Greece, http://www.ancientgreece.co.uk/menu.html. Open the door to the compelling world of Ancient Greece. The British Museum has compiled a collection of images and information on various aspects of Greek history such as the Acropolis, Athens, daily life, festivals and games, Sparta, war, and gods.

Harvard University. Digital Atlas of Roman and Medieval Civilizations, http://darmc.harvard.edu/icb/icb.do?keyword=k40248&pageid=icb.page188868. Harvard University allows students to tailor searches in order to access specific geopolitical and spatial cartographical representations of the Roman and medieval worlds.

Perseus Digital Library, http://www.perseus.tufts.edu/hopper/. Probably the largest website on Greece and Rome, with immense resources, hosted by Tufts University.

Chapter 8

Auboyer, Jeannine. *Daily Life in Ancient India.* London: Phoenix, 2002. Overview consisting of sections on social structures/religious principles; individual/collective existence; and royal and administrative existence. Multidisciplinary approach appropriate for most undergraduates.

Carter, John Ross, and Mahinda Palihawadana, trans. *The Dhammapada.* Oxford and New York: Oxford University Press, 1987. Erudite but accessible translation of one of the key texts in the Buddhist corpus. Students with some exposure to the introductory ideas of Buddhism will find it very useful in its step-by-step elucidation of a number of central concepts.

Chakravarti, Uma. *The Social Dimensions of Early Buddhism.* New Delhi: Oxford University Press, 1987. Thorough analysis, with extensive glossary, of the influence of the north Indian economic transition to peasant market farming on the social milieu of early Buddhism.

Diem-Lane, Andrea. *Ahimsa: A Brief Guide to Jainism.* Walnut, CA: MSAC Philosophy Group, 2016. Short, student-friendly guide to Jain concepts, history, and Jainism today.

Doniger, Wendy. *The Hindus: An Alternative History.* New York: Penguin, 2009. Vivid but controversial new interpretation of the history of Hinduism by one of the leading scholars of Indian history. The book's portrayals of Hindu history, particularly in the area between myth and history, have prompted a lawsuit in India, which resulted in the withdrawal of the book there by the publisher in early 2014.

Embree, Ainslee T. *Sources of Indian Tradition,* 2 vols, 2nd ed. New York: Columbia University Press, 1988. The latest edition contains a number of new selections useful for the study of social relations in addition to the older religious material. As with all of the works in this series, the level of writing is sophisticated, though accessible; the overviews are masterly; and the works are ably translated.

Keay, John. *India: A History.* New York: Grove, 2000. Lively, highly detailed narrative history, with a number of useful charts and genealogies of ruling houses. Sympathetic treatment of controversial matters.

Knott, Kim. *Hinduism: A Very Short Introduction.* Oxford and New York: Oxford University Press, 1998. Sound, brief discussion of modern Hinduism and its formative influences. Asks provocative questions such as "What is a religion?" and "Is Hinduism something more than the Western conception of religion?"

Nikam, N. A., and Richard McKeon, eds. and trans. *The Edicts of Asoka.* Chicago: University of Chicago Press, 1959. Slim but useful volume for those interested in reading the entire collection of Ashoka's Pillar, Cave, and Rock Edicts. Short, accessible introduction.

Willis, Michael. *The Archaeology of Hindu Ritual.* Cambridge, UK: Cambridge University Press, 2009. Best utilized by experienced students, this book uses site archaeology, Sanskrit documents, and studies of ancient astronomy to plot the development of Hinduism under the Guptas and their use of it in statecraft as they created their vision of a universal empire.

Wolpert, Stanley. *A New History of India*, 6th ed. Oxford and New York: Oxford University Press, 2000. The standard introductory work to the long sweep of Indian history. Evenly divided between the period up to and including the Mughals and the modern era. Good coverage of geography and environment, as well as social and gender issues. Good select bibliography arranged by chapter; highly useful glossary of Indian terms.

WEBSITE

Digital Library of India, http://www.dli.ernet.in. This online resource, hosted by the Indian Institute of Science, Bangalore, contains primary and secondary sources not only for history but also for culture, economics, literature, and a host of other subjects.

Chapter 9

Henricks, Robert C., trans. *Lao-Tzu, Te-Tao Ching. A New Translation Based on the Recently Discovered Ma-wang-tui Texts*. New York: Ballantine Books, 1989. Some of the intitial work done on the earliest extant Daoist texts, reinterpreting our understanding of philosophical Daoism.

Hinsch, Bret. *Women in Early Imperial China*. Lanham, MD: Rowman & Littlefield, 2002. Broad examination of the place of women, and transition of the place of women, during the crucial early Chinese dynasties.

Huang, Ray. *China: A Macro History*. Armonk, NY: M. E. Sharpe, 1997. Readable, entertaining, and highly useful one-volume history. Particularly good on the complex politics of the post-Han and Song–Yuan periods.

Keay, John. *China: A History*. New York: Basic Books, 2009. Adventurous and well-written general history of China from prehistory to the present. Especially good for students with some previous grounding in the essentials of Chinese history.

Lewis, Mark Edward. *The Early Chinese Empires: Qin and Han*. Cambridge, MA: Harvard University Press, 2007. Detailed exploration of the rise and adaptations of China's initial empires. Better for advanced students.

Qian, Sima. *Records of the Grand Historian*. Translated by Burton Watson. 3 vols., rev. ed. New York: Columbia University Press, 1993. Powerful translation of China's supreme historical work by one of its best interpreters. Includes material from the Qin and Han dynasties. Invaluable source for serious students.

Snow, Philip. *The Star Raft: China's Encounter with Africa*. Ithaca, NY: Cornell University Press, 1988. Important, accessible study of the little-known area of China's maritime trade with Africa from Han times to the epic fifteenth-century voyages of Zheng He and beyond.

Yao Xinzhong. *An Introduction to Confucianism*. Cambridge, UK: Cambridge University Press, 2000. Overview of the tradition of the *ru* as it evolved and its status today.

WEBSITES

Asian Topics for Asian Educators. "Defining 'Daoism': A Complex History," http://afe.easia.columbia.edu/cosmos/ort/daoism.htm. Looks at Daoism as a term, its use, and its practice in terms of morality, society, nature, and the self.

http://bulldog2.redlands.edu/Dept/AsianStudiesDept/index.html. *East and Southeast Asia: An Annotated Directory of Internet Resources*. One of the most complete guides to websites dealing with all manner of Chinese and East Asian history and society.

Chapter 10

The Arabian Nights. Translated by Husain Haddawy. New York: Norton, 1990. Translation of the critical edition by Muhsin Mahdi, which reconstitutes the original thirteenth-century text.

Barry, Michael. *Figurative Art in Medieval Islam and the Riddle of Bihazâd of Herât (1465–1535)*. Paris: Flammarion, 2004.

Chaudhuri, K. N. *Trade and Civilization in the Indian Ocean*. Cambridge, UK: Cambridge University Press, 1985. Discusses the historical evolution of the trade and its various aspects (sea route, ships, commodities, and capital investments).

Fryde, Edmund. *The Early Palaeologan Renaissance (1261–c. 1360)*. Leiden, the Netherlands: E. J. Brill, 2000. Detailed presentation of the main philosophical and scientific figures of Byzantium after the recovery from the Latin interruption.

Herrin, Judith. *Unrivalled Influence: Women and Empire in Byzantium*. Princeton, NJ: Princeton University Press, 2013. Detailed investigation by a leading Byzantine historian and engagegd feminist.

Hoyland, Robert. *In God's Path: The Arab Conquests and the Creation of an Islamic Empire*. Oxford and New York: Oxford University Press, 2014. A new history of Islamic origins, seeking to combine Christian and Islamic sources.

Khalili, Jim al-. *The House of Wisdom: How Arabic Science Saved Ancient Knowledge and Gave Us the Renaissance*. New York: Penguin, 2010. In spite of the somewhat overwrought title, an expertly written introduction to the golden age of Arabic science by a scientist.

Laiou, Angeliki E., and Cécile Morrisson. *The Byzantine Economy*. Cambridge, UK: Cambridge University Press, 2007. Comprehensive and well-researched study of ups and downs in the demography, productive capacity, and long-distance trade of Byzantium.

Lapidus, Ira. *Muslim Cities in the Later Middle Ages*. Cambridge, UK: Cambridge University Press, 1984. Seminal work and still the only study of Muslim urban society, although it should be supplemented by Shlomo D. Goitein's monumental study of Jews, *A Mediterranean Society* (1967–1993).

Rippin, Andrew. *Muslims: Their Religious Beliefs and Practices*, 2nd ed. London: Routledge, 2001. One of the best and most accessible introductions to the basic beliefs and practices of Islam, based on the reevaluation of Islamic origins also presented in this chapter.

Tyerman, Christopher. *God's War: A New History of the Crusades*. Cambridge, MA: Belknap, 2006. Persuasive revisionist history by a leading Crusade historian.

Whittow, Mark. *The Making of Byzantium, 600–1025*. Berkeley and Los Angeles: University of California Press, 1996. Revisionist study of the Byzantine struggle for survival in the early years.

WEBSITES

BBC—Religion: Islam. http://www.bbc.co.uk/religion/religions/islam/. A very basic overview of Islamic Civilization. Most websites on Islam and Islamic civilization are apologetic (pro-Muslim or pro-Christian), and earlier scholarly websites are no longer available.

Islamic Awareness. http://www.islamic-awareness.org/. This website, even though Islam-apologetic, is a fountain of early documents relevant for Islamic history.

Chapter 11

Bartlett, Robert. *The Making of Europe: Conquest, Colonization, and Cultural Change, 950–1350.* Princeton, NJ: Princeton University Press, 1993. Analyzes the expansion of Europe from a cultural perspective.

Berend, Norma, Przemyslaw Urbanczlyk, and Przemyslaw Wiszewski. *Central Europe in the High Middle Ages: Bohemia, Hungary and Poland, ca. 900–ca. 1300.* New York: Cambridge University Press, 2013. Learned and insightful study that explores frequently overlooked aspects of medieval Europe.

Brown, Peter. *The Rise of Western Christendom: Triumph and Diversity, A.D. 200–1000,* 2nd ed. Oxford, UK: Wiley-Blackwell, 2003. Traces the development of Christian Europe from the perspective of the church.

Grant, Edward. *The Foundation of Modern Science in the Middle Ages.* Cambridge, UK: Cambridge University Press, 1996. Seminal study of the contributions of medieval science to the scientific revolution of the seventeenth century.

Lawrence, C. H. *Medieval Monasticism: Forms of Religious Life in Western Europe in the Middle Ages,* 2nd ed. New York: Longman, 1984. Thorough survey of the development of the Western monastic tradition.

McKitterick, Rosamond. *Charlemagne: The Formation of a European Identity.* Cambridge, UK: Cambridge University Press, 2008. An examination of how Charlemagne's policies contributed to the idea of Europe.

Platt, Colin. *King Death: The Black Death and Its Aftermath in Late-Medieval England.* Toronto: University of Toronto Press, 1997. Riveting analysis of the effects of the Black Death on all aspects of society.

Riley-Smith, Jonathan, ed. *The Oxford Illustrated History of the Crusades.* Oxford and New York: Oxford University Press, 1995. A very useful and readable history of the crusading movement.

Turner, Denys. *Thomas Aquinas: A Portrait.* New Haven, CT: Yale University Press, 2013. Up-to-date biography of one of the greatest figures in medieval philosophy.

Wickham, Chris. *Medieval Europe.* New Haven, CT: Yale University Press, 2016. A scintillating and innovative study that presents new interpretations of important turning points in the development of medieval European civilization.

WEBSITES

British Library. Treasures in Full: Magna Carta, http://www.bl.uk/treasures/magnacarta/virtual_curator/vc9.html. An excellent website that makes available a digitized version of Magna Carta. Audio files answer many FAQs about the manuscript and its significance.

Howe, Jeffery. A Digital Archive of Architecture, http://www.bc.edu/bc_org/avp/cas/fnart/arch/gothic_arch.html. Jeffery Howe's Digital Archive of Architecture has a quick index reference guide, which links to images of both early and high Gothic architecture.

Chapter 12

Asif, Manan Ahmed. *A Book of Conquest: The Chachnama and Muslim Origins in South Asia.* Cambridge, MA: Harvard University Press, 2016. Comprehensive study of the pivotal story of deceit and conquest and the contentious legacy surrounding the initial Muslim forays into India.

Bulag, Uradyn Erden. *The Mongols at China's Edge: History and the Politics of National Unity.* Lanham, MD: Rowman & Littlefield, 2002. New historical overview of the Mongols through historical and anthropological lenses that seeks to demythologize their experience and interactions with China and central Asian peoples.

Chiu-Duke, Josephine. *To Rebuild the Empire: Lu Chih's Confucian Pragmatist Approach to the Mid-Tang Predicament.* Albany, NY: SUNY Press, 2000. Political and philosophical study of one of the Tang era's most important prime ministers and his attempts to retrieve Tang fortunes and actions in the beginning of the period's Confucian revival.

De Bary, William T., and Irene Bloom, eds. *Sources of Chinese Tradition,* 2nd ed., vol. 1. New York: Columbia University Press, 1999. Excellent introduction to major Chinese philosophical schools. Extensive coverage of Buddhism and Neo-Confucianism with accessible, highly informative introductions to the documents themselves.

Ebrey, Patricia Buckley, ed. *The Inner Quarters.* Berkeley and Los Angeles: University of California Press, 1993. Perhaps the best scholarly exploration of the roles of women in Song China.

Hansen, Valerie. *The Open Empire: A History of China to 1600.* New York: W. W. Norton, 2000. A fresh and accessible synthesis of pre-modern Chinese history.

Levathes, Louise. *When China Ruled the Seas: The Treasure Fleet of the Dragon Throne 1405–1433.* New York: Simon & Schuster, 1994. Delightful coverage of the voyages of Zheng He from 1405 to 1433. Particularly good on the aftermath of the voyages.

Robinson, Francis. *Islam and Muslim History in South Asia.* Oxford and New York: Oxford University Press, 2004. Compendium of essays and reviews by the author on a variety of subjects concerning the history and status of Islam in the subcontinent. Of particular interest is his response to Samuel Huntington's famous "clash of civilizations" thesis.

Singh, Patwant. *The Sikhs.* London: John Murray, 1999. Readable popular history of the Sikh experience to the present by an adherent. Especially useful on the years from Guru Nanak to the changes of the early eighteenth century and the transition to a more militant faith.

WEBSITES

Asian Topics in World History. "The Mongols in World History," http://afe.easia.columbia.edu/mongols/. With a timeline spanning 1000–1500, "The Mongols in World History" delivers a concise and colorful history of the Mongols' impact on global history.

Fordham University. Internet Indian History Sourcebook, http://www.fordham.edu/halsall/india/indiasbook.asp. One of the series of online "sourcebooks" by Fordham containing links to important documents, secondary literature, and assorted other web resources.

Fordham University. Internet East Asian History Sourcebook, http://www.fordham.edu/halsall/eastasia/eastasiasbook .asp. As with its counterpart above, this is one in the series of useful online sources and links put together by Fordham, in this case about East Asia, with particular emphasis on the role of China as a center of cultural diffusion.

Chapter 13

General

Holcombe, Charles. *A History of East Asia, From the Origins of Civilization to the Twenty-First Century.* Cambridge, UK: Cambridge University Press, 2011. A top one-volume history of China, Korea, and Japan, with an emphasis on the region's shared past.

Mann, Susan. *East Asia (China, Korea, Japan).* Washington, DC: American Historical Association, 1999. The second volume in the Women's and Gender History in Global Perspective series. Short, informative work with historiographic overviews and cross-cultural comparisons among the three countries named in the title. Critical annotated bibliographies on the use of standard texts in integrating women and gender into Asian studies.

Neuman, W. Lawrence. *East Asian Societies.* Ann Arbor, MI: Association For Asian Studies, 2014. Part of the AAS's "Key Issues in Asian Studies," this provides a short, accessible introduction to the region for beginning students.

Ramusack, Barbara N., and Sharon Sievers. *Women in Asia.* Bloomington: Indiana University Press, 1999. Part of the series Restoring Women to History. Far-ranging book divided into two parts, "Women in South and Southeast Asia" and "Women in East Asia." Coverage of individual countries, extensive chronologies, valuable bibliographies. Most useful for advanced undergraduates.

Korea

De Bary, William T., ed. *Sources of Korean Tradition,* vol. 1. Introduction to Asian Civilizations. New York: Columbia University Press, 1997. Part of the renowned Columbia series on the great traditions of East Asia. Perhaps the most complete body of accessible sources for undergraduates.

Korean Overseas Information Service. *A Handbook of Korea.* Seoul: KOIS, 1993. Wonderfully complete history, geography, guidebook, and sociology text. Excellent source, but students should keep in mind its provenance and treat some of its historical claims to uniqueness accordingly.

Seth, Michael J. *A Concise History of Korea.* 2nd ed. Lanham, MD: Rowman and Littlefield, 2016. Well-researched and comprehensive history of the Korean peninsula from Neolithic times to 2016. Covers both North and South Korea, though the South comes in for the most detailed treatment.

Japan

De Bary, William T., ed. *Sources of Japanese Tradition,* vol. 1. Introduction to Asian Civilizations. 2nd ed. New York: Columbia University Press, 2002. Like the volume above on Korea and the others in this series on India and China, the sources are well selected, the glossaries are sound, and the overviews of the material are masterful. As with the other East Asia volumes, the complexities of the various Buddhist schools are especially well drawn. Students with some previous experience will derive the most benefit from this excellent volume.

Murasaki Shikibu. *The Diary of Lady Murasaki.* Richard Bowring, trans. New York: Penguin, 1996. Capable translation of the court diary of the author of *The Tale of Genji* and an intimate glimpse into lives of the elite of Heian Japan.

Totman, Conrad. *A History of Japan.* Oxford, UK: Blackwell, 2000. Part of Blackwell's History of the World series. A large, well-balanced, and comprehensive history. More than half of the material is on the pre-1867 period, with extensive coverage of social history and demographics.

Vietnam

Steinberg, Joel David, ed. *In Search of Southeast Asia,* rev. ed. Honolulu: University of Hawaii Press, 1987. Extensive coverage of Vietnam within the context of an area study of Southeast Asia. Though weighted toward the modern period, very good coverage of agricultural and religious life in the opening chapters.

Taylor, Keith W. *The Birth of Vietnam.* Berkeley and Los Angeles: University of California Press, 1983. Comprehensive, magisterial volume on early Vietnamese history and historical identity amid the long Chinese occupation. Best for students with some background in Southeast Asian and Chinese history.

WEBSITES

Department of Prints and Drawings, British Museum, http://www.britishmuseum.org/the_museum/departments/prints_and_drawings.aspx. A comprehensive source for all manner of interests related to Asian studies.

Public Broadcasting Service, Hidden Korea, http://www.pbs.org/hiddenkorea/history.htm. Sound introduction to the geography, people, history and culture of Korea, with links to additional source material.

Cambridge Journals Online, Journal of Southeast Asian Studies, http://journals.cambridge.org/action/displayJournal?jid= SEA. Online version of the scholarly publication of the same name, features articles on the history, sociology, cultural studies, and literature of the region. It aims for scholarly but accessible presentations. Recommended for advanced students.

Chapter 14

Birmingham, David, and Phyllis M. Martin, eds. *History of Central Africa,* vol. 1. London: Longman, 1983. The first chapter, by Birmingham, provides an excellent summary of the history of Luba prior to 1450.

Collins, Robert O., and James M. Burns. *A History of Subsaharan Africa,* 2nd ed. Cambridge: Cambridge University Press, 2014. Authoritative history by two well-known Africanists, updated by James Burns after the death of Robert Collins.

Crummey, David. *Land and Society in the Christian Kingdom of Ethiopia: From the Thirteenth to the Twentieth Century.* Urbana: University of Illinois Press, 2000. The first book in which the rich land records of the church have been used for a reconstruction of agriculture and land tenure.

Horton, Mark, and John Middleton. *The Swahili: The Social Landscape of a Mercantile Society.* Oxford, UK: Blackwell, 2000. A study that gives full attention to the larger context of East Africa in which the Swahilis flourished. Middleton is the author of another important study, *The World of the*

Swahili: An African Mercantile Civilization (Yale University Press, 1992).

Huffman, Thomas N. *Mapungubwe: Ancient African Civilization on the Limpopo.* Johannesburg: Witwatersrand University Press, 2005. Short but illuminating summary of the archaeological record by a leading South African expert, although his interpretation of Zimbabwe in an earlier work (*Snakes and Crocodiles*, Witwatersrand University Press, 1996) is controversial.

Levtzion, Nehemia. *Ancient Ghana and Mali.* New York: Africana, 1980. Originally published London: Methuen, 1973. Standard history of ancient Ghana, Mali, and Songhay based on a thorough knowledge of the Arabic sources; a revision by David Conrad, Paulo Farias, Roderick J. McIntosh, and Susan McIntosh has been announced but has yet to appear.

Robinson, David. *Muslim Societies in African History.* Cambridge, UK: Cambridge University Press, 2004. Advertised as part of a series of new approaches, this book nevertheless presents a conventional view of Islam, albeit in its African context.

Trigger, Bruce. *History and Settlement in Lower Nubia.* Yale University Publications in Anthropology 69. New Haven, CT: Yale University Press, 1965. Chapter 9 is still the best overview of Nubian history, by a scholar with a broad understanding of early civilizations.

WEBSITES

Heilbrunn Timeline of Art History. "Ife (from ca. 350 B.C.)," http://www.metmuseum.org/toah/hd/ife/hd_ife.htm. An excellent introductory website hosted by the Metropolitan Museum of Art. It contains many links and presents clear overviews.

For a website by Patrick Darling, the principal archaeological investigator of the Nigerian earthworks, see http://cohesion.rice.edu/CentersAndInst/SAFA/emplibrary/49_ch09.pdf for a copy of a 1998 article.

Chapter 15

Bruhns, Karen Olsen, and Karen E. Stothert. *Women in Ancient America.* Norman: University of Oklahoma Press, 1999. Comprehensive account of women's role in daily life, religion, politics, and war in forager and agrarian–urban societies.

Brumfield, Elizabeth M., and Gary F. Feinman, eds. *The Aztec World.* New York: Abrams, 2008. Collection of expert short chapters on a variety of topics, richly illustrated.

Carrasco, Davíd. *The Aztecs: A Very Short Introduction.* Oxford and New York: Oxford University Press, 2012. Clear, compressed account by a specialist, containing all essential information.

D'Altroy, Terence. *The Incas.* 2nd ed., Hoboken, NJ: John Wiley and Sons, 2014. Well-organized, comprehensive, and up-to-date overview.

Hassig, Ross. *War and Society in Ancient Mesoamerica.* Berkeley and Los Angeles: University of California Press, 1992. Best study of the rising importance of militarism in Mesoamerican city-states, up to the Aztec Empire.

Julien, Catherine. *Reading Inca History.* Iowa City: University of Iowa Press, 2000. Ambitious "reading" of "genres" of memory in the available, mostly Spanish sources.

Malpass, Michael A. *Daily Life in the Inca Empire.* 2nd ed. Westport, CT: Greenwood, 2009. Clear, straightforward, and readable account of ordinary people's lives by a specialist.

Smith, Michael E., *The Aztecs,* 3rd ed. Hoboken, NJ: Wiley, 2013. Up-to-date, extensive account of all aspects of Inca history and civilization.

WEBSITE

Aztec History, http://www.aztec-history.com/. Introductory website, easily navigable, with links.

Chapter 16

Ágoston, Gábor. *Guns for the Sultan: Military Power and the Weapons Industry in the Ottoman Empire.* Cambridge, UK: Cambridge University Press, 2005. Thorough study, which is based on newly accessible Ottoman archival materials and emphasizes the technological prowess of Ottoman gunsmiths.

Casale, Giancarlo. *The Ottoman Age of Exploration.* Oxford and New York: Oxford University Press, 2010. Detailed correction, based on Ottoman and Portuguese archives, of the traditional characterization of the Ottoman Empire as a land-oriented power.

Casey, James. *Early Modern Spain: A Social History.* London: Routledge, 1999. Detailed, well-documented analysis of rural–urban and king–nobility tensions.

Elliott, John Huxtable. *Spain, Europe, and the Wider World: 1500–1800.* New Haven, CT: Yale University Press, 2009. A comprehensive overview, particularly strong on culture during the 1500s.

Glete, Jan. *War and the State in Early Modern Europe: Spain, the Dutch Republic, and Sweden as Fiscal–Military States, 1500–1660.* London: Routledge, 2002. A complex but persuasive construction of the forerunner to the absolute state. Unfortunately leaves out the Ottoman Empire.

Murphey, Rhoads. *Ottoman Warfare, 1500–1700.* New Brunswick, NJ: Rutgers University Press, 1999. Author presents a vivid picture of the Janissaries, their discipline, organization, campaigns, and voracious demands for salary increases.

Pamuk, Sevket. *A Monetary History of the Ottoman Empire.* Cambridge, UK: Cambridge University Press, 2000. Superb analysis of Ottoman archival resources on the role and function of American silver in the money economy of the Ottomans.

Ruiz, Teofilo R. *Spanish Society, 1400–1600.* London: Longman, 2001. Richly detailed social studies rewarding anyone interested in changing class structures, rural–urban movement, and extension of the money market into the countryside.

Subrahmanyam, Sanjay. *The Career and Legend of Vasco da Gama.* Cambridge, UK: Cambridge University Press, 1997. Focuses on the religious motivations of Vasco da Gama and the commercial impact of his journey to India.

WEBSITES

Frontline, "Apocalypse! The Evolution of Apocalyptic Belief and How It Shaped the Western World," PBS, 1995, http://www.pbs.org/wgbh/pages/frontline/shows/apocalypse/. The contribution by Bernard McGinn, University of Chicago, under the heading of "Apocalypticism Explained: Joachim of Fiore," is of particular relevance for the understanding of Christopher Columbus viewing himself as a precursor of Christ's Second Coming.

Islam: Empire of Faith: Timeline, http://www.pbs.org/empires/islam/timeline.html. Comprehensive and informative, this

PBS website on the Ottoman Empire examines the various facets of this Islamic culture such as scientific innovations, faith and its leaders.

Chapter 17

Biro, Jacquelin. *On Earth as in Heaven: Cosmography and the Shape of the Earth from Copernicus to Descartes*. Saarbrücken, Germany: VDM Verlag Dr. Müller, 2009. Short study establishing the connection between geography and cosmology in Copernicus. Uses the pathbreaking articles by Thomas Goldberg.

Black, Jeremy. *Kings, Nobles, and Commoners: States and Societies in Early Modern Europe—A Revisionist History*. London: I.B. Tauris, 2004. Available also electronically on ebrary; persuasive thesis, largely accepted by scholars, of a continuity of institutional practices in Europe across the sixteenth and seventeenth centuries, casting doubt on absolutism as being more than a theory.

Cañizares-Esguerra, Jorge. *Nature, Empire, and Nation: Explorations of the History of Science in the Iberian World*. Stanford, CA: Stanford University Press, 2006. A collection of essays that provides new perspectives on the history of science in early modern Iberia.

Geanakoplos, Deno John. *Constantinople and the West: Essays on the Late Byzantine (Palaeologan) and Italian Renaissances and the Byzantine and Roman Churches*. Madison: University of Wisconsin Press, 1989. Fundamental discussion of the extensive transfer of texts and scholars during the 1400s.

Jacob, Margaret C. *Scientific Culture and the Making of the Industrial West*. Oxford and New York: Oxford University Press, 1997. Widely cited short book emphasizing the connections among New Science, scientific societies, and the steam engine.

Margolis, Howard. *It Started with Copernicus: How Turning the World Inside Out Led to the Scientific Revolution*. New York: McGraw-Hill, 2002. Important scholarly study of the connection between the discovery of the Americas and Copernicus's formulation of a sun-centered planetary system.

Nexon, Daniel H. *The Struggle for Power in Early Modern Europe: Religious Conflict, Dynastic Empires and International Change*. Princeton, NJ: Princeton University Press, 2009. Charles Tilly–inspired reevaluation of the changes occurring in sixteenth- and seventeenth-century Europe.

Park, Katharine, and Lorraine Daston, eds. *The Cambridge History of Science*. Vol. 3, *Early Modern Science*. Cambridge, UK: Cambridge University Press, 2006. Voluminous coverage of all aspects of science, under the currently paradigmatic thesis that there was no dramatic scientific revolution in Western Christian civilization.

Rublack, Ulinka. *Reformation Europe*. Cambridge, UK: Cambridge University Press, 2006. Cultural history approach to the effects of Luther and Calvin on western Christians.

Schiebinger, Londa. *The Mind Has No Sex? Women in the Origins of Modern Science*. Cambridge, MA: Harvard University Press, 1989. A pioneering study presenting biographies and summaries of scientific contributions made by women. Discusses the importance of Marie Cunitz.

Wiesner-Hanks, Merry E. *Early Modern Europe, 1450-1789*. 2nd ed. Cambridge, UK: Cambridge University Press, 2013. Textbook in the Cambridge History of Europe series with a braod coverage of topics.

WEBSITES

Ames Research Center. "Johannes Kepler: His Life, His Laws and Times," http://kepler.nasa.gov/Mission/JohannesKepler/. This NASA website looks at the life and views of Johannes Kepler. It examines his discoveries, his contemporaries, and the events that shaped modern science.

Howard, Sharon. "Early Modern Resources," http://sharonhoward.org/earlymodern.html. Website with many links on the full range of institutional and cultural change.

Chapter 18

Alchon, Suzanne A. *A Pest in the Land: New World Epidemics in a Global Perspective*. Albuquerque: University of New Mexico Press, 2003. A broad overview, making medical history comprehensible.

Behringer, Wolfgang. *Witches and Witch-Hunts: A Global History*. Cambridge, UK: Polity, 2004. A well-grounded overview of the phenomenon of the fear of witches, summarizing the scholarship of the past decades.

Bulmer-Thomas, Victor, John S. Coatsworth, and Roberto Cortés Conde, eds. *The Cambridge Economic History of Latin America*. Vol. 1, *The Colonial Era and the Short Nineteenth Century*. Cambridge, UK: Cambridge University Press, 2006. Collection of specialized summary articles on aspects of Iberian colonialism.

Burkholder, Mark A., and Lyman L. Johnson. *Colonial Latin America*, 6th ed. Oxford and New York: Oxford University Press, 2008. A well-established text, updated multiple times.

Eastman, Scott, *Preaching Spanish Nationalism across the Hispanic Atlantic, 1759–1823*. Baton Rouge: Louisiana State University Press, 2012. Close look at the national reform debates in the Iberian Atlantic world at the close of colonialism.

Ekberg, Carl J. *French Roots in the Illinois Country: The Mississippi Frontier in Colonial Times*. Urbana: University of Illinois Press, 1998. Detailed, deeply researched historical account.

Peloso, Vincent. *Race and Ethnicity in Latin America*. Milton Park and New York: Routledge, 2014. Excellent presentation of the publicly enshrined, complex racial and ethnic identities during colonialism and since independence.

Socolow, Susan M. *The Women of Latin America*. Cambridge, UK: Cambridge University Press, 2000. Surveys the patriarchal order and the function of women within it.

Stein, Stanley J., and Barbara H. Stein. *Silver, Trade, and War: Spain and America in the Making of Early Modern Europe*. Baltimore: Johns Hopkins University Press, 2000. Covers the significance of American silver reaching as far as China.

Taylor, Alan. *American Colonies*. London: Penguin, 2001. History of the English colonies in New England, written from a broad Atlantic perspective.

Wood, Michael. *Conquistadors*. Berkeley and Los Angeles: University of California Press, 2000. Accessible, richly illustrated history of the conquest period.

WEBSITE

Conquistadors, http://www.pbs.org/conquistadors/. Wonderful interactive website that allows you to track the journeys made by the Conquistadors such as Cortés, Pizarro, Orellana, and Cabeza de Vaca. Learn more about their conquests in the Americas and the legacy they left behind them.

Chapter 19

Berlin, Ira. *Many Thousands Gone: The First Two Centuries of Slavery in North America.* Cambridge, MA: Harvard University Press, 1998. One of the most authoritative studies of antebellum chattel slavery by one of the era's leading historians.

Carney, Judith A. *Black Rice: The African Origins of Rice Cultivation in the Americas.* Cambridge, MA: Harvard University Press, 2001. Study which goes a long way toward correcting the stereotype that black slaves were unskilled laborers, and carefully documents the transfer of rice-growing culture from West Africa to the Americas.

Dubois, Laurent, and Julius S. Scott, eds. *Origins of the Black Atlantic: Rewriting Histories.* New York: Routledge, 2010. Book that focuses on African slaves in the Americas as they had to arrange themselves in their new lives.

Gray, Richard, and David Birmingham, eds. *Pre-Colonial African Trade.* London and New York: Oxford University Press, 1970. Collective work in which contributors emphasize the growth and intensification of trade in the centuries of 1500–1800.

Hall, Gwendolyn Midlo. *Slavery and African Ethnicities in the Americas: Restoring the Links.* Chapel Hill: University of North Carolina Press, 2005. Study that focuses on slaves in the Americas according to their regions of origin in Africa.

Heywood, Linda M., and John K. Thornton. *Central Africans, Atlantic Creoles, and the Foundation of the Americas.* Cambridge, UK: Cambridge University Press, 2007. Pathbreaking investigation of the creation and role of Creole culture in Africa and the Americas.

Iliffe, John. *Africans: The History of a Continent, 2nd ed.* Cambridge, UK: Cambridge University Press, 2007. Standard historical summary by an established African historian.

Kriger, Colleen E. *Cloth in West African History.* Lanham, MD Altamira, 2006. Detailed investigation of the sophisticated indigenous West African cloth industry.

LaGamma, Alisa. *Kongo: Power and Majesty.* New York: Metropolitan Museum of Art, 2015. Superbly illustrated exhibition catalogue, with articles by leading Africanists.

Oliver, Roland, and Anthony Atmore. *Medieval Africa, 1250–1800.* Cambridge, UK: Cambridge University Press, 2001. Revised and updated historical overview, divided into regions and providing detailed regional histories on the emerging kingdoms.

Stapleton, Timothy J. *A Military History of Africa.* Vol. 1, *The Precolonial Period: From Ancient Egypt to the Zulu Kingdom (Earliest Times to ca. 1870).* Santa Barbara, CA: Praeger, 2013. Summary of the historical evolution of West, East, Central, and South Africa.

Thornton, John. *The Kongolese Saint Anthony: Dona Beatriz Kimpa Vita and the Antonian Movement, 1684–1706.* Cambridge, UK: Cambridge University Press, 1998. Detailed biography of Dona Beatriz, from which the vignette at the beginning of the chapter is borrowed; includes a general overview of the history of Kongo during the civil war.

WEBSITES

British Museum. "Benin: An African Kingdom," www.british museum.org/PDF/british_museum_benin_art.pdf. In addition to offering a brief historical backdrop to the art of the Benin kingdom, the British Museum's PDF also depicts various artifacts taken by the British from the Royal Palace.

Voyages: The Atlantic Slave Trade Database, http://www.slave voyages.org/tast/index.faces. A large electronic website based at Emory University and sponsored by a number of American universities, presenting up-to-date demographic tables.

Chapter 20

Bernier, François. *Travels in the Mogul Empire, A.D. 1656–1668.* Translated by Archibald Constable. Delhi: S. Chand, 1968. One of many fascinating travel accounts by European diplomats, merchants, and missionaries.

Eaton, Richard M. *Essays on Islam and Indian History.* Oxford and New York: Oxford University Press, 2002. A compendium of the new scholarly consensus on, among other things, the differences between the clerical view of Islamic observance and its actual impact in rural India. Contains both historiography and material on civilizational and cultural issues.

Gommans, J. J. L. *Mughal Warfare: Indian Frontiers and Highroads to Empire 1500–1700.* New York: Routledge, 2002. Sound examination of the Mughal Empire as a centralizing state increasingly reliant on a strong military for border defense and extending its sway. Examination of the structure of Mughal forces and the organization and weapons of the military.

Hunt, Margaret R., and Philip J. Stern, eds. *The English East India Company at the Height of Mughal Expansion: A Soldier's Diary of the 1689 Siege of Bombay with Related Documents.* Boston and New York: Bedford/St. Martin's, 2016. Illuminating look at the interplay of Mughal and European actors during the reign of Aurangzeb through the eyes of James Hilton, an English East India Company soldier, whose diary had previously been unpublished.

Kearney, Milo. *The Indian Ocean in World History.* New York: Routledge, 2003. Long view of the history of Indian Ocean trade from ancient times. Particularly relevant in examining the vital period in which the Portuguese and later East Indian Companies come to dominate the trade.

Nizami, Khaliq A. *Akbar and Religion.* Delhi: IAD, 1989. Extensive treatment of Akbar's evolving move toward devising his din-i ilahi movement, by a leading scholar of Indian religious and intellectual history.

Richards, John F. *The Mughal Empire.* Cambridge, UK: Cambridge University Press, 1993. Comprehensive volume in the New Cambridge History of India series. Sophisticated treatment; best suited to advanced students. Extensive glossary and useful bibliographic essay.

Schimmel, Annemarie. *The Empire of the Great Mughals: History, Art, and Culture.* London: Reaktion, 2004. Revised edition of a volume published in German in 2000. Lavish illustrations, wonderfully drawn portraits of key individuals, and extensive treatment of social, family, and gender relations at the Mughal court.

Srivastava, M. P. *The Mughal Administration.* Delhi: Chugh, 1995. Solid overview and analysis of the development and workings of the Mughal bureaucracy. Best utilized by advanced students.

WEBSITES

Association for Asian Studies http://www. asian-studies.org/ As with other Asian topics, one of the most reliable websites is sponsored by the Association for Asian Studies, the largest professional organization for scholars of Asia.

BBC: Religions. "Mughal Empire (1500s, 1600s)" http://www
.bbc.co.uk/religion/religions/islam/history/mughal
empire_1.shtml. The Mughal Empire ruled most of India and
Pakistan in the sixteenth and seventeenth centuries. Learn
more about the religious divides and governance of Muslim
Mughals in a country with a majority of Hindu populace.

Chapter 21
China
Crossley, Pamela K. *A Translucent Mirror: History and Identity in
Qing Imperial Ideology.* Los Angeles: University of California
Press, 1999. Pioneering study of the transformation of Qing
self-image to one of leading a universal, multicultural empire.
De Bary, William T., and Irene Bloom, comps. *Sources of Chinese
Tradition*, 2 vols., 2nd ed. New York: Columbia University
Press, 1999. Thoroughgoing update of the classic sourcebook
for Chinese literature and philosophy, with a considerable
amount of social, family, and women's works now included.
Mungello, D. E. *The Great Encounter of China and West.* Lanham,
MD: Rowman & Littlefield, 1999. Sound historical overview
of the period marking the first European maritime expeditions into East Asia and extending to the height of the Canton
trade and the beginnings of the opium era.
Pomeranz, Kenneth. *The Great Divergence: China, Europe, and the
Making of the Modern World Economy.* Princeton, NJ: Princeton University Press, 2001. Pathbreaking work mounting the
strongest argument yet in favor of the balance of economic
power remaining in East Asia until the Industrial Revolution
was well under way.
Shuo Wang. "Manchu Women in Transition: Gender Relations
and Sexuality," in Stephen A. Wadley and Carsten Naeher,
eds. *Proceedings of the First North American Conference on
Manchu Studies.* Wiesbaden, Germany: Otto Harrassowitz
Verlag, 2006: 105–130. Pathbreaking study of the role of
Manchu women in Qing China in resistance to assimilation
and preserving cultural identity.
Spence, Jonathan. *The Memory Palace of Matteo Ricci.* New York:
Penguin, 1984. Highly original treatment of Ricci and the
beginning of the Jesuit interlude in late Ming and early Qing
China. Attempts to penetrate Ricci's world through the mis-
sionary's own memory techniques.

Japan
De Bary, William T., ed. *Sources of Japanese Tradition*, 2 vols. New
York: Columbia University Press, 1964. The Tokugawa era
spans volumes 1 and 2, with its inception and political and
philosophical foundations thoroughly covered in volume
1 and the Shinto revival of national learning, the later Mito
school, and various partisans of national unity in the face of
foreign intrusion covered in the beginning of volume 2.
Duus, Peter. *Feudalism in Japan*, 3rd ed. New York: McGraw-Hill,
1993. Updated version of a short, handy volume spanning
all of Japanese history to 1867, with special emphasis on the
shogunates. Good introduction on the uses and limitations
of the term "feudalism" with reference to Japan within a comparative framework.
Gordon, Andrew. *A Modern History of Japan from Tokugawa Times
to the Present.* Oxford and New York: Oxford University Press,
2009. One of the few treatments of Japanese history that spans

both the Tokugawa and the modern eras, rather than making
the usual break in either 1853 or 1867/1868. Both the continuity of the past and the novelty of the new era are therefore
juxtaposed and highlighted. Most useful for students with a
background at least equivalent to that supplied by this text.

WEBSITE
National Geographic. China's Great Armada, http://ngm.national
geographic.com/ngm/0507/feature2/map.html. Track the
voyages made by Zheng He to Southeast Asia, India, Arabia,
and Africa.

Chapter 22
Herb, Guntram H. *Nations and Nationalism: A Global Historical
Overview.* Santa Barbara, CA: ABC-Clio, 2008. Contains a
large number of articles on the varieties of ethnic nationalism
and culture and the proliferation of nationalism in Europe
and Latin America.
Israel, Jonathan I. *A Revolution of the Mind: Radical Enlighten-
ment and the Origins of Modern Democracy.* Princeton, NJ:
Princeton University Press, 2010. Israel is a pioneer of the
contemporary renewal of intellectual history, and his investigations of the Enlightenment tradition are pathbreaking.
Kaiser, Thomas E., and Dale K. Van Kley, eds. *From Deficit to Deluge:
The Origins of the French Revolution.* Stanford, CA: Stanford
University Press, 2011. Thoughtful reevaluation of the scholarly field that takes into account the latest interpretations.
Kitchen, Martin. *A History of Modern Germany: 1800 to the Present.* Hoboken, NJ: Wiley-Blackwell, 2011. A broadly conceived
historical overview, ranging from politics and economics to
culture.
Osterhammel, Jürgen. *The Transformation of the World: A Global
History of the Nineteenth Century.* Princeton, NJ: 2015. Celebrated evaluation of the myriads of changes and transformations characterizing the nineteenth century.
Rakove, Jack. *Revolutionaries: A New History of the Invention of
America.* Boston: Houghton Mifflin, 2010. A new narrative
history focusing on the principal figures in the revolution.
Riall, Lucy. *Risorgimento: The History of Italy from Napoleon to
Nation-State.* New York: Palgrave Macmillan, 2009. Historical summary, incorporating the research of the past half-
century, presented in a clear overview.
West, Elliott. *The Last Indian War: The Nez Perce Story.* Oxford
and New York: Oxford University Press, 2009. Vivid story
of the end of the US wars for the subjugation of the Native
Americans.
Wood, Gordon S. *The American Revolution: A History.* New
York: Modern Library, 2002. A short, readable summary
reflective of many decades of revisionism in the discussion of
the American Revolution.

WEBSITES
Liberty, Equality, Fraternity: Exploring the French Revolution, http://chnm.gmu.edu/revolution/. This website boasts
250 images, 350 text documents, 13 songs, 13 maps, and a timeline all focused on the French Revolution.
Nationalism Project, http://www.nationalismproject.org/. A
large website with links to bibliographies, essays, new books,
and book reviews.

Chapter 23

Adelman, Jeremy. *Sovereignty and Revolution in the Iberian Atlantic*, Princeton, NJ: Princeton University Press, 2006. A leading study in a group of recent works on the transatlantic character of colonial and postcolonial Latin America.

Brown, Matthew. *The Struggle for Power in Post-Independence Colombia and Venezuela*. New York: Palgrave Macmillan, 2012. Detailed history of the forces pulling for democracy as well as authoritarianism on the north coast of South America.

Bulmer-Thomas, Victor. *The Economic History of Latin America since Independence*, 2nd ed. Cambridge, UK: Cambridge University Press, 2003. A highly analytical and sympathetic investigation of the Latin American export and self-sufficiency economies, calling into question the long-dominant dependency theories of Latin America.

Burkholder, Mark, and Lyman Johnson. *Colonial Latin America*, 6th ed. New York: Oxford University Press, 2008. Overview, with focus on social and cultural history.

Dawson, Alexander. *Latin America since Independence: A History with Primary Sources*. New York: Routledge, 2011. Selection of topics with documentary base; for the nineteenth century covers the topics of the nation-state, caudillo politics, race, and the policy of growth through commodity exports.

Drake, Paul W. *Between Tyranny and Anarchy: A History of Democracy in Latin America*. Stanford, CA: Stanford University Press, 2009. The author traces the concepts of constitutionalism, autocracy, and voting rights since independence in clear and persuasive strokes.

Girard, Philippe, *The Slaves Who Defeated Napoléon: Toussaint Louverture and the Haitian War of Independence, 1801–1804*. Tuscaloosa: University of Alabama Press, 2011. Thoroughly researched study of the leader of the revolution, with a number of revisionist conclusions.

Hämäläinen, Pekka. *The Comanche Empire*. New Haven, CT: Yale University Press, 2008. A revisionist account that puts the extraordinary importance of the Comanche empire for the history of Mexico and the United States in the 19th century into the proper perspective.

Moya, Jose C., ed. *The Oxford Handbook of Latin American History*. Oxford and New York: Oxford University Press, 2011. Important collection of political, social, economic, and cultural essays by leading specialists on nineteenth-century Latin America.

Popkin, Jeremy D. *The Haitian Revolution and the Abolition of Slavery*. Cambridge, UK: Cambridge University Press, 2010.

Sanders, James E. *Vanguard of the Atlantic World: Creating Modernity, Nation, and Democracy in Nineteenth-Century Latin America*. Durham, NC: Duke University Press, 2014. Ambitious effort to evaluate the Latin American contributions to the creation of the modern state.

Sater, William F. *Andean Tragedy: Fighting the War of the Pacific, 1879–1884*. Lincoln: University of Nebraska Press, 2007. Close examination of this destructive war on the South American west coast.

Skidmore, Thomas. *Brazil: Five Centuries of Change*, 2nd ed. Oxford and New York: Oxford University Press, 2010. Short but magisterial text on the history of Brazil, with a detailed chapter on Brazil's path toward independence in the nineteenth century.

Wasserman, Mark, and Cheryl English Martin. *Latin America and Its People*, 2nd ed. New York: Pearson Longman, 2007.

Thematic approach, drawing general conclusions by comparing and contrasting the individual countries of Latin America.

WEBSITE

Casahistoria. "19th Century Latin America," http://www.casahistoria.net/latin_american_history19.html. Website on nineteenth-century Latin America, for students.

Chapter 24

China

Cohen, Paul. *Discovering History in China*. New York: Columbia University Press, 1984. Pivotal work on the historiography of American writers on China. Critiques their collective ethnocentrism in attempting to fit Chinese history into Western perspectives and approaches.

Fairbank, John K., and Su-yu Teng. *China's Response to the West*. Cambridge, MA: Harvard University Press, 1954. Though dated in approach, still a vitally important collection of sources in translation for the period from the late eighteenth century till 1923.

Kang, David C. *East Asia before the West: Five Centuries of Trade and Tribute*. New York: Columbia University Press, 2010. An excellent companion piece to D. E. Mungello's work covering the period from 1500 to 1800. Especially good on the Ming era.

Meyer-Fong, Tobie. *What Remains: Coming to Terms With Civil War in 19th Century China*. Stanford, CA: Stanford University Press, 2013. Extensive treatment of individual experiences during the world's bloodiest civil war, the Taiping movement.

Platt, Stephen R. *Autumn in the Heavenly Kingdom*. New York: Knopf, 2012. Reinterpretation of the Taiping era as global political and economic phenomena involving the curtailing of US cotton exports during its civil war, their effects on the British textile industry, and the loss of Chinese markets during the Taiping Rebellion.

Spence, Jonathan D. *The Search for Modern China*. New York: Norton, 1990. Extensive, far-reaching interpretation of the period from China's nineteenth-century decline in the face of Western imperialism, through its revolutionary era, and finally to its recent bid for global preeminence.

Japan

Keene, Donald. *Emperor of Japan: Meiji and His World, 1852–1912*. New York: Columbia University Press, 2002. Masterly treatment of Japan's modernizing emperor and his vast influence on Japan and Asia, by one of the twentieth century's finest translators and scholars of Japan.

Reischauer, Edwin O., and Albert M. Craig. *Japan: Tradition and Transformation*. Boston: Houghton Mifflin, 1989. Somewhat dated but still highly useful introductory text by two of the twentieth century's leading scholars of Japanese history.

Totman, Conrad. *Politics in the Tokugawa Bakufu, 1600–1843*. Berkeley: University of California Press, 1988. (Paperback edition with new preface and enhanced bibliography). Updated edition of Totman's breakthrough 1967 work. It remains one of the few highly detailed and deeply sourced monographs on the inner workings of the Tokugawa shogunate.

Walthall, Anne, and M. William Steele, *Politics and Society in Japan's Meiji Restoration: A Brief History with Documents*. New York: Bedford/St. Martin's, 2016. As with others in this series, a sound introduction for students with little or no background in the subject, accompanied by well-chosen documents.

WEBSITES

Association for Asian Studies, http://www.asian-studies.org/. This website of the Association for Asian Studies has links to sources more suited to advanced term papers and seminar projects.

Education about Asia, http://www.asian-studies.org/eaa/. This site provides the best online sources for modern Chinese and Japanese history.

Sino-Japanese War 1894–5, http://sinojapanesewar.com/. Packed with maps, photographs and movies depicting the conflict between Japan and China at the end of the nineteenth century, students can learn more about causes and consequences of the Sino–Japanese War.

Chapter 25

Gaudin, Corinne. *Ruling Peasants: Village and State in Later Imperial Russia*. DeKalb: Northern Illinois University Press, 2007. A close and sympathetic analysis of rural Russia.

Inalcik, Halil, and Donald Quataert, eds. *An Economic and Social History of the Ottoman Empire*. Vol. 2, *1600–1914*. Cambridge, UK: Cambridge University Press, 1994. A pioneering work with contributions by leading Ottoman historians on rural structures, monetary developments, and industrialization efforts.

Kasaba, Resat, ed. *The Cambridge History of Turkey*. Vol. 5, *Turkey in the Modern World*. Cambridge, UK: Cambridge University Press, 2008. An ambitious effort to assemble the leading authorities on the Ottoman Empire and provide a comprehensive overview.

Lieven, Dominic. *Empire: The Russian Empire and Its Rivals*. New Haven, CT: Yale University Press, 2002. Broad, comparative history of the Russian Empire, in the context of the Habsburg, Ottoman, and British Empires.

Massie, Robert K. *Catherine the Great: Portrait of a Woman*. New York: Random House, 2012. A comprehensive and insightful biography of one of the most fascinating women in history, whose policies, reforms, and personal life changed the course of Russian history.

Nikitenko, Aleksandr. *Up from Serfdom: My Childhood and Youth in Russia, 1804–1824*. Translated by Helen Saltz Jacobson. New Haven, CT: Yale University Press, 2001. Touching autobiography summarized at the beginning of the chapter.

Poe, Marshall T. *Russia's Moment in World History*. Princeton, NJ: Princeton University Press, 2003. A superb scholarly overview of Russian history, written from a broad perspective and taking into account a good number of Western stereotypes about Russia, especially in the nineteenth century.

Quataert, Donald. *Manufacturing in the Ottoman Empire and Turkey, 1500–1950*. Albany, NY: State University of New York Press, 1994. The author is still the leading American historian on workers and the early industrialization of the Ottoman Empire.

Riasanovsky, Nicholas, and Mark Steinberg. *A History of Russia*, 8th ed., 2 vols. Oxford and New York: Oxford University Press, 2011. A comprehensive, fully revised history, ranging from politics and economics to literature and the arts.

Uyar, Mesut, and Edward J. Erickson. *A Military History of the Ottomans: From Osman to Atatürk*. Santa Barbara, CA: Praeger Security International, 2009. A detailed, well-documented history of the Ottoman Empire from the perspective of its imperial designs and military forces, by two military officers in academic positions.

Zurcher, Erik J. *The Young Turk Legacy and Nation Building: From the Ottoman Empire to Atatürk's Turkey*. London: I. B. Tauris, 2010. Detailed yet readable account of how the Young Turk movement laid the foundation for Kemal Atatürk's Republic of Turkey.

WEBSITE

Russian Legacy. "Russian Empire (1689–1825)," http://www.russianlegacy.com/en/go_to/history/russian_empire.htm. Russian Legacy, a website devoted to the Russian Empire, organized as a timeline with links.

Chapter 26

Allen, Robert C. *The British Industrial Revolution in Global Perspective*. Cambridge, UK: Cambridge University Press, 2009. An in-depth analysis, well supported by economic data, not only of why the Industrial Revolution occurred first in Britain but also of how new British technologies carried industrialism around the world.

Dublin, Thomas, ed. *Farm to Factory: Women's Letters, 1830–1860*. New York: Columbia University Press, 1981. A fascinating collection of correspondence written by women who describe their experiences in moving from rural areas of New England to urban centers in search of work in textile factories.

Griffin, Emma. *Liberty's Dawn: A People's History of the Industrial Revolution*. New Haven, CT: Yale University Press, 2013. Riveting study of the impact of the Industrial Revolution on the lives of working men and women in Britain, as told in autobiographies and memoirs.

Headrick, Daniel R. *The Tools of Empire: Technology and European Imperialism in the Nineteenth Century*. Oxford and New York: Oxford University Press, 1981. A fascinating and clearly written analysis of the connections between the development of new technologies and their role in European imperialism.

Hobsbawm, Eric. *The Age of Revolution: 1789–1848*. London: Vintage, 1996. A sophisticated analysis of the Industrial Revolution (one element of the "twin revolution," the other being the French Revolution) that examines the effects of industrialism on social and cultural developments from a Marxist perspective.

More, Charles. *Understanding the Industrial Revolution*. London: Routledge, 2000. A comprehensive explanation of how theories of economic growth account for the development of the industrial movement in Britain.

Rosen, William. *The Most Powerful Idea in the World: A Story of Steam, Industry, and Innovation*. Chicago: University of Chicago Press, 2012. Absorbing history of the importance of steam technologies in the development of industrialism.

Roudinesco, Elisabeth, and Catherine Porter. *Freud: In His Time and Ours*. Cambridge, MA: Harvard University Press, 2016. A bold, comprehensive, and innovative analysis of one of the most influential—and complex—figures at the turn of the twentieth century.

Sperber, Jonathan. *Karl Marx: A Nineteenth-Century Life*. New York: W. W. Norton, 2013. A carefully researched biography that contextualizes Marx vis-à-vis the age of early industrialism and in comparison with other luminaries in the turbulent nineteenth century.

WEBSITES

Claude Monet: Life and Paintings, http://www.monetpainting.net/. A visually beautiful website which reproduces many of Monet's masterpieces; this site also includes an extensive biographical account of the famous painter's life and works. It also includes information about his wife Camille, his gardens at Giverny, and a chronology.

Darwin Online, http://darwin-online.org.uk/. This website has reproduced, in full, the works of Charles Darwin. In addition to providing digitized facsimiles of his works, private papers, and manuscripts, it has also added a concise biographical account and numerous images of Darwin throughout his life.

Einstein Archives Online, http://www.alberteinstein.info/. Fantastic and informative website that houses digitized manuscripts of Einstein's work. Also includes a gallery of images.

ThomasEdison.org, http://www.thomasedison.org/. Remarkable website that explores Thomas Edison's impact on modernity through his innovations and inventions. This site also reproduces all of Edison's scientific sketches, which are available to download as PDF files.

Chapter 27

Belich, James. Replenishing the Earth: The Settler Revolution and the Rise of the Anglo-World, 1783–1939. Oxford and New York: Oxford University Press, 2009. Important study by an Australian historian, focusing on the British settler colonies.

Chamberlain, M. E. The Scramble for Africa. New York: Routledge, 2013. Insightful account of the European colonization of Africa during the period 1870 to 1914.

Ferguson, Niall. Empire: The Rise and Demise of the British World Order and the Lessons for Global Power. New York: Perseus, 2002. Controversial but widely acknowledged analysis of the question of whether imperialism deserves its negative reputation or not.

Hobsbawm, Eric. The Age of Empire, 1875–1914. New York: Vintage, 1989. Immensely well-informed investigation of the climactic period of the new imperialism at the end of the nineteenth century.

Hochschild, Adam. King Leopold's Ghost: A Story of Greed, Terror, and Heroism in Colonial Africa. New York: Houghton Mifflin, 1998. A gripping exposé of Leopold II's brutal tactics in seizing territory and exploiting African labor in the Congo.

Jefferies, Matthew. Contesting the German Empire, 1871–1918. Malden, MA: Blackwell, 2008. Up-to-date summary of the German historical debate on the colonial period.

Münkler, Herfried. Empires:The Logic of World Domination from Ancient Rome to the United States. Cambridge, UK: Polity Press, 2007. Short but wide-ranging and historically well-informed analysis of the phenomena of empire and imperial hegemony in world history.

Vickers, Adrian. A History of Modern Indonesia, 2nd ed. Cambridge, UK: Cambridge University Press, 2013. Well-written account of Indonesia growing from heteregenous Dutch colonial islands into a modern nation state.

Singer, Barnett, and John Langdon. Cultured Force: Makers and Defenders of the French Colonial Empire. Madison: University of Wisconsin Press, 2004. Study of the principal (military) figures who helped create the French nineteenth-century empire.

Streets-Salter, Heather, and Trevor R. Getz, Empires and Colonies in the World: A Global Perspective. Oxford and New York: Oxford University Press, 2015. Particularly illuminating chapters on the new imperialism in the nineteenth century.

WEBSITES

The Colonization of Africa, http://exhibitions.nypl.org/africanaage/essay-colonization-of-africa.html. An academically based summary with further essays on African topics, as well as multimedia functions.

South Asian History—Colonial India, http://www.lib.berkeley.edu/SSEAL/SouthAsia/india_colonial.html. Very detailed website with primary documents and subtopics of nineteenth-century British India.

Chapter 28

Berend, Ivan T. An Economic History of Twentieth-Century Europe: Economic Regimes from Laissez-Faire to Globalization. Cambridge, UK: Cambridge University Press, 2006. Includes Europe-wide, comparative chapters on laissez-faire and state-directed economies, including deficit spending.

Bose, Sugata, and Ayesha Jalal. Modern South Asia: History, Culture, Political Economy. New York: Routledge, 2004. Well-informed analyses by two of the foremost South Asia specialists.

Clark, Christopher. The Sleepwalkers: How Europe Went to War in 1914. New York: HarperPerennial, 2014. One of a slew of new investigations into the origins of the war published to mark its centennial; emphasizes the Austrian–Serbian roots of the war.

Cohen, Adam. Imbeciles: The Supreme Court, American Eugenics, and the Sterilization of Carrie Buck. New York: Penguin, 2016.

Fritzsche, Peter. Life and Death in the Third Reich. Cambridge, MA: Harvard University Press, 2008. Book that seeks to understand the German nation's choice of arranging itself to Nazi rule.

Gelvin, James L. The Modern Middle East: A History, 4th ed. Oxford and New York: Oxford University Press, 2015. Contains chapters on Arab nationalism, British and French colonialism, and Turkey and Iran in the interwar period.

Gordon, Andrew. A Modern History of Japan: From Tokugawa Times to the Present, 2nd ed. Oxford and New York: Oxford University Press, 2009. Detailed overview of Japan's interwar period in the middle chapters.

Grasso, June M., J. P. Corrin, and Michael Kort. Modernization and Revolution in Modern China: From the Opium Wars to the Olympics, 4th ed. Armonk, NY: M. E. Sharpe, 2009. General overview with a focus on modernization in relation to the strong survival of tradition.

Martel, Gordon, ed. A Companion to Europe 1900–1945. Malden, MA: Wiley-Blackwell, 2010. Collective work covering a large variety of cultural, social, and political European topics in the interwar period.

Meade, Teresa A. A History of Modern Latin America: 1800 to the Present. Malden, MA: Wiley-Routledge, 2010. Topical discussion of the major issues in Latin American history, with chapters on the first half of the twentieth century.

Neiberg, Michael S. The Treaty of Versailles: A Concise Study. Oxford and New York: Oxford University Press, 2017. An assessment of the complexities attending the settlement of World War I, along with the consequences of its many flaws and failures.

Snyder, Timothy. Bloodlands: Europe between Hitler and Stalin. New York: Basic Books, 2010. Book that chronicles the horrific destruction left behind by these two dictators.

Wilson, Mark R. *Destructive Creation: American Business and the Winning of World War II*. Philadelphia: University of Pennsylvania Press, 2016. A thoroughly researched revisionist interpretation of the strained relationship between big business and the federal government as America mobilized for, and engaged in, World War II.

WEBSITES

BBC. World War One, http://www.bbc.co.uk/ww1, and World War Two, http://www.bbc.co.uk/history/worldwars/wwtwo/. The BBC's treatment of the causes, course, and consequences of both WWI and WWII from an Allied position.

Marxists Internet Archive. "The Bolsheviks," http://www.marxists.org/subject/bolsheviks/index.htm. A complete review of the Bolshevik party members, including biographies and links to archives which contain their works.

1937 Nanking Massacre, http://www.nanking-massacre.com/Home.html. A disturbing collection of pictures and articles tell the gruesome history of the Rape of Nanjing.

United States Holocaust Memorial Museum. Holocaust Encyclopedia, http://www.ushmm.org/wlc/en/article.php?ModuleId=10005151. The US Holocaust Memorial Museum looks back on one of the darkest times in Western history.

U.S. History, http://www.ushistory.org/us/. Maintained by Independence Hall Association in Philadelphia, this website contains many links to topics discussed in this chapter.

Chapter 29

Baret, Roby Carol. *The Greater Middle East and the Cold War: US Foreign Policy under Eisenhower and Kennedy*. London: I.B. Tauris, 2007. Thoroughly researched analysis of American policies in the Middle East, North Africa, and South Asia.

Birmingham, David. *Kwame Nkrumah: Father of African Nationalism*. Athens: University of Ohio Press, 1998. Short biography by a leading modern African historian.

Conniff, Michael L. *Populism in Latin America*. Tuscaloosa: University of Alabama Press, 1999. The author is a well-published scholar on modern Latin America.

Damrosch, David, David Lawrence Pike, Djelal Kadir, and Ursula K. Heise, eds. *The Longman Anthology of World Literature*. Vol. F, *The Twentieth Century*. New York: Longman/Pearson, 2008. A rich, diverse selection of texts. Alternatively, Norton published a similar, somewhat larger anthology of world literature in 2003.

De Witte, Ludo. *The Assassination of Lumumba*. Translated by Ann Wright and Renée Fenby. London: Verso, 2002. An admirably researched study of the machinations of the Belgian government in protecting its mining interests, with the connivance of CIA director Allen Dulles and President Dwight D. Eisenhower.

Goscha, Christopher E., and Christian F. Ostermann. *Connecting Histories: Decolonization and the Cold War in Southeast Asia, 1945–1962*. Stanford, CA: Stanford University Press, 2009.

Guha, Ramachandra. *India after Gandhi: A History of the World's Largest Democracy*. New York: Harper Collins, 2007. Highly readable, popular history with well-sketched biographical treatments of leading individuals, more obscure cultural figures, and ordinary people. Accessible to even beginning students.

Hasegawa, Tsuyoshi. *The Cold War in East Asia, 1945–1991*. Stanford, CA: Stanford University Press, 2011. A new summary, based on archival research by a leading Japanese historian teaching in the United States. New insights on the Soviet entry into World War II against Japan.

Herman, Arthur. *Joseph McCarthy: Reexamining the Life and Legacy of America's Most Hated Senator*. New York: Free Press, 2000. A fascinating study of the Wisconsin senator whose virulent campaign against communism launched decades of fear and reprisals in America during the Cold War era.

Jansen, Jan C., and Jürgen Osterhammel. *Decolonization: A Short History*. Princeton, NJ: Princeton University Press, 2017. Superb, analytical well-grounded summary of the decolonization process and its aftermath in the second half of the twentieth century.

Meredith, Martin. *The Fate of Africa: A History of the Continent since Independence*. Philadelphia: Perseus, 2011. A revised and up-to-date study of a fundamental analysis of Africa during the modern era.

WEBSITES

Economist. "The Suez Crisis: An Affair to Remember," http://www.economist.com/node/7218678. The *Economist* magazine looks back on the Suez Crisis.

NASA. "Yuri Gagarin: First Man in Space," http://www.nasa.gov/mission_pages/shuttle/sts1/gagarin_anniversary.html. In addition to information and video footage regarding Yuri Gagarin's orbit of the earth, students will also find information on America's space history.

Newseum. The Berlin Wall, http://www.newseum.org/berlinwall/. The Newseum's interactive website looks at what life was like on both sides of the Berlin Wall.

Chapter 30

Ash, Timothy Garton. *The Magic Lantern: The Revolution of '89 Witnessed in Warsaw, Budapest, Berlin, and Prague*. New York: Random House, 1999. A gripping first-hand account of the wave of anticommunist revolutions that rocked Eastern Europe after 1989.

Duara, Prasenjit, ed. *Decolonization: Perspectives from Now and Then*. London: Routledge, 2004. A leading scholar of China and postcolonial studies edits essays in this offering in the Rewriting Histories series on the fall of the colonial empires by scholars such as Michael Adas and John Voll and activists and leaders such as Frantz Fanon and Kwame Nkrumah.

Fanon, Frantz. *The Wretched of the Earth*. New York: Grove, 1961. One of the most provocative and influential treatments of theoretical and practical issues surrounding decolonization. Fanon champions violence as an essential part of the decolonization process and advocates a modified Marxist approach that takes into consideration the nuances of race and the legacies of colonialism.

Frieden, Jeffrey. *Global Capitalism: Its Fall and Rise in the Twentieth Century*. New York: W. W. Norton, 2006. Despite the title, a comprehensive history of global networks from the days of mercantilism to the twenty-first century. Predominant emphasis on twentieth century; highly readable, though the material is best suited for the nonbeginning student.

Gaddis, John Lewis. *The Cold War: A New History*. New York: Penguin, 2005. Though criticized by some scholars for his pro-American positions, America's foremost historian of the Cold War produces here a vivid, at times counterintuitive, view of the Cold War and its global impact. Readable even for beginning students.

Gitlin, Todd. *The Sixties: Years of Hope, Days of Rage*, rev. ed. New York: Bantam, 1993. Lively, provocative account of this pivotal decade by the former radical, now a sociologist. Especially effective at depicting the personalities of the pivotal period 1967–1969.

Goodwin, Doris Kearns. *Lyndon Johnson and the American Dream.* New York: St. Martin's Press, 1991. Insightful and probing study of President Johnson's character and personality, from its formation in his early years through his extensive political career.

Harmer, Tanya. *Allende's Chile and the Inter-American Cold War.* Chapel Hill: University of North Carolina Press, 2014. A reinterpretation of American determination to overturn Allende's leftist government and its subsequent results.

Liang Heng, and Judith Shapiro. *After the Nightmare: A Survivor of the Cultural Revolution Reports on China Today.* New York: Knopf, 1986. Highly readable, poignant, first-person accounts of people's experiences during the trauma of China's Cultural Revolution by a former husband-and-wife team. Especially interesting because China was at the beginning of its Four Modernizations when this was written, and the wounds of the Cultural Revolution were still fresh.

Raleigh, Donald J. *Soviet Baby Boomers: An Oral History of Russia's Cold War Generation.* Oxford and New York: Oxford University Press, 2012. A revealing and entertaining account of new social and cultural trends among Russia's youth, as told in a series of interviews.

Smith, Bonnie, ed. *Global Feminisms since 1945.* London: Routledge, 2000. Part of the Rewriting Histories series, this work brings together under the editorship of Smith a host of essays by writers such as Sara Evans, Mary Ann Tetreault, and Miriam Ching Yoon Louie on feminism in Asia, Africa, and Latin America, as well as Europe and the United States. Sections are thematically arranged under such headings as "Nation-Building," "Sources of Activism," "Women's Liberation," and "New Waves in the 1980s and 1990s." Comprehensive and readable, though some background in women's history is recommended.

WEBSITES

Cold War International History Project, http://www.wilson center.org/program/cold-war-international-history-project. Run by the Woodrow Wilson International Center for Scholars. Rich archival materials including collections on the end of the Cold War, Soviet invasion of Afghanistan, Cuban Missile Crisis, and Chinese foreign policy documents.

College of DuPage Library, http:codlibrary.org. Entering "Research guide to 1960s websites" in the search box yields a wide-ranging set of relevant topics.

Chapter 31

Chau, Adam Yuet, ed. *Religion in Contemporary China.* New York: Routledge, 2011. Collection of fascinating chapters on the revival of Daoist, Confucian, and Buddhist traditions and their adaption to middle-class modernity, with their proponents operating often in a gray zone between official recognition and suppression.

Daniels, Robert V. *The Rise and Fall of Communism in the Soviet Union.* New Haven, CT: Yale University Press, 2010. A magisterial summary of the communist period by a specialist.

Dillon, Michael. *Contemporary China: An Introduction.* New York: Routledge, 2009. Concise yet quite specific overview of the economy, society, and politics of the country.

Eichengreen, Barry. *Exorbitant Privilege: The Rise and Fall of the Dollar and the Future of the Monetary System.* Oxford and New York: Oxford University Press, 2011. The author is an academic specialist on US monetary policies, writing in an accessible style and presenting a fascinating picture of the role of something as prosaic as greenbacks.

Faust, Aaron M. *The Ba'thification of Iraq: Saddam Hussein's Totalitarianism.* Austin: University of Texas Press, 2015. Based on meticulous research among Ba'th Party documents, this study reveals how Saddam Hussein developed a totalitarian regime in Iraq, and why his dictatorship succeeded in gaining the loyalty of millions of Iraqis for nearly 25 years.

Gelvin, James L. *The Arab Uprisings: What Everyone Needs to Know.* Oxford and New York: Oxford University Press, 2012. Concise overview of the Arab Spring events with carefully selected background information.

Houghton, John. *Global Warming: The Complete Briefing.* 5th ed. Cambridge, UK: Cambridge University Press, 2015. One of the most authoritative summaries of all aspects of global warming.

Jacka, Tamara, Andrew Kipnis, and Sally Sargeson. *Contemporary China: Society and Social Change.* Cambridge, UK: Cambridge University Press, 2013. Ambitious sociological–historical study focusing on the many differences within Chinese society and the forces that drive change in contemporary China.

Meade, Teresa A. *A History of Modern Latin America: 1800 to the Present.* 2nd ed. Malden, MA: Wiley-Blackwell, 2016. The book is an excellent, comprehensive analysis and has a strong final chapter on recent Latin America.

Saxonberg, Steven. *The Fall: A Comparative Study of the End of Communism in Czechoslovakia, East Germany, Hungary, and Poland.* Amsterdam, The Netherlands: Harwood Academic, 2001. A well-informed overview of the different trajectories by an academic teaching in Prague.

Swanimathan, Jayshankar M. *Indian Economic Superpower: Fact or Fiction?* Singapore: World Scientific Publishing, 2009. A thoughtful evaluation of the pros and cons of economic growth in India, in concise overviews.

WEBSITES

BBC. Nelson Mandela's Life and Times, http://www.bbc.co.uk/news/world-africa-12305154. The BBC News looks back at the life and career of Nelson Mandela.

Environmental Protection Agency. Climate Change, http://www.epa.gov/climatechange/. The US Environmental Protection Agency's website on climate change reviews the threat to the world's climate and the implications of consistent abuse. The site also looks at various initiatives to help reverse some of the damage already done.

Sierra Club, http://sierraclub.org/. Balanced and informative environmental websites.

Credits

Stapleton Collection/Bridgeman Images, p. 612; Archives Charmet/Bridgeman Images, p. 614; Peter NEWark Pictures/Bridgeman Images, p. 616; Natural History Museum, London, UK/The Bridgeman Art Library International, p. 618.

Chapter 27: Chronicle/Alamy Stock Photo, p. 624; (a) Peter Horree/Alamy Stock Photo; (b) Granger Historical Picture Archive/Alamy Stock Photo, p. 626; LINE ART, p. 628; Bettmann/Getty Images, p. 629; Réunion des Musées Nationaux/Art Resource, NY, p. 632; Archives Charmet/Bridgeman Images, p. 633; © Hulton-Deutsch Collection/Getty Images, p. 635; Panos Pictures ASL00010DRC, p. 640; Courtesy of the Library of Congress, p. 644.

Chapter 28: Courtesy of the Library of Congress, p. 650; © Hulton-Deutsch Collection/Getty Images, p. 651; Hulton Archives/Getty Images, p. 657; Library of Congress LC-USW3-001543-D, p. 658; Fotosearch/Getty Images, p. 662; Bettmann/Getty Images, p. 663; Heritage Image Partnership Ltd/Alamy Stock Photo, p. 666; World History Archive/Alamy Stock Photo, p. 668; Courtesy of the Library of Congress, p. 671.

Chapter 29: Keystone/Getty Images, p. 679; Alfred Eisenstaedt/Getty Images, p. 681; © Bettmann/Getty Images, p. 685; © Rykoff Collection/Getty Images, p. 686; Library of Congress/Getty Images, p. 688; (a) © The Museum of Modern Art/Licensed by SCALA/Art Resource, NY. With permission of the Renate, Hans & Maria Hofmann Trust/Artists Rights Society (ARS), New York; (b) © 2009 Museum Associates/LACMA/Art Resource, NY. © 2017 The Willem de Kooning Foundation/Artists Rights Society (ARS), New York, p. 689; Lisa Larsen/Getty Images, p. 699; Courtesy of the Library of Congress, p. 700.

Chapter 30: © Alain DeJean/Sygma/Getty Images, p. 707; Historical/Getty Images, p. 709; Markku Vuorela/AFP/Getty Images, p. 711; © Bettmann/Getty Images, p. 714; India Today Group/Getty Images, p. 717; Bettmann/Getty Images, p. 720; CHAUVEL/Getty Images, p. 722; Courtesy of the Library of Congress, p. 727.

Chapter 31: Getty Images, p. 737; (a) str/Associated Press; (b) Xinhua, Liu Weibing/Associated Press, p. 741; Ali Atmaca/Anadolu Agency/Getty Images, p. 747; © Samuel Aranda /Getty Images, p. 748; Manish Swarup/Associated Press, p. 750; Louise Gubb/Getty Images, p. 751; Muzaffar Salman/Associated Press, p. 752; Peter Parks/Getty Images, p. 755.

Subject Index

Page numbers followed by *f* denote a figure, page numbers followed by *m* denote a map, and page numbers in italics denote a picture.

Aachen, 247
Abbasids, 215, 217, 219–20, 222, 223, 273–74
Abd al-Malik, 216–17, 219
Abdülhamit II, 582–83, 586
Abelard, Peter, 259
Abolition of slavery, 454, 520, 534, 536, 628; in Brazil, 532–33; in Great Britain, 637
Aboriginals (Australia), 13–15
Abortion, 715, 743
Absolutism, 371, 390, 398–401
Abstract expressionism, 688, 689
Abzu, 48
AC. *See* Alternating current
ACA. *See* Affordable Care Act
Academy of Florence, 240
Academy of Medicine (France), 509
Academy of Sciences (Paris), 386
Achaemenids, 120, 145–51, 147m, 158, 159, 161
Acheulian tools, 8, 9
Acropolis, 150
Adal, 437
Adelard of Bath, 259
Adena, 111, 112m
Admonitions for Women (Ban Zhao), 207
Adriatic Sea, 364–66
Advanced Research Projects Agency (ARPA), 752
Aeneid, The (Virgil), 165, 166
Aeschylus, 165
Aesthetics, in China, 208, 488
Affordable Care Act (ACA), 742–43
Afghanistan, 146, 174, 273, 458, 461, 463, 463; Alexander the Great in, 151; Great Britain and, 635; Soviet Union and, 707, 707–8, 711
AFL. *See* American Federation of Labor
Africa, 361m; agriculture in, 752; arts of, 332, 332–33, 333; chiefdoms in, 122, 122–43; China and, 752; Cold War in, 701–3; colonialism in, 636–40, 637m, 701–2; development in, 725–27; fossils from, 4–7; France and, 639–40; GDP of, 751; Great Britain and, 639–40; in Ice Age, 18; kingdoms of, 432–55; migrations from, 11, 12m; nation-states of, 694m, 701–3; Portugal and, 436, 701; in prehistory, 2, 4–26; railroads in, 639; scramble for, 636–40; slaves from, 434–48, 442m, 444m; Spain and, 701; state formation in, 316–36; symbols in, 11; Tang dynasty and, 276; transformations in, 751–52; witchcraft in, 432–33. *See also* East Africa; North Africa; Southern Africa; Sub-Saharan Africa; West Africa
African Americans, 520, 688, 714; Harlem Renaissance of, 656; lynchings of, 656, 657
African diaspora, 449–52, 451, 658–59
African National Congress (ANC), 727, 730–31

African spirituality, 130, 317, 329, 432–33
Afro-Eurasian world commercial system, 234–36, 235m
Agrarian-urban centers: in Americas, 98, 103–13; in Andes, 105–7, 106m; in Brazil, 411; in China, 75–96; in East Africa, 129–31; of eastern Mediterranean, 27–52, 29m; in Fertile Crescent, 28–31; in India, 53–74; in Mesoamerica, 108–13; in Mesopotamia, 27–52; of Middle East, 27–52, 29m; of prehistory, 3; in South Africa, 129–31; in sub-Saharan Africa, 123–31, 129m; in Vietnam, 309; in western Europe, 357; women of, 10
Agricultural estates (*haciendas*), 421–22, 540
Agriculture: in Africa, 752; in Amazonia, 111–12; in Americas, 103–13; in Andes, 342; of Assyrians, 42; in Brazil, 411, 532–33; in China, 77, 87–88; in Europe, 251–52; in Fertile Crescent, 50; in Great Britain, 600; in Han dynasty, 199, 202–3; in Japan, 301–2, 305; in Korea, 294, 295m; in Latin America, 546, 548; of Maya, 136, 341; in Ming dynasty, 477–78; of Mughals, 467; of Mycenaeans, 45; in New England, 425; in Nubia, 318; in Papua New Guinea, 114; in prehistory, 2–26; in Russia, 591; selective breeding in, 30–31; in Soviet Union, 665–66, 666; in Sparta, 149–50; in sub-Saharan Africa, 123–27
Aguinaldo, Emilio, 643–44
Ahimsa (nonviolence), 172
Ahmadinejad, Mahmoud, 746
Ahuramazda, 148, 159
AIM. *See* American Indian Movement
Ainu, 300
Airplanes: of CIA, 683; in Cuban Missile Crisis, 687; first built, 606
Akbar, Jalal ud-Din, 460m, 460–61, 462, 472
Akhenaten, 47, 47, 51–52
Akkadia, 35, 35m
Aksum, 120, 124m, 126–27, 127, 142, 320–21
Alamo, 537
Alaska, 20
Albania, 584, 712
Albigensians, 268–69
Aleppo, Syria, 732
Alexander I, 588
Alexander II, 591, 592, 596–97, 664
Alexander the Great, 65, 120, 150–51, 152m; Achaemenids and, 145–46; in India, 169–71
Alexander V, 264
Alexius I Comnenus, 228–29
Algebra, 163, 237
Algeria, 624–25, 634, 701
Ali, Muhammad (Egypt), 579, 582, 635
Allah, 216, 290
Allegory, 457
Allende, Salvador, 728
Alpaca, 104

Alphabet, 44, 44, 125
Altaics, 294, 457
Altar of Peace, 146
Alternating current (AC), 605
Alt-Right, 743
Altruism, in Buddhism, 179
Amazonia, 111–12, 355, 424
Ambassadors, The (James), 524
Amenemhet III, 40
American Civil War, 452, 520, 539
American Federation of Labor (AFL), 656
American Indian Movement (AIM), 715
American Indian Wars, 521
American Philosophical Society, 427
American Revolution, 501, 503–5
American System, 616
Americas, 97m; abolition of slavery in, 454; agrarian-urban centers of, 3, 98, 103–13; agriculture in, 103–13; animal domestication in, 104; Catholicism in, 426; chiefdoms in, 122, 122–43; city, city-states of, 354; climate of, 99–102, 100m; colonialism in, 407–31, 410m, 413m; Copernicus and, 404; culture of, 426–28; education in, 426–27; empires in, 337–55; ethnic groups of, 422–26, 423f; Eurasia and, 117; foraging in, 98–107; France and, 414–15; graves in, 103; hunting in, 98–107; hurricanes of, 101–3; irrigation in, 105; kingdoms in, 120; land bridges to, 19; migrations to, 17–23, 22m, 102–3; Monroe Doctrine for, 538–39; in Neolithic Age, 104–5; ocean currents of, 101–3; plantations in, 441–48; in prehistory, 97–113; rituals in, 103; rock art in, 103, 103; silver from, 419–21; slaves in, 441–48, 442m, 444m; social classes of, 422–26; sub-Saharan Africa and, 131; topography of, 99–102, 100m; wheat in, 421–22; wheel and, 104, 116, 117; women in, 424. *See also* Mesoamerica; North America; South America
Amerindians. *See* Native Americans
Amida (Buddha of the Pure Land), 207
Amistad, 542
Analects, 191–92
Anatolia, 28, 41, 46–47, 146–47, 159, 165, 216, 229; Byzantium and, 223, 227; Greece and, 662; Ottoman Empire and, 578, 583; Turks of, 363
Anaximander, 160
ANC. *See* African National Congress
Ancient Ghana, 316–17, 328–29
Andes, 111, 139–41, 140m; agrarian-urban centers of, 105–7, 106m; roads in, 104, 106; Tiwanaku of, 341–44, 342, 343m, 354; Wari of, 141, 343m, 343–44, 354. *See also* Inca
Anglican Church, 394, 397
Anglo-Saxons, 250

Angola, 701
Aniconism, 239
Animal domestication, 31, 50, 64, 94–95, 104, 318
Animal sacrifice, 162
An Lushan, 278
Anselm, St., 259
Anthony of Padua, St., 432, *440*
Antinomian group, 427
Antioch, siege of, 229
Anti-Semitism, 262, 678
Antonianism, *440*
Anzick-1 fossil, 23
Apaches, 418
Apartheid, in South Africa, 701, 726–27, *727*, 730–31
Aphorisms of Love (*Kama Sutra*) (Vatsyayana), 186
Apocalypse, 159, 161, 360
Apollo 11 Cave, 11, *11*
Aponte, José Antonio, 543
Appeasement, of Nazi Germany, 669
Aquinas, Thomas, 256, 267
Arabian Nights, 237
Arabs, 44, 217, 218*m*–19*m*, 270, 272, 661–62; in Algeria, 634; Byzantium and, 216; China and, 276; Christianity of, 215; Israel and, 717, 722, 722–24; Jews and, 695; in Mesopotamia, 215; Silk Road and, 185
Arab Spring, 745, 748–50, *752*, 752–53
Arafat, Yasir, 723
Aragon, 360
Archimedes, 163, 237, 384
Architecture: of Gothic cathedrals, *260*, 260–61; of Iran, *586*; of Islam, 239; of Mughals, 472–73; of Ottoman Empire, 375; of Roman Empire, 166; of Sasanids, 164, *164*; of south India, *177*
Ardashir, 154
Ardipithecus ramidus (Ardi), 6, 24
Argentina, 420, 424, 528–31, 546, 691; Dirty War in, 728–29; Falkland Islands and, 729
Aristocratic Republic, 535
Aristotle, 168, 237, 258–59, 267, 382, *384*
Arjuna, 66, 67
Armenia, 583, 665
Army of the Andes, 530
Arouet, François-Marie. *See* Voltaire
ARPA. *See* Advanced Research Projects Agency
Arthashastra (Kautilya), 65, 171
Articles of Confederation, 505
Artillery, 607
Art of War (Sun Zi), 65
Arts: of Africa, *332*, 332–33, *333*; of Americas, 426–27; Baroque, 381–83; of China, 208; of eastern Mediterranean, 48–49; of Greece, 165; of Habsburg dynasty, 376–77; of India, 186; Islam and, 237–39; of Japan, 304, 495–96, *496*, 572; of Latin America, 550; of Middle East, 48–49; of Ming dynasty, 489; modernity of, 619–20; of Mughals, 472; of Olmecs, 110, *110*; of Parthians, 163–64; of Renaissance, 382–83, *384*; of Roman Empire, 165–66; romanticism and, 523; of US, 656; after World War II, 688. *See also* Rock art
Aryans, 61–62, 68

Ascencio Padilla, Manuel, 528–29
Asceticism, 70–71, *71*, 177–78
Asháninka, 412
Ashante, 637–38, 702
Ashoka, 171–73, 184, 188
Asia, 185*m*; agrarian-urban centers of, 3; Cold War in, 696–701; hominins to, 8; land bridges to, 19; migrations from, 15–17. *See also* China; India; Japan; Korea; Southeast Asia
Asia Minor, 227
Al-Assad, Bashar, 743, 745, 749
Assemblies, in India, 65; in Mesopotamia, 32
Assembly line, 616, *616*
Assyrians, 42, 146–47
Astrolabe, 390
Astronomy, 163, 208, 237, 380, 383–84, 386, 470
Aswan High Dam, 695
Atahualpa, 410–11, *411*
Atatürk (Mustafa Kemal), 662
Atheism, 178, 619
Athens, 46, 148–50, 167–68
Atlantic system, for slave trade, 446–47, *447m*
Atomic bombs, at Hiroshima and Nagasaki, 675, *681*
Atum, 48
Augustine, St., 162, 245
Augustus, 154, *154*
Aurangzeb, 463–64, 469, 472, 473
Austen, Jane, 523
Australia, 12–15, 18, 631–32
Australopiths (*Australopithecus*), 6
Austria, 516, 517, 518, 669
Austria-Hungary, 583, 584, 651, 653, 654
Autarky, 660
Auto-da-fé, 376, *377*
Automobile, 606
Avatars, 181–82
Averroës (Ibn Rushd), 237
Avicenna (Ibn Sina), 237, 259
Avignon Papacy, 264
Ayub Khan, 697
Azerbaijan, 665
Aztecs, 344–46, *345*, 346*m*, *347*, 352, 352–53, 367, 408–9
Azurduy de Padilla, Juana, 528–29

Babi movement, 587
Babur, Zahir ud-Din Muhammad, 273, 458, 459*m*, *460*
Baby-boomer generation, 688, 715
Babylonia, 35, 35*m*, 36–37, 159
Bach, Johann Sebastian, 383
Bacon, Roger, 259
Bactria-Margiana Archaeological Complex (BMAC), 59, 63
Al-Baghdadi, Abu Bakr, 749
Baha'i faith, 587
Bakufu (tent government), 491
Balban, 274
Balfour Declaration, 661
Balkans, 363, 368, 592; Ottoman Empire and, 366, 372–73, 578, 584–86, 635; World War I and, 652
Balmaceda Fernández, José Manuel, 540, 552
Baltic states, 589, 712–13
Bambuk, 329
Bana, 272
Ban Biao, 207

Bandaranaike, Sirimavo, 679–80, 696
Bandung Conference, 698–99
Bangladesh, 696–97
Ban Gu, 207
Bank of England, 403
Banks, 266, 599, 657, 668
Al-Banna, Hasan, 695
Banner system, 48
Banpo Village, 77–79
Bantus, 129–30, 323
Bantustans, 730
Banu, Nadira, 472
Ban Zhao, 205, 207
Baojia, 286, 486
Barbados, 445
Barometer, 388
Baron, 250
Baroque arts, 381–83
Barrel vaults, 164, *164*
Baseball, 615
Basho, Matsuo, 496
Basilica, 260
Bathhouses, in Japan, 571
Battle of Adowa, 639
Battle of Agincourt, 262–63
Battle of Chaldiran, 366
Battle of Crécy, 262
Battle of Hastings, 250
Battle of Lepanto (Veronese), *371*
Battle of Manzikert, *228*, 228–29
Battle of Tours/Poitiers, 217, 246, 262
Battle on Santo Domingo (Sucholdoski), *502*
Bay of Pigs, 687
Beat Generation, 705–6
Beatles, The, 3, 706
Becquerel, Antoine, 617
Beethoven, Ludwig van, 523
Being, 160
Belgium, *40*, 638, 639, *651*, 702–3
Bell, Alexander Graham, 606
Benedict, St., 246
Benedictines, 255
Benin, 333, 439, *439*
Berbers, 217, 329, 634
Beringia Land Bridge, 19–20, 98
Berlin Airlift, 683
Berlin Wall, 687, 708, 712
Bhagavad Gita, 66, 67
Bharat, 181
Bhutto, Benazir, 680
Biafra, 726
Bible (Hebrew Bible, New Testament), 44, 223, 384–85, 393
Big business, industrialization and, 615–16
Bilal, 316
Bin Laden, Osama, 737
Bipedalism, of hominins, 6
Birth of a Nation, 452
Al-Biruni, 390
Bismarck, Otto von, *518*, 518–19
Black Death (plague), 236, 262, 263*m*, *264*, 283, 391, 477
Black Man's Burden, The (Morel), 647
Black pepper, 184–85
Black Sea, 578, 588
Blackshirts, 666
Black Volta River, 329
Blanc, Louis, 612
Blitzkrieg (lightning war), 669
Blombos Cave, 11

BMAC. *See* Bactria-Margiana Archaeological Complex
Boccaccio, Giovanni, 266
Bodhisattva, 179
Boers, 440, 726
Boko Haram, 752
Bolívar, Simón, 530, *534*, 534–35
Bolivia, 412, 419, 528–29, 535
Bolshevik Revolution, 680
Bolsheviks, 594, 653, 664–65
Bombay (Mumbai), 466, 626
Bonaparte, Louis-Napoleon. *See* Napoleon III
Bonaparte, Napoleon. *See* Napoleon Bonaparte
Boniface, St., 244
Boniface VIII, 264
Book of Hamza (*Hamzanama*), 472, 473
Book of History. See Shujing
Book of Kings (*Shahname*) (Firdosi), 164, 237
Book of Mencius (*Mengzi*) (Mencius), 192–93
Book of Odes, The. See Shijing
Book of Sentences (Lombard), 259
Book of Songs, The. See Shijing
Borana lunar calendar, 122
Bosnia-Herzegovina, 582, 584, 592, 652
Boston, 416
Boston Tea Party, 505
Bouazizi, Mohamed, 748, *748*
Bourbons, 414–15, 515–16
Bourgeoisie, 254, 610
Boxer Rebellion, 563–64, 673
Bradshaw paintings, 14–15, *15*
Brahe, Sophie, 386
Brahe, Tycho, 386
Brahma, 181
Brazil, 531–33; agriculture in, 411, 532–33; economy of, 729; federalism in, 532, 533; gold in, 415–16, *416*, 422, 443; Pedra Furada in, 103; plantations in, 422, 532, 533; populism in, 691; Portugal and, 411, 415–16; slave revolts in, 542–43; slaves in, 443; in Southern Cone, 529; sugarcane in, 411, 415, 443, 532–33
Breech-loading weapons, 607
Brezhnev, Leonid, 708, 709–10, 711
Brezhnev Doctrine, 710
Bride-price, 309
British East India Company, 465–66, 485–86, 505, 555–56, 625–28, *626*, 641
British Football Association, 615
Brontë, Anne, 523
Brontë, Charlotte, 523
Brontë, Emily, 523
Bronze Age, Bronze Age Collapse, 42, 63, 146, 301
Brown v. Board of Education, 714
Brunelleschi, Filippo, 382, *384*
Buddha of the Pure Land (Amida), 207
Buddhism, 178–80, *180*, 181*m*, 205; Ashoka and, 172; Beat Generation and, 705; caste system and, 185; in China, 179, 200–201, 207–8, 271, 276–88; Hinduism and, 272; Islam and, 219; in Japan, 179, 208, 293, 302, 306–8, 314; Kanishka and, 174; in Korea, 295, *296*, 299–300; in Ming dynasty, 489; Mongols and, 282; in Neo-Confucianism, 290; Nichiren, 307; Silk Road and, 183; in Tang dynasty, 279, 290; of Tibet, 483; in Vietnam, 309, 311, 312, 701; Zen, 208, 307–8, 314, 495
Buffalo, 521

Bulgaria, 582, 584, 592, 653, 681, 712
Bulgars, 223
Bullfights, 376
Bunraku, 495
Bunyoro kingdom, 436–37
Burial sites. *See* Gravesites
Burroughs, William, 705
Burundi, 638
Bush, George H. W., 736
Bush, George W., 736, 737
Bushido (Way of the Warrior), 304
Buyids, 323, 585
Bye industries, 254
Byzantium, *214*, 214–43, 225*m*, 226, 232–34, 233, 363; commonwealth of, *224*, 224–25; Crusades and, 257; Eastern Christianity in, 222–30; Fourth Crusade and, 240; iconoclasm in, 223–24, 238; icons of, 238–39, *239*; military in, 225–26; and Roman Empire, 216

Cahokia, 131, 338
Cahuachi, 141Calculating machine, 613
Calculus, 386
Calcutta, 466, 626
Calendar, 122, 129, 130, 134–35, 142–43
Calicoes, 668
Caliph, 216
Caliphates, 436
Calligraphy, 208, 304, *564*
Calvin, John, 394
Calvinism, 394, 396–97, 427
Cambodia, 183, 645, 722
Camel, 317
Canaanites (Phoenicians), 43–44, *44*, 153
Canada, 418, 503
Cannons, 373, 378, 488
Canoes, 19
Canon law, 213, 259
Canon of Medicine (Avicenna), 259
Canterbury Tales (Chaucer), 266
Canton system, of Qing dynasty, *484*, 484–85, 497–98
Cao Xueqin, 568
Capet, Hugh, 250
Capetians, 250
Capitalism, 612, 613, 645; in Chile, 728; in Europe, 253–54; in Great Depression, 657; in Japan, 569; in Soviet Union, 71
Capitalist democracy, 651, 677, 708, 733–54; Great Depression and, 666; of US, 657
Caral-Supe, 97, 105, 116
Caravel, 360, 362, 364
Caribbean, 414; abolition of slavery in, 454; Columbus to, 362; economy of, 545*m*; foraging in, 112–13; mercantilism in, 443; plantations in, 441–42; Spain and, 408, 419; urbanism in, 680–90, 690*m*
Caribs, 408
Carnegie, Andrew, 616
Carolingians, 246, 267
Carranza, Venustiano, 541
Cartels, 569, 615
Carter, Jimmy, 724, 725
Carthage, 153
Caste system: in Americas, 422–26; of India, 67–69, *68*, *69*, 71, 183–86, 275, 631; of Mughals, 469; in southern Africa, 437
Castile, 360–61
Castro, Fidel, 686–87

Catalan Atlas, 316
Çatal Hüyük, 46–47
Cataphracts, 147
Cathars, 268–69
Catherine II, the Great, 588
Catholicism: in Americas, 426; in China, 484, *484*; in France, 396, 507; Galileo and, 384–85; in Iberia, 375–77; in Italy, 667; in Latin America, 545, 549; in Mexico, 536; Native Americans and, 426; in Philippines, 643; in Poland, 685; in Renaissance, 383
Catholic Reformation, 383, 386, 389, 394–95, 426
Cattle, 440, 532
Cattle lords, 436–37
Caudillo, 534, 535, 539–40
Caves: in Americas, 103; Crô-Magnon from, 15; *Homo sapiens* in, 10. *See also* Rock art
Cavour, Camillo di, 517–18
Ceauşescu, Nicolae, 712–13
Celibacy, 226
Celluloid, 605
Central African Republic, 752
Central America. *See* Mesoamerica
Central Intelligence Agency (CIA), 683, 702, 703, 728
Centralized kingdoms, 390–93
Centralizing states, 371–74, 399; in England, 403; of Europe, 390–93, 392*m*; in Russia, 401
Cervantes, Miguel de, 379
Césaire, Aimé, 659
Cesspits, 58
Ceylon. *See* Sri Lanka
Chagatai, 457–58, 472
Chalcolithic Age (Copper Age), 33
Chalukyas, 175–76
Chamberlain, Neville, 669, 670
Chamorro, Violeta Barrios de, 728
Chan Buddhism, 208
Chandragupta, of Maurya Empire, 156, 170, 171–72, 178
Chandragupta I, of Gupta Empire, 4, 175*m*
Chandragupta II, of Gupta Empire, 174–75
Charaka Samhita, 187
Chariots, 41, *43*, 64, 75, *84*
Charlemagne, 245, 247, *247*, 248*m*
Charles I, 404
Charles IV, 262
Charles V, 359, 367, 368, 369, 373–74, 394, 409
Charles VII, 263
Charles X, 515
Chartism, 612–13
Châtelet, Gabrielle-Émilie du, 387–88
Chattel, slaves as, 441, 520
Chaucer, Geoffrey, 266
Chauvet Cave, 16
Chávez, Hugo, 754
Chavín de Huántar, 106–7, *107*
Chemicals, 605, 607
Cheng (First Emperor), 195–96, *196*, 209
Chennai (Madras), 626
Chernobyl nuclear accident, 712
Chernyshevsky, Nikolai, 597
Cheyenne, 418
Chiang K'ai-shek, 673–74, 692
Chiapas, 339
Chichén Itzá, 341, *341*

Chiefdoms: of Africa, *122*, 122–43; of Americas, *122*, 122–43; of Andes, 139–41, 140*m*; of central Africa, 327–28; of Mesoamerica, 338; of Mexican Basin, 338; of southern Africa, 436; of sub-Saharan Africa, 123–25

Chikamatsu, Monzaemon, 496

Childebert II, 246

Chile, 102, 347, 412, 419, 535, 551–52, 691, 728

China, 75, 83–84, 86, 89, 190–211, 484, 729; aesthetics in, 208; Africa and, 752; agrarian-urban centers of, 3, 75–96; agriculture in, 77, 87–88; Arabs and, 276; British East India Company in, 485–86, 555–56; Buddhism in, 179, 200–201, 207–8, 271, 276–88; Catholicism in, 484, *484*; chariots in, 75, *84*; children in, 720; Christianity in, 556, 559; client states in, 83; climate of, 76–77, 78*m*; communism in, 673, 692, 740–41; Communist Party in, 673–74, 718–19; compass from, 279, 390–91; Confucianism in, 191–92, 573; Cultural Revolution in, 718–19; culture of, 80, 90–93; earthquake detector in, 208, *208*; East Africa and, 131; economy of, 88–89, 719; European trade with, 253; factories in, 556; family in, 81, 89–90, 720; female infanticide in, 720; Four Modernizations in, 719–20; GDP of, 719, 733, 741, *741*; gender relations in, 89–90, 95–96; Great Depression in, 674; Great Leap Forward in, 693; Great Wall of, *190*, 197–98; greenhouse gases from, 755; *Homo sapiens in*, 77; Hundred Flowers campaign in, 693; in Ice Age, 18; import-substitution industrialization in, 735; India and, 183, 184–85, 207; industrialization in, 735, 757; Industrial Revolution and, 557; Japan and, 191, 313, 553–54, 553–74, 562, 563, 671–72, 674; Jesuits in, 484, *484*; kingdoms of, 120–21; Korea and, 294–95, 313, 481, 562; in Korean War, 683–84; land reform in, 198–99; Latin America and, 547; literature of, 288, 568; Longshan period of, 79; Mandate of Heaven in, 85, 95; merchants in, 88; modernity in, 553–74; Mongols in, 280–84, 284*m*; nation-state in, 692–93; Neo-Confucianism in, 213, 276–88; in Neolithic Age, 77–80; opium trade from, 555–56; oracle bones in, *90*, 90–91; Parthians and, 152; patriarchy in, 95–96; porcelain in, 208, 480–81, *481*, *482*; Portugal and, 484; pottery in, 208, 480–81, *481*, *482*; printing in, 208; railroads in, 674; religion in, 81, 90–93; responsibility system of, 719; rice in, 80, 477; science in, 208, 560–61, 568–69; ships of, 364, *365*, *557*; Silk Road in, 203–4, 204*m*–5*m*, 235; silver and, 479, 480*m*; social classes in, 81, 87, 88, 197; Southeast Asia and, 562; Soviet Union and, 692, 693, 718; Spring and Autumn period in, 90; stirrups in, *198*, 198–99; textile industry in, 601; Thermidorian Reaction by, 718; Tiananmen Square Massacre in, 720, *720*; topography of, 76–77, 78*m*; trade by, 89; Vietnam and, 191, 312, 314, 722; warfare in, 94; Warring States period in, 84, 86, 190, 193;

well-field system in, 88; West Africa and, 234–36; women in, 89–90, 95–96; World War I and, 653; writing in, 79, *90*, 90–93, 195–96, 207; Yellow River in, 76–81. *See also* Han dynasty; Ming dynasty; Qin dynasty; Qing dynasty; Shang dynasty; Song dynasty; Tang dynasty; Xia dynasty; Yuan dynasty; Zhou dynasty

Chinampas, 351

Chishti, Salim, 461, *462*

Cholas, 175–76, 272, 273

Cholera, 634

Christianity: African spirituality and, 432–33; of Arabs, 215; in Balkans, 368; canon of, 213; in China, 556, 559; church of, 162; of Creoles, 418; Crusades of, 227–31, 257–58, 359, 365; in Ethiopia, 320, *321*; in India, 628; Islam and, 219; Islam versus, 359–71; in Japan, 493; Latin, 245–49; Mughals and, 471; Nietzsche on, 619; in North Africa, 317–22; in Nubia, 317–18; origins of, 161–62; in Ottoman Empire, 579–80; in Qing dynasty, 498; of Roman Empire, 126, 155, 241; Spanish Inquisition and, 362; in sub-Saharan Africa, 636; Trinitarianism of, 216–17. *See also* Catholicism; Eastern Christianity; Western Christianity

Chronicles of Japan (Nihongi), 308

Chu nom (southern characters), 312

Churchill, Winston, 670, 680–81

CIA. *See* Central Intelligence Agency

Cistercians, 255

City, city-states: of Americas, 354; of East Africa, 323–28, 325*m*; of Greece, 46, 148–50; of Harappa, 60–61; of India, 53–61; of Mesopotamia, 33–34; of Mycenaeans, 45; of Syria, 43

City of God, The (St. Augustine), 162

"City of Victory" (Vijayanagar), 272

Civil Code (France), 508

Civilizing mission, 636

Civil Rights Act of 1964, 714

Civil rights movement (US), 714–18

Civil service (India), 629–31

Civil wars: American Civil War, 452, 520, 539; in England, 397; in France, 396; in Greece, 681; in Japan, 573–74; in Lebanon, 724; in Nigeria, 726; in Qing dynasty, 559; in Russia, 665; in Spain, 669; in Syria, 732, 745; Taiping Rebellion, 559, 559*m*, 573; in Yemen, 732–33; in Yugoslavia, 744

Cixi (Empress Dowager), 279, 291, 561

Classic of Documents. See Shujing

Classic of Filial Piety (Xiaojing), 206

Classic of the Way and Virtue, The (Daode Jing), 194

Cleisthenes, 149

Cleitus, 145–46

Clement V, 264

Clement VII, 264

Client states (China), 83

Climate: of Americas, 99–102, 100*m*; of China, 76–77, 78*m*; of Japan, 300, 301*m*; of Korea, 293; of Mesoamerica, 101; of North America, 99–101

Climate change: Australian Aboriginals and, 14; in eastern Mediterranean, 31; global warming and, 754–56; hominins and, 5;

in Middle East, 31; Nazca and, 141; Neanderthals and, 20; in Neolithic Age, 30; Plague of Justinian and, 156; in prehistory, 3; Teotihuacán and, 138. *See also* Ice Age

Clinton, Bill, 736

Clinton, Hillary, 743

Clive, Robert, 626

Clothing: of *Homo sapiens*, 10; in Ice Age, 19

Clovis (Frankish king), 245–46

Clovis points, 20, 23, 102

Coal mines, *611*, 611–12

Code of Manu, 184

Codex Justinianus, 157

Coercive Acts (Intolerable Acts), 505

Coffee, 532–33, 546, 641

Cold War, 649, 680–88, 682*m*; in Africa, 701–3; in Asia, 696–701; climax of, 708–14; counterculture in, 705–6; NAM and, 679–80, 696, 698–99; Six-Day War and, 723; Vietnam War and, 721

Colombia, 419, 424, *534*, 535, 691, 753–54

Colonialism: in Africa, 636–40, 637*m*, 701–2; in Americas, 407–31, 410*m*, 413*m*; defined, 625; in North America, 416–19, 417*m*; in Southeast Asia, 640–45, 642*m*

Columbian Exchange, 419, 420–21, 421*m*

Columbus, Christopher, 362, 408

Comanches, 418, 537–38

COMECON. *See* Council for Mutual Economic Assistance

Commanderies (China), 197

Commedia dell'arte, 383

Committee of Public Safety, in French Revolution, 507

Committee of Union and Progress (CUP), 583–84

Common Era: Greece in, 174, 186; Han dynasty in, 191; India in, 66, 173, 271; Japan in, 301; Nubia in, 317; Teotihuacán in, 137

Commonwealth: of Byzantium, *224*, 224–25; of Islam, 215, 222*m*

Commonwealth of Independent States, 714

Commune, 526–27

Communes (*mirs*), 591

Communism: in China, 673, 692, 740–41; in Cuba, 686–87; in Eastern Europe, 710*m*; goulash, 709; in Greece, 681; industrialization and, 677; Italian resistance to, 666; McCarthy and, 684; modernity of, 676; in Russia, 651; in Soviet Union, 664–66; supremacist nationalism and, 677; in Vietnam, 700–701, 720–22, 740–41

Communist Manifesto, The (Marx and Engels), 613

Communist Party: in China, 673–74, 718–19; in France, 660; in Poland, 710, 712; in Soviet Union, 664–65

Companion to Urania (Urania propitia) (Cunitz), 380

Compass, 279, 390–91

Computers, 649

Comte, Auguste, 523–24

CONADEP. *See* National Commission on the Disappearance of Persons

Concert of Europe, 515, 517, 633–34

Concordat of Worms, 255

Concubines, in Japan, 571

Confederate States of America, 520
Confessions (Augustine), 162
Confucianism, 90; in China, 191–92, 573; in Han dynasty, 196, 206; Islam and, 219; in Japan, 191, 306; in Korea, 295; reciprocity in, 210; in Song dynasty, 271; in Tang dynasty, 279; in Vietnam, 310, 312; on women, 204. *See also* Neo-Confucianism
Congo (Zaire), 40, 130, 638, 639, 702–3
Congress of Berlin, 582, 583, 592
Congress of Vienna, 515, 516m, 589
Conrad III, 257
Constantine I, the Great, 155–56, 166
Constantine XI, 365
Constantinople, 359, 364, 366; Crusades and, 230, 257; Russia and, 587, 590
Constitutional Government Party (Seiyukai), 571
Constitutionalism: in England, 401–3; ethnic nationalism and, 514, 677; in France, 502; Hobbes on, 390; in Italy, 517; in Japan, 571, 604; in Latin America, 529–41, 543–45, 663; in Mexico, 541; in Ottoman Empire, 582; in Russia, 590, 595
Consumerism, 654, 688
Containment, of Soviet Union, 681
Continental Association, 505
Continuous-flow production, 616, 616
Cook, James, 631
Coolies, 547–48
Copernicus, Nicolaus, 383–84, 386, 404
Copper Age (Chalcolithic Age), 33
Coptic Christianity, 126, 162, 317, 320
Cordilleras, 99
Coricancha, 351
Corliss steam engine, 605
Corn, 108–9, 136, 477
Corn Laws (England), 522
Coronation, 246
Corporate state, 666
Corpus Iuris Civilis (Justinian), 259
Corsairs, 358
Cortés, Hernán, 408, 408–9, 410m
Cossack Brigade, 587
Costa Rica, 691
Cottage industries, 600
Cotton, 446; in Brazil, 532; calicoes of, 668; from England, 586, 600; from India, 600; in Mexico, 537; slaves for, 519–20; from US, 601, 602
Council for Mutual Economic Assistance (COMECON), 683
Council of Clermont, 229
Council of Constance, 266, 268
Council of Nicaea, 155
Council of Pisa, 264
Council of Trent, 394
Counterculture, 705–6
Courtesans, in Japan, 571
Cowboys (*gauchos*), 530, 531
Creation myths, 48
Creed, Christian, 226–27
Creoles, 412, 414, 415, 423; African diaspora and, 449; in Argentina, 529–31; in Brazil, 531–33; Christianity of, 418; in Mexico, 535–41; in New Granada, 534; patriarchy of, 424
Crete, 34
Cricket, 615
Crimea, 588, 740

Crimean War, 581, 590, 635
Criollo, 550
Crô-Magnon, 15
Cromwell, Oliver, 397–98
Crusades, 227–31, 257–58, 359, 365; First, 227, 254, 257, 258m; Fourth, 227, 240, 257; Second, 230, 257; Third, 230, 257
Ctesiphon, 164
Cuauhtémoc, 409
Cuba, 686–87, 690, 728; slave revolts in, 542, 542–43
Cuban Missile Crisis, 649, 687m, 687–88, 708
Cubism, 620
Cultivation system, 641
Cultural nationalism, of Germany, 514
Cultural Revolution (China), 718–19
Culture: African diaspora and, 449–52, 451; in Americas, 426–28; by Australian Aboriginals, 13–15; in China, 80, 90–93; of Eastern Christianity, 382; in eastern Mediterranean, 46–49; in Europe, 688; in Greece, 151, 165; in Gupta Empire, 174; in High Middle Ages, 258–60; in India, 66–71, 271–75; industrialization and, 617–20; of Islam, 236–40; in Japan, 308, 572, 688; in Korea, 299–300; in Latin America, 549–50; of Meroë, 125–26; in Middle East, 46–49; in Ming dynasty, 287–88, 489; in North America, 688; in Oceania, 114–15, 116; of Parthians, 163–64; in Qing dynasty, 568–69; in Roman Empire, 165–66; in Russia, 590–91; in US, 654–59; in Vietnam, 310–12; of Western Christianity, 258–60; after World War II, 688; in Yellow River, 76–81; in Zhou dynasty, 91–93. *See also* Arts; Enlightenment
Cuneiform writing, 34
Cunitz, Maria, 380, 386
CUP. *See* Committee of Union and Progress
Curie, Marie, 617
Cuzco, 346–47, 351, 354, 411
Cyprus, 582
Cyrus II the Great, 146–47
Czar (tsar), 401, 587
Czechoslovakia: Prague Spring in, 709–10; Velvet Revolution in, 712
Czech Republic, 16, 16

Da Gama, Vasco, 362–63, 369, 437
Daimyo, 304, 308, 314
Dai Viet (Great Viet), 310–11
Dalai Lama, 483
Dante Alighieri, 266
Daode Jing (*The Classic of the Way and Virtue*), 194
Daoism, 193–94, 205, 219, 312, 489; in Neo-Confucianism, 290
Daoxue, 287
Dapenkeng, 79–80
Darwin, Charles, 618, 618
Daughters of Liberty, 504–5
David, 44
Da Vinci, Leonardo, 382
Dawes Plan (US), 668
Death in the Snow (Makovsky), 595
Decembrist Revolt, 590
Declaration of Independence, 505, 580
Declaration of the Rights of Man and of the Citizen, 507, 580

Decolonization. *See* Nation-states
Decretum (Gratian), 259
Dede Korkut, 237–38
De Gaulle, Charles, 700
De Klerk, Frederik Willem, 727
De Kooning, Willem, 689
De la Cruz, Juana Inés, 430–31
Delhi, 273–74, 275m
Demesne, 250
Democracy: in Athens, 149, 167–68; in India, 697; in Latin America, 691; of Mycenaeans, 46. *See also* Capitalist democracy
Demoiselles d'Avignon, Les (Picasso), 620, 620
Deng Xiaoping, 718, 719, 729
Denmark, 394, 518
Department of Commerce and Labor, US, 522
Descartes, René, 389–90, 512–13
Descent of Man, The (Darwin), 618
Description of Africa (Leo Africanus), 359
Détente, 649, 708
Deutero-Isaiah (Second Isaiah), 159
Deval, Pierre, 624
Devotion: in Byzantium, 238; in Hinduism, 176, 180–82; in Sufism, 236; in Western Christianity, 256
Devşirme, 372
Dharma, 66, 67–69, 172, 184
Di, 91
Dialectic, 523
Dialectic materialism, 613
Díaz, Porfirio, 539–40
Dickens, Charles, 524
Diderot, Denis, 512, 513
Diepkloof Rock Shelter, 11
Diggers, in England, 404–5
Dinga, 316
Dinh Bo Linh, 310
Diocletian, 155
Dirigibles, 606
Dirty War, in Argentina, 728–29
Divine Comedy, The (Dante), 266
Divine wind (*kamikaze*), 303
Dmanisi Cave, 8
Dollar regime, of US, 734–35, 757
Dome of the Rock, 216
Domestication of animals. *See* Animal domestication
Dominic (Saint), 256
Dominican Republic, 112
Dominicans, 256; in China, 484
Donatello, 382
Donation of Constantine, 226–27
Don Quixote (Cervantes), 379
Doré, Gustave, 612
Dorgon, 481
Dream of the Red Chamber, The (*Hong Lou Meng*) (Cao Xueqin), 568
Dreamtime, 14
Duarte, Eva, 691
Dubček, Alexander, 710
DuBois, W. E. B., 659
Du Fu, 279
Dulles, Allen, 686
Duma, 595
Dura-Europos, 162
Dutch United East India Company (VOC), 641
Dutch West India Company, 440
Dyes: from chemicals, 605; indigo, 445–46, 477

Dylan, Bob, 706
Dynamite, 605; for artillery, 607

Early Dynastic Period (Egypt), 38
Early humans. *See* Agrarian-urban centers;
    Prehistory
Earthquake detector, 208, *208*
East Africa: agrarian-urban centers of, 129–31;
    Ardi in, 6; Borana lunar calendar, 122;
    city, city-states in, 323–28, 325*m*;
    colonialism in, 638–39; genocide in,
    638–39; government in, 324; hominins
    in, 5; *Homo sapiens* in, 9; Indonesia and,
    130, *130*; Islam in, 436; Italy and, 667;
    migrations from, 25; ships of, 365;
    Swahili city-states, 323–28; trade by,
    130–31; urbanism in, 324
East Asia. *See* China; Japan
Easter, 256
Easter Island, 115
Eastern Christianity, *593*; in Byzantium, 222–30;
    Crusades and, 257; height of, 231–36;
    iconoclasm and, 223–24; in Kiev, 240;
    Russia and, 401; Western Christianity
    and, 226–27
Eastern Europe: Christianity in, 201; Cold War
    in, 687; communism in, 710*m*; foragers
    in, 28; fossils from, 8; Germany and, 514,
    652, 669; Jews in, 254, 662; Ottoman
    Empire and, 394. *See also* Russia; Soviet
    Union
Eastern Mediterranean: agrarian-urban centers
    of, 27–52, 29*m*; Arabs in, 185; chariots in,
    41; climate change in, 31; culture of,
    46–49; foraging in, 28–31; horses in, 41;
    in Ice Age, 29; multiethnic/multireligious
    interactions in, 40–46; religion in,
    46–49; Roman Empire and, 153; science
    in, 49; topography of, 28–29
Eastern Syriac Church, 162
Eastern Zhou period, 85–86
East Germany (German Democratic Republic),
    684–85, 712; Berlin Wall and, 687
Ebert, Friedrich, 667
Economy: of African slave trade, 446–48; of
    Brazil, 729; of Caribbean, 545*m*; of
    China, 88–89, 719; Enlightenment and,
    513; in Europe, 266; in Han dynasty,
    201–2, 202*m*; of India, 182–83, 275; of
    Japan, 305, 493–95, 569–71; of Latin
    America, 541–49, 545*m*; of Mughals,
    467–68; of Nazi Germany, 669; in Qing
    dynasty, 566–67; in Vietnam, 311
Ecuador, 104, 347, 424, 535, 691
Edessa, 257
Edict of Milan, 260
Edison, Thomas, 614
Education: in Americas, 426–27; Catholic
    Reformation and, 426; desegregation of,
    714; in Japan, 571; in Russia, 588; of
    women, 430–31
Edward III, 262
Edwin Smith Papyrus, 49
Egypt: Achaemenids and, 146, 147; Arab
    Spring in, 748–49; arts of, 49; Black
    Death in, 236; Coptic Christianity in,
    162; creation myth of, 48; Early Dynastic
    Period in, 38; East Africa and, 131; Great
    Britain and, 635, *635*, 662; Hittites and,
    41–42; India and, 184–85; irrigation in,

233; Judaism in, 235; kingdoms of, 34, 37,
    38–40, 39*m*, 41–42, 47, 51–52; Mamluks
    in, 227, 231–32, *232*; mathematics in, 49;
    medical science in, 49; Middle Kingdom
    of, 40; Muslim Brotherhood in, 723;
    Napoleon in, 578; as nation-state, 695–
    96; New Kingdom of, 37, 41–42, 47; Nile
    River of, 28, 31–32, 317–20; Old
    Kingdom of, 38–40, 39*m*, 51–52; Persians
    in, 216; Phoenicians and, 43–44;
    polytheism in, 47; SNSs in, 753; Sunni
    Islam in, 230; women in, 37; World War I
    and, 662; in Yom Kippur War, 723–24
Eiffel, Alexandre Gustave, 615
Eightfold Path, of Buddhism, 178–79
Einstein, Albert, 386, 617–18
Eisai, 307
Eisenhower, Dwight D., 684, 686, 701, 714
Elamite-Dravidian language, 56
Electricity, 605, 614–15
Electrons, 617
Elements (Euclid), 163, 384
Eliot, George, 524
Elizabeth I, 397
Elmina, *438*, 446
El Mirador, 133, *133*
El Niño, 101–3
El Paraíso, Peru, 105–6
El Salvador, 728
Emancipation Edict (Russia), 591, 596–97
Empires, 120–43; in Africa, *122*, 122–43; in
    Americas, 337–55; capitalism and, 645; of
    China, 190–211; critics of, 647; exports
    from, 646; of France, 660–61; of Great
    Britain, 633–34, 660–61; of India,
    169–89; of Islam, 214–43; of Japan,
    565–66, 566*m*; military and, *632*, 632–33;
    in 1914, 634*m*; of nineteenth century,
    624–47; religion of, 121; religious
    civilizations from, 213; of Russia, 576–97,
    589*m*, 633–34; weapons and, *632*, 632–33;
    of western Eurasia, 145–68; World War I
    and, 660–61, 661*m*. *See also* Colonialism;
    Kingdoms; *specific empires*
Empress Dowager (Cixi), 279, 291, 561
Empress Wu (Wu Zetian), 279, 279, 290–91
Encyclopédie (Diderot), 512, *513*
Enfield rifles, 628
Engels, Friedrich, 612, 613
England: Brazil and, 532; Calvinism in, 397;
    Caribbean and, 414; civil war in, 397;
    constitutionalism in, 401–3; cotton from,
    586, 600; Cromwell and, 397–98; in
    Crusades, 257; Diggers in, 404–5;
    fifteenth century political reorganization
    in, 265; Glorious Revolution in, 398, 403,
    503, 641; in Hundred Years' War, 262–63;
    Japan and, 492; laws in, 250–51;
    mercantilism of, 443; nation-state of, 522;
    Native Americans and, 504; New
    Sciences in, 385, 386; ninth century
    political recovery in, 250–51; North
    America and, 416, 503–5, 504*m*;
    plantations and, 422; in Seven Years' War,
    419, 503, 625; slaves and, 443, 444–46,
    445; Three Kingdoms, 397; tobacco and,
    446; trade by, 446–47; Western
    Christianity to, 244
English Football League, 615
Enheduanna, 27

Enlightenment, 356, 389, 501, 688; atheism of,
    619; economy and, 513; ethnic
    nationalism and, 513–14; in Germany,
    514; Haiti and, 511; in Japan, 596; Latin
    America and, 529; literature of, 513;
    morality of, 512–13; music of, 513;
    Napoleon Bonaparte and, 508;
    philosophy of, 512–13; romanticism and,
    523; Russia and, 577, 588
Enmebaragesi of Kish, 35
Entente Cordiale, 640
Enuma Elish, 48
Environment: modernity and, 754–56. *See also*
    Climate; Topography
Epic of Gilgamesh, 47–48
Erasmus, Desiderius, 382
Erdoğan, Recep Tayyip, 746–47, *747*
Eritrea, 667
Erligang, 87
Estancias (estates), 531
Estates-General, 250
Estonia, 712
Étatism, 662
Ethiopia, 127, 320–22, 322*m*, 667; Christianity
    in, 320, *321*; *Homo sapiens* in, 9; Lucy in,
    4–5, 6, *6*; Portugal and, 437–38
Ethnic cleansing, in Yugoslavia, 744
Ethnic nationalism: constitutionalism and,
    514, 677; Enlightenment and, 513–14; in
    Greece, 579; in Italy, 517–18; in Ottoman
    Empire, 583
Etruscans, 153, 166
Eucalyptus, 13
Eucharist, 226
Euclid, 163, 384
Eugenics, 656–57
Euphrates River, 28, 31–32, 152
Eurasia: Americas and, 117; China and, 83;
    empires of, 145–68; in Ice Age, 18; Meroë
    and, 126; Neanderthals in, 20; sub-
    Saharan Africa and, 121; trade in, 274*m*
Euripides, 165, 168
Europe: agriculture in, 251–52; banks in, 266;
    Black Death in, 262, 263*m*, *264*;
    capitalism in, 253–54; centralizing states
    of, 390–93, 392*m*; China and, 484;
    colonialism by, 407–31, 410*m*;
    counterculture in, 705–6; culture of, 688;
    economy in, 266; in 1871, 519*m*; famine
    in, 261; 1560, 368*m*; firearms in, 371;
    Jesus of Nazareth and, 256, *256*; Jews in,
    254; kingdoms of, 404; knitting in, 255;
    languages of, 266; Latin America and,
    548; literature of, 266; Middle East and,
    632–36; migrations and, 15–17, 610,
    610*m*; of Napoleon Bonaparte, 510*m*; in
    1914 and 1923, 655*m*; Ottoman Empire
    and, 625; philosophy in, 267; printing in,
    382; religion in, 254–58; Renaissance in,
    381–90; rock art in, 15; in 1648, 400*m*;
    social classes in, 254; taxes in, 404; trade
    in, 252–53, 253*m*, 265–66; uprisings in,
    516–17, *517*; urbanism in, 254; Western
    Christianity in, 244–69; World War II in,
    669–71, 672*m*. *See also* Eastern Europe;
    Western Europe
Evans, Mary Ann (George Eliot), 524
Ewuare, 439
" Exaltation of Inanna, The" (Enheduanna), 27
Exceptionalism, 357

Existentialism, 688
Explorer I, 68
Explosives, 605, 607
Exports: from Brazil, 729; from empires, 646; from Latin America, 545–49, 551, 754; of Ottoman Empire, 586; to US, 735; from Vietnam, 645
Extraterritoriality, 558
Ezana, 126

Factories: in China, 485, 556; in Great Britain, 600–601; in Latin America, 549; in Russia, 593 2; steam engine in, 621
Factory Act, 613
Factory towns, 612, *612*
Falkland Islands, 729
Family: in China, 81, 89–90, 720; in Confucianism, 192; in India, 66–70, 183–86; in Japan, 305–6; in Latin America, 549–50; in Ming dynasty, 285–86, 485–87; of Mughals, 469–70; in Qing dynasty, 485–87, 567; in Russia, 591
Family planning, in India, 697
Famine: in Europe, 261; in India, 697; in Ireland, 522; in Russia, 591, *591*
Faraday, Michael, 605
Far from the Madding Crowd (Hardy), 619
Fascism, in Italy, 666–67
Fatehpur Sikri, 461, 472
Fatimids, 222, 227
February Revolution (Russia), 653
Federalism, in Brazil, 532, 533
Federal Reserve Act, 522
Federal Trade Commission Act, 522
Federation of the Equator, 532
Female infanticide, 286, 720
Feminism, 614, 716–17
Ferdinand I, 369
Ferdinand II, 360, 362, 398
Ferdinand IV, 252
Fernando VII, 529, 536
Fertile Crescent, 28–31, 50
Fertilizers, 251, 605
Festivities: of Habsburg dynasty, 376; of Ottoman Empire, 375
Feudalism: in China, 86; of Franks, 249, 249f; in Prussia, 401. *See also* Serfdom
Fichte, Johann Gottlieb, 514
Filioque, 226–27
Final Solution, 670
Finland, 589
Firdosi, 237
Firearms, 378; centralizing states and, 391–92; in England, 403; in Europe, 371; of European centralize states, 392; French Revolution and, 506; in Japan, 492; in Middle East, 371; in Ming dynasty, 488; of Mughals, 458; of Native Americans, 416; of Russia, 401; samurai and, 492
First Balkan War, 584–86
First Crusade, 227, 254, 257, 258m
First Emperor (Cheng), 195–96, *196*, 209
First New Chronicle and Good Government, The (Poma de Ayala), 427
First Opium War, 554, 556, 557–58, 558m, 564
First Republic of Cartagena, 534
First War of Independence (India), 628, *629*
Flaubert, Gustave, 524
Flintlocks, 392, *402*, 416
Flores Island, Indonesia, 25–26

Flying buttresses, 261
Flying shuttle, 600
Food: from African diaspora, 449–50; famine of Europe and, 261; French Revolution and, 506; in Japan, 494, *494*; in Oceania, 117; Pure Food and Drug Act, 522; in Soviet Union, 665
Foot binding, 285
Foraging: in Americas, 98–107; in Andes, 111; in Australia, 13; in Caribbean islands, 112–13; in eastern Mediterranean, 28–31; by *Homo sapiens*, 9; in Mesoamerica, 111; in Middle East, 28–31; by Neanderthals, 15; in prehistory, 3; in sub-Saharan Africa, 130
Fortunate Edict, 581–82
Forty-Seven Ronin, The (Chikamatsu), 496
Fossils: from Africa, 4–7, 8; from Georgia, 8; of hominins, 6–7; of *Homo erectus*, 8; of *Homo sapiens*, 21; Lucy, 4–5
Foucault, Michel, 379
Fourier, Charles, 612
Four Modernizations, in China, 719–20
Four Noble Truths, of Buddhism, 178–79
Fourteen Points, 654
Fourth Crusade, 227, 240, 257
Frame Breaking Act (England), 622
France: absolutism in, 398–401; Africa and, 639–40; Algeria and, 624–25, 634, 701; Americas and, 414–15, 515–16; Bourbons of, 414–15, 515–16; Calvinism in, 394, 396; Cambodia and, 645; Canada and, 418, 503; Caribbean and, 414; Catholicism in, 396, 507; Chauvet Cave in, 16; Civil Code of, 508; civil war in, 396; constitutionalism in, 502; in Crimean War, 581, 590; in Crusades, 257; East India Company of, 465–66; empires of, 660–61; fifteenth century political reorganization in, 265; Great Depression in, 660; Haiti and, 508–9; in Hundred Years' War, 262–63; Japan and, 565–66; Laos and, 645; Lascaux Cave in, 16, *17*; Mamluks and, *632*; mercantilism of, 443; Mexico and, 538–39; monasteries in, 255; Nazi Germany and, 669; New Sciences in, 385, 386; ninth century political recovery in, 250–51; in North America, 416; Ottoman Empire and, 580–81, 624–25; republics of, 507; in Seven Years' War, 419, 503, 625; Sino-Japanese War and, 563; slaves and, 443; Suez Canal and, 696; Third Republic of, 519, 526–27; Thirty Years' War and, 398; Tunisia and, 636; Vichy government in, 670; Vietnam and, 644–45, 700–701; West Africa and, 638; women in, 614; in World War I, 648, *651*, 660; World War II in, 669–70
Franciscans, 256, 360, 484
Francis I, 394
Francis of Assisi, St., 256
Franco, Francisco, 669
Franco-Prussian War, 518, 635
Franklin, Benjamin, 427
Franks, 245–49, 249f
Franz Ferdinand, 652
Frederick I, 251, 257
Frederick II, the Great, 401
French League of Women's Rights, 614

French Revolution, 502, 503, 506–9, *507*; Enlightenment and, 501; Russia and, 587, 588–89
Freud, Sigmund, 618
FSLN. *See* Sandinista National Liberation Front
Fugitive Slave Act, 452
Fu Hao, 75, 83–84, 89
Fulton, Robert, 601

Gagarin, Yuri, 686
Galen, 259
Galileo, Galilei, 260, 384–85
Gandhi, Indira, 680
Gandhi, Mohandas, 663, *663*, 697
Ganges River, 62, *71*, 170, 273
Gaozu (Liu Bang), 196–97
Garibaldi, Giuseppe, 518
Garvey, Marcus, 659
Gasoline, 606
Gatling Gun, 608
Gauchos (cowboys), 530, *531*
Gaul, 245–49
Gautama, Siddhartha, 178
Gay Liberation Front (GLF), 715
Gays. *See* Homosexuals
Gaza Strip, 745
GDP. *See* Gross domestic product
Gender relations: of Australian Aboriginals, 13; in China, 89–90, 95–96; in Han dynasty, 204–5; of *Homo sapiens*, 10; of Inca, 352; in India, 68–70, 186; in Middle East, 35–38; in Ming dynasty, 285–86; of Mughals, 469–70; in US, 688. *See also* Women
Genghis Khan, 230, 281–82, 457–58
Genji Monogatari (*Tale of Genji*) (Murasaki), 292
Genoa, 360
Genocide: in Cambodia, 722; in East Africa, 638–39; ethnic cleansing, in Yugoslavia, 744; of Jews, 670, *671*, 677–78; in Rwanda, 737
Genro, 565
Geoglyphs, of Nazca, 141, 143
Geography (Ptolemy), 383
Geometry, 163
Georgia (nation-state), 8, 578, 665, 740
Georgia (US state), 446, 454–55
Gerbert of Aurillac, 258
German Confederation, 516–17
German Democratic Republic. *See* East Germany
Germany: Bismarck and, *518*, 518–19; cultural nationalism of, 514; East Africa and, 639; Eastern Europe and, 514, 652, 669; Enlightenment in, 514; industrialization in, 604, 616; Iran and, 746; Japan and, 565–66; Ming dynasty and, 563; Morocco and, 640; New Sciences in, 385, 386; ninth century political recovery in, 251; Protestant Reformation in, 393–94; Russia and, 653; Sino-Japanese War and, 563; steel from, 604, 616; Thirty Years' War in, 398; Weimar Republic in, 667–68; women in, 614. *See also* Nazi Germany; World War I; World War II
Gestapo, 669, 678
Ghana, 637–38, 751; as nation-state, 702. *See also* Ancient Ghana

Ghazan, 242
Ghaznavids, 273
Ghost Dance, 521
GI Bill, 688, *688*
Gibraltar, 252
Gilgamesh, 47, 48
Ginsberg, Allen, 705
Glasnost (Soviet Union), 710, 711–12
GLF. *See* Gay Liberation Front
Global balance of trade, 735*m*
Globalization: poor countries and, 740; US and, 735–36
Global warming, 754–56, 756*m*, 758
Glorious Revolution (England), 398, 403, 503, 641
Glyphic script, 136, *137*
Göbekli Tepe, 46
Go-Daigo, 303–4, 489
Goethe, Johann Wolfgang von, 513
Gold: in Australia, 631–32; in Brazil, 415–16, *416*, 422, 443; in Chile, 412, 419; in Colombia, 419; in Hispaniola, 441–42; of Incas, 411; Mali and, 330–31; of Songhay Empire, 434; in West Africa, 359
Golden Horde, 281
Golden Horn, 364
Goodyear, Charles, 605
Gorbachev, Mikhail, 710, 711–12
Gorham's Cave, 16
Gothic cathedrals, *260*, 260–61
Gouache, 472
Goulash communism, 709
Government: in Confucianism, 192, 206; Daoism and, 194; in East Africa, 324; in Harappan, 58–59; in Ming dynasty, 286; of Mongols, 281
Government of India Act, 663
Gowon, Yakubu, 725
Granada, 362, 369
Gran Colombia, 535
Grand Canal, in China, 200
Grasslands (*pampas*), 424, 530
Gratian, 259
Gravesites: in Americas, 103; in China, 83–84, 89; of Chishti, *462*; for First Emperor of Qin dynasty, 196, *196*; in Greece, *165*; of *Homo sapiens*, 11; of Inca, 337; in Japan, 302; in Moche Valley, 139; of Neanderthals, 15; of Paracas, 141
Gray, Tom, 4
Great Awakening, 428
Great Britain: abolition of slavery in, 637; Afghanistan and, 635; Africa and, 639–40; agriculture in, 600; Australia and, 631–32; banks in, 599; chartism in, 612–13; in Crimean War, 581, 590; Egypt and, 635, *635*, 662; empire of, 633–34, 660–61; factories in, 600–601; Falkland Islands and, 729; Ghana and, 702; Greece and, 680–81; India and, 625–31, 627*m*, 629, 630*m*, 662–63; industrialization in, 599–603, 602*m*, 615; Industrial Revolution in, 599–603, 621; Israel and, 694; Kenya and, 702; National Society for Women's Suffrage in, 614; nation-states of, 522; Nazi Germany and, 669; Ottoman Empire and, 579, 581; Qing dynasty and, 554–67; railroads in, 601; Russia and, 634–35; Sudan and, 635; Suez Canal and, 662, 696; textile industry

in, 600; urbanism in, 610; West Africa and, 637–38; World War I and, 648, 653, 659–60; World War II and, 669–70, 671. *See also* England
Great Depression, 657–59, 660, 663–64, 666, 667, 674
Great Enclosure, 327
Greater East Asia Co-Prosperity Sphere, 675
Great Famine (Ireland), 522
Great Game, 634–35
Great Leap Forward (China), 693
Great Plains, Native Americans of, 418
Great Pyramid, of Khufu, 38–40, *40*
Great Reform (*Taika*), 302
Great Reform Bill (England), 522
Great Viet (Dai Viet), 310–11
Great Wall of China, *190*, 197–98, 209
Great Zimbabwe, 327, *327*
Greece, 149*m*; Achaemenids and, 146–51; Anatolia and, 662; arts of, 48–49; city, city-states of, 46, 148–50; civil war in, 681; communism in, 681; culture of, 151, 165; ethnic nationalism in, 579; graves in, *165*; Great Britain and, 680–81; Italy and, 382; Judaism and, 161; literature of, 165; Mycenaeans of, 42, 44–46, 48–49; Normans in, 228; Ottoman Empire and, 579; Persia and, 146–51; Phoenicians and, 43–44; Roman Empire and, 166; Sea Peoples from, 42; World War I and, 653
Greek philosophy, 160
Greenhouse gases, 734, 754–56, 758
Gregory I, 244–47
Gregory VII, 255
Gromyko, Andrei, 709
Gross domestic product (GDP): of Africa, 751; of China, 719, 733, 741, *741*; in Latin America, 546; of Russia, 740
Grosseteste, Robert, 259
Guatemala, 108, 339, 424, 691
Gudit, 320
Guericke, Otto, von, *388*
Guerrero, Vicente, 536
Guilds, 254
Guillotin, Joseph Ignace, 509
Guillotine, 508–9
Guinea Bissau, 752
Gulag system (Russia), 687
Gülen, Fethullah, 747
Gulf of Tonkin Resolution, 720–21
Gulf Stream, 101
Guncotton, 607
Gunpowder, 280–81, 378, 506, 628
Gunpowder empires, 470
Gupta Empire, 156, 170, 174–75, 175*m*, 271
Gustavus II Adolphus, 398
Gu Yanwu, 488
Gypsies (Roma), 669, 671

Habsburgs, 367–71, 398, 401; in Austria, 517; centralizing state of, 371–74; natural sciences and, 385; Ottoman Empire and, 577–78; Russia and, 577, 588; in Spain, 375–77
Haciendas (agricultural estates), 421–22, 540
Hadar AL 288-1 (Lucy), 4–5, 6, *6*
Haiku, 496
Haiti, 112, 449, 502–3, 508–11, 529
Haitian Revolution, 501, 503, 508
Hakkas, 559, 567

Halifax Gibbet, 508
Halo, 238
Hamas, 745–46
Hammurabi, 35, 36–37
Hamzanama (Book of Hamza), 472, *473*
Han dynasty (China), 85, 191, 196–99, 197*m*; agriculture in, 199, 202–3; Confucianism in, 206; decline of, 199; economy in, 201–2, 202*m*; gender relations in, 204–5; historians in, 206–7; Korea and, 294; ships of, 364; technology of, 203, *203*; Vietnam and, 310; women in, 204–5
Han Fei, 193, 195
Han-gul, 299
Hanseatic League, 265, 391
Hanshu (*The History of the Former Han*) (Ban Biao and Ban Gu), 207
Hara-kiri (ritual suicide), 304
Harappa, 53–62, 54, 57*m*, 59, 72–74
Hardy, Thomas, 619
Hariri, al-, 233, 236, 237
Harlem Renaissance, 656, 658–59
Harsha Vardhana, 271–72, 272*m*
Harvard College, 427
Hasmonean, 161
Hausa, 726
Hausaland, 436
Hawaii, 115
Hay, John, 563
Headmen, 197
Heaven, 91–92, 161, 206
Heavenly Buddha (Mahayana), 179–80, 312
Heavenly Kingdom of Great Peace (*taiping tianguo*), 559
Hebrew Bible, 44, 223, 384–85
Hegel, Georg Wilhelm Friedrich, 523, 597, 613
Heian period (Japan), 292–93, 302, 303, 303*m*, *304*
Hellenism, 151, 161
Helots, 150
Henry II, 250–51
Henry III of Navarre, 396
Henry IV, 255
Henry the Navigator, 360, 437
Henry VI, 251
Henry VIII, 394
Heraclitus, 160, 216
Herder, Johann Gottfried, 514
Herero, 639
Hertz, Heinrich Rudolf, 606
Herzl, Theodore, 662
Hesiod, 165, 382
Heyerdahl, Thor, 118
Hezbollah, 745, 746, 749
Hidalgo y Costilla, Miguel, 536, *536*
Hidden Twelfth Imam (Ismail), 366
Hideki, Tojo, 675
Hideyoshi, Toyotomi, 476–77, 481, 490, *490*, 491*m*
Hierankopolis, 38
Hieroglyphic writing, 38, *38*, 125
High Middle Ages, 258–60
Himyar, 127
Hindenburg, Paul von, 668
Hinduism, 70; Buddhism and, 272; devotional branches of, 176, 180–82; Gupta Empire and, 174–75; in India, 631–32, 696–97; Islam and, 219, 271, 289–90; Mughals and, 471; polytheism of, 471; Rajarajeshwara Temple, 273; sexuality in, 186; Sikhism and, 275; of south India, 272

Hippies, 706, 715

Hirobumi, Ito, 553, 570

Hiroshima, 675, *681*

Hispaniola, 409, 414, 420, 441–42

History of the Former Han, The (*Hanshu*) (Ban Biao and Ban Gu), 207

Hitler, Adolf, 62, 657, 668–70

Hittites, 41–42, 45, 120

HLA. *See* Human leukocyte antigen

Hobbes, Thomas, 389–90, 618–19

Hobbits, of Flores Island, 25–26

Ho Chi Minh, 700, 701

Hofmann, Hans, *689*

Hohenzollern, 401

Holocaust, 670, *671*, 677–78

Holy Christian League, 369

Holy Roman Empire, 251, 257, 367, 369, 398, 401

Holy Rule (St. Benedict), 246

Holy war (*jihad*), 220, 229, 359, 378, 438, 583, 638

Homer, 165

Homestead Act, 521

Hominins, 5–8; bipedalism of, 6; climate change and, 5; in East Africa, 5; of Flores Island, Indonesia, 25–26; fossils of, 6–7; in savanna, 6; tools of, 6–7

Homo erectus, 5, 6–7, 8, 15, 25

Homo floresiensis, 25–26

Homo neanderthalensis (Neanderthals), 15–17, 20–21, 25

Homo sapiens, 9–26; in caves, 10; in China, 77; foraging by, 9; fossils of, 21; hunting by, 9, 19; in Ice Age, 17–23, *18m*; migrations by, 11–17, *12m*

Homosexuals: civil rights for, 715; Nazi Germany and, 669, *671*

Honduras, 753

Hong Lou Meng (*The Dream of the Red Chamber*) (Cao Xueqin), 568

Hongwu (Zhu Yuanzhang), 283–84, 296

Hong Xiuquan, 559

Hong xue (redology), 568

Hoover, Herbert, 657–58

Hopewell, 111, *112m*

Hoplites, 147

Horace, 165

Horned God, *59*

Horses: of Achaemenids, 147; in China, 198–99; in eastern Mediterranean, 41; in Europe, 252; in Middle East, 41; in north India, 64

Horus, 38

Household slavery, 438

House of Chosen Women, 352

House Un-American Activities Committee, 684

Howl and Other Poems (Ginsberg), 705

Huainan zi, 206

Huang Zongxi, 488

Hughes, Langston, *657*, 658, *659*

Huguenots, 396

Hui Neng, 208

Huitzilpochtli, 344

Humanism, 382

Human leukocyte antigen (HLA), 118

Human sacrifice, by Aztecs, 345, 352, 352–53

Humayun, 458–59, *461*

Humboldt Current, 102

Hundred days' reform, of Ming dynasty, 563

Hundred Flowers campaign (China), 693

Hundred Years' War, 262–63

Hungary, 685, *685*

Huns, 156

Hunting: in Americas, 98–107; in Australia, 13; in Caribbean islands, 112–13; by *Homo sapiens*, 9, 19; in Ice Age, 19; by Inuit, 111

Hurricanes, 101–3

Hurston, Zora Neale, 658

Husák, Gustáv, 710, 712

Huss, John, 264, 266

Hussein (Algerian Ottoman ruler), 624

Hussein, Saddam, 725, 736–37

Hutchinson, Anne, 427

Hutu, 437, 737

Hu Yaobang, 720

Iberia: Arabs in, 217; Berbers in, 217; Catholicism in, 375–77; Islam in, 370–71; land grants in, 371–72; Napoleon Bonaparte in, 529; natural sciences of, 385; *Reconquista of*, 359; ships of, 365. *See also* Portugal; Spain

Ibn Battuta of Tangier, 283

Ibn Khaldun, Abd al-Rahman, 237

Ibn Qasim, Muhammad, 270–71

Ibn Rushd (Averroes), 237

Ibn Sina (Avicenna), 237, 259

Ibn Taymiyya, Taqi al-Din, 242–43

Ibn Tughluq, Muhammad ("Muhammad the Bloody"), 274

ICBM. *See* Intercontinental ballistic missile

Ice Age, 17–23, *18m*; eastern Mediterranean in, 29; hunting in, 19; Japan and, 300; land bridges in, 19–20, 98; Middle East in, 29

Iconoclasm: in Byzantium, 223–24, 238; Eastern Christianity and, 223–24

Icons, of Byzantium, 238–39, *239*

Ieyasu, Tokugawa, 490–93, 497–98, 564–65

Ife, 332

Igbo, 726

Ijebu, 333

Iliad (Homer), 165

Ilkhans, 282

Illustrated Gazetteer of the Maritime Countries (Wei Yuan), 568

IMF. *See* International Monetary Fund

Immigration. *See* Migrations

Imperialism. *See* Empires

Import-substitution industrialization, 533; in Chile, 552; in China, 735

Impression, Sunrise (Monet), 620

Impressionism, 619–20

Inca, 337, 346–49, *348m*; empire of, 350–53; gender relations of, 352; Habsburgs and, 367; mummies of, 352–53; roads of, 349, *349*; Spain and, 409–11, *411*, 427

Incandescent light bulb, 615

Indentured laborers, 443, 547

Index of Prohibited Books, 395

India: abolition of slavery in, 628; agrarian-urban centers of, 3, 53–74; Alexander the Great in, 151, 169–70; Arabs and, 272; Arabs in, 270; arts of, 186; black pepper and, 184–85; British East India Company in, 625–28, 626, 641; caste system of, 67–69, *68*, 69, 71, 183–86, 275, 631; China and, 207; Christianity in, 628; city, city-states of, 53–61; civil service in, 629–31; in Common Era, 66, 173, 271;

cotton from, 600; culture of, 66–71, 271–75; da Gama to, 362–63, 369; economy of, 182–83, 275; empires of, 169–89; European trade with, 253; family in, 66–70, 183–86; family planning in, 697; First War of Independence in, 628, *629*; gender relations in, 68–70, 186; Great Britain and, 625–31, *627m*, 629, *630m*, 662–63; Gupta Empire of, 156, 170, 174–75, *175m*, 271; Harappa in, 53–62, 54, *57m*, 59, 72–74; Hinduism in, 631–32, 696–97; industrialization in, 757; Islam in, 272–75, 631–32, 663, 696–97; kingdoms of, 120–21; Latin America and, 547; literature of, 186; *mahajanapadas of*, 64–65; mathematics in, 187; Mauryans of, 170–87, *173m*; medical science in, 187; Mediterranean and, 164; Mehrgarh in, 56–57; middle class in, 750, *750*; Middle East and, 164; monsoon system of, 54–56, *55m*; in NAM, 680, 696, 698, *700*; as nation-state, 662–63, 696–99; Portugal and, 363; religion of, 54, 70–71; republics of, 189; Sasanids and, 164; science in, 187; Seven Years' War and, 625; sexuality in, 69–70; ships of, 365, *365*; spice trade of, 438, 465; Suez Canal and, 662; taxes in, 182–83, 628; textile industry in, 601; topography of, 54–56, 55m; trade by, 183, 184–85, 363, 468, *468m*; Vedas of, 63–64, 70–71, 176–80; Vietnam and, 310; warfare in, 65–66; women in, 68–70. *See also* Mughals; North India; South India

Indian Ocean, *361m*; Islam in, 369; migration in, 114

Indian Removal Act, 521

Indigo, 445–46, 477

Indo-Aryans, 63

Indonesia: East Africa and, 130, *130*; *Homo floresiensis* in, 25–26; land bridges to, 19; migration from, 114; in NAM, 680, 696; Netherlands and, 640–41; Portugal and, 640–41

Indulgences, 393, 394

Indus River, 56, 72–73, 215

Industrialization: big business and, 615–16; cartels and, 615; in Chile, 551–52; in China, 735, 757; communism and, 677; critics of, 612–13; culture and, 617–20; 1871-1914, *603m*, 603–9; in Germany, 604, 616; in Great Britain, 599–603, *602m*, 615; in India, 757; in Japan, 604; in Latin America, 663, 689–91, 754; leisure and, 615; migrations and, 610, *610m*; modernity and, 617–20; monopolies and, 615; in Ottoman Empire, 586; reforms for, 613; in Russia, 587–95, 604; science and, 617–19; 1750-1870, 599–603; 1750-1914, 598–622; social classes and, 610–12, 621; socialists and, 612–13; sports and, 615; in Turkey, 746–47; urbanism and, 609–10, 614–15; in US, 602–3, 616; voting rights and, 612; of weapons, 607–9; women and, 613, *613*. *See also* Import-substitution industrialization

Industrial Revolution, 357; China and, *557*; in Great Britain, 599–603, 621, 626; Japan and, 572; Latin America and, 546; Russia and, 577–78

Indus Valley: Achaemenids and, 147; Harappa in, 57*m*, 57–61
Infanticide, 286, 720
Information technology (IT), 736
Ingenious Gentleman Don Quixote of La Mancha, The (Cervantes), 379
Inquiry into the Nature and Causes of the Wealth of Nations (Smith, Adam), 513
Institutionalization, 459
Institutional Revolutionary Party (Partido Revolucionario Institucional) (PRI), 663–64
Intercontinental ballistic missile (ICBM), 686, 708
Internal combustion engine, 605
International Monetary Fund (IMF), 739–40
Interpretation of Dreams,The (Freud), 618
Intolerable Acts (Coercive Acts), 505
Inuit, 111
"Investiture Controversy," 255
Ionia, 147, 150
Iran: Achaemenids of, 120, 145–51, 147*m*, 158, 159, 161; architecture of, 586; hostage crisis in, 725; Islamic Revolution in, 585, 725; Israel and, 746; Mahmud of Ghazna and, 273; Parthians and, 151; shahs of, 586–87, 725; Silk Road in, 235; Syria and, 749; transcendence in, 159; Twitter Revolution in, 753. *See also* Persians
Iran-Iraq War, 725
Iraq: Iran and, 725; US and, 736–37
Ireland, 522
Iron: in China, 92, 201; in Meroë, 124
Iron Age, 42
Iroquois, 418
Irrigation: in Americas, 105; in Egypt, 233; in Japan, 305; in Nubia, 318; by Paracas, 140
Isabella, 360, 362
ISIS. *See* Islamic State in Iraq and al-Sham
Islam (Muslims): agriculture and, 252; in ancient Ghana, 329; aniconism of, 239; Byzantium and, 214–43; caste system and, 275; versus Christianity, 359–71; commonwealth of, 215, 222*m*; in Constantinople, 359; Crusades and, 229–30; culture of, 236–40; in East Africa, 436; empire of, 214–43; in Ethiopia, 438; five religious duties of, 220; formation of, 215–22; height of civilization, 231–36; Hinduism and, 219, 271, 289–90; in Iberia, 370–71; in India, 272–75, 631–32, 663, 696–97; in Indian Ocean, 369; in Indonesia, 641; in Italy, 257; in Jerusalem, 257; Jesus of Nazareth and, 162; *jihad* of, 220, 229, 359, 378, 438, 583, 638; laws of, 220; literature and, 237–39; miniatures of, 238–39; Mongols and, 282; in Nigeria, 726; in North Africa, 317–22; in Nubia, 319–20; in Pakistan, 697; in Philippines, 643; philosophy and, 236–37; in Red Sea, 369; Russification of, 592; science and, 236–37; in Sicily, 257; Sikhism and, 275; in slave revolts, 543; in southern Africa, 323–28; in Spain, 257, 371; theology of, 218–19; Umayyads and, 216–17; in West Africa, 328–33, 434, 638; in western Mediterranean, 257; women in, 214–15. *See also* Byzantium;

Mughals; Ottoman Empire; Shiite Islam; Sunni Islam
Islamic Government, The, 725
Islamic Revolution (Iran), 585, 725
Islamic State in Iraq and al-Sham (ISIS), 749–50
Islamification, of Mughals, 463
Islamism, 744–45
Islamization, 748
Ismail (Hidden Twelfth Imam), 366
Israel: Arabs and, 717, 722, 722–24; Egypt and, 696; Gaza Strip and, 745; Iran and, 746; as nation-state, 694–95; Palestine and, 694–95
Israelites, 44, 159, 220
Isthmus Declaration, 153
IT. *See* Information technology
Italy: Byzantium and, 226; Catholicism in, 667; constitutionalism in, 517; East Africa and, 639; ethnic nationalism in, 517–18; European trade and, 252; fascism in, 666–67; Great Depression in, 667; Greece and, 382; Islam in, 257; Normans in, 228, 257; supremacist nationalism in, 666–67; World War I and, 653
Iturbide, Agustín de, 536–37
Itzcóatl, 345

Jacobite Church, 162
Jahan, Nur, 469, 469
Jahangir, 461–63, 469, 469
Jainism, 171, 177–78, 178, 185
Jama Masjid, 473
James, Henry, 524
Jamestown, 416–18, 445
Janissaries, 372, 579
Japan, 300–308; agriculture in, 301–2, 305; arts of, 304, 495–96, 496, 572; Buddhism in, 179, 208, 293, 302, 306–8, 314; calligraphy in, 564; capitalism in, 569; China and, 191, 313, 553–74, 562, 671–72, 674; Christianity in, 493; civil war in, 573–74; climate of, 300, 301*m*; Confucianism in, 191, 306; constitutionalism in, 571, 604; culture of, 308, 572, 688; economy of, 305, 493–95, 569–71; empire of, 565–66, 566*m*; Enlightenment in, 596; family in, 305–6; firearms in, 492; food in, 494, 494; Heian period in, 292–93, 302, 303, 303*m*, 304; India and, 183; industrialization in, 604; Jomon period of, 301–2; Korea and, 294, 476–77, 490, 566; land bridges to, 19, 300; languages of, 292; literature of, 292; Meiji in, 493, 564–66, 569–72; military of, 498, 671–72; modernity in, 553–74, 570*m*; nation-state of, 565; Neo-Confucianism in, 492, 495, 498, 565; Netherlands and, 492, 498–99; political parties in, 571; pottery in, 301, 301; railroads in, 569, 570; religion in, 306–8; Russia and, 565–66, 593–94; science in, 560–61, 572; seclusion of, 492, 498–99; shogunates of, 303–4; social classes in, 571; Southeast Asia and, 675; supremacist nationalism in, 651, 671–72; Tang dynasty and, 276; telegraph in, 569; theater in, 495–96, 572; topography of, 300, 301*m*; trade by, 497–99; unification of, 489–90; urbanism of, 493*m*, 493–94;

US and, 565; women in, 495, 571; World War I and, 653; Yayoi period in, 302. *See also* World War II
Japan Current, 102, 293
Jefferson, Thomas, 505
Jenné-jeno, 143
Jerusalem, 216, 227, 257, 321; Crusades and, 229, 230; Jesus in, 161–62; Neo-Babylonia and, 159
Jesuits, 415, 426, 438, 484, 484
Jesus of Nazareth, 155, 161–62, 223, 238, 254, 256, 256, 426
Jews and Judaism, 159; animal sacrifice of, 162; anti-Semitism and, 262, 678; Arabs and, 695; in Egypt, 235; in Europe, 254; genocide of, 670, 671, 677–78; Islam and, 220; Nazi Germany and, 668, 677–78; in Ottoman Empire, 579–80; in Palestine, 161, 661–62; in Persia, 155; Portugal and, 362; in Russia, 593; saviors of, 677–78
Jinnah, Muhammad Ali, 663
Joan of Arc, 263
John (King of England), 251
Johnson, James Weldon, 658
Johnson, Lyndon B., 709, 714, 721–22
John XII, 251
Jomon period (Japan), 301–2
Jousts, 376
Juárez, Benito, 538
Judah, 44
Judaism. *See* Jews and Judaism
Julius Caesar, 154
Juntas, 534
Junzi, 192
Jurchens, 280
Justinian I, the Great, 156–57, 204, 259

Kabuki, 496, 572
Kaddaba teeth, 5, 6
Kahun Papyrus, 49
Kailsantha Temple, 177
Kalakmul, 132
Kalinga, 172
Kama Sutra (Aphorisms of Love) (Vatsyayana), 186
Kamikaze (divine wind), 303
Kana system, 308, 312, 313
Kanchipuram, 272
Kandinsky, Wassily, 689
Kanem-Bornu, 436
Kangxi, 482
Kang Youwei, 563
Kanishka, 174
Kannon, 307
Kant, Immanuel, 512–13, 523
Karma, 178
Karman, Tawakkol, 732–33
Karma-samsara, 71
Kasa-Vubu, Joseph, 703
Kashmir, 697
Katipunan, 643
Kautilya of Magadha, 65, 171
Kennedy, John F., 687–88, 701, 714
Kennedy, Robert, 716
Kennewick Man, 23
Kenseito (Liberal Party), of Japan, 571
Kenya, 122, 131, 702
Kepler, Johannes, 380, 386
Kerosene, 605

Kerouac, Jack, 705
KGB, 687
Khalijis, 274
Kharijis, 323, 329
Khartoum, 123
Khmer Rouge, 722
Khmers, 183
Khoi, 440
Khomeini, Ayatollah Ruhollah, 585, 725
Khosrow I, 157–58
Khosrow II, 216
Khrushchev, Nikita, 680, 685–88, 692, 693, 708, 718
Khubilai Khan, 281–82, *283*
Khufu, 38–40, *40*
Khurram (Shah Jahan), 456–57, 463
Khwarizmi, al-, Muhammad ibn Musa, 237
Khyber Pass, 76, 463
Kibbutz, 722
Kiev, 225, 240
Kim Jong-un, 758
King, Martin Luther, Jr., *714*, 716
Kingdom of Poland, 588, 589
Kingdoms: of Africa, 432–55; of Alexander the Great, 150–51; in Americas, 120; of central Africa, 324–28; centralized, 390–93; of China, 120–21; of Crete, 34; of Egypt, 34, 37, 38–40, *39m*, 41–42, 47, 51–52; of Europe, 404; of India, 120–21; in Mediterranean, 120; in Mesoamerica, 120, 131–39; of Mesopotamia, 34–36; in Middle East, 120; of north India, 272; in Nubia, 317–18; religious civilizations from, 213; of southern Africa, 324–27; of south India, 175–76; in sub-Saharan Africa, 120, 123–25, *435m*
King List (Mesopotamia), 34–35
King of kings: of Achaemenids, 148; Alexander the Great as, 146; Ardashir as, 154; Ctesiphon as capital of, 152; Khosrow II as, 216
King's Peace of 386 BCE, 150
Kipling, Rudyard, 647
Knitting, 255
Koguryo kingdom (Korea), 294–95
Kojiki (Records of Ancient Matters), 308
Kokoro (Natsume Soseki), 572
Kokutai (national polity/essence), 650, 671
Komnenos dynasty (Byzantium), 234
Kongo, 432–33, 439–40, *440*, 449
Kon-Tiki, 118
Korea, 293–300; agriculture in, 294, *295m*; Buddhism in, 295, *296*, 299–300; China and, 191, 294–95, 313, 481, 562; climate of, 293; Confucianism in, 191, 295; culture of, 299–300; Japan and, 476–77, 490, 566; land bridges to, 19; land reform in, 297–98; literacy in, 299; marriage in, 299; Neo-Confucianism in, 297, 298; North Korea, 746, 758–59; printing in, 298–99; religion in, 299–300; rocket launcher of, *280*; Sino-Japanese War and, *562*, 563; Tang dynasty in, 276; topography of, 294, *295m*; women in, 298–99; writing in, 299; Yuan dynasty and, 281
Korean War, 683–84
Koryo kingdom (Korea), 296–97, *297m*
Kosok, Paul, 143
Krakatau, 156

Krishna, 66, 67, 182
Ku Klux Klan, 656, *657*
Kulaks, 665
Kurdish, 230, 366, 583, 747, 750
Kushans, 174
Kushites, 122
Kuwait, 736

Labor assignments (*repartimiento*), 414, 420
Labor Party (Australia), 632
Labor unions, in US, 656
Lady Ji, 89
Lahori, Ustad Ahmad, 472
Laissez-faire, 513
Land bridges, 19–20, 98, 300
Land grants: in Brazil, 411; in Iberia, 371–72; in Ottoman Empire, 371–72
Land-labor grants, 408
Land reform: in China, 198–99; in Colombia, 691; in Cuba, 690; in Korea, 297–98; in Mexico, 540, 541; in Ottoman Empire, 582; in Philippines, 643
Langland, William, 266
Languages: of China, 191, 207; of Creoles, 449; of Europe, 266; of Japan, 292; Mughals and, 472; Proto-Indo-European, 63; of sub-Saharan Africa, 130; of Toltec, 338. *See also* Writing
Laos, 645, 722
Lao Tzu (Laozi) , 193–94
Lapita, 114–15, 116
Lascaux Cave, in France, 16, *17*
Last Judgment, 366
Lateen sail, 253
Latin America: agriculture in, 546, 548; Catholicism in, 545, 549; constitutionalism in, 529–41, 543–45, 663; culture of, 549–50; democracy in, 691; economy of, 541–49, *545m*; Enlightenment and, 529; expansion of, 753–54; exports from, 545–49, 551, 754; factories in, 549; family in, 549–50; GDP in, 546; Great Depression in, 663–64; independence in, 529–41, 551; industrialization in, 663, 689–91, 754; Industrial Revolution and, 546; literature in, 550; migrations in, *547*, 547–48; nation-states of, *538m*; in nineteenth century, 528–52; populism in, 691; proxy wars in, 728–29; republics of, 542; urbanism in, 680–90, *690m*; women in, 549–50; World War I and, 663–64; World War II and, 690. *See also* Caribbean; Mesoamerica; South America
Latin Christianity, 245–49
Latin Empire, 227, 238
Latvia, 712
La Venta, 110
Lawrence, T. E., 661
Laws: of Babylonia, 36–37; in England, 250–51; in High Middle Ages, 259; of Islam, 220; in Japan, 302; in Korea, 297; of Mauryans, 172; of Roman Empire, 153, 157, 242; of Sumer, 37
League of Nations, 654, 667
Lebanon: civil war in, 724; Hezbollah in, 745
Lebensraum (living space), 653, 669–70
Legalism, Confucianism and, 193
Legge, James, 190
Legionaries, 153

Leibniz, Gottfried Wilhelm, 386
Leisure, industrialization and, 615
Le Loi, 311
Lenin, Vladimir Ilyich, 594, 645, 653, 664–65
Leo III, 247
Leo IX, 226
Leopold II, 638, 639
Leo Africanus (al-Wazzan, al-Hasan Ibn Muhammad), 358–59
Leo X, 358
Lesbians. *See* Homosexuals
Levallois tools, 8, 9
Leviathan (Hobbes), 390
Liang Qichao, 563
Li Bai, 279
Liberal Party (Kenseito), 571
Liberia, 751–52
Library of Alexandria, science at, 163
Libya (Tripolitania), 639, 667, 748
Li dynasty (Vietnam), 310
Li Er (Lao Tzu/Laozi), 194
Life lease, 578
Life of Harsha (Bana), 272
Light bulb, 615
Lightning war (*Blitzkrieg*), 669
Li Hongzhang, 553, 561, 563
Lijia, 486
Lin Biao, 719
Lincoln, Abraham, 520
Linear A writing, of Minoans, 40
Linear B writing, of Mycenaeans, 45
Lin Zexu, 556, *557*
Li Shimin, 200
Li Si, 193, 195, 196
Literacy: in Japan, 571; in Korea, 299; in New England, 426
Literature: of China, 288, 568; of Enlightenment, 513; of Europe, 266; of Greece, 165; of Habsburg dynasty, 376–77; of India, 186; Islam and, 237–39; of Japan, 292, 308; in Latin America, 550; in Ming dynasty, 488; modernity in, 619; of Mughals, 471–72; novel, 288, 308, 568; poetry, 208, 237, 266, 279, 304, 308, 496, 513, 568; realism and, 524; of Roman Empire, 165–66; romanticism and, 523; of Russia, 591
Lithuania, 712
Little Ice Age, 391
Liu Bang (Gaozu), 196–97
Liu Shaoqi, 693, 718
Living space (*Lebensraum*), 653, 669–70
Livingstone, David, 636
Locke, John, 389–90
Lodis, 274
Lombard, Peter, 259
Lombards, 247
London Working Men's Association, 612–13
Long Depression, 522
Long March, in China, 674–75
López, Francisco Solano, 531
Longshan period (China), 79
Lord of Sipán, 139
Lord of the Rings (Tolkien), 26
Lords Proprietors, of Barbados, 445
Lorentz, Hendrik, 617
Lothal, 60, *61*
Lotus Sutra, 207, 306–7
Louisiana, 418
Louisiana Purchase, 521

Louisiane, La, 418
Louis-Philippe, 516
Louis the Pious, 248
Louis VII, 257
Louis XIII, 398
Louis XIV, 396, 398–401
Louis XVI, 506
Louis XVIII, 515–16
Loyola, Ignatius, 395
Luba kingdom, 327–28, 328m
Lucy (Hadar AL 288-1), 4–5, 6, 6
Luddites, 622
Lumumba, Patrice, 703
Lunyu, 191–92
Lusitania, 653
Luther, Martin, 393–94
Lynchings, of African Americans, 656, 657

MacArthur, Douglas, 684
Macaulay, Thomas B., 628
Macedonia, 120, 150–51, 583
Machiavelli, Niccolò, 373, 382
Machine gun, 607, 608
Madame Bovary (Flaubert), 524
Madero, Francisco, 540–41
Madras (Chennai), 626
Magellan, Ferdinand, 642
Magic Flute, The (Mozart), 513
Maginot Line, 669
Magna Carta, 251
Magneto ignition system, 606
Maguey, 137
Magyars, 248
Mahabharata, 66, 66, 180–81
Mahajanapadas, 64–65
Mahal, Mumtaz, 456
Maharajas, 65
Mahavira, 171
Mahayana (Heavenly Buddha), 179–80, 207, 312
Mahdi (rightly guided leader), 584
Mahmud of Ghazna, 273
Maize, 108–9
Maji-Maji rebellion, 638–39
Makovsky, Vladimir Yegorovich, 595
Malaria, 636
Malaysia, 19
Mali, 329, 330–32, 434–36
Malinche, 408, 408
Malinke, 331
Mami Wata, 451
Mamluks, 227, 230, 360, 632; in Egypt, 231–32, 232; Nubia and, 317, 320; Ottoman Empire and, 366, 578–79
Manchuria, 83, 278, 293, 482, 671–72, 674
Manchus, 48, 481, 567
Mandate of Heaven, 85, 95, 192, 206, 302
Mandates, 661
Mandela, Nelson, 727, 731, 751, 751
Manet, Édouard, 539
Manichaeism, 269
Manorialism, 249, 249f
Manumission, 445
Man'yoshu (*The Ten Thousand Leaves*), 308
Mao Zedong, 673–74, 684, 692–93, 741; Cultural Revolution of, 710–19
Maps: of Renaissance, 390–91, 391; of Waldseemüller, 384, 385
Mapuche, 412
Mapungubwe, 325–27, 326

Maqamat (al-Hariri), 233, 236, 237
Maracaibo, 424
Marajó, 111–12
Marathas, 464–65, 474
Marathon, 150
Marconi, Guglielmo, 606
Marcus, Siegfried, 606
Marduk, 48, 147
Marie Antoinette, 507
Marius, 153–54
Maronites, 724
Maroons, 452
Marriage: of Australian Aboriginals, 14; in India, 186; in Japan, 306; in Korea, 299; in Middle East, 36–37; in Qing dynasty, 567; same-sex, 715
Marshall Plan, 681–83
Martel, Charles ("the Hammer"), 217, 246
Martial Emperor (Wudi), 312
Martin V, 266
Marx, Karl, 379, 612, 613, 664
Marxism, 594, 719, 728, 753–54
Master Kong, 191
Matchlock musket, 392, 458
Mathematical Principles of Natural Philosophy (Newton), 386
Mathematics: in China, 208; in eastern Mediterranean, 49; in Egypt, 49; in High Middle Ages, 258, 259; in India, 187; Islam and, 237; at Library of Alexandria, 163; of Maya, 116; in Middle East, 49; of Mughals, 470
Matriarchal clans, 301
Matrilineal clans, 301
Matrilocal marriage, 299
Mau Mau movement (Kenya), 702
Mauryan Empire, 170–74, 173m, 184, 188
Maxim, Hiram, 607, 608
Maximilian, 539, 539
Maya, 113, 116, 120, 131–36, 132m; agriculture of, 136, 341; ball game of, 134, 134–35; collapse of, 136; writing of, 133, 136, 137; on Yucatán Peninsula, 132–33, 339–41
Mazdak, 157
McCarthy, Joseph, 684
McKay, Claude, 658
McMahon-Hussein correspondence, 661
McNamara, Robert, 721
Meat Inspection Act, 522
Mecca, 366, 463
Medea (Euripides), 168
Medes, 146–47
Medical science, 259, 610; in Egypt, 49; in India, 187; Islam and, 237
Medici, Giovanni Leone di, 358
Mediterranean, 361m, 368m; India and, 164; kingdoms in, 120; Middle East and, 145–68; ships in, 364; trade in, 252–53, 253m. *See also* Eastern Mediterranean; Western Mediterranean
Megasthenes, 171
Mehmet II, the Conqueror, 363, 364–66, 366, 373
Mehrgarh, 56–57
Meiji (Mutsuhito), in Japan, 493, 564–66, 569–72
Meiji Constitution, 571, 604
Mein Kampf (Hitler), 670
Meluha, 59–60
Menander, 173

Mencius, 190, 192–93
Mengzi (*Book of Mencius*) (Mencius), 192–93
Mensheviks, 594
Mercantilism, in Caribbean, 443
Merchants, in China, 88
Mercury, in Peru, 412
Meroë, 120, 124–26, 125m, 131, 142
Merovingians, 245–46, 267
Mesoamerica, 340m; agrarian-urban centers of, 108–13; Aztecs of, 344–46, 345, 346m, 347, 352, 352–53, 367, 408–9; calendar in, 122; chiefdoms in, 338; climate in, 101; foraging in, 111; kingdoms in, 120, 131–39; pottery in, 105
Mesopotamia, 5, 28, 31–32, 42, 47, 49, 151, 159, 215; Achaemenids and, 147; agrarian-urban centers of, 27–52; city, city-states in, 33–34; kingdoms of, 34–35
Messiah, 159, 366
Mestizos, 423–24, 534, 535
Metternich, Klemens von, 515
Mexican-American War, 564
Mexican Basin, 338, 344–45, 350m
Mexican Revolution, 536, 536–41, 537
Mexico: abolition of slavery in, 536; agrarian-urban centers of, 108; Catholicism in, 536; Comanches and, 537–38; constitutionalism in, 541; corn from, 108; Creoles in, 535–41; France and, 538–39; independence of, 535–41, 536; labor assignments in, 414; land reform in, 540, 541; migrations in, 537; Native Americans in, 424, 535, 537–38; political parties in, 663–64, 753; radiocarbon dating in, 122; as republic, 536–37; Spain and, 407–11; Teotihuacán in, 136–39, 138m, 338–41; Texas and, 537; uprising in, 536; urbanism in, 663; US and, 537–38, 539m
Michael I Cerularius, 226, 227
Michelangelo, 382
Midden, 104
Middle class, 254, 386, 599; in England, 503; Enlightenment and, 512; in France, 660; in India, 750, 750; in Japan, 305, 494, 495; in Mexico, 540; in US, 688
Middle East, 655m; agrarian-urban centers of, 3, 27–52, 29m; arts of, 48–49; Assyrians and, 42; chariots in, 41; climate change in, 31; divorce in, 37; Europe and, 632–36; firearms in, 371; foraging in, 28–31; gender relations in, 35–38; hominins to, 8; horses in, 41; in Ice Age, 29; India and, 164; Islamism in, 744–45; kingdoms in, 120; marriage in, 36–37; Mediterranean and, 145–62; monism in, 158–62; monotheism in, 158–62; multiethnic/multireligious interactions in, 40–46; nation-states of, 693–96, 694m; Ottoman Empire in, 577; patriarchy in, 35–38; property rights in, 36; Roman Empire and, 153; science in, 49; Seljuk Turks in, 257; ships of, 365; sub-Saharan Africa and, 142–43; Tang dynasty and, 276; topography of, 28–29; wars in, 10; women in, 36–38
Middle Kingdom (Egypt), 40
Middle Passage, for slave trade, 447–48
Migrations, 548m; from Africa, 11, 12m; to Americas, 17–23, 22m, 102–3; in

Argentina, 531; from Asia, 15–17; to Australia, 12–15; from East Africa, 25; Europe and, 15–17, 610, 610m; by *Homo sapiens*, 11–17, 12m; industrialization and, 610, 610m; in Latin America, 547, 547–48; in Mexico, 537; in Oceania, 113m, 113–15, 115; from South Africa, 12–15; to US, 656

Military: of Alexander the Great, 169; of Andes, 106; of Argentina, 530; of Aztecs, 345–46; of Brazil, 531, 729; in Byzantium, 225–26; of China, 718; desegregation of, 714; of Egypt, 749; empires and, 632, 632–33; of England, 397; of European centralized kingdoms, 391–92; of Incas, 348–49; in Israel, 722; in Italy, 667; in Japan, 498; of Japan, 671–72; of Kongo, 440; in Mesopotamia, 34, 35; in Middle East, 146; in Ming dynasty, 488; of Nazi Germany, 669; of Nubia, 123; of Ottoman Empire, 372; of Persians, 217; of Prussia, 402; of Russia, 401; of Shang dynasty, 82, 87, 89; of US, 714, 736

Military orders, Portugal, 360

Millet, 77

Mines Act of 1842, 613

Ming dynasty (China), 265, 284–89, 477–89, 478m; Africa and, 324; culture of, 287–88, 489; family in, 285–86, 485–87; gender relations in, 285–86; hundred days' reform in, 563; Korea and, 296–97; Neo-Confucianism in, 287, 479–80, 488; trade in, 479, 479m, 480–81, 481m, 484, 484–85

Miniatures, in Islamic Civilization, 238–39

Minoans, 40, 48–49

Minutemen, 505

"Minute on Education" (Macaulay), 628

Mirs (communes), in Russia, 591

Mit'a, 347–48, 547

Mithridates II, the Great, 151–52

Moche Valley, in Peru, 139–40

Moctezuma II, 409

Model Parliament, 251

Modernity and modernism: of arts, 619–20; of capitalist democracy, 677, 733–54; in China, 553–74; of communism, 676; defined, 688; environmental limits of, 754–56; industrialization and, 617–20; in Japan, 570m, 553–74; in literature, 619; in music, 620; New Sciences and, 705; in Ottoman Empire, 578, 583; in philosophy, 619; in religion, 619; in Russia, 587–95; in Soviet Union, 664–66; in supremacist nationalism, 666–75; in US, 654–59; World War I and, 648–49, 651–64; World War II and, 649

Mo Di, 210–11

Mohenjo-Daro, 54, 58

Moldboard, in Europe, 251

Molucca Islands, 272

Monasteries: in France, 255; in Japan, 306; in Western Christianity, 246

Monet, Claude, 620

Money economy, 371

Mongolia, 200, 281

Mongols, 230, 284m, 296; Abbasids and, 273–74; in China, 280–84, 284m; Ibn Taymiyya and, 242–43; Mughals and, 457–58; Ottoman Empire and, 363; Qing

dynasty and, 482–83; Silk Road and, 265; Song dynasty and, 270–91; in Vietnam, 236, 310

Monism, 121, 146, 212; of Greek philosophy, 160; in Middle East, 158–62; Upanishads and, 176–77

Monochrome painting, 495, 496

Mononobu, Hishikawa, 477

Monopolies, 615

Monotheism, 146; of Achaemenids, 158; in Middle East, 158–62; polytheism to, 160–61; in Roman Empire, 155

Monroe Doctrine, 538–39

Monsoon system, 54–56, 55m

Montana, Anzick-1 fossil from, 23

Montenegro, 582, 584, 592

Moquegua, 342–43

Morel, Edward D., 647

Morisco, 369, 370–71

Morocco, 10, 358, 366–67, 436, 640

Morrison, Jim, 706

Morse, Samuel F. B., 606

Most-favored nations, 558, 558m

Mothers of Plaza de Mayo, 29

"Mourning Chen Tao" (Du Fu), 279

Mozambique, 701

Mozart, Wolfgang Amadeus, 513

Muawiya, 216

Mubarek, Hosni, 753

Mugabe, Robert, 726

Mughals, 273, 274–75, 282, 456–75, 461; administrative personnel of, 466–67; Afghanistan and, 463, 463; agriculture of, 467; architecture of, 472–73; arts of, 472; astronomy of, 470; caste system of, 469; economy of, 467–68; family of, 469–70; gender relations of, 469–70; gunpowder and, 281; Hinduism and, 471; history and politics of, 457–66; literature of, 471–72; mathematics of, 470; ministries of, 466; religion and, 470–71, 474; Revolt of the Sons of, 461; Safavids and, 471; science of, 470; Sikhism and, 464, 474, 475; Silk Road and, 467; social classes of, 468–70; taxes of, 469; women of, 469–70

Muhammad (Prophet), 218–20, 316, 324, 584

Mukhtar, Umar, 639

Mulattoes, 423–24; in Argentina, 530

Mumbai (Bombay), 466, 626

Mummies, of Inca, 352–53

Musa, Mansa, 316, 331

Music: from African diaspora, 449–50; of Enlightenment, 513; modernity in, 620; in Renaissance, 382–83; romanticism and, 523; in Tang dynasty, 278

Muslim Brotherhood, in Egypt, 723

Mussolini, Benito (Il Duce), 666–67; Nazi Germany and, 668

Mutsuhito (Meiji), in Japan, 493, 564–66

Mycenaeans, 42, 44–46, 48–49

NAACP, 659

Nabobs, 626, 627

Nagasaki, 675, 681

Nagy, Imre, 685

Nahuatl, 338, 408

Naia, 23

Nakbé, 133

NAM. *See* Non-Aligned Movement

Nama, 639

Namibia, 639; Apollo 11 Cave in, 11, 11

Nanak, 275

Nanda, Mahapadama, 170

Napata, 124

Napoleon Bonaparte, 507; in Egypt, 578; Enlightenment and, 508; Europe of, 510m; in Iberia, 529; Russia and, 508, 587, 588–89

Napoleon III, 516, 518, 539, 580, 590, 615, 645

Naram-Sin of Akkad, 35, 42

Nasser, Gamal Abdel, 680, 695–96

Nataputta, Nigantha, 177

National Commission on the Disappearance of Persons (CONADEP), in Argentina, 729

National Organization of Women (NOW), 716

National polity/essence (*kokutai*), 650, 671

National Rifle Association, 743

National Security Strategy of 2002, of US, 736

National Society for Women's Suffrage, in Great Britain, 614

Nation-states: of Africa, 694m, 701–3; of Asia, 696–701; China as, 692–93; Congress of Vienna and, 515, 516m; from Great Britain Empire, 522; India as, 662–63, 696–99; Israel as, 694–95; Japan as, 565; of Latin America, 538m; of Middle East, 693–96, 694m; origins of, 503–11; of South America, 534–35; of Southeast Asia, 700–701; from Soviet Union, 712–14; US as, 519–22, 520m

Native Americans, 23, 424–25; American Indian Wars with, 521; in Argentina, 531; Catholicism and, 426; civil right movement for, 714–15; Declaration of Independence and, 505; England and, 504; Indian Removal Act for, 521; Jesuits and, 415, 426; in Mexico, 535, 537–38; in North America, 416–18; as slaves, 412, 415; smallpox and, 408, 414, 441; tobacco and, 445; writing of, 425

NATO. *See* North Atlantic Treaty Organization

Natufians, 30

Naturalism, 47

Natural sciences, of Iberia, 385

Natural selection, 618

Navigation Acts, 446

Navigation systems, for ships, 253, 279

Navy: of Achaemenids, 147; of England, 403; of Ming dynasty, 285, 287; of Ottoman Empire, 369–70; of Sparta, 150

Nazca, 141, 143

Nazi Germany, 668–69; Aryans and, 62; Jews and, 677–78; Soviet Union and, 669, 670; US inspirations for, 657

Ndongo, 439–40, 449

Neanderthals (*Homo neanderthalensis*), 15–17, 20–21, 25

Négritude, 659

Nehru, Jawaharlal, 696, 697

Neo-Assyria, 3, 42, 120, 165

Neo-Babylonia, 44, 147, 159

Neo-Confucianism, 290; in China, 213, 276–88; ethics of, 560–61; in Japan, 492, 495, 498, 565; in Korea, 297, 298; in Ming dynasty, 287, 479–80, 488; samurai and, 495

Neolithic Age (New Stone Age), 30; Americas in, 104–5; China in, 77–80; Mehrgarh in, 56; Vietnam in, 308–9

Neo-Platonists, 382
NEP. *See* New Economic Policy
Netherlands: Calvinism in, 394, 396–97;
    Caribbean and, 414; colonialism of, 641;
    East India Company of, 465–66;
    Indonesia and, 640–41; Japan and, 492,
    498–99; mercantilism of, 443; New
    Sciences in, 385, 386; in North America,
    416; South Africa and, 440; war of
    independence of, 396–97
Newcomen, Thomas, 388, 604
New Deal, 658–59
New Economic Policy (NEP), in Soviet Union,
    665
New England, 425–26; Protestantism in, 427;
    witchcraft in, 427, 428
New Granada, 533–34
New Harmony, 612
New imperialism, 625
New Kingdom (Egypt), 37, 41–42, 47
New Lanark, 612
New Model Army, 397
New Sciences (Scientific Revolution), 356, 381,
    383–90, 387m, 705; in Germany, 385,
    386; in North America, 427; philosophy
    and, 389–90; social impact of, 386–89;
    women and, 386–88
Newspapers, 568, 647
New Stone Age. *See* Neolithic Age
Newton, Isaac, 386, 617
New Zealand, 115
Ngangas, 432–33
Ngo Dinh Diem, 701
NGOs. *See* Non-governmental organizations
Nguyen Van Thieu, 720
Nicaea, 257
Nicaragua, 728
Nicene Creed, 155
Nichiren, 307
Nicholas I, 590, 592
Nicholas II, 592–95, 593, 653
Nietzsche, Friedrich, 619
Niger, 143
Nigeria, 726, 752
Niger River, 329
Nightingale, Florence, 590
Nihongi (*Chronicles of Japan*), 308
Nikitenko, Aleksander, 576
Nile River, 28, 31–32, 317–20
Nineteenth Amendment, 656
Nirvana, 178–79
Nixon, Richard, 719, 722, 728, 734
Nkomo, Joshua, 726
Nkrumah, Kwame, 702
Nobel, Alfred Bernhard, 605
Nobunaga, Oda, 489, 490
Noh, 495, 572
Nomads, 33; in China, 83, 198, 280; of North
    India, 173–74; of Persia, 146; Roman
    Empire and, 155–58, 158m; in sub-
    Saharan Africa, 129–30
Non-Aligned Movement (NAM), 679–80, 696,
    698–99, 700
Non-governmental organizations (NGOs), 740
Nontariff autonomy, 558
Nonviolence (*ahimsa*), 172
Norman Conquest, 252, 262
Normans, 226, 228, 250, 257
North Africa: Christianity in, 317–22; Islam in,
    317–22; in 1914 and 1923, 655m;

Ottoman Empire in, 577; Portugal and,
    359–60; trade in, 318–19, 319m
North America, 340m; climate of, 99–101;
    colonialism in, 416–19, 417m;
    counterculture in, 705–6; culture of, 688;
    England and, 416, 503–5, 504m; Inuit in,
    111; Native Americans in, 416–18; New
    Sciences in, 427; slaves in, 444–46, 445;
    topography of, 99–101. *See also* United
    States
North Atlantic Treaty Organization (NATO),
    683, 740
North Dynasty (China), 200
Northern Expedition, 673–74
North India, 63–64, 67m, 73, 172m; Alexander
    the Great in, 170–71; kingdoms of, 272;
    Mauryans of, 170–73, 173m; nomads of,
    173–74; sultanates of, 273–74, 275m
North Korea, 746, 758–59
North Sea, 364
Novel, 288, 308, 568
NOW. *See* National Organization of Women
Nubia, 123–24, 317–20
Nuclear Test Ban Treaty, 688, 708
Nuclear weapons: Cuban Missile Crisis and,
    649, 687m, 687–88, 708; Einstein and,
    618; at Hiroshima and Nagasaki, 675,
    681; in North Korea, 758–59. *See also*
    Cold War

Obama, Barack, 736, 742
Obregón, Álvaro, 541
Ocean currents, of Americas, 101–3
Oceania, 97m; culture of, 114–15, 116; food in,
    117; migrations in, 113m, 113–15, 115
Octavian, 154
October Manifesto, 594–95
Odyssey (Homer), 165
Office of Strategic Services (OSS), 683
Official nationality, in Russia, 590
Ogé, Vincent, 502–3
Oglethorpe, James, 446, 454–55
Ohio Company of Virginia, 419
OHL. *See* Supreme Army Command
Oil, 605, 616, 691, 708, 717, 723, 734–35
Old Kingdom (Egypt), 38–40, 39m, 51–52
Oldovan tools, 6, 8
Old Stone Age (Paleolithic Age), 6
Olmec, 108–11, 116
Olympic Games, 148, 615
Omanis, 638
*On the Origin of Species by Means of Natural
    Selection* (Darwin), 618
On the Road (Kerouac), 705
OPEC. *See* Organization of the Petroleum
    Exporting Countries
Operation Colombo, 728
Opium, 555–56, 556m, 557; First Opium War,
    554, 556, 557–58, 558m, 564; Second
    Opium War, 560
Oracle bones, 90, 90–91
Oracles, 148
Oral tradition, of Mali, 331
Organization of the Petroleum Exporting
    Countries (OPEC), 717, 734
Organization of Work, The (Blanc), 612
Orinoco River, 112, 424
Orrorin femurs, 5
Ortega, Daniel, 728
Orthodox Catholic Church, 162

Ortíz, Alonso, 406–7
Osman, 363
OSS. *See* Office of Strategic Services
Osuke, Hibata, 564
Otto I of Saxony, 251
Ottoman Empire, 362–71, 367m, 633–34;
    Adriatic Sea and, 364–66; Anatolia and,
    578, 583; architecture of, 375; Balkans
    and, 366, 372–73, 578, 584–86, 635;
    cannon of, 373; centralizing state of,
    371–74; constitutionalism in, 582; in
    Crimean War, 581, 590; decentralization
    in, 578; decline of, 580m–81m, 583–85;
    East Africa and, 639; Egypt in, 635;
    Europe and, 625; exports of, 586;
    festivities of, 375; France and, 624–25;
    gunpowder and, 281; Habsburg dynasty
    and, 367–71; Habsburgs and, 577–78;
    industrialization in, 586; land grants in,
    371–72; modernity in, 578, 583; Morocco
    and, 366–67; navy of, 369–70; Palestine
    and, 590; Persia and, 366–67; Portugal
    and, 369; reforms in, 578, 596; Russia
    and, 576–97, 625; Safavids and, 366–67,
    369–70; self-strengthening in, 583;
    theater in, 375; trade by, 369; World War I
    and, 648, 652, 654
Over London by Rail (Doré), 612
Owen, Robert, 612
Oxford Calculators, 260
Oyo, 332–33

Pachacuti, 347
Pacific Ocean: El Niño in, 101–3; Mexican-
    American War and, 564; World War II in,
    675–76, 676m. *See also* Oceania
Paekche kingdom (Korea), 294–95
Pahlavi, Muhammad Reza, 725
Pakistan, 174, 680, 696–97
Palace-states, of Minoans, 40
Paleolithic Age (Old Stone Age), 6. *See also*
    Prehistory
Palestine, 159, 161, 216, 661–62, 742; Israel
    and, 694–95; Ottoman Empire and, 590
Palestine Liberation Organization (PLO),
    723–24, 745
Pallavas, 175–76
Pampas (grasslands), 424, 530
Pan-African movement, 659
Panama, 535, 605
Panama Canal, 535
Pandyas, 175–76
Pan-Slavism, 592, 652
Pantheon, 166
Papacy: crisis of, 264, 265m; and Investiture
    Controversy, 255; Protestant
    Reformation and, 393; of Western
    Christianity, 246–47
Papal States, 517, 518
Paper, 201, 382, 605
Papin, Denis, 388, 604
Papua New Guinea, 114
Paracas, 140–41
Paraguay, 420, 529, 531, 753
Pardos, 534
Pargana, 467
Paris: Academy of Sciences in, 386; redesign of,
    615
Paris Agreement, 758
Parliament, 251

Parthians, 120, 151–54, 163–64
Partido Revolucionario Institucional
        (Institutional Revolutionary Party)
        (PRI), 663–64
Pascal, Blaise, 388
Passion plays, 376
Pastoral Symphony (Beethoven), 523
Patriarchy: in China, 95–96; of Creoles, 424; of
        Eastern Syriac Church, 162; in Middle
        East, 35–38; in Russia, 591; in Vedas, 63
Patricians, 323
Paul, Mary, 598–99
Paul of Tarsus, 162
Pax mongolica, 265
Pax romana, 154
Peace Preservation Law of 1925, in Japan, 671
Pearl Harbor, 675
Pearl River, 77
Peasants' Revolt, 262, 394
Pedra Furada, 103
Pedro I, 532
Pedro II, 532
Pedro IV, 433
Pelesets (Philistines), 44
Peloponnesian War, 150
People's Liberation Army, of China, 674, 692,
        719
People's War, in China, 573
Pepin III, the Short, 246, 247
Perestroika, 711, 711–12
Perón, Juan, 29, 691
Perpetual Peace (Kant), 512
Perry, Matthew C., *564*, 565, 604
Persians: East Africa and, 131; Greece and,
        146–51; Mongols and, 282; Mughals and,
        465; Ottoman Empire and, 366–67;
        recovery of, 156–58; religion in, 155;
        Roman Empire and, 151–58, 215, 216;
        silk and, 204; trade by, 234. *See also*
        Achaemenids; Parthians; Safavids;
        Sasanids
Persians, The (Aeschylus), 165
Peru, 104, 412, 419–20, *422*, 534, 691; Caral-
        Supe in, 97, 105; Chile and, 535; El Niño
        and, 102; El Paraíso, 105–6; exports of,
        546; Moche Valley in, 139–40; Native
        Americans of, 424; Nazca of, 141, 143;
        Paracas in, 140–41; Polynesia and, 118;
        Spain and, 407–11; Wari in, 343–44. *See
        also* Inca
Peter I, the Great, 401, 587, 588
Petrarch, Francesco, 266
Petronius, 266
Phalanxes, 147
Phallic stones, 60
Phan Boi Chau, 645
Pharisees, 161
Philip I, 257, 370
Philip II, 150–51, 376–77, 396, 427, 642
Philip IV, 250, 264
Philip VI, 262Philippines, 479, 641–44, *644*
Philosophy: Byzantium and, 240; of
        Enlightenment, 512–13; in Europe, 267;
        Islam and, 236–37; modernity in, 619;
        New Sciences and, 389–90; romanticism
        and, 523
Phoenicians (Canaanites), 43–44, *44*, 153
Photography, *524*
Physics, 163, 237, 384–85, 386
Picasso, Pablo, 620, *620*

Piedmont, 517–18
Piérola, Nicolás de, 535
Piers Plowman (Langland), 266
Pietism, 514
Pillow Talk (Shonagon), 292
Pinochet, Augusto, 728
Piracy, 625; in East Africa, 638; in Qing
        dynasty, 555–56
Pizan, Christine de, 266
Pizarro, Francisco, 409–11
Plague. *See* Black Death
Plague of Justinian, 156*m*, 156–57
Planck, Max, 617
Plantations: in Americas, 441–48; in Brazil,
        422, 532, 533; in Caribbean, 441–42;
        England and, 422; for rubber, 647; Spain
        and, 422; for sugarcane, 442–43
Platform of the Sixth Patriarch, The (Hui Neng),
        208
Plato, 160, 237, 240, 382, *384*
Plessy v. Ferguson, 714
PLO. *See* Palestine Liberation Organization
Plow, 251
Plymouth, 416
Poe, Edgar Allan, 523
Poetry, 208, 237, 266, 279, 304, 308, 496, 513,
        568
Poetry Classic. See Shijing
Poland, 589, 592, 685, 712; Solidarity Union
        in, 709–10, *711*; World War II in, 669–70
Political parties: in Australia, 632; in France,
        660; in India, 663; in Italy, 666; in Japan,
        571; in Mexico, 663–64, 753; of Russian
        abortive revolution of 1905, 594; in US,
        742–43
Politics (Aristotle), 168, 382
Pollack, Jackson, *689*
Polo, Marco, 282–83
Pol Pot, 722
Polynesia, 115, *115*, 118
Polytheism, 46–47; of Achaemenids, 148; in
        Aksum, 126; challenges to, 159–61; of
        Hinduism, 471; of Maya, 133–34; to
        monotheism, 160–61
Poma de Ayala, Guamán, 427, *427*
Pompeii, 166
Pompey, 154
Pontius Pilate, 162
Poopó, Lake, 342
Population growth: 1700-1900, 608*m*–9*m*,
        609–10; in sub-Saharan Africa, 701
Populism: in Latin America, 663, 691; of Tea
        Party movement, 742
Porcelain: in China, 208, 480–81, *481*, *482*; in
        Japan, 494; in Song dynasty, 288, *288*
Portugal: Africa and, 436, 701; Benin and, 439,
        439; Brazil and, 411, 415–16; China and,
        484; East Africa and, 639; Ethiopia and,
        437–38; India and, 363; Indonesia and,
        640–41; Japan and, 492; Jews and, 362;
        Kongo and, 439–40, *440*; mercantilism
        of, 443; North Africa and, 359–60;
        Ottoman Empire and, 369; ships of, 365;
        slaves and, 438–40; spice trade of, 465;
        West Africa and, 437–38
Positive Philosophy, The (Comte), 523
Positivism, 524, 533
Postcolonialism, 733
Postimpressionism, 620
Postmodernism, 733

Potatoes, 477
Potosí, 419–20, 422
Pottery: in China, 208, 480–81, *481*, *482*; in
        Japan, 301, *301*, 494; in Mesoamerica,
        105; in South America, 105; of
        Teotihuacán, 138
Powell, Adam Clayton, 698–99
Power loom, 600
Powhatan confederacy, 416–18
Prague Spring, 709–10
Predestination, 394
Prehistory, 7*m*; from Africa, 2, 4–26; agrarian-
        urban centers of, 3; agriculture of, 2–26;
        in Americas, 97–113; climate change in,
        3; foraging in, 3; ocean travel in, 21–23;
        technology of, 2. *See also* Hominins;
        Neolithic Age; Paleolithic Age
Presentism, 441
PRI. *See* Partido Revolucionario
        Institucional
Priest-rulers, of Olmec, 109–10
Prince, The (Machiavelli), 382
Printing, 382; in China, 208; in Japan, 307; in
        Korea, 298–99; Protestant Reformation
        and, 393
Privateers, 443
Progressive era, in US, 521–22
Protestant Reformation, 357, 383, 393–94,
        395*m*
Proto-Davidian language, 58
Proto-Indo-European language, 62–63
Proto-Mediterraneans, 58–59
Proxy wars, in Latin America, 728–29
Prussia, 401, *402*, 507, 516, *518*, 518–19
Psychoanalysis, 618
Ptolemy, 163, 383
Pueblo (tribe), 131, 338
Pueblo Revolt, 537
Pure Food and Drug Act, 522
Puritans, 397
Puruchuco, 337
Pu Songling, 489
Putin, Vladimir, 740
Pu-Yi, 672

Qaddafi, el-, Muammar, 748
Qadesh, 41–42
Qaeda, al-, 737, 753
Qajars dynasty, 586–87
Qianlong, 483*m*, 483–84, 554–55
Qin dynasty, (early China) 194–96, 195*m*;
        First Emperor of, 195–96, *196*; Korea
        and, 294; Vietnam and, 309–10
Qing dynasty (early modern China), 477–89;
        banner system of, 48; Canton system in,
        483*m*, 484–85, 497–98; Christianity in,
        498; civil war in, 559; culture of, 568–69;
        economy in, 566–67; family in, 485–87,
        567; Great Britain and, 554–67; marriage
        in, 567; Mongols and, 482–83; pirates in,
        555–56; race for concessions in, 563, *563*;
        Republican Revolution against, 673;
        self-strengthening in, 553, 560–61, 567;
        trade in, 479, 479*m*, 480–81, 481*m*, 555
Quantum theory, 617
Que, 75–76
Quebec, 416, 418
Quetzalcoatl, 352
Quinine, from Indonesia, 641
Quipu, 98, 105, 348

Quotations from Chairman Mao Zedong (Mao Zedong), 718

Quran, 214, 220, 221, 456, 584; aniconism and, 239; Iranian Islamic Revolution and, 725; ISIS and, 749

Race for concessions, in Qing dynasty, 563, *563*

Racism, from slavery, 454

Radioactivity, 617

Radiocarbon dating, 97, 99, 122

Railroads: in Africa, 639; in Argentina, 531; in China, 674; in Great Britain, 601; Harappa and, 53; in Italy, 517; in Japan, 569, 570; in Ottoman Empire, 583; Trans-Siberian Railroad, 566, 593; in US, 60, 520–21

Rain-forest kingdoms, of West Africa, 332–33

Raj, 629

Rajarajeshwara Temple, *273*

Rajputs, 175, 273, 474

Ramadan War, 717, 723–24

Ramayana, 66, 180–81

Rape of Nanjing, 674–75

Raphael, 382, *384*

Rastafarians, 322

Rayon, 605

Raziya, 273

Reagan, Ronald, 711, 717

Realism (art), 523–24, *524*

Realpolitik, 517, *518*

Reciprocity, 192, 210, 342, 344–45, 347, 352, 354

Recoil cylinder, for artillery, 607

Reconquista, 257, 359, 362

Record of the World (Xu Jiyu), 568

Records of Ancient Matters (*Kojiki*), 308

Records of the Grand Historian, The (*Shiji*) (Sima Qian), 207, 294

Red Eyebrow Revolt, 198–99

Redology (*hong xue*), 568

Red Sea, 127, 369, 437

Reformation. *See* Protestant Reformation

Regency, 460

Reichstag fire, 668

Reign of Terror, in French Revolution, 507, 508–9

Religion: Akbar and, 464–65; canon law of, 213, 259; in China, 81, 90–93; in eastern Mediterranean, 46–49; of empires, 121; in Europe, 254–58; in Harappa, 59, 60; of India, 54, 70–71; in Japan, 306–8; in Korea, 299–300; in Middle East, 46–49; in Ming dynasty, 489; modernity in, 619; Mongols and, 282; Mughals and, 470–71, 474; in Persia, 155; schism in, 178; science and, 618–19; in Shang dynasty, 91; of slaves, 450–51, *451*; in Tang dynasty, 276–79; of Teotihuacán, 138–39, *139*; in Vietnam, 311–12; in Zhou dynasty, 91–93. *See also specific religions*

Religious civilizations: comparability of, 212–13; from kingdoms, 213; uniqueness of, 212

Renaissance, 357; arts of, 382–83, *384*; Byzantium and, 363; Catholicism in, 383; in Europe, 381–90; Harlem, 656, 658–59; maps of, 390–91, *391*; music in, 382–83; theater in, 383

Repartiemiento (labor assignments), 414, 420

Republican Revolution, against Qing dynasty, 673

Republics: of Brazil, 531–33; of ancient Rome, 153–54; of France, 507; of India, 189; of Latin America, 542; of Mexico, 536–37; of Mycenaeans, 46; of Vietnam, 645

Responsibility system (China), 719

Restoration War (Japan), 565

Revivalism, 428

Revolt of the Sons, of Mughals, 461

Revolver, 607

Rhapta, 131

Rhind Mathematical Papyrus, 49

Rhodes, Cecil, 639

Rhodesia, 726

Ricci, Matteo, 484, *484*

Rice, 64, 80, 305, 422, 445–46, 477

Richard I, 257

Richard II, 264

Rifled musket, 607

Rifles, 607, 628

Rift Valley, *4, 6*, 322, 438

Rightly guided leader (Mahdi), 584

Rig-Veda, 62, 63, 73

Rikyu, Sen-no, 308

Rio de Oro, 639, 701

Rio Grande do Sul, 532

Ritual pollution, 184

Ritual suicide (*hara-kiri*), 304

Rivera, Diego, *536*

Rizal, José, 643

Roads: of Achaemenids, 148; in Andes, 104, 106; in China, 200; of Hopewell, 111; of Inca, 349, *349*; in Qin dynasty, 195; in Tang dynasty, 278

Rock art, 14–17, *25, 46*, 103, *103*

Rocket launcher, of Korea, *280*

Roe v. Wade, 715

Rojdi, 59

Roma (Gypsies), 669, *671*

Roman Empire, 120; Byzantium and, 216; Christianity of, 126, 155, 241; culture of, 165–66; Islam and, 215; laws of, 153, 157, 242; literature of, 165–66; Meroë and, 126; monotheism in, 155; nomads and, 155–58, 158*m*; Parthians and, 151–54; Persia and, 151–58, 215, 216; recovery of, 156–58; Sasanids and, 154–58; ships of, 364, *365*; state religions of, 155, 240; trade by, 234

Romania, 582, 653, 681, 712–13

Roman Peace (*pax romana*), 154

Romanticism, 523

Roosevelt, Franklin D., 657–58

Roosevelt, Theodore, 522, 535

Rouhani, Hasan, 746

Rousseau, Jean-Jacques, 512

Royal Society of London, 386

Rubber, 605, 641, 647

Rumelia, 584, 592

Russia, 401, 402*m*; abortive revolution of 1905, 594–95, *595*; Balkans and, 592; Baltics and, 589; civil war in, 665; communism in, 651; Constantinople and, 587, 590; constitutionalism in, 595; constitutional nationalism in, 590; in Crimean War, 581, 590; culture of, 590–91; empires of, 576–97, 589*m*, 633–34; factories in, 593 2; famine in, 591, *591*; February Revolution

in, 653; French Revolution and, 587, 588–89; GDP of, 740; Georgia and, 578, 740; Germany and, 653; golden age of, 590–91; Great Britain and, 634–35; gulag system of, 687; industrialization in, 587–95, 604; Iran and, 587; Iranian Cossack Brigade of, 587; Japan and, 565–66, 593–94; Jews in, 593; literature of, 591; Ming dynasty and, 563; modernity in, 587–95; Napoleon Bonaparte and, 508, 587, 588–89; in nineteenth century, 588–91; Ottoman Empire and, 576–97, 625; reforms in, 591–92; serfdom in, 576, 591, *591*; Syria and, 749; World War I and, 648, 652–53

Russification, 592

Russo-Japanese War, 593–94

Russo-Ottoman War, 590, 592

Rutherford, Ernest, 617

Rwanda, 638, 737

SA. *See Sturmabteilung*

Saadids, 366

Sabotage, 600

Sacraments, 264

Sadat, el-, Anwar, 724

Sadler Report, 613

Safavids, 281, 585, 586–87; Mughals and, 461, 462, 471; Ottoman Empire and, 366–67, 369–70

Safra, 214–15

Saint-Simon, Henri de, 612

Saladin (Salah al-Din), 230, 257

Salem witch trials, 428

Salons, for New Sciences, 387

Salt, 201, 440

SALT II, 711

Salt March, 663

Samarkand, 45

Same-sex marriage, 715

Samudragupta, 174

Samurai, 304, *305*, 308, 492, 495, 565

Sandinista National Liberation Front (FSLN), 728

Sanitation, 614–15

San Lorenzo, 109

San Martín, José de, 529, 530, 534–35

Sanskrit, 63, 70, 472

Santa Anna, Antonio López de, 537–38

Sanusiyya Brotherhood, 639

Sargon of Akkad, 27, 35

Sasanids, 120, 127, 164, 222, 241; Islam and, 215; Roman Empire and, 154–58

Satellites, 68, 686

Saul, 44

Savanna, *6*, 129

Savery, Thomas, 604

Sayyids, 274

Schism: in religion, 178; Western Schism, 263, 265*m*

Schoenberg, Arnold, 620

Scholasticism, 258

Schutzstaffel (SS), 669

Science and technology: in China, 208, 560–61, 568–69; in East Asia, 560–61; in eastern Mediterranean, 49; in Han dynasty, 203, *203*; in High Middle Ages, 259–60; in India, 187; industrialization and, 617–19; Islam and, 236–37; in Japan, 560–61, 572; at Library of Alexandria, 163; in

Middle East, 49; in Ming dynasty, 287–88, 488; of Mughals, 470; religion and, 618–19. *See also* New Sciences
Scientific management, 616
Scientific Revolution. *See* New Sciences
Scientific socialism, 613
Scotland, 393–94, 522
Scotus, John Duns, 267
Scramble for Africa, 636–40
SDI. *See* Strategic Defense Initiative
Sea Peoples, from Greece, 42
Sebastião I, 440
Second Balkan War, 577
Second Coming of Jesus, 426
Second Crusade, 230, 257
Second Industrial Revolution, 603*m*, 603–9, 610, 621
Second Isaiah (Deutero-Isaiah), 159
Second Opium War, 560
Second Reform Act (England), 522
Second Temple, 159, 161
Secret History of the Mongols, 282
Seiyukai (Constitutional Government Party), 571
Seko, Mobutu Sese, 703
Selective breeding, 30–31
Seleucids, 151, 161
Seleucus Nikator, 65, 169–70, 171
Self-rule (*swaraj*), 663
Self-strengthening: in Ming dynasty, 553, 560–61, 567; in Ottoman Empire, 583
Seljuk Turks, 227–29, 257
Sendler, Irene, 678
Senghor, Léopold, 659
Sepoy, 626
September 11, 2001 terrorist attack, 737, 737
Serbia, 582, 592, 652
Serfdom, in Russia, 576, 591, 591
Seven Years' War, 419, 474, 503, 625
Sewer system, 58, 137, 350
Sexuality: in Buddhism, 205; of Empress Wu, 291; in Hinduism, 186; in India, 69–70
Sexual revolution, 715
Seyon, Amda, 322
Shahinshahs. *See* King of kings
Shah Jahan (Khurram), 456–57, 463
Shahjahanabad, 472, 473
Shahname (Book of Kings) (Firdosi), 164, 237
Shahs, of Iran, 586–87, 725
Shakas, 174
Shakespeare, William, 383
Shakti, 182
Shangdi, 90, 91
Shang dynasty (China), 75–76, 79, 82–84, 83*m*, 84, 89; bronzes of, 91; religion in, 91; Xia dynasty and, 94
Shapur II, 155
Sharecroppers, 32–33
Sharia, 220, 242–43, 463, 752
Sharifian descent, 324
Shaw, George Bernard, 619
Shenbao, 568
Shi, 88
Shiite Islam, 221–22, 584–85; Humayun and, 459; Iranian Islamic Revolution and, 725; Messiah of, 366; Ottoman Empire and, 366–67
Shiji (The Records of the Grand Historian) (Sima Qian), 207, 294

Shijing (The Book of Odes, Poetry Classic, The Book of Songs), 89, 92–93, 95–96
Shikibu, Murasaki, 292
Shinto (way of the gods), 302, 306–8
Ships, 253, 279, 364, 364–65, 365, 601; of China, 557; of Genoa, 360; for slave trade, 447–48, 448. *See also* Navy
Shiraz, 323–24
Shiva, 174, 180, 181–82
Shogun, 489
Shogunates, of Japan, 303–4
Shoguns, of Japan, 303–4
Shonagon, Sei, 292
Shotoku (Prince), 302
Shujing (Book of History, Classic of Documents), 80, 81, 82, 84, 85
Siam. *See* Thailand
Siberia, 17–23, 22*m*, 111
Sicily, 251, 252, 257
Sikhism, 275, 290, 464, 474, 475
Silk, 201, 204, 279, 297, 605
Silk Road, 76, 152, 183, 185, 276, 467; in China, 203–4, 204*m*–5*m*, 235; Mongols and, 265; Samarkand on, 45; Wudi and, 198
Silla kingdom (Korea), 294–95
Silver, 411, 412, 440; from Americas, 419–21; China and, 479, 480*m*; in Ottoman Empire, 372–73; in Peru, 419–20, 422
Sima Qian, 207, 294
Sima Tan, 207
Sinan, 375
Sinicizing, 198, 310, 312
Sino-Japanese War, 553, 562, 563, 565
Sino-Soviet Split, 693, 708, 718
Sioux, 418
Sirleaf, Ellen Johnson, 751–52
Six-Day War, 723
Six Dynasties period (China), 200
Slave revolts, 452, 453*m*; in Brazil, 542–43; in Cuba, 542, 542–43; in Haiti, 502–3, 510–11, 529
Slaves and slavery: from Africa, 434–48, 442*m*, 444*m*; in Americas, 441–48, 442*m*, 444*m*; Atlantic system for, 446–47, 447*m*; in Brazil, 443; as chattel, 441, 520; for cotton, 519–20; Declaration of Independence and, 505; England and, 443, 444–46, 445; France and, 443; household, 438; of Kharijis, 323; in Louisiana, 418; in Middle East, 35; Middle Passage for, 447–48; Native Americans as, 412, 415; in North America, 444–46, 445; on plantations, 422; Portugal and, 438–40; racism from, 454; religion of, 450–51, 451; resistance by, 450–52; of Roman Empire, 153; ships for, 447–48, 448; in sub-Saharan Africa, 438–39; Turks as, 222, 227; in US, 519–20; in Vietnam, 311. *See also* Abolition of slavery
Slavs, 223, 363; in Nazi Germany, 670, 671; pan-Slavism and, 592, 652
Smallpox, 408, 410, 414, 441
Smith, Adam, 513, 517
Smith, Ian, 726
Smoot-Hawley Tariff of 1930, 658
SNSs. *See* Social networking sites
Soccer, 615
Social classes: of Americas, 422–26; in China, 81, 87, 88, 197; in Europe, 254; of

Frankish feudalism, 249, 249*f*; of India, 67–69, 68, 69, 71; industrialization and, 610–12, 621; in Japan, 571; in Korea, 297, 298; of Mughals, 468–70. *See also* Caste system; Middle class
Social Contract (Rousseau), 512
Social Darwinism, 618, 647
Social networking sites (SNSs), 752, 752–53
Social Security Act, 658
Social stratification, 82
Society of Friends of Blacks, 502
Society of Harmonious Fists, 564
Solidarity (Poland), 709–10, 711
Solomon, 44
Solomonid dynasty (Ethiopia), 322
Somalia, 667
Somoza García, Anastasio, 728
Song dynasty (China): Confucianism in, 271; gunpowder from, 280–81; Mongols and, 270–91; porcelain in, 288, 288
Songhay Empire, 434–36, 637
Soninke, 331
Sons of Liberty, 505
Sophocles, 165
Soseki, Natsume, 572
South Africa, 11, 12–15, 129–31, 751; apartheid in, 701, 726–27, 727, 730–31; Netherlands and, 440
South America: nation-states in, 534–35; Orinoco River in, 112; pottery in, 105; topography of, 101
South Carolina, 445–46
South dynasty, in China, 200
Southeast Asia, 309*m*; China and, 562; colonialism in, 640–45, 642*m*; India and, 183, 184–85; Japan and, 675; nation-states in, 700–701; Tang dynasty and, 276; trade in, 468*m*
Southern Africa, 323–28, 436–37
Southern characters (*chu nom*), 312
Southern Cone, 529
South India, 175–76, 177, 272
South Sudan, 640, 752
Soviet Union: Afghanistan and, 707, 707–8, 711; agriculture in, 665–66, 666; Baltics and, 712–13; Bulgaria and, 681; capitalism in, 71; China and, 692, 693, 718; collapse of, 708–14; communism in, 664–66; Communist Party in, 664–65; Congo and, 703; containment of, 681; Cuba and, 686–87; East Germany and, 685–86; Egypt and, 696; Hungary and, 685, 685; Israel and, 694–95; modernity in, 664–66; nation-states from, 712–14; Nazi Germany and, 669, 670; Nicaragua and, 728; Poland and, 669, 685; Romania and, 681; satellites of, 68, 686; World War I and, 648; Yom Kippur War and, 723. *See also* Cold War
Spain, 422, 443; Africa and, 701; Caribbean and, 408, 419; civil war in, 669; East Africa and, 639; Habsburg dynasty in, 375–77; Inca and, 409–11, 411, 427; Islam in, 257, 371; Japan and, 492; Mexico and, 407–11; Nazi Germany and, 669; Netherlands and, 396–97; Peru and, 407–11; Philippines and, 641–44
Spanish-American War, 643, 644
Spanish Inquisition, 362
Sparta, 46, 148–50

Spartacus, 153
Spears, 9, 13, 102–3, 301
Spencer, Herbert, 618
Spice trade, 438, 465, 642
Spinning jenny, 600
Spinning mule, 600
Spinoza, Baruch, 389
Spiritual Guide, in Iran, 725
Sports, industrialization and, 615
Spring and Autumn Chronicles, 84
Spring and Autumn period, in China, 90
Sputnik, 686, *686*
Squinches, 164
Sri Lanka (Ceylon), 131, 679–80, 696
Srivijaya, 272
SS. *See Schutzstaffel*
Stagflation, 717
Stalin, Joseph, 664, 665–66, 669, 680, 681–82, 684
Stamp Act, 504–5
Standard Oil Company, 616
Stanley, Henry Morton, 638
START. *See* Strategic Arms Reduction Talks/ Treaty
Star Wars, 711
State religions, 121; of Roman Empire, 155, 240; of Sasanids, 241
Steam engine, 388–89, 600, 601, 604–5, *605*, 621
Steel, 604–5, 616
Stirrups, *198*, 198–99
Stoics, 161
Strait of Tiran, 695–96
Strange Tales from the Make-Do Studio (Pu Songling), 489
Strategic Arms Reduction Talks/Treaty (START), 711
Strategic Defense Initiative (SDI), 711
Striation, 294
Stuarts, 397, 403
Sturmabteilung (SA), 669
Subaltern, 631
Sub-Saharan Africa, 121, 129–30, 636; agrarian-urban centers of, 123–31, *129m*; agriculture in, 123–27; Americas and, 131; kingdoms in, 120, 123–25, *435m*; Middle East and, 142–43; nation-states in, 701–3; population growth in, 701; slaves in, 438–39
Sucholdoski, January, *502*
Sudan, 635, 640, 737
Suez Canal, *624*, 662, 685, 696
Suffragettes, 614, 715
Sufism, 236, 471, 472
Sugarcane, 442–43; in Africa, 437; in Brazil, 411, 415, 443, 532–33; in China, 477; in Cuba, 542; in Indonesia, 641; in Latin America, 546; in Louisiana, 418; in Philippines, 642; in South Carolina, 445–46
Suger (Abbot), 261
Sui, 200–201
Suiko (Empress), 302
Sukarno, 680, 696
Süleyman I, the Magnificent, 366, 367, 373
Sultanates, of north India, 273–74, *275m*
Sumeria, 37
Sumptuary laws, 286
Sundiata, 335–36
Sungbo's Eredo, 332–33

Sunna, 218
Sunni Islam, 221–22, 230, 236, 366, 463, 584–85
Sun religion, of Egypt, 47, *47*
Sun Yat-sen, 673
Sun Zi, 65
Supremacist nationalism, 677; in Italy, 666–67; in Japan, 651, 671–72; modernity in, 666–75
Supreme Army Command (OHL), in Germany, 667
Sur, Sher Khan, 459–60
Surrealism, *689*
Sustainability, 754
Swahili city-states, 323–28
Swaraj (self-rule), 663
Sweden, 394, 398
Switzerland, 393–94
Syllabary, 292
Sylvester II, 258
Symbols: in Harappa, 60; of *Homo sapiens*, 10–11; syllabary, 292
Symphonie fantastique (Berlioz), 523
Synagogues, 161, *162*
Syria, 43, 44, 215, 216, 227, 230; Arab Spring in, 749; Byzantine and, 216; civil war in, 732, 745; Crusades in, 229, 257; Hittites in, 41–42; Jacobite Church in, 162; in Lebanese civil war, 724; Neo-Assyrians in, 165; Ottoman Empire and, 579; Turkey and, 743

Taif Agreement, 724
Taiho Code, 302
Taika (Great Reform), 302
Tailor's Rebellion, 543
Taíno, 112–13, 408
Taiping Rebellion (Qing dynasty), 559, *559m*, 573
Taiping tianguo (Heavenly Kingdom of Great Peace), 559
Taisho Democracy (Japan), 671
Taiwan, 114
Taj Mahal, *456*, 456–57, 472
Takauji, Ashikaga, 303–4, 489
Tale of Genji (Genji Monogatori) (Shikibu), 292
Taliban, 737, 745, 753
Tamerlane (Timur), 274, 282, 363, 457–58, *458m*
Tamils, 176
Tamil Tigers, 679–80
Tang dynasty (China), 200–201, 271, *277m*; music in, 278; poetry in, 279; religion in, 276–79; ships of, 365; trade in, 279–80
Tanjore, 272
Tantra, 182
Tanzania, 638
Tanzimat, 579
Tariffs, 183, 601, 658
Tatars, 588
Tatsukichi, Minobe, 650–51
Tawantinsuyu, 346
Taxes: in Aksum, 126; in Europe, 404; of European centralized kingdoms, 392–93; French Revolution and, 506; in Han dynasty, 199; in India, 182–83, 628; of Maya, 135; in Ming dynasty, 479; of Mughals, 467; in Nubia, 320; in Roman Empire, 154; of Stamp Act, 504–5. *See also* Tariffs

Tax farming, 235, 372–73, 479, 581
Tea, 279, 307, 505, 641
Tea Party movement, 742
Technology. *See* Science and technology
Tecumseh, 521
Telegraph, 540, 569, 606–7
Telephone, 606, 613
Ten Hours Act, 613
Tennessee Valley Authority, 658
Tenochtitlán, 350m, 350–51, *351*, 354, 409, 410m
Tenskwatawa, 521
Tent government (*bakufu*), 491
The Ten Thousand Leaves (Man'yoshu), 308
Teosinte, 104, 108–9
Teotihuacán, 136–39, *138m*, *139*, 338–41
Tesla, Nikola, 605
Tet Offensive, 721–22
Teutonic Knights, 391
Texas, 537
Textile industry, 600–601; Luddites and, 622; women in, *598*, 613
Thackeray, William Makepeace, 524
Thailand (Siam), 645
Thales, 160
Thambo, Oliver, 731
Thatcher, Margaret, 717
Theater: of Habsburg dynasty, 376–77; in Japan, 495–96, 572; in Ottoman Empire, 375; in Renaissance, 383
Theogony (Hesiod), 165
Theory of Harmony (Schoenberg), 620
Theory of relativity, 617
Theravada, 179–80, 207, 312
Thermidorean Reaction, by China, 718
Third Coalition, 589
Third Crusade, 230, 257
Third Empire, 669
Third Republic (France), 519, 526–27
Thirty Years' War, 380, 397, 398, *399*
Thrace, 583
Three Kingdoms period: in China, 200; of England, 397
Tiamat, 48
Tiananmen Square massacre, 720, *720*
Tiantai, 207
Tibet, 281, 282, 483
Tigris River, 28, 31, 42
Tikal, 132, 138–39
Timbuktu, 331, 434
Timur (Tamerlane), 274, 282, 363, 457–58, *458m*
Timurids, 282, 458, 464, 466–69
Titicaca, Lake, 342, 347
Tito, Josip Broz, 681, 696, 744
Tiwanaku, 341–44, *342*, *343m*, 354
Tlaxcala, 345
TNT, 607
Toba, 200
Tobacco, 422, 445, 446, 477
Tokko, 671
Tokugawa. *See* Ieyasu, Tokugawa
Tolkien, J. R. R., 26
Toltecs, 338–41
Tools: of hominins, 6–8, *8*; of *Homo erectus*, 8; of *Homo sapiens*, 10; of Neanderthals, 16
Topkapı Palace, 365, 374, *375*
Topography: of Americas, 99–102, *100m*; of Australia, 12–13; of China, 76–77, *78m*; of eastern Mediterranean, 28–29; of

India, 54–56, 55m; of Japan, 300, 301m; of Korea, 294, 295m; of Middle East, 28–29; of North America, 99–101; of South America, 101
Tories, 403
Torricelli, Evangelista, 388
Total war, 652
Toumaï skull, 5
Tour de France, 615
Toussaint Louverture, François-Dominique, 510–11
Trade: Afro-Eurasian world commercial system, 234–36, 235m; by Aksum, 127; by ancient Ghana, 328–29; in Asia, 185m; by Assyrians, 42; by Australian Aboriginals, 14; in Caribbean, 443; by China, 89; by East Africa, 130–31; by England, 446–47; in Eurasia, 274m; in Europe, 252–53, 253m, 265–66; global balance of, 735m; by Harappa, 59–60; by India, 183, 184–85, 363, 468, 468m; by Japan, 497–99; by Mali, 331; by Mauryans, 172; in Mediterranean, 252–53, 253m; in Ming dynasty, 479, 479m, 480–81, 481m, 484, 484–85; by Mycenaeans, 45; in North Africa, 318–19, 319m; in Nubia, 318–19; by Ottoman Empire, 369; by Persia, 234; by Phoenicians, 43–44; in Qing dynasty, 479, 479m, 480–81, 481m, 555; in Red Sea, 369; by Roman Empire, 234; in Southeast Asia, 468m; by south India empires, 176; in Tang dynasty, 279–80; by Teotihuacán, 137, 138; from textile industry, 601; by Toltecs, 339; in Vietnam, 311; in Yuan dynasty, 281
Trade forts, for African slave trade, 438
Trail of Tears, 521
Transcendence, 159, 160–61, 167, 332; Buddhism and, 179; Daoism and, 194; Islam and, 236; Jainism and, 178; Upanishads and, 176
Trans-Siberian Railroad, 566, 593
Treaty of Brest-Litovsk, 653
Treaty of Kadesh, 42
Treaty of Kanagawa, 565
Treaty of Nanjing, 557–58, 558m
Treaty of Paris, 263
Treaty of Shimonoseki, 554
Treaty of Tianjin, 565
Treaty of Verdun, 248
Treaty of Versailles, 654
Tres Zapotes, 110
Tribute mission system, of Neo-Confucianism, 498
Trinitarianism, of Christianity, 216–17
Triple Intervention, 565–66, 594
Tripolitania. See Libya
Trotsky, Joseph, 664–65
Truman, Harry S, 675, 681–83, 714
Truman Doctrine, 681
Trump, Donald, 743
Trung Nhi, 310
Trung Trac, 310
Tsar (czar), 401, 587
Tsetse fly, 129, 439
Tughluqs, 274–75, 276
Tulans, 338–39
Tundra, 19, 111
Tunisia, 636, 748, 748–49
Túpac Amaru, 337

Turkey, 742, 746–47, 747; Kurdish and, 747; Syria and, 743; World War I and, 662
Turkistan, 157, 273
Turks, 222; of Anatolia, 363; Mughals and, 457; Seljuk, 227–29, 257. See also Ottoman Empire
Turner, Nat, 452
Tutenkhaten, 51–52
Tutsi, 437, 737
Tuxen, Laurits Regner, 593
Twelve Tablets, of Roman Empire, 153
Twitter Revolution, in Iran, 753
Typewriter, 613

Uaxactún, 138–39
Ubaids, 31, 47
Ukiyo-e, 564, 572
Ukraine, 592, 665, 740
Umar, Al-Hajj, 638
Umayyads, 215, 216–17, 223, 252, 317
Umma, 220
UN. See United Nations
Unction, 246
Union of German Women's Organizations, 614
Union of Soviet Socialist Republics. See Soviet Union
United Arab League, 696
United Nations (UN), 680, 694, 723, 724, 736–37, 738m, 746
United States (US), 519–22, 520m; American Civil War, 452, 520, 539; American Revolution, 501, 503–5; Chile and, 728; civil rights movement in, 714–18; computers in, 649; consumerism in, 654, 688; cotton from, 601, 602; culture of, 654–59; Dawes Plan of, 668; dollar regime of, 734–35, 757; early years of, 505–6; entertainment in, 654; exports to, 735; gender relations in, 688; globalization and, 735–36; Great Depression in, 657–59; industrialization in, 602–3, 616; Iran and, 746; Iraq and, 736–37; ISIS and, 749–50; Japan and, 565; in Korean War, 683–84; labor unions in, 656; Mexico and, 537–38, 539m; migrations to, 656; military of, 714, 736; modernity in, 654–59; Monroe Doctrine of, 538–39; Nicaragua and, 728; in 1990s, 733–40; Panama Canal and, 535; Philippines and, 643–44, 644; political parties in, 742–43; Progressive era in, 521–22; railroads in, 60, 520–21; satellites of, 68; security commitments of, 738–39, 739m; slaves in, 519–20; textile industry in, 602; Truman Doctrine of, 681; Vietnam and, 701, 720–22, 721m; women in, 656, 715; World War I and, 653–59; World War II and, 670–71, 675–76, 676m; Yom Kippur War and, 723. See also Cold War
United States Steel Corporation, 616
Universities, in High Middle Ages, 258–59
Upanishads, 71, 176–77
Urania propitia (Companion to Urania) (Cunitz), 380
Urban II, 257
Urbanism and urbanization: in Caribbean, 680–90, 690m; in East Africa, 324; in Europe, 254; in Great Britain, 610; industrialization and, 609–10, 614–15; in

Japan, 493m, 493–94; in Latin America, 680–90, 690m; of Mayans, 341; in Mexico, 663; in Ming dynasty, 477–78; in sub-Saharan Africa, 701
Urban VI, 264
Uruguay, 529, 530
Uruk, 33, 48
Urukagina, 36
US. See United States
Usury, 394
Utamaro, Kitagawa, 496
Utari, 300
Uzbeks, 461

Vacuum, 388, 388
Vajjian Confederacy, 65
Vanity Fair (Thackeray), 524
Varangian Guard, 225, 226, 234
Vatsyayana, 186
Vedas, 63–64, 70–71, 176–80
VE Day (Victory in Europe Day), 671
Velvet Revolution (Czechoslovakia), 712
Venezuela, 421, 535, 691, 754
Venus, 16, 16
Vernacular, 266
Veronese, Paolo, 371
Vesuvius, Mount, 166
Vichy government, 670
Victor Emanuel II, 518
Victory in Europe Day (VE Day), 671
Vietcong, 701, 721
Vietnam, 308–12; agrarian-urban centers of, 309; Buddhism in, 309, 311, 312, 701; China and, 191, 312, 314, 722; communism in, 720–22, 740–41; Confucianism in, 191; France and, 644–45; Han dynasty and, 310; India and, 183; Mongols in, 236, 310; as nation-state, 700–701; as republic, 645; Tang dynasty in, 276; US and, 720–22, 721m; Yuan dynasty and, 281
Vietnam War, 720–22, 721m; student demonstrations against, 716–17
Vijayanagar ("City of Victory"), 272
Vikings, 248, 364
Villa, Francisco "Pancho," 536, 540, 541
Viracocha, 347
Virgil, 165, 166
Virgin Mary, 426, 472
Vishnu, 174, 180, 181–82
Visigoths, 156, 217
A Visit to the Yoshiwara (Mononobu), 477
Vita Kimpa, Dona Beatriz, 432–33, 440
Vivaldi, Antonio, 383
Vladimir I, 225
VOC. See Dutch United East India Company
Voltaire, 387
Von Guericke, Otto, 388
Voodoo, 428, 450–51
Voting rights, 520, 612, 614, 656, 715
Voting Rights Act of 1965, 714
Vulcanization, of rubber, 605

Waldseemüller, Martin, 384, 385
Wales, 522
Wałęsa, Lech, 710, 711, 712
Wang Anshi, 279–80
Wang Chong, 208
Wang Mang, 198–99
Wang Yangming, 287, 488

Wari, 141, 343*m*, 343–44, 354
War of Paraguay, 533
War of the Pacific, 535
Warring States period (China), 84, 86, 190, 193
Warsaw Pact, 683, 710
Washington, George, 505
Washington Consensus, 738–39
Water frame, 600
Watt, James, 604–5
Way of the gods (Shinto), 302, 306–8
Way of the Warrior (*bushido*), 304
Wazzan, al-, al-Hasan Ibn Muhammad (Leo Africanus), 358–59
Weapons, 607–9, *632*, 632–33; of Aztecs, 345–46, *347*; of European centralized kingdoms, 392; ICBM, 686, 708; of Incas, 349; in Ming dynasty, 488; of Mughals, 470; in Qing dynasty, 568; of Russia, 401; of Spain, 411; spears of early man, 9, 13, 102–3, 301. *See also* Nuclear weapons
Weapons of mass destruction, in Iraq, 737
Wedgwood, Josiah, 481
Weimar Republic, 667–68
Wei Yuan, 568
Well-field system, in China, 88
Wen Bo, 89
Wesley, Charles, 428
Wesley, John, 428
West Africa, 330*m*, 359, 637–38, 647; China and, 234–36; Islam in, 328–33, 434, 638
West African Mail, 647
Western Christianity, 244–69, 258–60, 367; Byzantium and, 240; Crusades and, 257; Eastern Christianity and, 226–27; Gothic cathedrals of, *260*, 260–61; Mamluks and, 360
Western Europe: agrarian-urban centers of, 357; expansion of, 358–79; ships of, 365
Western Mediterranean, 153, 257
Western Schism, 263, 265*m*
Western Zhou period, 85–86
What Is to Be Done? (Chernyshevsky, Lenin), 597
Wheat, 421–22
Wheel, 104, 116, 117
Whigs, 403
White Lotus, 554
"The White Man's Burden" (Kipling), 647
White Nile, 640
White Revolution, 725
White Shaman, 103, *103*
Wilhelm I, 518
William I of Aquitaine, 255
William of Ockham, 267
William of Orange, 641
William the Conqueror, 250
Wilson, Woodrow, 653–54
Windmills, 252
Winstanley, Gerrard, 405
Wireless telegraph, 606–7
Witchcraft, 130, 427, 428, 432–33
Witte, Sergei, 593

Women: African American, 656; in agrarian-urban centers, 10; in Americas, 424; in Argentina Dirty War, 29; in Athens, 167–68; of Australian Aboriginals, 13; Buddhism of, 205; in Byzantium, *226*; in China, 89–90, 95–96; civil rights for, 715; in coal mines, *611*, 611–12; education of, 430–31; in Egypt, 37; feminism and, 614, 716–17; in France, 614; in Germany, 614; in Han dynasty, 204–5; of Inca, 352; in India, 68–70; industrialization and, 613, *613*; in Islam, 214–15; in Japan, 495, 571; in Korea, 298–99; in Latin America, 549–50; in Mexican Revolution, *537*; in Middle East, 36–38; in Ming dynasty, 286, 486–87; of Mughals, 469–70; New Sciences and, 386–88; in Russia, 591; in Sparta, 150; in Tang dynasty, 279; Ten Hours Act for, 613; in textile industry, *598*, 613; in US, 656, 715; in Vietnam, 311; voting rights for, 614, 656, 715
Wong Kon, 29
Woodstock Festival, 715
Wool, 104, 600
Works of Mencius, The (Legge), 190
World Trade Center, 737, *737*
World War I: Belgium in, *651*; empires and, 660–61, 661*m*; France and, 648, *651*, 660; German reparations for, 667–68; Great Britain and, 648, 653, 659–60; Latin America and, 663–64; machine guns in, 608; modernity and, 648–49, 651–64; Ottoman Empire and, 639, 652; US and, 653–59
World War II: atomic bombs in, 675, *681*; culture after, 688; in Europe, 669–71, 672*m*; in France, 669–70; Great Britain in, 669–70, 671; Japan in, 675–76, 676*m*; Latin America and, 690; modernity and, 649; in Pacific Ocean, 675–76, 676*m*; Palestine and, 694–95; in Poland, 669–70; US in, 670–71, 675–76, 676*m*
Wounded Knee, 521, 715
Wright, Richard, 698–99
Wright brothers, 606
Writing: of Achaemenids, 148; in China, 79, 90, 90–93, 195–96, 207; in Harappa, 53–54, *54*; in Korea, 299; of Maya, 133, 136, *137*; of Native Americans, *425*; of Olmec, 110–11; by Phoenicians, 44; of Teotihuacán, 137; in Vietnam, 312
Writs, 251
Wudi (Martial Emperor), 197–98, 312
Wu Ding, 75, 83, 89, 90
Wu Sangui, 481
Wu Zetian (Empress Wu), 279, *279*, 290–91
Wycliffe, John, 264

Xesspe, Toribio Mejia, 143
Xia dynasty (China), 80–81, 94
Xiaojing (*Classic of Filial Piety*), 206
Xiongnu, 174
X-rays, 617
Xuan Zang, 207, 272–73

Xu Jiyu, 568
Xunzi, 193
Xu Qinxian, 720

Yahweh, 159, 161
Yamato, 302
Yangban, 492
Yang Jian, 200
Yang Zhu, 210–11
Yangzi River, 77, 200
Yanukovych, Viktor, 740
Yasht, 155, 159
Yayoi period (Japan), 302
Yellow fever, 636
Yellow Hat sect, 282
Yellow River, 76–81, 200
Yemen, 127, 130, 732–33
Yi dynasty (Korea), 297
Yoga, 71
Yom Kippur War, 717, 723–24
Yongle, 285
Yongzheng, 482
Yoritomo, Minamoto, 303
Yoruba, 726
Younger Dryas, 30
Young Ottomans, 582
Young Turks, 583–84
Yuan dynasty (China), 281–84, 288
Yuan Shikai, 673
Yucatán Peninsula: Maya on, 132–33, 339–41; Native Americans of, 424; Teotihuacán on, 136–39, 138*m*
Yuezhi, 174
Yugoslavia, 681, 696, 744

Zacuto, Abraham, 390
Zaghlul, Saad, 662
Zagwe dynasty (Ethiopia), 320–21
Zaibatsu (cartels), 569
Zaire. *See* Congo
Zanzibar, 638
Zapata, Emiliano, *536*, 540, 541, *541*
Zemstvos, 591
Zen Buddhism, 208, 307–8, 314, 495
Zeng Guofan, 561
Zenki, Imad al-Din, 229–30
Zeppelin, Ferdinand von, 606
Zheng He, 287, 324
Zhou dynasty (China), 84–94, 85*m*, *94*; agriculture in, 87–88; culture of, 91–93; economy in, 88–89; Korea and, 294; Qin dynasty and, 194–95; religion in, 91–93; trade in, 89; well-field system in, 88; women in, 89–90
Zhu Xi, 287
Zhu Yuanzhang (Hongwu), 283–84, 296
Zimbabwe, 726
Zionism, 662
Zoroastrians, 148, 155, 157, 159–60, *160*; Cathars and, 269; Islam and, 219; Judaism and, 161; of Sasanids, 241
Zulu, 726–27